DOS 6.0
Handbook

DOS 6.0 Handbook

Jack Nimersheim

BANTAM BOOKS
NEW YORK • TORONTO • LONDON • SYDNEY • AUCKLAND

DOS 6.0 Handbook
A Bantam Book / May 1993

All rights reserved.
Copyright © 1993 by Jack Nimersheim
Cover design Copyright © 1993 by Bantam Books
Interior design by Nancy Sugihara
Produced by The LeBlond Group

No part of this book may be reproduced or transmitted
in any form or by any means, electronic or mechanical,
including photocopying, recording, or by any information
storage and retrieval system, without permission from the publisher.
For information address: Bantam Books

Throughout this book, tradenames and trademarks of some companies
and products have been used, and no such uses are intended to convey
endorsement of or other affiliations with the book.

ISBN 0-553-37229-7

Published simultaneously in the United States and Canada

Bantam Books are published by Bantam Books, a division of Bantam Doubleday Dell Publishing Group, Inc. Its trademark, consisting of the words "Bantam Books" and the portrayal of a rooster, is Registered in U.S. Patent and Trademark Office and in other countries. Marca Registrada, Bantam Books, 1540 Broadway, New York, New York 10036.

PRINTED IN THE UNITED STATES OF AMERICA

0 9 8 7 6 5 4 3 2 1

Contents

Acknowledgments xv
Preface xvii

Part I MS-DOS, A Tour de Force

1 Welcome to the Trenches 3

What Is MS-DOS? 4
The Myriad Faces of DOS 5
Hardware 7
    The System Unit 8
    Secondary Storage Devices 12
    PC Keyboards 14
    Monitors and Display Adapters 17
    Additional Hardware Options 18
PC Software 20
    System Software 20
    Application Software 21
    Utilities 21
Data 22

2 Getting to Know You: A Brief Introduction to DOS 23

Easy DOS It 23
Using the DOS Command Line 25
    Internal vs. External DOS Commands 25
    Filters, Switches, Options, and Parameters 26
    Structuring DOS Commands 27
Using the DOS Shell 28
    Starting the DOS Shell 31
    The DOS Shell Display 31

Navigating the DOS Shell   32
Changing the Active Area   32
Displaying the DOS Shell Pull-down Menus   33
Requesting Help in the DOS Shell   34
Dialog Boxes   35
A Mouse in the DOS House   36
Quitting the DOS Shell   37

Getting Help with DOS   38

Using the /? Switch   38
DOS Help Finally Comes of Age   39
Elements of the Help Display   40
Navigating the Help Display   40
Requesting Help for a Command   41
Searching Help on a Topic   43
Exiting Help   45

3 Working with Disks   47

Don't "Dis" Your Disks   48
Disks: The Ultimate Office Organizer   48

Floppy Disks vs. Hard Disks   49
How Disks Work   50
Preparing a Disk for Use   51

Formatting a Disk (The FORMAT Command)   53

FORMAT Parameters and Command Switches   53
Formatting a System Disk   54

Analyzing a Disk (The CHKDSK Command)   56

CHKDSK Parameters and Command Switches   57
Running CHKDSK   57
Including a File Analysis in Your CHKDSK Report   58
Detecting Bad Sectors with CHKDSK   59
Recovering Lost Clusters   59

Labeling a Disk (The LABEL Command)   61

LABEL Parameters   61
Limitations on Volume Label Names   61
Running LABEL   61

Checking a Volume Label (The VOL Command)   62

VOL Parameters   62
Running VOL   62

Duplicating Disks (The DISKCOPY and DISKCOMP Commands)   63

DISKCOPY Parameters and Command Switches   63
Running DISKCOPY   63
DISKCOMP Parameters and Command Switches   65
Running DISKCOMP   65

Restoring Accidentally Formatted Disks (The UNFORMAT Command) 66
- UNFORMAT Parameters and Command Switches 67
- Running UNFORMAT 67
- Limitations on Using UNFORMAT 68
- Partitioning a Hard Disk (The FDISK Command) 68
- FDISK Switches 69
- Running FDISK 69

4 Working with Directories 73

The Organizational Man (and Woman, of Course) 73
- Creating Order from Chaos 74
- Designing a Logical Directory Structure 74
- The Path-Finder 76

Creating Directories (The MKDIR or MD Command) 77
- MKDIR Parameters 78
- Using MD 78

Displaying the Contents of a Directory (The DIR Command) 78
- DIR Parameters and Command Switches 79
- Using DIR 80
- Using DIR Switches 81

Changing Active Disk Drives 84

Clearing Your Display (The CLS Command) 84

Changing Active Directories (The CHDIR or CD Command) 85
- CHDIR Parameters 85
- Using CHDIR 85
- Using CD on Other Drives 87

Customizing Your System Prompt (The PROMPT Command) 89
- PROMPT Parameters 89
- Using PROMPT 89
- Special PROMPT Symbols 90

Displaying a Disk's Directory Structure (The TREE Command) 92
- TREE Parameters and Command Switches 92
- Using TREE 92

Removing Directories (The RMDIR or RD Command) 93
- RMDIR (RD) Parameters 94
- Using RMDIR (RD) 94

Removing Entire Directory Trees (The DELTREE Command) 95
- DELTREE Parameters and Command Switches 96
- Using DELTREE 96

Fooling DOS (The APPEND and SUBST Commands) 97
- SUBST Parameters and Command Switches 98
- Using SUBST 99

viii CONTENTS

  Removing a SUBST Assignment 99
  APPEND Parameters and Command Switches 100

5 Working with Files 103

 The Ghost of Christmas Presents 103
 File Types 104
 DOS Says: Do It My Way 105
  File Naming Conventions 106
  Path Notation 108
 Copying Files (The COPY Command) 108
  COPY Parameters and Command Switches 108
  Using COPY 109
  Using COPY to Create a File 111
 Viewing the Contents of a File (The TYPE Command) 112
  TYPE Parameters 112
  Using TYPE 113
 Organizing Long Listings (The MORE Filter) 114
  MORE Parameters 114
  Using the MORE Filter 114
 Deleting Files (The DEL and ERASE Commands) 115
  DEL Parameters and Command Switches 116
  A Few Words to the Wise 116
  Using DEL 116
  Using Function Keys with DOS Commands 117
  Erasing Multiple Files 118
  Gone, but Not Forgotten 119
 Recovering Deleted Files (The UNDELETE Command) 119
  UNDELETE Parameters and Command Switches 119
  Levels of UNDELETE Protection 120
 Comparing Files (The FC Command) 123
  FC Parameters and Command Switches 123
  Using FC 124
 Renaming Files (The RENAME or REN Command) 124
  REN Parameters 125
  Using REN 125
 Verifying File Copies (The VERIFY Command) 126
  VERIFY Parameters 126
 Moving Files (The MOVE Command) 127
  MOVE Parameters 127
  Using MOVE 127
  Renaming Directories with MOVE 128

Copying Files from Multiple Directories (The XCOPY Command)   129
   XCOPY Parameters and Command Switches   129
   Using XCOPY   130

6 Working with Devices and Drivers   133

What Is a Device?   134
DOS Devices   135
Redirecting Input and Output   135
   Redirecting Output to the System Printer   135
   Redirecting Output to a File   136
The DOS Device Drivers   137
   Using Device Drivers   138
   The CONFIG.SYS File   138
Using ANSI.SYS   140
Using SETVER   142
   SETVER Parameters and Command Switches   143

7 Have It Your Way: Fine-Tuning Your System   147

Setting MS-DOS 6.0 in Stone (The DELOLDOS Command)   147
Creating CONFIG.SYS   149
Creating and Modifying Text Files (Using EDIT)   151
   Starting EDIT   151
   EDIT Parameters and Command Switches   151
   Using EDIT   152
Contents of CONFIG.SYS   154
Improving Disk Performance (The FILES, BUFFERS, and SMARTDRV Commands)   156
   Increasing Disk BUFFERS   156
   Increasing FILES   158
Using Double-Buffering with SMARTDRV   158
Creating a Virtual Disk (The RAMDRIVE Command)   160
Increasing the Number of Drives on Your System (The LASTDRIVE Command)   161
Making the Most of Memory (The HIMEM, DOS, EMM386, MEMMAKER, and DEVICEHIGH Commands)   162
   A Brief History of Memory   162
   HIMEM.SYS   166
Loading DOS High (The DOS Command)   168
Mega-Memory Management (The EMM386.SYS Device Driver)   168
   Let DOS Do It (The MemMaker Utility)   171
Moving Up to Upper Memory (The DEVICEHIGH Command)   180
   DEVICEHIGH Parameters and Command Switches   181

CONTENTS

CONFIG.SYS Cornucopia (Miscellaneous CONFIG.SYS Commands)   181

> There Are More Programs in Heaven and Earth, Horatio... (The INSTALL Command)   181
> INSTALL Parameters   182
> By the Numbers (The NUMLOCK Command)   182

What Is AUTOEXEC.BAT?   183

> Batch-ing It   183

The Pathfinder (The PATH Command)   184

> Some Like It Warm (Warm Booting Your System)   187
> A Matching Set (The SET Command)   187

The DIRCMD Variable   188
Claiming the High Ground (The LOADHIGH or LH Command)   189

8   Play It Safe: Protecting Your Data   191

Don't Neglect that Data   191
A New Face for an Old Friend (The MSBACKUP Utility)   192

> MSBACKUP Parameters and Command Switches   193
> Running MSBACKUP   193
> Creating an MSBACKUP Setup File   201
> Saving an MSBACKUP Setup File   205
> Ending an MSBACKUP Session   207

Gone, but Not Forgotten (The BACKUP and RESTORE Commands)   207

> The BACKUP Command   208
> The RESTORE Command   210

Modifying File Attributes (The ATTRIB Command)   212

> ATTRIB Parameters and Command Switches   212
> Using ATTRIB   213

Keeping Your System Healthy (The VSAFE Utility)   215

> VSAFE Parameters and Command Switches   216
> Using VSAFE   216
> Do You Need VSAFE?   218

9   The Age of Automation: Batch Files and Other Conveniences   219

Using Batch Files   219

> How a Batch File Works   221
> Batch File Commands   221

Creating a Batch File   222

> Replaceable Parameters (The % Sign)   224
> Testing Conditions (The IF Command)   225

CONTENTS **xi**

  Branching within a Batch File (The GOTO Command) 226
 Offering Users a Choice (The CHOICE Command) 227
  Miscellaneous Notes on MYFORMAT.BAT 227
  Running a Batch File 228
 DOS Doesn't Forget (The DOSKEY Utility) 230
  DOSKEY Parameters and Command Switches 230
  Using DOSKEY 230
  Recalling Command Lists 231
  Using the Command List 232
  Creating Macros with DOSKEY 232
  Including Special Characters in a Macro 233
  Saving Macros 234

10 Where No DOS Has Gone Before: New MS-DOS 6.0 Features 235

 Placing Your Digital Ducks in a Row (The DEFRAG Command) 236
  Contiguous vs. Noncontiguous Files 236
  Why Files Become Noncontiguous 237
  What DEFRAG Accomplishes 237
  DEFRAG Command Syntax 237
  DEFRAG Parameters and Command Switches 237
  Using DEFRAG 238
 A PC Two-fer (The DBLSPACE Utility) 242
  How Data Compression Works 243
  Setting Up DBLSPACE 244
  Using the DoubleSpace Tools 250
  Running DBLSPACE from the Command Line 252
 Opening Up the "Black Box" (The MSD Utility) 253
  MSD Parameters and Command Switches 253
 More Than Meets the Eye (Setting Up Multiple Configurations) 256
 A Personal Question (Using **?** in Your CONFIG.SYS File) 257
  Menu Magic (The INCLUDE, MENUCOLOR, MENUDEFAULT, MENUITEM, and SUBMENU Commands) 258
  Choices within Choices (Using the **F5** *and* **F8** *Function Keys)* 261

Part II   Command Reference

Command Reference 265

Appendix A Installing MS-DOS 6.0   507

What You Will Need   507
Write-Protecting Floppy Disks   507
    Write-Protecting 5.25" Disks   508
    Write-Protecting 3.5" Disks   508
    Write-Protecting Your MS-DOS 6.0 Distribution Disks   510
Getting Ready   510
    The MS-DOS 6.0 Setup Utility   511
    Installing MS-DOS 6.0 on a New System   512
    Upgrading to MS-DOS 6.0 from a Previous Version   512
Reverting to a Previous Version of DOS   522

Appendix B Going Graphic: An Introduction to the DOS Shell   523

Starting the DOS Shell   523
    The DOS Shell Display   524
Navigating the DOS Shell   525
    Running the DOS Shell from the Keyboard   525
    Using the DOS Shell with a Mouse   525
Switching the DOS Shell to a Graphic Display   526
Selecting Items on the DOS Shell Display   527
    Viewing Storage Requirements for Multiple Files   529
    Canceling a Multiple File Selection   530
Task Switching   530
    What Is Task Switching?   530
    Enabling Task Switching   531
    Adding Programs to the Task List   531
    Removing Programs from the Task List   533
    Ending Task Switching   535
Working with Program Groups   536
    What Are Program Groups?   536
    The Initial Program Groups   536
    Creating a Program Group   537
    Running a Program   541
    Modifying a Program Group Item   543
    Removing a Program Group Item   544

Appendix C Glossary   547

Index   555

For Stan Veit, editor emeritus of *Computer Shopper*, one massive, monthly computer magazine. Stan started accepting articles and reviews from an unproved writer named Nimersheim in 1988. Those initial sales evolved into a full-time career that has since produced 18 books and over 600 articles, reviews, columns, and other assorted items. So, thank or blame Stan, as you see fit. And, as always, for Susan and Jason, my wife and son. Without their presence in my life, those previously listed accomplishments would mean nothing.

Acknowledgments

No one book is the exclusive product of one person. Sure, my name is the only name on this book's cover, but a lot of people helped me bring it from initial idea to final product. They include:

Ron Petrusha at Bantam Doubleday Dell. Ron's sense of humor is so dry, it requires a weekly dusting. But Ron dusted it off regularly as I worked on this project — which, I believe, helped stop both of us from going crazy.

Ralph Roberts, friend and fellow writer. Ralph offered invaluable assistance when things did not go quite as planned. Thanks, pal.

Several editors at several computer magazines who extended several deadlines for columns and other assignments as the dreaded deadline crunch loomed on the horizon. Without their understanding, I would not have completed this book in time. Thanks, all.

And, finally, Susan and Jason, my wife and six-year-old son. They stayed out of what little remains of my hair long enough for me to write the 600-plus pages that follow. But they were always there when I needed them. These two make it all worthwhile.

Preface

In many ways, MS-DOS and I have grown up together — if one can begin "growing up" at age 32. That's how old I was when I purchased my first DOS computer. The year was 1982, and that seminal system came with MS-DOS 1.0, the first version of MS-DOS released.

In 1983, Microsoft released MS-DOS 2.0. That same year, although my full-time profession was that of a social worker, I started writing technical documents during my off-hours for a variety of software companies. Version 2.0's ability to recognize a hard disk aided me in these efforts immensely.

In 1985, I upgraded to MS-DOS 3.1. That was also the year I sold my first review to a computer magazine.

By 1987, I had graduated to MS-DOS 3.3, the most stable and impressive DOS version available at the time. By 1987 I had also quit my position at a local community center and was writing full-time for a living, mixing technical writing and submissions to the popular PC press to scrape out a meager living. The technical writing still comprised the majority of that living.

MS-DOS 4.0 came out in late 1989, just as I was completing my first book on this now familiar operating environment. That book went on to spend 12 months on Waldenbooks' top-20 best-seller list for computer titles. DOS 4.0 went on my hard disk long enough to write about it, and then was deleted. I didn't like this particular version of DOS and elected instead to return to 3.3. I did like the idea of having written a best-selling computer book, so much so, in fact, that I shifted over to writing for the popular press full-time.

In 1991, Microsoft released MS-DOS 5.0. I revised my DOS book accordingly. This time, the company got it right. MS-DOS 5.0 was an impressive upgrade. I told my readers so in the three monthly columns I was then writing for different computer magazines.

Now, it is 1993. DOS takes another major step forward. MS-DOS 6.0 is not quite the revolutionary product MS-DOS 5.0 was, but it's still a darn impressive upgrade. Enough so that when Bantam Doubleday Dell called and asked me if I wanted to write a book about the newest DOS, it took me a full five seconds to say: "You bet I would." You're holding the consequence of that conversation in your hands. It is the eighteenth computer book I've written, and the fourth one that deals with DOS.

As I said, DOS and I have grown up together. It's been a long and rewarding friendship, one I hope lasts quite a bit longer.

Jack Nimersheim
January, 1993
Vevay, Indiana

Part I

MS-DOS, A Tour de Force

Chapter 1

Welcome to the Trenches

Welcome to the trenches. That's a good title for our first chapter together, which is designed primarily to introduce the basics of the MS-DOS operating environment. You see, it's down there, in the trenches of DOS, that all of the real work gets done on your computer.

Store shelves and magazine advertisements are filled with computer programs designed to run on an IBM-compatible personal computer, or PC. Some, called word processors, help you enter and edit text; others, the electronic spreadsheets, help you crunch numbers; still others, the database managers, concentrate on collating general information. And there are more. Many of these programs are quite good; others leave a lot to be desired. But they all have one thing in common: Each of them requires MS-DOS to work properly.

MS-DOS is like the foundation of a building. Even though you may not see it, it's always there holding things up, keeping things together, stopping everything from falling apart. Without DOS, your computer would be nothing more than an expensive paperweight, taking up valuable space on what's already, no doubt, a very crowded desktop.

But what is DOS? What is it designed to do? And how does DOS do the voodoo that it do so well? (Yes, I realize that last sentence is a grammatical nightmare. As I pointed out in my Introduction, however, I plan to have a little fun with this normally dull subject matter. So, bear with me, even through the bad puns, okay?)

In this chapter, I'll answer these and other fundamental questions about MS-DOS. I'll examine exactly what role DOS plays in your day-to-day PC operations. I'll discuss — very briefly, I promise — the various types of equipment over which DOS takes charge each time you turn on your computer. Finally, I'll introduce some important terms and concepts you'll need to be familiar with as you go about the important business of using DOS on your PC.

So, settle back and buckle up. We've got a lot of ground to cover.

What Is MS-DOS?

The term MS-DOS is an acronym, one of those marvelous "nonwords" the computer industry seems to relish sneaking into the English language on an almost daily basis. MS-DOS, the acronym, stands for Microsoft Disk Operating System, Microsoft being the name of the company that created this now ubiquitous product.

All computers, from the most massive mainframe to the puniest palmtop, require some kind of disk operating system to work properly. Several exist: Apple Macintosh computers use a disk operating system called System 7. Many mainframes and minicomputers — and an ever-growing number of PCs — run under UNIX, an operating system that contributed significantly to DOS during the latter's formative stages. Several other systems rely on a proprietary operating system, one designed exclusively for their specific hardware components. In short, there are dozens of operating systems out there, each possessing its own unique strengths and weaknesses.

The most popular disk operating system, however, is MS-DOS. It controls an estimated 70 million personal computers worldwide. And this number continues to increase at a phenomenal rate, as more and more "regular folks" sign up for the PC revolution.

In fact, MS-DOS so dominates the PC industry that, figuratively speaking, it has kidnapped the generic term "DOS." Tell someone familiar with personal computers that you own a DOS system, and I'll bet you dollars to doughnuts that he or she immediately assumes you're talking about an IBM-compatible personal computer running under the MS-DOS operating system.

So, we've established that MS-DOS is an acronym for Microsoft Disk Operating System. Don't let the somewhat narrow nature of this nomenclature fool you, however. MS-DOS is much more than a system that operates disks. In truth, DOS controls virtually everything that happens in, around, and near your personal computer. Not one pixel could light up on your display, not one letter could be transmitted from your keyboard, not one bit of data could be manipulated in memory without DOS making itself available to organize all of this activity.

If you think I'm exaggerating, try the following experiment. Open up a brand new package of floppy disks, place one in whichever disk drive on your computer is identified as A and then turn on your system. After a few seconds, you'll see a message similar to the one below:

```
Non-system disk or disk error
Replace and press any key when ready
```

Even a computer — which, as you'll soon see, is an extremely ignorant device — is smart enough to recognize that it needs DOS.

Each time you start your system, DOS takes control. Like an electronic policeman during rush hour, it supervises traffic at the heart of a very busy intersection, controlling any and all equipment connected to your PC (see Figure 1.1).

When you type a sentence at your keyboard, DOS transmits that sentence to the monitor, allowing you to admire your handiwork. When you print a document, DOS assumes responsibility for guaranteeing that your peerless prose is sent to the appropriate port. When you request a particular piece of information, DOS seeks that information out and delivers it to whatever destination you've specified.

Without DOS, none of these events would happen. Knowing that they will occur, and that they will do so in a predictable fashion, allows you to use a personal computer productively.

The Myriad Faces of DOS

Now that I have explained how critical DOS is, let me lay a bombshell: There are many versions of DOS, each one of which differs slightly from the rest. I'm not alluding here to the various operating systems mentioned earlier –- System 7, UNIX and the like — I'm talking about MS-DOS itself.

You see, DOS has been around for a long time. It was first introduced in 1981, along with IBM's original PC. That initial version of DOS was called MS-DOS 1.0.

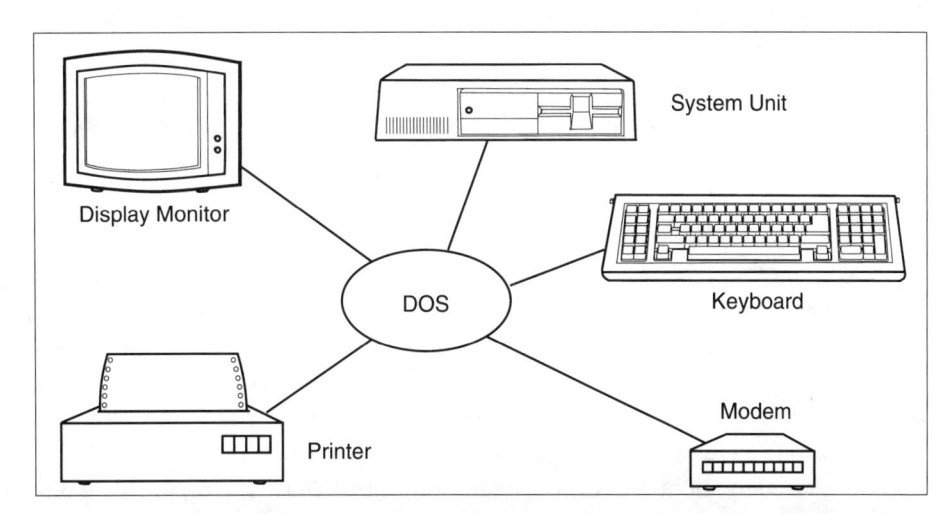

Figure 1.1 DOS functions like an electronic traffic cop, coordinating the activities of the various components attached to your PC.

> **Note:** MS-DOS 1.0 had an electronic "twin" named PC-DOS 1.0, a version of DOS that IBM licensed directly from Microsoft. MS-DOS and PC-DOS were basically the same operating system, however, so we'll treat them as a single entity.

DOS has gone through many changes since then. Some have been major, some minor. At regular intervals, DOS was improved enough to warrant a new version number. DOS 1.0 begat DOS 2.0, which begat DOS 2.1, which, in turn, begat DOS 3.0, and so on, up the numeric scale. Amidst much fanfare, Microsoft recently released MS-DOS 6.0, the latest in a long line of upgrades to its premier product.

All of which brings me to a critical conundrum: With all of the different releases of DOS currently in use, which version should I cover in this book?

The quick answer to this question is: all of them. Certain functions are available in every version of DOS, from DOS 1.0 right on up through the newest DOS release, MS-DOS 6.0. For example, there has always been a DOS DIR command, the command you use to display information about the files stored on your disks. Consequently, when I discuss the DIR command later in this book, that discussion will be of interest to all DOS users.

Other DOS functions are not so universal. The ability to use a DOS=HIGH statement to load portions of DOS into a specific area of your computer's memory was not added to DOS until the release of MS-DOS 5.0. For anyone reading this book who owns DOS 4.1 or earlier, therefore, our discussion of loading DOS into high memory, while educational, will have no practical value unless and until you upgrade to DOS 5.0 or higher. Likewise, DOS did not offer any kind of virus protection until the newly released MS-DOS 6.0. Even MS-DOS 5.0 users are out of luck on this one.

> **Note:** Throughout this book, whenever appropriate, I'll include information about the specific version of DOS in which a given command or function first appeared.

As you've probably deduced from the previous paragraph, each new generation of DOS includes more — and more impressive — features than its electronic ancestors. For this reason, it's usually a good idea to keep your system current by changing over to the most recent DOS version. (Microsoft makes doing so relatively painless by offering upgrades at a reduced price to registered users of previous DOS releases.)

But enough about the various permutations of DOS. Trying to figure out the logic behind software numbering conventions can be detrimental to your mental health. It's time to discuss, specifically, how DOS works. We'll begin this discussion by describing the various physical components of your PC system that fall under DOS's control.

Hardware

Hardware is a broad-brush term that applies to the physical, tangible components of a personal computer — those items you can "touch," to state it as nontechnically as possible. Various types of hardware — listed below — perform different functions within your total PC environment.

- the system unit
- secondary storage devices
- the keyboard
- display hardware (including monitor and video card)
- printer
- modem
- mouse
- additional peripherals

Figure 1.2 shows a typical MS-DOS system, which includes a number of items. Let's take a look at what these various items are, examine the kind of hardware components they generally contain, and discuss the specific operations this hardware performs.

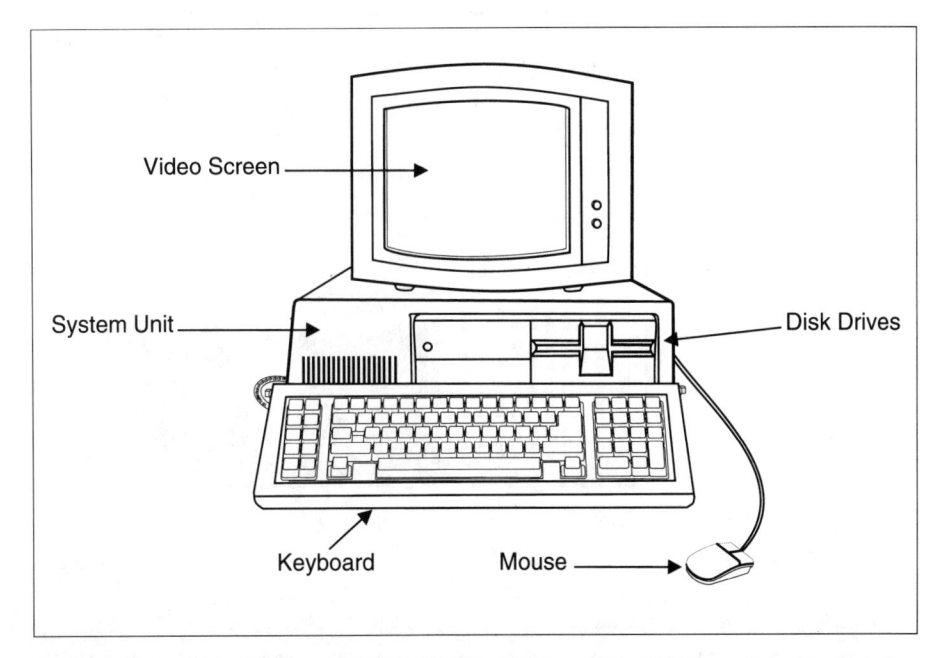

Figure 1.2 Your PC can include a variety of hardware components.

✔ **Note:** I realize you didn't buy this book to become an expert on PC hardware. Nevertheless, a basic understanding of the various items DOS is responsible for controlling will help you use your PC more effectively. I promise I'll keep the following discussion as short and as painless as possible.

The System Unit

The system unit houses several important components of an MS-DOS personal computer (Figure 1.3). These include:

- the motherboard
- the Central Processing Unit, or CPU
- system memory (RAM and ROM)
- the Basic Input/Output System, or BIOS
- input/output (I/O) ports
- expansion slots
- secondary storage devices (floppy disks, hard disk, tape devices, CD-ROM devices, and so forth)

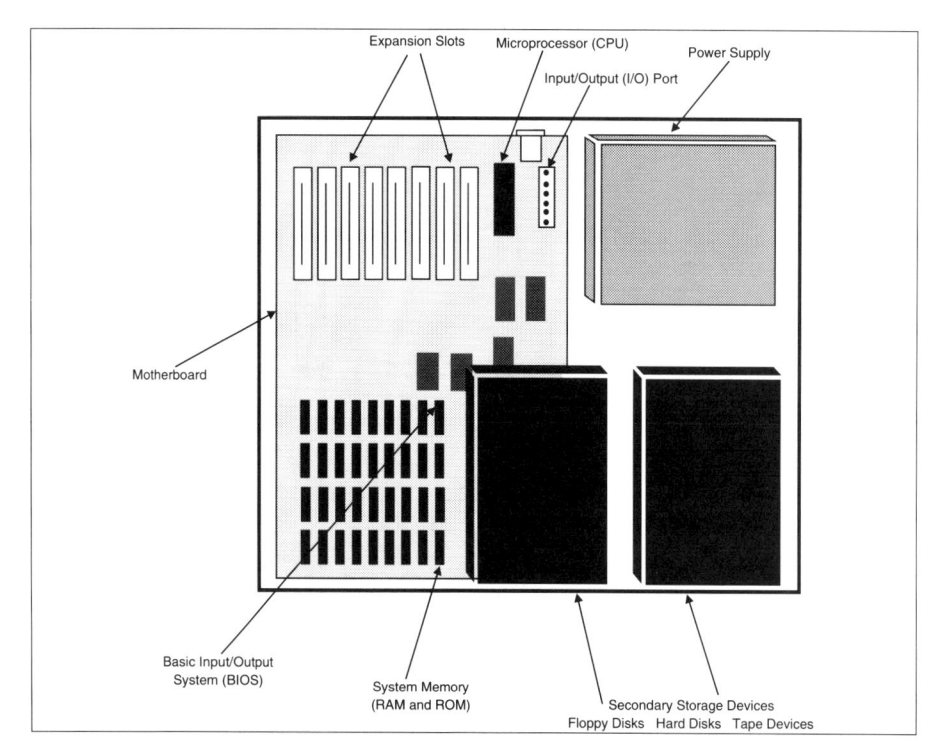

Figure 1.3 There's a lot of power packed within a PC's system unit.

Motherboard

Look inside your computer and you'll probably see a rectangular, green circuit board. This board, called the motherboard (Figure 1.4), contains a number of items critical to the operation of your PC.

A computer's random access memory (RAM), for example, is usually installed directly on the motherboard, although some system designs incorporate RAM that is mounted on a separate expansion card. The special slots that accept such cards — called, logically enough, expansion slots — are another item commonly found on the motherboards.

> ✓ **Note:** Most industry analysts believe that IBM's decision to include expansion slots on the motherboard of the original IBM PC played a large part in that system's early success. I'll explain why in a few paragraphs.

Central Processing Unit (CPU)

Stated simply, the central processing unit, or CPU, is the "brains" behind your PC. Manufacturers etch literally hundreds of thousands of transistors and printed circuits onto the CPU, a single chip no larger than a matchbook. It is these circuits that, in turn, define the operations a computer can perform, based on instructions it receives from the programs you run.

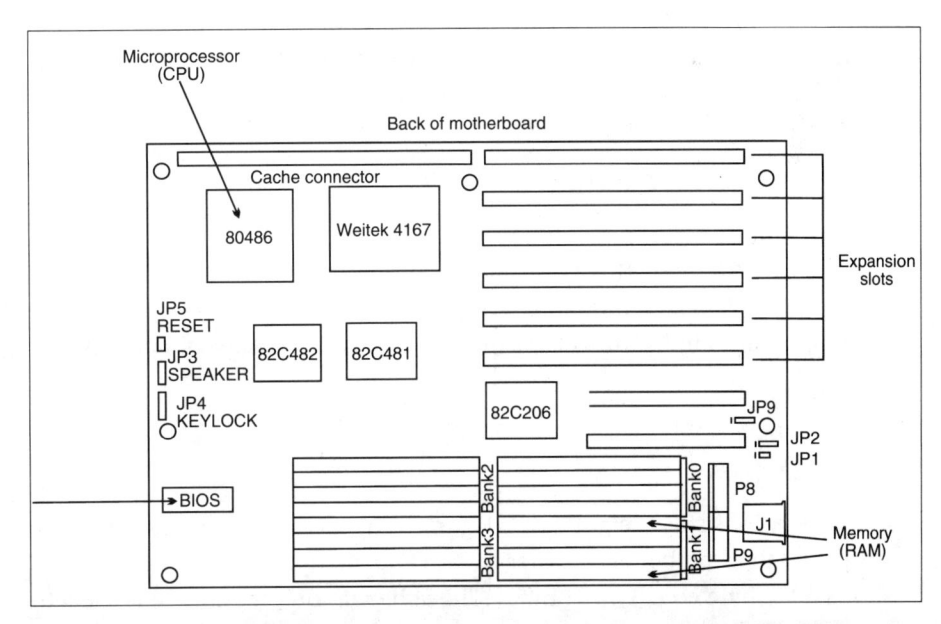

Figure 1.4 The motherboard contains several critical components of a personal computer.

Like all operating systems, DOS was designed to work with a particular kind of CPU — specifically, those belonging to the Intel 80xxx family of microprocessors. For many years, Intel was the only company that made this particular type of CPU. Today, several other manufacturers (Cyrix and AMD, to name but two) produce microprocessors that work like the various 80xxx chips. DOS also will run on computers that are built around one of the these compatible CPUs.

The original IBM PC/XT model, as well as the so-called "clone" machines that worked like a PC/XT, contained either an Intel 8088 or 8086 microprocessor as its CPU. Second-generation AT systems were built around Intel's 80286 chip; 386 computers use the 80386 or 80386SX. (Are you beginning to see a pattern emerge, here?) The most advanced DOS systems currently available incorporate Intel's i486 chip. Intel already has announced an even newer CPU. For trademark reasons, however, the company is dropping its traditional numbering scheme. This new chip, which once would have been called the 586, has been dubbed the Pentium Processor. So much for patterns.

As is the case with software, a higher microprocessor number (086 vs. 286 vs. 386) indicates a more recent, and therefore more advanced, CPU. Newer microprocessors offer features not found in earlier, lower numbered models from the same CPU "family."

> ✔ *Note:* As I stated earlier, DOS will run on any member of the Intel 80xxx family of microprocessors or a compatible chip from another manufacturer. As you'll learn in subsequent chapters, however, not all DOS commands work on all CPUs. Certain advanced features offered in newer versions of DOS require a 386 or higher system.

System Memory (RAM and ROM)

If you think of a CPU as the brains behind your PC, memory corresponds to the amount of "muscle" this brain has at its disposal. The more memory that is installed in your PC, the more powerful it is, and by extension, the more it's capable of accomplishing. PC memory is measured in three basic units:

- bytes
- kilobytes
- megabytes

A byte consists of eight bits. (Figuratively speaking, a bit is an electronic "switch" that can be set to either an "on" or "off" position.)

One kilobyte equals 1024 bytes. The abbreviation for kilobyte is the letter K, as in 1K. The kilobyte notation is commonly used to indicate how much memory is required to run a given program or perform a specific function.

One megabyte equals 1024 kilobytes (1024K). A simple calculation reveals that a megabyte contains more than a million bytes (1024 x 1024 = 1,048,576). One common use of the megabyte notation, abbreviated MB, is to indicate the size of a mass storage device. A 120MB hard disk, for example, is capable of storing 120 megabytes (more than 122,000K) of data.

System memory is divided into two distinct types:

- RAM
- ROM

The contents of RAM, an abbreviation for random access memory, constantly change during processing. As you use your PC, information is continuously moved into (written to) and out of (read from) RAM, as needed. RAM is sometimes called volatile memory, because its contents are lost whenever you turn off your PC.

The contents of ROM, an abbreviation for read-only memory, remain constant. Once information has been coded within ROM, a process that usually occurs before these chips are installed in your PC, it cannot be changed. ROM is generally used to hold the "permanent" instructions your PC requires to function properly. (The BIOS chip, described next, is one example of ROM.)

The Basic Input/Output System (BIOS)

The BIOS is a special ROM chip — remember, ROM stands for read-only memory — containing the basic instructions your PC uses to coordinate the activities of its various hardware components. If an application requests that a file be saved to disk, instructions contained in the BIOS chip specify how this save operation should occur. Each time a program displays information to your monitor, BIOS coordinates this task also. How similar a given system's BIOS instructions are to those used in IBM personal computers determines the level of compatibility that system maintains with the so-called IBM standard.

Input/Output Ports

One of the BIOS's primary responsibilities is managing your computer's input/output (I/O) ports. I/O ports are electronic doorways, so to speak, through which information is transferred to and from various devices.

If a program attempts to read a file, for example, your PC must know where to find the disk on which that file is stored — not its physical location, but the resources your computer sets aside to coordinate its activities. This location is represented by that disk's I/O port — the specific memory addresses through which all of its input and output operations take place.

✔ ***Note:*** Which I/O ports are already in use and which ones remain free is a critical consideration whenever you add a new piece of equipment to your system.

Expansion Slots

As mentioned earlier, many analysts believe IBM's decision to include expansion slots on the motherboard of the original IBM PC contributed greatly to that computer's early success. Expansion slots allow you to modify your computer to such a degree that, over time, it could evolve into a totally different system than the one you purchased originally.

Do you need more memory? That's easily taken care of by installing a new memory board in an open expansion slot. Would you like to replace your EGA monitor with a high-resolution VGA display? Once again, no problem. Simply remove your old EGA card from its expansion slot and replace it with one that supports VGA. By allowing you to "pick and choose" the various components installed on your PC, expansions slots provide you with an incredible amount of flexibility, much more than is available with so-called closed systems.

Secondary Storage Devices

As stated earlier, the contents of random access memory (RAM) change constantly. Furthermore, any information contained in RAM is lost each time you shut down your system. If RAM were the only place available to store programs and data, therefore, using a PC would not be very practical. You'd be forced to begin all of your work all over again each time you turned on your computer.

✔ ***Note:*** This notion is not as absurd is it sounds. The very first personal computer I ever purchased had no storage capabilities beyond RAM. Each time I turned on this machine, I had to enter completely any instructions I wanted it to execute, even if I was doing exactly the same kind of work I'd done the last time I used it. Talk about an argument against nostalgia. Few of us industry "old-timers" possess any desire to return to those "good old days."

Secondary storage devices allow you to preserve (store) a copy of your programs and data before turning off your PC. A partial list of secondary storage devices available for MS-DOS computers would include:

- floppy disks
- hard disks
- tape devices

- RAM cards
- bubble memory
- CD-ROMs
- Write-Once Read-Many (WORM) devices
- erasable optical disks

By far the most prevalent secondary storage devices in use today are the first two listed above, floppy disks and hard disks. They are the ones we'll discuss here.

Floppy Disks

Floppy disks, also called removable disks, come in all shapes and sizes. There are 5.25" disks, generally designed to hold either 360K or 1.2 megabytes of data. There are 3.5" disks, which can be formatted to store 720K or 1.44MB of data. Other kinds of floppy disks exist, but these are the two main types used on MS-DOS systems. Floppy disk drives — the devices that hold removable disks — are almost always accessible from the front panel of your PC's system unit. (See Figure 1.5.)

The biggest advantage associated with floppy disks is that they are transportable. You can remove a floppy disk from one PC and use it in a similar drive on a second unit. The biggest disadvantages associated with floppy disks are their limited storage space and lack of speed.

Figure 1.5 You can insert and remove floppy disks using disk drives that are generally accessible from the front of your system unit.

Hard Disks

Unlike floppy disks, hard disks are permanently mounted within the system unit. (Removable hard disks exist, but most PCs include the stationary type.) Some hard disks are mounted so that their front panel is visible from outside the system unit. It is more common, however, for the hard disk to be completely enclosed, safely hidden away from prying eyes and hands (see Figure 1.6).

Hard disks hold an amazing amount of information compared to a floppy disk. A 60MB hard disk, for example, can be used to store over 150 times the amount of data that will fit on a 360K floppy disk. Hard disks are also much faster than their floppy counterparts.

The biggest drawback associated with hard disks is that, because they are mounted permanently within your system unit, it's not always easy to share the files they contain with other users. Given their size, speed, and convenience, however, hard disks have become the de facto standard for disk storage. It's rare these days to find a PC system advertised that does not include a hard disk.

PC Keyboards

You use the keyboard to communicate with your PC. If you've ever used a typewriter, you should feel right at home with most PC keyboards. The fundamental design of a PC keyboard adheres to the QWERTY layout (the standard typewriter keyboard layout), used by most typewriter companies, as illustrated in Figure 1.7.

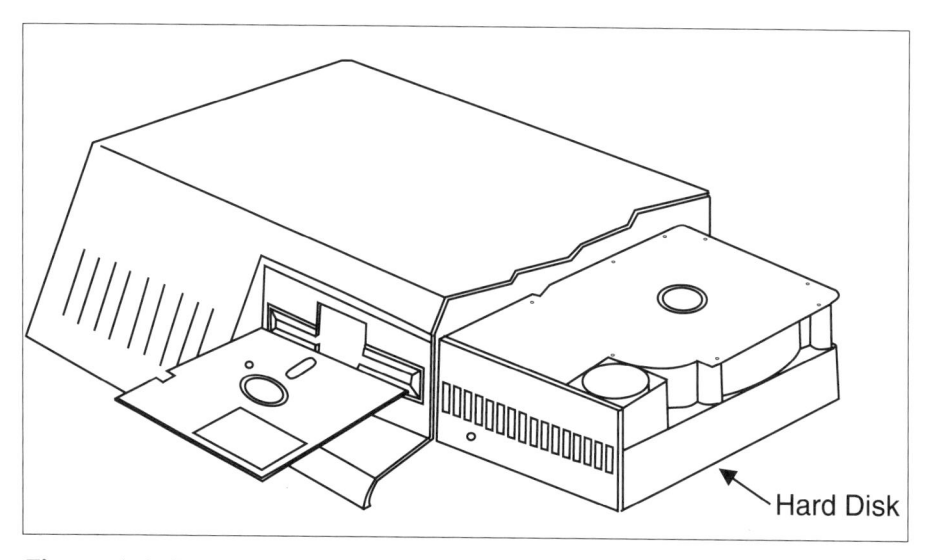

Figure 1.6 Hard disks are mounted, usually permanently, within the system unit.

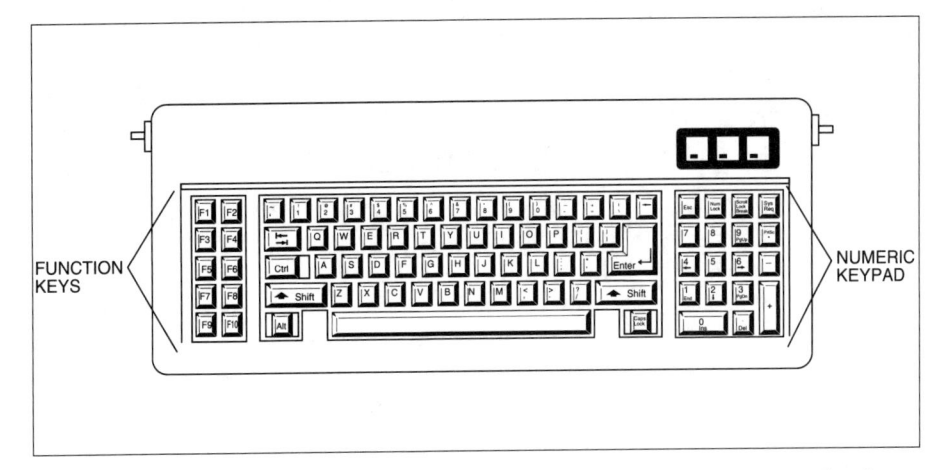

Figure 1.7 A PC keyboard is similar, but not identical to the keyboard found on a standard typewriter.

Function Keys

Though similar, PC and typewriter keyboards are not identical to one another. A PC keyboard contains several keys designed to simplify computer-specific operations.

Immediately obvious are the function keys that appear on computer keyboards. Depending on the type of keyboard you have, it will include ten or twelve function keys, labeled F1 through F10 (or alternately, F1 through F12). Many applications, including DOS, let you use these function keys to quickly initiate a wide range of predetermined operations.

Older PC keyboards positioned the function keys vertically, just to the left of the alphanumeric keys, as shown in Figure 1.7. Most newer keyboards arrange them in a horizontal row above the number keys, a design illustrated in Figure 1.8.

Shift Keys

Any experienced typist will be familiar with the Shift key. Traditional typewriters use the Shift key to differentiate between lowercase and uppercase letters, numbers and punctuation marks, etc. The Shift keys on a PC keyboard, located on either side of the central part of the keyboard and sometimes identified by an arrow pointing upwards, serves this same purpose.

A PC keyboard includes two keys that are similar to the Shift key, marked Ctrl and Alt. Many applications allow these keys to be depressed along with other keys to quickly enter certain commands or perform specific operations. Each key on a PC keyboard, therefore, can theoretically be used in four different ways:

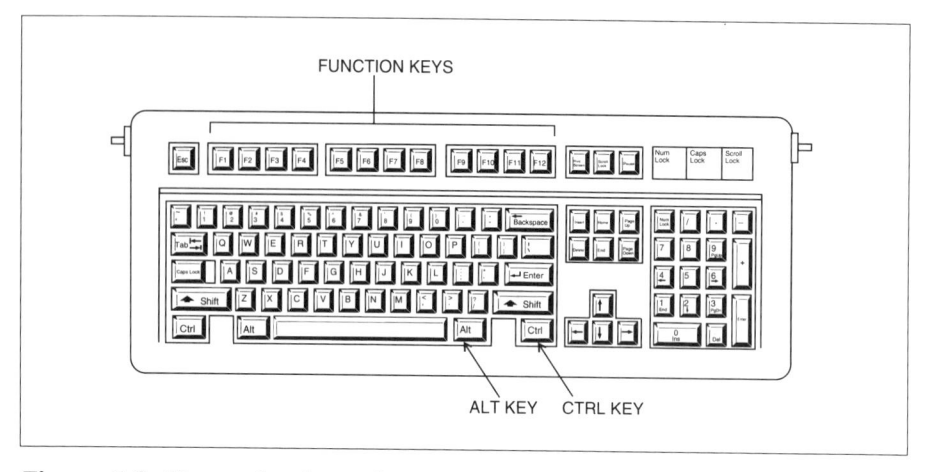

Figure 1.8 Newer keyboards arrange the function keys in a horizontal row above the number keys.

- by itself
- in a shifted position
- combined with the Ctrl key
- combined with the Alt key

✔ *Note:* As a convenience to the user, some newer PC keyboards include two Ctrl and Alt keys, one each positioned on either side of the alphanumeric keys. As is true with the two Shift keys, the second Ctrl and Alt keys duplicate their counterparts located on the opposite side of the keyboard.

The Numeric Keypad

Given the number of people who use their computers primarily for "number crunching," it only makes sense to incorporate an ersatz calculator into the design of a PC. Most PC keyboards contain a keypad that allows quick and easy entry of numbers and basic mathematical operations.

✔ *Note:* Two noticeable exceptions to this general rule are laptop and notebook computers. To reduce space requirements, a simulated numeric keypad often is "embedded" within the alphanumeric keys of such systems.

In addition to the numbers 0 through 9 and various mathematical symbols (+, -, *, /, =), the numeric keypad includes several keys used to perform specific operations. What a given key accomplishes is normally determined by the application program you are running at the time. On most word processors, for example, the Ins key is used to alternate between insert and overstrike mode. (Don't be overly concerned if you're unfamiliar with these specific terms; the critical concept here is that each key can serve different functions.)

System Keys

We'll close out our informal tour of the PC keyboard with a brief description of several special system keys found on most PC keyboards. As with the function keys, these system keys initiate a variety of computer-related activities.

The CapsLock key works much like Shift-Lock does on a traditional typewriter keyboard. Pressing CapsLock sets the alphabetic keys A through Z to uppercase mode — that is, to produce capital rather than lowercase letters by default. With CapsLock engaged, you use the Shift key to enter lowercase letters.

The NumLock key performs a similar function for the numeric keypad. With NumLock engaged, the keypad generates numeric values by default. Pressing Shift and a number key with NumLock active generates the alternate sequence for each key. For example, entering Shift-9 with NumLock active is the same as pressing the PgUp key without NumLock engaged.

> *Note:* NumLock only affects the numeric keypad. It does not affect the horizontal row of number keys positioned above the alphanumeric section of the keyboard.

The PrtSc (or Print Screen) key provides a quick and easy way to reproduce the current contents of the display on your system printer.

Monitors and Display Adapters

Do you like confusion? Well, step right up, because I have some for you. Nowhere is the diversity of PC marketplace more apparent — and potentially more confusing — than in the myriad of monitors and display adapters it supports. No fewer than six major display "standards" have surfaced for MS-DOS systems since the IBM PC was first introduced in 1981. These include, in the order of their development and initial release:

- MDA (Monochrome Display Adapter)
- CGA (Color Graphics Adapter)
- Hercules (and compatible) monochrome graphics
- EGA (Enhanced Graphics Adapter)
- VGA (Video Graphics Array)
- SVGA (Super VGA)

MDA is a monochrome, text-only display introduced with the original IBM PC. The others add graphics capabilities, with all but one — the Hercules — also supporting color.

The biggest difference between the various color graphics standards is their display resolutions. Each subsequent standard produced a more detailed image than its predecessors by increasing the number of pixels — individual points of light — an image contained. The rule here is simple: The more recent the display type, the better picture it produces. An EGA display, for example, generates an image that is 640 pixels (horizontal) × 350 pixels (vertical). With the introduction of VGA, these numbers increased to 640 × 480 pixels.

This may not sound like much of an improvement. Keep in mind, however, that the total number of pixels on a screen — and, by extension, the maximum resolution of its display — is calculated by multiplying these two figures together. An EGA display, therefore, contains only 224,000 individual pixels (640 multiplied by 350), while a VGA screen increases this number nearly one-half again, to 307,200 pixels (640 × 480). SVGA ups the ante even more with its 800 × 600 pixel array, for a total display resolution of almost one-half million (480,000) pixels. Thanks to the recent move toward graphical user interfaces (GUIs) like Microsoft Windows, newer, even more impressive color display standards continue to evolve.

Additional Hardware Options

The components described previously (the system unit, disk storage, keyboard, and display) can be found on almost all PC systems. Additional hardware options abound primarily because, as explained earlier, the inclusion of expansion slots on most MS-DOS computers greatly simplifies adding new features to your PC.

Printers

A printer lets you generate a permanent copy of your work. After pulling together their basic system, this is the optional piece of hardware users usually buy first.

PC printers come in three basic types:

- dot matrix printers
- daisy wheel printers
- laser printers

You can pick up a dot matrix printer for under $200. They are relatively fast; the quality of their output, however, leaves something to be desired.

Daisy wheel printers, on the other hand, produce documents that, for all intent and purposes, look as polished as any page printed on an electric typewriter. (This shouldn't surprise you. The print mechanisms used by these two products are identical.) Like an MDA display, however, daisy wheel printers are limited to printing text only. If the work you do requires printing graphic images, a daisy wheel printer simply won't cut it.

Several years ago, laser printers took the PC world by storm. Combining near-typeset quality with full graphics capabilities, laser printers have changed forever the way people use their PCs. The street prices for inexpensive (but still impressive) laser printers have fallen below $750. This isn't chicken feed, to be sure. It is, however, well within the budgetary constraints of many users.

Mice

The mouse is another PC peripheral that's recently come into its own. A mouse is a small pointing device that complements the keyboard as you use certain applications. Rolling the mouse around a flat surface causes a pointer on your monitor screen to move in a corresponding manner. Mice are especially convenient when you're working in a graphics-based environment like Windows, which relies heavily on "point and click" operations. To select an option in a graphics-based environment, you simply "point" the cursor at the appropriate item, then "click" a mouse button.

> **Note:** DOS 4.0 and newer DOS releases can be configured to allow a mouse to be used to initiate many DOS operations, rather than limiting mouse usage to specific application programs.

There are many variations on the basic mouse theme. Other pointing devices that can be used with your PC include a trackball (an upside-down mouse that operates while stationary), a mouse pen (it looks like a pen but works like a mouse), pen tablets (substitutes a stylus and electronic pad for pen and paper), and joysticks (similar to those used in computer games), among others.

Modems

A modem puts your PC in touch with other computers, using standard phone lines. The technical explanation of how a modem works is quite complicated. What a modem can do, however, is easy to explain: Adding a modem to your PC places the world, quite literally, at you fingertips. After you install a modem, it can be used to exchange files with other PC users, send and receive electronic mail, participate in "real-time" conferences with people from around the globe, and download software from bulletin boards and on-line information services. A modem even allows you to shop electronically, from the privacy of your own living room.

These are but a few of the additional hardware components available for MS-DOS systems. Only you can decide how many and which ones you might need — or merely want. All have their practical applications. Many, like a modem, are also extremely fun to use. Regardless of the hardware options you choose, responsibility for making them work properly lies primarily on DOS's electronic shoulders.

PC Software

Software turns your computer into a powerful productivity tool. As is true with hardware, DOS coordinates the software you use on your system. Software is so dependent on the operating system under which it is running, in fact, that programs designed for one operating system cannot be used with any other operating system. This is why, for example, you can't run DOS programs on a Macintosh computer.

The popularity of the MS-DOS operating system — those 70 million-plus users spend a lot of money on software — has resulted in literally thousands of DOS application programs entering the marketplace. These include word processors, spreadsheets, database managers, communication programs, graphics applications, desktop publishing programs, contact managers, personal information managers, appointment managers, integrated packages, programming languages, games, sales tracking tools, and more utilities than you can shake a mouse at. The one thread that ties all these programs together is DOS. It's always present, monitoring a program's activities, coordinating its operations.

> ✓ **Note:** In truth, DOS itself is really software. It just happens to be a program whose primary responsibility is to ensure that other programs run properly.

The software available for MS-DOS systems can be grouped into three main categories:

- system software
- application software
- utilities

System Software

Simply put, this is DOS. It is the software that manages your system. As stated in the previous note, DOS is nothing more than software, a series of programs and special commands that allow you to take control of your PC. As you work, you, an application program or, in some cases, DOS itself executes these commands when necessary. We'll examine the various programs comprising DOS throughout this book. Right now, however, I would like to mention three very important ones: IO.SYS, MSDOS.SYS, and COMMAND.COM.

> ✔ ***Note:*** The first two filenames listed here are used by Microsoft in its retail release of MS-DOS. Comparable programs also exist in other versions of DOS — IBM's licensed PC-DOS, licensed versions from other manufacturers, etc. — if you own one of them. Their actual filenames, however, will differ, depending upon which manufacturer has licensed the particular version of DOS you use.

Your PC's BIOS (remember, Basic Input/Output System) seeks out IO.SYS and MSDOS.SYS each time you start your system. If the BIOS routine finds these files, they're automatically loaded into system memory, thus laying the groundwork for DOS to run on your PC. The third file, COMMAND.COM, is DOS's command processor, the program responsible for coordinating any DOS operations that you request or, alternately, are initiated from within other application programs. Your computer will not start successfully unless IO.SYS and MSDOS.SYS are stored in the root directory of your boot drive during system startup.

Application Software

Application software are programs designed to perform specific tasks. You use a word processor, for example, primarily to edit text (or, "process words," in the esoteric language we call computerese — hence, the name). Similarly, a database manager makes it relatively easy to manage data. (See, none of this stuff is really that difficult to understand; it just seems that way sometimes.) As stated earlier in this section, literally thousands of application programs are sold that run under MS-DOS.

Utilities

Some people would argue that utilities should fall under system software. In the early days of DOS, when it was the only set of programs you could use to perform many DOS operations, this may have been a valid argument. Since then, however, hundreds of third-party utility programs have appeared that, to varying degrees, modify and, in some cases, improve upon the basic DOS commands. For example, there are special utility programs that allow you to "tweak" bad sectors on a disk and return them to active use, a capability DOS lacks. DOS contains utilities, to be sure (and you'll encounter many of them as we progress). Not all utilities, however, are part of DOS. For this reason, I've chosen to lump these third-party programs together and call them utilities.

Data

One final category of files that fall under DOS's domain deserves special mention. The information you generate with your PC is the most valuable resource you have. If something happens to an application program, you can always reinstall and rerun it. Even if DOS itself becomes corrupted, it can be restored. However, information — or data, to use the more common term — is irreplaceable. That phone directory of important customers you created with your database manager may lead to success or failure, but it isn't worth a plug nickel if you can't get to it when you need to. That important report you're composing with a popular word processor represents a considerable investment of time, energy, and expertise that can't be mimicked by even the most powerful application software. In short, data is the pot of gold that's buried at the rainbow's end of all your PC operations.

Oh, yeah. As you work, you store your data on disks, as files. And what assumes responsibility for managing and maintaining these data files? DOS, of course.

Are you beginning to see how important DOS is? I hope so. It is, as I mentioned at the beginning of this chapter, the foundation that supports all of your other PC activites. In the next chapter, I'll start explaining how you build that foundation as we begin examining specific DOS commands and operations.

Chapter 2

Getting to Know You: A Brief Introduction to DOS

Very shortly, you're going to begin learning about the individual DOS commands. There are more than 120 of them in MS-DOS 6.0; fewer in earlier versions. The exact number depends on how much "earlier" that earlier version appeared. As I pointed out in the previous chapter, Microsoft keeps improving DOS, adding new commands and features to each new release as the company strives to keep its premier operating system competitive and current.

Before you and DOS can become intimate friends, however, you first need to be introduced to one another. That's what this chapter is all about. Rather than diving immediately into specific commands, we're going to spend the next few pages getting our feet wet, so to speak, by examining the various ways you can communicate with DOS. We'll also see how DOS itself is always ready to offer assistance, should you ever require it.

Easy DOS It

It is now — easy that is. Once upon a time, DOS demanded a lot from its followers, more than many uninitiated users felt comfortable giving. In the early days of the PC revolution, there was only one way to tell DOS what you wanted to accomplish. This involved entering commands at the DOS system prompt, a truly daunting example of calculated obscurity.

The following command, for example, was required before you could perform a simple task such as copying a file called QBASIC.EXE from the DOS directory on drive C to a directory called BASIC on a floppy disk in drive A:

```
COPY C:\DOS\QBASIC.EXE A:\BASIC\
```

Worst of all, this command had to be entered *exactly* as it appears above. If you made one typographical error, the copy operation would be aborted or — only slightly more desirable — either the wrong file would be duplicated or the copy you were creating of that file would end up in the wrong place, possibly with the wrong name.

As this simple example illustrates, DOS was a harsh taskmaster back then. And early versions of DOS did not provide much assistance with the harsh tasks they expected you to perform. Either you knew what you were doing, or you didn't. Ironically, experienced PC users appreciate DOS's "bare-bones" design. Once you memorize the DOS commands, they offer the fastest way to accomplish a wide range of activities on your computer. Type in a short (even if potentially confusing) command, hit the Enter key, and DOS takes over, quickly and efficiently doing whatever it was that you requested it to do. For the PC neophyte, however, mastering the DOS commands could be a daunting experience indeed. Beginning with MS-DOS 4.0, Microsoft added two important features to DOS that make it much easier for inexperienced users to master this powerful operating system:

- the DOS Shell
- on-line Help for DOS commands

As mentioned in the previous chapter, DOS is really a collection of commands and special programs that you can use to control and manage your PC environment. From this perspective, DOS is not that different from any other computer program — a word processor or spreadsheet, for example.

What sets DOS apart from such programs — called *applications*, to differentiate them from an operating environment like DOS — is that it includes programs designed to help other programs run on your PC. If every application had to include all the "low-level" routines DOS uses to communicate with the various hardware components of your system, the computer industry would exist in a state of utter chaos. (Some people believe this to be the case currently. Trust me, however. Things could be worse, much worse.) DOS removes from the shoulders of applications the need to do this. Rather than starting from scratch, therefore, application programs designed to run under DOS can concentrate on their strong points (editing and formatting text with a word processor, crunching numbers with an electronic spreadsheet, and so forth), while turning over to DOS primary responsibility for coordinating the basic operations of the computer on which they are running.

A second advantage to DOS being a separate entity is that it also allows you to take direct control of your PC. After learning how to enter and use the various DOS commands, for example, you can copy a file from your hard disk to a floppy disk in drive A, as illustrated in the previous example, or send the contents of a file directly to your printer without having to load a second program to accomplish this.

Using the DOS Command Line

As stated earlier, the fastest and most efficient way to execute a DOS command is by entering it directly at the DOS system prompt. I'll concentrate primarily on this method throughout the remainder of this book as we examine and experiment with specific DOS commands. Before getting started, however, it will help if you understand how these commands are structured.

Internal vs. External DOS Commands

There are two kinds of DOS commands:

- internal DOS commands
- external DOS commands

DOS automatically loads its internal commands into memory each time you turn on your PC. Doing so makes them available at any time, from anywhere on your system. An external DOS command, on the other hand, is a separate program file that must be loaded into memory from disk, each time it is executed.

A partial listing of the DOS internal commands includes:

- COPY — used to copy files from one disk to another
- CHDIR or CD — used to change to a different default directory
- DATE — used to view and/or reset the system date recorded in your computer
- DEL — used to delete files from a disk
- DIR — used to display a listing of files on a disk
- MKDIR or MD — used to create a new directory on a disk
- PATH — used to allow you to quickly access programs not in the currently active, or default, directory
- REN — used to rename a disk file
- RMDIR or RD — used to remove an empty directory from a disk
- TIME — used to view and/or reset the system time recorded in your computer
- TYPE — used to display the contents of a file

People tend to use internal DOS commands frequently as they work within DOS. For this reason, it's quite convenient to have them immediately available in memory.

A partial listing of DOS external commands includes:

- CHKDSK — used to check the contents and status of a disk
- DISKCOMP — used to compare the contents of two disks
- FDISK — used to partition a hard disk, prior to formatting
- FORMAT — used to prepare a disk to store files
- MODE — used to change the settings of your display and a serial port and configure your printer

Normally, you'll use the external DOS commands less frequently than their internal counterparts. By not loading them into memory automatically, DOS reduces its RAM requirements, thereby freeing up more memory for other programs.

> *Note:* Like most conveniences, this one carries with it a caveat. In order to execute an external command, DOS must be able to locate the corresponding file. This means it must either be stored in the current directory or in a directory that's included in a PATH statement. (Don't worry, you'll learn what a PATH statement is and how to create one in Chapter 4, "Working With Directories.")

Filters, Switches, Options, and Parameters

A DOS command can be as simple or as complex as you want or need. At their simplest, DOS commands can consist of a single word, as in the following example, which displays an unstructured listing of files in the current directory:

```
DIR
```

This same directory command, however, could be structured to send to a printer attached to the LPT1 device on your system a listing of all BAT (batch) files located in the BATCH subdirectory of your drive C hard disk, sorted by file size, using the following command:

```
DIR C:\BATCH\*.BAT /O:S >PRN
```

> *Note:* Once again, don't panic if that second command looks like a some sort of foreign correspondence to you at this point. You'll be entering equally complex commands — and understanding exactly what they accomplish — by the time you reach the end of this book.

To support such complex operations, most DOS commands allow you to specify one or more command modifiers called filters, switches, options, and parameters. In the above DIR command, for example, the **/O:S** switch was used to organize the resulting list in ascending order, by file size. The **>PRN** redirection option then transferred the resulting file list to a printer rather than the monitor, as would normally happen when you enter a DIR command.

Structuring DOS Commands

Once we begin entering DOS commands — which we'll do in just a few paragraphs — you'll need some way of knowing what to type, in order to initiate a specific procedure. For this reason, I'll use the following conventions to explain the actual DOS commands you'll be entering throughout this book. Don't worry. I'm going to keep this extremely simple.

Commands and Values

I'll use boldface, uppercase letters to list those items that must be entered exactly as shown. This includes actual DOS commands and any specific switches required to perform a particular activity, as in the following example:

DIR

> ✔ ***Note:*** When you're entering commands on the command line, DOS does not differentiate between uppercase and lowercase letters. **DIR** and **dir** are both the same command, as far as DOS is concerned. To avoid confusion, though, I use uppercase letters to print any commands incorporated into the exercises this book contains.

Variables

Variables — values that can change depending upon what we want to accomplish — will be shown in italics, as in the following example:

DIR *filename*

In this example, the *filename* variable would be used to identify the file or group of files for which you want to see a **DIR** listing.

Optional Command Parameters

I'll enclose optional command parameters in braces, as shown in the following examples:

DIR [*disk:*][*\directory*][*\filename*]

Optional parameters are not required for a command to run. Adding an optional parameter, however, changes what happens when the command is executed. As the previous example illustrates, the DIR command can be entered alone or with a specific disk, directory, or files for which you want to see a file listing.

Keys

Any special keys you need to press will be identified by their keyboard name and shown in boldface, as in the following example, which includes instructions to press the Enter key on your keyboard:

Type **DIR >PRN**.
Press **Enter**.

Key Combinations

Some DOS procedures require that you press more than one key at the same time. Should this be the case, I'll use a plus sign (+) to separate the individual keys that must be pressed concurrently, as in the following example:

Press **Shift+F1**.

To execute this command you would hold down the Shift key while pressing the F1 function key.

That's it. Pretty simple, eh? As you'll soon realize, that word — simple — describes most DOS operations. I mean it. I know you've probably heard how difficult computers are to use, how hard it is to master DOS. But do you remember when your parents (or friends, or driving instructor, or whoever) told you this same thing about driving? And if you're like most people, those first few times behind the steering wheel were challenging, indeed. Today, however, chances are that you cruise the highways with little or no thought given to the actual steps required to start and maneuver a car. Turn the key, shift into gear, and off you go.

That's pretty much what it's like when you're learning DOS. At first, everything seems confusing and complicated. I'd be lying if I told you otherwise. The more you work in DOS, however, the easier it gets. And after a while, once you've mastered some basic concepts, instinct takes over just as it did when you were learning how to drive a car. After a while, you'll be touring the PC highways like a seasoned pro.

Using the DOS Shell

Beginning with MS-DOS 4.0, Microsoft added a new feature to DOS that makes it even easier to settle in behind the wheel of your PC, so to speak. This feature, the DOS Shell, gives DOS a new and friendlier face — literally. Rather than simply trying to describe how working within the DOS Shell differs from using the traditional DOS system prompt, let me show you.

Though DOS has evolved in several important ways since its initial release, one aspect of DOS has remained etched in electronic stone: its so-called *user interface*. From the first time the very first DOS user first turned on that first IBM PC, DOS's primary method for communicating with the outside world (meaning you) has been its drive letter system prompt — the legendary "C greater than" symbol on most systems. Figure 2.1 shows this traditional DOS system prompt. It's the C that you see at the bottom of the screen.

To be honest, there's a lot to like about the DOS system prompt. It puts you totally and directly in charge of your PC. Since it forces you to tell DOS exactly what to do, DOS does exactly what you want it to. Nothing more. Nothing less. There are no fancy icons, no frivolous pictures and no pre-existing procedures to confuse the issue. For the neophyte user, however, the system prompt's minimalist design can be infuriating. Let's face it, that "naked" C> system prompt doesn't exactly provide much information about how DOS works. For years, therefore, desperate voices within the PC community begged, "Please, give us an easier way." Starting with MS-DOS 4.0, Microsoft did.

MS-DOS versions 4.0 and higher (this includes MS-DOS 5.0 and the recently released MS-DOS 6.0) offer a feature called the DOS Shell, a graphical user interface (or GUI, pronounced "gooey") designed to simplify initiating many PC operations. If you don't believe the DOS Shell differs radically from the traditional DOS system prompt, check out Figure 2.2, which shows a typical DOS Shell display.

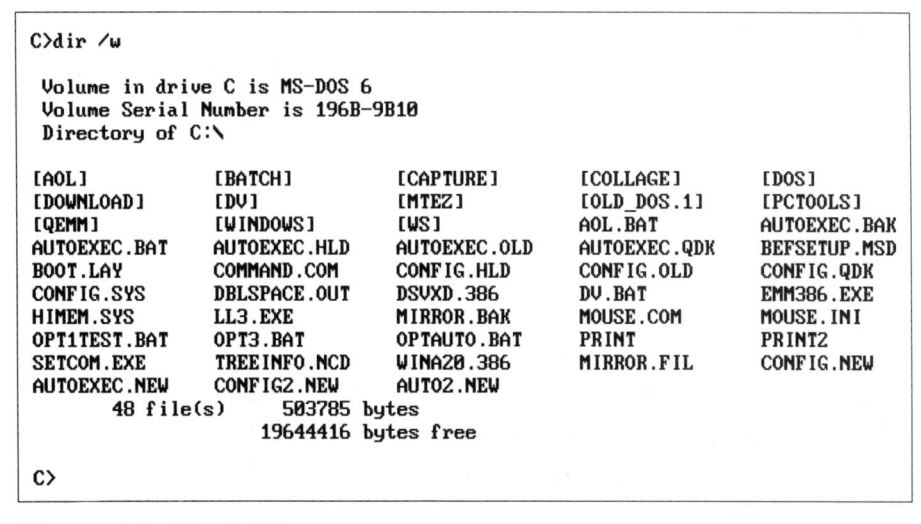

```
C>dir /w

 Volume in drive C is MS-DOS 6
 Volume Serial Number is 196B-9B10
 Directory of C:\

[AOL]            [BATCH]          [CAPTURE]        [COLLAGE]        [DOS]
[DOWNLOAD]       [DV]             [MTEZ]           [OLD_DOS.1]      [PCTOOLS]
[QEMM]           [WINDOWS]        [WS]             AOL.BAT          AUTOEXEC.BAK
AUTOEXEC.BAT     AUTOEXEC.HLD     AUTOEXEC.OLD     AUTOEXEC.QDK     BEFSETUP.MSD
BOOT.LAY         COMMAND.COM      CONFIG.HLD       CONFIG.OLD       CONFIG.QDK
CONFIG.SYS       DBLSPACE.OUT     DSVXD.386        DV.BAT           EMM386.EXE
HIMEM.SYS        LL3.EXE          MIRROR.BAK       MOUSE.COM        MOUSE.INI
OPT1TEST.BAT     OPT3.BAT         OPTAUTO.BAT      PRINT            PRINT2
SETCOM.EXE       TREEINFO.NCD     WINA20.386       MIRROR.FIL       CONFIG.NEW
AUTOEXEC.NEW     CONFIG2.NEW      AUTO2.NEW
       48 file(s)       503785 bytes
                      19644416 bytes free

C>
```

Figure 2.1   The DOS system prompt

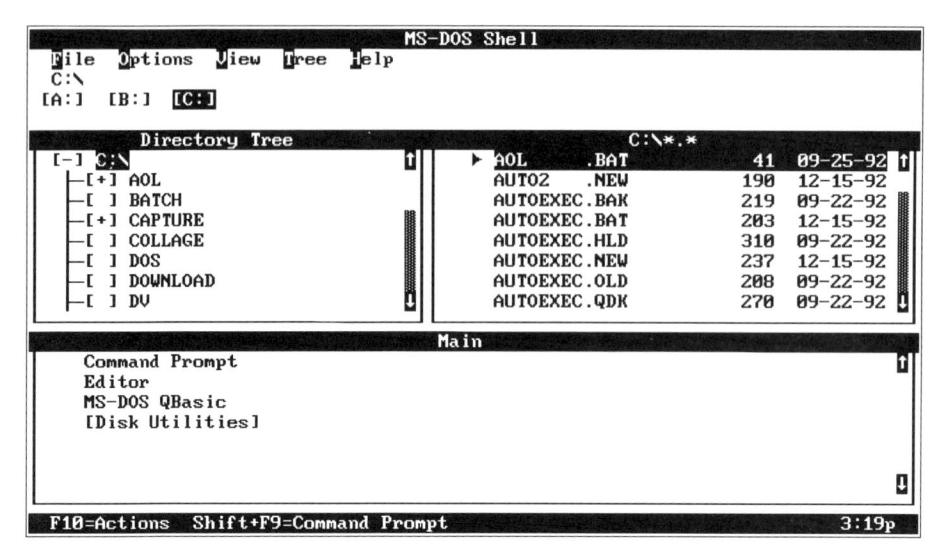

```
                          MS-DOS Shell
 File  Options  View  Tree  Help
 C:\
 [A:]   [B:]   [C:]
         Directory Tree                        C:\*.*
 [-] C:\                           ▶ AOL      .BAT       41   09-25-92
  ├─[+] AOL                          AUTO2    .NEW      190   12-15-92
  ├─[ ] BATCH                        AUTOEXEC.BAK      219   09-22-92
  ├─[+] CAPTURE                      AUTOEXEC.BAT      203   12-15-92
  ├─[ ] COLLAGE                      AUTOEXEC.HLD      310   09-22-92
  ├─[ ] DOS                          AUTOEXEC.NEW      237   12-15-92
  ├─[ ] DOWNLOAD                     AUTOEXEC.OLD      208   09-22-92
  ├─[ ] DV                           AUTOEXEC.QDK      270   09-22-92
                              Main
 Command Prompt
 Editor
 MS-DOS QBasic
 [Disk Utilities]


 F10=Actions  Shift+F9=Command Prompt                         3:19p
```

Figure 2.2 The DOS Shell

To better understand the difference between using the DOS system prompt and working in the DOS Shell, consider what happens when you place a telephone call and end up connected to that curse of modern communications, a voice-mail system. You know the kinds of systems I'm talking about, the ones where a disembodied voice comes on the line and says: "Thank you for calling X-Y-Z Incorporated. If you would like to speak to someone in Sales, press 1. If you would like to speak to someone in Marketing, press 2. If you would like to speak to someone in Billing, press 3..." and so forth.

As frustrating as this is, imagine how much worse it would be if you were given no instructions at all, but instead were expected to figure out on your own the next action required to reach the party with whom you wished to speak. (Of course, this assumes that you'll want to speak to anyone in a company that relies exclusively on machines to serve its customers. I usually don't.) It would be pretty frustrating, to say the least. Well, frustration is exactly what many people feel when they're initially confronted with the C> system prompt.

The DOS Shell assumes the role of that disembodied voice in the voice-mail system; it guides you through the DOS labyrinth. Rather than forcing you to enter long and often convoluted commands in a very precise manner, with little assistance, the DOS Shell transforms most DOS operations into interactive procedures. It does so by requesting any information DOS requires to perform a specific activity. To see what I mean, let's enter the DOS Shell and examine, in a very cursory way, how it works.

✔ > *Note:* I'm making two assumptions here. One is that you've already installed MS-DOS on your computer. If you haven't, stick a bookmark in this page and flip back to Appendix A, "Installing MS-DOS." Once you've completed that critical step, rejoin me here. You'll then be able to follow along as I demonstrate some of the conveniences offered by DOS Shell.
>
> My second assumption is that you're using MS-DOS version 4.0 or higher. If you're not, you're out of luck. Earlier releases of DOS did not include the DOS Shell. (This is another argument for upgrading to the newest DOS version, MS-DOS 6.0., which not only includes the DOS Shell but also a number of other useful features we'll examine throughout the remaining chapters of this book.)

Starting the DOS Shell

What you see each time you start your computer depends on how you instructed DOS to set itself up during installation:

- If you specified that the DOS Shell was to be loaded automatically at system startup, then you will see a screen similar to the one shown in Figure 2.2.
- If you did not tell DOS to run the DOS Shell automatically, then you will need to start it manually, after DOS completes its startup procedures and displays the system prompt.

To start the DOS Shell from the system prompt:

Type **DOSSHELL**.
Press **Enter**.

This loads the DOS Shell and displays a screen similar to the one shown in Figure 2.2.

✔ > *Note:* Figure 2.2 shows the DOS Shell display with MS-DOS 6.0 running on my computer. Undoubtedly, what you see on your monitor will differ somewhat from this figure. Specifically, other directories and filenames will be listed in your DOS Shell display. Also, the DOS Shell that shipped with MS-DOS 4.0 differs slightly from the DOS Shell included with MS-DOS 5.0 and MS-DOS 6.0.

The DOS Shell Display

The DOS Shell display is divided into several sections. These include:

- *Menu bar* — used to select and display the DOS Shell pull-down menus
- *Drive listing* — used to select the active disk drive
- *Directory tree* — used to display and select directories on the active drive.

- *File listing* — used to select and work with files stored in the current directory.
- *Program group window* — used to to select and run programs and utilities you've set up using the DOS Shell.
- *Status line* — shows the current time, as well as displaying any special commands currently available in the DOS Shell.

As mentioned earlier, our initial tour of the DOS Shell is meant to be a cursory one, at best. The majority of this book is designed to demystify working from the DOS system prompt. For now, we'll only hit the highlights of working in the DOS Shell. Appendix B, "Going Graphic: An Introduction to the DOS Shell," contains additional information about working in this relatively recent addition to DOS.

Navigating the DOS Shell

Several keys allow you to move around the DOS Shell display. These include:

- the arrow keys — used to move the highlight bar within the currently active portion of the display
- the Enter key — used to select a highlighted option
- the Esc key — used to cancel a selected option
- the Tab key — used to switch between the different areas of the DOS Shell display
- the PgUp key — used to view previous sections of information that are too large to fit in a single display window
- the PgDn key — used to view subsequent sections of information that are too large to fit in a single display window

Let's see how some of these keys work.

Changing the Active Area

We'll begin by making the file listing the active portion of the DOS Shell display:

Press **Tab** twice.

Certainly, nothing dramatic happened. If you were paying close attention, however, you probably noticed that a small arrow moved first to directory tree, then to the file listing, where it now points at the first filename in that portion of the DOS Shell display.

Next, we'll move the highlight bar to a different filename:

Press **Down Arrow** twice.

If all went as planned — and there's no reason it shouldn't have — the third filename in your file listing is highlighted, as illustrated in Figure 2.3. (Once again, remember that the actual filename highlighted on your display probably will be different than the one shown here.) With this file selected, let's look at another DOS Shell feature, its pull-down menus.

Displaying the DOS Shell Pull-down Menus

Most DOS Shell activities are initiated through pull-down menus. As a rule, you select a DOS Shell pull-down, as well as the options it contains, by entering a *mnemonic* command.

Mnemonic

Mnemonic refers to a single letter that provides some indication of the command with which it is associated. The Alt+F key combination, for example, is a mnemonic command used to display the DOS Shell File menu.

Using the File menu as an example, let's see how to display a DOS Shell menu:

Press **Alt+F**.

Remember, this notation indicates that you need to press more than one key at the same time. In this case, it's telling you to hold down the Alt key while pressing F.

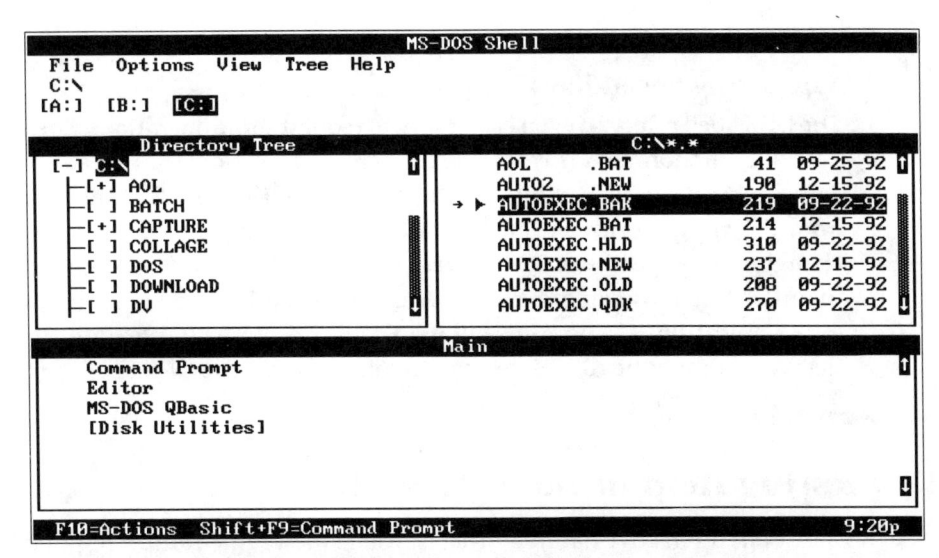

```
                          MS-DOS Shell
 File  Options  View  Tree  Help
 C:\
 [A:]   [B:]   [C:]
           Directory Tree                         C:\*.*
   [-] C:\                           AOL     .BAT      41  09-25-92
    ─[+] AOL                         AUTO2   .NEW     190  12-15-92
    ─[ ] BATCH                    → ► AUTOEXEC.BAK    219  09-22-92
    ─[+] CAPTURE                     AUTOEXEC.BAT    214  12-15-92
    ─[ ] COLLAGE                     AUTOEXEC.HLD    310  09-22-92
    ─[ ] DOS                         AUTOEXEC.NEW    237  12-15-92
    ─[ ] DOWNLOAD                    AUTOEXEC.OLD    208  09-22-92
    ─[ ] DV                          AUTOEXEC.QDK    270  09-22-92
                              Main
    Command Prompt
    Editor
    MS-DOS QBasic
    [Disk Utilities]


 F10=Actions   Shift+F9=Command Prompt                        9:20p
```

Figure 2.3 Using the keyboard to navigate the DOS Shell

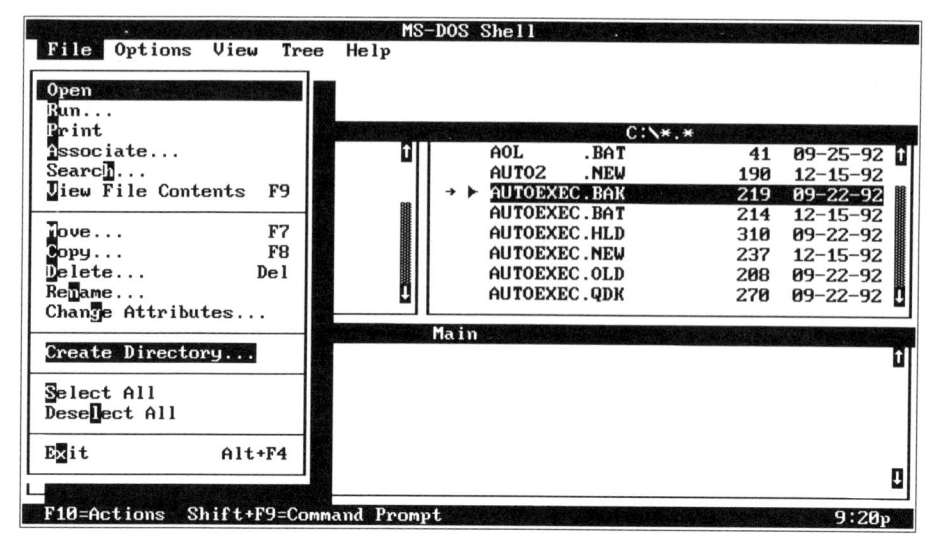

```
                        MS-DOS Shell
 File  Options  View  Tree  Help
┌─────────────────────────┐
│Open                     │
│Run...                   │                    C:\*.*
│Print                    │
│Associate...             │ │   AOL      .BAT      41   09-25-92
│Search...                │ │   AUTO2    .NEW     190   12-15-92
│View File Contents    F9 │→►  AUTOEXEC.BAK      219   09-22-92
│                         │    AUTOEXEC.BAT      214   12-15-92
│Move...              F7  │    AUTOEXEC.HLD      310   09-22-92
│Copy...              F8  │    AUTOEXEC.NEW      237   12-15-92
│Delete...            Del │    AUTOEXEC.OLD      208   09-22-92
│Rename...                │    AUTOEXEC.QDK      270   09-22-92
│Change Attributes...     │
├─────────────────────────┤            Main
│Create Directory...      │
│                         │
│Select All               │
│Deselect All             │
├─────────────────────────┤
│Exit             Alt+F4  │
└─────────────────────────┘
 F10=Actions  Shift+F9=Command Prompt                      9:20p
```

Figure 2.4 You use pull-down menus to initiate most DOS Shell operations.

The Alt+F key combination displays the File menu shown in Figure 2.4. This menu contains the DOS Shell options that allow you to manage the files stored on your disks. Notice that each of the File options contains a highlighted letter. These letters indicate the key you would press to select a specific option from the File menu. This early in the game, you may not recognize what kind of activity each of these options represents. That's okay, though. The DOS Shell itself stands ready to provide this information.

> *Tip:* Using Speed Keys
>
> The DOS Shell offers an even easier way to request some operations. Speed keys are function keys (F1, F2, etc.), other special keys (Del, Esc, etc.) or key combinations that allow you to bypass the DOS Shell menus and immediately perform certain activities such copying or deleting files, changing the appearance of the directory tree, exiting the DOS Shell, and so forth. When available, a speed key is listed on a DOS Shell menu next to the operation it is used to initiate. Figure 2.4, for example, indicates that you can use the Alt+F4 key combination to exit the DOS Shell.

Requesting Help in the DOS Shell

Because of its interactive nature — that is, you request something, it responds — the DOS Shell makes certain assumptions about what operation it is you are attempting to perform. As an added bonus, this interactive design also allows the DOS Shell to provide, on demand, information about how a specific operation works. This is called *on-line, context-sensitive help*, in the PC vernacular. For example, to request additional information about the currently highlighted option on the DOS Shell File menu:

Press **F1**.

This displays a DOS Shell Help message shown in Figure 2.5. Because the Open option on the File menu was highlighted when you pressed F1, the DOS Shell displays information about this operation. (This explains why the DOS Shell Help system is described as being context-sensitive; the on-line portion of that description should be relatively easy to figure out.)

To remove the Open help message:

Press **Esc**.

Dialog Boxes

Standard DOS — that is, the DOS system prompt — is a *reactive* command processor. As I've pointed out several times, it depends entirely on the commands you input to determine what it is you wish to accomplish. By contrast, as I've also mentioned previously, the DOS Shell can make certain assumptions about your intentions and even provide assistance when possible. It is, to use the term I introduced at the time, *interactive* in nature. To see what I mean:

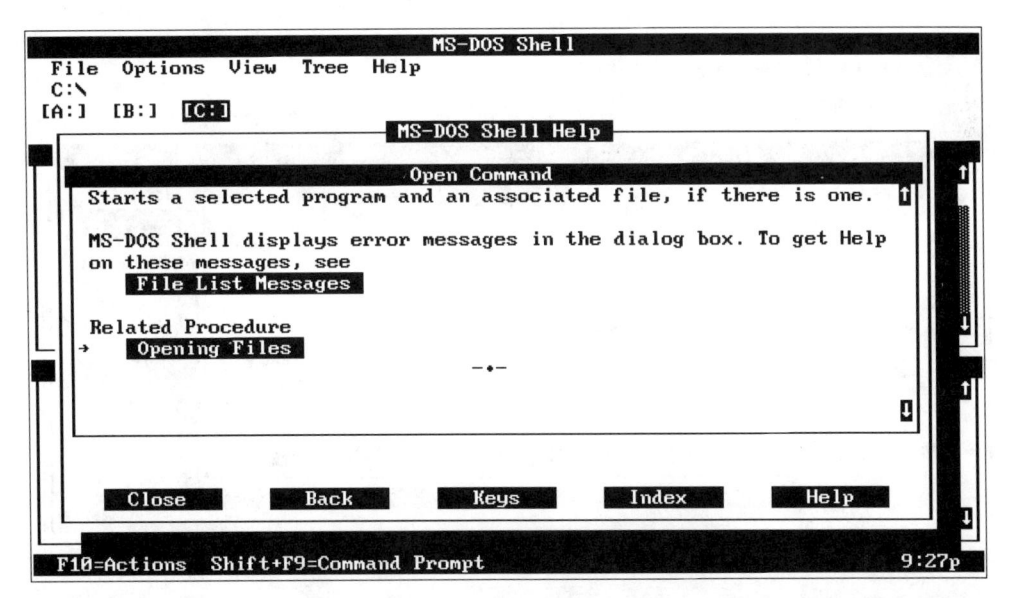

```
                          MS-DOS Shell
 File    Options   View   Tree    Help
 C:\
 [A:]   [B:]   [C:]
                         ┌─── MS-DOS Shell Help ───┐
                         │      Open Command       │
                         │ Starts a selected program and an associated file, if there is one. │
                         │                         │
                         │ MS-DOS Shell displays error messages in the dialog box. To get Help │
                         │ on these messages, see  │
                         │   File List Messages    │
                         │                         │
                         │ Related Procedure       │
                         │ → Opening Files         │
                         │                         │
                         │        —•—              │
                         │                         │
                         │                         │
                         │  Close   Back   Keys   Index   Help │
                         └─────────────────────────┘
 F10=Actions   Shift+F9=Command Prompt                              9:27p
```

Figure 2.5 The DOS Shell provides context-sensitive help for many of its operations.

If necessary, press **Alt+F** to redisplay the File menu.
Press **Down Arrow** until the **Copy** option is highlighted.
Press **Enter**.

This displays the Copy File dialog box shown in Figure 2.6. The DOS Shell uses dialog boxes to gather any information it requires to complete a requested operation. In this case, for example, the dialog box is asking you to identify two items:

- You use the **From:** prompt to identify the file you want to copy.
- You use the **To:** prompt to identify where you want this file copied to.

You'll also notice that the the name of the currently highlighted file already has been inserted into the **From:** field (AUTOEXEC.BAK in Figure 2.6). This is another example of the DOS Shell's interactive design. It assumes, unless told otherwise, that you want the specified operation to be carried out on the currently selected file.

To remove the Copy File dialog box:

Press **Esc**.

A Mouse in the DOS House

Although the DOS Shell is easy to manage from your keyboard, it's even easier to use if your system includes a mouse. Selecting options in the DOS Shell with a mouse is a simple, two-step "point-and-click" operation:

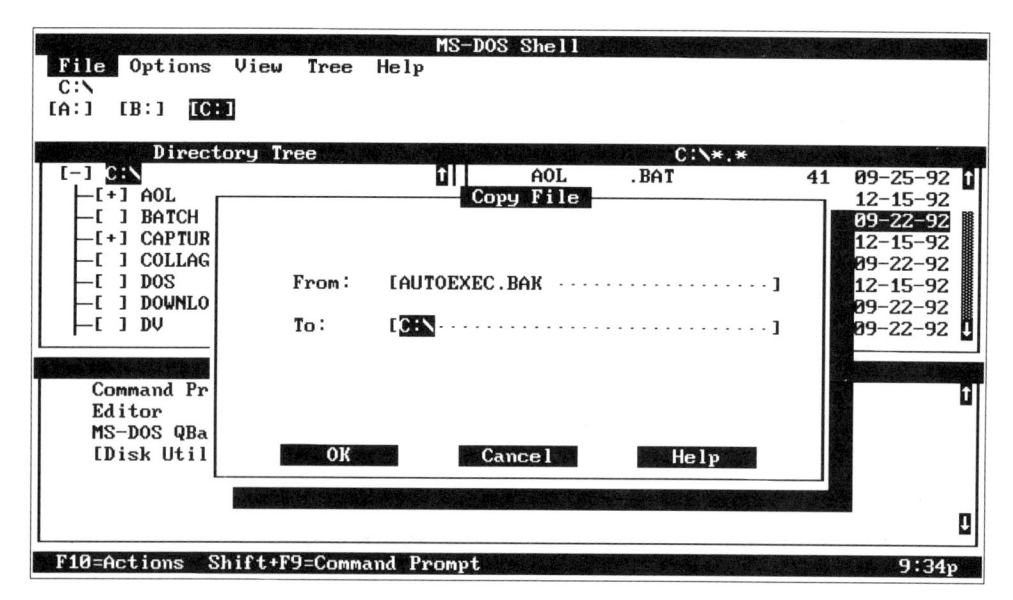

```
                         MS-DOS Shell
 File  Options  View  Tree  Help
  C:\
 [A:]  [B:]  [C:]
          Directory Tree                       C:\*.*
 [-] C:\                        ↑        AOL      .BAT      41  09-25-92 ↑
   ├[+] AOL                         ┌─ Copy File ─┐           12-15-92
   ├[ ] BATCH                       │             │           09-22-92
   ├[+] CAPTUR                      │             │           12-15-92
   ├[ ] COLLAG                      │             │           09-22-92
   ├[ ] DOS              From:  [AUTOEXEC.BAK ············]   12-15-92
   ├[ ] DOWNLO                                                 09-22-92
   └[ ] DV               To:    [C:\ ······················]  09-22-92

  Command Pr                                                              ↑
  Editor
  MS-DOS QBa
  [Disk Util        ┌─ OK ─┐      ┌─ Cancel ─┐      ┌─ Help ─┐

                                                                          ↓
 F10=Actions   Shift+F9=Command Prompt                            9:34p
```

Figure 2.6 The DOS Shell uses dialog boxes to gather the information it requires to complete an operation.

1. Move your mouse around until an on-screen arrow is pointing at the option you wish to select.
2. Click (that is, press and release) the left mouse button.

✔ *Note:* Before you can use a mouse with the DOS Shell, you'll need to load its device driver into your computer's memory.

Device Driver

This term refers to special programs that allow MS-DOS to recognize and control a specific piece of equipment, such as a mouse, a scanner, a CD-ROM device, and the like. Such devices usually include the required device driver on a disk that accompanies them. Chapter 6, "Working with Devices and Drivers," contains more information about how drivers work and how you load them into memory.

Once the DOS Shell knows that a mouse is connected to your system, it can be used to perform the following mouse-related activities:

Point	Maneuvering your mouse until the onscreen mouse pointer points to an item on the DOS Shell display
Click	Pressing and releasing the mouse button
Click on	Pointing to an item on the screen and then clicking the mouse button
Double-click	Pressing and releasing the mouse button twice in quick succession
Drag	Holding down the mouse button as you move the pointer around the DOS Shell display

Most people who use a mouse find it to be more intuitive and convenient than controlling a computer exclusively from the keyboard.

Quitting the DOS Shell

As stated earlier, my primary goal in this book is to help you get the most bang for your buck out of your computer, using the various features available in DOS. Although the DOS Shell provides a practical way to familiarize yourself with DOS's basic commands and capabilities — and some people may even find it possible to work exclusively from within the DOS Shell — tapping the true

38   DOS 6.0 HANDBOOK

power of DOS requires that you know how to execute DOS commands directly. Now that we've covered some of the more fundamental aspects of the DOS Shell, therefore, let's leave this graphics-based interface and return to the unadorned yet unbelievably powerful system prompt.

To exit the DOS Shell:

Press **Alt+F** to display the **File** menu.
Press **X** to select the **Exit** option.

> ✔ ***Note:*** Remember, anyone interested in exploring the DOS Shell further can do so by flipping back to Appendix B, "Going Graphic: An Introduction to the DOS Shell."

Getting Help with DOS

Several times already, I've alluded to the fact that DOS traditionally left users hanging, offering little in the way of information as to how specific operations are performed. (Of course, I'm speaking primarily of users working at the "naked" DOS system prompt. As you saw in the previous section, the context-sensitive Help feature is readily available, quite literally, at your fingertips whenever you're working in the DOS Shell.) Little by little, over the past few DOS releases, Microsoft has been working to eliminate this frustration.

Using the /? Switch

MS-DOS 5.0 introduced the HELP command, which could be used to request that DOS display a listing of commands, along with a brief description of what each one accomplished. MS-DOS 5.0 also allowed you to enter a command followed by a question mark switch, in the following format:

```
DIR /?
```

DOS does not execute commands that are followed by the question mark switch (/?). Rather, it recognizes this switch as a request to display more information about how a command works, what it does, and how it is entered. MS-DOS 6.0 also supports the question mark switch. To see what I mean, try the following:

Type **DIR /?**.
Press **Enter**.

Your screen should now resemble Figure 2.7. Notice that the information contained in this screen pertains specifically to DIR, the command you entered along with the /? switch. Take a moment to examine the information Figure 2.7 contains. It includes:

```
Displays a list of files and subdirectories in a directory.

DIR [drive:][path][filename] [/P] [/W] [/A[[:]attribs]] [/O[[:]sortord]]
    [/S] [/B] [/L] [/C]

  [drive:][path][filename]   Specifies drive, directory, and/or files to list.
  /P        Pauses after each screenful of information.
  /W        Uses wide list format.
  /A        Displays files with specified attributes.
  attribs   D  Directories         R  Read-only files         H  Hidden files
            S  System files        A  Files ready to archive  -  Prefix meaning "not"
  /O        List by files in sorted order.
  sortord   N  By name (alphabetic)        S  By size (smallest first)
            E  By extension (alphabetic)   D  By date & time (earliest first)
            G  Group directories first     -  Prefix to reverse order
            C  By compression ratio (smallest first)
  /S        Displays files in specified directory and all subdirectories.
  /B        Uses bare format (no heading information or summary).
  /L        Uses lowercase.
  /C        Displays file compression ratio if on a compressed drive.

Switches may be preset in the DIRCMD environment variable.  Override
preset switches by prefixing any switch with - (hyphen)--for example, /-W.

C>
```

Figure 2.7 The /? switch allows you to request information about a specific DOS command.

- a description of what the DIR command accomplishes
- the correct command syntax for entering the DIR command, including any filters, switches, options, or parameters it supports
- a brief description of these various command elements
- an additional comment explaining that the default format of directory listings can be overridden with the DIRCMD variable

Okay, so maybe this single message screen doesn't include *all* of the information someone just learning DOS needs to use the DIR command effectively. But it sure beats nothing, which is exactly what DOS offered in the way of assistance before adding the /? switch to its command structure. Anyone who purchased MS-DOS 5.0 was bound to appreciate this new feature. And the news gets even better for MS-DOS 6.0 users.

DOS Help Finally Comes of Age

Beginning with MS-DOS 6.0, it's finally possible to request *comprehensive* information on virtually every DOS command. The key to this capability is DOS's new and vastly improved HELP command. How improved is Help in DOS 6.0? To find out:

Type **HELP**.
Press **Enter**.

Your screen should now resemble Figure 2.8. At first glance, this appears to be little more than a simple command listing. In actuality, though, it's an electronic

40   DOS 6.0 HANDBOOK

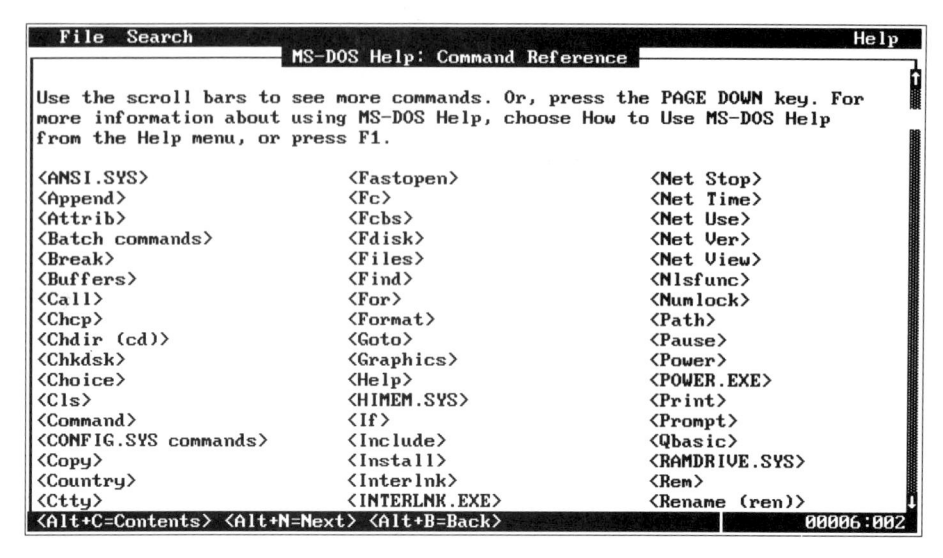

```
┌─ File  Search ──────────────────────────────────────────── Help ─┐
│                      MS-DOS Help: Command Reference              │
├──────────────────────────────────────────────────────────────────┤
│ Use the scroll bars to see more commands. Or, press the PAGE DOWN key. For │
│ more information about using MS-DOS Help, choose How to Use MS-DOS Help    │
│ from the Help menu, or press F1.                                 │
│                                                                  │
│ <ANSI.SYS>              <Fastopen>            <Net Stop>         │
│ <Append>                <Fc>                  <Net Time>         │
│ <Attrib>                <Fcbs>                <Net Use>          │
│ <Batch commands>        <Fdisk>               <Net Ver>          │
│ <Break>                 <Files>               <Net View>         │
│ <Buffers>               <Find>                <Nlsfunc>          │
│ <Call>                  <For>                 <Numlock>          │
│ <Chcp>                  <Format>              <Path>             │
│ <Chdir (cd)>>           <Goto>                <Pause>            │
│ <Chkdsk>                <Graphics>            <Power>            │
│ <Choice>                <Help>                <POWER.EXE>        │
│ <Cls>                   <HIMEM.SYS>           <Print>            │
│ <Command>               <If>                  <Prompt>           │
│ <CONFIG.SYS commands>   <Include>             <Qbasic>           │
│ <Copy>                  <Install>             <RAMDRIVE.SYS>     │
│ <Country>               <Interlnk>            <Rem>              │
│ <Ctty>                  <INTERLNK.EXE>        <Rename (ren)>>    │
├──────────────────────────────────────────────────────────────────┤
│<Alt+C=Contents> <Alt+N=Next> <Alt+B=Back>              00006:002 │
└──────────────────────────────────────────────────────────────────┘
```

Figure 2.8 MS-DOS 6.0 includes a comprehensive Help system.

doorway through which lies a wealth of information on almost any activity that can be performed using the various DOS commands.

Elements of the Help Display

The main Help display resembles the DOS Shell in that it is divided into several sections. These include:

- *Menu bar* — used to select and display the pull-down Help menus
- *Message window* — used to display the initial command listing and any subsequent information you request on a specific command or DOS procedure
- *Status line* — shows the keyboard commands used to navigate Help quickly

Navigating the Help Display

Several keyboard commands are available to navigate Help. These include:

- **the arrow keys** — used to move the cursor within the currently active portion of the display
- **Enter** — used to select a highlighted command or option
- **Esc** — used to remove a menu or cancel a requested operation
- **Tab** — used to move across columns within the message window
- **PgUp** — used to view previous sections of information that are too large to fit in a single display window
- **PgDn** — used to view subsequent sections of information that are too large to fit in a single display window

- **Alt+F** — used to display the pull-down File menu
- **Alt+S** — used to display the pull-down Search menu
- **Alt+H** — used to display the pull-down Help menu
- **Alt+C** — used to return to the initial command listing shown in Figure 2-8
- **Alt+N** — used to recall the next screen in a Help sequence
- **Alt+B** — used to move back one screen in the current sequence of Help messages

Requesting Help for a Command

Notice that, at the top of Figure 2.8, the Help display is identified as a Command Reference. That's an apt description. As I mentioned earlier, you use this display to request comprehensive information on virtually any DOS operation. A few quick keystrokes will give you a basic idea of how the MS-DOS 6.0 Command Reference feature works. Try the following:

Press **PgDn** to display the next section of the command listing in the Help message window.
Use **Down Arrow** to highlight the DIR command.
Press **Enter**.

Figure 2.9 shows the initial Help message for the DIR command. This first screen contains some of the same information that was revealed when you used the /? switch earlier to request help with DIR (see Figure 2-7). Notice, however, that the Command Reference expands upon much of the information included in that earlier message. Notice, also, that two additional Help categories are available for DIR:

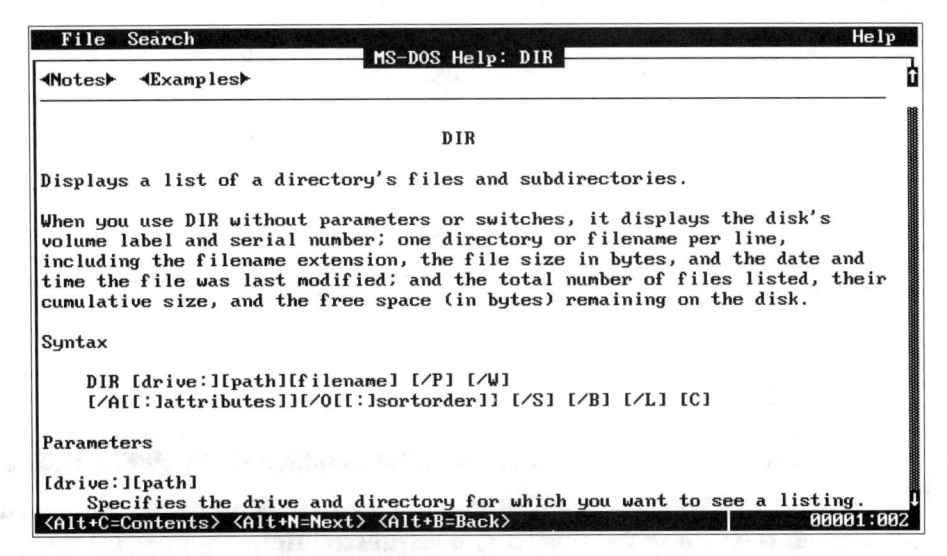

```
 File  Search                                                      Help
                         MS-DOS Help: DIR
 ◄Notes► ◄Examples►
 ─────────────────────────────────────────────────────────────────────
                                   DIR

 Displays a list of a directory's files and subdirectories.

 When you use DIR without parameters or switches, it displays the disk's
 volume label and serial number; one directory or filename per line,
 including the filename extension, the file size in bytes, and the date and
 time the file was last modified; and the total number of files listed, their
 cumulative size, and the free space (in bytes) remaining on the disk.

 Syntax

     DIR [drive:][path][filename] [/P] [/W]
     [/A[[:]attributes]][/O[[:]sortorder]] [/S] [/B] [/L] [C]

 Parameters

 [drive:][path]
     Specifies the drive and directory for which you want to see a listing.
 <Alt+C=Contents> <Alt+N=Next> <Alt+B=Back>                    00001:002
```

Figure 2.9 The initial DIR Help message

- Notes — used to display specific information about what a command accomplishes, how it works, and any special restrictions you need to be aware of relating to that command
- Examples — used to display actual examples of the command entered to accomplish specific tasks

And there's still one more convenient feature associated with the Command Reference. To see this last feature, Press **PgDn** several times, until you reach the last screen of the initial DIR message. (Go ahead and read some of the intermediate information, if you want. I'll wait.)

After pressing **PgDn** four or five times, your screen will resemble Figure 2.10. Notice the section at the bottom of this screen, following the Related Command heading. This information appears with any commands for which it is appropriate. When available, it contains a brief description of any DOS commands that perform a task related to the one for which you have requested Help. Better still, DOS makes it easy to request additional information on these related commands, when they're available. To see how:

Press **Tab** to move the cursor to the **TREE** command in the Related Command section.
Press **Enter**.

Selecting a related command causes DOS to display automatically information about that command, as illustrated in Figure 2.11. This feature, called *hypertext*,

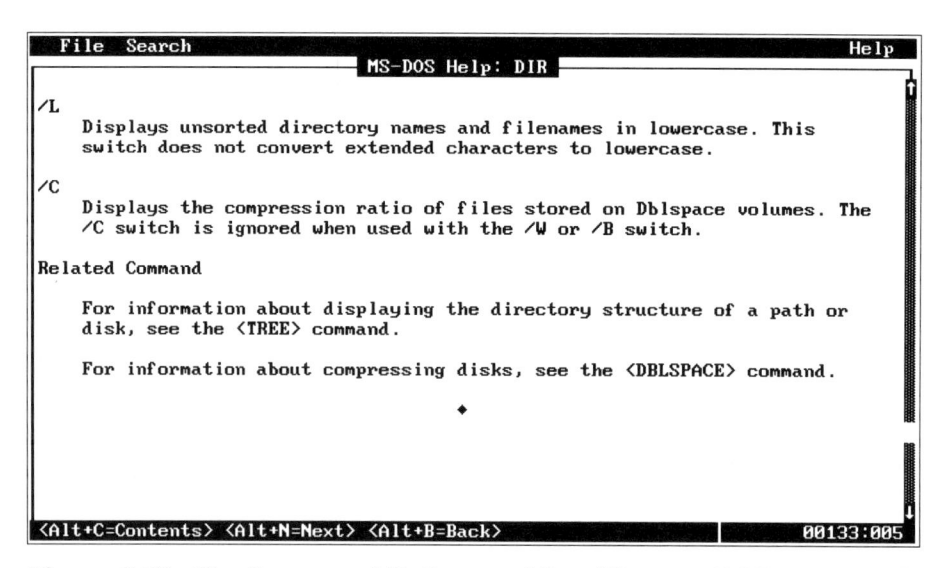

```
┌─File  Search─────────────────────────────────────────────────Help─┐
│                      ┌─MS-DOS Help: DIR─┐                          │
│ /L                                                                 │
│     Displays unsorted directory names and filenames in lowercase. This
│     switch does not convert extended characters to lowercase.
│ /C
│     Displays the compression ratio of files stored on Dblspace volumes. The
│     /C switch is ignored when used with the /W or /B switch.
│ Related Command
│
│     For information about displaying the directory structure of a path or
│     disk, see the <TREE> command.
│
│     For information about compressing disks, see the <DBLSPACE> command.
│
│                                  ♦
│
│
│
│
│
│ <Alt+C=Contents> <Alt+N=Next> <Alt+B=Back>              00133:005 │
└────────────────────────────────────────────────────────────────────┘
```

Figure 2.10 The Command Reference identifies any DOS commands related to the one for which you requested Help.

allows you to follow a thread through the Help Command Reference until you find the information you're looking for on a specific activity.

Any science fiction fans out there looking for a way to picture how hypertext works need look no further than that mainstay of modern sci-fi plotting, the wormhole. Just as a wormhole allows fictional spaceships to instantly reach distant galaxies, hypertext lets you travel from one location to another without having to traverse the normal distance between the two. Think about it: With your screen displaying information about the DIR command, you could have requested information about the TREE command by pressing Alt+C and returning to the main Help command list. Selecting TREE from within the Related Command section of the DIR command, however, took you immediately to the TREE Command Reference, bypassing this intermediate step.

Searching Help on a Topic

The new MS-DOS 6.0 Help feature also lets you initiate an organized search for information on a specific topic. Suppose, for example, that you are looking for the DOS command that allows you to recover your data, should you ever accidentally format a hard disk.

✔ *Note:* For now, don't worry about what all of this technical gobbledygook means, if you don't already know. You'll learn how to format disks in the next chapter, which is called, appropriately enough, "Working with Disks."

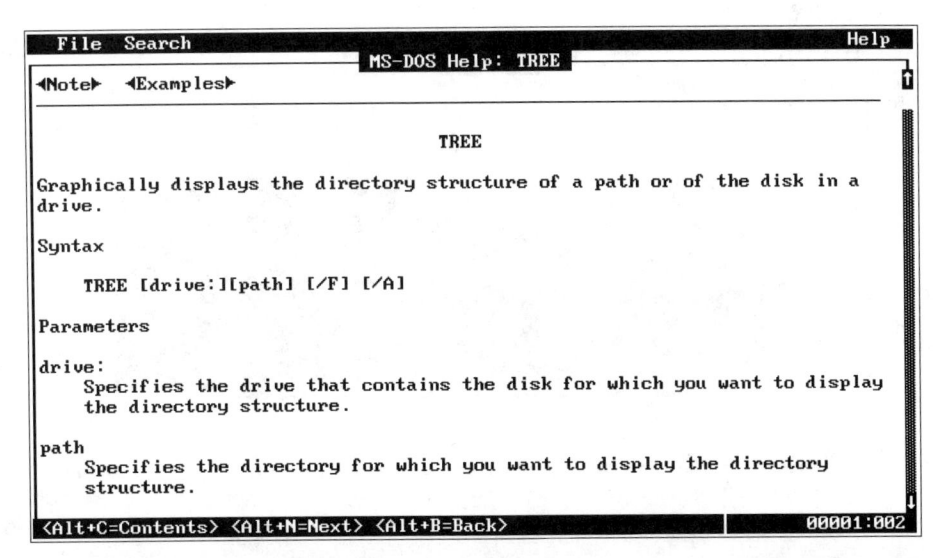

Figure 2.11 Built-in linkages make it easy to request additional information about related commands.

One way to find out this information would be to examine every DOS command that references the phrase "hard disk." Let's do this.

Press **Alt+S** to display the Search menu.
Press **F** to select the Find option.

Help displays the Find dialog box, shown in Figure 2.12. You use this dialog box to enter the word or phrase you want DOS to look for within the Help Command Reference. To display information relating to hard disks:

Type **hard disk**.
Press **Enter** to accept OK and initiate the search.

A few seconds later, you'll see a message screen containing information pertaining to the UNDELETE command. This could be the command we're looking for, but let's assume it's not. To find the next occurrence of "hard disk" in the Command Reference:

Press **Alt+S** to display the Search menu.
Press **R** to select the Repeat Last Find option.

The next occurrence of "hard disk" Help finds is in the UNFORMAT command, as shown in Figure 2.13. Offhand, I'd say we've found the information we were looking for, wouldn't you?

Those of you already familiar with DOS may be surprised that the first appearance of "hard disk" that Help located was way back in the U section of the DOS commands. What about commands like FORMAT and FDISK, to name

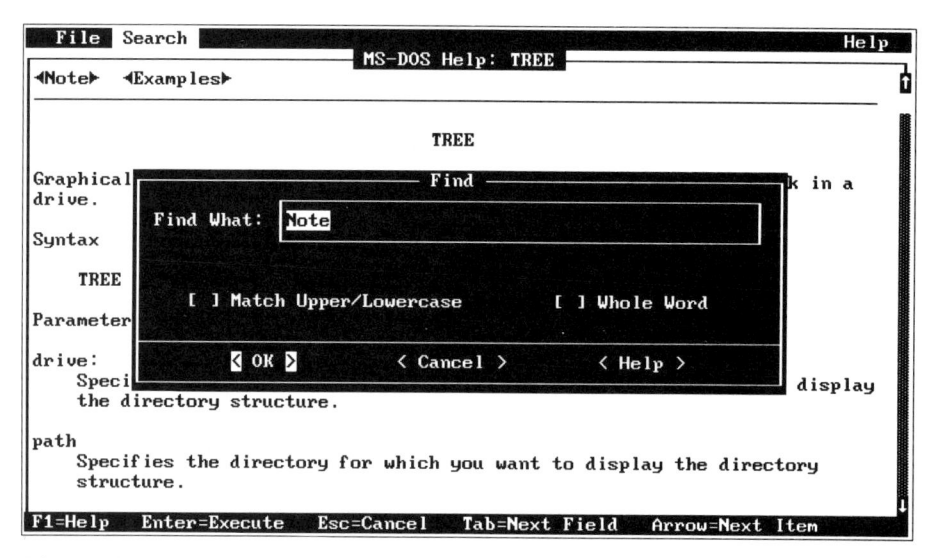

Figure 2.12 The Find option lets you search the Command Reference for specific information.

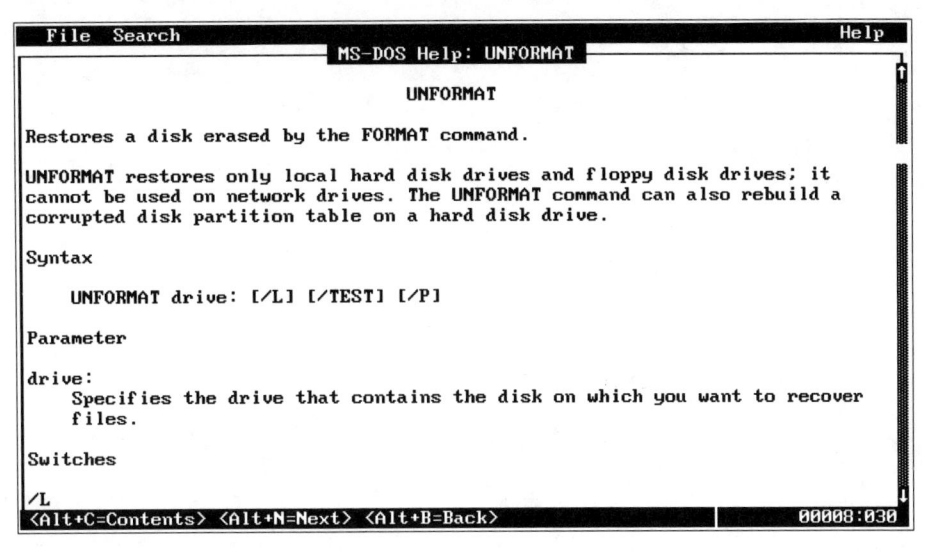

```
 File  Search                                                    Help
                    ┌─ MS-DOS Help: UNFORMAT ─┐
                               UNFORMAT
 Restores a disk erased by the FORMAT command.

 UNFORMAT restores only local hard disk drives and floppy disk drives; it
 cannot be used on network drives. The UNFORMAT command can also rebuild a
 corrupted disk partition table on a hard disk drive.

 Syntax

     UNFORMAT drive: [/L] [/TEST] [/P]

 Parameter

 drive:
     Specifies the drive that contains the disk on which you want to recover
     files.

 Switches

 /L
 <Alt+C=Contents>  <Alt+N=Next>  <Alt+B=Back>             00008:030
```

Figure 2.13   You use the Repeat Last Find option to display the next occurrence of the specified word or phrase.

but two? The explanation to this one is simple. Whenever you initiate a Search, Help starts alphabetically from whatever command is currently displayed. Once you realize that Help started looking there, it's no longer surprising that UNDELETE was the first command it found that referenced "hard disk."

> *Tip:* Help Speed Keys
> The eagle-eyed among you probably noticed the F3 notation next to the Repeat Last Find option. Like the DOS Shell, Help also provides speed keys that let you quickly perform specific activities. No doubt you'll become familiar with these as you use Help.

Exiting Help

As you can see, the new Help feature in MS-DOS 6.0 is an invaluable ally in your efforts to learn about DOS. Of course, the truly invaluable aspects of DOS surface when you begin actually using all those commands we've been requesting Help for in this section. That's exactly what we'll do in the next chapter. But first, let's leave Help and return to the DOS system prompt. To exit Help:

Press **Alt+F** to display the **File** menu.
Press **X** to select the **Exit** option.

Chapter 3

Working with Disks

As I pointed out in Chapter 1, the DOS in MS-DOS stands for *disk operating system*. Given this fact, I can't think of a more logical place to begin our hands-on examination of MS-DOS than with those commands that perform disk-related operations. (I'm not often accused of being logical, so enjoy it while it lasts.) And the most logical place to begin this beginning is by explaining what disks are, what they do, and how they work.

This chapter and the two that follow form a trilogy of sorts, with each chapter examining a different aspect of how DOS helps you organize and manage the information stored on your disks. This chapter introduces and describes the various DOS commands used to manipulate individual disks and the drives associated with them. In Chapter 4 we move down one level in a typical disk/file structure and examine those DOS commands that allow you to create and manage directories — smaller sections of a disk that make it easier to keep track of your program and data files. Finally, in Chapter 5, we'll look at the commands DOS provides to help you manage the individual files stored in the directories that exist on the disks that we'll discuss in this chapter.

> ✔ **Note:** I realize that this early in the game, all of this may sound complicated. Trust me, it isn't. Come back and reread the previous paragraph after you finish Chapter 5, and I can assure you that it will make perfect sense.

Don't "Dis" Your Disks

Disks are arguably the most critical component of any computer system. Come to think of it, there really *isn't* any argument with that statement. Disks *are* the most critical component of any computer system. Why? Because disks contain the programs and, even more important, the data files that together comprise the most valuable asset on your PC.

If a monitor stops working, you can always replace it. If a keyboard fails, you simply plug in a new one. Were your system unit to melt down tomorrow into an unrecognizable slag heap, other computers are lined up on the showroom shelves waiting to take its place. (Furthermore, given the speed with which PC technology advances, chances are those "other computers" would offer far more power at a much lower price than the one they'd supplant.)

To be sure, each of these disasters would be an inconvenience. And recovering from any one of them would require reaching down into your pocket and pulling out some hard-earned shekels to purchase the appropriate piece of new equipment. But hardware is replaceable. As a general rule, it's also possible to reinstall the application programs that generate your data, although doing so can be a frustrating and time-consuming proposition.

Should an irreplaceable data file ever be irrevocably destroyed, however... well, let's just say that this would be a true catastrophe, in every sense of the word. The reliability of your disks is all that stands between you and this potential disaster. Adding to their importance is the fact that, without disks, your PC would be more trouble to use than it's worth.

Disks: The Ultimate Office Organizer

As pointed out in Chapter 1, the contents of your computer's memory are erased each time it's turned off. Without some method of saving the work you've performed that day, therefore, you would have to start all over again each time you restarted your PC.

Enter the ever-so-humble yet oh-so-critical computer disk. It is what allows you to preserve and, even more important, organize your program and data files.

Compare your computer system to a typical office. Within this imaginary office, the system unit itself is not unlike a desk or other workspace. It's where you organize the various items you'll work with during a typical day.

If you're like most people, one of the first things you do each morning is gather together on your desktop any information required to begin that day's first project. The PC analog of this activity is loading programs and data files into your computer's memory. (Extending this metaphor back a step, turning on your computer compares to unlocking your office door at the beginning of the day.)

But where do you find all of this information? Chances are your desk has drawers. Your office probably contains a file cabinet or two (or five, if it's as cluttered as mine), as well. These various locations, which allow you to organize and store the materials you work with over the course of a normal day — assuming there is such a thing as a "normal" day — correspond to the disks and disk drives within your personal computer.

Floppy Disks vs. Hard Disks

Chapter 1 contained a brief discussion of how floppy disks and hard disks differ from one another. There are advantages and disadvantages associated with each.

Floppy disks are limited in how much data they can hold. They are, however, quite portable. It's easy to take a floppy disk out of one computer and transfer it, along with any files it contains, to a similar disk drive on another computer.

By contrast, a hard disk can store vast quantities of information. Today's 60-, 120- and 240-megabyte hard disks hold several hundred times as much data as a floppy disk. Unlike their highly mobile counterparts, however, most hard disks are mounted permanently inside a computer's system unit. Consequently, it's not always easy to transfer files between the hard disks of different computers.

Hard disks possess one undeniable and extremely attractive advantage over their floppy counterparts: They're fast. The speeds with which information can be transferred to and from a hard disk (referred to as its access rate, a value measured in milliseconds) puts to shame the performance of any floppy disk currently on the market.

Considering the amount of information people manage with their PCs, and given that one of the primary attractions of a personal computer is that it allows you to work more quickly, it should come as no surprise that hard disks — with their larger capacity and superior speed — have become the storage medium of choice among today's demanding PC users. The odds are quite high, therefore, that your computer includes a hard disk. Hard disks so dominate today's PC marketplace, in fact, that I'll be working under this assumption throughout the chapters that follow, as we discuss DOS commands relating to disk operations.

> ✔ *Note:* This doesn't mean that I plan to ignore anyone whose computer lacks a hard disk. There are millions of people out there who get along perfectly well relying exclusively on floppy disks. More and more, though, DOS itself has come to incorporate features targeted primarily at the hard disk user. It only makes sense, therefore, that a book on DOS would reflect this bias.

How Disks Work

Chapter 1 contained a brief discussion of bits, bytes, and other electronic esoterica pertaining to the manner in which a computer represents information. Expanding upon this discussion will help you understand how disks work, as well.

Bit

Bit is an abbreviation for *b*inary dig*it*. A bit corresponds to the current status of an electronic switch or other device. The term *binary* reflects the fact that this device can be set to one of two discrete states, commonly identified as off or on. *Digit* is loosely derived from the tradition of representing these two states with the numeric digits zero (0) and one (1) — off and on, respectively.

Byte

A byte consists of multiple bits, usually seven or eight. The pattern of the bits contained in a byte can be used to represent specific information. For example, the ASCII code, a code recognized by most personal computers, uses the eight-bit byte 01000001 to represent an uppercase A. Referring back to the previous definition of bits, this notation indicates that the eight "switches" within a byte that correspond to an uppercase A in the ASCII code would be configured in the following sequence:

off-on-off-off-off-off-off-on

Any device or material capable of existing in one of two discrete states can represent information as bits and, by extension, bytes. Within a computer's memory chips this is accomplished with tiny electronic switches that can be turned on and off. Disks achieve the same thing, but instead rely on the polarity of a magnetic field. Polarizing the field one way indicates an on bit; reverse the polarity and — symbolically speaking, at least — you've turned that bit off. For this reason, computer disks are referred to as magnetic storage devices. (I realize that I've provided only a basic and extremely nontechnical explanation of how bits and bytes are recorded on a disk. For our purposes, however, it will suffice.)

A disk drive's read/write head works much like the record/playback mechanism in a traditional tape recorder. Writing data to a disk corresponds to what happens when you record music on a tape, except for the critical difference that only binary digits, not analog tones, get recorded. Likewise, the process of reading data from a disk resembles playing back music previously recorded (stored) on an audio tape.

DOS assumes primary responsibility for coordinating all of this activity. (And believe me, during the course of an average day, the activity level of a disk drive is high indeed.) It keeps track of where specific information is stored on a disk; DOS then helps your computer find and retrieve this information, when necessary. The manner in which DOS organizes the data stored on a disk leads directly to our next topic.

Preparing a Disk for Use

All disks — 3.5" floppy disks, 5.25" floppy disks, and hard disks of every size — begin their electronic life as a tabula rasa, or blank slate. In this respect, they resemble the blank cassette tapes you would purchase to record music with a traditional tape recorder. In its initial blank state, a disk is about as useful as wings on a pig; in other words, not very. Before you can use a disk to store data, it must be prepared to work properly with your computer. This process is called formatting.

Earlier in this chapter I compared disks to the traditional filing cabinets used in most places of business. Returning to this analogy for a few moments will help explain how formatting prepares a disk to be used on your PC.

It would be wonderful if you could unpack a filing cabinet and immediately begin storing your important documents in it. Unfortunately, this isn't normally the case. A much more likely scenario is that your new filing cabinet will require some initial preparation before you can use it to store and retrieve information. For example, you may have to assemble your filing cabinet, as was the case with one I purchased recently. I had to physically build the framework and drawers that ultimately held my files. Symbolically speaking, this is similar to what happens when you use DOS to format a disk.

> ✓ *Note:* Of course, many stores sell preassembled filing cabinets. Likewise, it's possible to purchase preformatted disks. And most manufacturers now prepare the hard disks installed in their systems prior to shipping them.

The DOS FORMAT command constructs its metaphorical drawers out of sectors and tracks, as illustrated in Figure 3.1. Once this structure exists, DOS can use it to keep track of the files a disk contains.

The precise size and placement of the sectors and tracks on a disk vary, depending on the type of disk being formatted. Luckily, you don't have to concern yourself with such details. DOS assumes full responsibility for maintain-

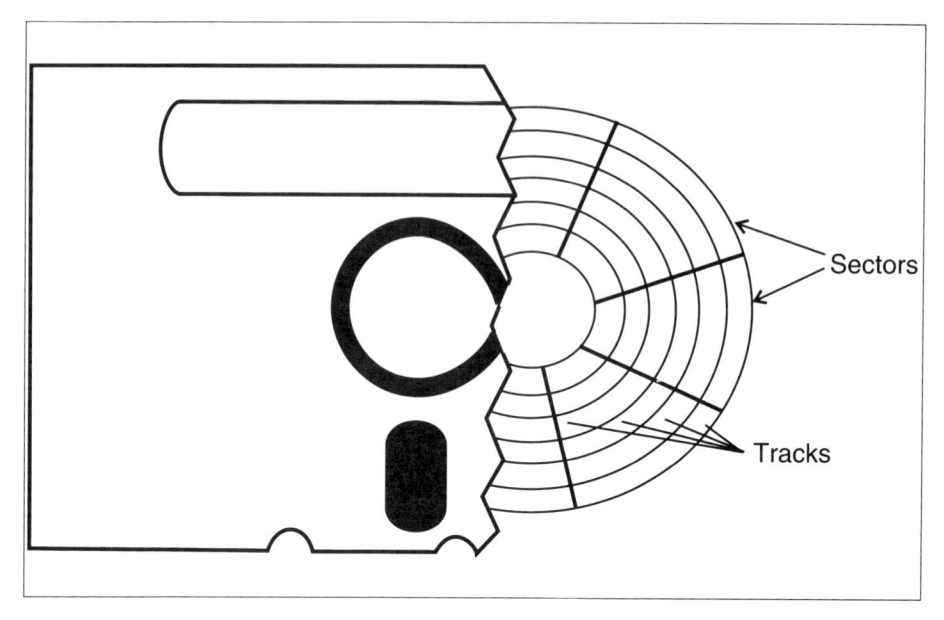

Figure 3.1 During formatting, DOS creates sectors and tracks on a disk.

ing a record of how the sectors and tracks are laid out on a particular disk. DOS creates two additional items on a disk during formatting:

- the disk directory
- the file allocation table, or FAT

Let's return once again to our imaginary filing cabinet to get an idea of how these two items work. Most people attach some sort of identifying tag or card to the front of the individual drawers in a filing cabinet. This allows them to identify, at a glance, the general type of information each drawer contains. During formatting, DOS magnetically encodes disks with a similar "index," called the disk directory.

Finally, if you look inside the individual drawers of a file cabinet, you'll often find some type of dividers. Most commonly, they are arranged in alphabetical order. The purpose of these dividers is to help someone quickly find a specific file a given drawer contains. DOS creates a comparable organizational tool on a disk during formatting. It is called the file allocation table, or FAT. The FAT contains information about how many sectors and tracks a given file occupies. The FAT also tells DOS where the first part of each file is stored on a disk.

Now that you know in theory at least what happens when you format a disk, let's see exactly how this is done.

Formatting a Disk (The FORMAT Command)

The correct syntax for entering a FORMAT command is:

```
FORMAT drive: [/V[:label]] [/Q] [/U] [/F:size][/B|/S]
FORMAT drive: [/V[:label]] [/Q] [/U] [/T:tracks /N:sectors] [/B|/S]
FORMAT drive: [/V[:label]] [/Q] [/U] [/1] [/4] [/B|/S]
FORMAT drive: [/Q] [/U] [/1] [/4] [/8] [/B|/S]
```

FORMAT Parameters and Command Switches

You can format a disk in a number of different ways. For example, if you plan to use a disk to start your computer, that disk must include the three system files required to load DOS into memory: IO.SYS, MSDOS.SYS, and COMMAND.COM. If a disk will only be used to store program and data files, these three system files can be eliminated, which frees up more space for your other files.

Like most DOS commands, FORMAT allows you to use parameters and switches to indicate exactly how you want a disk formatted. FORMAT accepts the following parameters and command switches:

drive: is the letter of the drive containing the disk you want to format.

/1 formats a disk for use in a single-sided floppy disk drive.

/4 formats a standard 360K double-sided, double-density floppy disk in a 1.2MB high-density disk drive.

/8 formats a 5.25" disk to contain 8 sectors per track.

/B formats the disk but leaves enough space to allow that disk to accept the three system files for any version of MS-DOS.

/F:*size* is used to specify the size (data storage capacity) of the disk being formatted. (The /F: switch is only available in DOS versions 4.0 and higher.) The following list describes the valid size parameters you can use with the /F switch:

  160 or 160K or 160KB
   160K, single-sided, double-density, 5.25" disk
  180 or 180K or 180KB
   180K, single-sided, double-density, 5.25" disk
  320 or 320K or 320KB
   320K, double-sided, double-density, 5.25" disk
  360 or 360K or 360KB
   360K, double-sided, double-density, 5.25" disk
  720 or 720K or 720KB
   720K, double-sided, double-density, 3.5" disk
  1200 or 1200K or 1200KB or 1.2 or 1.2M or 1.2MB

1.2MB, double-sided, quadruple-density, 5.25" disk
1440 or 1440K or 1440KB or 1.44 or 1.44M or 1.44MB
1.44MB, double-sided, quadruple-density, 3.5" disk
2880 or 2880K or 2880KB or 2.88 or 2.88M or 2.88MB
2.88MB, double-sided, extra-high-density, 3.5" disk

/N:*sectors*   specifies the number of sectors per track. (Cannot be used with the /F: switch.)

/Q   tells DOS to perform a quick format on the disk.

/S   automatically copies the DOS system files on a disk following formatting.

/T:*tracks*   specifies the number of tracks that should be created on this disk. (Cannot be used with the /F: switch.)

/U   specifies an unconditional format operation for a floppy or hard disk.

/V[:*label*]   allows you to specify a volume label for the disk being formatted.

As you can see, formatting a disk is a potentially confusing procedure. As a rule, however, you'll use only a few of the switches listed above. These include the /F:, /Q, /S, /U and /V options. The first command syntax shown at the beginning of this section indicates the correct way to enter these most commonly used FORMAT switches.

> **Note:** Most of the remaining switches were used in earlier versions of DOS to indicate how sectors and tracks should be arranged on a disk.

Most of the time you'll only need to format either a system or nonsystem disk designed to work with the disk drive on which it was initially formatted. This greatly simplifies matters, especially when you're first learning DOS. To see what I mean, let's prepare a few disks on your system, using the most common FORMAT options.

> **Caution:** Formatting a disk destroys any data that disk previously contained. Make certain, therefore, that any work disks you use during the following exercises do not contain important program or data files.

Formatting a System Disk

You add the /S switch to the FORMAT command to create a system disk — that is, a disk that can be used to start your PC. To format a system disk:

```
(C:\) FORMAT A: /S
Insert new diskette for drive A:
and press ENTER when ready...
```

Figure 3.2 DOS prompts you to insert a disk for a FORMAT operation.

Place the disk to be formatted in drive A.
Type **FORMAT A: /S**.
Press **Enter**.

> ✔ *Note:* When using the /S switch, it must be the last format option included on the command line.

DOS responds by requesting that you insert a disk in the specified drive, as shown in Figure 3.2. After inserting this disk as instructed, pressing Enter begins the format operation. What happens next depends on which version of DOS you are using:

- DOS versions 3.1 and earlier display the following message:

    `"Formatting..."`

- DOS versions 3.2 and 3.3 provide a little more information by displaying and updating information about the current head and cylinder location during the FORMAT operation.

- DOS versions 4.0 and higher report on their progress in a way real people like you and me can actually understand: They list and update the percentage of the FORMAT operation that has been completed, as shown in Figure 3.3.

Because you included the /S switch in this command, FORMAT automatically transfers the DOS system files to the disk in drive A. What happens next also depends on which version of DOS you have:

```
(C:\) FORMAT A: /S
Insert new diskette for drive A:
and press ENTER when ready...

Checking existing disk format.
Saving UNFORMAT information.
Verifying 1.2M
 19 percent completed.
```

Figure 3.3 Newer versions of DOS provide useful information about the FORMAT operation.

- Before completing the FORMAT operation, DOS versions 4.0 and higher automatically ask you to identify this disk with a Volume label, displaying the prompt:

    "Volume label (11 characters, ENTER for none)?"

    If you are using one of these DOS versions:

    Press **Enter**.

- DOS versions 3.3 and earlier bypass the Volume prompt.

As the final step in a format operation, all versions of DOS display the "Format another (Y/N)?" prompt shown in Figure 3.4. This prompt is DOS's way of asking whether you want to format additional disks before it returns you to the system prompt. For now:

Type **N** and press **Enter**.

The disk in drive A is now formatted as a system disk. It has been magnetically encoded with tracks, sectors, a disk directory, and a file allocation table. Additionally, the three system files for your version of DOS were automatically transferred to this disk following formatting. DOS provides an easy way to verify whether this indeed happened.

Analyzing a Disk (The CHKDSK Command)

The DOS CHKDSK command lets you analyze the contents of a disk. During this analysis, DOS checks to make sure that there are no problems with the disk itself

```
(C:\) FORMAT A: /S
Insert new diskette for drive A:
and press ENTER when ready...

Checking existing disk format.
Saving UNFORMAT information.
Verifying 1.2M
Format complete.
System transferred

Volume label (11 characters, ENTER for none)?

   1213952 bytes total disk space
    132096 bytes used by system
   1081856 bytes available on disk

       512 bytes in each allocation unit.
      2113 allocation units available on disk.

Volume Serial Number is 1E4F-18E5

Format another (Y/N)?
```

Figure 3.4 DOS allows you to format multiple disks with a single FORMAT command.

or any files it contains. If no problems exist, CHKDSK returns a report on the status of the disk. Should a problem be discovered, CHKDSK gives you an opportunity to recover the questionable data.

The correct syntax for entering a CHKDSK command is:

CHKDSK [*drive:*][*pathname*][*filename*] [**/F**] [**/V**]

CHKDSK Parameters and Command Switches

CHKDSK accepts the following parameters and command switches:

drive: is the letter of the drive containing the disk you want to check.

pathname is the name of a directory or subdirectory on which you want a partial CHKDSK operation performed.

filename is the name of a specific file for which CHKDSK should generate a status report.

/F causes CHKDSK to attempt to correct any errors it detects on the disk being analyzed.

/V causes CHKDSK to display the name of each file on the target drive during execution.

Running CHKDSK

Let's go ahead and run CHKDSK on the disk you formatted in the previous exercise. To analyze your system disk and display the names of any files it contains:

Type **CHKDSK A: /V**.
Press **Enter**.

The **A:** parameter causes CHKDSK to analyze the floppy disk currently in drive A. The /V switch tells CHKDSK to include filenames in its report. After completing its analysis, CHKDSK displays a report similar to the one shown in Figure 3.5.

✔ *Note:* Your screen may differ slightly from Figure 3.5, depending on which version of DOS you're using and what type of disk you formatted. The CHKDSK report shown here was generated by MS-DOS 6.0 with a 5.25" 1.2MB disk.

Because it was just formatted, the system disk is almost empty, a fact reflected in Figure 3.5. Note, however, that there are the two hidden files CHKDSK says it found. Those files, IO.SYS and MSDOS.SYS, are the two DOS system files, the files that load DOS into memory during system startup.

```
(C:\) CHKDSK A: /V
Volume Serial Number is 1E4F-18E5
Directory A:\
A:\IO.SYS
A:\MSDOS.SYS
A:\COMMAND.COM

   1213952 bytes total disk space
     78336 bytes in 2 hidden files
     53760 bytes in 1 user files
   1081856 bytes available on disk

       512 bytes in each allocation unit
      2371 total allocation units on disk
      2113 available allocation units on disk

    655360 total bytes memory
    552688 bytes free

(C:\)
```

Figure 3.5 CHKDSK analyzes a disk and returns information about its contents.

In addition to the file listing, CHKDSK reveals the following information about a disk:

- the total amount of storage space it contains following formatting
- how much of this space is currently being used (CHKDSK breaks this information down by file type, e.g., hidden and user files.)
- how much free storage space remains available on the disk
- how the disk is organized, based on allocation units (An allocation unit is a group of sectors in which DOS stores individual sections of a file.)
- the total amount of memory recognized by DOS as being installed in your system
- how much of this memory is currently unused

✔ *Note:* Once again, not all of this information is included in the CHKDSK report generated by all versions of DOS. DOS versions 3.3 and earlier, for example, do not include the file allocation section.

Including a File Analysis in Your CHKDSK Report

Let's run CHKDSK again and use the *filename* parameter to request additional information:

Type **CHKDSK A:COMMAND.COM /V**.
Press **Enter**.

This time CHKDSK adds the following line to the end of the previous report:

```
All specified file(s) are contiguous.
```

This message indicates that the file you specified, COMMAND.COM, is contiguous. That's a fancy word meaning that DOS did not have to break COMMAND.COM up into several segments stored in nonsequential allocation units. (I'll explain how files become noncontiguous in a few pages. Then, in Chapter 10, "Where No DOS Has Gone Before," I'll show you a new feature of MS-DOS 6.0, the DEFRAG command that allows you to correct this situation.)

Detecting Bad Sectors with CHKDSK

I'm going to pull a fast one on you. I'm going to run CHKDSK on a disk you don't have. But I'll do so after formatting a double-density (360K) diskette as a system disk in a high-density (1.2MB) drive. This process is guaranteed to generate formatting errors. (Keep in mind, I'm a trained professional. You should never try this at home.) Figure 3.6 contains the results of my little experiment.

Notice that a new item, bad sectors, has been added to the resulting CHKDSK report. We can use this new twist on the old CHKDSK command to expand upon how DOS uses the file allocation table mentioned earlier in this chapter.

During formatting DOS verifies whether the sectors it creates are, indeed, usable. If they are, all is well and DOS considers the format to have been 100 percent successful. Should problems arise, however, DOS identifies the troublesome sectors and marks them as being "bad" (that is, unusable) in the disk's file allocation table. Ever the vigilant operating system, DOS will not attempt to store data on any bad sectors whenever a file is saved to this "damaged" disk. (Don't worry, the disk can still be used. It just won't hold as much information — that is, bytes of data — as it would if all of its sectors had been formatted successfully.)

Recovering Lost Clusters

The final CHKDSK feature I'm going to discuss, the /F switch, is difficult to demonstrate, primarily because DOS tends to be such a reliable operating system.

```
(C:\) CHKDSK A:
Volume Serial Number is 163E-1DD3

    1213952 bytes total disk space
    1067520 bytes in bad sectors
     146432 bytes available on disk

        512 bytes in each allocation unit
       2371 total allocation units on disk
        286 available allocation units on disk

     655360 total bytes memory
     552688 bytes free

(C:\)
```

Figure 3.6 CHKDSK can detect bad sectors during a disk analysis.

Despite playing fast and loose with disk read/write operations for the better part of the past hour or so, I have been unable to generate a single lost file cluster. (Like I said, DOS is dependable.) Consequently, I'm forced to describe, rather than demonstrate, how the /F switch works.

Lost clusters occur when DOS gets "bewildered," for want of a better term. As I mentioned earlier, clusters are groups of sectors. Whenever possible, DOS stores a file in contiguous sectors, which follow one another physically on a disk. Over time, however, files that start out contiguous can become fragmented — spread out among noncontiguous groups of sectors or clusters. Generally, this happens because not enough contiguous sectors remain open to hold the entire file.

But remember, DOS is extremely reliable; 99.99 percent of the time, it manages to keep track of where the different clusters that make up a noncontiguous file are located without a hitch. It's that .01 percent (or thereabouts) potential for error that you need to watch out for. When it strikes, DOS loses its place, so to speak, and you end up with something called *lost clusters*. Including the /F switch in a CHKDSK command may allow you recover some of the contents of a corrupt file if this happens.

Whenever CHKDSK discovers lost clusters on a disk, it displays a message similar to the following:

```
Ten lost clusters found in 3 chains.
Convert lost chains to files (Y/N)?
```

> ✔ **Note:** The number of lost clusters and chains will vary, depending on how many file errors CHKDSK discovers.

Answering Y (Yes) to this prompt instructs CHKDSK to take the data in the fragmented clusters and save it to one or more files, using the following naming convention: FILE0000.CHK, FILE0001.CHK, FILE0002.CHK, and so forth. Someone who knows what they're doing may then be able to recover the data these files contain. Whether and how you can accomplish this depends on the type of file that was corrupted. For some files, like an ASCII text file, it's relatively easy. For formatted program or data files, it may involve manually modifying data in the corrupted file at the bit level — something else "you should not try at home," unless you know exactly what you're doing.

If you use a hard disk, it's a good idea to run CHKDSK regularly. Doing so only takes a few seconds and will help guard against the inevitable loss of data that occurs when a file is corrupted.

WORKING WITH DISKS   61

Tip: Running CHKDSK
Some people recommend that you run CHKDSK every time you start your computer. I can't say I agree. Given the reliability of DOS, I would suggest that every three or four days is more than adequate.

Labeling a Disk (The LABEL Command)

You may recall that, after it formatted your system disk, DOS paused and requested whether you wanted to enter a volume label. At that time, we declined. Let's do this now, using the LABEL command. The correct syntax for entering a LABEL command is:

LABEL [*drive:*][*label*]

LABEL Parameters

LABEL accepts the following parameters:

drive: is the letter of the drive containing the disk you want to label.

label   specifies the new volume label.

Assigning a volume label to a disk is similar to attaching a paper label with some identifying name or phrase on the outside of that disk. A name entered with the LABEL command, however, is actually stored on the disk where it remains unless and until you change it.

Limitations on Volume Label Names

A volume label may contain as many as 11 characters and may include spaces. Consecutive spaces are interpreted as a single space.

Caution: A volume label may not include the following characters:

* ? / \ | . , ; : + = [ ] ( ) & ^ "

Running LABEL

To assign a volume label to the system disk created earlier in this chapter:

Type **LABEL A:MS-DOS 6**.
Press **Enter**.

Hmmm. About all DOS did was spin the disk in drive A for a few seconds and return you to the system prompt. It doesn't look as if much happened, does it? Luckily, there's an easy way to check what, if anything, we accomplished.

Checking a Volume Label (The VOL Command)

The VOL command instructs DOS to display the volume label assigned to a disk, along with its DOS-generated serial number. The correct syntax for entering a VOL command is:

`VOL [drive:]`

VOL Parameters

VOL accepts the following parameter:

drive: is the letter of the drive containing the disk for which you want DOS to display the volume label and serial number.

Running VOL

Let's check how successful our earlier LABEL command was. To verify that a volume label was added to the system disk in drive A:

Type **VOL A:**.
Press **Enter**.

Yup, it was. DOS returns a message similar to the following:

```
Volume in drive A is MS-DOS 6
Volume Serial Number is 163E-1DD3
```

> *Tip:* Label On Disk
>
> Even the highest quality paper labels deteriorate over time. Storing an identifying name directly on a disk allows you to keep track of its contents. And with some imagination, it's not too difficult to work around LABEL's 11-character limitation. For example, you could use the following label to identify a disk containing your 1992 tax information: 92 TAX DATA. Or, try this next one for a quarterly budget projection: BUDG QTR1. True, neither of these will win you the Pulitzer Prize for creative writing; they should be enough to spark your memory, however, should you ever need to check a disk's content.

> **Note:** DOS versions 4.0 and later automatically assign a serial number to a disk during formatting. The serial number for your disk will differ from the one shown above.

Duplicating Disks (The DISKCOPY and DISKCOMP Commands)

As you'll see in Chapter 5, "Working with Files," DOS provides a number of ways to transfer the contents of your disks to a different location. Generally, this involves creating copies of a file or group of files, a process that can be performed easily with the contents of either a floppy or hard disk. There may be times, however, when you want to create an exact replica of a floppy disk — clone it, so to speak. The DISKCOPY command allows you to do this. The correct syntax for entering a DISKCOPY command is:

```
DISKCOPY [drive1: [drive2:]] [/1] [/V]
```

DISKCOPY Parameters and Command Switches

DISKCOPY accepts the following parameters and command switches:

- *drive1*: is the drive containing the disk you want to make a copy of, called the source disk.
- *drive2*: is the drive containing the disk you want to copy to, called the target disk.
- /1 instructs DISKCOPY to copy only the first side of a disk.
- /V instructs DISKCOPY to verify that the information is copied correctly.

Running DISKCOPY

How you enter the DISKCOPY command depends on how many and what kinds of disk drives are installed on your system. To run DISKCOPY on a system with a single floppy disk drive:

Type **DISKCOPY A: A:**.
Press **Enter**.

To run DISKCOPY on a system with two floppy disk drives of the same type:

Type **DISKCOPY A: B:**.
Press **Enter**.

> **Caution:** The second DISKCOPY method shown above will work only on similar disk drives. If your system has two drives but they do not use disks of the same size (that is, they are not both either a 5.25" or 3.5" drive), you'll need to use the single-drive method, the first command shown above.

After DOS loads the DISKCOPY program into memory, it will instruct you to insert a SOURCE and, in some cases, a TARGET diskette in the appropriate disk drive, as shown in Figure 3.7.

> **Note:** Figure 3.7 contains the message DOS displays for a single-drive DISKCOPY operation. If you are using two drives for DISKCOPY, DOS begins by telling you to insert both the SOURCE and TARGET diskettes in the appropriate drives.

The SOURCE disk is the disk you are copying from, in this case, the system disk we formatted earlier. Conversely, the TARGET disk is the disk you are copying to — a blank work disk, for our purposes here.

If necessary:

Place the system disk created earlier in drive A.

On a dual-floppy system, you must also:

Place a second work disk in drive B.

Then:

Press **Enter**.

This begins the DISKCOPY operation. If you're working with a single drive, DOS will pause from time to time and display one of the following messages:

```
Insert TARGET diskette in drive A:
Press any key to continue . . .
```

or

```
Insert SOURCE diskette in drive A:
Press any key to continue . . .
```

```
(C:\) DISKCOPY A: A:
Insert SOURCE diskette in drive A:
Press any key to continue . . .
```

Figure 3.7 DOS explains how to perform a DISKCOPY.

> **Note:** How many times you'll have to swap disks depends on the type of disk being copied and how much free memory your system has.

After it has finished duplicating the system disk, you'll see the following prompt:

```
Copy another diskette (Y/N)?
```

For now:

Press **N**.

Do you want to see if we were successful? No problem. All we have to do is run DISKCOMP, a complementary command to DISKCOPY. The correct syntax for entering a DISKCOMP command is:

DISKCOMP [*drive1*: [*drive2*:]] [/1] [/8]

DISKCOMP Parameters and Command Switches

DISKCOMP accepts the following parameter and command switches:

drive1: is the drive containing one of the floppy disks you want compared.

drive2: is the drive containing the second floppy disk.

/1 instructs DISKCOMP to compare only the first sides of the disks, even if the disks are double-sided and the drives can read double-sided disks.

/8 instructs DISKCOMP to compare only the first 8 sectors per track, even if the disks contain 9 or 15 sectors per track.

> **Note:** DISKCOMP works only with floppy disks. It cannot be used with a hard disk. If you specify a hard disk drive for *drive1* or *drive2*, DISKCOMP displays the following error message:
>
> ```
> Invalid drive specification
> Specified drive does not exist or is non-removable
> ```

Running DISKCOMP

As was true of DISKCOPY, the way you enter the DISKCOMP command depends on how many and what kinds of disk drives are installed on your system. To compare two disks on a single floppy disk drive:

Type **DISKCOMP A: A:**.
Press **Enter**.

To compare two disks in separate drives:

Type **DISKCOMP A: B:**.
Press **Enter**.

Once again, DOS provides instructions for the DISKCOMP operation, telling where and when to insert the necessary disks. Go ahead and follow these instructions until DISKCOMP is finished, at which point, if the two disks were identical, you'll see the following message:

```
Compare OK
Compare another diskette (Y/N)?
```

For now:

Press **N**.

> ✓ *Note:* If differences exist between the two disks, DOS displays messages during the DISKCOMP operation that identify those tracks and sectors that are not identical.

Now that we've created this second system disk — a true clone of the first disk you formatted — let's destroy it. (Don't worry. We're doing so for a good purpose.)

First, make sure the copy of your system disk created with DISKCOPY is in drive A, then:

Type **FORMAT A:**.
Press **Enter**.

DOS begins formatting the disk in drive A. When the Volume label prompt appears:

Press **Enter**.

When the Format another prompt appears:

Type **N** and press **Enter**.

I cautioned you earlier that formatting a disk destroys any data it previously contained. Well, it's true confessions time. As you'll see in the next section, I fudged somewhat when I issued that warning.

Restoring Accidentally Formatted Disks (The UNFORMAT Command)

Beginning with MS-DOS 5.0, DOS allows you, in some cases, to recover the data a disk held previously, even after it has been reformatted. The correct syntax for entering an UNFORMAT command is:

```
UNFORMAT drive: [/L] [/TEST] [/P]
```

UNFORMAT Parameters and Command Switches

UNFORMAT accepts the following parameter and command switches:

drive: is the drive containing the disk on which you want to perform an UNFORMAT operation.

/L   instructs DOS to display a list of every file and subdirectory UNFORMAT finds on the target disk before restoring its contents.

/TEST   instructs DOS to display a report indicating how UNFORMAT would re-create the target disk, but does not initiate an UNFORMAT operation.

/P   instructs DOS to send any messages generated by UNFORMAT to a printer connected to LPT1.

Running UNFORMAT

Let's see if UNFORMAT can work its magic on the duplicate disk we just formatted:

Type **UNFORMAT A:**.
Press **Enter**.

DOS displays the following message:

```
Insert disk to rebuild in drive A:
and press ENTER when ready.
```

If necessary, insert the duplicate system disk we created earlier in drive A, then:

Press **Enter**.

After performing a few checks, DOS displays the somewhat lengthy message shown in Figure 3.8.

As you can see, DOS takes special care to make certain that you indeed want to restore the disk's previous contents. We do. So:

Press **Y**.

DOS chugs along for a few seconds. First, DOS tries its darndest to rebuild the disk directory and FAT. If this works, it then attempts to recover any files the disk previously contained. Finally, DOS reports back to you either that the UNFORMAT operation was successful or not. Because we just formatted our disk, the UNFORMAT command should have worked; the less interim activity, the better the chances of recovery.

```
(C:\) UNFORMAT A:

Insert disk to rebuild in drive A:
and press ENTER when ready.


Restores the system area of your disk by using the image file created
by the MIRROR command.

        WARNING !!         WARNING !!

This command should be used only to recover from the inadvertent use of
the FORMAT command or the RECOVER command.  Any other use of the UNFORMAT
command may cause you to lose data!  Files modified since the MIRROR image
file was created may be lost.

Searching disk for MIRROR image.

The last time the MIRROR or FORMAT command was used was at 10:23 on 12-18-92.

The MIRROR image file has been validated.

Are you sure you want to update the system area of your drive A (Y/N)?
```

Figure 3.8 Newer versions of DOS allow you to "unformat" a disk.

Limitations on Using UNFORMAT

As impressive as UNFORMAT is, it ain't perfect. There are times when you simply won't be able to recover earlier data from a formatted disk. Limitations on the UNFORMAT command include:

1. UNFORMAT cannot restore a disk that was formatted using the /U switch.
2. UNFORMAT cannot be used to restore data on network drives.
3. UNFORMAT cannot completely recover fragmented files — files whose contents are stored in discontiguous sectors of a disk. Should it encounter a fragmented file, UNFORMAT pauses and asks whether you want recover the first part of the file or delete it altogether.

Despite its inherent weaknesses, however, UNFORMAT is a welcome addition to DOS's arsenal. You'll realize just how valuable UNFORMAT is the first time you accidentally reformat an important disk.

Partitioning a Hard Disk (The FDISK Command)

We're about to wade into some highly technical and fairly dangerous waters, so pay close attention, please. I mentioned earlier how a brand new disk resembles a blank slate. What you may not realize is that hard disks start out even more blank than their floppy counterparts.

Formatting a floppy disk is all that's required to get it ready for use. A brand new hard disk, however, needs additional preparation to be functional. It must be divided into partitions and, if appropriate, logical drives, before it can be formatted successfully. Most manufacturers take care of this little chore before shipping their products out the door. And, indeed, if you've been able to follow along with the various exercises in these past two chapters, your hard disk was partitioned long before you ever started using it. For those who couldn't, MS-DOS 6.0 initiates disk partitioning as part of its installation routine. (See Appendix A, "Installing MS-DOS 6.0," for more information on DOS installation.) It's unlikely, however, that you'll ever need to do this yourself.

Nevertheless, you may decide to install a second hard disk on your system or, more likely, restructure the *logical drives* that currently exist. The FDISK command allows you to do this.

Logical drive

A logical drive is a drive that does not exist physically. Usually, a logical drive consists of a portion of a large disk drive that DOS recognizes as a separate entity; it is assigned its own drive letter. You could, for example, set aside 30MB of a 120MB hard disk to create a logical drive. If the original 120MB drive was drive C on a system containing a single hard disk, DOS would assign this new (and, remember, nonexistent) drive the next available drive letter, D. Also, the storage capacity of drive C would be reduced by 30 megabytes, the size you specified for drive D in the above example.

The correct syntax for running the FDISK command is:

FDISK [/STATUS]

FDISK Switches

FDISK accepts the following switch:

/STATUS   displays information about the partitions on your computer's hard disk(s) without actually running the FDISK program.

Running FDISK

FDISK works only on hard disks physically installed on your computer. It cannot be used on a "false" drive created with the SUBST command, which allows a subdirectory to be treated as if it were a separate disk drive. Nor will it work on a network drive. FDISK *can* be used to perform the following tasks:

- creating a primary MS-DOS partition
- creating an extended MS-DOS partition
- setting a partition to active
- deleting a partition
- displaying partition data
- selecting the next hard disk for partitioning, if a system has multiple hard disks

> **Caution:** FDISK has the potential of destroying all the data on your hard disk. For this reason, you should never experiment with the FDISK command.

If I could, I'd punctuate the previous warning with a giant, red skull and crossbones. I can't. So I'll simply repeat: YOU SHOULD NEVER EXPERIMENT WITH THE FDISK COMMAND!!! There. That should do it. This chapter is about disk-related DOS commands, however, and FDISK is one of them. So, let me gingerly introduce you to it.

> **Caution:** Yes, I'm warning you again. Do not perform the following exercise! It has the potential of destroying all the data on your hard disk, including DOS! ('nuff said?)

When the user runs the FDISK program by typing FDISK and pressing Enter, DOS loads the FDISK program into system memory, a process which takes a few seconds, and then displays the menu shown in Figure 3.9. This menu lists the various FDISK options available to configure your hard disk for DOS operations.

As I mentioned earlier, you may at some point decide to divide a single, large disk drive into smaller logical drives. To accomplish this you would select option 1 from the FDISK menu: "Create DOS partition or Logical DOS Drive." Selecting this option displays the second-level FDISK menu shown in Figure 3.10.

```
                    MS-DOS Version 6
                  Fixed Disk Setup Program
               (C)Copyright Microsoft Corp. 1983 - 1993

                         FDISK Options

Current fixed disk drive: 1

Choose one of the following:

1. Create DOS partition or Logical DOS Drive
2. Set active partition
3. Delete partition or Logical DOS Drive
4. Display partition information


Enter choice: [1]




Press Esc to exit FDISK
```

Figure 3.9 FDISK options

```
            Create DOS Partition or Logical DOS Drive
Current fixed disk drive: 1

Choose one of the following:

1. Create Primary DOS Partition
2. Create Extended DOS Partition
3. Create Logical DOS Drive(s) in the Extended DOS Partition



Enter choice: [1]




Press Esc to return to FDISK Options
```

Figure 3.10 Creating logical drives lets you divide a large hard disk into smaller, more manageable segments.

FDISK is an interactive program. It walks you through each step required to create, delete, or examine partitions and logical drives. But, as I implied earlier — and I'll say specifically, here — you should never use FDISK unless you know exactly what you're doing!

We've covered a lot of territory in this chapter. In the process, you've seen some of the commands DOS uses to fulfill its primary objective of being a *disk operating system*. Still, we've only scratched the surface of what DOS allows you to do with your disks and the files they contain. In the next chapter we'll examine those DOS commands used to create and manage an extremely useful organizational tool, disk directories.

Chapter 4

Working with Directories

In this chapter, as promised, we move down one level within the three-tiered structure mentioned at the beginning of Chapter 3. It is the second part of the "trilogy" I mentioned at that time.

Now that you've learned how to prepare disks for use, along with being introduced to some additional procedures that allow you to examine and maintain those disks, we can begin designing a structure that helps you organize the information they ultimately will contain. DOS assists you in this effort through its ability to create, organize, and manage directories and subdirectories. This chapter introduces you to the DOS commands used to perform directory-related activities.

The Organizational Man (and Woman, of Course)

The ever increasing size and reduced price of hard disks have made them an invaluable component of any personal computer. It's a fact of PC life: You can never have too large a hard disk. Let's be honest. Today's applications are disk hogs. It's not unusual for a program's files to consume 5 to 10 megabytes of disk space following installation. And this doesn't take into account the additional storage requirements for the data files these programs require to actually accomplish something. The good news is that hard disks have never been more affordable.

I remember when I initially contemplated adding a hard disk to one of my first computers in 1982. A local store was willing to part with a 5MB model for a song, relatively speaking. Lamentably, his song and mine, based on my financial situation at the time, were in two different keys. That whopping 5MB hard disk would have set me back to the tune of just under $1,000.

What a difference a decade makes. Flip through the pages of any computer magazine on the racks today and you'll find a dozen ads offering 130MB hard drives priced anywhere between $250 and $300. More than twenty-five times the storage capacity of that 1982 model, at less than one third its cost! I think it's fair to say that the price of mass storage has dropped dramatically over the past ten years or so.

As rosy as this picture is, one aspect of having access to almost unlimited disk space can be a real thorn your side. If you compare the typical floppy disk to an electronic closet in which you store valuable digital possessions, today's multi-megabyte hard disks assume the proportions of a gigantic warehouse. Today's hard disks are large enough to hold literally thousands of files. Imagine the difficulty involved in finding one lone piece of data within this cavernous abyss.

Clearly, what's needed is some practical method of organizing the files a large disk contains. That's where DOS's ability to create and manage directories and subdirectories comes in.

Creating Order from Chaos

To visualize the advantages inherent in setting up a DOS directory structure, consider a written outline. Most of us learned early in our education how an outline could help bring order to an otherwise chaotic undertaking. When used properly, an outline allows you to break down large and elaborate projects into smaller and more manageable components.

A written outline contains multiple headings. Items are associated in some way with the heading under which they appear. The directories and subdirectories on a hard disk reflect this same general structure, as illustrated in Figure 4.1.

The topmost level in a disk directory structure is called the *root directory*. DOS creates this root directory automatically during disk formatting. The responsibility then falls on your shoulders to use the various directory-related commands to design an organized structure of directories and subdirectories running off the root directory in much the same way that you add headings and subheadings to a written outline.

Designing a Logical Directory Structure

The key word in the previous sentence is *organized*. A poorly organized written outline confuses, rather than clarifies. To be truly useful, an outline must flow

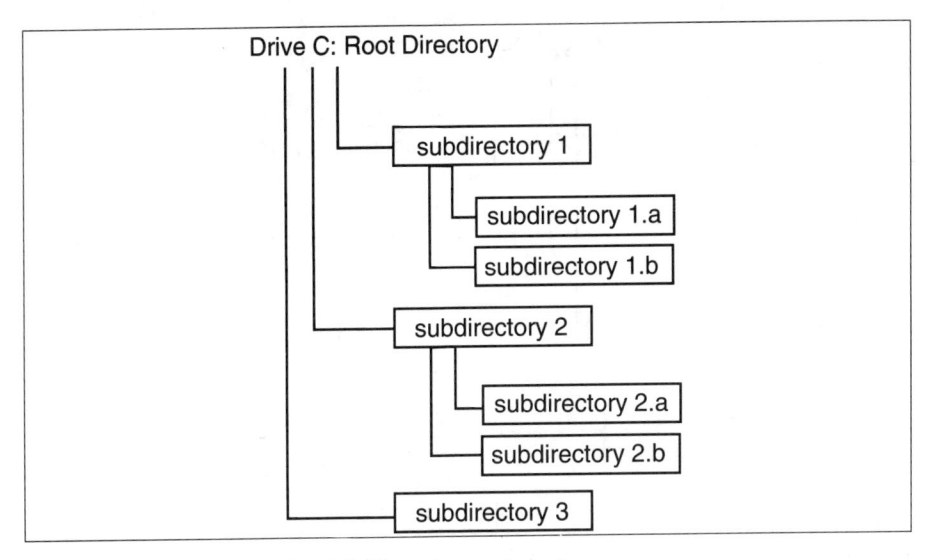

```
┌─────────────────────────────────────────────────────────┐
│              Drive C: Root Directory                    │
│              │  │ │                                     │
│              │  │ └──┬─────────────────┐                │
│              │  │    │  subdirectory 1 │                │
│              │  │    └─────────────────┘                │
│              │  │         │ ┌───────────────────┐       │
│              │  │         ├─│ subdirectory 1.a  │       │
│              │  │         │ └───────────────────┘       │
│              │  │         │ ┌───────────────────┐       │
│              │  │         └─│ subdirectory 1.b  │       │
│              │  │           └───────────────────┘       │
│              │  └──┬─────────────────┐                  │
│              │     │ subdirectory 2  │                  │
│              │     └─────────────────┘                  │
│              │           │ ┌───────────────────┐        │
│              │           ├─│ subdirectory 2.a  │        │
│              │           │ └───────────────────┘        │
│              │           │ ┌───────────────────┐        │
│              │           └─│ subdirectory 2.b  │        │
│              │             └───────────────────┘        │
│              └──┬─────────────────┐                     │
│                 │ subdirectory 3  │                     │
│                 └─────────────────┘                     │
└─────────────────────────────────────────────────────────┘
```

Figure 4.1 A typical DOS directory structure

logically, moving smoothly from topic to topic and defining clearly any associations that exist between the headings and subheadings it contains. The same holds true for a DOS directory structure. You can't simply begin creating directories randomly and then expect order to arise magically from such a haphazard approach.

One common method for organizing the directories and subdirectories on a disk is to gather together similar program and data files and place them in the same directory or, alternately, within a group of related subdirectories. For example, suppose that your hard disk contains Windows, Microsoft's popular graphics-based operating environment. During installation, Windows places its main program files in a directory running off the root directory that it names, logically enough, WINDOWS. It then proceeds to create two additional subdirectories running off this WINDOWS directory, assigning them the names SYSTEM and TEMP.

Windows does all of this automatically, without your intervention. It's easy to see how taking the same approach would allow you to organize your personal files. For example, I might elect to store the program files for my word processor in a first-level directory called WORD. Next, I could create two subdirectories running off this WORD directory, calling them BOOKS and ARTICLES. These two additional subdirectories would be where I'd store my data files for — you guessed it — book and article assignments, respectively.

Using this same logic, it would be relatively easy to create directories and subdirectories for all my other programs and data files, as well. Figure 4.2 illustrates the directory structure that would result from such an approach.

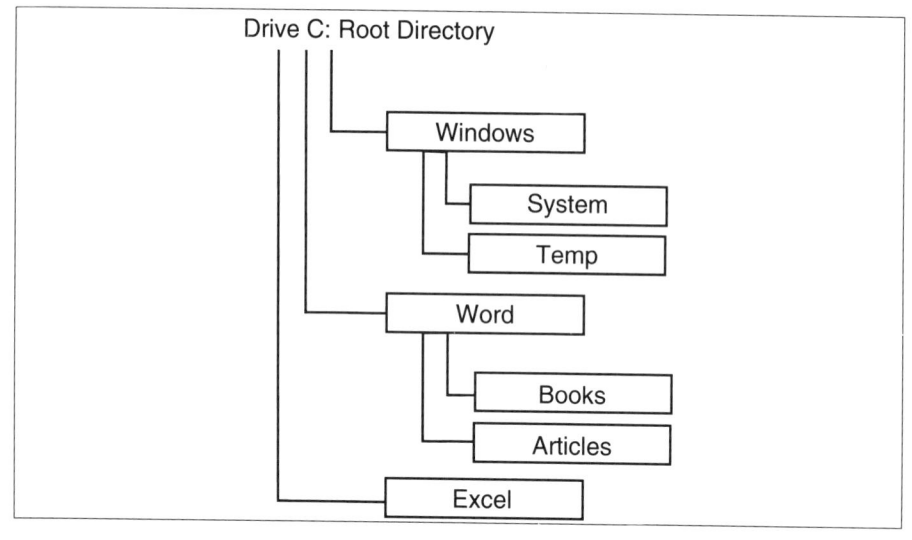

```
                Drive C: Root Directory
                │
                ├── Windows
                │        ├── System
                │        └── Temp
                ├── Word
                │        ├── Books
                │        └── Articles
                └── Excel
```

Figure 4.2 One useful approach is to group related files together within your directory structure.

> *Tip:* **Append Subdirectories**
>
> Most applications resemble Windows in that, during installation, they automatically create a directory into which they copy their program files. Why not build upon this foundation? Appending additional subdirectories to the initial program directory, which can then be used to store its data files, will result in a well-organized and easy-to-manage hard disk directory structure.

The Path-Finder

DOS relies on a precise notation, called a *path*, to identify where a specific file can be found within a disk's directory structure. The path information for a file consists of the drive letter and any directories or subdirectories leading to its location. The drive letter must be followed by a colon (:) and individual directory names separated with a backslash (\). I'll use the word processing program mentioned in the previous section to demonstrate how this works.

For the sake of this example, let's assume that the actual word processing program is a file called WRITE.EXE. If this were the case and this file was stored on drive C, its location could be identified using the following path notation:

```
C:\WORD\WRITE.EXE
```

By extension, then, the complete path notation for a data file called CHAP04.TXT that's stored in the subdirectory set aside for book-related projects would be:

`C:\WORD\BOOKS\CHAP04.TXT`

If you think about it, the individual elements within this path notation function much like road signs, pointing DOS toward its final destination. In essence, they provide the following "directions" to DOS:

1. Start out on the root directory of drive C (**C:**).
2. Move down one level to the WORD directory (**WORD**).
3. Drop down another level to a directory called BOOKS (**BOOKS**).
4. That's where you'll find a file called **CHAP04.TXT**.

> *Tip:* **Elements in a Path Statement**
> **How many individual elements must be included in a path statement is determined by where you're located within a disk's directory structure at the time. If you are working in the WORDS directory of drive C, for example, you could eliminate C:\WORD\ from the previous example. Instead, you can indicate that the CHAP04.TXT exists in the BOOKS directory by entering BOOKS\CHAP04.TXT. Because the WORDS directory on drive C: is the current directory, the C:\WORD is implied. (Once again, we can draw a comparison between this situation and road signs that provide directions. No signs are needed to point someone toward the road on which they're currently traveling.)**

Now that you have a basic idea of how DOS directories can help you organize the files stored on your disks, let's go ahead and create one.

Creating Directories (The MKDIR or MD Command)

You use the DOS MKDIR (MaKe DIRectory) command, which can be shortened to MD, to create new directories on a disk. The correct syntax for entering a MKDIR command is:

`MKDIR [drive:]path`

or

`MD [drive:]path`

MKDIR Parameters

MKDIR accepts the following parameters:

drive: is used to specify the drive on which the new directory is being created. (This parameter is not required if the directory you are creating is on the current drive.)

path is used to specify the complete path name for the new directory.

> ✔ **Note:** The maximum length of any single path from the root directory to the final directory is 63 characters, including the required backslashes (\).

Using MD

When we formatted our MS-DOS 6.0 floppy work disk in the previous chapter, we included the /S switch in the FORMAT command. This installed the necessary DOS files on the disk. But so far, all that the disk contains are two hidden system files (IO.SYS and MSDOS.SYS) and COMMAND.COM, the DOS command processor, all of which are stored on the root directory of drive A. A quick MD command will allow us to add a new directory to this disk.

To create a directory called TEST on the floppy disk in drive A:

Type **MD A:\TEST** and press **Enter**.

As with a number of previous commands, not much seemed to happen. To verify that our MD operation was successful, I'll need to introduce yet another DOS command designed to help you keep track of your directories and, by extension, any files they contain.

Displaying the Contents of a Directory (The DIR Command)

In the previous chapter we used the CHKDSK command to get a general idea of a disk's contents. As a rule, however, you'll want much more than a "general idea" of what's going on in your PC. Rather, you'll need specific information about the directories and files a disk contains. The DOS DIR (DIRectory) command provides this.

The correct syntax for entering a DIR command is:

```
DIR [drive:][path][filename] [/P] [/W]
[/A[[:]attributes]][/O[[:]sortorder]] [/S] [/B] [/L] [/C]
```

DIR Parameters and Command Switches

DIR accepts the following parameters and command switches:

drive: is the drive containing the disk for which you want to see a directory listing.

path   is the directory path for which you want to see a directory listing.

filename   is used to specify a particular file or group of files for which you want to see a directory listing.

/P   instructs DOS to display a directory listing one screen at a time. DOS prompts you to press any key to continue the listing.

/W   instructs DOS to display the listing in wide format, showing filenames only.

/A: instructs DOS to display only the names of directories and files that match the attributes you specify.

attributes   is used with the /A switch to identify what type of files you want included in the directory listing; valid attributes include:

- H   Hidden files
- -H   Files that are not hidden
- S   System files
- -S   Files other than system files
- D   Directories
- -D   Files only (not directories)
- A   Files ready for archiving (backup)
- -A   Files that have not changed since the last backup
- R   Read-only files
- -R   Files that are not read-only

/O: instructs DOS to display the names of the directories and files in the specified sort order.

sortorder   is used with the /O switch to identify the order in which you want a directory listing sorted; valid sort orders include:

- N   In alphabetic order by name
- -N   In reverse alphabetic order by name (Z through A)
- E   In alphabetic order by extension
- -E   In reverse alphabetic order by extension (Z through A)
- D   By date and time, earliest first
- -D   By date and time, latest first
- S   By size, smallest first
- -S   By size, largest first
- G   With directories grouped before files

	-G	With directories grouped after files
	C	By compression ratio, lowest first
	-C	By compression ratio, highest first
/S		instructs DOS to list every occurrence of the specified filename within the specified directory and any subdirectories it contains.
/B		instructs DOS to list only filenames and extensions, one per line, but does not include heading information and file summaries.
/L		converts the directory listing to lowercase.
/C		used to view information on the compression ratio of files stored on DBLSPACE volumes. (Chapter 10, "Where No DOS Has Gone Before," contains information about DBLSPACE volumes.)

I think it's safe to say that DIR is the most complex DOS command we've encountered up to this point. It's also a command you'll use quite frequently as you work on your PC. Finally, it's a command that allows us to introduce a number of other useful DOS tools. So, let's spend a couple minutes seeing just how DIR works.

Using DIR

We'll begin with a basic DIR command that will show us the contents of our MS-DOS 6.0 floppy disk.

Type **DIR A:** and press **Enter**.

Your screen should now resemble Figure 4.3. Notice that a new file appears to have been added to this disk: There's COMMAND.COM, which we saw in the previous chapter; but a second listing for something called TEST also appears. It looks slightly different than the COMMAND.COM listing, though, doesn't it?

```
(C:\) MD A:\TEST

(C:\) DIR A:

Volume in drive A is MS-DOS 6
Volume Serial Number is 1E4F-18E5
Directory of A:\

COMMAND  COM     53405 12-06-92   6:00a
TEST          <DIR>      12-19-92  12:17p
        2 file(s)        53405 bytes
                       1081344 bytes free

(C:\)
```

Figure 4.3 **The DIR command can be used to display the contents of a disk.**

For one thing, it's lined up a little differently; also, instead of the number following COMMAND.COM, it includes the notation DIR enclosed in brackets (< >). The explanation for the first difference, the lack of numbers following the filename, will have to wait until the next chapter, "Working with Files," when we look more closely at what files are and how DOS manages them. The second difference, however, is easy to explain: The enclosed notation — <DIR> — following TEST identifies it as a directory. Do you want to verify this? We can, you know, by entering a second, simple DIR command.

Using DIR Switches

Try the following:

Type **DIR A: /A:D**.

Your screen should now resemble Figure 4.4. Adding the /A:D switch to the previous DIR command accomplished two things:

1. The **/A:** switch told DOS that you wanted to see only those files that possessed certain attributes.
2. The **D** attribute is the attribute switch DOS uses to identify directories.

The resulting directory listing, therefore, contains only one item, the TEST directory you created on drive A. Now, let's try a different set of switches.

Type **DIR A: /A:A-D /O:N /W**.
Press **Enter**.

```
(C:\) DIR A:

Volume in drive A is MS-DOS 6
Volume Serial Number is 1E4F-18E5
Directory of A:\

COMMAND  COM      53405 12-06-92   6:00a
TEST         <DIR>      12-19-92  12:17p
        2 file(s)       53405 bytes
                      1081344 bytes free

(C:\) DIR A: /A:D

Volume in drive A is MS-DOS 6
Volume Serial Number is 1E4F-18E5
Directory of A:\

TEST         <DIR>      12-19-92  12:17p
        1 file(s)           0 bytes
                      1081344 bytes free

(C:\)
```

Figure 4.4 Command switches let you modify the appearance and contents of a directory listing.

That was a fairly complex command, containing several DIR switches. The results are shown in Figure 4.5. Let's break this command down into its component parts to see what we accomplished.

1. The **/A:A-D** combination did two things. First, it instructed DOS to include all files that have not changed since the last time the contents of this disk were backed up. (We'll discuss backing up disks in Chapter 8, "Playing It Safe: Protecting Your Data.") Because this is a new disk that has never been backed up, DOS listed all of the files it contains, including the two normally hidden DOS system files. Adding -D, the second attribute switch, instructed DOS to limit this listing to files only. That's why the TEST directory doesn't appear.

2. The **/O:N** switch instructed DOS to organize this directory in alphabetical order, by name.

3. Finally, the **/W** switch instructed DOS to display this listing in wide format. This shows only filenames, placing them horizontally across the display, thus allowing a single screen to contain more files.

The previous example also illustrates how easy it is to combine multiple switches in a single DIR command. Notice that you did not separate the two attribute switches with a space.

Using Wildcards with DIR

I'm going to get a little tricky here, so stay with me. Try the following:

```
TEST          <DIR>       12-19-92   12:17p
       2 file(s)         53405 bytes
                       1081344 bytes free

(C:\) DIR A: /A:D

 Volume in drive A is MS-DOS 6
 Volume Serial Number is 1E4F-18E5
 Directory of A:\

TEST          <DIR>       12-19-92   12:17p
       1 file(s)             0 bytes
                       1081344 bytes free

(C:\) DIR A: /A:A-D /O:N /W

 Volume in drive A is MS-DOS 6
 Volume Serial Number is 1E4F-18E5
 Directory of A:\
COMMAND.COM      IO.SYS           MSDOS.SYS
       3 file(s)       130923 bytes
                       1081344 bytes free

(C:\)
```

Figure 4.5 You can mix and match DIR parameters and switches.

Type **DIR A:*.SYS /A:H /L**.
Press **Enter**.

The most obvious difference between this listing and the ones we've seen previously is that including the /L switch instructed DOS to display the resulting filenames in lowercase letters (see Figure 4.6). Of even more interest, however, is the asterisk (*), which I inserted into the *filename* section of the command. What is it used for, and what did it accomplish? Allow me to explain.

The asterisk is one of two available DOS wildcard characters that can be used to simplify the process of entering a wide range of DOS commands, including DIR:

- When included in a filename, an asterisk (*) indicates that any character can occupy that position or any of the remaining positions within the filename or file extension.

- When included in a filename, a question mark (?) indicates that any character can occupy that position.

Basically, the asterisk (*) replaces all characters in a DOS filename either up to the period separating its filename and extension (as was the case in the previous exercise), or from where the asterisk is entered to the end of the extension portion of a DOS filename. In essence, the * wildcard tells DOS: Perform the current operation on any file(s) matching this partial description, regardless of the character(s) that follow the asterisk.

```
         1 file(s)         0 bytes
                    1081344 bytes free

(C:\) DIR A: /A:A-D /O:N /W

 Volume in drive A is MS-DOS 6
 Volume Serial Number is 1E4F-18E5
 Directory of A:\

COMMAND.COM     IO.SYS          MSDOS.SYS
         3 file(s)     130923 bytes
                    1081344 bytes free

(C:\) DIR A:*.SYS /A:H /L

 Volume in drive A is MS-DOS 6
 Volume Serial Number is 1E4F-18E5
 Directory of A:\

io       sys      40038 12-06-92   6:00a
msdos    sys      37480 12-06-92   6:00a
         2 file(s)      77518 bytes
                    1081344 bytes free

(C:\)
```

Figure 4.6 The DOS wildcards lets you select specific filenames for inclusion in a DIR listing.

The **?** wildcard differs from an asterisk in that it is used to replace a single character within either the filename or extension portion of a file.

> *Note:* Although I've introduced them in this section on DIR, wildcards can be used with most DOS commands. In fact, we'll use them throughout this book. So, take a moment to make sure you understand how * and ? are used to specify characters within a filename.

> *Tip:* **Combining Wildcards**
> It's perfectly "legal" to combine both DOS wildcards within a single command. Doing so allows you to identify quite explicitly which files you want included in a DIR listing.

You'll encounter many more examples of DIR in the next chapter, "Working with Files." As I stated earlier, it's a powerful and frequently used command. We still have a lot of ground to cover relating to directories, however, so let's move on. (Well, after two more brief detours.)

Changing Active Disk Drives

Until now you've been forced to include the *drive* parameter in all of our exercises. That's because we've been working from drive C, but requesting information about the disk in drive A. A short and sweet command will eliminate this inconvenience.

Type **A:** and press **Enter**.

This makes drive A the active drive. Like I said, short and sweet. Enjoy it. Few DOS commands are this simple to learn and use. Well, come to think of it, there is one other one. And it provides our second brief detour.

Clearing Your Display (The CLS Command)

In addition to being short and sweet, the CLS command is also extremely useful. It gives you a way eliminate the clutter that fills up your monitor after you've executed several DOS commands in quick succession, as we've done. So, try the following:

Type **CLS** and press **Enter**.

Stated simply, the CLS (CLear Screen) command clears your monitor and returns the system prompt to the top left-hand corner of the display screen. Now that we have a clean visual slate to work with, let's return to the main topic of this chapter: DOS directories.

Changing Active Directories (The CHDIR or CD Command)

Just as it's possible to change active disk drives, you can also choose to work from within a different directory. The correct syntax for switching active directories is:

CHDIR [*drive:*][*path*][*..*]

or

CD [*drive:*][*path*][*..*]

CHDIR Parameters

CHDIR (or CD) accepts the following parameters:

drive: is used to specify the drive for which you want to change the active directory. (This parameter is not required if the directory you want to make active is in the current drive.)

path   is used to specify the complete path name for the directory you want to make active.

..   is a "shortcut" parameter that tells DOS you want to move up one level in your directory structure to the parent directory of the current directory.

Using CHDIR

Right now you should be working in the root directory of the floppy disk in drive A. (Remember, we made drive A the active drive a short time ago.) There's an easy way to check this:

Type **CD** and press **Enter**.

When entered by itself without parameters, the CD command instructs DOS to display the current directory (in this case A:\) and return you immediately to the system prompt. This should be what happened on your monitor. Next, we'll change to a different directory:

Type **CD TEST** and press **Enter**.

86   DOS 6.0 HANDBOOK

Not much happened, did it? Once again, DOS returned you to the same A> system prompt you've been seeing throughout the previous exercises. But, try the following:

   Type **CD** and press **Enter**.

DOS indicates that the previous command did, indeed, move you down one level to the A:\TEST directory. To verify this a second way:

   Type **DIR** and press **Enter**.

Your screen should now resemble Figure 4.7, which shows a directory listing for the TEST directory on drive A. According to Figure 4.7 there are two files in TEST. What are they? To explain away this mystery:

   Type **CD..** and press **Enter**.
   Type **DIR** and press **Enter**.

You should now be looking at something you've seen a couple times already — specifically, a directory listing for the root directory of drive A. "Wait a minute," I can almost hear you saying. "I thought I needed to specify the directory I wanted to make active for the CD command to work properly. What the heck did you just do?"

   I confess. I cheated. You see, I *did* specify a directory. I just did so with a double-period, a special "shorthand" notation DOS lets you use to simplify the process of entering certain commands.

   Look again at Figure 4.7. When you entered the DIR command, you probably expected this directory to be empty. I mean, what possibly could be in TEST, considering we just created it a few minutes ago? But it wasn't empty, was it? Instead, DIR revealed that two files, (. <**DIR**> and .. <**DIR**>) were in TEST. As the

```
A>CD
A:\

A>CD TEST

A>CD
A:\TEST

A>DIR

 Volume in drive A is MS-DOS 6
 Volume Serial Number is 1E4F-18E5
 Directory of A:\TEST

 .            <DIR>     12-19-92  12:17p
 ..           <DIR>     12-19-92  12:17p
         2 file(s)          0 bytes
                      1081344 bytes free

A>
```

Figure 4.7 By default, DOS carries out commands on the active directory.

<DIR> notation indicated, these two "files" are really directories. But what directories are they?

I guess that's enough anticipation. It's time to clear up your confusion. DOS uses these two shorthand notations to indicate the following items:

- **. <DIR>**   This is the directory in which you are working, also called the current or *default directory*.

- **.. <DIR>**   This is the directory one level above the current directory, also referred to as the *parent directory*.

When you entered the **CD..** command earlier, DOS interpreted this to mean "move up one level in the directory structure," relative to where we were working at the time. Consequently, it moved us out of the TEST directory and into TEST's "parent," the root directory on drive A.

Using CD on Other Drives

Including the *drive* parameter with a CD command allows you to change the current directory on a drive other than the one you're using at the time. Try the following:

Type **CD TEST** and press **Enter**.
Type **CD C:\DOS** and press **Enter**.
Type **C:** and press **Enter**.
Type **CD** and press **Enter**.
Type **CD A:** and press **Enter**.

Follow me as I explain what you accomplished in the previous exercise:

1. The CD TEST command changed the current directory on drive A back to the TEST directory created earlier. Because drive A was the active drive, you didn't need to include a *drive* parameter in this command.

2. Including the C: *drive* parameter in the second command, CD C:\DOS, instructed DOS to change the current directory on drive C from its root directory to a directory called DOS. (MS-DOS automatically created this directory as part of its installation routine.) Including the *drive* parameter in this command informed DOS that you wanted to change the current directory on a drive other than the active drive, which is currently drive A.

3. The third command made drive C the active drive.

4. The final two commands instructed DOS to identify the current directory on drives C and A, respectively. If all went as planned — and there's no reason to doubt that it did — your screen should now resemble Figure 4.8, which shows the previous command sequence and DOS's response to each.

```
A>DIR

 Volume in drive A is MS-DOS 6
 Volume Serial Number is 1E4F-18E5
 Directory of A:\

COMMAND  COM       53405 12-06-92   6:00a
TEST            <DIR>       12-19-92  12:17p
        2 file(s)       53405 bytes
                       1075712 bytes free

A>CD TEST

A>CD C:\DOS

A>C:

C>CD
C:\DOS

C>CD A:
A:\TEST
```

Figure 4.8 Drive parameters let you perform many DOS commands on drives other than the active drive.

As this exercise demonstrates, DOS remembers the current directory for one drive, even if you're working on a different drive. This explains why it responded to the final command (CD A:) by telling you that TEST is the current directory on drive A.

There are some very real benefits associated with DOS's penchant for keeping track of such details. To see what I mean, try the following:

Type **COPY LABEL.EXE A:** and press **Enter**.
Type **A:** and press **Enter**.
Type **DIR** and press **Enter**.

✓ *Note:* I realize that I've not yet introduced you formally to the COPY command included in the previous exercise. This brings up a problem any author faces when writing a book about DOS. Its various functions are so interrelated that fully exploring one topic sometimes requires that you perform an operation out of sequence — that is, before the time is appropriate to explain all of its nuances. I promise, I'll try to keep such incidents to a minimum. (And rest assured, we'll examine the COPY command more thoroughly in the next chapter, "Working with Files".)

The DIR command reveals that the TEST directory on drive A, which was previously empty, now contains a file called LABEL.EXE. (If you're curious, this is the program DOS runs whenever you execute the LABEL command introduced in the previous chapter.) Because DOS remembered that TEST was the current directory on drive A, you did not have to include a *drive* parameter to identify it as the directory to which you wanted the LABEL.EXE file copied. Instead, DOS placed LABEL.EXE there automatically.

As the exercises in this section have demonstrated, the CD command (or, in its longer form, the CHDIR command) allows you to move around directories and subdirectories. Over the course of time, you'll almost certainly create a directory structure that reflects your personal work habits. It's comforting to know that CD is available to help you navigate this potential PC maze with relative ease.

Customizing Your System Prompt (The PROMPT Command)

Although DOS has allowed us to navigate the maze mentioned above, it's failed to provide us with much information about our location at any given time. On several occasions so far, we've used the CD or DIR command to verify our current position within the directory structure, but having to repeatedly ask DOS for this information quickly becomes tedious. Luckily, there's a simple way to eliminate this problem: the PROMPT command, which allows you to change the appearance of the MS-DOS system prompt. The correct syntax for entering a PROMPT command is:

PROMPT [*text*]

PROMPT Parameters

PROMPT accepts the following parameter:

> *text*   specifies any text or other information you want included in your system prompt.

Using PROMPT

By default, DOS generates a pretty blasé system prompt — the infamous C> symbol PC users have complained about for years. The good news is that you can change this default prompt to almost anything you want. To see what I mean:

> Type **PROMPT It's time for a change!**.
> Press **Enter**.

DOS changes the system prompt with the specified text string, as shown in Figure 4.9. Although this new prompt is a bit more entertaining than the default C> prompt, it still doesn't provide much information about what's actually happening inside your PC. To accomplish this, I'll need to introduce yet another feature of the prompt command.

```
C:\DOS

C>CD A:
A:\TEST

C>COPY LABEL.EXE A:
        1 file(s) copied

C>A:

A>DIR

 Volume in drive A is MS-DOS 6
 Volume Serial Number is 1E4F-18E5
 Directory of A:\TEST

.            <DIR>      12-19-92   12:17p
..           <DIR>      12-19-92   12:17p
LABEL   EXE        9390 12-06-92    6:00a
        3 file(s)       9390 bytes
                     1071616 bytes free

A>PROMPT It's time for a change!

It's time for a change!
```

Figure 4.9 You can change the appearance of your DOS system prompt.

Special PROMPT Symbols

DOS allows you to include special symbols within a PROMPT that are designed to display useful information about your PC environment. These include:

Characters	Resulting Prompt Information
$q	the = character
$$	$ character
$t	the current time
$d	the current date
$p	the currently active disk drive and directory
$n	the default drive
$v	the version number of your DOS release
$g	a greater than symbol (>)
$l	a less than symbol (<)
$b	a pipe character (|)
$_	a linefeed/carriage return
$s	a blank space
$e	ASCII escape code (code 27)
$h	Backspace (used to delete a character that has been written to the prompt command line)

These various symbols can be used by themselves or in combination with the *text* parameter to create a truly useful system prompt. For example, try the following experiment:

Type **PROMPT The current directory is $p $s**.
Press **Enter**.

As Figure 4.10 illustrates, including these two symbols in the PROMPT command instructed DOS to include the name of the currently active subdirectory (**$p**), followed by a blank space (**$s**), in the system prompt. The accompanying text string explains what this information represents. To see what I mean:

Type **C:** and press **Enter**.

The customized system prompt reflects the fact that you're now working in the DOS directory on drive C. You can make your system prompt as simple or as complex as you want. Should things get complicated, DOS even makes it easy to return to the default DOS prompt. To do this:

Type **PROMPT** and press **Enter**.

Voila! DOS returns to its familiar (and much maligned) C> prompt. Are you beginning to understand how useful the PROMPT command can be? With a little experimentation you'll be able to create a system prompt that provides precisely the information you want to see. For now, however, let's specify a relatively simple prompt that I find informative, yet not overly cluttered:

```
C>CD A:
A:\TEST

C>COPY LABEL.EXE A:
        1 file(s) copied

C>A:

A>DIR

 Volume in drive A is MS-DOS 6
 Volume Serial Number is 1E4F-18E5
 Directory of A:\TEST

.            <DIR>      12-19-92  12:17p
..           <DIR>      12-19-92  12:17p
LABEL    EXE      9390  12-06-92   6:00a
        3 file(s)       9390 bytes
                     1071616 bytes free

A>PROMPT It's time for a change!

It's time for a change!PROMPT The current directory is $p $s

The current directory is A:\TEST
```

Figure 4.10 A customized prompt can include useful information about your system.

Type **PROMPT ($p) $s**.
Press **Enter**.

Your prompt should now display the name of the current directory, enclosed in parentheses.

> ✔ *Note:* DOS stores any changes you make to the system prompt in memory. If you turn your computer off and then back on again, therefore, you'll be returned to the default system prompt. Consequently, you may want to make a note of the previous command. In Chapter 9, "The Age of Automation: Batch Files and Other Conveniences," you'll learn how to customize the system prompt automatically each time you start your computer.

Displaying a Disk's Directory Structure (The TREE Command)

As you saw earlier, the DIR command provides a convenient way to request a listing of any subdirectories running off a single directory. But what if you want to see the directory structure of an entire disk? The TREE command provides a convenient way to do this. The correct syntax for entering a TREE command is:

```
TREE [drive:][path] [/F] [/A]
```

TREE Parameters and Command Switches

TREE accepts the following parameters and command switches:

- *drive*: is the drive containing the disk for which you want to display a directory tree.
- *path* is the directory for which you want to display a TREE listing.
- /F instructs DOS to display the names of the files in each directory.
- /A instructs TREE to use text characters, rather than graphic characters, to display the lines linking subdirectories. (Use this switch with nongraphic display cards.)

Using TREE

Before we actually see how TREE works, let's expand the directory structure on our MS-DOS 6.0 floppy disk:

Type **A:** and press **Enter**.

This makes drive A the active drive.

WORKING WITH DIRECTORIES

Type **MD TEST2**.

This creates a second directory running off the TEST directory that you created earlier.

Type **MD TEST2\TEST3** and press **Enter**.

This adds another directory to the work disk, one more level down, running off the TEST2 subdirectory created in the previous step. So, let's see what we've accomplished:

Type **CLS** and press **Enter** to clear your screen.
Type **CD..** and press **Enter** to return to the root directory.
Type **TREE** and press **Enter**.

Figure 4.11 shows the resulting display. This screen lists each of the directories running off the root directory, graphically depicting their relationship to one another. Now, try the following:

Type **TREE /F** and press **Enter**.

This time, in addition to listing the directories on drive A, DOS includes the names of any files each directory contains, as shown in Figure 4.12. As you can see, TREE provides a convenient way to view the contents of your disks.

Removing Directories (The RMDIR or RD Command)

Like most things in life, DOS directories tend to outlive their usefulness. A directory you create to store the data files for a specific project is no longer needed once that project has been completed. In order to avoid cluttering up your hard disk over time, therefore, it only makes sense to get rid of it. The RMDIR (or RD) command allows you to do this. The correct syntax for entering a RMDIR command is:

```
(A:\TEST) MD TEST2

(A:\TEST) MD TEST2\TEST3

(A:\TEST) CD..

(A:\) TREE
Directory PATH listing for Volume MS-DOS 6
Volume Serial Number is 1E4F-18E5
A:.
└──TEST
    └──TEST2
        └──TEST3

(A:\)
```

Figure 4.11   A sample directory tree

```
(A:\TEST) MD TEST2\TEST3

(A:\TEST) CD..

(A:\) TREE
Directory PATH listing for Volume MS-DOS 6
Volume Serial Number is 1E4F-18E5
A:.
└──TEST
    └──TEST2
        └──TEST3

(A:\) TREE /F
Directory PATH listing for Volume MS-DOS 6
Volume Serial Number is 1E4F-18E5
A:.
│   COMMAND.COM
│
└──TEST
    │   LABEL.EXE
    │
    └──TEST2
        └──TEST3

(A:\)
```

Figure 4.12 The /F switch instructs DOS to include files in your directory listing.

```
RMDIR [drive:]path
```

or

```
RD [drive:]path
```

RMDIR (RD) Parameters

RMDIR (RD) accepts the following parameter:

drive:path   is the DOS path notation for the directory you want to remove.

Using RMDIR (RD)

The RD command is fairly straightforward. To see how it works, try the following:

Type **RD TEST\TEST2\TEST3** and press **Enter**.
Type **TREE** and press **Enter**.

Your TREE listing should now show only two subdirectories running off the drive A root directory, TEST and TEST2, indicating that the previous RD command successfully removed TEST3.

We're just about finished examining the DOS directory-related commands. So, go ahead and get rid of all the TEST directories. A single RD command should accomplish this.

Type **RD TEST** and press **Enter**.

WORKING WITH DIRECTORIES 95

It appears that we have a small problem. DOS, which has been very cooperative up to this point, doesn't seem willing to execute the previous command. Instead, it displays the error message shown in Figure 4.13 and returns you to the system prompt. There is a simple and very logical explanation for this: DOS is merely being cautious.

When you ask DOS to remove a directory, it assumes that you're making this request because any items previously stored in that directory are no longer needed and have, therefore, been erased. For this reason, the RD command works only on empty directories. The error message shown in Figure 4.13 is DOS's way of telling you that it found something in the TEST subdirectory — either files, additional directories, or both.

One way around this obstacle is to go into TEST and eliminate everything it contains. When you're dealing with a single directory, as we are now, this isn't difficult to do. But what if the project you've finished is a large one, involving dozens of files and several directories? Would it not be more convenient if there was a way of eliminating the entire structure with a single command? It would, and, beginning with MS-DOS 6.0, there is.

Removing Entire Directory Trees (The DELTREE Command)

Utilities have been available for years that allow you to delete a directory and any files it contains with a single command. By adding the DELTREE command

```
Directory PATH listing for Volume MS-DOS 6
Volume Serial Number is 1E4F-18E5
A:.
│   COMMAND.COM
│
└───TEST
    │   LABEL.EXE
    │
    └───TEST2
        └───TEST3

(A:\) RD TEST\TEST2\TEST3

(A:\) TREE
Directory PATH listing for Volume MS-DOS 6
Volume Serial Number is 1E4F-18E5
A:.
└───TEST
    └───TEST2

(A:\) RD TEST
Invalid path, not directory,
or directory not empty

(A:\)
```

Figure 4.13 For some reason, DOS refuses to remove the specified directory.

to MS-DOS 6.0, Microsoft has finally caught up with the competition. The correct syntax for entering a DELTREE command is:

```
DELTREE /Y [drive:]path
```

DELTREE Parameters and Command Switches

DELTREE accepts the following parameter and command switches:

drive:path is the DOS path notation for the directory you want to remove, along with any files it contains.

/Y instructs DOS to delete these items automatically — that is, without requiring additional confirmation.

Using DELTREE

Now that we've been introduced to the DELTREE command, let's see if we can get rid of that pesky TEST directory.

Type **DELTREE TEST** and press **Enter**.

This time, rather than refusing outright to follow our instructions, DOS displays the following prompt:

```
Delete directory "TEST" and all its subdirectories? [yn]
```

DOS seems willing to cooperate with us this time — albeit, begrudgingly. Let's go ahead and give our official okay to the DELTREE operation:

Type **Y** and press **Enter**.

To see if we succeeded:

Type **TREE** and press **Enter**.

This time, as Figure 4.14 clearly shows, the DELTREE operation was successful. All subdirectories below the root directory of drive A have been deleted.

> *Caution:* Microsoft had a logical reason for waiting so long to catch up to the competition in this area. Potentially destructive commands such as DELTREE must be used with caution. A carelessly entered DELTREE command could erase weeks, even months, of work in a matter of seconds. For this reason, I strongly advise that you think carefully and know precisely what you want to accomplish before using DELTREE.

```
(A:\) TREE
Directory PATH listing for Volume MS-DOS 6
Volume Serial Number is 1E4F-18E5
A:.
└───TEST
    └───TEST2

(A:\) RD TEST
Invalid path, not directory,
or directory not empty

(A:\) HELP

(A:\) DELTREE TEST
Delete directory "TEST" and all its subdirectories? [yn] y
Deleting TEST...

(A:\) TREE
Directory PATH listing for Volume MS-DOS 6
Volume Serial Number is 1E4F-18E5
A:.
No sub-directories exist

(A:\)
```

Figure 4.14 DELTREE removes directories and files with a single command.

Fooling DOS (The APPEND and SUBST Commands)

As I've pointed out several times already, personal computers have evolved over the years. So, too, has DOS. For the most part, this is good. Today's consumer can buy more power at a lower price than those of us who were here at the beginning of the PC revolution ever dreamed possible. The problem is that this evolution has not occurred in a vacuum.

Sure, recent PC buyers enjoy all the benefits offered by true state-of-the-art equipment. But a lot of people continue to rely on hardware and software they purchased years ago — and there's nothing wrong with this. If an older system still does what someone wants it to do, why replace it? For example, I have a friend who wrote thirteen best-selling science fiction novels on a first-generation, dual-floppy IBM PC. Not even a PC/XT, mind you, but the original IBM PC. And this original, dual-floppy IBM PC — which helped him write hundreds of short stories in addition to those thirteen novels — had a mere 256K of RAM.

Only recently did my friend upgrade to a 33MHz 386 system with a hard disk. Part of me believes he still yearns for the "good ole days" when he didn't have to scour 200MB of stored data to find a particular file. He doesn't regret his recent upgrade, mind you. He loves the speed and convenience with which he now can work. Nevertheless, there are moments when I'm sure my friend misses collaborating with that old and prolific electronic partner.

Progress, however, exacts its own price. When MS-DOS 1.0 was released, hard disks were not yet common on personal computers. Consequently, this early version of DOS did not include some contemporary commands, whose primary purpose was to help you control and manage large disks. By extension, therefore, neither did some early application programs. At this point, my friend the science fiction writer reenters our story — which does have a point, I assure you. You see, his favorite word processor is one of those early programs. And while my friend was willing to replace his hardware, he was not about to abandon the software that he used on the road to success. Most writers, including this one, lean toward superstition. Once you find a word processor you're comfortable with, it becomes almost an extension of yourself. Needless to say, you think long and hard before switching to another one.

Normally, this doesn't present a problem. With my friend's program, however, it did. His trusted word processor could not take full advantage of DOS's ability to manage hard disk operations; specifically, it lacked the code required to access subdirectories. Consequently, he would have to forgo the capability to organize and store his data files in multiple directories on his new hard disk — unless, of course, he could "fool" DOS (and, by extension, his word processor) into believing those subdirectories were something else. A pair of DOS commands allowed him to do precisely that.

The SUBST command lets you substitute a drive letter for a directory path. After running SUBST, you can access any file in the original directory path by referring to the drive letter to which that path was assigned. The correct syntax for entering a SUBST command is:

SUBST [*drive1*: [*drive2*:]*path*] [/D]

SUBST Parameters and Command Switches

SUBST accepts the following parameters and command switches:

drive1: is the drive letter representing a virtual drive you want to associate with a path.

drive2: is the physical drive that contains the path you want reassigned to a drive letter.

path is the path that you want to assign to a virtual drive.

/D is used to delete a virtual drive — that is, to disassociate a directory path from the drive letter to which it was assigned with a SUBST command

> **Caution:** The following commands should never be used on drives that have been reassigned with a SUBST command:
>
> | | | | |
> |---|---|---|---|
> | *ASSIGN | FORMAT | FDISK | RECOVER |
> | BACKUP | DISKCOMP | LABEL | RESTORE |
> | CHKDSK | DISKCOPY | *MIRROR | SYS |
> | DEFRAG | | | |
>
> *Commands from DOS 5.0 and earlier versions

> **Caution:** The *drive1* parameter must be within the range specified by the LASTDRIVE command. (See Chapter 7, "Have It Your Way: Fine-Tuning Your System," for more information on LASTDRIVE.) If you specify a drive letter outside the LASTDRIVE range, DOS displays the following error message:
>
>   Invalid parameter - drive1:

Using SUBST

Suppose, for example, that my friend wanted to store the files for a new novel he's writing in a directory on drive C called NEWNOVEL. To accomplish this, he could use a SUBST command to assign that subdirectory to the drive letter A, which normally identifies a floppy disk that his word processor recognizes as a valid drive. The following command would accomplish this:

SUBST A: C:\NEWNOVEL

His word processor now could access files in the NEWNOVEL directory. How? Well, all he does is "lie" to the program by telling it to use drive A. DOS, which also falls for this little fib, looks for any files he requests in the NEWNOVEL directory on drive C. He fools DOS, DOS fools his word processor and, best of all, no one's hurt by his chicanery.

Removing a SUBST Assignment

Of course, at some point he may need to use drive A — the real drive A, not the *virtual drive* SUBST created using his NEWNOVEL directory. This would be the case, for example, if he wanted to copy files from his hard disk to a floppy disk. Before doing so, he could change his system back to normal with the following command:

```
SUBST A: /D
```

This returns drive letter A to its original assignment, the first floppy disk drive on a system.

The second command able to help my friend is APPEND. It can be used to allow a program to open data files in a directory or group of directories as if they were stored in the current directory.

A familiar metaphor for how APPEND works is the call forwarding feature provided by many of today's phone systems. Just as call forwarding allows your phone to find you when you're not at home, APPEND automatically lets DOS find the data files stored in an APPENDed directory, regardless of where they are actually located. The correct syntax for entering an APPEND command is:

```
APPEND [[drive:]path[;...]] [/X[:ON|:OFF]][/PATH:ON|/PATH:OFF] [/E]
```

APPEND Parameters and Command Switches

APPEND accepts the following parameter and command switches:

[drive:]path	is used to identify the drive and directory that you want to APPEND to the current directory. (To specify multiple drives and paths, separate individual entries with a semicolon.)
;	is used to cancel the existing list of APPENDed directories.
/X:ON	DOS maintains a PATH setting, which defines the directories through which DOS will search for a program file (that is, a file ending with an extension of .COM, .EXE, or .BAT) if it cannot find the file in the current directory. APPEND, on the other hand, ordinarily determines the directories that DOS will search for data files. But the /X:ON switch is used to temporarily add APPENDed directories to the current PATH, so that DOS will search these directories for both program files and data files.
/X:OFF	indicates that APPENDed directories are not added to the current path, and will not determine where DOS searches for program files. In this case, the APPENDed directories will be searched only when DOS cannot find a data file in the current directory.
/PATH:ON	If you enter the name of a data file along with its path as the parameter to some command, the setting of the /PATH switch determines what DOS will do if it cannot find the file in a specified path. /PATH:ON tells DOS that if it cannot find the file, it should then search the APPENDed directories. This is how DOS ordinarily behaves.

/PATH:OFF   In contrast to /PATH:ON, /PATH:OFF tells DOS that if it cannot find the file in the specified path, it should not search any APPENDed directories. Instead, DOS will simply return a "File Not Found" error message.

/E   assigns the list of APPENDed directories to an environment variable named APPEND.

The primary difference between SUBST and APPEND is that SUBST assigns a "permanent" drive letter to a directory while APPEND always associates the specified directories with the current one. If you change directories, files in any APPENDed directories accompany you to this new location.

Be aware, however, that some penalties accompany this power. APPEND should be used carefully as it can "get confused" easily. What if two different files with the same name exist in the current *and* an APPENDed directory? Which one do you want when you tell DOS to look for a file with this name? When DOS goes to save a new file, where should it be stored? In the current or an APPENDed directory?

The best advice I can give you is to read carefully the section on APPEND in Part II of this book. Then read, just as carefully, any information you can find on APPEND in the *MS-DOS User's Guide*. APPEND is both potentially useful and potentially harmful. Make certain, therefore, that you know *how* to use it before you attempt to use it.

Earlier versions of DOS included two additional commands that allowed you to "fool" DOS into thinking one thing was something else. These two commands, ASSIGN and JOIN, disappeared in the recently released MS-DOS 6.0.

ASSIGN did for disks what SUBST does for directories; it allowed you to assign a new drive letter to a disk drive. JOIN worked exactly the opposite of SUBST; it was used to assign a directory name to a disk drive. In essence, both of these older commands have been supplanted by capabilities now available with either SUBST or APPEND.

We're two-thirds of the way through our trilogy of related topics. In the previous chapter we looked at disk-related commands. This chapter examined how DOS allows you to manage directories. In Chapter 5, the final part of our trilogy, we'll discuss what is perhaps the most critical element of your PC operations: the program and data files stored in the directories you create for your disks.

Chapter 5

Working with Files

As you've seen throughout the previous four chapters, DOS controls a number of important elements within your PC environment. None, however, is more critical than the main topic of this chapter: the program and data files stored on your disks.

Files form the backbone of your PC activities. Stated simply, your computer would be little more than a high-tech paperweight if it could not find, manage, and access files. Your PC looks in files when seeking the instructions, or *programs*, it uses to help you complete any tasks you set out to accomplish. Files also contain the information, or *data*, that allows these programs to produce the desired results.

This chapter introduces the various DOS commands used to manage your disk files. Before actually placing fingers to keyboard and experimenting with these file-related commands, however, it's probably a good idea to examine the various types of files found on a typical PC system.

Familiar situations often help us to explain unfamiliar concepts. Coincidentally, I have the perfect analogy to explain how PC files work.

The Ghost of Christmas Presents

I sat down to write this chapter the week after Christmas. Still threatening to bury our home at the time was the pile of toys received by my six-year-old child, Jason. And an awful lot of the toys bore that dreaded disclaimer: "Some assembly required." So it came to pass that I spent most of my waking hours in the days following Christmas, well, *assembling*. This activity involves reading poorly written instructions that attempt to explain how to combine inadequately identified parts into a working whole. Add to that the fact that this all occurs under the tutelage of an impatient six-year-old querying at intervals of approximately every ten nanoseconds, "Is it ready yet?"

But, enough kvetching. My purpose in relating this personal tale is to provide you with a familiar example of how a computer uses files. A computer works pretty much the same way I did as I assembled my son's Christmas presents. (Although, honesty once again forces me to admit, a computer works much more efficiently and with many fewer false starts than I experienced.) To begin with, a computer requires instructions to accomplish something. These instructions take the form of a program, which is a series of specially coded commands describing precisely what it is a computer is expected to accomplish and exactly how it should go about accomplishing this. Most computer programs also use data — the "parts" with which a program works as it goes about its assigned task.

When all the pieces are assembled properly on your PC, programs and data come together to produce the desired results. For example, a spreadsheet (program) and the numbers (data) it is instructed to manipulate combine to generate error-free, attractively formatted financial reports.

But where do these programs and data come from? And how do they get from wherever they start out to your computer? This is where files enter the PC picture.

File Types

Your PC, an admittedly incredible machine that performs impressive feats, is actually pretty stupid. It can only count to one (remember the binary method introduced in the first chapter?), and it literally forgets almost everything it knows whenever you're not using it. That's because the memory in your computer is *volatile*, meaning that its contents cannot be maintained without a constant electrical current. Each time you turn off a computer, everything you were working on disappears, lost in the electronic ether.

This means you must find some method for preserving your ongoing projects between sessions, some way to make the programs and data you require readily accessible at the start of a new day. Files provide this capability.

Most of the files you use on your PC will fall into one of two categories:

- program files
- data files

> ✔ *Note:* To be sure, you'll encounter other kinds of PC files, as well, the more you use DOS and your PC. For the current discussion, however, I'll concentrate on program and data files.

You've already seen program files in action. We've worked with several of them in the previous two chapters. The FORMAT command we used to prepare the floppy disk we've been working with is one example. When you entered the FORMAT command, DOS loaded into your computer's memory a program called FORMAT.EXE, which was stored on your hard disk. Your PC then executed the coded instructions that this FORMAT.EXE program contains.

You may not realize it, but you've also encountered data, similar to that which all PC programs need to work properly. It wasn't much data, to be sure, but it was data used by a program, nonetheless. When you formatted that initial floppy disk, for example, you entered the following command:

```
FORMAT A: /S
```

In this procedure, FORMAT was the actual command required to initiate the desired formatting operation — to read in the FORMAT.EXE program file, as it were. The other items, the **A:** drive designator and the **/S** switch specifying a system disk, represented two pieces of data that FORMAT needed to perform the way you wanted it to — that is, by preparing a disk in drive A (A:) to include the DOS system files (/S).

This, in a nutshell, is how virtually all PC operations work: Responding to your commands, DOS loads and executes a program, or, as is the case with the internal DOS commands, executes a program already in memory. This program, in turn, uses some form of data to determine precisely what you wish to accomplish.

When executing most DOS commands, you'll enter all the required data directly from the keyboard, as you did with the FORMAT command above. It's much more common, however, for a program to load data from an external file. This is especially true with large application programs — word processors, spreadsheets, database managers, and the like — which tend to require more data than you'd want to enter by hand each time you run them.

DOS Says: Do It My Way

Any request for a file, whether it comes directly from you entered at the keyboard or from within an application program running on your PC, must pass muster with DOS before it will be acted upon. In other words, DOS must recognize what is being requested as a valid filename and, just as important, it must know where that file can be found.

DOS applies specific conventions to each of these tasks. Let's begin by looking at what DOS recognizes as a valid filename.

File Naming Conventions

DOS filenames are divided into two parts:

- the filename
- an optional extension

Take a look at the following filename:

```
MYFILE.DAT
```

The portion of this filename preceding the period, MYFILE, is its filename. The portion following the period, DAT, is the extension.

A set of strict rules govern how a filename is structured and what it can contain. These include:

1. The filename portion may be no more than eight characters long.
2. The extension portion may not exceed three characters.
3. You must use a period (.) to divide the filename from the extension.
4. The filename portion is mandatory.
5. The extension is optional, as is the period if no extension is used.
6. Neither the filename nor the extension portion of a DOS filename may contain blank spaces.
7. The following characters may not be used in either the filename or extension portion of the filename: . " / \ [ ] |< > + : = ; ,

DOS demands strict adherence to the seven rules listed above when naming your files. Over the years, additional, less formal file naming conventions have evolved, as well. Primary among these is the accepted practice of using the extension portion of a filename to indicate the file's contents — what kind of data it contains.

The following list includes some of the more commonly used file extensions and contains a brief description of the type of file each one usually indicates:

EXE An executable program: A program that, when the filename portion of its name is entered at the system prompt, actually loads and executes a series of commands.

COM A second extension used to identify executable programs.

BAT A batch file: A batch file is a text file that contains commands and other instructions you want DOS to execute whenever it is run. Although it executes commands, a batch file is not, technically speaking, an executable file like an EXE or COM file. (You'll learn more about batch files in Chapter 9.)

SYS A system file or device driver: A file containing the instructions DOS needs to modify its default operations or, alternately, recognize a particular piece of equipment such as a mouse, CD-ROM device, scanner, and so forth.

DRV A second extension used to identify some device drivers.

TXT A text file: A file that contains text only, rather than executable code.

ASC An ASCII file: A file containing only characters recognized within the American Standard Code for Information Interchange. (In reality, an ASCII file is just a specific kind of text file.)

BAK A backup file: The BAK extension is used by many applications to identify a second copy of a data file, usually as it existed just prior to the most recent save operation.

BIN A binary file: Binary files commonly contain the information that a specific program needs to run properly.

INI Initialization files: These are used to store the initial settings for a particular program. A file called DOSSHELL.INI, for example, contains the default settings for the DOS Shell.

FNT A font file: A file containing the typefaces normally used by a word processor or desktop publishing program.

HLP A help file: A file containing the messages displayed when you request information about a program using its on-line Help feature.

ZIP A file compressed using a utility program called PKZIP. Compressed files preserve all of the information contained in the original file, but take up less storage space. ZIPped files subsequently must be expanded using a utility called PKUNZIP before they can be executed or, alternately, the data they contain loaded into an application program.

ARC A file compressed using ARC, another popular compression utility.

Many DOS application programs also apply special naming conventions to the files they create or use. PC Paintbrush files, for example, are commonly referred to as PCX files, since they are created using the default three letter file extension PCX. Windows uses the file extension DLL to identify files containing special code that tells a program how to exchange data with other Windows-based applications. Other programs employ additional naming conventions for their data files.

As a rule, ignoring these conventions will not influence the way DOS operates. They do, however, provide a convenient way to organize the program and data files your disks contain. (The three exceptions to this general rule are EXE, COM, and BAT files. A file must use one of these three extensions if it is an executable or a batch file.)

Path Notation

You may need to include a file's path notation with its name so that DOS can identify the disk drive and directory in which the specific file you're looking for is located. An analogy to this is the way in which the prefix North or South is often used to identify a specific location. For example, North America and South America are two different continents, even though they share the name America. Similarly, the following two notations would indicate two different files, even though the files themselves share the same filename:

```
C:\WORD\PERSONAL\LETTER.TXT
C:\WORD\BUSINESS\LETTER.TXT
```

> ✓ *Note:* We discussed how DOS uses path notations in the previous chapter. Review that information if you find the above explanation confusing.

Keep these rules and conventions in mind as we discuss the various commands DOS provides to help you manage your program and data files. I'll begin that discussion by formally introducing a command you've already used, although I didn't tell you exactly how it worked at the time.

Copying Files (The COPY Command)

We've already seen the COPY command in action. You used it in the previous chapter to copy the LABEL.EXE file from the DOS directory of your hard disk to the TEST directory on the floppy system disk we formatted in Chapter 3. (Remember, this chapter and the two that preceded it form a trilogy covering interrelated topics. Now that the pieces are coming together, hopefully you are beginning to see what I mean)

The basic syntax for entering a COPY command is:

COPY [/A|/B] [*drive1*:][*path1*] [/A|/B] [*drive2*:][*path2*] [/V]

COPY Parameters and Command Switches

COPY accepts the following parameters and command switches:

drive1: is the drive containing the files you plan to copy.

path1 is the complete filename, including directory path, of the file(s) being copied.

drive2: is the drive (or other device) you want to copy files to

path2	is the directory path and, if necessary, filename of the target file(s)
/A	instructs DOS to terminate the COPY operation once it encounters an end-of-file marker in an ASCII file.
/B	identifies a non-ASCII (binary) file transfer, which instructs DOS to ignore any end-of-file markers it encounters and base its copy on the number of corresponding bytes contained in the source file.
/V	instructs DOS to verify that all sectors written to the target disk are recorded properly.

Using COPY

At its most basic level, COPY allows you to duplicate files. Consider it the PC analog of a copy machine. In the previous chapter, for example, we used COPY to duplicate the LABEL.EXE file on a disk in drive A. Of course, a subsequent DELTREE command erased this duplicate file, leaving our floppy work disk somewhat barren. Let's correct this situation.

If necessary, type **A:** and press **Enter** to make drive A the active drive.

Type **CD ** and press **Enter** to ensure that the root directory is the current directory in drive A.

Type **MD\TEST** and press **Enter** to re-create the TEST subdirectory we removed in the previous chapter.

Type **CD TEST** and press **Enter** to make this the current directory.

Okay, now we've pretty much rebuilt the practice structure that the DELTREE command wiped out earlier. So, let's practice a little bit.

Type **COPY C:\DOS\ANSI.SYS** and press **Enter**.
Type **COPY C:\CONFIG.SYS ..** and press **Enter**.
Type **COPY ..\COMMAND.COM COMMAND.BAK** and press **Enter**.
Type **COPY C:*.INI *.HLD** and press **Enter**.
Type **COPY C:*.FLP** and press **Enter**.

That's should be enough. Now, let's analyze the results of all this activity. Your screen should resemble Figure 5.1. Notice that DOS reports the results of each COPY operation. It even informs you when it can't find the specified source file, as indicated by the following message that appears after the last COPY command:

```
File not found - C:\????????.FLP
```

I confess, I threw a lot of variations on the basic COPY theme at you in the above command sequence. To see what actually made its way to our TEST directory:

Type **DIR** and press **Enter**.

110   DOS 6.0 HANDBOOK

```
(A:\) CD TEST
(A:\TEST) COPY C:\DOS\ANSI.SYS
        1 file(s) copied
(A:\TEST) COPY C:\CONFIG.SYS ..
        1 file(s) copied
(A:\TEST) COPY ..\COMMAND.COM COMMAND.BAK
        1 file(s) copied
(A:\TEST) COPY C:\DOS\*.INI *.HLD
C:\DOS\DOSSHELL.INI
C:\DOS\QBASIC.INI
        2 file(s) copied
(A:\TEST) COPY C:\*.FLP
File not found - C:\????????.FLP
        0 file(s) copied
(A:\TEST)
```

Figure 5.1 Sample COPY commands

Figure 5.2 shows a listing of the files copied to the TEST directory. Hmmm. Some simple math indicates something isn't right. According to DOS, a total of 5 files were copied. But I only see four actual files in Figure 5.2, not counting the two directory symbols. What happened? I'll answer that perplexing question in a few paragraphs. First, though, let's see what was copied, how it was copied and what, if anything, happened during the COPY operation.

1. The first COPY command duplicated a file called ANSI.SYS in TEST, just as you'd expect it to. No surprises here.
2. COMMAND.BAK was created with the third COPY command. But how? Well, I used the double-period (..) directory indicator to copy COMMAND.COM from the parent directory of TEST, the root directory of drive A. (Remember this symbol from Chapter 4?) I renamed it COMMAND.BAK in the process by specifying this as the name of the target file.

```
(A:\TEST) DIR

 Volume in drive A is MS-DOS 6
 Volume Serial Number is 1E4F-18E5
 Directory of A:\TEST

.            <DIR>     12-21-92   7:12p
..           <DIR>     12-21-92   7:12p
ANSI     SYS      8959 12-06-92   6:00a
COMMAND  BAK     53405 12-06-92   6:00a
DOSSHELL HLD     16922 12-15-92  10:06a
QBASIC   HLD       132 12-20-92   5:01p
        6 file(s)     79418 bytes
                     999936 bytes free

(A:\TEST)
```

Figure 5.2 Several files were copied to the TEST directory.

3. The fourth COPY command utilized a wildcard character (*), also introduced in the previous chapter, to copy all files with the extension INI from the DOS directory of drive C to TEST, renaming them with an HLD extension in the process.

That covers the first, third, and fourth COPY commands. But what did that second command accomplish? Where's the CONFIG.SYS file? To answer this:

Type **CD ..** and press **Enter**.
Type **DIR** and press **Enter**.

There it is, in the root directory of drive A, as shown in Figure 5.3. But how did it get there? Once again, the parent directory symbol (..) came into play. This time, however, I used it as the *drive2* parameter to specify that I wanted COPY to place a duplicate of the CONFIG.SYS file on drive C in the parent directory of TEST.

As these few examples illustrate, COPY is an incredibly useful and flexible command. But we're not finished yet.

Using COPY to Create a File

The COPY command can do much more than simply copy files between disks. It also can copy input from virtually any DOS device and direct the output to another device. You can use this capability of the COPY command, for example, to create a new file directly from the keyboard, using the following command syntax:

`COPY CON [`*drive:*`][`*pathname*`]`

The CON parameter in this command is the device name DOS assigns your keyboard. In essence, therefore, this COPY command is telling DOS: "Take what

```
(A:\TEST) CD..

(A:\) DIR

 Volume in drive A is MS-DOS 6
 Volume Serial Number is 1E4F-18E5
 Directory of A:\

COMMAND  COM     53405 12-06-92   6:00a
TEST         <DIR>       12-21-92   7:12p
CONFIG   SYS       229 12-17-92   2:53p
        3 file(s)        53634 bytes
                        999936 bytes free

(A:\)
```

Figure 5.3 Wildcards and other tools let you do some pretty creative copying.

I type at the keyboard and copy it to the file specified by **drive:pathname**." To see what I mean, try the following:

Type **COPY CON AUTOEXEC.BAT** and press **Enter**.
Type **DATE** and press **Enter**.
Type **TIME** and press **Enter**.
Type **PROMPT I started the system from drive** A and press **Enter**.
Press **Ctrl+Z**.
Press **Enter**.

> ✔ *Note:* Remember, the notation used in the second-to-last line indicates a key combination — that is, pressing more than one key concurrently. This command indicates that you should hold down the Ctrl key and press Z. DOS uses this key combination to specify an end-of-file marker. The ^Z on your display reveals that DOS recognized the Ctrl+Z sequence. (The ^ indicates that the Ctrl key was pressed.)

When you've finished, the display should resemble Figure 5.4, which shows the full sequence used to create a file called AUTOEXEC.BAT. To see if this little experiment succeeded, let's call upon another file-related DOS command.

Viewing the Contents of a File (The TYPE Command)

The TYPE command lets you display the contents of a file. The correct syntax for entering a TYPE command is:

TYPE [*drive:*][*path*]*filename*

TYPE Parameters

Type accepts the following parameter:

[*drive:*][*path*]*filename*   indicates the full name, including path information, of the file you want to view.

```
(A:\) COPY CON AUTOEXEC.BAT
DATE
TIME
PROMPT I started the system from drive A
^Z
        1 file(s) copied

(A:\)
```

Figure 5.4   The COPY CON command provides a method for creating files directly from your keyboard.

Using TYPE

You can use the TYPE command to verify that the previous COPY CON operation was successful. First, clear the display. Then, to view the contents of AUTOEXEC.BAT:

Type **CLS** and press **Enter**.
Type **TYPE AUTOEXEC.BAT** and press **Enter**.

If all went as planned, your screen should contain the same commands entered earlier into AUTOEXEC.BAT:

```
DATE
TIME
PROMPT I started the system from drive A
```

> ✓ *Note:* Ctrl+Z, the end-of-file marker, is a "nonprinting" character; it does not show up on your display. That's why you don't see a line in AUTO-EXEC.BAT corresponding to the Ctrl+Z command.

I realize I threw two new commands at you in this AUTOEXEC.BAT file, DATE and TIME. They're so straightforward, however, that they don't require much explanation. In a nutshell, DATE lets you view and, optionally, reset the date recorded in your system clock. TIME allows you to do the same two things with the time recorded in your system clock. (DOS uses these two values to generate the date and time information included in directory listings, which you've seen several times already throughout the previous exercises.) That's it.

As the previous example demonstrates, TYPE provides a convenient way to see what's in your files. There are, however, limitations on how useful TYPE is. To see what I mean, try the following:

Type **TYPE COMMAND.COM** and press **Enter**.

Although the contents of the specified file, COMMAND.COM, were displayed on your screen, the results contained only gibberish. Why? TYPE is designed to display text files; that is, files stored in ASCII format as, obviously, AUTO-EXEC.BAT was. Consequently, TYPE is not able to display executable files, files stored in binary format that contain program code. Because COMMAND.COM does, indeed, contain program code, TYPE could not handle it. The result is all those impressive but illegible characters in Figure 5.5, commonly referred to as garbage. Despite its limitations, TYPE is useful when all you want to do is view the contents of a text file — even a long text, when it's used in conjunction with MORE, another DOS command.

```
(A:\) TYPE AUTOEXEC.BAT
DATE
TIME
PROMPT I started the system from drive A

(A:\) TYPE COMMAND.COM
⊖]§`×§  ╥* uɳ à‡                            ♪⯑d ▲ɳ. .◆⯑♪⯑Y ▲ɳ. ⯑♪⯑N ▲ɳ.
.⯑⯑♪⯑C ▲ɳ. .▶⯑⯑9 ▲ɳ. .¶⯑⯑/ ▲ɳ. .†⯑⯑% ▲ɳ. .⌐⯑⯑← ▲ɳ. . ⯑⯑◄ ▲ɳ. .$⯑⯑ ▲ɳ. .(⯑£.Ç>4⯑
⯑⯑ s♥⯑
(A:\)
```

Figure 5.5 TYPE can only be used to view ASCII (standard text) files.

Organizing Long Listings (The MORE Filter)

I introduced the concept of command filters in Chapter 2. Aside from that quick reference, however, I didn't really explain much. I'll rectify that now.

Filters are used to modify how a DOS command is executed. For example, the MORE filter causes DOS to display command output one screen at a time. The correct syntax for using the MORE filter is:

   command-name | **MORE**

or

   MORE <[*drive:*][*path*]*filename*

MORE Parameters

MORE accepts the following parameters:

   command-name   is used to specify the command that supplies information you want to display one screen at a time.

   [drive:][path]filename   is the location and name of a file that supplies data you want to display.

Using the MORE Filter

To use the MORE filter with a DOS command, you add it to the end of the command line, separating the command and MORE filter with the DOS pipe symbol (|). To see what this accomplishes, try the following:

Type **CD TEST** and press **Enter**.
Type **TYPE DOSSHELL.HLD | MORE** and press **Enter**.

DOS begins displaying the contents of DOSSHELL.HLD, a file you copied earlier into the TEST directory. However, DOSSHELL.HLD is a long file. Using the MORE filter causes DOS to pause after displaying the first 23 lines of the file (see Figure 5.6). The -- More -- prompt at the bottom of this figure screen indicates that DOS is waiting for you to press a key to resume the file listing. So:

```
EGA.INI/VGA.INI
*************** WARNING ********************
This file may contain lines with more than 256
characters. Some editors will truncate or split
these lines. If you are not sure whether your
editor can handle long lines, exit now without
saving the file.

Note: The editor which is invoked by the
      MS-DOS 5.0 EDIT command can be used
      to edit this file.
*************** NOTE ***********************
Everything up to the first left square bracket
character is considered a comment.
********************************************
[savestate]
screenmode = text
resolution = low
startup = filemanager
filemanagermode = shared
sortkey = name
pause = disabled
explicitselection = disabled
-- More --
```

Figure 5.6 The MORE filter lets you display long files one screen at a time.

Press any key.

After the next section of DOSSHELL.HOLD has been displayed, MORE will pause a second time and redisplay the -- More -- prompt again. Pressing any key resumes the directory listing. This cycle will be repeated until the entire file has been displayed, at which time you are returned to the system prompt.

Of course, if you're viewing an extremely long file, this could take a while. Luckily, DOS provides a special keystroke to interrupt commands that are already underway. For example, to interrupt this file display:

Press **Ctrl+C**.

DOS suspends the TYPE operation and returns you to the system prompt.

> ***Caution:*** MORE works by creating a temporary file on the active disk. It then uses this file to store information until it is displayed. MORE cannot create this file if the active disk is write-protected or does not have enough free space.

Deleting Files (The DEL and ERASE Commands)

As with directories, files also become outdated over time. And it makes no sense to take up valuable storage space with unneeded files. The DEL command allows you to delete unwanted files from your disks. The correct syntax for entering a DEL command is:

DEL `[drive:][path]filename [/P]`

or

ERASE `[drive:][path]filename [/P]`

> ✔ *Note:* DEL and ERASE accomplish the same thing. The very first DOS release offered only an ERASE command, a carryover from the UNIX operating system upon which DOS was based. The DEL command, which is shorter and therefore more convenient to use, entered the picture not long thereafter. Microsoft kept the ERASE command to maintain compatibility with the initial version of DOS and it's been around ever since.

DEL Parameters and Command Switches

DEL accepts the following parameters and command switches:

drive:path   is the location of the file or set of files you want to delete.

filename   is the name of the file or set of files you want to delete.

/P   instructs DOS to prompt you for confirmation before deleting the specified file or files.

A Few Words to the Wise

The DEL command is as dangerous as it is useful. Even experienced PC users have been known to inadvertently erase important files with a carelessly entered DEL command. And, yes, I'm one of them. I still shudder when I recall an incorrectly structured DEL command that, after I pressed Enter, proceeded to wipe out every file in my hard disk's DOS directory. It wasn't a pretty sight. The good news is that one such incident generally suffices to teach you a very valuable lesson: Look before you let DEL do its thing. If you don't, there may not be much to see after it's finished.

Nevertheless, I'm now going to bait Beelzebub, so to speak, and have you erase some of the practice files created in the previous exercises.

Using DEL

Deleting a single file is a relatively straightforward proposition. You simply follow the DEL command with the name of the file you want to erase. For example, to erase the ANSI.SYS file located in the TEST directory on drive A:

Type **DEL A:\TEST\ANSI.SYS** and press **Enter**.

Unlike when you originally copied this file, DOS offers no hint as to whether the DEL operation was successful. There's no "1 file(s) deleted" or similar message to let you know that everything worked as planned. But a quick DIR command lets you check the results. In fact, DOS even provides a way to request this listing quickly, while ensuring that the returned directory covers only those files erased with the previous DEL command. But before we do that, let's sidetrack to learn about function keys.

Using Function Keys with DOS Commands

Function keys originally appeared on mainframe computers. Their availability allowed application programmers to incorporate shortcuts into their software, which made it possible to initiate a specific operation merely by pressing the appropriate function key. IBM wisely incorporated this convenience into the design of its original PC. Function keys have been a mainstay of the PC industry ever since. In fact, several "standard" uses for specific function keys have evolved during the intervening years. Today, for example, most PC application programs let you use the F1 function key to request on-line help.

DOS also endows the function keys with some useful capabilities. The DOS *User's Guide* includes a complete explanation of what each function key does when you're working in DOS. Unfortunately, it's filled with references to templates and editing keys and tools and a lot of other impressive words that tend to confuse what are, in all honesty, relatively straightforward procedures. Allow me to clear up the confusion. The following list includes the most commonly used DOS function keys and describes what each accomplishes.

- *F1* Pressing the F1 function key sends a single letter from the most recently entered DOS command to your display screen.

- *F2* Pressing the F2 function key lets you automatically reenter the last DOS command, up to a specified character.

- *F3* Pressing the F3 function key recalls any characters remaining in the DOS command line used to execute the most recent DOS operation.

- *F7* Pressing the F7 function key displays a list of recently executed commands. (A special utility called DOSKEY must be loaded into memory for the F7 shortcut to work. You'll learn about DOSKEY in Chapter 9, "The Age of Automation.")

- *F9* Pressing the F9 function key lets you choose a previously entered command based on a line number reference displayed with the F7 key. (The F9 shortcut also requires that the DOSKEY utility be loaded into memory.)

Now let's use one of these function key shortcuts to see whether our earlier delete operation succeeded:

Type **DIR** .
Press the **Spacebar**.
Press the **F3** function key.
Press **Enter**.

As Figure 5.7 illustrates, the above sequence replaced the DEL command issued in the previous exercise with a DIR command. Notice also that DOS reported back that it could not find any file matching the specified filename, thus verifying that our DEL command worked.

Erasing Multiple Files

You can use DOS wildcard characters to erase multiple files with a single DEL command. To see how this works:

If necessary, type **CD \TEST** and press **Enter** to make TEST the current directory.
Type **DEL *.HLD** and press **Enter**.

Then, to check the results:

Type **DIR**.
Press the **Spacebar**.
Press the **F3** function key.
Press **Enter**.

Once again, DOS returns a "File not found" message, indicating that the DEL operation was successful.

In case you're curious, the previous sequence erased the DOSSHELL.HLD and QBASIC.HLD files we created with the COPY command earlier in this chapter. So they're gone, right? Well, yes and no. That ambivalent answer leads to a brief explanation of what happens when you erase a file.

```
(A:\TEST) DEL A:\TEST\ANSI.SYS

(A:\TEST) DIR A:\TEST\ANSI.SYS

 Volume in drive A is MS-DOS 6
 Volume Serial Number is 1E4F-18E5
 Directory of A:\TEST

File not found

(A:\TEST)
```

Figure 5.7 Function key shortcuts simplify entering DOS commands.

Gone, but Not Forgotten

When you delete a file, DOS does not actually eliminate all of the data that file contained. Rather, it modifies the disk directory, replacing the initial character in the erased file's name with a question mark (?), which tells DOS not to include this name in subsequent directory listings. DOS also updates the disk's file allocation table (FAT) to reflect the fact that any sectors previously occupied by the deleted file are now free — that is, available to store new data.

What does all of this magnetic maneuvering mean? Basically, it indicates that all of the data the erased file contained remains somewhere on your disk. DOS has merely developed a case of self-induced amnesia, causing it to forget, in essence, where the data is located. In some cases, however, this condition may only be temporary.

Recovering Deleted Files (The UNDELETE Command)

With early versions of DOS, deleted files were lost forever. (Well, that's not quite true. For years, other companies have offered special utilities that allowed you to recover erased files.) Starting with MS-DOS 5.0, however, Microsoft once again caught up to the competition and incorporated this ability into MS-DOS by adding an UNDELETE command to the DOS arsenal. The correct syntax for entering an UNDELETE command is:

```
UNDELETE[[drive:][path]filename] [/DT|/DS|/DOS]
UNDELETE [/LIST|/ALL|/PURGE[drive]|/STATUS|/LOAD|/U
|/S[:drive]|/Tdrive[-entries]]
```

UNDELETE Parameters and Command Switches

UNDELETE accepts the following parameters and command switches:

drive:path	is the location of the file or set of files you want to recover.
filename	is the name of the file or set of files you want to recover.
/DT	instructs DOS to recover only those files listed in a deletion-tracking file.
/DS	instructs DOS to recover only those files contained in a SENTRY directory.
/DOS	instructs DOS to recover only those files that are internally listed as deleted by MS-DOS.

/LIST	instructs DOS to list any deleted files on the current disk that it determines can be recovered, but does not initiate an UNDELETE operation.
/ALL	instructs DOS to recover automatically any deleted files it can, without user intervention.
/PURGE[:*drive*]	instructs DOS to delete the contents of the SENTRY directory on the specified drive.
/STATUS	instructs DOS to display the type of delete protection set up for each drive.
/LOAD	is used to load the terminate-and-stay-resident (TSR) portion of UNDELETE.
/U	is used to remove the TSR portion of UNDELETE from memory.
/S[:*drive*]	enables the Delete Sentry level of protection and loads the TSR portion of the UNDELETE program, using the settings defined in the UNDELETE.INI file.
/T*drive*[-*entries*]	enables the Delete Tracker level of protection and loads the TSR portion of the UNDELETE program.

Levels of UNDELETE Protection

UNDELETE lets you choose from three different levels of protection:

1. Delete Sentry: This is the highest level of protection DOS offers against data loss. Using Delete Sentry virtually guarantees that you'll be able to recover deleted files. You activate Delete Sentry by including the **/S** switch with an UNDELETE command.

2. Delete Tracker: The Tracker method provides an intermediate level of protection. It can recover lost data, as long as the request to restore a file is made within a reasonable amount of time. You activate Delete Tracker by including the **/T** switch with an UNDELETE command.

3. The third and least effective method of protection is to use the UNDELETE command only when you are attempting to restore a file. This method is available automatically and does not require that you load the TSR portion of UNDELETE into memory.

> ✔ **Note:** The TSR portion of UNDELETE used with the Sentry and Tracker methods requires approximately 14K of memory.

With the addition of UNDELETE to its command structure, DOS acquired the capability to protect against accidental loss of data in either a preventive or responsive manner. Using the /S or /T switch, you can load UNDELETE into memory as a TSR program. Once in memory, UNDELETE creates a tracking log in which it keeps a record of all file deletions. It also manages disk activity to protect the information that a deleted file contained, preventing it from being overwritten with new data. How long DOS reserves disk sectors depends on which protection level you choose, Sentry or Tracker.

The alternative to preinstalling UNDELETE into memory is to run the UNDELETE program only when you wish to recover a deleted file. When used in this manner, UNDELETE looks for directory entries that begin with a question mark (?). UNDELETE then analyzes the contents of any disk sectors assigned to these files to see if any data they originally contained has been overwritten. If it has, UNDELETE informs you that the file cannot be recovered. If the original contents of the file have not been modified, UNDELETE prompts you to replace the leading question mark with a new first letter for the filename.

> *Tip:* **Using UNDELETE**
>
> **Although the UNDELETE command will usually recover deleted files, it can guarantee success only if no subsequent disk write operations have used the disk sectors that the file originally occupied. For this reason, whenever possible, you should run UNDELETE immediately after a file is erased.**

Given that we just deleted the two HLD files from our TEST directory, UNDELETE should be able to recover them. Let's see.

Type **UNDELETE *.HLD** and press **Enter**.

DOS responds with the message shown in Figure 5.8. Because no Delete Tracking file exists, UNDELETE scans TEST, the current directory, looking for any filenames beginning with a question mark. It finds two. Furthermore, UNDELETE determines that the original data in both of these files remain available, meaning that they can be recovered. To recover the first file:

Type **Y**.

UNDELETE then displays the following prompt, requesting you to replace the question mark with a valid filename character:

```
Enter the first character of the filename.
```

At this prompt:

```
(A:\TEST) UNDELETE *.HLD

PC Shell - Stand-Alone Undelete   V6
(C) Copyright 1990   Central Point Software, Inc.
Unauthorized Duplication Prohibited.

Directory: A:\TEST
File Specs: *.HLD

    Delete Tracking file not found.

    DOS Directory contains    2 deleted files.
    Of those,    2 files may be recovered.

Using the DOS Directory.

       ?OSSHELL HLD     16922 12/15/92 10:06a   ...A
Do you want to undelete this file? (Y/N)
```

Figure 5.8 UNDELETE can often recover accidentally erased files.

Type **D**.

UNDELETE reports back that file recovery was successful and moves on to **?BASIC.HLD**, the second file matching our request, as shown in Figure 5.9. We won't restore this file.

Type **N**.

A quick DIR command will let you see whether UNDELETE recovered the DOSSHELL.HLD file.

Type **DIR** and press **Enter**.

```
PC Shell - Stand-Alone Undelete   V6
(C) Copyright 1990   Central Point Software, Inc.
Unauthorized Duplication Prohibited.

Directory: A:\TEST
File Specs: *.HLD

    Delete Tracking file not found.

    DOS Directory contains    2 deleted files.
    Of those,    2 files may be recovered.

Using the DOS Directory.

       ?OSSHELL HLD     16922 12/15/92 10:06a   ...A
Do you want to undelete this file? (Y/N)
Y
Enter the first character of the filename.
D
File successfully undeleted.

       ?BASIC   HLD       132 12/20/92 15:01p   ...A
Do you want to undelete this file? (Y/N)
N
```

Figure 5.9 DOS reports on the success or failure of the UNDELETE operation.

```
(A:\TEST) DIR

 Volume in drive A is MS-DOS 6
 Volume Serial Number is 1E4F-18E5
 Directory of A:\TEST

 .            <DIR>        12-21-92   7:12p
 ..           <DIR>        12-21-92   7:12p
 COMMAND  BAK        53405 12-06-92   6:00a
 DOSSHELL HLD        16922 12-15-92  10:06a
         4 file(s)          70327 bytes
                          1009152 bytes free

(A:\TEST)
```

Figure 5.10 UNDELETE restores the erased file to your directory listing.

There it is, back in the TEST directory, along with a file called COMMAND.BAK (see Figure 5.10). Hmmm. It's been a while since we created these files. I can't remember exactly what COMMAND.BAK is? I think it's a copy of COM-MAND.COM, but I'm not sure. Is there a simple way to find out? (Would I even ask this question if there weren't?)

Comparing Files (The FC Command)

You can use the FC command to compare the contents of two files and then have DOS report any differences that exist between them. The correct syntax for entering an FC command is:

FC [/A] [/C] [/L] [/LB*n*] [/N] [/T] [/W] [/*nnnn*]
[*drive1*:][*path1*]*filename1* [*drive2*:][*path2*]*filename2*

or, to compare binary files:

FC /B [*drive1*:][*path1*]*filename1* [*drive2*:][*path2*]*filename2*

FC Parameters and Command Switches

FC accepts the following parameters and command switches:

[*drive1:*][*path1*]*filename1*	is the complete name, including path information, for the first file you want to compare.
[*drive2:*][*path2*]*filename2*	is the complete name, including path information, for the second file you want to compare.
/A	instructs DOS to abbreviate the results of an ASCII comparison. By default, FC displays all lines that are different. The /A switch instructs FC to display only the first and last lines for each set of differences.

/C	instructs FC to ignore the case of letters. With the /C switch selected, for example, FC considers a and A to be the same.
/L	instructs DOS to compare the two files in ASCII mode.
/LB*n*	specifies how many lines you want to use for an internal line buffer, which FC uses to store consecutive lines in which differences exist.
/N	instructs DOS to display line numbers for reference during an ASCII comparison.
/T	instructs DOS to suppress the default FC procedure of expanding tabs to spaces during an ASCII file comparison.
/W	instructs DOS to compress tabs and spaces during the comparison.
/*nnnn*	specifies how many consecutive lines must match before FC considers the two files it is comparing to be resynchronized.
/B	instructs DOS to compare the files in binary mode.

Using FC

That's a lot of parameters and switches, many of them highly technical in nature. As a rule, however, you'll use FC to perform a quick comparison of two files, just to see if they are the same. Let's do this to determine if COMMAND.BAK is, as I suspect, a copy of COMMAND.COM, the DOS system file in the parent directory of TEST.

Type **FC COMMAND.BAK ..\COMMAND.COM**.
Press **Enter**.

FC begins by reading the specified files into memory, without executing them. It then compares their contents, line by line, to see if any differences exist. Finally, it reports the results of this comparison, as shown in Figure 5.11. In this case, no differences exist, so COMMAND.BAK is indeed a copy of COMMAND.COM. It would be nice if there were some way to change its name, to avoid future confusion. Of course, there is.

Renaming Files (The RENAME or REN Command)

The correct syntax for entering a REN command is:

```
(A:\TEST) DIR

 Volume in drive A is MS-DOS 6
 Volume Serial Number is 1E4F-18E5
 Directory of A:\TEST

 .            <DIR>      12-21-92    7:12p
 ..           <DIR>      12-21-92    7:12p
 COMMAND  BAK      53405 12-06-92    6:00a
 DOSSHELL HLD      16922 12-15-92   10:06a
         4 file(s)       70327 bytes
                       1009152 bytes free

(A:\TEST) FC COMMAND.BAK ..\COMMAND.COM
Comparing files COMMAND.BAK and ..\COMMAND.COM
FC: no differences encountered

(A:\TEST)
```

Figure 5.11 You use FC to compare the contents of two files.

    RENAME *[drive:][path]filename1 filename2*

or

    REN *[drive:][path]filename1 filename2*

REN Parameters

REN accepts the following parameters:

[drive:][path]filename1	is the complete name, including path information, for the file you want to rename.
filename2	is the new name you want assigned to the file or group of files you want to rename.

Using REN

To avoid future confusion, let's go ahead and rename the COMMAND.BAK file to COMMAND.COM.

    Type **REN COMMAND.BAK COMMAND.COM**.
    Press **Enter**.

DOS does not report the results of a REN command. Once again, however, you could use the DIR command to see whether COMMAND.BAK has been renamed. Go ahead and do this, if you want.

    There are a couple of limitations you should be aware of when using RENAME. First of all, it does not allow you to specify a new drive or path for the renamed file. Files can only be renamed within the directory on which they are already located. Second, the new name you assign to a file cannot match that of another file in the current directory. DOS automatically aborts a RENAME operation if a file with *filename2* already exists in the current directory.

> *Tip:* **Wildcards and RENAME**
> DOS supports the use of wildcards (* and ?)with the RENAME command. This lets you rename groups of files having similar filenames with a single REN command.

Verifying File Copies (The VERIFY Command)

Earlier, you saw how to use the FC command to determine if two files are identical to one another. An ancillary use for FC is to check whether a COPY operation was successful; after copying a file, you could compare its contents to the original. However, executing two DOS commands each time you copy a file just to ensure that COPY didn't malfunction in some manner is not overly efficient. An alternative is to include the /V (verify) switch with every COPY command you execute. But what if you were to forget this switch? Certainly, the odds are against that particular COPY operation failing. Still, Murphy's Law states: "Anything that can go wrong, will go wrong."

Luckily, there is a way to force DOS to verify all file copies. It's done with a single command that you run once and then forget about. That command is VERIFY. The correct syntax for entering a VERIFY command is:

VERIFY [ON|OFF]

VERIFY Parameters

VERIFY accepts the following parameters:

ON   instructs DOS to enable file verification.

OFF   instructs DOS to disable file verification.

> *Note:* Entering VERIFY with no command switch causes DOS to report on the current status of file verification, that is, whether verification is enabled (ON) or disabled (OFF).

> **Tip:** Automatic Verification
> To ensure that copy verification is always in effect, try including a VERIFY ON statement in an AUTOEXEC.BAT file. Doing so enables file checking automatically, each time you start your system. (You'll learn many other things that can be accomplished with a well-designed AUTOEXEC.BAT file in Chapter 9.)

Moving Files (The MOVE Command)

The COPY command provides a convenient way to replicate (i.e., clone) a file. Moving a file, however, has not always been as easy. In the past, this process involved two separate commands. First, you had to COPY the file to a new disk or directory; then, you had to use the DEL command to delete the file from its original location. The MOVE command, new to MS-DOS 6.0, eliminates this inconvenience by allowing you to relocate a file with a single command. The correct syntax for entering a MOVE command is:

```
MOVE [drive:][pathname][filename1]
     [drive:][pathname][filename2]
```

MOVE Parameters

MOVE accepts the following parameters:

[drive:][pathname]filename1   is the complete name, including path information, for the file you want to move.

[drive:][pathname]filename2   is the complete name, including path information, if necessary, for the new location to which you want this file moved.

Using MOVE

Just for the heck of it, let's try moving the DOSSHELL.HLD file one level up in our current directory structure, from the TEST directory to the root directory of drive. To do this:

Type **MOVE DOSSHELL.HLD** ...
Press **Enter**.
Type **DIR** and press **Enter**.
Type **DIR ..** and press **Enter**.

As Figure 5.12 illustrates, the MOVE command relocated DOSSHELL.HLD from the TEST directory to the root directory of drive A.

```
 Volume in drive A is MS-DOS 6
 Volume Serial Number is 1E4F-18E5
 Directory of A:\TEST

 .            <DIR>       12-21-92   7:12p
 ..           <DIR>       12-21-92   7:12p
 COMMAND  COM        53405 12-06-92   6:00a
         3 file(s)         53405 bytes
                         1009152 bytes free

(A:\TEST) DIR..

 Volume in drive A is MS-DOS 6
 Volume Serial Number is 1E4F-18E5
 Directory of A:\

 COMMAND  COM        53405 12-06-92   6:00a
 TEST         <DIR>       12-21-92   7:12p
 CONFIG   SYS          229 12-17-92   2:53p
 AUTOEXEC BAT           54 12-21-92   8:58p
 DOSSHELL HLD        16922 12-15-92  10:06a
         5 file(s)         70610 bytes
                         1009152 bytes free

(A:\TEST)
```

Figure 5.12 The MOVE command reduces moving a file to a single operation.

Renaming Directories with MOVE

As an added bonus, MOVE can be used to rename directories, another capability you previously had to look outside MS-DOS to find. To see how this works:

Type **CD ..** and press **Enter** to move to the root directory.

Type **MOVE A:\TEST A:\NEWTEST** and press **Enter**.

Type **DIR** and press **Enter**.

As Figure 5-13 illustrates, MOVE renamed the TEST directory to NEWTEST, as instructed.

```
(A:\TEST) CD..

(A:\) MOVE A:\TEST A:\NEWTEST
a:\test => a:\newtest [ok]

(A:\) DIR

 Volume in drive A is MS-DOS 6
 Volume Serial Number is 1E4F-18E5
 Directory of A:\

 COMMAND  COM        53405 12-06-92   6:00a
 NEWTEST      <DIR>       12-21-92   7:12p
 CONFIG   SYS          229 12-17-92   2:53p
 AUTOEXEC BAT           54 12-21-92   8:58p
 DOSSHELL HLD        16922 12-15-92  10:06a
         5 file(s)         70610 bytes
                         1009152 bytes free

(A:\)
```

Figure 5.13 MOVE can also be used to rename directories.

> ✓ **Note:** When using MOVE to assign a new name to a directory, you must be located in a directory other than the one you want to rename. Attempting to rename the directory you're working in causes DOS to abort the MOVE operation and display the following error message:
>
> ```
> Permission denied
> ```

Copying Files from Multiple Directories (The XCOPY Command)

As I've pointed out several times, DOS continues to evolve. Many new commands added to recent versions of DOS perform operations that were missing from previous versions; MOVE, UNDELETE, UNFORMAT, and others come immediately to mind. The COPY command, which has been a part of DOS since its initial release, has one major shortcoming. It can be used only to duplicate files located in the same directory. Prior to the release of MS-DOS 3.3, copying files from multiple directories required multiple COPY commands, even if all of the directories involved were connected to one another within a disk's directory tree. XCOPY eliminates this restriction by allowing you to copy files from multiple directories with a single command. The correct syntax for entering an XCOPY command is:

XCOPY *source [destination]* [/A|/M] [/D:*date*] [/P] [/S [/E]] [/V] [/W]

XCOPY Parameters and Command Switches

XCOPY accepts the following parameter and command switches:

source is the name and location of any files you want to copy. (When using XCOPY, this parameter must include either a drive letter or a path.

destination identifies where you want to copy the files to. (This parameter can include a drive letter and colon, a directory name, a filename, or any combination of these items.)

/A instructs DOS to copy only source files that have their archive file attributes set, but does not update this attribute as part of the XCOPY operation.

/M instructs DOS to copy source files that have their archive file attributes set and, unlike the /A switch, updates each file's attribute after it is copied.

/D:*date*   instructs DOS to copy only those files that have been modified on or after the specified date.

/P   instructs DOS to prompt you before each file is copied.

/S   instructs DOS to copy specified files located in any subdirectories running off the current directory or a directory specified in the source parameter, unless the subdirectory is empty. (This is the switch that endows XCOPY with its most impressive capability. Omitting this switch causes XCOPY to work like the COPY command, in that it will only copy files from a single directory.)

/E   instructs DOS to re-create all subdirectories in *source*, even if they are empty.

/V   instructs DOS to verify that the sectors written to the target disk are recorded properly.

/W   instructs DOS to display the following message before initiating the XCOPY operation:

```
Press any key to begin copying file(s)
```

Using XCOPY

We're about to achieve something very impressive in three short commands. Are you ready? All right, let's go.

Type **MD C:\TEST** and press **Enter**.

Type **XCOPY *.* C:\TEST /S** and press **Enter**.

Okay, so at first glance maybe it doesn't look like anything impressive happened. To see how erroneous first impressions can be, try the following:

Type **C:** and press **Enter**.

Type **CD \TEST** and press **Enter**.

Type **TREE /F** and press **Enter**.

What you're looking at is a complete reproduction of the directory tree from the work disk we've been using in drive A (see Figure 5.14). XCOPY not only duplicated the files in the root directory of A (which is where we were when we entered the XCOPY command), adding the **/S** switch to the XCOPY command also caused it to create and replicate the contents of the NEWTEST subdirectory. True, our work disk only had one subdirectory on it, but XCOPY could have handled a directory tree a dozen levels deep just as easily.

```
COMMAND.COM
CONFIG.SYS
AUTOEXEC.BAT
DOSSHELL.HLD
NEWTEST\COMMAND.COM
        5 File(s) copied

(A:\) C:

(C:\) CD TEST

(C:\TEST) TREE /F
Directory PATH listing for Volume MS-DOS 6
Volume Serial Number is 1991-76A1
C:.
    │   COMMAND.COM
    │   CONFIG.SYS
    │   AUTOEXEC.BAT
    │   DOSSHELL.HLD
    │
    └───NEWTEST
            COMMAND.COM

(C:\TEST)
```

Figure 5.14 XCOPY reproduces an entire directory tree with a single command.

✓ *Note:* The only thing missing from this "clone" of our work disk are the two DOS system files, IO.SYS and MSDOS.SYS. Older versions of XCOPY could copy all files — even hidden and system files — to a destination disk, if instructed to do so. This is a capability fraught with potential perils, however. Wisely, Microsoft dropped this capability from the XCOPY program, beginning with MS-DOS 6.

Tip: XCOPY Is Faster
Because XCOPY reads multiple files into memory, it's actually faster to use for file duplication than the COPY command. So, use it. I tend to rely on XCOPY exclusively when copying files.

This about wraps up our examination of the DOS commands used to perform file-related tasks. Once again, we've covered a lot of ground. As I stated at the beginning of this chapter, though, files form the backbone of your PC operations. Knowing how to manage them is critical to using DOS effectively.

We've also come to the end of the trilogy that began with Chapter 3. Starting in the next chapter, we move away from the "nuts and bolts" of disks and files and begin looking at some of the more ephemeral aspects of DOS. Specifically, we'll see how to use device drivers to expand DOS's capabilities and enhance its performance.

Chapter 6

Working with Devices and Drivers

With this chapter we begin looking beyond the basic DOS commands used to manage your disks and any the files they contain. As I stated in Chapter 1, DOS assumes almost total responsibility for your *entire* PC system.

As important as they are, disks and files represent only a portion of that system — one of the more important portions, to be sure, but a mere portion, nonetheless. Other items found on virtually every computer include memory, a display, a keyboard, and one or more communication ports. And such items define only the most rudimentary PC system. Beyond these components, the possibilities are nearly infinite.

One of the major attractions associated with MS-DOS systems is their flexibility. From the beginning, DOS computers were designed to be customized. The PC you purchase initially can be viewed as nothing more than a foundation. Over time it's possible to build upon this foundation, adding such useful and exotic devices as a mouse, a modem, a printer, a sound card, a scanner, a tape drive, a CD-ROM device, and many more. DOS allows you to construct — electronic brick by electronic brick, so to speak — the perfect PC, one that's designed to meet your personal requirements.

Immediately following installation, DOS knows how to control the primary components of any personal computer: its keyboard, display, memory, disk drives, communication ports, and so forth. Should you decide to customize your system to incorporate devices beyond this basic setup, however, you'll need to inform DOS of their presence and, even more important, provide the information required to manage them properly. In this chapter we'll look at how to use device drivers to modify your initial PC configuration.

What Is a Device?

A device, quite simply, is anything that allows your PC to communicate with the outside world. Devices can be divided into three main categories:

- input devices
- output devices
- input/output devices

Which category a specific device falls into depends on how it is used. A device that transfers information exclusively into your computer is called an input device; a device that transfers information out of your computer is called an output device; and as you've probably surmised, input/output devices can move information in either direction — that is, into or out of your PC. Familiar input devices include:

- keyboards
- mice
- scanners
- joysticks
- trackballs
- touch-sensitive input pads
- CD-ROM devices

Familiar output devices include:

- monitors
- printers
- audio speakers

Familiar input/output devices include:

- memory
- floppy disk drives
- hard disks
- tape drives
- modems
- sound boards (if they include recording capabilities)
- network cards
- WORM (write-once read-many) devices

> ✓ ***Note:*** It may have surprised you to see memory included in this last category. Strictly speaking, however, memory is also a device, one that DOS constantly moves information into and out of. In fact, as you'll discover in the next chapter, DOS includes several device drivers that are designed to help your PC use its memory more efficiently.

To repeat, DOS itself contains all of the instructions required to manage many of these components — keyboards, disk drives, memory, etc. Other devices, such as a modem, can be controlled directly by the appropriate application program; still others, however, require you to make special instructions, called device drivers, available to DOS before they will work properly.

One popular input device, for example, is a mouse. When available, this particular PC peripheral can be used to move a cursor around the display, select menu items in a graphics-based environment such as Windows, and perform a variety of other useful and convenient operations. Before DOS can control the movements of a mouse, though, you need to load its device driver — usually a file called MOUSE.EXE, MOUSE.COM or MOUSE.SYS — into memory. (You'll learn how to install device drivers in the next chapter, "Have It Your Way: Fine-Tuning Your System.")

DOS Devices

DOS assigns device names to those items it controls directly. When you direct output to a printer attached to your first parallel port, for example, DOS transfers data to LPT1, the device name DOS assigns to that particular parallel port, using command sequences a printer recognizes. If your PC includes a second parallel port, DOS assigns it the device name LPT2. Chances are your system also has one or more serial ports; DOS assigns these ports device names, as well: COM1, COM2, and so forth. Even your keyboard and monitor share a device name: CON, short for console.

In fact, DOS assigns virtually every hardware component on your system its own device name. This name, in turn, corresponds to the memory address through which instructions for that device are coordinated. The advantage device names possess over actual addresses will become obvious in the next section.

Redirecting Input and Output

This name game that DOS plays has some practical repercussions. Using the appropriate procedures, you can instruct DOS to send input and output *away* from its normal destination to a different device, a process called *redirection*. You don't have to know the actual address with which that device is associated, either.

Redirecting Output to the System Printer

The default destination of a directory listing, for example, is your monitor. The previous two chapters contained several examples of this. But let's say that, instead, you wanted to print the contents of a directory. Is this possible? Yes, and it's not even that difficult. All you have to do is include a greater than symbol (>) in the appropriate place within the command for which you want input or output redirected.

Let's try redirecting a directory listing of all files stored in the DOS directory to the system printer — which DOS identifies as a device called PRN — rather than to your monitor, as would normally happen. To see how this works:

Type **DIR C:\DOS /W > PRN** and press **Enter**.

> *Caution:* The previous exercise requires that you have a printer connected to the first parallel port (LPT1) on your PC. This printer should be turned on and set to "on-line." If you do not have a parallel printer, or if your printer is connected to a port other than the PRN device, the previous command sequence will cause DOS to display the following error message:
>
> ```
> Write fault error writing device PRN
> Abort, Retry, Ignore, Fail?
> ```
>
> Should this happen, pressing **A** (Abort) or **F** (Fail) will return you to the DOS system prompt.

If all went as planned, your printer should have spewed forth a page containing a listing of all the files copied to your DOS directory during installation. This happened because you used the redirection symbol (>) to deflect the output of the DIR command away from the monitor, its normal output device, to PRN, your default system printer.

Redirecting Output to a File

Extending the concept of redirection to its logical conclusion, it's easy to extrapolate that, if DOS perceives a disk drive as a device, it also should be able to redirect output to a file created on that device. It can, as the following exercise will demonstrate:

Type **DIR C:\DOS /W > FILELIST.TXT** and press **Enter**.
Type **TYPE FILELIST.TXT** and press **Enter**.

The first command redirects a listing of all files in the DOS directory to a file named FILELIST.TXT. The second command displays the contents of this newly created file on your monitor.

At a slightly higher technical level, redirection is the process that permits one computer to control a second computer over a telephone line or network connection. Input entered into the first computer is redirected over this connection, causing the second computer to respond. Admittedly, this is a simplistic explanation of how remote access and networking work. My objective, however, is to demonstrate how potentially powerful device redirection can be.

The DOS Device Drivers

DOS provides other device-related tools, as well. Microsoft includes a number of device drivers with MS-DOS 6.0. These were copied from the distribution disks onto your hard disk when you installed DOS on your PC. In this section we'll examine the purpose of these device drivers and how they are used. The following device drivers are supplied with MS-DOS 6.0:

ANSI.SYS	modifies display attributes, cursor movements, and key assignments.
CHKSTATE.SYS	is used exclusively by MS-DOS 6.0's new memory management utility, MEMMAKER.EXE.
DBLSPACE.SYS	is used exclusively by DOS to manage DBLSPACE, the disk-compression utility added to MS-DOS 6.0. (We'll discuss the DBLSPACE utility in Chapter 10.)
DISPLAY.SYS	prepares your system to display international characters.
DRIVER.SYS	allows DOS to access drive types it does not normally support.
EGA.SYS	allows the DOS Shell to support task switching when used with an EGA display.
EMM386.EXE	manages memory beyond the 640K conventional RAM on systems that have an 80386 or higher CPU. (We'll discuss how you use EMM386.EXE in the next chapter.)
HIMEM.SYS	manages extended memory on systems that have an 80286 or higher CPU. (This is also discussed in the next chapter.)
INTERLNK.EXE	redirects disk drive and printer activity on networked PCs.
POWER.EXE	reduces power consumption on laptop or notebook computers that conform to the Advanced Power Management (APM) specifications.
RAMDRIVE.SYS	creates a virtual hard drive in system memory (another topic covered in Chapter 7).

SETVER.EXE   loads the MS-DOS version table into memory. (This table may allow you to use programs that otherwise would not run under MS-DOS 6.0.)

SMARTDRV.EXE   creates a disk cache in extended memory. (Chapter 7 again.)

> ✔ *Note:* MS-DOS 6.0 includes two additional files that, although they appear to be device drivers based on the SYS extension in their filenames, do not function as such. COUNTRY.SYS and KEYBOARD.SYS contain data used by the COUNTRY and KEYB commands, respectively. They cannot be loaded directly by DOS, as true device drivers can.

Using Device Drivers

Although device drivers are programs in the strict sense of that word, to execute them it is necessary to use procedures different from the normal commands that are used to run other applications. You cannot run a DOS device driver by entering its program name at the DOS system prompt, as is the case, for example, when you enter a FORMAT command to run the executable program FORMAT.EXE. Instead, you load a device driver into memory during system startup by including the appropriate DEVICE or DEVICEHIGH statement in a special file called CONFIG.SYS.

> ✔ *Note:* The above rule holds true even when the name of the device driver ends with an EXE file extension — for example, EMM386.EXE and POWER.EXE. The EXE file extension would seem to imply that these are executable programs. They aren't. Like all other DOS device drivers, they also must be loaded into memory from within a CONFIG.SYS file.

The CONFIG.SYS File

You've encountered the CONFIG.SYS file previously in name only, so let me take a few minutes now to explain what it is. You'll learn the actual procedures used to create or modify CONFIG.SYS in the next chapter, "Have It Your Way: Fine-Tuning Your System."

Each time you turn on your computer, DOS looks for two special files, CONFIG.SYS and AUTOEXEC.BAT, in the root directory of the *boot disk*. If either of these two files exists, DOS automatically executes any commands or statements it contains as part of its normal startup procedure. Among other items, the CONFIG.SYS file provides a way to load device drivers into memory, making them available to DOS as you use your system. (During system startup, AUTO-EXEC.BAT automatically executes commands that you would otherwise have to enter manually at the system prompt. Creating or modifying an AUTOEXEC.BAT file is another topic we'll cover in then next chapter.)

Boot disk

This disk contains the three files required to load DOS into system memory (IO.SYS, MSDOS.SYS, and COMMAND.COM). On a floppy disk system, this disk must be inserted into drive A before you turn on the computer. If your PC includes a hard disk, DOS uses drive C as the default startup disk unless it finds a floppy disk containing the DOS system files in drive A.

Figure 6.1 shows the contents of the CONFIG.SYS file on my own 386 system. Notice that I've set up the first part of this file to load three of the DOS device drivers mentioned earlier: SETVER.EXE, HIMEM.SYS, and EMM386.EXE. At this point, don't worry about the exact procedures this entails. I'll get to that in the next chapter. For now, focus your attention on what some of the most commonly used DOS device drivers allow you to accomplish. Notice that I said "some," not "all." DOS itself takes care of setting up two of its device drivers, CHKSTATE.SYS and DBLSPACE.SYS, when you execute other commands, so there's no need to cover them here. Other DOS device drivers support functions that are either beyond the scope of this book (for example, INTERLNK.EXE is used to redirect input and output on a PC connected to a network) or used too infrequently to warrant discussion here. EGA.SYS is an example of the latter. And because most systems today include a VGA display, there's no need to explain how this particular device driver allows you to configure the DOS Shell for an EGA monitor. Likewise, DRIVER.SYS was created primarily to let older PCs access

```
(C:\) TYPE CONFIG.SYS
DEVICE=C:\DOS\SETVER.EXE
DEVICE=C:\DOS\HIMEM.SYS
DEVICE=C:\DOS\EMM386.EXE ram WIN=DD00-DFFF WIN=DA00-DCFF
dos=high,umb
BUFFERS=30,0
FILES=30
LASTDRIVE=E
FCBS=4,0
STACKS=9,256

SHELL=C:\DOS\COMMAND.COM C:\DOS\  /p

(C:\)
```

Figure 6.1 You load DOS device drivers using a special file called CONFIG.SYS.

high-density 3.5" floppy disk drives, a capability that's built into the BIOS of newer systems. With these caveats in mind, let's move on.

Using ANSI.SYS

The ANSI.SYS device driver lets you modify the performance of your keyboard and monitor using escape codes established by the American National Standards Institute (ANSI). Certain applications require that ANSI.SYS be loaded into memory to work properly. Should this be the case, the program's documentation will indicate this, usually as part of its system requirements or installation instructions.

You also may be forced to load ANSI.SYS if your computer or any programs you use have trouble recognizing the additional keys found on a 101-key keyboard. Should this happen, loading ANSI.SYS with its /K switch causes DOS to ignore the troublesome keys.

Most people, however, load ANSI.SYS voluntarily to customize some aspect of their display or keyboard, based on personal preferences. One popular use of ANSI.SYS, for example, is to change the color of the default DOS display from the normal color scheme of white letters on a black background. Once ANSI.SYS is loaded, you can accomplish this using the following PROMPT command:

`PROMPT ($p) $s$e[`*a;ff;bb*`m`

The details of this command are as follows:

PROMPT	is the PROMPT command introduced in Chapter 4.
($p)$s	maintains the directory/space prompt currently displayed on your screen (If you don't include a valid prompt code with this command, the screen colors will change but no visible prompt will be displayed.)
$e[	is a required notation indicating that DOS should interpret what follows as an ANSI escape code.
a	is an optional attribute code.
ff	is the ANSI code used to specify the desired foreground color.
*bb*m	is the ANSI code used to specify the desired background color.

Table 6.1 contains the valid attribute, foreground, and background color codes recognized by ANSI.SYS.

Using the values in Table 6.1, the following command would change the default display colors to white letters on a blue background:

`PROMPT ($p) $s$e[37;44m`

Table 6.1 ANSI Display Color and Attribute Codes

Attribute (*a*)	Effect
0	All attributes off
1	Bold on
4	Underscore (use with IBM-monochrome adapters only)
5	Blink on
7	Reverse video on

Color	Foreground code (*ff*)	Background code (*bb*)
Black	30	40
Red	31	41
Green	32	42
Yellow	33	43
Blue	34	44
Magenta	35	45
Cyan	36	46
White	37	47

ANSI codes can also be used to assign a text value to a key. Suppose, for example, that you wanted DOS to display a file listing for the current directory each time you pressed the F11 function key, a key largely ignored by DOS. The following command sequence would accomplish this:

```
PROMPT ($p) $s$e[0;133;"DIR";13p
```

The following values are represented within this command sequence:

PROMPT ($p) $s   retains the directory/space prompt.

$e[prepares DOS to receive a series of ANSI escape codes.

0;133   is the ANSI code representing the F11 function key.

"DIR"   is the text string you want DOS to substitute for the default F11 key sequence. (You must enclose text strings in quotation marks, as shown here.)

13p   is the ANSI escape code that represents the Enter key. (Including this value completes the DIR command.)

The DOS *User's Guide* contains a complete listing of the ANSI escape codes assigned to each key on your PC's keyboard. With a little bit of imagination, you can use ANSI.SYS to establish a truly personal and creative DOS interface.

(Remember, you'll learn how to include an ANSI.SYS statement within your CONFIG.SYS file in the next chapter.) Before moving on, let's look at one more extremely useful device driver that's included with MS-DOS 6.0.

Using SETVER

As noted, MS-DOS 6.0 is a radically different operating environment from its initial release, DOS 1.0, that appeared in 1981. Over the years, application programs also have been upgraded to reflect DOS's improved capabilities. Today's high-end applications simply won't run under earlier DOS versions that don't support the specific functions they require to work properly. For compatibility reasons, therefore, these programs check for the installation of a particular DOS version before they attempt to start. This is why the system requirements listed for a program often include a statement such as "For DOS 2.1 or higher."

Sometimes, however, this strategy can backfire. If a particular program looks for specific DOS versions, a newer DOS release may prevent it from being loaded successfully. Suppose, for example, that a program is designed to look for DOS versions 3.0 - 5.0. How will such a program react with it finds DOS 6.0 running on your computer? Many will run just fine. Others, however, may balk at this discrepancy, sailing off into electronic limbo even though there is no real conflict between the program and MS-DOS 6.0. A hybrid device driver/executable program called SETVER.EXE may solve this problem, should it ever arise on your system.

SETVER keeps a list of programs in a special file called, appropriately enough, the SETVER table. Each entry in this table contains an application's name and the version of DOS for which it was designed. SETUP, the MS-DOS 6.0 installation utility automatically incorporates into a CONFIG.SYS file a statement that loads the device driver portion of SETVER.EXE into memory. It also creates an initial SETVER table containing the appropriate DOS versions for many popular application programs. To view the contents of this initial table:

Type **SETVER |MORE** and press **Enter**.

Figure 6.2 shows the first part of the initial SETVER table. (Including the MORE filter in the previous command causes DOS to pause after an entire screen of information has been displayed.) Notice, for example, that SETVER configures DOS to report to Excel, Microsoft's popular Windows-based spreadsheet program, that you are running version 4.10. Version 4.10 is also the DOS version SETVER identifies as being appropriate for Word for Windows. You probably won't recognize every program in this list, but they all need to find a version of MS-DOS other then 6.0 to run properly. Go ahead check out some of the other program names, as you page through the remainder of the initial SETVER table.

```
WIN200.BIN       3.40
WIN100.BIN       3.40
WINWORD.EXE      4.10
EXCEL.EXE        4.10
HITACHI.SYS      4.00
MSCDEX.EXE       4.00
REDIR4.EXE       4.00
NET.EXE          4.00
NETWKSTA.EXE     4.00
DXMA0MOD.SYS     3.30
BAN.EXE          4.00
BAN.COM          4.00
MSREDIR.EXE      4.00
METRO.EXE        3.31
IBMCACHE.SYS     5.00
REDIR40.EXE      4.00
DD.EXE           4.01
DD.BIN           4.01
LL3.EXE          4.01
REDIR.EXE        4.00
SYQ55.SYS        4.00
SSTDRIVE.SYS     4.00
ZDRV.SYS         4.01
-- More --
```

Figure 6.2   During installation, MS-DOS 6.0 creates an initial SETVER table.

All of this is well and good, and it demonstrates an amazingly cooperative attitude on the part of Microsoft not to leave applications in the dust as DOS gallops down the road of increased capabilities. But what if one of your favorite programs causes problems and is not included in the SETVER table?

For example, I was in the middle of writing a book about GeoWorks Ensemble when I initially installed MS-DOS 5.0 on my computer. The first time I tried to run Ensemble after upgrading to that version, my system froze, locking up so completely that I had to perform a warm boot by pressing the reset button to get up and running again. Clearly, Ensemble had trouble running under DOS 5.0.

Luckily, like MS-DOS 6.0, DOS 5.0 provided the SETVER command. (It was the first DOS release to do so.) Fortunate, too, is the fact that SETVER allows you to add new programs to the initial table, using the following command syntax:

SETVER *[drive:path] [filename [n.nn]] [/D] [/QUIET]*

SETVER Parameters and Command Switches

SETVER accepts the following parameter and command switches:

drive:path   is used to specify the location of the SETVER.EXE file.

filename   is used to specify the name of the program file (usually an .EXE or .COM file) that you want to add to the version table.

n.nn is used to indicate the version of MS-DOS (for example, 3.3 or 4.01) that MS-DOS 6.0 reports to the specified program each time it is run.

/D instructs SETVER to delete the version table entry for the specified program file.

/QUIET suppresses the message DOS normally displays when it deletes an entry from the version table.

> **Caution:** You cannot include the wildcard characters (* or ?) in the *filename* when entering a SETVER command.

To see what this accomplishes, try the following experiment:

Type **SETVER GEOS.EXE 4.01** and press **Enter**.

DOS responds with the series of message shown in Figure 6.3. Much of this message screen is a case of corporate C.Y.A. Microsoft is cautioning you that it cannot guarantee the performance of the specified program under MS-DOS 6.0. (The company includes in the initial SETVER table only those applications that it has verified will work with its latest and greatest DOS.) The message further states, however, that DOS did, indeed, update the SETVER table. To verify this:

Type **SETVER** and press **Enter**.

You'll see that the following entry has been appended to the SETVER table:

```
GEOS.EXE        4.01
```

The message in Figure 6.3 further states that you'll need to restart your system before this change takes effect. That's because DOS creates an active version table in memory each time the device driver portion of SETVER is loaded into memory from CONFIG.SYS. Even though GEOS.EXE now shows up in the SETVER listing, it was not there when you last started your computer. If you were a GeoWorks Ensemble user, you'd have to reboot your system, thus causing DOS to create a new SETVER table, one that includes the GEOS.EXE entry. That, in turn, would allow our little digital sleight-of-hand to take effect, letting you run Ensemble under MS-DOS 6.0. (And, yes, this technique worked for me. I was able to load Ensemble under DOS 5.0 and complete the previously mentioned book.)

WORKING WITH DEVICES AND DRIVERS   145

```
(C:\) SETVER GEOS.EXE 4.01

WARNING - Contact your software vendor for information about whether a
specific program works with MS-DOS version 6.0. It is possible that
Microsoft has not verified whether the program will successfully run if
you use the SETVER command to change the program version number and
version table. If you run the program after changing the version table
in MS-DOS version 6.0, you may lose or corrupt data or introduce system
instabilities. Microsoft is not responsible for any loss or damage, or
for lost or corrupted data.

Version table successfully updated
The version change will take effect the next time you restart your system

(C:\)
```

Figure 6.3 You can add new programs to the initial SETVER table.

Tip: For GEOS Users

You may need to insert this line — GEOS.EXE 4.01 — in your SETVER table and not even realize it. America Online, a popular commercial information system, relies on the GEOS graphics interface for one version of its proprietary access software. (There's also a version that runs under Windows.) If you have the GEOS-based version, you'll have to update the SETVER table after installing MS-DOS 6.0 before you'll be able to go back on-line with America Online.

If your system does not include GeoWorks Ensemble (or the GEOS interface with America Online), the following command can be used to remove GEOS.EXE from the updated SETVER table:

Type **SETVER GEOS.EXE /D** and press **Enter**.

Once again, DOS reports that the version table has been updated and that the change will take effect the next time you start your computer.

As you can see, DOS's ability to use device drivers lets you add a variety of capabilities and features to this already powerful operating environment. Device drivers allow you to incorporate additional hardware, both familiar and exotic, into your PC arsenal. In the next chapter, you'll learn how to create the CONFIG.SYS file that, in turn, installs device drivers into memory each time you start your computer.

Chapter 7

Have It Your Way: Fine-Tuning Your System

If you've been working your way through this book linearly — reading each chapter in order, performing any exercises it contains as you go along — you now have a functional, if admittedly fundamental, DOS environment set up on your PC. That's because, until now, we've pretty much let DOS call all the shots. This situation is about to change.

In this chapter we begin examining those DOS commands and procedures that allow you to take control of your PC and turn it into a lean, mean computing machine. No longer will we be content to possess a "generic" system, one that's designed to be all things to all people. Instead, we're going to start milking your system for all it's worth.

We'll make certain the memory installed in your computer is being used efficiently. We'll make it possible for DOS to find easily those programs you run most often. We'll take whatever steps we can to speed up read/write operations on your disk drives. Ultimately, we'll even automate those activities you perform regularly, reducing them to a single keystroke. In short, we'll tweak to peak performance the various components of your PC.

Setting MS-DOS 6.0 in Stone (The DELOLDOS Command)

I'm about to make the critical assumption that MS-DOS 6.0 has performed as expected throughout the previous six chapters. If it has, chances are it will continue to do so. And if this is the case, you're ready to free up valuable storage space by removing from your hard disk whatever version of DOS was superseded by MS-DOS 6.0. This seems like a logical place to begin the process of bringing your PC up to peak performance.

> ***Caution:*** Running DELOLDOS eliminates the possibility of restoring an earlier version of DOS using the "uninstall" disk created by Setup when you installed MS-DOS 6.0 on your computer. Should you still harbor any doubts as to the reliability of MS-DOS 6.0, therefore, skip the following exercise. You can always run DELOLDOS at some later time, after you feel totally comfortable working in MS-DOS 6.0.

To erase from your hard disk those files associated with a previous version of DOS:

Type **DELOLDOS** and press **Enter**.

DOS responds with the warning message shown in Figure 7.1, which reiterates the Caution above that running DELOLDOS makes it impossible to remove MS-DOS 6.0 from your system and recover your previous DOS version. If you're satisfied that MS-DOS 6.0 works reliably on your computer:

Press **Y**.

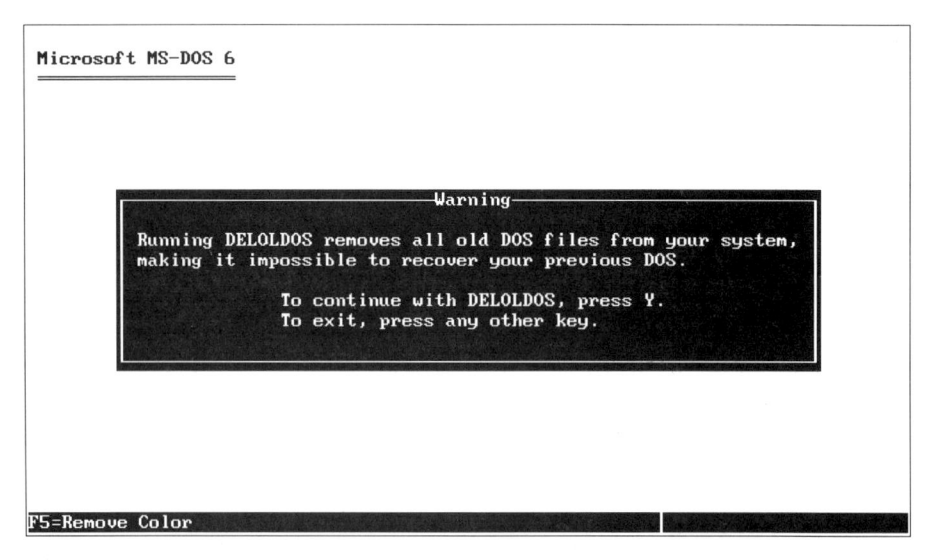

```
Microsoft MS-DOS 6

                          ─Warning─
     Running DELOLDOS removes all old DOS files from your system,
     making it impossible to recover your previous DOS.

              To continue with DELOLDOS, press Y.
              To exit, press any other key.


F5=Remove Color
```

Figure 7.1 MS-DOS 6.0 lets you decide when you're satisfied with its performance.

If you want to keep all of your options open, pressing any key but Y at the previous warning message aborts DELOLDOS and returns you to the system prompt with no damage done. Keep in mind, however, that the files associated with that previous DOS release will continue to consume anywhere from 1MB to possibly 4MB of storage space on your hard disk until they are removed.

If you pressed Y, after a few seconds you'll see the message shown in Figure 7.2, indicating that DELOLDOS has erased the files associated with your previous version of DOS. (Setup copied these files to a directory called OLD_DOS.1 when you upgraded your system to this newest DOS release.) Congratulations! MS-DOS 6.0 is now a permanent weapon in your PC arsenal. So let's begin tuning up that weapon to meet its most demanding specifications.

Creating CONFIG.SYS

To be honest, the name of this section is a misnomer. If you just finished installing MS-DOS 6.0 on your system, you already have a CONFIG.SYS file. Setup, the MS-DOS 6.0 installation utility, automatically created it for you. To verify this:

Type **TYPE CONFIG.SYS** and press **Enter**.

Figure 7.3 shows the CONFIG.SYS file Setup created on my computer. There isn't much there, to be sure. The few lines this initial CONFIG.SYS does contain, however, represent the first faltering steps in a journey toward making your PC run as efficiently as possible.

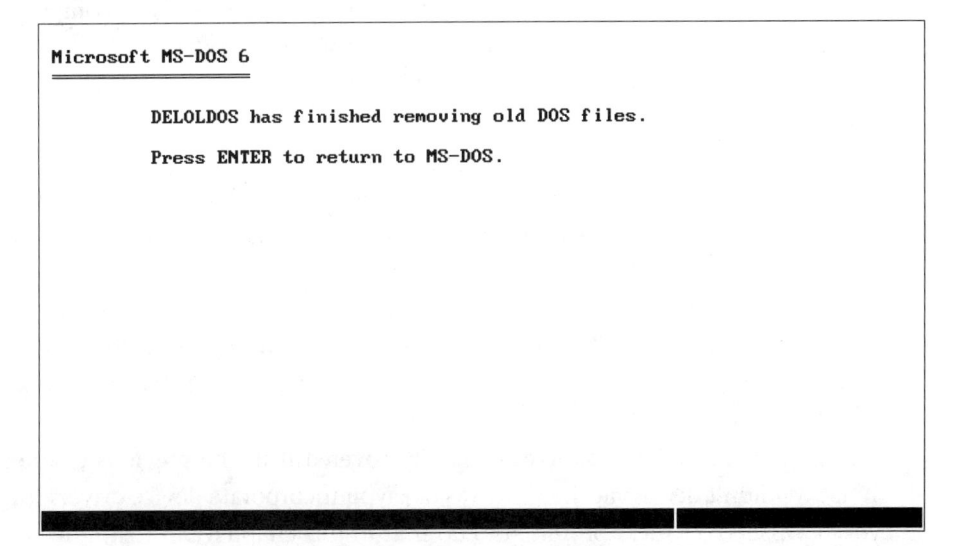

```
Microsoft MS-DOS 6

        DELOLDOS has finished removing old DOS files.
        Press ENTER to return to MS-DOS.
```

Figure 7.2   DELOLDOS removes your old DOS files.

```
C:\>TYPE CONFIG.SYS
DEVICE=C:\DOS\SETVER.EXE
DEVICE=C:\DOS\HIMEM.SYS
DOS=HIGH
FILES=30
SHELL=C:\DOS\COMMAND.COM C:\DOS\  /p

C:\>
```

Figure 7.3 As part of the MS-DOS 6.0 installation, Setup creates a CONFIG.SYS file.

> ✔ *Note:* Don't be concerned if your CONFIG.SYS file differs somewhat from Figure 7.3. Setup determines what to include in this initial file based on a preliminary analysis of the resources available on the computer on which MS-DOS 6.0 is being installed. For example, I installed DOS on a 386SX system with 3MB of extended memory. As I'll explain in a few paragraphs, this configuration supports the HIMEM.SYS device driver, which DOS uses to manage extended memory. Because it detected extended memory on my system, Setup included in my CONFIG.SYS file a statement that loads HIMEM.SYS into RAM. (It's the second DEVICE statement in Figure 7.3.) If your computer does not have extended memory, Setup will not add this statement to your CONFIG.SYS file.

I explained briefly in the previous chapter how CONFIG.SYS works. I'll expand on that explanation now. In a world of specialized PC files, CONFIG.SYS may just be the most specialized file of all. Each time you turn on your computer, DOS checks to see whether a CONFIG.SYS file exists in the root directory of your boot disk — the disk DOS uses to load itself into system memory. If DOS finds a CONFIG.SYS file, it executes any statements it contains. DOS then proceeds to ignore CONFIG.SYS completely until the next time you boot your system.

Don't let CONFIG.SYS's lack of contribution to your day-to-day operations fool you, however. It is an invaluable tool, one that allows you to customize your PC to an amazing extent. How? Among other things, CONFIG.SYS is where you install those device drivers we discussed in the previous chapter. And device drivers, in turn, can actually modify the way in which your PC operates — what hardware it supports, how it manages memory, how quickly specific operations take place, and so forth.

But all of that is old hat. We've already covered it in the previous chapter. What we didn't discuss at the time was *how* you incorporate device drivers into your CONFIG.SYS file. I promised to do that in this chapter. But first, I need to introduce you to another feature of MS-DOS 6.0, its full-screen editor.

Creating and Modifying Text Files (Using EDIT)

For the longest time, DOS lacked a utilitarian text editor. Early DOS users were forced to rely either on Edlin, a completely moronic line editor that shipped with older versions of DOS, or invest in a separate word processor that would allow them to create and modify text files. Most people opted for the second approach. Edlin may have been free, but it was so difficult to learn and so clumsy to use that its price — in time and effort — was still too high.

Microsoft finally eliminated this frustration in May, 1991, when it started shipping MS-DOS 5.0. In addition to Edlin, DOS 5.0 included a full-screen text editor called, appropriately enough, EDIT. Needless to say, DOS users were ecstatic. So much so, in fact, that Edlin has disappeared completely from MS-DOS 6.0. Few, if any, will mourn its passing.

EDIT can be used to create and modify ASCII files — files that contain text conforming to the American Standard Code for Information Interchange, or ASCII, format. CONFIG.SYS is an ASCII file; therefore, EDIT can be used to modify CONFIG.SYS.

> *Tip:* Is It ASCII?
> You can use the TYPE command to tell whether a file is stored in ASCII format. If the results of a TYPE command are legible, chances are you're dealing with an ASCII file. If a TYPE command generates "garbage" — on-screen gibberish that makes little sense — then the file you attempted to display probably contains non-ASCII characters, meaning that it can't be modified with EDIT.

Starting EDIT

The correct syntax for starting EDIT is:

EDIT [[*drive:*][*path*]*filename*] [/B] [/G] [/H] [/NOHI]

EDIT Parameters and Command Switches

EDIT accepts the following parameters and command switches:

drive:path   specifies the location of the file you want to edit.

filename   specifies the name of the file you want to edit. If *filename* already exists, EDIT opens it and displays its contents on the screen. If

	the file does not exist, EDIT creates a new file using the specified name and location.
/B	instructs DOS to run EDIT in black and white. This option is especially useful if the Editor screen is difficult to read on a monochrome monitor or on the LCD display found in most laptop and notebook computers.
/G	instructs DOS to provide the fastest screen updating for a CGA monitor.
/H	instructs EDIT to display the maximum number of lines possible for your monitor.
/NOHI	lets you to run EDIT on a monitor that only displays 8 colors. By default, EDIT is set up to use 16 colors.

> ***Caution:*** EDIT needs the MS-DOS QBasic programming language, a file called QBASIC.EXE, to work properly. For this reason, QBASIC.EXE must be in the current directory, included in your search path, or located in the same directory as the file EDIT.COM. If you've deleted QBASIC.EXE to free up space on your hard disk, therefore, you won't be able to use EDIT.

We'll use EDIT to examine and, if possible, modify the contents of the initial CONFIG.SYS file created by Setup. To begin this process:

Type **EDIT CONFIG.SYS** and press **Enter**.

This starts EDIT and loads the specified file, CONFIG.SYS, into memory for editing, as shown in Figure 7.4.

Using EDIT

EDIT resembles the DOS Shell, which I discussed briefly in Chapter 2. Like the DOS Shell, EDIT uses an interactive design; it allows you to select commands, options, and preferences with pull-down menus and dialog boxes. To see what I mean:

Press **Alt+F**.

The **Alt+F** key combination displays the pull-down File menu shown in Figure 7.5. This menu contains several options used to perform file-related operations — opening a file, saving a file, printing a file, and the like. Other pull-down menus include:

Edit (Alt+E)	contains the options used to delete, copy and move blocks of text.

FINE-TUNING YOUR SYSTEM 153

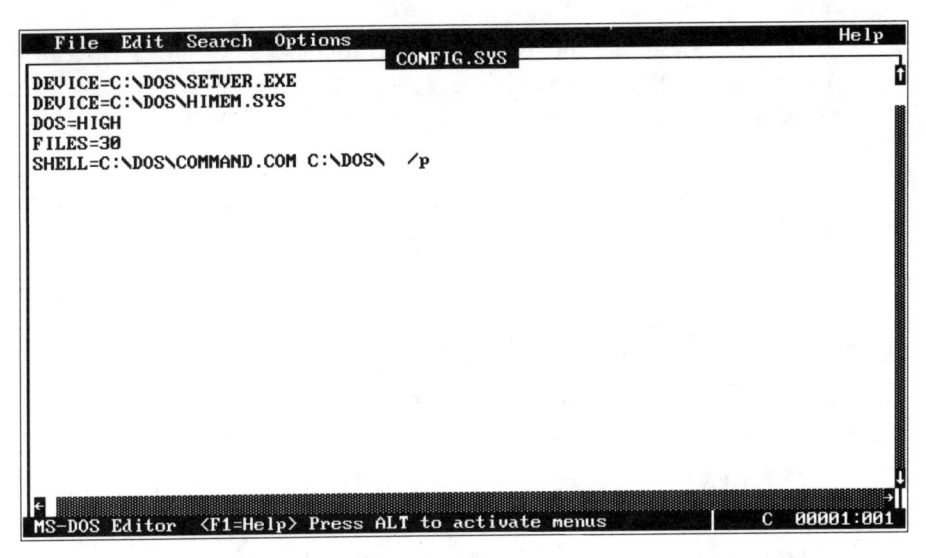

```
 File  Edit  Search  Options                                    Help
                         CONFIG.SYS
DEVICE=C:\DOS\SETVER.EXE
DEVICE=C:\DOS\HIMEM.SYS
DOS=HIGH
FILES=30
SHELL=C:\DOS\COMMAND.COM C:\DOS\  /p




 MS-DOS Editor   <F1=Help> Press ALT to activate menus    C  00001:001
```

Figure 7.4 MS-DOS 6.0 includes a full-screen text editor.

    Search (Alt+S)   contains the options used to find a specified word or phrase and, optionally, replace it with different text.

    Options (Alt+O)   used to change display colors and specify the path containing the EDIT Help files, if this path is different from the one in which the EDIT program is stored.

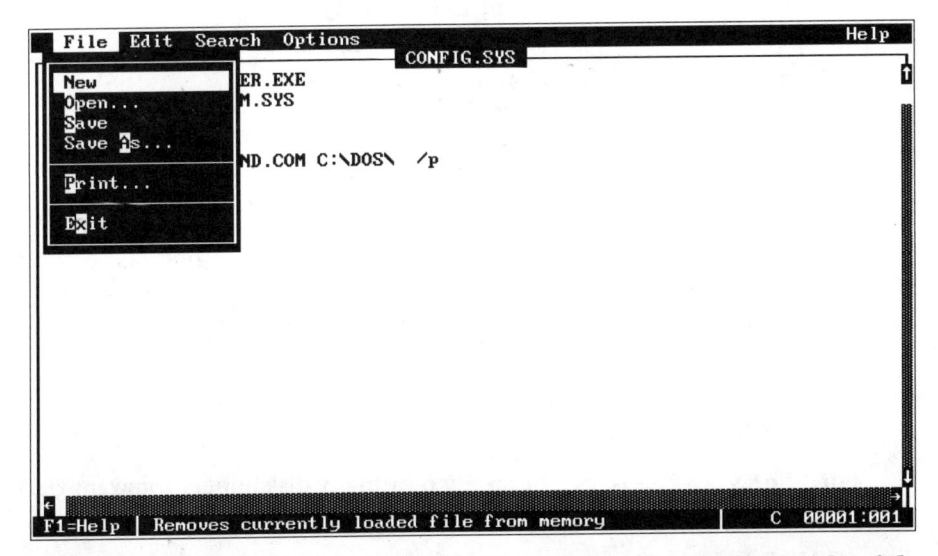

```
 File  Edit  Search  Options                                    Help
                         CONFIG.SYS
 ┌─────────────┐
 │ New         │ ER.EXE
 │ Open...     │ M.SYS
 │ Save        │
 │ Save As...  │ ND.COM C:\DOS\  /p
 │ Print...    │
 │ Exit        │
 └─────────────┘




 F1=Help | Removes currently loaded file from memory      C  00001:001
```

Figure 7.5 EDIT's interactive design makes it simpler to work with your files.

> ✔ **Note:** As the last item above implies, EDIT includes an on-line Help feature. As was true in the DOS Shell, pressing the F1 function key displays Help messages containing information about using EDIT.

For all its useful buzzers and bells, however, EDIT's primary purpose is to let you modify text in an ASCII file. So let's get to it.

Contents of CONFIG.SYS

My initial CONFIG.SYS file (Figure 7.4) already contains five useful statements. These are:

SETVER.EXE   is used to load the device driver portion of the SETVER.EXE program, which was discussed in the previous chapter.

HIMEM.SYS   is used to load HIMEM.SYS, a device driver that allows DOS to manage extended memory. (Remember, Setup included this statement in my CONFIG.SYS file because it detected the presence of extended memory in my system.)

DOS=HIGH   is used to load a portion of DOS itself into high RAM, a special section of memory just above the 1MB memory address at which extended memory begins, thus making more memory available to my application programs. (Once again, Setup inserted this statement based on its analysis of my 386 system.)

FILES   is used to specify the number of files DOS can have open at any given time.

SHELL   is used to specify the name and location of the command interpreter you want DOS to use (COMMAND.COM is the default DOS command interpreter.)

Notice that the last three items in my CONFIG.SYS file were not included in the list of device drivers introduced in the previous chapter. That's because they are not device drivers — they are commands. CONFIG.SYS can do much more than load device drivers.

Additional commands that can be executed exclusively from within CONFIG.SYS include:

BUFFERS   is used to specify how many disk buffers you want DOS to set up for read/write operations.

COUNTRY   is used to modify how DOS displays dates, times, and currencies, among other items.

FINE-TUNING YOUR SYSTEM 155

DEVICE is used to actually load device drivers into memory.

DEVICEHIGH is used to load device drivers into upper memory, a section of memory between 640K and the 1MB address at which extended memory begins.

DRIVPARM is used to modify the default parameters for an existing disk drive.

FCBS is used to specify the number of file control blocks DOS can have open at any given time.

INSTALL is used to install memory-resident programs into RAM during system startup.

LASTDRIVE is used to specify the highest drive letter DOS can access on your system.

NUMLOCK is used to specify the initial state of your keyboard's NUM-LOCK key.

STACKS is used to specify how DOS should handle hardware interrupts.

SWITCHES is used to set several miscellaneous options on your system, including how DOS handles a 101-key keyboard and whether or not DOS allows you to bypass the STARTUP command by pressing the F5 or F8 function key.

Additionally, three commands can be executed either from within CONFIG.SYS or directly from the DOS system prompt. These include:

BREAK tells DOS how frequently and when to check for a BREAK (Ctrl+C) keystroke, which can be used to abort certain operations.

REM is used to identify a remark — a statement that should not be executed but is included in CONFIG.SYS for informational purposes only.

SET is used to display information about and, if necessary, modify certain aspects of the DOS environment.

Starting with MS-DOS 6.0, DOS allows you to define multiple configurations for your system. During startup, you can select the one you want to use for the current session. You accomplish this by using the following CONFIG.SYS commands, which we'll discuss in greater detail in Chapter 10:

INCLUDE
MENUCOLOR
MENUDEFAULT
MENUITEM
SUBMENU

That's an awful lot of information you can cram into a CONFIG.SYS file. And remember, you'll use CONFIG.SYS to load device drivers, as well — both the DOS device drivers introduced in the previous chapter and any device drivers required for additional hardware items from other manufacturers that you add to your PC. As was true with the DOS device drivers, however, some of these CONFIG.SYS commands are so specialized or so technical that most people will never need them. Still, several can be useful in almost any PC environment. These are the ones we'll concentrate on here as we begin using EDIT to modify your CONFIG.SYS file.

Improving Disk Performance (The FILES, BUFFERS, and SMARTDRV Commands)

The PC industry tends to place a lot of emphasis on CPU speed. Flip through any computer magazine and you'll find page after page of advertisements touting the "latest and greatest" systems that run at 20MHz, 25MHz, 33MHz, 50MHz and up. When it comes to judging the power of a PC, it seems that even the fastest CPU is never fast enough.

But CPU speed reveals only half the story, if that much, when it comes to indicating how quickly your computer can actually get something accomplished. Equally important is the performance of your hard disk. Including three simple commands in your CONFIG.SYS file can increase the efficiency of your disk operations dramatically.

Increasing Disk BUFFERS

DOS uses disk buffers, special storage areas set up in memory, to hold temporarily data moving to and from a disk. If a program requests a piece of data from a disk file, DOS processes this request and moves the desired data from the file to a disk buffer. DOS then transfers the data to memory, at which point it is ready to be processed by the requesting application.

Each time an application asks for specific data, DOS first checks to see whether that data is already stored in a disk buffer, where it may have been placed during a previous request. If DOS discovers the requested information in one of its buffers, it passes the data immediately to the application. Doing so eliminates the need to perform an additional disk read and, therefore, saves some time.

Logically, then, one can assume that, the larger the buffer area, the greater the likelihood that DOS will find data in the buffer to satisfy repetitive requests.

This is indeed the case — up to a point. If the size of the buffer grows too large, then DOS will spend more time searching this temporary storage area than it would have taken to read the data from a file directly. Should this happen, you've reached a point of diminishing returns.

How large a buffer area you start out with depends on how much memory is installed in your PC. The default value for computers with 512K of RAM or more is 15 buffers, each of which holds approximately 532 bytes of data, or enough memory to hold a total of around 7,984 bytes of data. On machines with less memory — and these are becoming exceedingly rare — DOS sets aside fewer buffers, although the size of each remains 528 bytes.

So, how many buffers should you set up on your system? The most commonly recommended number, barring a special circumstance, is 20, five more than the default used by DOS. The "special circumstance" is if you use an application that requires more, a fact that will be stated somewhere in its documentation, which usually accompanies the installation instructions.

The correct syntax for including a BUFFER statement in CONFIG.SYS is:

BUFFERS=*n*[,*m*]

BUFFERS accepts the following parameters:

n   is a value, 1 through 99, specifying how many disk buffers you want created at system startup.

m   is a value, 0 through 8, specifying how many buffers you want created in a secondary buffer cache.

With this information in hand, let's use EDIT to add a BUFFERS statement to your CONFIG.SYS file.

Use the arrow keys to move the cursor down three or four lines in CONFIG.SYS (A logical place to insert a BUFFERS statement is immediately before the FILES statement, if one exists.)

Type **BUFFERS=20** and press **Enter**.

This adds the appropriate BUFFERS statement to CONFIG.SYS. The next time you start your system, DOS will create 20 buffers in memory.

> ✓ *Note:* The secondary buffer is most useful on slower, first-generation PCs, systems with an 8088 or 8086 CPU. Anyone with a computer that uses a newer processor (an 80286 or higher) will achieve better results by ignoring the secondary buffer and using SMARTDRV.EXE to create a disk cache, instead. We'll discuss SMARTDRV.EXE in a few paragraphs.

Keep in mind that each buffer you create requires approximately 532 bytes of memory. The more buffers you have, therefore, the less memory DOS will be able to use for your applications.

> *Tip:* **Loading DOS High**
> Later in this chapter you'll learn how to use the DOS=HIGH command to load portions of DOS itself into the high memory area, or HMA. Loading DOS High offers a second beneficial side-effect: It allows DOS to create its buffers in the HMA, if enough unused memory exists there to do so. This, in turn, frees up additional memory in conventional RAM for your applications.

Increasing FILES

By default, DOS allows eight files to be open concurrently. If it receives requests for data from more files than this, DOS must close one file before opening an additional file to fulfill the latest request. Here again, therefore, increasing the number of files DOS can access at any given time to a number larger than the default can improve disk performance. The correct syntax for including a FILES statement in CONFIG.SYS is:

`FILES=x`

FILES accepts the following parameter:

x is a value, 8 through 255, specifying how many files you want DOS to be able to access concurrently.

As Figure 7.4 illustrates, Setup automatically increases the FILES setting when it installs DOS. The value Setup specifies, 30, is a commonly recommended number and should not need to be changed.

Using Double-Buffering with SMARTDRV

Left to its own devices (pun intended), DOS operates linearly. When you tell DOS to do something, DOS does it, even if following your instructions requires that it interrupt another and perhaps more important activity. Consequently, DOS may interrupt calculations and other operations quite frequently in order to read and write data to and from disk files.

One way to eliminate the inefficiency of such an approach is to create a disk cache. A disk cache is a block of memory where DOS can store temporarily data being transferred from disk to RAM or vice versa. When disk caching is in effect,

DOS performs the actual data transfer during "idle times," that is, when it is least likely to interrupt other activities.

Normally, you create a disk cache by including the appropriate SMARTDRV command in your AUTOEXEC.BAT file, a procedure we'll discuss later in this chapter. Certain hard disk controllers, however, require that you implement double-buffering, a process that involves including the SMARTDRV command in both your CONFIG.SYS and AUTOEXEC.BAT files. If your hard disk controller requires double-buffering, you'll need to add the following statement to your CONFIG.SYS file:

```
DEVICE=C:\DOS\SMARTDRV.EXE /DOUBLE_BUFFER
```

Of course, the next logical question is: How do you know if your hard disk controller requires double-buffering? DOS provides a relatively reliable (if admittedly convoluted) way to determine this, using the steps listed below. (This technique includes commands and procedures you've not yet encountered, so you may find it somewhat confusing at this time. Don't worry. You can always come back and perform the following steps later, once we have examined the various commands it contains.)

1. Add the following command to your CONFIG.SYS file, if necessary:

   ```
   DEVICE=C:\DOS\SMARTDRV.EXE /DOUBLE_BUFFER
   ```

2. Add the following command to your AUTOEXEC.BAT file, if necessary:

   ```
   C:\DOS\SMARTDRV.EXE
   ```

3. Type **MEMMAKER** and press **Enter**.

4. Follow the on-screen instructions to have MemMaker optimize how your computer uses memory.

5. Type **MEM /C /P** and press **Enter** to verify that your system is using upper memory.

6. Type **SMARTDRV** and press **Enter** to display information about how the disk cache is set up on your system.

7. If "yes" appears under the Buffering column in any line of the subsequent screen display, your hard disk controller requires double-buffering and you will need to leave the SMARTDRV command in CONFIG.SYS. If "no" appears in every line under the Buffering column, you can remove the SMARTDRV command from CONFIG.SYS.

Adding the appropriate BUFFERS, FILES, and SMARTDRV statements to your CONFIG.SYS file can have a dramatic impact on disk performance. This, by extension, improves the efficiency of virtually all your PC operations. And speaking of topics "virtual," there's one additional disk-related trick that you can perform in CONFIG.SYS, one that creates a disk drive, of sorts, the speed of which will astound you.

Creating a Virtual Disk (The RAMDRIVE Command)

The RAMDRIVE.SYS device driver lets you simulate in memory the functions of a hard disk. Because this simulated disk does not exist physically — you cannot touch it — it is called a *virtual disk drive*. And because it is electronic rather than mechanical in nature, a virtual disk drive operates much faster than its physical counterpart.

That's the good news. The bad news is that, because it's created in volatile RAM, information stored on a virtual drive is lost whenever you turn off or reboot your computer. You must make certain, therefore, that you transfer any critical information stored on a virtual drive to a real disk before ending a session.

The correct syntax for including a RAMDRIVE statement in CONFIG.SYS is:

```
DEVICE=[drive:][path]RAMDRIVE.SYS [DiskSize SectorSize [NumEntries]] [/E|/A]
```

RAMDRIVE accepts the following parameter and command switches:

- *drive:path*   specifies the location of the RAMDRIVE.SYS file.
- *DiskSize*   specifies, in a range between 4K and 32767K, how many kilobytes of memory you want designated as a RAM drive. The default size of a RAM disk is 64K.
- *SectorSize*   configures your RAM drive to emulate a particular type of disk drive by specifying a sector size in bytes.
- *NumEntries*   specifies, in a range between 2 and 1024, the number of files and directories that can exist in the RAM drive's root directory.
- /E   instructs DOS to create the RAM drive in extended memory. (You must load HIMEM.SYS from your CONFIG.SYS file to create a RAM drive in extended memory.)
- /A   instructs DOS to create the RAM drive in expanded memory. (You must install an expanded memory manager, such as EMM386.EXE, from your CONFIG.SYS file to create a RAM drive in expanded memory.)

Suppose, for example, that you wanted to create a 1MB RAM disk in extended memory. Adding the following command to your CONFIG.SYS file would accomplish this:

```
DEVICE=C:\DOS\RAMDRIVE.SYS 1024 /E
```

DOS assigns to a RAM disk the next available drive letter. For example, if your system has a single hard disk, drive C, the RAM disk would become drive D. Once a virtual disk drive exists, you use it just as you would any hard disk.

One practical way to take advantage of a RAM disk is as a temporary location to which you copy the program files for an application that performs frequent disk accesses. Some word processors, for example, load external files — called overlays — to perform specific operations. The increased speed of a RAM disk would allow such programs to run noticeably faster. Also, because the RAM disk would contain program files only — no data files — you eliminate the risk of losing valuable information should your system ever freeze up or be turned off accidentally before you had a chance to save your work. Including in an AUTOEXEC.BAT file those commands required to copy the application files to your RAM disk would create the desired environment each time you turned on or restarted your system.

> *Tip:* **Should You Create a RAM Disk?**
> In truth, there's little advantage to creating a RAM disk unless your system includes enough extended or expanded memory to make doing so practical. Creating a virtual disk in conventional RAM steals memory away from your application programs.

Increasing the Number of Drives on Your System (The LASTDRIVE Command)

For DOS to use a RAM disk — or any device, for that matter — it must be able to find it. Normally, this is no problem. By default, DOS sets aside the resources to recognize up to five devices: two floppy disks, drives A and B; and three other devices, drives C through E. But what if your system already has this many devices? Wouldn't any RAM disk you create fall outside DOS's domain, so to speak? Yes, they would, but DOS provides an easy way around this potential problem.

Including a LASTDRIVE statement in a CONFIG.SYS file increases the number of devices DOS recognizes by setting aside additional device identifiers during system startup. This one's easy. Adding the following statement to your CONFIG.SYS file, for example, would let DOS recognize ten devices, assigned letters A through J:

```
LASTDRIVE=J
```

That's all there is to it. Not everything about setting up CONFIG.SYS has to be complicated and technically obscure. Unfortunately, our next topic is. However, it also covers one of the most impressive and potentially useful features of CONFIG.SYS: it's ability to get the most out of any memory installed on your computer.

Making the Most of Memory (The HIMEM, DOS, EMM386, MEMMAKER, and DEVICEHIGH Commands)

This quintet of commands, if used properly, can increase dramatically the amount of conventional RAM available to your application programs. Given today's memory-hungry applications, this can be a real godsend, especially if your system includes a number of devices that without advanced memory management would pick away at conventional RAM like a vulture dining on carrion. To understand why this is so, you need to know a little something about how DOS's ability to use memory has evolved.

A Brief History of Memory

Microsoft designed DOS initially to recognize only the first 640K of memory installed on a computer. That was it. No more. No less. This 640K block of memory is commonly identified by a name that you've encountered several times already in this chapter: *conventional RAM*.

In Microsoft's defense, I should point out that, when DOS was first released, 640K seemed like an incredible amount of memory. After all, the personal computers that antedated DOS systems got along quite well with only 64K of memory to work with, one-tenth the amount DOS was designed to access. Certainly, most people at the time figured 640K of RAM was more memory than anyone would ever want or need.

Unfortunately, most of these same people failed to recognize an undeniable truism about computers: Memory is like a vacuum; leave it unoccupied, and something inevitably rushes in to fill it. That "something" is programmers — programmers who can't resist cramming more and more features into their programs, features that in turn demand more and more memory to work properly.

Exacerbating this problem was the PC community's penchant for incorporating more and more exotic devices into their computers. As we've already seen, virtually every piece of equipment you tack onto a PC requires a device driver to run properly. And every device driver you install consumes at least a little bit of RAM. The device driver that controls a mouse, for example, uses anywhere from 7K to 15K of memory, depending on what type of mouse it is. DOS's own SMARTDRV.EXE disk cache program, which we discussed earlier, also eats up 15K of RAM. And what if you should decide to add a CD-ROM device to your

PC? Well, be prepared to sacrifice a whopping 75K or so of memory to take advantage of this particular convenience.

So it came to pass that powerful programs and proliferating devices ran a collision course with one another. The white line delineating their demolition derby was the 640K memory address beyond which DOS could not reach. Within a year or two after DOS's initial release, therefore, users started crashing into what has since been dubbed the infamous 640K DOS barrier.

But the PC industry is nothing if not creative. And over time, it developed two creative solutions to this problem: extended and expanded memory.

Extended Memory

Extended memory is any RAM installed above the 1MB memory address. (I realize I just leaped over a fairly sizable gap in memory, namely, those addresses between 640K and 1MB. Don't worry. We'll come back to them in a few paragraphs.) Although DOS itself cannot access directly extended memory, it can be employed for other uses.

From the beginning, extended memory could serve as an ersatz virtual disk drive, if you will, in which data could be stored. Very early on, programs like Lotus 1-2-3 took advantage of this capability, allowing users to create spreadsheet files larger than was possible before. Then, Microsoft added to DOS a device driver called VDISK that allowed you to create a fully functional virtual disk drive (similar to what RAMDRIVE accomplishes now) in extended memory. Finally, a loosely organized consortium of software manufacturers got together and designed something called the DOS extender — a mini-operating system of sorts that, when tacked on top of DOS, would permit it to perform at least certain limited operations within extended memory.

DOS still could not break through the 640K barrier, but at least some useful activity was now permitted beyond the previously insurmountable 1MB memory address where extended memory begins.

Expanded Memory

Expanded memory is also extra memory that's installed in a PC. Physically — if this word can be applied to something as ephemeral as memory locations — it too exists beyond the realm of the 1MB memory address. But expanded memory serves a very special function from atop its lofty peak. Its sole purpose is to "fool" DOS into thinking that it's still chugging along within that 640K called conventional RAM, while making much more memory than is available for your PC operations. I'm not going to get too technical here, but this is accomplished through an incredible feat of digital sleight-of-hand.

Basically, an expanded memory manager constantly shuffles discrete chunks of RAM in and out of DOS's reach. Each of these chunks can contain different information — program code or data — but at any given time, DOS recognizes only those portions of RAM to which the expanded memory manager has granted it direct access. The rest is suspended in limbo somewhere, symbolically speaking, waiting for its turn to feed at the DOS trough.

For the brief instant it has control over a chunk of expanded memory, DOS treats that memory as if it were "real" RAM located between 0K and 640K. Then, faster than DOS can realize, the expanded memory manager swaps this chunk of expanded memory out DOS's reach and replaces it with another one, which DOS then proceeds to process as if *it* had always existed within the boundaries of conventional RAM. The technical name for this process, where memory normally beyond DOS's control is associated with addresses DOS can recognize and manage, is *memory mapping*.

Perhaps a "real-world" analogy would help you visualize how memory mapping works. Consider animation, a process by which individual drawings merge with one another so rapidly that our eyes and brains are "fooled" into thinking we're observing continuous, fluid movements. Memory mapping works in a similar fashion. The individual chunks of expanded memory are turned over to and removed from DOS's control so swiftly and seamlessly that DOS doesn't realize what's going on. It's "fooled" into thinking everything that's happening is happening within conventional RAM.

The result of all this digital manipulation is that expanded memory allows DOS to handle tasks that require much greater amounts of RAM than what it was originally designed to control. As I stated earlier, this is quite an incredible feat, one that effectively broke DOS out of the doldrums imposed on it by the 640K DOS barrier.

As you'll soon discover, MS-DOS 6.0 includes several features designed to take full advantage of extended and expanded memory. But first, let's see if we can plug up that "sizable gap," the one between the 640K address beyond which DOS overextends itself and the 1MB address at which extended memory begins.

Upper Memory

There's nothing magical or mystical about the 640K memory address that defines DOS's limits. In truth, the decision to restrict DOS to this much memory was arrived at somewhat capriciously. IBM, when it contracted with Microsoft to develop an operating environment for its new PC, instructed the company to, in essence, keep its hands off the upper 384K of the whopping 1MB of memory that Intel's then-revolutionary 8088 CPU — the heart of that seminal IBM personal computer — could manage. Thus was born the infamous DOS 640K barrier. (1024K–384K=640K. Get it?)

Some of this reserved memory was drafted into service immediately for a number of critical operations such as controlling the display, managing disk drives, and so forth. According to Big Blue, however, the vast majority of it needed to be withheld for unspecified "future uses."

The funny thing is, over a decade into the future IBM envisioned in 1981, very little of this 384K memory block, now referred to as *upper memory*, is being used. Most of it just sits there, idle, while DOS makes do as best it can with its meager allotment of 640K. MS-DOS 6.0 provides a number of tools that let you put this upper memory to work for you. We'll get to them in a minute, but before we do, there's one more minor memory-related topic to discuss.

HMA (The High Memory Area)

The first 64K block of RAM just beyond the 1MB address at which extended memory begins is called the high memory area, or HMA. HMA is unique in that it can be used to load a portion of the DOS code, along with other items, in an area of memory outside of conventional RAM, thus freeing up additional memory for application programs.

To review: the RAM installed in your computer can be divided into several different kinds of memory. Table 7.1 lists these various memory types, followed by the locations associated with each.

Hopefully the foundation I've laid has provided you with a basic understanding of how PC memory works. This, in turn, will allow you to stand on slightly firmer ground when we begin examining the various MS-DOS 6.0 commands that are designed to help you use efficiently the memory installed in your PC.

> ✓ **Note:** None of the memory-management techniques outlined in the following sections will work on so-called first-generation PCs — computers built around Intel's 8088 or 8086 CPU. If you own such a system, you're out of luck, at least insofar as DOS is concerned. You may be able to buy an expanded memory board that includes its own expanded memory manager, but DOS itself offers no assistance in putting your PC's memory to good use.

Table 7.1 Types of Memory and Locations

Type of Memory	Location
Conventional RAM	0K - 640K
Upper Memory Blocks	640K - 1MB
Extended Memory	1MB and up
High Memory Area (HMA)	First 64K of extended memory
Expanded Memory	Additional memory that's mapped to DOS

HIMEM.SYS

HIMEM.SYS provides the foundation on which DOS builds almost all of its memory-management capabilities. HIMEM.SYS must be installed for DOS to be loaded high; it also must be installed for EMM386.EXE to work its digital magic on a 386 or 486 system, and HIMEM.SYS must be installed before a DEVICE-HIGH statement can be used to load device drivers into upper memory. So if your computer has a 286 or higher CPU and Setup did not automatically add a HIMEM.SYS statement to your CONFIG.SYS file, this is the very first memory-related command you need to learn about.

The correct syntax for including a HIMEM.SYS statement in CONFIG.SYS is:

```
DEVICE=[drive:][path]HIMEM.SYS [/A20CONTROL:ON|OFF]
[/CPUCLOCK:ON|OFF] [/EISA] [/HMAMIN=m] [/INT15=xxxx]
[/NUMHANDLES=n] [/MACHINE:xxxx] [/SHADOWRAM:ON|OFF] [/VERBOSE]
```

HIMEM.SYS accepts the following parameters and switches:

drive:path	specifies the location of the HIMEM.SYS file. You can omit the drive and path information if HIMEM.SYS is stored in the root directory of your startup drive.
/A20CONTROL:ON|OFF	specifies whether HIMEM should take control of the A20 line. (The A20 handler gives your computer access to the high memory area, or HMA).
/CPUCLOCK:ON|OFF	specifies whether HIMEM should manage the clock speed of your computer.
/EISA	is used only on an EISA (Extended Industry Standard Architecture) system with more than 16MB of RAM to allocate all available extended memory.
/HMAMIN=*m*	specifies how many kilobytes of memory an application must have for HIMEM to give that application use of the high memory area (HMA).
/INT15=*xxxx*	is a value ranging from 64 to 65535 that allocates the amount of extended memory (in kilobytes) to be reserved for the Interrupt 15h interface.
/NUMHANDLES=*n*	is a value ranging from 1 to 128 that specifies the maximum number of extended-memory block (EMB) handles that can be used simultaneously.
/MACHINE:*xxxx*	specifies what type of computer you are using.
/SHADOWRAM:ON|OFF	tells HIMEM whether to enable or disable shadow RAM, if it is available on your computer.

/VERBOSE   instructs HIMEM.SYS to display status and error messages as it is loaded into memory from the CONFIG.SYS file. You may abbreviate /VERBOSE as /V. An alternative method of displaying status messages is to depress the ALT key as HIMEM.SYS is loaded.

HIMEM normally detects the type of system on which it is being installed automatically. If it can't, HIMEM uses the default system type: IBM AT or compatible. Should you have trouble loading HIMEM, try choosing a system type from the following list, substituting the codes or number values listed in the following table for *xxxx*, following the /MACHINE switch.

at	1	IBM AT or 100% compatible
ps2	2	IBM PS/2
ptlcascade	3	Phoenix Cascade BIOS
hpvectra	4	HP Vectra (A & A+)
att6300plus	5	AT&T 6300 Plus
acer1100	6	Acer 1100
toshiba	7	Toshiba 1600 & 1200XE
wyse	8	Wyse 12.5 Mhz 286
tulip	9	Tulip SX
zenith	10	Zenith ZBIOS
at1	11	IBM PC/AT (alternative delay)
at2	12	IBM PC/AT (alternative delay)
css	12	CSS Labs
at3	13	IBM PC/AT (alternative delay)
philips	13	Philips
fasthp	14	HP Vectra
ibm7552	15	IBM 7552 Industrial Computer
bullmicral	16	Bull Micral 60
dell	17	Dell XBIOS

As you can see, a HIMEM.SYS statement can be quite convoluted. Luckily, most of these special switches are designed to be used only if you have trouble installing HIMEM.SYS on your system. In most cases, the following extremely simple statement, placed at the beginning of your CONFIG.SYS file, will work just fine:

```
DEVICE=C:\DOS\HIMEM.SYS
```

If it doesn't, then you'll need to experiment with the alternatives. Try starting with the /MACHINE switch. It will eliminate the majority of problems that surface when HIMEM.SYS tries to take command of a system that's not 100 percent compatible with the IBM standard.

Loading DOS High (The DOS Command)

It's ability to load portions of itself into the high memory area is by far one of DOS's most useful memory management features. Doing so frees up from 45K to more than 60K of additional conventional RAM for application programs. As an added attraction, using the optional UMB switch with the DOS command allows you to load some terminate-and-stay-resident (TSR) programs and other device drivers into the HMA.

The correct syntax for entering the DOS command is:

DOS=[HIGH|LOW][,UMB|,NOUMB]

DOS accepts the following command switches:

HIGH|LOW instructs DOS whether it should load a portion of itself into the HMA (HIGH) or load all of itself into conventional RAM (LOW).

UMB|NOUMB instructs MS-DOS either to manage upper memory blocks (UMB) or not manage them (NOUMB).

Tip: **Load HIMEM.SYS First**
The DOS command requires that HIMEM.SYS or another extended memory manager be loaded into memory first. If you plan to load DOS High, therefore, make sure a HIMEM.SYS statement precedes it in your CONFIG.SYS file.

If you attempt to load DOS High and no HMA is available, the following message appears:

```
HMA not available
Loading DOS low
```

Note: Loading DOS High offers the additional benefit of allowing disk buffers to be placed in the HMA rather than conventional RAM, thus freeing up even more additional memory for your application programs.

Mega-Memory Management (The EMM386.SYS Device Driver)

If you're impressed with the MS-DOS 6.0 memory management features introduced up to this point, hold onto your hat. You ain't seen nothin' yet, especially if you own a 386 or 486 system.

The passing of the torch from the first-generation 8086 CPU to its immediate offspring, the 80286, was considered a respectable step toward more powerful PCs. In comparison, the birth of the 80386 chip represented a quantum leap into the future of personal computing. And the subsequent introduction of the 486 held us steady on this course.

But disregard its faster speed. Forget its ability to address more memory. (Both of which, by the way, are no small accomplishments.) The true benefit associated with using a 386 CPU — and, by extension the 486 — is being able to take advantage of its ability to run in *virtual 8086* mode. This technological breakthrough can be summed up in a single sentence: The 386 CPU can set aside discrete blocks of memory and configure each of them to emulate an independent 8086-based computer.

Think about that for a moment. Bounce it off a few synapses. Then, seriously consider its ramifications. That 386 or 486 system sitting on your desk is no longer just a single machine. With enough memory, it can function as two, three, four...however many computers you desire. And each one of these computers-in-a-computer can be running a separate program. Further, every one of these programs will function reliably, without running headlong into any of the others, causing the kinds of system crashes that plagued anyone who ever used an 80286-based PC.

It only makes sense that Microsoft would come up with a device driver designed to take advantage of the newfound capabilities of the CPU: EMM386.EXE, the DOS expanded memory emulator. EMM386.EXE converts extended memory into expanded memory. It also provides access to the upper memory area, replacing the UMB switch of the DOS command.

The correct syntax for including an EMM386.EXE statement in CONFIG.SYS is:

```
DEVICE=[drive:][path]EMM386.EXE [ON|OFF|AUTO] [memory]
[MIN=size] [W=ON|W=OFF] [Mx|FRAME=address|/Pmmmm]
[Pn=address] [X=mmmm-nnnn] [I=mmmm-nnnn] [B=address]
[L=minXMS] [A=altregs] [H=handles] [D=nnn] [RAM=mmmm-nnnn]
[NOEMS] [NOVCPI] [HIGHSCAN] [VERBOSE] [WIN=mmmm-nnnn] [NOHI]
[ROM=mmmm-nnnn] [NOMOVEXBDA] [ALTBOOT]
```

Obviously, EMM386.EXE is even more technically adroit than HIMEM.SYS was. Once again, however, several of the parameters and switches shown above are designed for extremely high-end users, folks who truly know their way around the ole' memory banks. To list all of the EMM386.SYS parameters and switches here would really muddy the waters. (You will find a complete explanation of these in Part II, *Command Reference*, however.) So, for our purposes here I'll just hit the high spots.

drive:path		specifies the location of the EMM386.EXE file.
[ON|OFF|AUTO]		activates or deactivates the EMM386.EXE device driver. The ON parameter activates expanded memory support; the OFF parameter deactivates expanded memory support. The AUTO parameter configures EMM386.EXE to auto mode. (In auto mode, EMM386.EXE enables expanded memory support and upper memory block support only when a program calls for it.)
memory		specifies, in kilobytes, the maximum amount of extended memory that you want EMM386.EXE to convert to expanded/Virtual Control Program Interface memory (EMS/VCPI). The default value for *memory* is all free extended memory.
M*x*		specifies the address at which you want DOS to establish a page frame for managing EMS, using the following codes as *x* to specify the corresponding memory address:

1	C000h
2	C400h
3	C800h
4	CC00h
5	D000h
6	D400h
7	D800h
8	DC00h
9	E000h
10	8000h
11	8400h
12	8800h
13	8C00h
14	9000h

You should only use values in the range 10 through 14 if your computer has at least 512K of installed RAM.

X=*mmmm-nnnn*	excludes the address range specified by the hexadecimal notation *mmmm-nnnn* from EMM386.EXE control.
I=*mmmm-nnnn*	makes the hexadecimal address *mmmm-nnnn* range available to EMS386.EXE for an EMS page or UMBs.
L=*min*XMS	ensures that the amount of extended memory specified in kilobytes with *min* will still be available after you load EMM386.EXE. The default value of *min* is 0.

RAM=*mmmm-nnnn* specifies that you want the hexadecimal range of segment addresses *mmmm-nnnn* configured as upper memory blocks (UMBs). Using the RAM switch by itself without specifying *mmmm-nnnn* causes EMM386.EXE to use all available extended memory.

NOEMS instructs EMM386 to grant access to the upper memory area but does not convert extended memory to expanded memory.

WIN=*mmmm-nnnn* removes the range of addresses specified by the hexadecimal notation *mmmm-nnnn* from control of EMM386.EXE and reserves it for use by Windows.

NOHI prevents EMM386.EXE from loading into the upper memory area.

> **Note:** As I pointed out earlier, EMM386.EXE will not load properly unless a HIMEM.SYS statement appears in your CONFIG.SYS prior to the line that installs EMM386.EXE.

Don't worry if all of this technobabble seems intimidating. Clearly, EMM386.EXE can test the technical aptitude of all but the most knowledgeable users. Luckily, DOS provides an alternative to tweaking EMM386 manually. To see what it is, let's leave EDIT and return to the system prompt for a few moments. To close EDIT:

Press **Alt+F** to display the pull-down File menu.
Press **X** to select Exit.

Because we changed your CONFIG.SYS file during this session, EDIT displays the prompt box shown in Figure 7.6, asking if you want to save your modifications. To do this:

Press **Enter** to accept Yes.

EDIT saves the modified file and returns you to the DOS system prompt. From here we can run a special utility, MemMaker, that *automatically* configures EMM386.SYS to work properly with your computer.

Let DOS Do It (The MemMaker Utility)

MemMaker automatically optimizes your system's memory, based on extensive analysis of its physical components and, in some cases, the software you use. It accomplishes this in three primary ways:

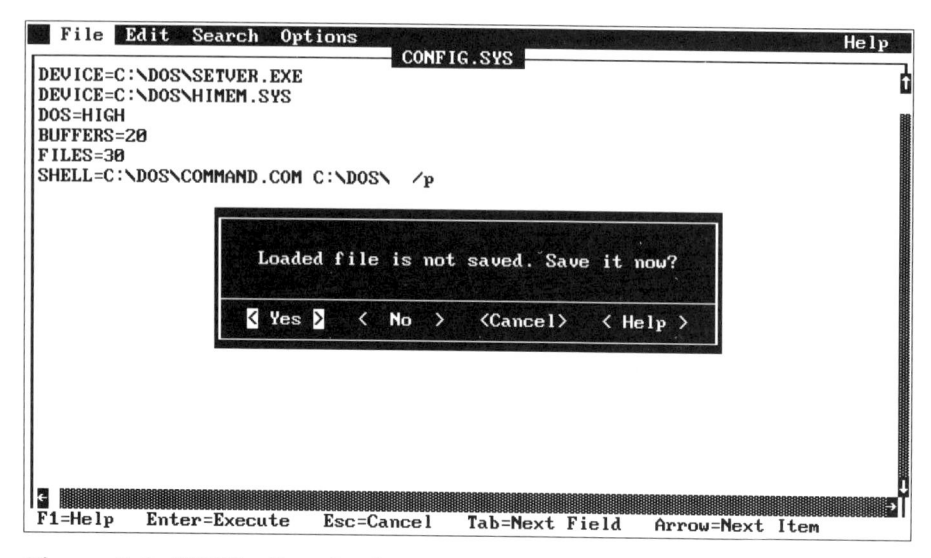

```
 File Edit  Search  Options                                    Help
                       CONFIG.SYS
DEVICE=C:\DOS\SETVER.EXE
DEVICE=C:\DOS\HIMEM.SYS
DOS=HIGH
BUFFERS=20
FILES=30
SHELL=C:\DOS\COMMAND.COM C:\DOS\  /p

              ┌─────────────────────────────────────┐
              │  Loaded file is not saved. Save it now? │
              │                                         │
              │   ◄ Yes ►   < No >   <Cancel>   < Help > │
              └─────────────────────────────────────┘




F1=Help   Enter=Execute   Esc=Cancel   Tab=Next Field   Arrow=Next Item
```

Figure 7.6 EDIT asks whether you want to save your modifications.

1. MemMaker analyzes how much and what type of memory you have. It then then incorporates into CONFIG.SYS those statements required to use this memory most efficiently.
2. MemMaker uses two special commands, DEVICEHIGH and LOADHIGH, to load automatically into upper memory any device drivers or programs that can be placed there. This frees additional memory for your application programs.
3. If MemMaker finds Windows on your hard disk, it automatically adjusts DOS's EMM386.EXE settings for maximum Windows performance.

For nontechnical users, MemMaker provides an easy way to take advantage of any MS-DOS 6.0 memory management features supported by their systems. Experienced users may want to let MemMaker perform the first steps towards improving their system's performance and then fine-tune the results.

✔ *Note:* MemMaker can be run only on computers with an 80386 or 80486 CPU on which at least 1MB of extended memory has been installed.

The correct syntax for running the MEMMAKER command is:

MEMMAKER [/B] [/BATCH] [SESSION] [/SWAP:*drive*] [/T] [/UNDO] [/W:*size1,size2*]

MEMMAKER accepts the following command switches:

/B   used when a monochrome monitor isn't displaying MEM-MAKER correctly.

/BATCH	causes MEMMAKER to run unattended, using the default values for all of its operations.
/SESSION	is exclusive to MEMMAKER during the memory optimization process.
/SWAP:*drive*	specifies the letter of the drive you used to boot your system.
/T	disables the detection of IBM Token Ring networks.
/UNDO	allows you to reverse any changes made by MEMMAKER and revert to your previous system configuration (This switch is provided as a "failsafe" device, should you encounter any problems after running MEMMAKER.)
/W:*size1,size2*	specifies how much upper memory DOS should reserve for Windows translation buffers. MEMMAKER normally sets aside two 12K regions of upper memory for Windows translation buffers. On non-Windows systems, specifying /W:0,0 prevents MEMMAKER from using this memory.

> ✔ **Note:** If any errors occur during processing, MEMMAKER creates a special file, MEMMAKER.STS, containing information about any problems it encountered. The contents of this file can be viewed using the DOS EDIT program. Before aborting, MEMMAKER restores your previous CONFIG.SYS and AUTOEXEC.BAT files.

Don't let all those switches intimidate you. MemMaker is extremely easy to use — a real "no-brainer" — even if this is the first time you've ever set fingers to a PC keyboard. How easy? Well, try the following:

Type **MEMMAKER** and press **Enter**.

Figure 7.7 shows the initial MemMaker display. This screen provides a brief explanation of what MemMaker accomplishes, along with instructions on how the program is used. The former may be quite technical, but the latter is an exercise in simplicity.

1. As MemMaker runs, you're presented with a number of options. For each option, MemMaker displays the default selection as highlighted text. (You can't see it on the accompanying screen shot, but the word **Continue** following the "Continue or Exit?" prompt is highlighted and will be on your display.)
2. To accept the highlighted option, simply press **Enter**.
3. Pressing **Spacebar** cycles you through any selections that are available for a given prompt.

4. When MemMaker displays the option you want, press **Enter** to select that option.

That's all there is to it. With these simple instructions in hand, we're ready to let MemMaker start optimizing your system.

> *Tip:* **An Easy Out**
>
> **MemMaker provides one additional and very important option whenever it pauses for user input. Pressing F3 at any input prompt exits the program and returns your system settings to whatever they were before you started MemMaker. Should any instructions or options presented by MemMaker confuse you, exit the program. You can always rerun it after finding out more information about the topic in question.**

To continue running MemMaker:

Press **Enter**.

The next screen, shown in Figure 7.8, lets you select the mode in which you want MemMaker to run. Your two options are:

- Express Setup
- Custom Setup

When run in Express mode, MemMaker automatically uses its default values for all program options. The Express Setup is the more logical choice for inexperi-

```
Microsoft MemMaker

Welcome to MemMaker.

MemMaker optimizes your system's memory by moving memory-resident
programs and device drivers into the upper memory area. This
frees conventional memory for use by applications.

After you run MemMaker, your computer's memory will remain
optimized until you add or remove memory-resident programs or
device drivers. For an optimum memory configuration, run MemMaker
again after making any such changes.

MemMaker displays options as highlighted text. (For example, you
can change the "Continue" option below.) To cycle through the
available options, press SPACEBAR. When MemMaker displays the
option you want, press ENTER.

For help while you are running MemMaker, press F1.

                Continue or Exit? Continue
ENTER=Accept Selection   SPACEBAR=Change Selection   F1=Help   F3=Exit
```

Figure 7.7 MemMaker helps you optimize your system's performance.

```
Microsoft MemMaker

There are two ways to run MemMaker:

Express Setup optimizes your computer's memory automatically.

Custom Setup gives you more control over the changes that
MemMaker makes to your system files. Choose Custom Setup
if you are an experienced user.

           Use Express or Custom Setup? Express Setup




ENTER=Accept Selection   SPACEBAR=Change Selection   F1=Help   F3=Exit
```

Figure 7.8 MemMaker lets you choose between its Express or Custom Setup.

enced users. You may want to choose Custom Setup, however, if one of the following conditions applies to your situation:

1. You want to control the changes MemMaker makes in your CONFIG.SYS and AUTOEXEC.BAT files.
2. You don't run any applications that use expanded memory.
3. You use Windows but don't run any DOS applications from within this GUI.
4. You want to prevent MemMaker from transferring certain device drivers or TSR programs from conventional RAM into upper memory.
5. You want to prevent MemMaker from aggressively scanning your upper memory.

The last reason listed would apply if, for example, your system freezes up after you run MemMaker in Express mode. Such a problem could indicate a conflict between your computer's architecture and the way in which MemMaker configures upper memory. You could rerun MemMaker using the UNDO switch, then run it a third time, choosing Custom mode to give you more control over how it analyzes upper memory.

For this initial MemMaker pass, go ahead and select Express Setup. To do this:

Press **Enter**.

The one thing MemMaker can't determine automatically is whether you run any programs that require expanded memory. So, as Figure 7.9 illustrates, it asks. If you know you use an application program that requires expanded memory:

Press **Spacebar** to change the highlighted option to **Yes**.
Press **Enter**.

> ✔ *Note:* Because the fax software on my system uses expanded memory, I have to choose the **Yes** option, but you should pick whichever option is appropriate for your software.

If you're not certain of the answer or you know that none of your applications require expanded memory:

Press **Enter**.

MemMaker requires at least two system restarts to test all of the variables that can influence memory optimization. Prior to each restart, it displays a message similar to the one in Figure 7.10. Notice that this message instructs you how to recover successfully, should MemMaker have trouble starting your system automatically. You simply turn off your system, then turn it back on again. What could be easier? To initiate the second phase of MemMaker's optimization process:

Press **Enter**.

```
Microsoft MemMaker

  If you use any programs that require expanded memory (EMS), answer
  Yes to the following question.  Answering Yes makes expanded memory
  available, but might not free as much conventional memory.

  If none of your programs need expanded memory, answer No to the
  following question.  Answering No makes expanded memory unavailable,
  but can free more conventional memory.

  If you are not sure whether your programs require expanded memory,
  answer No.  If you later discover that a program needs expanded
  memory, run MemMaker again and answer Yes to this question.

  Do you use any programs that need expanded memory (EMS)? No




ENTER=Accept Selection   SPACEBAR=Change Selection   F1=Help   F3=Exit
```

Figure 7.9 You can choose whether MemMaker should set up EMM386 to convert extended memory into expanded memory.

FINE-TUNING YOUR SYSTEM   177

```
Microsoft MemMaker

    MemMaker will now restart your computer.

    If your computer doesn't start properly, just turn it off
    and on again, and MemMaker will recover automatically.

    If a program other than MemMaker starts after your computer
    restarts, exit the program so that MemMaker can continue.

         * Remove any disks from your floppy-disk drives and
           then press ENTER. Your computer will restart.




ENTER=Continue
```

Figure 7.10   As part of its optimization process, MemMaker must restart your system.

During its first system startup, MemMaker tests a variety of configurations on your computer. After selecting the one it thinks is most appropriate, MemMaker pauses a second time and displays the message screen shown in Figure 7.11, informing you that is will once again restart your system. As this figure points out, pay attention to the messages displayed during this second startup and note any that indicate potential problems or conflicts that arise with the configuration MemMaker chose. To restart your system:

```
Microsoft MemMaker

    MemMaker will now restart your computer to test the new memory
    configuration.

    While your computer is restarting, watch your screen carefully.
    Note any unusual messages or problems. If your computer doesn't
    start properly, just turn it off and on again, and MemMaker
    will recover automatically.

    If a program other than MemMaker starts after your computer
    restarts, exit the program so that MemMaker can continue.

         * Remove any disks from your floppy-disk drives and
           then press ENTER. Your computer will restart.


ENTER=Continue
```

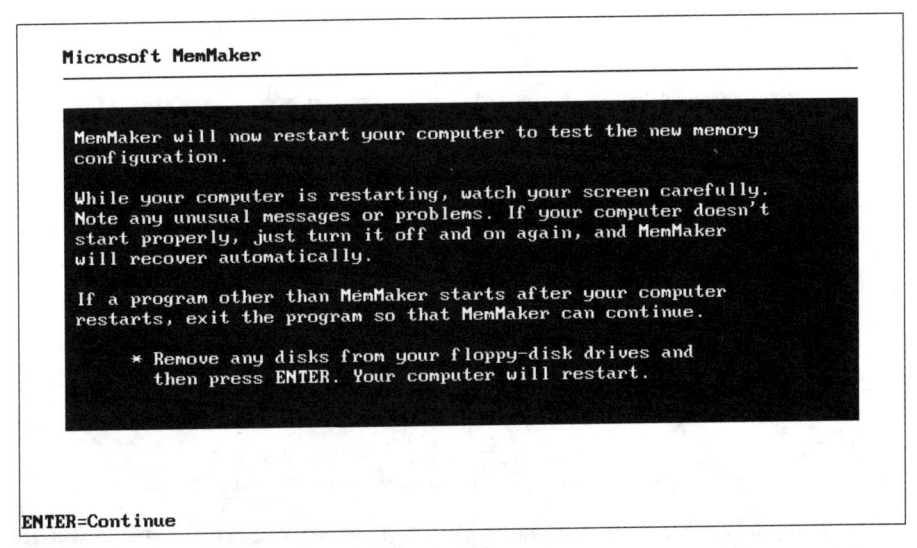

Figure 7.11   MemMaker automatically tests your new startup routines.

Press **Enter**.

Figure 7.12 shows the final message MemMaker displays as part of its system optimization process. Basically, MemMaker is asking if you noticed any problems during the previous restart. If you did, press **Spacebar** to select **No** in response to the "Does your system appear to be working properly?" prompt. If everything went as expected — and chances are it did:

Press **Enter** to accept the **Yes** response.

Before returning you to the system prompt MemMaker displays a report similar to the one shown in Figure 7.13, indicating the results of its optimization efforts. On my system, for example, it reported a loss of 2,448 bytes in conventional memory. However, a gain of over 90K in upper memory — a fact also reflected in Figure 7-13 — more than compensates for this loss. Let's see what modifications MemMaker made in my startup routine to accomplish this feat:

Press **Enter** to exit MemMaker.
When the system prompt appears, type **TYPE CONFIG.SYS**.
Press **Enter**.
When the system prompt reappears, type **TYPE C:\DOS\CONFIG.UMB**.
Press **Enter**.

MemMaker automatically saved your initial CONFIG.SYS to a file called CONFIG.UMB in the DOS directory. The above command sequence uses the TYPE command to display both the current and previous contents of CONFIG.SYS

```
Microsoft MemMaker


  Your computer has just restarted with its new memory configuration.
  Some or all of your device drivers and memory-resident programs
  are now running in upper memory.

  If your system appears to be working properly, choose "Yes."
  If you noticed any unusual messages when your computer started,
  or if your system is not working properly, choose "No."

  Does your system appear to be working properly? Yes










ENTER=Accept Selection   SPACEBAR=Change Selection   F1=Help   F3=Exit
```

Figure 7.12   You can tell MemMaker if any problems surfaced during system restart.

```
Microsoft MemMaker

MemMaker has finished optimizing your system's memory. The following
table summarizes the memory use (in bytes) on your system:

                            Before        After
Memory Type                 MemMaker      MemMaker      Change

Free conventional memory:   558,928       556,480       -2,448

Upper memory:
    Used by programs              0           688          688
    Reserved for Windows          0             0            0
    Reserved for EMS              0        65,536       65,536
    Free                          0        92,576

Expanded memory:            Disabled      Enabled

Your original CONFIG.SYS and AUTOEXEC.BAT files have been saved
as CONFIG.UMB and AUTOEXEC.UMB. If MemMaker changed your Windows
SYSTEM.INI file, the original file was saved as SYSTEM.UMB.

ENTER=Exit   ESC=Undo changes
```

Figure 7.13 MemMaker reports on the results of its memory optimization.

(see Figure 7.14). A comparison of the two will reveal any changes MemMaker made to your startup routine.

✔ *Note:* The last line of Figure 7.14 was included in my CONFIG.SYS to give me access to the screen capture program I used to reproduce the sequence of figures that accompanied the previous MemMaker exercises.

```
C:\>TYPE CONFIG.SYS
DEVICE=C:\DOS\HIMEM.SYS
DEVICE=C:\DOS\EMM386.EXE RAM HIGHSCAN
BUFFERS=20,0
FILES=30
DOS=UMB
LASTDRIVE=E
FCBS=4,0
DEVICEHIGH /L:1,12048 =C:\DOS\SETVER.EXE
DOS=HIGH
SHELL=C:\DOS\COMMAND.COM C:\DOS\ /p
INSTALL C:\COLLAGE\SNAP.exe c:\CAPTURE /T

C:\>TYPE \DOS\CONFIG.UMB
DEVICE=C:\DOS\SETVER.EXE
DEVICE=C:\DOS\HIMEM.SYS
DOS=HIGH
BUFFERS=20
FILES=30
SHELL=C:\DOS\COMMAND.COM C:\DOS\ /p
INSTALL C:\COLLAGE\SNAP.exe c:\CAPTURE /T

C:\>
```

Figure 7.14 You can compare the current and previous contents of CONFIG.SYS.

Two items in the modified CONFIG.SYS file (the upper listing in Figure 7.14) deserve mention:

1. Notice that MemMaker automatically added to CONFIG.SYS the statement used to install the EMM386.EXE memory manager, including the appropriate command switches for my system.

2. MemMaker moved the SETVER command down. Previously, it was the first statement in CONFIG.SYS. It also replaced the DEVICE command previously used to load the SETVER.EXE device driver with one you've not yet encountered. (It is no coincidence that this command, DEVICEHIGH, is the topic of our next discussion.)

One more comment about tweaking your memory before we move on. MemMaker adjusts your CONFIG.SYS and AUTOEXEC.BAT files based on their contents at the time. If you're like most people, you'll modify your PC environment from time to time — add a new piece of hardware here, remove another there. Should these changes also involve adding or removing device drivers, it's a good idea to rerun MemMaker once the situation stabilizes. That way, you'll always know you have the most efficient memory configuration for your current setup.

Moving Up to Upper Memory (The DEVICEHIGH Command)

You've encountered the DEVICE command several times already. As I explained in the previous chapter, this is the command used in CONFIG.SYS to load device drivers into memory during system startup. So, what's DEVICEHIGH doing in the SETVER statement? Obviously, it's connected with the DEVICE command. But how? And even more important, how do the two differ from one another?

The DEVICE command loads device drivers into the conventional RAM, that 640K of memory DOS uses to run programs. Left to its own devices (Ouch!) therefore, the DEVICE command demands a trade-off. Each driver you load consumes memory that could otherwise be made available to your applications. Robbing Peter to pay Paul, in a sense. If either the EMM386.EXE memory manager or a DOS=UMB command can free enough memory between 640K and 1MB (that block of RAM that comprises the upper memory blocks discussed earlier), this needn't be the case. When upper memory is available, the DEVICEHIGH command allows you to specify that a device driver is loaded there, rather than in conventional RAM.

The correct syntax for entering a DEVICEHIGH command is:

DEVICEHIGH [*drive:*][*path*]*filename* [*dd-parameters*]

Or, you can use the following command to specify the region(s) of upper memory into which you want a device driver loaded:

```
DEVICEHIGH= [[/L:region1[,minsize1][;region2[,minsize2]]
[/S]] [drive:][path]filename [dd-parameters]
```

DEVICEHIGH Parameters and Command Switches

DEVICEHIGH accepts the following parameters and command switches:

drive:path	specifies the location of the device driver you want to load into the upper memory area.
filename	specifies the name of the device driver you want to load into the upper memory area.
dd-parameters	passes to DEVICEHIGH any command line information required by the device driver being loaded.
/S	shrinks the UMB to its minimum size while the driver is loading.
/L:region1,minsize1 ;region2,minsize2	forces DOS to load a device driver into one or more specific regions of memory.

A DEVICEHIGH command can be simple or complicated. My advice, if you're just starting out, is: Keep it simple — depend on the first DEVICEHIGH syntax listed above. It's easy and foolproof. If there isn't enough upper memory available when you issue this command, DOS automatically loads the device driver in conventional RAM, just as it would if you had used a standard DEVICE command. As you become more familiar with upper memory blocks, you can always tweak your CONFIG.SYS file to load drivers into specific memory areas.

CONFIG.SYS Cornucopia (Miscellaneous CONFIG.SYS Commands)

We're almost finished with our examination of the various commands and statements that you can include in a CONFIG.SYS file. In fact, we only have two quickies to go.

There Are More Programs in Heaven and Earth, Horatio... (The INSTALL Command)

There was a time when you could only load device drivers from CONFIG.SYS. Any executable programs you wanted to use had to be run either through an AUTOEXEC.BAT file (which we'll examine in a few paragraphs) or from the command prompt following system startup. This is no longer the case. The

INSTALL command, which first appeared in MS-DOS 5.0, allows you to load memory-resident programs directly from your CONFIG.SYS.

One advantage associated with using this technique is that, because they bypass COMMAND.COM and are loaded directly into memory, programs installed from CONFIG.SYS use less RAM. (The explanation for this has to do with the manner in which COMMAND.COM creates an environment for every program you run, a process that requires a small amount of additional memory.)

The correct syntax for entering an INSTALL command is:

```
INSTALL=[drive:][path]filename [command-parameters]
```

INSTALL Parameters

INSTALL accepts the following parameters:

drive:path	specifies the location of the program you want to run in the upper memory area.
filename	specifies the name of the program that you want to run in the upper memory area.
command-parameters	is used to enter any command parameters required by the program specified with *filename*.

Caution: Some programs may not run properly when loaded with an INSTALL statement.

Look back at Figure 7.14 and you'll notice that I used an INSTALL command to load the screen capture program I mentioned earlier. Doing so reduced its memory requirements by 1K. This isn't much, I realize, but in the PC purse, where memory is one of your most valuable assets, a K saved is a K earned.

By the Numbers (The NUMLOCK Command)

This one's about as easy as they get. You use the NUMLOCK command to specify the initial state of the numeric keypad on your computer's keyboard. By default, DOS activates the number keys on the numeric keypad. Inserting the following statement into your CONFIG.SYS file turns off the number keys during system startup, allowing you to use the numeric keypad for cursor movement instead:

```
NUMLOCK=OFF
```

That's it.

We've covered a lot of territory in this initial discussion of CONFIG.SYS, and we'll leave it for now and move on to AUTOEXEC.BAT, the second file that allows you to modify the default DOS environment each time you turn on your computer. CONFIG.SYS will be back for a return engagement in the final chapter of this book when we examine MS-DOS 6.0's newfound ability to define multiple configurations for your PC during system startup.

What Is AUTOEXEC. BAT?

A couple of seconds after CONFIG.SYS finishes working its digital magic is when AUTOEXEC.BAT steps in to put the finishing touches on the fine-tuning of your DOS environment.

To understand what an AUTOEXEC.BAT file is, all you need to do is break the name down into its component parts. AUTOEXEC.BAT is an *auto*matically *exec*uted *bat*ch file.

Stated simply, if DOS discovers an AUTOEXEC.BAT file in the root directory of your startup disk, it automatically executes any commands this file contains before advancing you to the system prompt. This description, of course, leads directly to a second question. Namely, what is a batch file?

Batch-ing It

The concept of batch processing has its roots in the seminal days of computers. Not today's sleek, smart, state-of-the-art personal computers, mind you, but the vast, vacuum-tube-filled, monolithic monstrosities that fired the first digital shots in the so-called computer revolution. Back then, you didn't turn on a computer and begin typing instructions into a keyboard like you do today. Rather, you interacted with a computer by feeding a stack of punch cards into a device that could make some sense out of the patterns of holes these card contained. The computer translated those patterns into the commands or data values that allowed these archaic automatons to actually accomplish something useful.

As you can imagine, in the days of punch cards, performing even a relatively simple operation was an inconvenient and tedious undertaking. A truly complicated task required piles of punch cards — hundreds, sometimes thousands of them. Early on, someone decided to call this technique batch processing, a sobriquet derived from the rather large "batch" of cards required to accomplish all but the most simple tasks using an early computer.

Some frustrated users may argue differently, but we have made progress since those PC pioneer days. (Although I'm not totally convinced that some of the more esoteric "alternate input devices" I've seen out there represent true technological advancement.) At least we no longer rely on punch cards to communicate with our computers.

DOS does, however, support batch processing of a sort. It's still possible to start a "stack" of commands running, figuratively speaking, and then let your computer take over from there. Today, however, you accomplish this with a batch file, not a batch of punch cards. A batch file is an ASCII file containing one or more commands you normally would enter at the system prompt. When a batch file is run, DOS executes these commands as if you had typed them in at your keyboard.

At this point, however, I'm going to table any comprehensive discussion of batch files until Chapter 9, "The Age of Automation: Batch Files and Other Conveniences." Instead, for the remainder of this chapter, I'll concentrate on introducing a few, simple commands that, when included in AUTOEXEC.BAT, add a touch of convenience to your PC operations.

The Pathfinder (The PATH Command)

The PATH command allows you to specify a search path DOS can use to find the files associated with any commands you enter or programs you try to run. To understand why a PATH command can be useful, you need to know what happens when you ask DOS to execute a command you enter.

When you press Enter after typing in a command, it sends DOS off on a predetermined course of action, which is comprised of a series of four steps that determines whether on not DOS can execute your command successfully:

1. The first thing DOS does is check to see whether the command you entered is an internal DOS command — one of the commands loaded into memory each time you turn on or restart your system. (COPY and DIR are two examples of internal commands.) If it is, DOS immediately fulfills your request.

2. If you have not entered an internal command, DOS next tries to find the file associated with your command in the current directory. (This must be an executable file — a file with the file extension EXE, COM, or BAT.) If DOS finds the appropriate file, it executes your command.

3. If it can't find the required file in the default directory, DOS still doesn't give up. Rather, it begins an organized search of all the directories assigned to the PATH variable in your DOS environment, starting with the first directory listed. If the appropriate file exists in any of the directories to which PATH gives DOS access, it executes your command.

4. If, after all of this searching, DOS fails to find the file that allows it to execute your command, it displays a "Bad command or filename" message and returns you to the system prompt.

Three of these four steps are fairly straightforward. But what's that PATH variable mentioned in step 3? And even more important, where does it come from?

First, the PATH variable: It is defined, logically enough, by entering a PATH command. The correct syntax for entering a PATH command is:

PATH [;] [[*drive:*]*path*[;...]]

PATH accepts the following parameter and command switch:

drive:path specifies the drive, directory, and subdirectory you want DOS to search when it tries to find a command file.

; used by itself, a semicolon clears the PATH variable, causing MS-DOS to search only the current directory for executable files, including external DOS commands. The semicolon is also used to separate the individual entries when multiple directories are included in a PATH command.

> ***Caution:*** The maximum length of the PATH command is 127 characters. If your search path requires more directories than this limit allows, use the SUBST command to substitute logical drive names for some directories.

> ***Tip:*** First Come, First Served
> How quickly DOS finds a file is influenced by how early in the PATH variable the directory containing that file appears. Remember, DOS searches your directories in the order in which they are listed within the PATH command. An efficient technique, therefore, is to place those directories containing frequently used files near the beginning of the PATH command.

Like virtually all DOS commands, PATH can be executed either at the system prompt or from within a batch file. One way to ensure that the same search path exists whenever you use your computer is to add the appropriate PATH statement to your AUTOEXEC.BAT file, which we'll do in the following exercise to help prepare you for the information covered in subsequent chapters.

Make certain that you are at the system prompt in the root directory of your startup disk.

Type **MD \BATCH** and press **Enter**.

Type **EDIT AUTOEXEC.BAT** and press **Enter**.

You should now be looking at the contents of a file called AUTOEXEC.BAT. (This file did not magically appear on your hard disks. It was created by Setup when you first installed MS-DOS 6.0.) Figure 7.15 shows the contents of a very basic AUTOEXEC.BAT file, which is the initial AUTOEXEC.BAT file that Setup creates on a new disk.

As you can see, Setup has already placed a PATH statement in this file. It did this so that DOS would be able to find any files it needed to execute external commands. We're going to expand our search path to include a second directory: the BATCH directory created in the previous exercise. While we're at it, let's also make the PROMPT format we established in Chapter 4 our default system prompt. To do this:

Use the arrow keys to position the cursor after **PROMPT** in the current PROMPT statement.

Use the **DEL** key to remove the current prompt specifications.

Type **($p) $s**.

Use the arrow keys to position the cursor after **C:\DOS** in the current PATH statement.

Type ;C:**BATCH**.

Press **Alt+F** to display EDIT's pull-down File menu.

Press X to select **Exit**.

When EDIT asks if you want to save the file, press **Enter** to specify **Yes**.

This closes down Edit and returns you to the system prompt. We must perform one more step before the changes we made to AUTOEXEC.BAT will take effect.

Figure 7.15 You can use EDIT to modify AUTOEXEC.BAT.

In the process, you'll learn about another useful DOS feature, the ability to "warm-boot" your system.

Some Like It Warm (Warm Booting Your System)

Modifications made to an AUTOEXEC.BAT or CONFIG.SYS file don't take effect until the next time you start your system. One way to do this is to turn your computer off and then back on again. However, there is a second, more convenient way to accomplish this; it's called a *warm boot*, and it involves a simple combination keystroke:

Press **Ctrl+Alt+Del**.

> **Caution:** A warm boot mimics turning off your computer in a second way, as well. It erases any programs and data previously stored in memory. For this reason, you should never restart a PC arbitrarily. Make certain that you have exited all your applications and saved any important data files prior to initiating a warm boot, just as you would before turning off your computer.

The Ctrl+Alt+Del key combination tells DOS that you want to restart your computer without actually turning it off. DOS complies, which in turn incorporates into your default PC environment the modifications we made to AUTOEXEC.BAT in the previous exercise. One way you'll be able to verify this is by looking at your system prompt. It should now be displayed using the format specified in your modified AUTOEXEC.BAT file, (C:\), rather than the earlier format of C>.

There's also an easy way to see if the BATCH directory has been added to your PATH variable, and this leads directly into our next topic.

A Matching Set (The SET Command)

Eagle-eyed readers no doubt noticed that another command was included in the AUTOEXEC.BAT file that we edited in the previous section:

```
SET TEMP=C:\DOS
```

The SET command is used to display information about your DOS environment or, if desired, to modify it. The correct syntax for entering a SET command is:

SET [*variable*=[*string*]]

SET accepts the following parameters:

variable   identifies the environment variable you want to set or modify.

string   specifies the string you want associated with *variable*.

Environment variables allow you to modify certain elements of your DOS environment — hence, the name. For example, customizing the system prompt, as we did earlier, causes DOS to store the new setting in a variable called, appropriately enough, PROMPT. In a short while you'll learn how to use another variable, DIRCMD, to specify a default format for your directory listings. Many programs use environment variables to identify where to find certain information they require to run properly.

Entering the SET command by itself, with no variables, causes DOS to display the current environment. To see what I mean:

Type **SET** and press **Enter**.

As Figure 7.16 indicates, DOS accepted our new search path. DOS will now search through the BATCH directory, if it can't find an executable file it needs in either the current or DOS directories.

Now we're going to return to EDIT and add two more lines to AUTOEXEC.BAT. I'll explain in a moment what they accomplish.

Type **EDIT AUTOEXEC.BAT** and press **Enter**.
Use the arrow keys to position the cursor at the end of the current AUTOEXEC.BAT file.
Type **SET DIRCMD=/O:N /P** and press **Enter**.
Type **LH DOSKEY**.
Press **Alt+F** to display EDIT's pull-down File menu.
Press **X** to select **Exit**.
When EDIT asks if you want to save the file, press **Enter** to specify **Yes**.
Press **Ctrl+Alt+Del** to warm boot your system.

As promised, I'll now explain what we did in the preceding exercise.

The DIRCMD Variable

Why tell you about something when I can show it to you? After all, as they say, one picture is worth a thousand words. So, let's get a picture of what one of the commands we added to AUTOEXEC.BAT accomplished:

```
(C:\) SET
COMSPEC=C:\DOS\COMMAND.COM
PROMPT=($p) $s
PATH=C:\DOS;C:\BATCH
TEMP=C:\DOS

(C:\)
```

Figure 7.16   When used by itself, the SET command displays a profile of your environment settings.

Type **CD \DOS** and press **Enter**.
Type **DIR** and press **Enter**.

Your display should now resemble Figure 7.17. You probably recognize this as a directory listing, but it's not your typical, helter-skelter, run-on-forever display listing. Its contents are sorted by filename. And it automatically paused after a full screen of information was displayed.

Astute readers will recognize this as the DIR format specified by /O:N /P, the DIR command switches we included in the DIRCMD statement added to AUTOEXEC.BAT in the previous exercise. The DIRCMD variable lets you choose a new default format DOS should use for your directory listings. For now, let's interrupt this display listing and move on to the next and final topic relating to the AUTOEXEC.BAT file.

Press **Ctrl+C**.

Claiming the High Ground (The LOADHIGH or LH Command)

The other new command introduced in the previous exercise was LH, an abbreviation for LOADHIGH. LOADHIGH works like a hybrid DEVICEHIGH/INSTALL command, both of which were introduced earlier in this chapter. It installs memory-resident programs into unused upper memory blocks (UMBs). Unlike DEVICEHIGH and INSTALL, though, which can only be used in a CONFIG.SYS file, LOADHIGH can be entered at the system prompt or from within a batch file.

```
Volume in drive C is MS-DOS 6
Volume Serial Number is 199C-54D2
Directory of C:\DOS

.            <DIR>         09-17-92   8:21p
..           <DIR>         09-17-92   8:21p
ANSI     SYS       8959   12-06-92   6:00a
APPEND   EXE      10774   12-06-92   6:00a
APPNOTES TXT       9058   12-06-92   6:00a
ATTRIB   EXE      11165   12-06-92   6:00a
AUTOEXEC UMB         54   12-30-92  10:13a
CHKDSK   EXE      12058   12-06-92   6:00a
CHKSTATE SYS      41536   12-06-92   6:00a
CHOICE   COM       1754   12-06-92   6:00a
COMMAND  COM      53405   12-06-92   6:00a
CONFIG   UMB        166   12-30-92  10:07a
COUNTRY  SYS      17066   12-06-92   6:00a
DBLSPACE BIN      65402   12-06-92   6:00a
DBLSPACE EXE     294330   12-06-92   6:00a
DBLSPACE HLP      35851   12-06-92   6:00a
DBLSPACE INF       1546   12-06-92   6:00a
DBLSPACE SYS        217   12-06-92   6:00a
DEBUG    EXE      15715   12-06-92   6:00a
Press any key to continue . . .
```

Figure 7.17 You use the DIRCMD variable to format your directory listings.

The correct syntax for entering a LOADHIGH command is:

`LOADHIGH|LH` `[drive:][path] filename [parameters]`

Or, you can use the following command to specify the region(s) of upper memory into which you want a memory-resident program loaded:

`LOADHIGH|LH=` `[[/L:region1[,minsize1][;region2[,minsize2]]...]`
`[/S]] [drive:][path]filename [parameters]`

LOADHIGH accepts the following parameters and command switches:

drive:path	specifies the location of the memory-resident program you want to load into the upper memory area.
filename	specifies the name of the program you want to load into the upper memory area.
parameters	passes to LOADHIGH any command line information required by the program being loaded.
/S	shrinks the UMB to its minimum size while the driver is loading.
/L:*region1,minsize1 ;region2,minsize2*	forces DOS to load a program into one or more specific regions of memory.

All of this may look familiar, and it should. The command syntax and parameters for LOADHIGH are exactly the same as those used by DEVICEHIGH. So, too, is my advice. Start out simple, using the basic LOADHIGH or LH command, and then refine your program placement as you learn more about the memory architecture of your system.

> ✔ **Note:** By the way, don't concern yourself now with exactly *which* TSR program we loaded into upper memory during the previous exercise. It will be made clear in Chapter 9, "The Age of Automation."

We've traveled through a lot of territory in this chapter. Much of it was quite technical in nature. All of it will help you customize your PC environment to match your personal preferences. You're beginning to take ownership of your computer and it's natural to want to protect that which you own. Protecting your PC and the files it contains is a topic we'll cover in the next chapter.

Chapter 8

Play It Safe: Protecting Your Data

Hardware components, as you know by now, are not the most critical items associated with your PC. Should something happen to your system units, keyboards, monitors, modems, printers, they can all be replaced. Nor are the application programs stored on your hard or floppy disks the most critical elements. A damaged program also can be restored to health, should this ever be necessary.

The real jewels in your computer's crown are your data files. They are unique, a cornucopia of individual information that's exclusively yours. Possessing little or no value to anyone else, they're an invaluable component of your PC operations. Given this fact, it's amazing how cavalierly many people treat this often irreplaceable asset. One story comes to mind that illustrates this.

Don't Neglect that Data

When I was a computer consultant, one of my clients was a company that kept voluminous and extremely detailed customer records stored on their then state-of-the-art IBM AT 80286-based computer. At any given time, records on 25,000 to 30,000 transactions were stored on their 40MB hard drive, and each record consisted of something like 23 fields or individual pieces of information. Every record, in turn, was linked to one or more ancillary database files containing invoice codes, transaction histories, special billing instructions, and so forth.

When I installed this system, I took special precautions to set up a completely automated backup routine to protect this important information. With a single keystroke, my client could take a "snapshot" of these files for safekeeping. I also stressed how critical it was that this "shapshot" be kept current. The backup disks represented an electronic insurance policy, one that could restore the client's operations to full service should disaster ever befall the original files.

Disaster did indeed strike, and unexpectedly, as disaster often will. And of course it struck in the middle of my client's busiest billing period.

Needless to say, my client called in a panic. "No problem," I assured him, putting on my best consultant's voice. "Just grab the latest backup disks and I'll walk you through the steps required to restore your files to pristine performance. We can do it over the phone." There was a long pause on the other end of the line. He had backed up his data religiously, every day for the first month or so after I installed his system. A couple of months later he decided that his miracle machine was working so reliably that he didn't need to back up his files more than once a week.

By the time I received his phone call, the most current data he had in his possession was at least three months old and, therefore, three months out of date. He spent the next month — or, more correctly, two of his administrative assistants spent the next month — reentering from paper records information that could have been restored in minutes had he only followed the three basic rules of data protection:

1. Back up
2. Back up
3. Back up

Now, I'm not implying that everyone has to back up the entire contents of their hard disks daily. They don't. In all honesty, I don't, nor do most people I know. This strict a regimen is necessary only if the contents of your files change dramatically every day, and if the loss of a single day's worth of data will have a detrimental impact on your operations, as was the case with this particular client.

What I am saying is that you need to take whatever steps are appropriate to protect your data against accidental or — as you'll see in a while, deliberate — loss or damage. DOS provides a number of valuable tools to assist you in this effort, starting with the ability to make archive copies of the files on your hard disk.

A New Face for an Old Friend (The MSBACKUP Utility)

Every release of DOS since version 2.0 — the first version of DOS to recognize hard disks — has allowed you to create archive copies of your files. In fact, every release of DOS since version 2.0 has relied on essentially the *same* program to accomplish this — BACKUP.

BACKUP worked, to be sure. But it was a difficult program to learn and a clumsy program to use. MS-DOS 6.0 eliminates these problems by replacing BACKUP with a menu-driven, interactive file archiving utility called MSBACKUP. The correct syntax for entering a MSBACKUP command is:

```
MSBACKUP [setup_file] [/BW|/LCD|/MDA]
```

MSBACKUP Parameters and Command Switches

MSBACKUP accepts the following parameter and command switches:

- *setup_file* identifies the setup file containing the parameters you want applied to the current backup operation.

- /BW instructs DOS to run MSBACKUP using a black-and-white display scheme.

- /LCD instructs DOS to run MSBACKUP using a video mode compatible with laptop displays.

- /MDA instructs DOS to run MSBACKUP using a monochrome display adapter.

Notice that the parameter and every switch associated with MSBACKUP is optional. Like the BACKUP command, MSBACKUP can be run exclusively from the command line, using the *setup_file* parameter listed above to control its operations. Unlike BACKUP, however, MSBACKUP can also be run interactively to create the actual configuration files associated with the *setup_file* parameter. In fact, you *must* run MSBACKUP in interactive mode at least once to create an initial *setup_file*. So, let's do that.

Running MSBACKUP

To start the MSBACKUP utility:

Type **MSBACKUP** and press **Enter**.

Because this is the first time you've run MSBACKUP, DOS displays the Alert shown in Figure 8.1. Basically, DOS is telling you that MSBACKUP must be provided certain information about your system before it will run. To begin this process:

Press **Enter**.

MSBACKUP responds with the Video and Mouse Configuration dialog box shown in Figure 8.2. This is the first in a series of dialog boxes MSBACKUP uses to record your preferences and, in some cases, perform hardware tests to determine how it should run on your system. As the Setup utility did when you installed

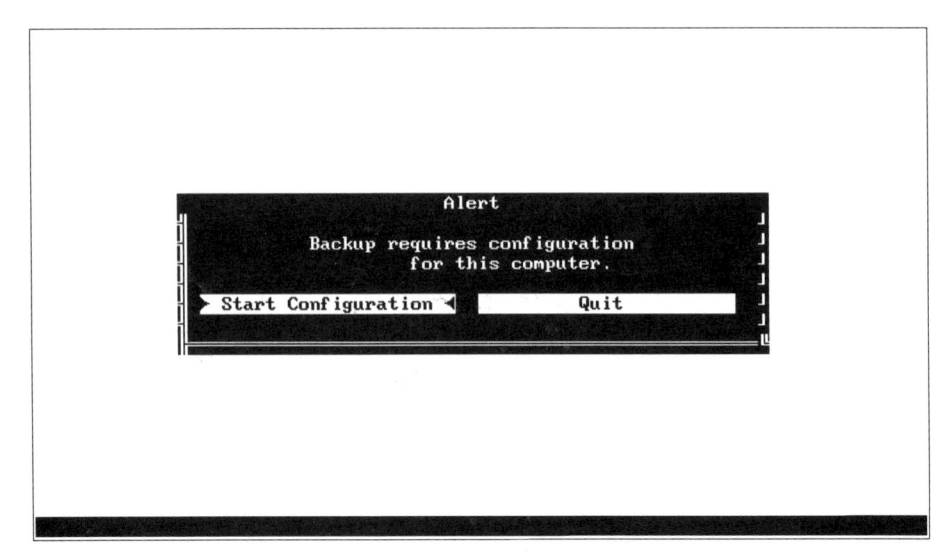

Figure 8.1 You must configure MSBACKUP to work properly on your system.

MS-DOS 6.0, MSBACKUP suggests initial values for its configuration file based on an analysis of your hardware. Unless a glaring incompatibility surfaces, it's probably a good idea to accept the recommended settings the first time you run MSBACKUP. Later, if you want, you can modify your configuration based on personal preferences. To accept the suggested Video and Mouse Configuration settings:

Press **Enter**.

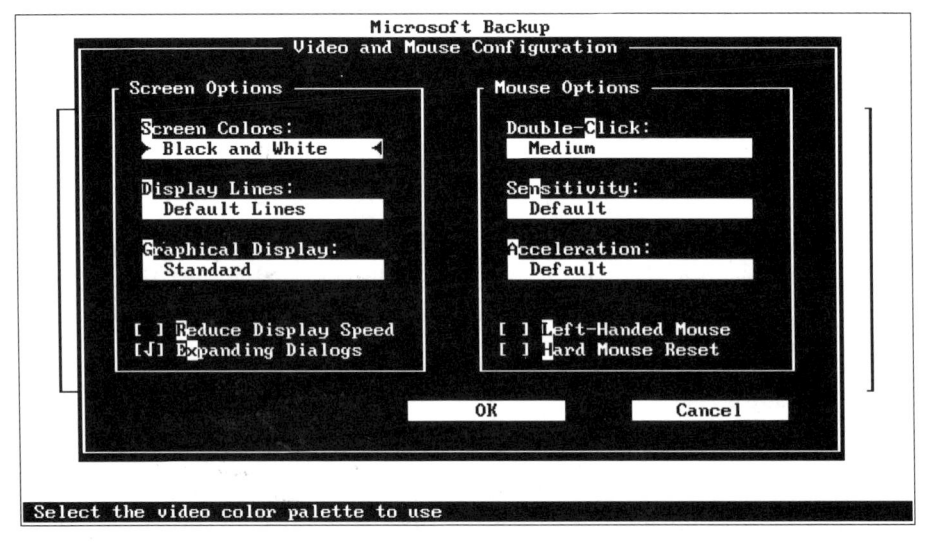

Figure 8.2 You select the appropriate settings for your hardware.

Tip: **Backing Out of MSBACKUP**
You can abort the initial MSBACKUP configuration at any time. To do this, simply use the TAB key to highlight the Cancel option and press Enter. This returns you to the initial MSBACKUP screen shown in Figure 8.1, from which you can select the Quit option. Be aware, however, that the next time you try to run MSBACKUP, it will force you to perform the initial configuration before disk archiving will be permitted.

MSBACKUP advances to its first hardware test (see Figure 8.3). This test determines the method MSBACKUP will use to detect when you change disks in your floppy disk drive during archiving. (The older BACKUP program required that you press Enter to tell DOS a new disk had been inserted into the target drive.) To initiate this test:

If necessary, remove any floppy disks from your disk drives.
Press **Enter** to accept the **Start Test** option.

Don't let the grinding sound coming out of your system alarm you. It's just MSBACKUP's way of analyzing what kind of floppy disk drives are installed on your system. MSBACKUP displays the results of this analysis using the message box shown in Figure 8.4. Check to see if the listed drive types match your hardware. If they do:

Press **Enter**.

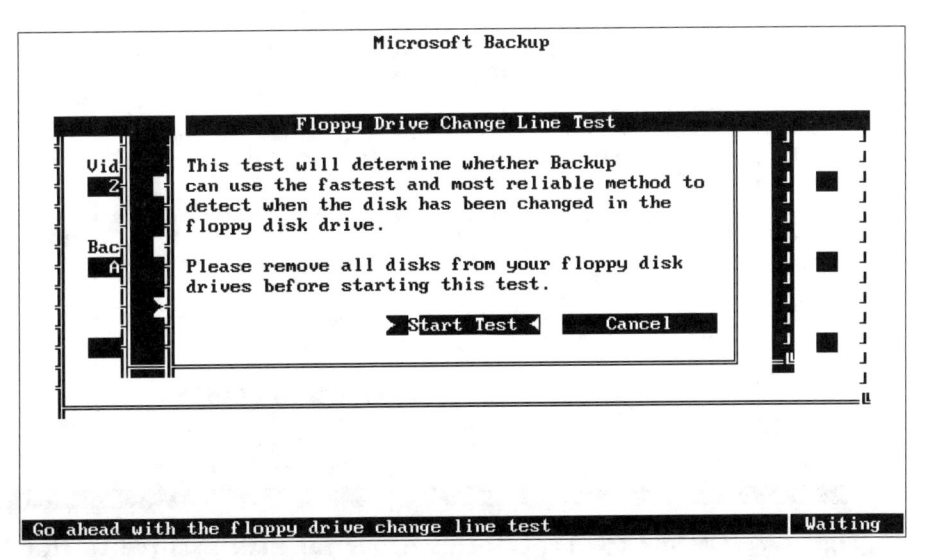

Figure 8.3 Testing hardware for performance and compatibility.

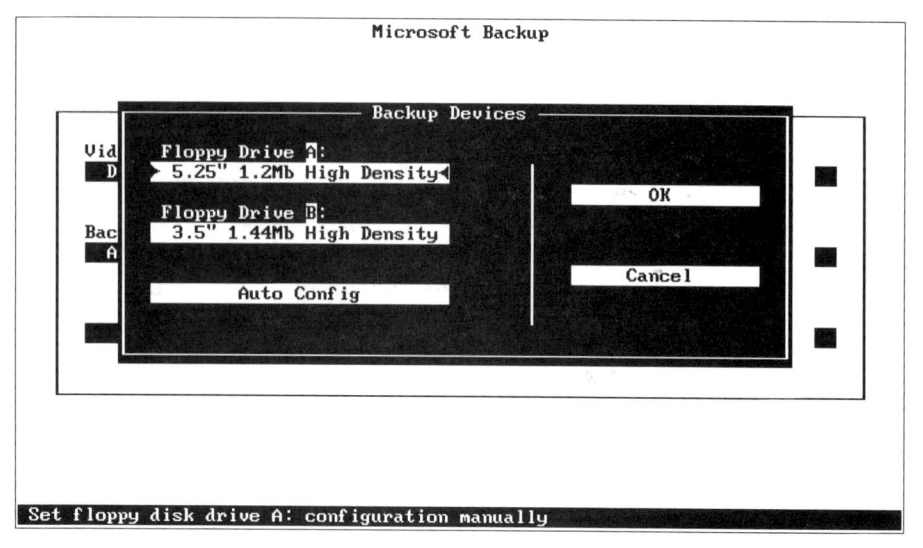

Figure 8.4 MSBACKUP determines what kind of floppy disk drives you have.

Next, MSBACKUP analyzes your memory and hard disk, after which it displays the Floppy Disk Compatibility Test screen shown in Figure 8.5. This message indicates that MSBACKUP is preparing to perform a partial backup, which it uses to verify that it has created an archive configuration that's compatible with your hardware.

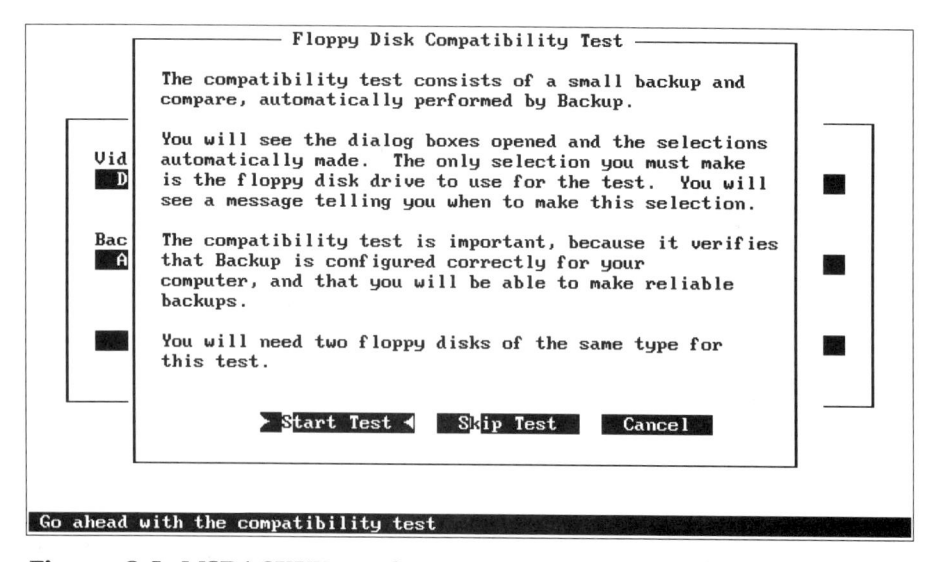

Figure 8.5 MSBACKUP performs a partial disk archive to test its configuration.

PLAY IT SAFE: PROTECTING YOUR DATA **197**

> *Caution:* You'll need two floppy disks of the same type to complete this phase of MSBACKUP's initial configuration. Make certain neither of these two disks contains important data, as their contents will be altered during testing.

To initiate the partial backup:

Press **Enter** to accept the **Start Test** option.

When the next message box appears informing you that MSBACKUP is about to request that you identify the disk drive it should use for this test:

Press **Enter**.

MSBACKUP automatically proceeds through a number of preliminary steps, after which it displays the dialog box shown in Figure 8.6. You use this dialog box to select a target drive for the partial backup. To select the default, drive A, using its highest density:

Press **Enter**.

If you want to use drive B or one of the other choices, which let you specify a disk density different from each drive's default, simply press the highlighted letter or number associated with that option. For example, to select drive B:

Press **B**.
Press **Enter**.

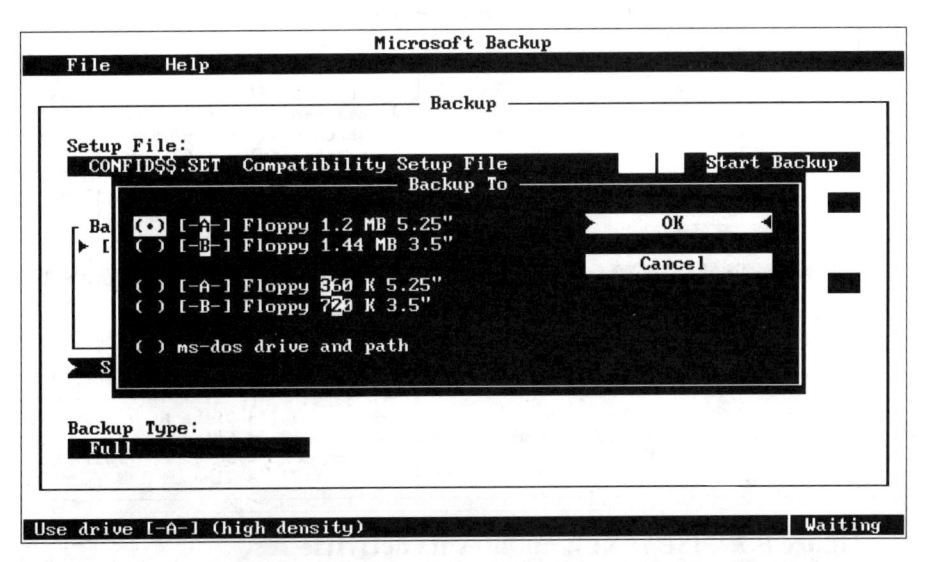

Figure 8.6 You select a target drive for the partial backup.

Once again, MSBACKUP whizzes through a series of automated steps. At the appropriate time it pauses and prompts you to insert a disk in the selected drive. When this happens:

Insert the first disk as instructed and press **Enter**.

MSBACKUP automatically senses the disk's presence and begins the actual test archive. This takes a minute or so, during which you'll see a screen similar to the one shown in Figure 8.7, which MSBACKUP uses to report on its progress. At the appropriate time, it will request that you insert the second disk. When this happens:

Insert the second disk as instructed.

When the test archive has been completed, you'll see a message similar to the one shown in Figure 8.8. This message, which you'll see each time you run MSBACKUP, contains information about the just-completed backup. After reviewing the contents of this message:

Press **Enter** accept **OK**.

More automated steps follow, nonc of which need concern you at this point. As part of this initial compatibility test, MSBACKUP uses its Compare option to analyze the results of the previous backup operation. Figure 8.9 shows the message that MSBACKUP displays in preparation for this test.

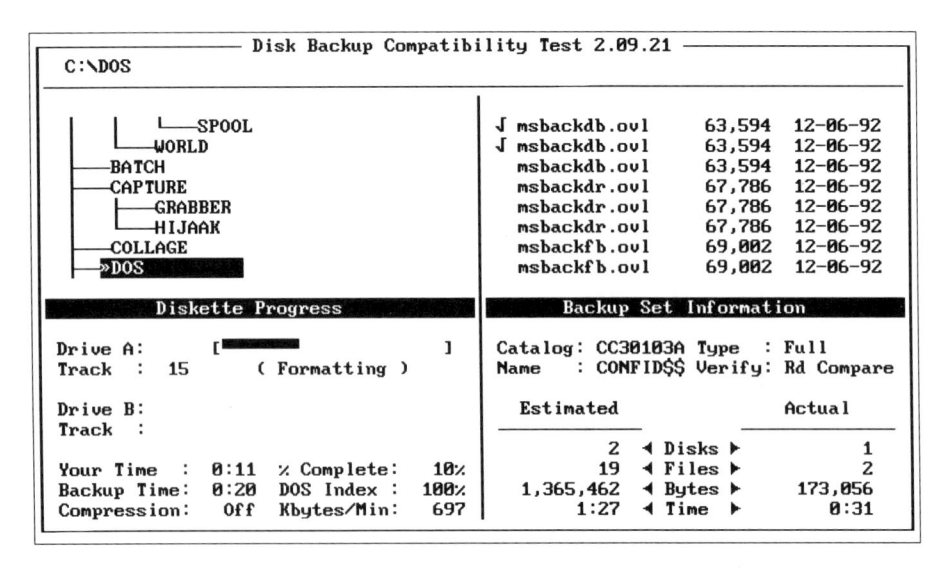

```
┌─────────────── Disk Backup Compatibility Test 2.09.21 ───────────────┐
│ C:\DOS                                                                │
│                                                                       │
│          └──SPOOL              √ msbackdb.ovl    63,594   12-06-92    │
│          └──WORLD              √ msbackdb.ovl    63,594   12-06-92    │
│       ──BATCH                    msbackdb.ovl    63,594   12-06-92    │
│       ──CAPTURE                  msbackdr.ovl    67,786   12-06-92    │
│          └──GRABBER              msbackdr.ovl    67,786   12-06-92    │
│          └──HIJAAK               msbackdr.ovl    67,786   12-06-92    │
│       ──COLLAGE                  msbackfb.ovl    69,002   12-06-92    │
│       »DOS                       msbackfb.ovl    69,002   12-06-92    │
│                                                                       │
│──────── Diskette Progress ────────┬──── Backup Set Information ───────│
│                                                                       │
│ Drive A:    [████████████████]    Catalog: CC30103A Type  : Full      │
│ Track  :  15      ( Formatting )  Name   : CONFID$$ Verify: Rd Compare│
│                                                                       │
│ Drive B:                             Estimated            Actual      │
│ Track  :                                                              │
│                                          2  ◄ Disks ►         1       │
│ Your Time    :  0:11  % Complete:  10%  19  ◄ Files ►         2       │
│ Backup Time:   0:20  DOS Index :  100%  1,365,462 ◄ Bytes ► 173,056   │
│ Compression:   Off   Kbytes/Min:  697       1:27  ◄ Time  ►    0:31   │
└───────────────────────────────────────────────────────────────────────┘
```

Figure 8.7 MSBACKUP updates its activities.

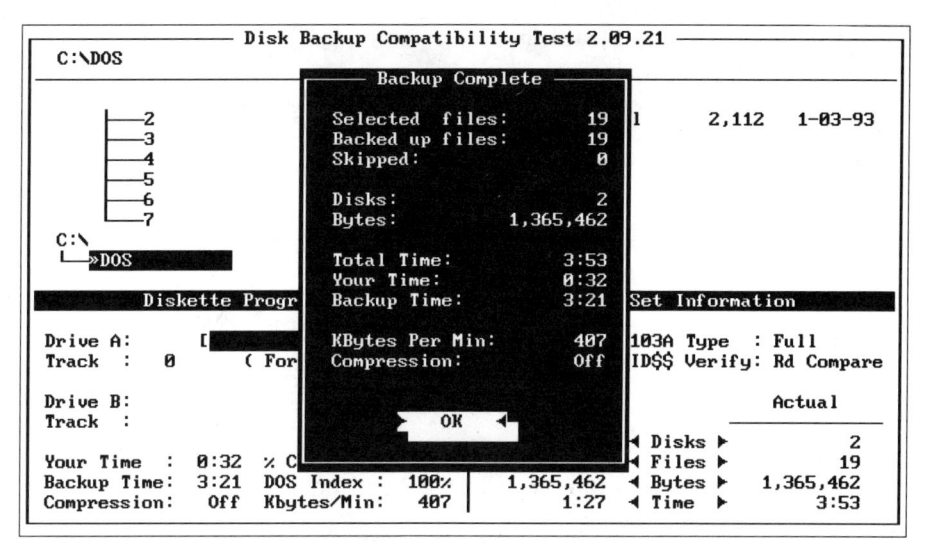

```
┌─────────────── Disk Backup Compatibility Test 2.09.21 ───────────────┐
│ C:\DOS                                                                │
│            ┌──── Backup Complete ────┐                                │
│      ─2    │                         │                                │
│      ─3    │ Selected files:    19   │l     2,112    1-03-93          │
│      ─4    │ Backed up files:   19   │                                │
│      ─5    │ Skipped:            0   │                                │
│      ─6    │                         │                                │
│      ─7    │ Disks:              2   │                                │
│ C:\        │ Bytes:        1,365,462 │                                │
│   ▶DOS     │                         │                                │
│            │ Total Time:      3:53   │                                │
│            │ Your Time:       0:32   │                                │
│    Diskette Progr│ Backup Time: 3:21 │Set Information                 │
│ Drive A:  [      │ KBytes Per Min: 407│103A Type  : Full              │
│ Track :   0  ( For│ Compression:   Off│ID$$ Verify: Rd Compare        │
│ Drive B:         │                   │              Actual            │
│ Track :          │         OK ◀      │                                │
│                  └───────────────────┘  ◀ Disks ▶             2       │
│ Your Time  : 0:32  % C                  ◀ Files ▶            19       │
│ Backup Time: 3:21  DOS Index :  100%  1,365,462  ◀ Bytes ▶  1,365,462│
│ Compression: Off   Kbytes/Min:  407        1:27  ◀ Time  ▶      3:53 │
└──────────────────────────────────────────────────────────────────────┘
```

Figure 8.8   MSBACKUP reports on the results of its test archive.

Notice that MSBACKUP is requesting you to insert the first disk of a specified backup set (CC30103A.FUL, in Figure 8.9). MSBACKUP gives each catalog file a unique name that helps you identify a backup set. Each character in the catalog name contains information about a particular backup set. The following catalog name, CC30103A.FUL, describes the elements of our partial backup reading from left to right:

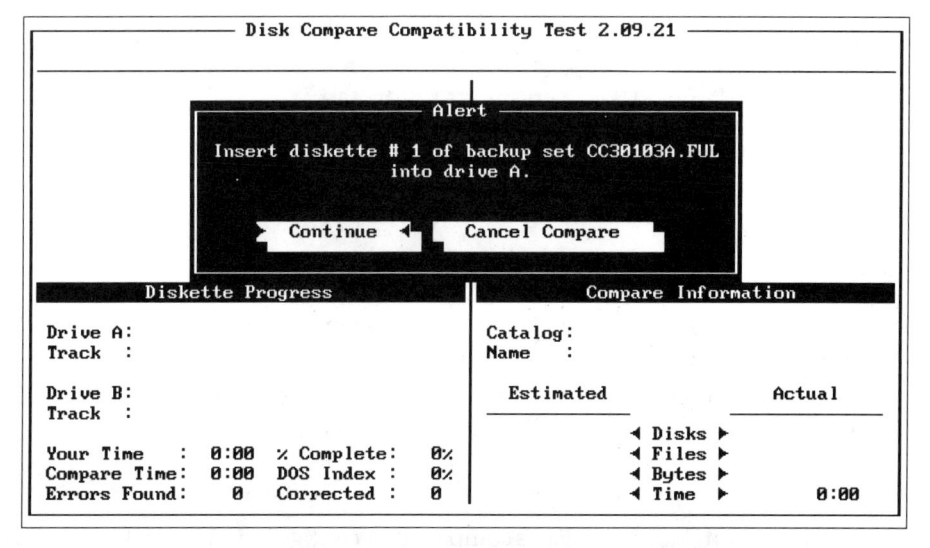

```
┌─────────────── Disk Compare Compatibility Test 2.09.21 ──────────────┐
│                                                                       │
│              ┌──────────── Alert ────────────┐                        │
│              │ Insert diskette # 1 of backup set CC30103A.FUL │       │
│              │              into drive A.                     │       │
│              │                                                │       │
│              │    Continue  ◀     Cancel Compare              │       │
│              └────────────────────────────────────────────────┘       │
│        Diskette Progress          ║     Compare Information           │
│ Drive A:                          ║ Catalog:                          │
│ Track  :                          ║ Name   :                          │
│                                   ║                                   │
│ Drive B:                          ║   Estimated         Actual        │
│ Track  :                          ║                                   │
│                                   ║   ◀ Disks ▶                       │
│ Your Time   : 0:00  % Complete:  0%│  ◀ Files ▶                       │
│ Compare Time: 0:00  DOS Index  :  0%│  ◀ Bytes ▶                      │
│ Errors Found:   0   Corrected  :  0 │  ◀ Time  ▶            0:00      │
└──────────────────────────────────────────────────────────────────────┘
```

Figure 8.9   MSBACKUP tests the results of its analysis.

Character(s)	Meaning
C	is the first drive backed up in this set, drive C in our example.
C	is the last drive backed up in this set. If only one drive was backed up, this letter would be the same as the first drive that was backed up, as in our example.
3	is the last digit of the year, as determined by the system date. In the example, the year is 1993.
01	is the month the backup set was created. In the example, the month is January (01).
03	is the day of the month the backup set was created. In the example, the date is the 3rd.
A	is the position in the sequence of this backup. If more than one backup of the same drive(s) is performed on the same day and the Keep Old Backup Catalogs option is set to On, MSBACKUP assigns a letter from A to Z to indicate the order in which the backups were performed (A is the first backup you created that day, B is the second, C the third, and so on). If the Keep Old Backup Catalogs option is set to Off, this alternates between A and B.
FUL	is the type of backup performed, where: FUL indicates a full backup INC indicates an incremental backup DIF indicates a differential backup

To allow MSBACKUP to perform its restore test:

Remove the second disk from your disk drive and replace it with the first disk from this test archive.

Press **Enter**.

Once again, MSBACKUP moves merrily on its way, automatically testing the process of restoring the files backed up previously. And once again, you'll be prompted to insert the second disk at the appropriate time. Following the restore process, you'll see another report screen similar to the one in Figure 8.8. After reviewing the information contained in this report:

Press **Enter**.

At this point, MSBACKUP has completed its configuration analysis, after which it displays the following message:

```
                          Microsoft Backup
  File    Help

                      ┌─── Backup 2.09.21 ───┐
                      │                      │
                      │  ▶ Backup ◀  Restore │
                      │                      │
                      │   Compare   Configure│
                      │                      │
                      │         Quit         │
                      │                      │
                      └──────────────────────┘


  Back up your hard disks and network drives
```

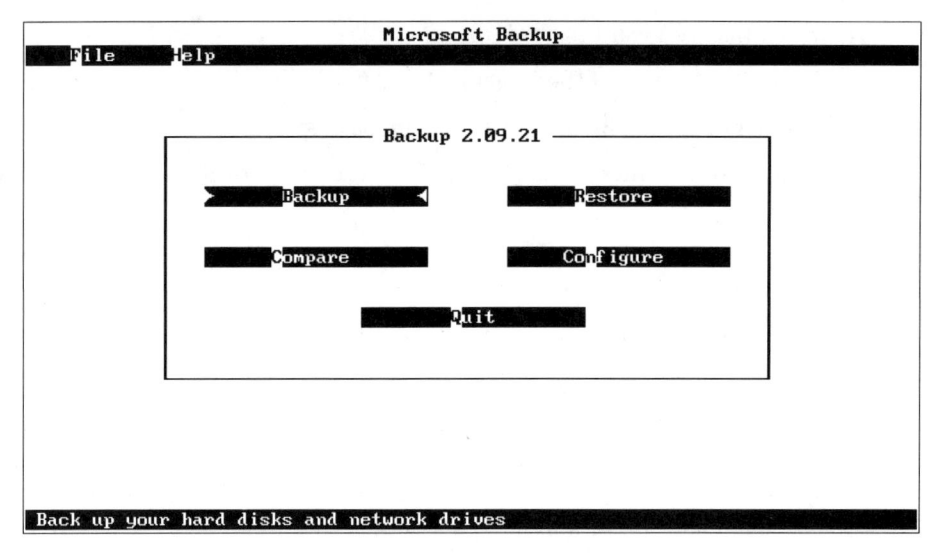

Figure 8.10 The MSBACKUP Options menu

```
The compatibility test completed successfully.
You can now make reliable disk backups.
```

When this message appears:

Press **Enter.**

When the Configure dialog box reappears:

Press **Tab** to highlight the **OK** option.
Press **Enter.**

Figure 8.10 shows the Options menu that is displayed each time you run MSBACKUP, following initial configuration testing. You use this menu to select the activity you want to perform using MSBACKUP. Options include:

Backup   backs up files from hard disks and network drives to a floppy disk drive.

Compare   compares the original and archive files to ensure that a backup was successful.

Restore   restores archived files from a backup disk to the hard drive.

Configure defines hardware settings for your MSBACKUP environment.

Creating an MSBACKUP Setup File

MSBACKUP uses setup files to define the parameters for a specific backup operation. Among other settings, the setup file includes information about:

202   DOS 6.0 HANDBOOK

- which files you want backed up
- the letter and type of the target disk drive
- whether or not MSBACKUP verifies the backup files
- whether or not files are compressed on the target disk during the backup operation
- whether MSBACKUP prompts you before copying data to diskettes that were used for a previous backup
- whether the target disks are formatted during each backup operation

You create a setup file by selecting settings from the main Backup options screen. After identifying the settings you want, you use the Save Setup As option on the pull-down File menu to store these settings in a setup file. To perform a backup using the settings in a particular setup file, insert that file's name as the *setup_file* parameter in an MSBACKUP command. If you enter the MSBACKUP command without a *setup_file* parameter, DOS automatically loads the settings contained in a file called DEFAULT.SET.

Setup files are identified with a SET extension, for example, MYDATA.SET. When you name a setup file, you must use this extension as part of its filename. To see how this works:

Press **B** to select Backup.

Figure 8.11 shows the Backup options screen, which is used to select the settings listed earlier. The Select Files option, for example, lets you identify the files you want to back up. Try the following:

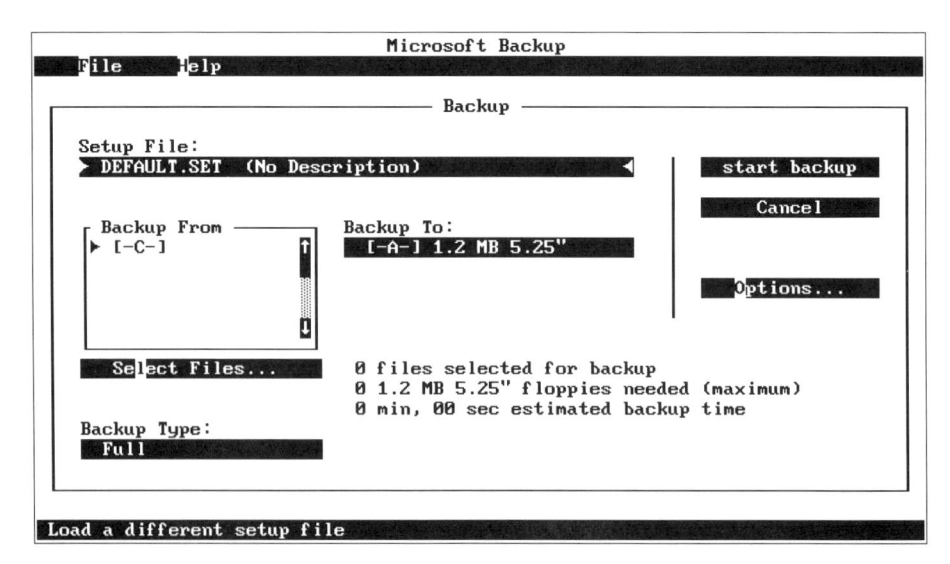

```
                      Microsoft Backup
 File  Help
                         ┌─ Backup ─┐
 Setup File:
 ► DEFAULT.SET  (No Description)           ◄        start backup

                                                      Cancel
 ┌ Backup From ─┐   Backup To:
 ► [-C-]            [-A-] 1.2 MB 5.25"
                                                      Options...


   Select Files...     0 files selected for backup
                       0 1.2 MB 5.25" floppies needed (maximum)
                       0 min, 00 sec estimated backup time
 Backup Type:
   Full

 Load a different setup file
```

Figure 8.11 The main Backup options screen

PLAY IT SAFE: PROTECTING YOUR DATA 203

Press **L** to choose Select Files.

Figure 8.12 shows the screen you use to select files for a backup operation. Files can be selected individually, by shared traits (file extension, date ranges, attributes, etc.), or as entire directories and subdirectories.

When you first open the Select File screen, the highlight bar is placed in its directory listing, a window on the left-hand side of the display containing a directories tree for the current drive. You can use the arrow keys to move the highlight bar to a different directory. As you highlight a directory, the names of the files it contains are listed in a file window on the right-hand side of the Select File display. The Tab key can be used to move the highlight bar to a different section of the display. To see what I mean:

Press **Down Arrow** until the DOS directory is highlighted in your directory tree.

Press **Tab**.

This selects the DOS directory and moves the highlight bar to its file listing, as shown in Figure 8.13. Use the Spacebar to select a highlighted file for inclusion in the current backup. For example, to select two specific files from the DOS directory:

Press **Spacebar**.

Press **Down Arrow** twice.

Press **Spacebar**.

```
┌─────────────────── Select Backup Files ───────────────────┐
│ [-C-]                                                      │
│ C:\*.*                                                     │
│ C:\                    │ ansi     .txt   13,959  12-27-92  5:44a ....│
│   ─AOL                 │ ansi2    .txt      925  12-27-92  5:45a ....│
│       ─DOCUMENT        │ ansi3    .txt      998  12-27-92  5:45a ....│
│       ─FONT            │ aol      .bat       41   9-25-92  8:20p ....│
│       ─SYSAPPL         │ autoexec .bat      182   1-01-93  5:56a ...a│
│       ─SYSTEM          │ autoexec .hld      182   1-01-93  5:56a ....│
│           ─QFORMS      │ backup2  .bak    5,585  12-31-92  6:12p ....│
│           ─SPOOL       │ backup2  .txt    5,376  12-31-92  6:14p ....│
│       ─WORLD           │ befsetup .msd   21,141  12-28-92 10:20a ....│
│   ─BATCH               │ command  .com   53,405  12-06-92  6:00a r...│
│   ─CAPTURE             │ config   .hld      162   1-01-93  5:56a ....│
│ Total Files:    847 [    21,883 K]  Selected Files:    0 [       0 K]│
│ [ Include ]  [ Exclude ]  [ Special ]  [ Display ]  [ OK ] [ Cancel ]│
│ Select entire directories with right mouse button or Spacebar        │
└──────────────────────────────────────────────────────────────────────┘
```

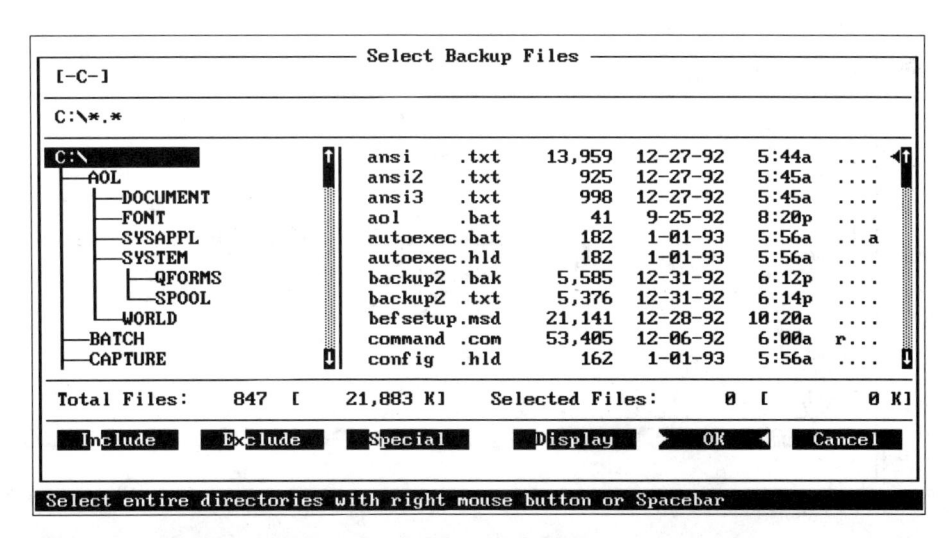

Figure 8.12 From the Select Backup Files screen you can select the files that you want to back up.

204 DOS 6.0 HANDBOOK

```
┌─────────────────── Select Backup Files ───────────────────┐
│ [-C-]                                                      │
│ ─────────────────────────────────────────────────────────  │
│ C:\DOS\*.*                                                 │
│                                                            │
│    ├─SYSAPPL         ansi     .sys    8,959  12-06-92  6:00a ...a │
│    ├─SYSTEM          append   .exe   10,774  12-06-92  6:00a ...a │
│    │  ├─QFORMS       appnotes .txt    9,058  12-06-92  6:00a ...a │
│    │  └─SPOOL        attrib   .exe   11,165  12-06-92  6:00a ...a │
│    └─WORLD           autoexec.umb        54  12-30-92 10:13a ...a │
│  ├─BATCH             cc21231a.ful    2,048  12-31-92  8:21p ...a │
│  ├─CAPTURE           cc21231b.ful    2,048  12-31-92  8:25p ...a │
│  │  ├─GRABBER        cc30101a.ful    2,048   1-01-93  5:41a ...a │
│  │  └─HIJAAK         chkdsk   .exe  12,058  12-06-92  6:00a ...a │
│  ├─COLLAGE           chklist  .ms      108   1-02-93  7:51p ...a │
│  ├─DOS        ◄      chkstate.sys   41,536  12-06-92  6:00a ...a │
│                                                            │
│ Total Files:   847 [   21,883 K]  Selected Files:   0 [   0 K] │
│                                                            │
│  ▐ In╞clude  ▐ E╞xclude  ▐ S╞pecial  ▐ D╞isplay  ▶ OK ◀  Cancel │
│ ────────────────────────────────────────────────────────── │
│ Select files with right mouse button or Spacebar           │
└────────────────────────────────────────────────────────────┘
```

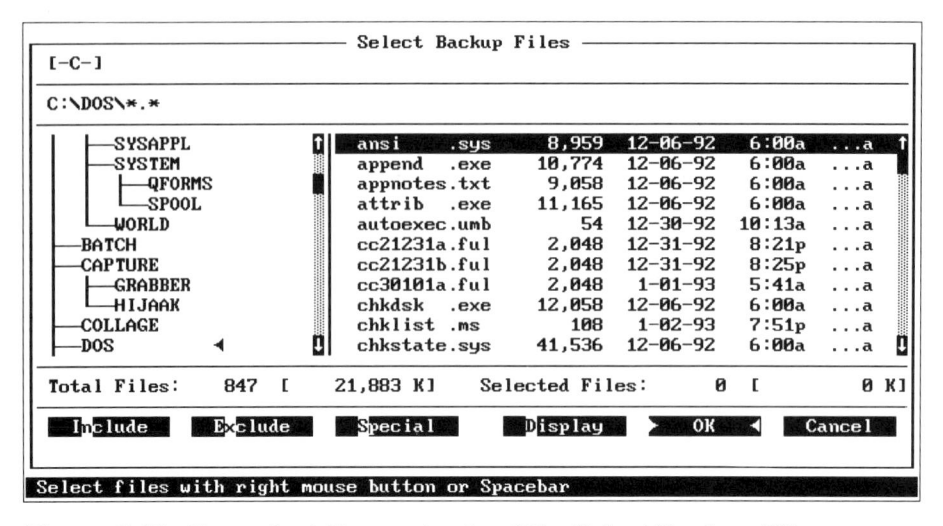

Figure 8.13 You select the contents of the Select Backup Files screen.

MSBACKUP places a check mark to the left of any selected filenames, as shown in Figure 8.14. A status line just below the directory listing and file window indicates how many files have been selected, along with their combined size. (The status line in Figure 8.14, for example, indicates 2 files totaling 19K.) Using the arrow keys and Spacebar in this manner, along with the special selection buttons running across the bottom of the Select File display, you can create a complete listing of those files you want to back up. When all desired files have been selected:

```
┌─────────────────── Select Backup Files ───────────────────┐
│ [-C-]                                                      │
│ ─────────────────────────────────────────────────────────  │
│ C:\DOS\*.*                                                 │
│                                                            │
│    ├─SYSAPPL       √ ansi     .sys    8,959  12-06-92  6:00a ...a │
│    ├─SYSTEM          append   .exe   10,774  12-06-92  6:00a ...a │
│    │  ├─QFORMS       appnotes .txt    9,058  12-06-92  6:00a ...a │
│    │  └─SPOOL      √ attrib   .exe   11,165  12-06-92  6:00a ...a │
│    └─WORLD           autoexec.umb        54  12-30-92 10:13a ...a │
│  ├─BATCH             cc21231a.ful    2,048  12-31-92  8:21p ...a │
│  ├─CAPTURE           cc21231b.ful    2,048  12-31-92  8:25p ...a │
│  │  ├─GRABBER        cc30101a.ful    2,048   1-01-93  5:41a ...a │
│  │  └─HIJAAK         chkdsk   .exe  12,058  12-06-92  6:00a ...a │
│  ├─COLLAGE           chklist  .ms      108   1-02-93  7:51p ...a │
│  ├─»DOS       ◄      chkstate.sys   41,536  12-06-92  6:00a ...a │
│                                                            │
│ Total Files:   847 [   21,883 K]  Selected Files:   2 [  19 K] │
│                                                            │
│  ▐ In╞clude  ▐ E╞xclude  ▐ S╞pecial  ▐ D╞isplay  ▶ OK ◀  Cancel │
│ ────────────────────────────────────────────────────────── │
│ Select files with right mouse button or Spacebar           │
└────────────────────────────────────────────────────────────┘
```

Figure 8.14 MSBACKUP marks any files selected for the current backup operation.

Press **Enter** to select OK.

This returns you to the main Backup options screen shown in Figure 8.11. Choose Options to identify specific activities you want MSBACKUP to perform as it backs up the selected files.

Press **O** to select Options.

Figure 8.15 shows the settings available from the Options screen. As was true in the Select Files screen, you use the arrow keys and Spacebar to activate and deactivate specific settings. For example, to tell MSBACKUP to verify archive files but not compress the data during a backup:

Press **Spacebar** to activate the Verify option.
Press **Down Arrow** to move the cursor to the Compress option.
Press **Spacebar** to deactivate the Compress option.
Press **Enter** to select OK.

Saving an MSBACKUP Setup File

Using procedures similar to this, you select any parameters you want applied to the current backup. Once MSBACKUP is configured exactly as you want it, saving the current settings allows you to recall them instantly for future sessions. To do this:

Press **Alt+F** to display the File menu.
Press **A** to select the Save File As option.

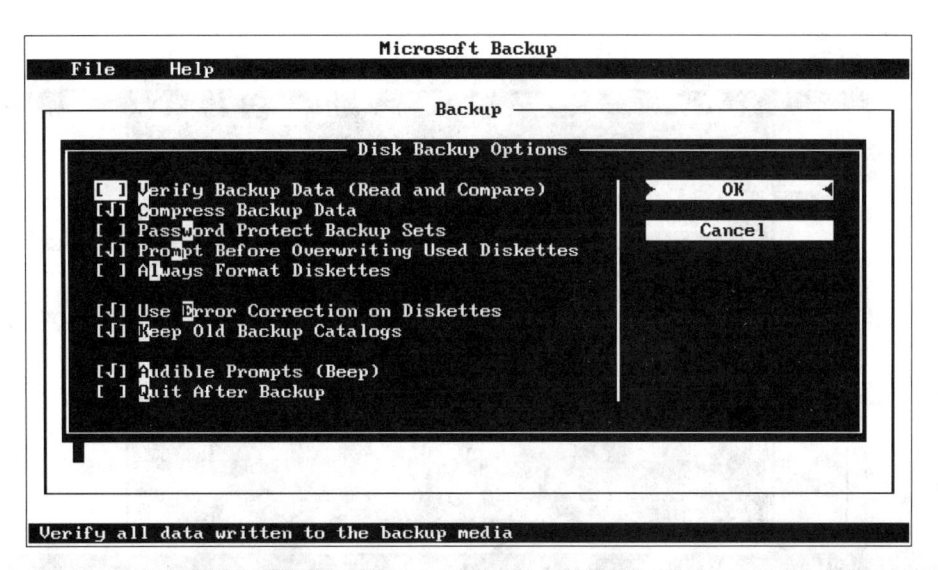

Figure 8.15 MSBACKUP offers a variety of options for controlling a backup procedure.

MSBACKUP displays its Save Setup File dialog box, shown in Figure 8.16. You use this dialog box to assign a name and optional description to the file containing the current MSBACKUP settings.

> Type **TEST.SET**.
> Press **Tab** to move to the Description field.
> Type **Save two files in DOS**.
> Press **Enter**.

MSBACKUP saves your current configuration to a file called TEST.SET and returns you to the main Backup options display. Notice that the Setup File field now contains the name and description entered in the previous exercise (see Figure 8.17). Once TEST.SET exists, it can be entered with an MSBACKUP command as the *setup_file* parameter to initiate automatically a backup using its configuration.

> *Tip:* A Backup Each Day...
> To save time as you safeguard your most valuable PC resource, try creating an MSBACKUP configuration that's designed to archive only those data files that change regularly on your system. Running this backup at the end of each day protects you against data loss but eliminates the need to back up unnecessarily large numbers of files on a daily basis.

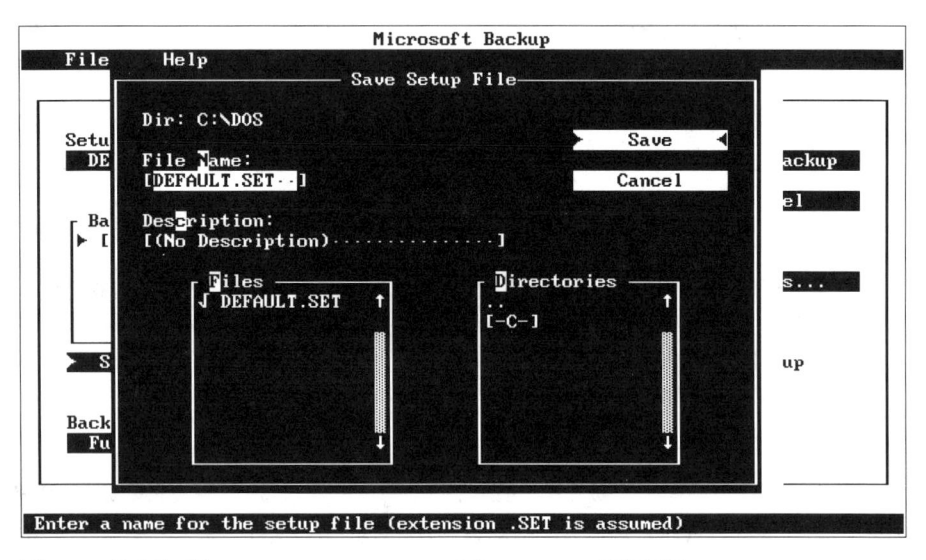

Figure 8.16 You can save your settings to a SET file.

Ending an MSBACKUP Session

MSBACKUP's interactive design adds an elegant touch to what was once a tedious chore. You really should familiarize yourself with all the features of MSBACKUP. Doing so will allow you to create setup files that let you "pick and choose" from a variety of backup procedures. For now, let's exit MSBACKUP. After all, we still have a few more security-related features of MS-DOS 6.0 to check out. To exit MSBACKUP:

Press **Alt+F** to display the File menu.
Press **X** to select the Exit option.

This closes down the MSBACKUP utility and returns you to the DOS system prompt.

> ***Caution:*** Because of the manner in which they are stored, the files on an MSBACKUP archive disk cannot be used for normal PC operations. Before you can incorporate these archive files into your day-to-day activities, they must be reconstructed in standard DOS format using MSBACKUP's Restore procedure.

Gone, but Not Forgotten (The BACKUP and RESTORE Commands)

As stated earlier, the MS-DOS 6.0 MSBACKUP utility replaces the BACKUP and RESTORE commands included in previous versions of DOS. And although this

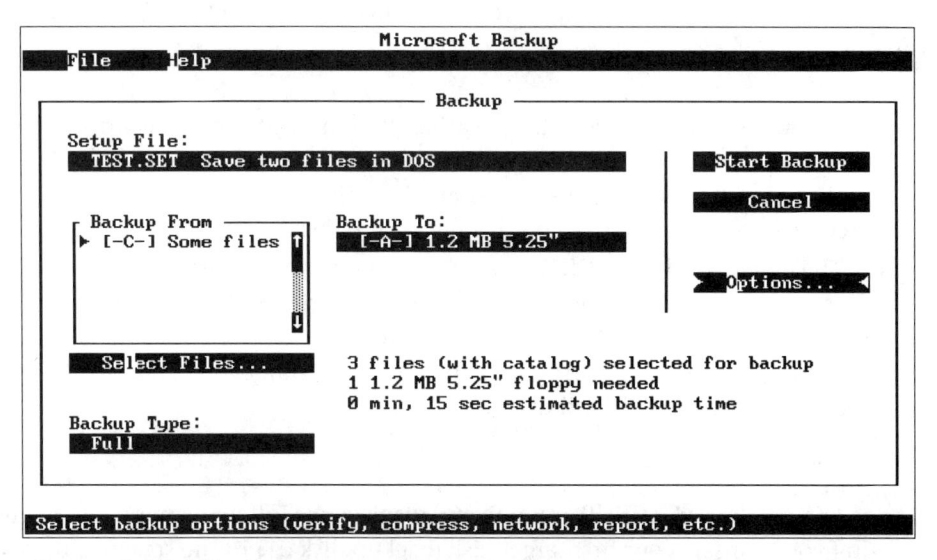

Figure 8.17 The Backup screen reflects your changes.

book concentrates primarily on this newest DOS release, millions of people still are using an earlier version of DOS. Therefore, the BACKUP command may be gone from MS-DOS 6.0, but it's not forgotten; in fact, MS-DOS 6.0 still supports the RESTORE command. This permits people upgrading to MS-DOS 6.0 from a previous release to transfer files archived with an earlier DOS release back onto their hard drive, should this ever be necessary. So, for those readers not yet using MS-DOS 6.0, the following is a brief explanation of how both BACKUP and RESTORE work.

The BACKUP Command

The BACKUP command was used in versions of DOS prior to MS-DOS 6.0 to create archive copies of files stored on your hard disk. The correct syntax for entering a BACKUP command is:

```
BACKUP [drive1:][path][filename][drive2:][command options]
```

BACKUP accepts the following parameters and command switches:

drive1:	is the drive letter of the disk containing the file(s) to be backed up.
path	is the name of a directory or subdirectory containing the files you want to archive.
filename	is the name of any files you want to archive.
drive2:	is the target drive — the drive containing the disk(s) on which you want the specified file(s) to be archived.
command options	is one of the BACKUP options described in Table 8.1.

If you have DOS version 3.2 or earlier, you must format disks prior to using them as target disks with the BACKUP command. Starting with MS-DOS 3.3, this preliminary step is no longer necessary. The **/f:** option formats a target disk as archive files are transferred to it from the hard disk.

The easiest kind of BACKUP operation to perform is a total archive, where all files existing on *drive1*, including any subdirectories it contains, are duplicated on the target disk. Essentially, this procedure creates a "clone" of your entire hard disk structure. The following command archives to target disks in drive A all files located on the drive C hard disk:

```
BACKUP C: A: /S
```

DOS loads the BACKUP program and displays the following message, instructing you to insert your first target disk (backup disk 01) in the specified drive:

Table 8.1 BACKUP Command Options

Option	Function
/s	Backs up any subdirectories associated with the specified path.
/m	Backs up only those files that have been altered since the previous backup.
/a	Appends any files being archived with the current BACKUP operation to those already stored on the backup disks.
/d:*date*	Archives only those files that have been modified on or after the specified date.
/t:*time*	Archives only those files that have been modified since the specified time.
/l:*filename*	Creates a log file called filename.
/f:*size*	Causes the target disk in *drive2* to be formatted to the specified size.

```
Insert backup diskette 01 in drive A:

Warning! Files in the target drive
A:\ root directory will be erased
Strike any key when ready
```

Pressing any key initiates the BACKUP procedure. As it copies files to the target disk, BACKUP lists their names on your display. If more than a single disk is required to hold the specified files, BACKUP prompts you to remove the current target disk at the appropriate time and replace it with another disk. BACKUP repeats this sequence until all specified files have been archived on target disks.

As already mentioned, DOS versions DOS 3.3 and higher allow you to format your target disks during a BACKUP operation by adding the **/f:** switch to a BACKUP command. DOS 3.3 automatically uses the default format for the target disk drive. MS-DOS versions 4.0 through 5.0 allow you to specify how the target disk should be formatted, using the following command syntax:

```
BACKUP C: A: /S /F:size
```

Table 8.2 shows the valid **/f:** options that can be included in the BACKUP command, along with the format associated with each.

You may not always want or need to back up all the files on your hard disks. In fact, selective backups are the quickest and most convenient way to protect critical data files without also archiving applications, which change only rarely. The following command updates archive disks by copying only those files in a directory called MYDATA that have been modified since the previous BACKUP operation was performed:

Table 8.2 BACKUP Format Codes

/f: size	Resulting format
160	160K single-sided 5.25" disk
180	180K single-sided 5.25" disk
320	320K double-sided 5.25" disk
360	360K double-sided 5.25" disk
720	720K double-sided 3.5" disk
1.2	1.2 megabyte high-density 5.25" disk
1.44	1.44 megabyte high-density 3.5" disk

```
BACKUP C:\MYDATA\*.* A: /M /A
```

The **/M** switch in this command instructs DOS to back up modified files only. The **/A** switch tells DOS to append the modified files to the target disks, thus preserving the archive files it already contains.

If you think about the previous exercises, you'll realize that the new MSBACKUP utility does everything the original BACKUP command could; however, it greatly simplifies the process of specifying how a backup should occur. It also possesses some features BACKUP lacked: MSBACKUP lets you select files with disparate filenames, something that was virtually impossible with BACKUP. If you switch to MS-DOS 6.0, therefore, I strongly recommend that you also switch to MSBACKUP for your archiving activities.

The RESTORE Command

Microsoft also maintained the RESTORE in MS-DOS 6.0 so that you can access those files you backed up in an earlier version of DOS.

The RESTORE command transfers files that were archived with the BACKUP program back onto your hard disk. The syntax RESTORE uses is similar to that of a BACKUP command. It is:

```
RESTORE [drive1:][path][filename][drive2:][command options]
```

RESTORE accepts the following parameters and command switches:

drive1 is a required drive letter, indicating the drive containing the archived file(s) to be restored.

drive2 is the target drive — the hard disk to which the archived file(s) should be restored.

PLAY IT SAFE: PROTECTING YOUR DATA 211

path   is the name of a directory or subdirectory that originally contained the files being restored.

filename   is the name of any files you want to restore.

command options   is one of the BACKUP options described in Table 8.3.

The following describes a couple of commonly used RESTORE techniques to familiarize you with this command, should you ever require it.

The following command would use a target disk in drive A to restore to drive C any files originally archived from its MYDATA subdirectory:

```
RESTORE A: C:\MYDATA\*.*
```

Unless you tell it to do otherwise, RESTORE goes about its business uninterrupted, overwriting any files that already exist on the target disk with their archived versions. Normally, this works. But if some of the files residing on the MYDATA subdirectory of the hard disk in the previous example were versions newer than those stored on an archive disk, you might not want to replace them during the RESTORE operation. In such a case, include the **/p** switch in a RESTORE command, and RESTORE will pause if it encounters any files on the hard disk that have been modified since the last BACKUP was performed. The following command would accomplish this, so that you have time to decide whether to replace the newer files in the MYDATA directory with their archived counterparts:

TABLE 8.3 RESTORE Command Options

Option	Function
/s	Restores any subdirectories associated with the specified path.
/m	Restores only those files modified since the last backup.
/b:*date*	Restores only those files that have been modified on or before the specified date.
/a:*date*	Restores only those files that have been modified on or after the specified date.
/l:*time*	Restores only those files last modified at or later than the specified time.
/p	Causes RESTORE to display a special prompt whenever it encounters a file on the target disk that has changed since the last backup or is marked as a read-only file. You are then given the option of either replacing the existing version or telling RESTORE to bypass that file.
/n	Restores only those files that are not already present on the target disk.

```
RESTORE A: C:\MYDATA\*.* /p
```

Suppose, for example, that there was a file called MYBUDGET.DAT already in the MYDATA subdirectory of the target disk, one that had been updated since you performed your last BACKUP operation. RESTORE would display the following message before overwriting the newer version:

```
Warning! File MYBUDGET.DAT
was changed after it was backed up
Replace the file (Y/N)?
```

This prompt offers you two options:

1. Responding Yes (Y) replaces the newer version of MYBUDGET.DAT with the archived copy.
2. Responding No (N) preserves the newer version on the target disk and resumes the RESTORE operation at the next file.

Obviously, MSBACKUP, the older BACKUP, and its complementary RESTORE command provide valuable safeguards against lost data by allowing you to recover damaged files using archive disks. But is there any way to protect your files against such damage in the first place? Is there some method to prevent their being accidentally overwritten or erased? Yes, there is — within certain limitations. How you accomplish this is the topic of our next section.

Modifying File Attributes (The ATTRIB Command)

The ATTRIB command is used to assign attributes to a file. You can choose from four attributes:

Hidden	Used to stop a file from showing up in DIR listings.
System	Used to identify system files.
Read-only	Files assigned a read-only attribute can be read into memory, but DOS will not allow them to be modified and saved back to disk.
Archive	DOS uses this attribute to identify files that have been modified since the last time they were backed up.

The correct syntax for entering an ATTRIB command is:

```
ATTRIB [+R|-R] [+A|-A] [+S|-S] [+H|-H][[drive:][path]
filename] [/S]
```

ATTRIB Parameters and Command Switches

ATTRIB accepts the following parameters and command switches:

drive:path   specifies the location of the file(s) you want to process.

filename   specifies the name of the file(s) you want to process.

+R   sets the read-only file attribute .

-R   clears the read-only attribute and assigns read/write status to a file.

+A   assigns the archive attribute to a file.

-A   clears the archive file attribute.

+S   assigns the system attribute to a file.

-S   clears the system file attribute.

+H   assigns hidden status to a file or group of files.

-H   removes the hidden-file attribute.

/S   instructs DOS to process files in the current directory and any subdirectories it contains.

Using ATTRIB

Entering an ATTRIB command by itself lets you view the attribute settings of all files in the current directory. Try the following:

If necessary, type **CD ** and press **Enter** to move to the root directory of your hard disk.

Type **ATTRIB |MORE** and press **Enter**.

This displays a listing of any files stored in your root directory, along with the attributes assigned to each file (see Figure 8.18). I included the MORE filter in the previous command so that DOS would pause after ATTRIB displayed a complete screen of files.

Notice that DOS has taken the appropriate steps to protect critical files. For example, DOS automatically assigns to its two system files, IO.SYS and MSDOS.SYS, system (S), hidden (H) and read-only (R) status. Another file that's marked read-only is COMMAND.COM, the DOS command interpreter. Although not foolproof, setting COMMAND.COM to read-only status helps protect your PC against potentially destructive code that's designed to infiltrate and, in some cases, modify your system. (We'll discuss these programs, called computer viruses, that contain this pernicious code in a few paragraphs.)

What do these attributes accomplish? To find out, try the following:

Type **DEL IO.SYS** and press **Enter**.
Type **DEL COMMAND.COM** and press **Enter**.

The first command, with which you attempted to erase the DOS IO.SYS system file, returned the following message:

```
File not found
```

The second command, if it worked properly, should have deleted COMMAND.COM and returned a different message:

```
Access denied
```

Each of these messages reflects how DOS responds to a specific file attribute. In the first case, DOS reported that it couldn't find the requested file because IO.SYS is a hidden file. In the second instance, DOS found the file but refused to erase it because COMMAND.COM is a read-only file; deleting a file requires modifying its contents on your disk, and the read-only attribute prevents this from happening.

> *Tip:* **Protect from Erasure**
>
> As the second example illustrates, you can use the ATTRIB command to ensure that important files on your disk are not erased accidentally. Simply assign the read-only attribute to any files that you want to protect in this manner. This approach only works with program files. You wouldn't want to assign read-only status to a data file; doing so would prevent an application from updating the information it contains.

```
         SHR     C:\IO.SYS
         SHR     C:\MSDOS.SYS
                 C:\PRINT
                 C:\PRINT2
     A           C:\DSVXD.386
         R       C:\WINA20.386
     A   R       C:\MIRROR.FIL
     A           C:\AOL.BAT
     A           C:\DV.BAT
         R       C:\COMMAND.COM
     A   SHR     C:\MIRORSAV.FIL
     A   R       C:\MIRROR.BAK
     A           C:\BEFSETUP.MSD
     A           C:\CONFIG.HLD
     A           C:\TREEINFO.NCD
     A           C:\DBLSPACE.OUT
     A           C:\CONFIG.SYS
     A           C:\AUTOEXEC.BAT
     A           C:\ANSI.TXT
     A           C:\ANSI2.TXT
     A           C:\ANSI3.TXT
     A           C:\AUTOEXEC.HLD
     A           C:\MSBACKUP.BAK
  -- More --
```

Figure 8.18 You can request a listing of attributes assigned to files in a directory.

Now, try the following:

Type **ATTRIB -A *.*** and press **Enter**.

This command removes the Archive attribute from all files in the current directory, with two noticeable exceptions. DOS reports back that it did not reset the Archive attribute for the two hidden DOS system files, IO.SYS and MSDOS.SYS. In order to change any other attributes for these files, you must eliminate their Hidden status. If you reenter the ATTRIB | MORE command executed earlier, you would see that the Archive setting has been removed from any files to which it was previously attached.

Keeping Your System Healthy (The VSAFE Utility)

Ironically, just prior to sitting down to write this section on computer viruses, I came down with a virus of my own. And just as this microscopic invader debilitated me, a computer virus can bring your system to its "knees."

A computer virus is a program whose sole purpose is to disrupt your PC. Some viruses are relatively benign. They may simply take over your computer long enough to display a "cute" message on the monitor like "Gotcha!" or some similar taunt. Other viruses are truly malicious; they actually destroy the data on your hard disk.

The people who write viruses generally distribute them by hiding the destructive code within a file that appears quite harmless. It may be lurking within a utility that you download off a local bulletin board or hidden in a seemingly innocuous file on a disk that someone gives you, which contains the latest and greatest shareware programs they've picked up from various sources. No matter how you pick up a virus, once it finds its way into your system, you have a real problem.

Utilities designed to guard your computer against a virus have been available for years. But you always had to pay extra for such utilities. Previously, DOS itself offered no virus protection; MS-DOS 6.0, however, does. Microsoft includes VSAFE, a virus-detection utility licensed from Central Point Software with MS-DOS 6.0. VSAFE is a memory-resident program that constantly monitors your computer for any indication that a virus is present. If VSAFE detects any activity that indicates a potential virus attack, it displays a message warning you of its discovery. The correct syntax for starting the VSAFE utility is:

```
VSAFE /[option[+|-] ...] [/NE] [/NX] [/Ax] [/Cx] [/N] [/D] [/U]
```

VSAFE Parameters and Command Switches

VSAFE accepts the following parameters and command switches:

option [+|-] uses one of the following values to specify how VSAFE should perform virus checking:

> 1 Issues a warning if a virus attempts to format a hard disk; the default setting is "on."
>
> 2 Issues a warning if a program attempts to stay in memory; the default setting is "off."
>
> 3 Automatically prevents a program from writing to disk; the default setting is "off."
>
> 4 Performs a virus check each time you load an executable file; the default setting is "on."
>
> 5 Checks the boot sector of all your disks for viruses; the default setting is "on."
>
> 6 Issues a warning whenever a program attempts to write to the boot sector or partition table of your hard disk; the default setting is "on."
>
> 7 Issues a warning whenever a program attempts to write to the boot sector of a floppy disk; the default setting is "off."
>
> 8 Issues a warning whenever an attempt is made to modify an executable file; the default setting is "on."

/NE instructs VSAFE not to monitor expanded memory.

/NX instructs VSAFE not to monitor extended memory.

/A*x* specifies a hot key for VSAFE, using the Alt key in combination with whatever key is specified by *x*.

/C*x* specifies a hot key for VSAFE, using the Ctrl key in combination with whatever key is specified by *x*.

/N allows network drivers to be loaded after VSAFE is started.

/D disables checksumming as a protection technique.

/U removes the TSR portion of VSAFE from memory.

Using VSAFE

Protecting your system against viruses is like juggling: On the one hand, you want to have VSAFE monitor the activities usually associated with a virus attack; on the other, you don't want this checking to interfere with your normal PC

PLAY IT SAFE: PROTECTING YOUR DATA   217

operations. The default settings for the VSAFE parameters guard against the most common types of viruses without overly burdening your system. Notice, for example, that the default setting for the 3 parameter, which detects disk-write activity, is off. This allows you to work without VSAFE issuing a warning each time you try to save a file to disk. Unless you have an overriding reason to configure VSAFE otherwise, therefore, you should be able to use its default settings.

To load VSAFE into memory:

Type **VSAFE** and press **Enter**.

DOS loads VSAFE into memory, after which it displays the message shown in Figure 8.19. Once VSAFE is loaded, you can modify its program settings by calling up a special Control window, using the program's hot key, which is the Alt+V key combination.

Press **Alt+V**.

Now I'd like to show you what happens next, but I can't. Calling up the VSAFE Control window temporarily suspends all system interrupts, including the one that allows my screen capture program to work. What you should be looking at is a message box listing the various VSAFE warning options, along with the current setting for each. Pressing the number associated with a given option toggles its setting on and off. After reviewing the VSAFE dialog box:

Press **Esc** to return to the system prompt.

As you probably noticed, with the Control window displayed, you can use an Alt+U key combination to remove VSAFE from memory. You can also unload VSAFE directly from the system prompt, using the /U switch. To remove VSAFE from memory:

Type **VSAFE /U** and press **Enter**.

```
        VSafe (tm)

    Copyright (c) 1991-1992
 Central Point Software, Inc.
        Hotkey:    <Alt><V>

VSafe successfully installed.
VSafe is using  7K of conventional memory,
                0K of XMS memory,
                64K of EMS memory.
(C:\)
```

Figure 8.19   VSAFE reports its presence in memory.

Do You Need VSAFE?

Virus protection is like life insurance: You don't really need it until you need it. Some people are at greater risk of virus infection than others. If you download files from local and largely unpoliced bulletin board systems regularly or accept disks without knowing where they came from, there could be a virus out there with your name on it just waiting to wreak havoc in your computer. If, on the other hand, you take the appropriate precautionary steps — only downloading programs from reputable on-line systems, only accepting disks from people you know and trust — you're already protecting yourself against the most common methods used to distribute these truly malevolent programs.

The best way to guard against the devastating effects of a virus attack, however, is to follow the three simple rules of data protection specified earlier in this chapter:

1. Back up
2. Back up
3. Back up

This ounce of prevention will save you more than a pound of anxiety, should anything ever happen to your irreplaceable data files.

Chapter 9

The Age of Automation: Batch Files and Other Conveniences

Automation: It's what computers do best. A computer excels at taking a repetitive task and reducing it to a few, simple steps. In the grand scheme of things, automated assembly lines can churn out products with little or no human intervention. It makes it possible for a small group of employees to keep the turbines of a mammoth power plant turning, providing electricity for millions of people.

But automation offers advantages on a smaller scale, as well. To return to the context of this book, DOS provides two valuable tools that are designed to help you automate your PC operations: batch files and the DOSKEY utility.

Using Batch Files

You've already seen a batch file in action. In Chapter 7 we modified the contents of AUTOEXEC.BAT, a special batch file that DOS executes each time you start your computer. As I explained then, a batch file is an ASCII file containing one or more commands that you normally would execute from the DOS system prompt. Including these commands in a batch file, however, means they can be executed automatically, each time that batch file is run.

To understand what this means, let's examine the contents of a batch file that I use to start my word processor at the beginning of each day. Figure 9.1 shows the contents of this batch file, which I call WRITE.BAT. Briefly, this batch file accomplishes the following tasks:

```
(C:\) TYPE \BATCH\WRITE.BAT
@ECHO OFF
CLS
MARK LC
LCPOPUP
CD \WS
WF
D:
CD \LIGHT
LIGHT
ENVI A
C:
CD \WS
WS
RELEASE LC

(C:\)
```

Figure 9.1 Batch files let you automate complex procedures.

1. The first line in this batch file uses a special batch command, ECHO, to suppress the display on any commands it contains. (You'll learn about the DOS batch commands in a few paragraphs.)

2. The second line in this batch file uses a CLS command to clear the screen.

3. Next, a special utility called MARK is loaded to identify a temporary memory location, which DOS can use to keep track of my memory-resident programs.

4. Next, the batch file loads a special print utility, LCPOPUP, which provides me with greater control over my laser printer.

5. The **CD\WS** command changes to the directory on my hard disk in which I have stored the program files for WordStar, my word processor.

6. Then WordFinder (**WF**), WordStar's thesaurus program is loaded. (You don't believe we writers think up all these words on our own without any help, do you?)

7. The next two lines change the active drive to drive D and make a directory called LIGHT the active directory.

8. The following two lines load Borland's Turbo Lightning (an interactive spell checker and thesaurus program that helps me keep errors to a minimum) and configure this program to run properly with WordStar.

9. Having completed all of this preliminary work, my batch file is finally ready to switch back to the WS directory on drive C and run WordStar, which is exactly what the next three lines accomplish.

10. DOS runs the final line of this batch file after I exit WordStar. It uses RELEASE, a companion utility to the MARK program mentioned earlier, to remove from RAM those memory-resident programs I use to set up my word processing environment.

Without a batch file, I would have to enter each of these fourteen commands manually whenever I sat down to write. How inconvenient would this be? Inconvenient enough that I probably wouldn't enjoy writing half as much as I do now. With this batch file at my disposal, however, I only have to type in its name, WRITE, and press the Enter key. At that point, DOS takes over and takes care of everything else.

How a Batch File Works

The easiest way to understand how a batch file works is to compare its contents to those steps you would normally perform to accomplish something from your keyboard. Each line in a batch file corresponds to a single DOS command that you would enter to initiate the desired activity. Running a batch file causes DOS to read and execute the contents of that file, rather than accepting keyboard input.

In my WRITE.BAT file, for example, DOS begins by reading in the first line, **@ECHO OFF**. DOS interprets the carriage return at the end of this line the same way it would the Enter key — it executes the previous command. When it's finished with the first line, DOS automatically advances to the second line of the batch file, which it "reads" and executes — once again, just as if you were typing this command at the keyboard. Unless you tell it to do otherwise (and, as you'll learn shortly, you can), DOS continues this process until every line in the batch file has been read and executed.

Whenever a batch file turns control of your PC over to an application program, as when WRITE.BAT issued the **WS** command, it suspends its own execution until you exit that application. Normally, this would return you to the system prompt. If an application is started from within a batch file, however, the batch file resumes execution at precisely the place where it left off, automatically advancing to the line immediately following the one used to run your application. This feature allows you to design incredibly complex batch files that can enter and exit multiple programs, moving automatically from one to the next, until each of the steps required to complete a specific task has been performed.

Batch File Commands

By itself, the ability to execute DOS commands is a powerful and useful tool. But DOS takes this process a step further by allowing you to include in a batch file special commands that provide even greater control over how it functions. Some of these commands determine what you see during execution of a batch file. Others can be used to influence which operations a batch file performs, depending on specified conditions or, in some cases, user input. Table 9.1 contains a listing of the various batch file commands supported by MS-DOS 6.0.

TABLE 9.1 DOS Batch File Commands

Command	Function
CALL	Used to run one batch file from within another batch file, without ending execution of the first file (The CALL command is not available in releases of DOS prior to version 3.3.).
CHOICE	Used to display a prompt and then initiate a specified action, based on the value returned by user input. (This command is not available in versions of DOS prior to 6.0.)
ECHO	Used to turn on or off screen echo, which determines whether commands within a batch file are displayed on your monitor during execution.
FOR	Used to execute a command on each file in a set of files.
GOTO	Used to direct DOS to a line within a batch file identified with a specified label.
IF	Tells DOS to perform a command only if a specified condition is met.
PAUSE	Pauses execution of a batch file until the user presses any key.
REM	Used to include nonexecuting comments into a batch file.
SHIFT	Used to increase the number of replaceable parameters that can be used in a batch file.

Some of these commands — FOR and GOTO, among others — will look familiar to anyone who's ever done any programming. Others are unique to batch-file operations; SHIFT and CHOICE fall into the latter category. All provide incredible flexibility when designing and creating batch files. So, let's do just that: design and create a batch file.

Creating a Batch File

First, we'll use the CD command to move to the BATCH directory we created in Chapter 7. To do this:

Type **CD \BATCH** and press **Enter**.

> ✓ *Note:* If you didn't create a BATCH directory in that earlier exercise, use the MD command to do so now.

Remember, a batch file is an ASCII file — it contains standard text characters. Consequently, you can use the DOS EDIT program, also introduced in Chapter 7,

BATCH FILES AND OTHER CONVENIENCES **223**

to create or modify a batch file. We'll use EDIT to create a batch file that's designed to let you specify the manner in which you want to format a disk for a floppy disk drive.

> ✔ ***Note:*** The following exercise assumes that your system includes two floppy disk drives, A and B.

To create a batch file called MYFORMAT.BAT:

Type **EDIT MYFORMAT.BAT** and press **Enter**.

This loads the DOS text editor. Notice that the filename you specified, MYFORMAT.BAT, is listed above the now empty input window. We'll use this window to enter the text that ultimately will comprise our special batch file.

Type **@ECHO OFF** and press **Enter**.
Type **CLS** and press **Enter**.
Type **if "%1" == "A:" goto adisk** and press **Enter**.
Type **if "%1" == "a:" goto adisk** and press **Enter**.
Type **if "%1" == "B:" goto bdisk** and press **Enter**.
Type **if "%1" == "b:" goto bdisk** and press **Enter**.
Type **goto warn** and press **Enter**.
Type **rem Format routine for drive A** and press **Enter**.
Type **:adisk** and press **Enter**.
Type **choice Are you formatting a system disk** and press **Enter**.
Type **if errorlevel 2 goto dataa** and press **Enter**.
Type **if errorlevel 1 goto systema** and press **Enter**.
Type **:systema** and press **Enter**.
Type **format a: /s** and press **Enter**.
Type **goto end** and press **Enter**.
Type **:dataa** and press **Enter**.
Type **format a:** and press **Enter**.
Type **goto end** and press **Enter**.
Type **rem Format routine for drive B** and press **Enter**.
Type **:bdisk** and press **Enter**.
Type **choice Are you formatting a system disk** and press **Enter**.
Type **if errorlevel 2 goto datab** and press **Enter**.
Type **if errorlevel 1 goto systemb** and press **Enter**.
Type **:systemb** and press **Enter**.
Type **format b: /s** and press **Enter**.
Type **goto end** and press **Enter**.
Type **:datab** and press **Enter**.
Type **format b:** and press **Enter**.
Type **goto end** and press **Enter**.

Type **:warn** and press **Enter**.
Type **echo You must enter a drive letter** and press **Enter**.
Type **echo for this batch file to run properly** and press **Enter**.
Type **pause** and press **Enter**.
Type **:end** and press **Enter**.

Your screen should resemble Figure 9.2, which shows the final portion of the MYFORMAT.BAT file in the EDIT display. In this file we used several of the batch commands available in MS-DOS 6.0. Before discussing what these commands accomplish, we'll save MYFORMAT.BAT to disk. To do so:

Press **Alt+F** to display the pull-down File menu.
Press **X** to select the Exit option.
When EDIT asks if you want to save the file, press **Enter** to select **OK**.

> ✔ *Note:* You can use the TYPE command to verify whether this batch file was created successfully.

Replaceable Parameters (The % Sign)

You can use a percentage symbol (%) to specify up to ten replaceable parameters in your batch files. DOS substitutes any parameter appended to the end of the command entered to start a batch file for the corresponding percentage symbol within that batch file. Parameters are substituted in ascending order, i.e., the first parameter on the command line is substituted for %1, the second parameter on

```
File  Edit  Search  Options                                      Help
                          MYFORMAT.BAT
goto end
:dataa
format a:
goto end
rem Format routine for drive B
:bdisk
choice Are you formatting a system disk
if errorlevel 2 goto datab
if errorlevel 1 goto systemb
:systemb
format b: /s
goto end
:datab
format b:
goto end
:warn
echo You must enter a drive letter
echo for this batch file to work properly
pause
:end

MS-DOS Editor   <F1=Help> Press ALT to activate menus        00035:001
```

Figure 9.2 You create MYFORMAT.BAT with the EDIT program.

the command line is substituted for %2, the third for %3, and so forth, through %9.

> ✔ ***Note:*** I realize this only provides for nine options. If necessary, DOS uses %0 as a dummy parameter to signify the drive name and filename you enter to start the batch file.

In our MYFORMAT.BAT file, whatever drive you specify after entering the MYFORMAT command will be substituted for %1 when the batch file executes. If you enter the command line **MYFORMAT A:** or **MYFORMAT a:**, therefore, the batch file branches to the routine we've called "adisk," which formats a disk in drive A. Conversely, entering the command line **MYFORMAT B:** or **MYFORMAT b:** causes the batch file to branch to the routine named "bdisk," which formats a disk in drive B.

> ✔ ***Note:*** Notice that there are two "goto" statements for each branch. This allows MYFORMAT to test for the drive letter in either uppercase or lowercase letters. If a drive other than drive A or B is specified, or if the user enters no drive parameter after MYFORMAT, the batch file advances to the "warn" section, which informs the user that a drive letter is required.

Testing Conditions (The IF Command)

Lines 3 through 6 in the MYFORMAT.BAT file use an IF command to test a specified condition; in this case to find out what the user entered as a %1 parameter following the MYFORMAT command. There are two possible outcomes:

1. If the result of this test is TRUE — if the user entered one of the four valid responses (A, a, B or b) — DOS executes the remainder of the IF statement.
2. If this test returns a FALSE condition — the user entered no value or a value other than the four letters listed above — the rest of the command is ignored and the batch file automatically advances to the next line.

The correct syntax for using an IF command is:

```
IF "string1"=="string2" command
```

An IF command accepts the following parameters:

string1   indicates the first condition being tested.

==   is a mandatory double equal sign used in conjunction with the IF statement when testing two conditions.

string2   indicates the second condition being tested.

command indicates the command you want DOS to execute if an IF test returns a TRUE value.

Branching within a Batch File (The GOTO Command)

The GOTO command lets you change the order in which statements within a batch file are executed. As I explained earlier, DOS normally moves through a batch file sequentially, executing each line then moving on to the one that follows it. A GOTO statement allows you to specify which portion of a batch file should be executed next, usually based on the result of a test performed within a statement; for example, the MYFORMAT.BAT file used GOTO commands in conjunction with IF statements to determine which disk contains the disk being formatted. The correct syntax for using a GOTO command is:

GOTO *label*

A GOTO command accepts the following parameter:

label specifies the label used to identify the next section of the batch file you want DOS to execute.

In MYFORMAT.BAT, eight branch labels are specified: adisk, bdisk, systema, dataa, systemb, datab, warn, and end. Each of these eight routines serves a different purpose:

- **adisk** is used to format a disk in drive A, if the replaceable parameter included with a MYFORMAT command is either A: or a:.
- **bdisk** is used to format a disk in drive B, if the replaceable parameter included with a MYFORMAT command is either B: or b:.
- the two **system** branches indicate that the disk in the specified drive should be formatted as a system disk.
- the two **data** branches indicate that the disk in the specified drive should be formatted as a nonsystem disk.
- **warn** is used to inform the user that he or she must include a drive letter with the MYFORMAT command.
- **end** is used to jump to the end of MYFORMAT.BAT.

The ability to branch lets you design a batch file that performs any one of several different functions, depending on which subroutines it calls. Subroutines within a batch file are identified with a single line consisting of a colon (:), followed by the branch label. For example, the branch subroutine within MYFORMAT.BAT used to format a system disk in drive B begins with the line **:systemb**. DOS branches to this subroutine if the user answers Y to the **choice** prompt immediately preceding it.

Offering Users a Choice (The CHOICE Command)

The CHOICE command is a batch command new to MS-DOS 6.0. It allows you to identify the subroutine DOS should branch to within a batch file, based on specific user input. The correct syntax for using a CHOICE command is:

CHOICE [/C[:*keys*] [/N] [/S] [/T[:]*c,nn*] [*text*]

A CHOICE command accepts the following parameters and switches:

/C:*keys* identifies allowable keys in the response. DOS displays any keys specified in brackets [ ], followed by a question mark. If no *keys* are specified, CHOICE defaults to Y/N.

/N instructs DOS not to display the *keys* prompt or, alternately, Y/N.

/S instructs DOS to make CHOICE case-sensitive — the user must enter his/her response in uppercase or lowercase letters as specified by *keys*.

/T:*c,nn* instructs DOS to pause for *nn* seconds before defaulting to the *c* response. *nn* indicates a number of seconds in a range from 0 to 99.

text indicates any text you want displayed before the prompt specified by *keys* or Y/N.

A CHOICE statement returns an errorlevel to DOS, based on valid responses. DOS assigns an errorlevel value of 1 to the first response specified by *keys*, 2 to the second response, 3 to the third, and so on. (In the default Y/N response, Y returns an error level value of 1.) Testing this errorlevel allows you to control program branching.

MYFORMAT.BAT uses a CHOICE statement to determine if it should include the DOS system files on the formatted disk.

Miscellaneous Notes on MYFORMAT.BAT

I've used several additional batch file techniques to refine MYFORMAT.BAT. These include:

1. A **goto end** statement was inserted at the end of any conditional tests. Doing so prevents MYFORMAT.BAT from automatically moving on to the next step if the conditions being met are not matched.
2. Both the **adisk** and **bdisk** subroutines also end with a **goto end** statement for the same reason. After the desired format operation is completed, the batch file automatically advances to **end**, returning you to the DOS system prompt.

3. The **rem** command was used to include nonexecuting statements that clarify the purpose of a particular subroutine within MYFORMAT.BAT. This technique is especially helpful for long batch files that include branching.

4. Whenever possible, include instructions or messages that help other users execute your batch files. Notice, for example, the **warn** subroutine which was used to tell users that they have to include a drive letter with the MYFORMAT command.

> *Tip:* **Clear It Up**
> **Make it a habit to include a CLS command at the beginning of every batch file. Doing so clears the screen of any previously displayed messages, instruction, etc., making it easier for a user to keep track of what's going on in the current sequence of commands.**

Running a Batch File

Now that we have this batch file, let's see how it works.

Type **MYFORMAT** and press **Enter**.

Hmmm. It didn't work. Or did it? If all went as planned, DOS should have cleared the screen and then displayed the following message:

```
You must enter a drive letter
for this batch file to work properly
Press any key to continue...
```

This is the **warn** subroutine kicking in, which happened based on DOS not finding a replaceable parameter to insert as the %1 variable. Let's try again.

Press any key to abort the current execution of MYFORMAT.BAT. Type **MYFORMAT B:** and press **Enter**.

This time things look a little more promising. DOS again clears the screen and displays the following prompt:

```
Are you formatting a system disk[Y,N]?
```

Bingo! Obviously our first IF statement worked, as did the CHOICE command associated with the **bdisk** portion of MYFORMAT.BAT. To continue our test:

Press **Y**.

DOS resumes execution of MYFORMAT.BAT, displaying the following message:

```
Insert new diskette for drive B:
and press ENTER when ready...
```

So far, so good. As you probably guessed, this message was generated by the FORMAT program. (It must have been, since we did not specify it anywhere within our batch file.) Notice that DOS automatically inserted the appropriate drive letter into the FORMAT message — again, based on the replaceable parameter entered with the original MYFORMAT command. So, let's see what happens.

Insert a blank or reusable diskette in drive B.
Press **Enter**.

This starts DOS merrily on its way, formatting the floppy disk you placed in drive B. When DOS prompts you for a volume label:

Press **Enter**.

When formatting is completed, your screen should resemble Figure 9.3. (The statistics listed for your formatted disk may differ from the ones shown here, depending on what type of disk drive you have.) Notice that DOS did indeed transfer the system files to the formatted disk, as requested in the **systemb** subroutine of MYFORMAT.BAT. At this **Format another (Y/N)?** prompt:

Type **N** and press **Enter**.

This exits MYFORMAT.BAT and returns you to the DOS system prompt. Congratulations! You just programmed and ran your first batch file.

Batch files provide a convenient way to automate complex DOS operations. For simpler tasks, you may want to familiarize yourself with a second DOS automation tool, the DOSKEY utility.

```
Are you formatting a system disk[Y,N]?Y
Insert new diskette for drive B:
and press ENTER when ready...

Checking existing disk format.
Saving UNFORMAT information.
Verifying 1.44M
Format complete.
System transferred

Volume label (11 characters, ENTER for none)?

   1457664 bytes total disk space
    132096 bytes used by system
   1325568 bytes available on disk

       512 bytes in each allocation unit.
      2589 allocation units available on disk.

Volume Serial Number is 3B25-18E6

Format another (Y/N)?
```

Figure 9.3 MYFORMAT.BAT formats the disk in drive B, per your instructions.

DOS Doesn't Forget (The DOSKEY Utility)

In MS-DOS 5.0, Microsoft introduced a new and extremely useful utility to DOS. On the surface, DOSKEY doesn't appear to be that impressive. The "official" explanation of what DOSKEY does according to the on-screen Help system is: "[The DOSKEY command] loads into memory the Doskey program, which recalls MS-DOS commands." But, don't let this deceptively modest description fool you. This elegant little program, which consumes only 3K of memory to load and run, offers advantages far beyond its obvious ability to "recall MS-DOS commands."

The correct syntax for running DOSKEY is:

DOSKEY [/REINSTALL] [/BUFSIZE=*size*] [/MACROS|/M] [/HISTORY|/H] [/INSERT|/OVERSTRIKE] [*macroname*=[*text*]]

DOSKEY Parameters and Command Switches

DOSKEY accepts the following parameters and command switches:

macroname=	creates a DOSKEY macro that can be used to carry out one or more DOS commands.
text	includes any commands you want executed by the macro specified with *macroname*.
/REINSTALL	installs a second copy of the DOSKEY program over one that is already running.
/BUFSIZE=*size*	creates a buffer of the specified size, in the range of 256 bytes to 512 bytes, which DOSKEY can then use to store commands and macros.
/MACROS or /M	displays a list of all current DOSKEY macros.
/HISTORY or /H	displays a list of all commands stored in memory.
/INSERT|/OVERSTRIKE	switches between insert and overstrike mode when you're entering new text into a command line or macro.

Using DOSKEY

Once you load DOSKEY into memory — which we did automatically from the AUTOEXEC.BAT file created in Chapter 7 — it maintains a history of the most recently entered DOS commands. To see how this works:

Press the **Up Arrow** key.

BATCH FILES AND OTHER CONVENIENCES 231

✔ ***Note:*** If nothing happens when you press Up Arrow, try loading DOSKEY manually by entering a DOSKEY command at the system prompt.

DOSKEY recalls the most recent command you executed. If you've followed the order of the exercises in this book, this would be the MYFORMAT B: command entered in the previous exercise.

Now, you may be thinking, big deal. You could have accomplished the same thing with the F3 function key, as explained in Chapter 5. That's true. But try accomplishing the following with F3.

Press the **Up Arrow** key a second time.

This moves DOSKEY one step back in your stack of stored commands, displaying the ill-fated MYFORMAT command you entered before the successful MYFORMAT B: command in the previous section. Each time you press Up Arrow, DOSKEY recalls the command you executed just prior to the last one displayed. Once a command you're looking for appears, you can reexecute that command by pressing **Enter**. You also can modify a command displayed with DOSKEY to change its function slightly. When you execute this new command, it in turn becomes the first command in the DOSKEY stack.

Recalling Command Lists

If the command you're looking for was executed a while back, looking for it by repeatedly pressing the Up Arrow key can be more trouble that it's worth. Fortunately, there is an easier way.

Press the **F7** function key.

The F7 key recalls all commands currently stored in the DOSKEY command stack. Figure 9.4 shows the command list F7 recalled on my system. (As you can see, I've been quite busy while writing these past few pages.) Notice that each command is identified by a corresponding line number. I'll explain how you use this line number in a few moments. DOSKEY uses the MORE filter to pause this list after a complete screen is displayed. To see the next portion of the command listing:

Press any key.

The default DOSKEY buffer holds approximately 45 commands, depending on the length of each one. You can increase the size of this buffer by using the /BUFFER switch described earlier.

```
(C:\BATCH)
 1: HELP
 2: EDIT MYFORMAT.BAT /B
 3: MYFORMAT
 4: EDIT MYFORMAT.BAT /B
 5: MYFORMAT
 6: EDIT MYFORMAT.BAT /B
 7: HELP
 8: HELP IF
 9: WS
10: MYFORMAT
11: MYFORMAT B:
12: MYFORMAT
13: MYFORMAT B:
14: CD BATCH
15: EDIT MYFORMAT.BAT
16: HELP CHOICE
17: EDIT MYFORMAT.BAT /B
18: MYFORMAT B:
19: MYFORMAT B:
20: FORMAT B:
21: MYFORMAT B:
22: HELP CHOICE
23: CD BATCH
-- More --
```

Figure 9.4 You use the F7 key to recall the DOSKEY command stack.

Using the Command List

Once you know the line number associated with a previously entered command, you can use the F9 function key to recall it. In Figure 9.4, for example, line 17 contained **EDIT MYFORMAT.BAT /B**, the command I used to load the EDIT program and create MYFORMAT.BAT in the previous section. (The /B switch allowed me to capture this screen in monochrome.) To recall this command, I could:

Page through the command list to return to the system prompt.

Press the **F9** function key.

DOS displays the following prompt:

`Line number:`

To recall the line 17 command, I would:

Type **17** and press Enter.

DOS redisplays the requested line. Pressing Enter a second time would execute this command.

Creating Macros with DOSKEY

The final DOSKEY capability we'll examine is perhaps its most impressive. You can use DOSKEY to create customized macros, routines that run automatically each time you enter their corresponding names. To see what I mean:

BATCH FILES AND OTHER CONVENIENCES 233

```
Volume in drive C is MS-DOS 6
Volume Serial Number is 199C-54D2
Directory of C:\

AUTOEXEC BAT          196 01-03-93   5:34p
CONFIG   SYS          177 01-03-93   5:30p
AUTOEXEC HLD          182 01-01-93   5:56a
CONFIG   HLD          162 01-01-93   5:56a
BACKUP2  TXT         5376 12-31-92   6:14p
BACKUP2  BAK         5585 12-31-92   6:12p
MSBACKUP TXT         2048 12-31-92   6:04p
MSBACKUP BAK         1125 12-31-92   6:00p
MIRROR   FIL        59904 12-31-92   5:44p
BEFSETUP MSD        21141 12-28-92  10:20a
ANSI3    TXT          998 12-27-92   5:45a
ANSI2    TXT          925 12-27-92   5:45a
ANSI     TXT        13959 12-27-92   5:44a
HOLD         <DIR>        12-23-92   7:55a
TEST         <DIR>        12-22-92   7:43p
MIRROR   BAK        59904 12-08-92   8:45a
DSVXD    386         5741 12-06-92   6:00a
WINA20   386         9349 12-06-92   6:00a
COMMAND  COM        53405 12-06-92   6:00a
Press any key to continue . . .
```

Figure 9.5 DOSKEY commands can be stored as macros.

Press **Esc** to clear the command line.
Type **DOSKEY DATEDIR=DIR /O:-D /P** and press **Enter**.

It doesn't look like anything happened. Don't worry; something did. To see what:

Type **CD ** and press **Enter** to return to the root directory.
Type **DATEDIR** and press **Enter**.

DOS automatically executes the macro recorded earlier, displaying the contents of my root directory, sorted by date, pausing after each screen (see Figure 9.5).

Including Special Characters in a Macro

DOSKEY even lets you include special characters in a macro to perform specific operations. The following special characters control command operations when defining a macro:

$G or $g	Use either of these characters to redirect output to a device or file, instead of to the screen. When used in a macro, this character is equivalent to the DOS redirection symbol (>).
GG or gg	Use either of these double characters to append output to an existing file, rather than create a new file that replaces the older one. These characters are equivalent to the DOS append redirection symbol (>>).
$L or $l	Use either of these characters to read input from a file or a device other than the keyboard. This character is equivalent to the DOS input redirection symbol (<).

$B or $b	These characters replace the DOS pipe symbol (|) in a macro.
$T or $t	Use these characters to separate multiple commands while creating macros or typing commands on the DOSKEY command line.
$1 through $9	These characters are similar to replaceable parameters in that they allow you to include user-specified command line information in a macro.
$*	This character also resembles the replaceable parameters $1 through $9, with one important difference: Everything you type on the command line following the macro name is substituted for the $*, within the macro.
$$	This character is used to include a dollar sign character ($) in a macro. (A double dollar sign is required to prevent DOS from interpreting the dollar sign as one of its special characters.)

Saving Macros

Because DOS stores macros in memory, any macros you create will be lost when you turn off your computer. Fortunately, it's easy to save your current macros to a file for future use. A single command accomplishes this:

Type **DOSKEY /MACROS MYMACS.BAT** and press **Enter**.

This creates a file called MYMACS.BAT containing any macros you created during the current session. Go ahead and use a TYPE command to verify this, if you like.

If you really want to get fancy, you can call this file into EDIT and insert DOSKEY at the beginning of each line. Because you gave it a BAT extension, running this file the next time you started your system would reload into memory any macros it contains.

And, if you really want to make friends and impress technodweebs, try adding the following line to your AUTOEXEC.BAT file:

MYMACS

This runs the MYMACS.BAT file, loading all of your customized macros automatically each time you turn on your PC.

Batch files and DOSKEY are valuable allies in your efforts to master DOS. Both can be used to create a PC environment that complements your work habits.

Chapter 10

Where No DOS Has Gone Before: New MS-DOS 6.0 Features

This chapter was both the most fun and the most frustrating to write, as is often the case when enumerating the details about a major software upgrade. Let me explain.

The information in the previous nine chapters applies to virtually every release of DOS, with some exceptions. For example, the DELTREE command described in Chapter 4 is new to MS-DOS 6.0, as is the MOVE command introduced in Chapter 5; and the MSBACKUP utility covered in Chapter 8 replaces the BACKUP command found in earlier DOS releases. In most cases, however, these represent new ways to perform familiar activities. (You could always write a batch file that accomplished the same thing as MOVE or DELTREE, for example. The availability of these new commands simply eliminates the need to take matters into your own hands, as it were.) Describing them and placing them within the context of other DOS operations, therefore, is relatively easy for anyone conversant with previous DOS versions.

Striking out into new territory is another matter entirely. It's fun because, well, because any new experience *should* be fun. It's also frustrating for a very pragmatic reason. Ideally, a book about a new software product should be available at the same time as the software. Therefore, the book must be written three to four months before all of the final touches have been put on the software to allow for publishing and printing processes. For this reason, inconsistencies — albeit minor — are bound to exist between what appears in the book and what you ultimately get — in this case — with MS-DOS 6.0.

God willing and the bugs don't byte, however, any such inconsistencies will remain minor: maybe a missing command parameter here or a new switch added there; or sometimes, a message screen will be revised to more closely adhere to the King's English; or, the order in which options appear in a dialog box will be altered for arcane reasons at which we can only guess. In some cases, however, the differences may be more conspicuous. For this reason, in this chapter more than others, pay special attention as you work through the exercises. Compare my instructions and figures to those that you see on your screen; verify that they are *identical* to one another. If differences exist, analyze the discrepancies and adjust your responses, as appropriate. As I stated earlier, they'll probably be marginal, so this should not present any major problems. Forewarned is forearmed. Now, let's begin to examine some of the new capabilities built into in MS-DOS 6.0.

Placing Your Digital Ducks in a Row (The DEFRAG Command)

To understand what DEFRAG accomplishes, you first must know a little about how DOS stores files on a disk. Chapter 3 briefly described that, during formatting, DOS creates tracks and sectors on a disk. To review: DOS uses the disk directory and file allocation table (or FAT), also created during formatting, to keep track of where the files a disk contains are located. The term contiguous was used to indicate how the various parts of a file are stored on a disk. That brief explanation is expanded below.

Contiguous vs. Noncontiguous Files

Think of a contiguous file as the groove in a phonograph record. (You do remember records, don't you?) When you place a phonograph needle on a record, it travels along this groove smoothly, in a continuous "line," so to speak.

A contiguous file is like that record groove. All of the sectors it occupies follow one another directly. When you access a contiguous file, therefore, the heads on a disk drive move smoothly from one sector to the next, reading in data.

Conversely, sectors in a noncontiguous file do not follow one another. Instead, they can be scattered over a disk. To access a noncontiguous file, the heads of a disk drive must follow an oblique route, skipping from one location to another, much like the ball bearing in those toy mazes many of us had, where the goal was to maneuver the ball to the center of the maze by following a roundabout route. A disk drive has no trouble finding all of the data in a noncontiguous file, to be sure, but the gyrations it must go through to do so are extremely inefficient.

Why Files Become Noncontiguous

Whenever possible, DOS attempts to store files in contiguous sectors. When you first start using a disk — that is, shortly after it's formatted and, therefore, largely empty — DOS has no trouble doing so. It has a lot of contiguous unused sectors from which to choose.

Over time, however, as files are added to and deleted from a disk, this becomes more difficult until, ultimately, DOS is forced to begin storing files in noncontiguous sectors. To repeat, this doesn't prevent DOS from finding a file's contents, but it does have an effect on how much time is required to gather all the pieces together. Compare that smooth phonograph groove with the maze and you'll understand why this is so.

What DEFRAG Accomplishes

In essence, a noncontiguous file is fragmented, with its contents spread all over a disk. DEFRAG reorganizes fragmented files into contiguous sectors. This, in turn, improves system performance.

DEFRAG Command Syntax

The correct syntax for entering a DEFRAG command is:

DEFRAG [*drive:*] [/F] [/S[:]*order*] [/B] [/SKIPHIGH] [/H] [/LCD] [/BW] [/G0]

or

DEFRAG [*drive:*] [/U] [/B] [/SKIPHIGH] [/H] [/LCD] [/BW] [/G0]

DEFRAG Parameters and Command Switches

DEFRAG accepts the following parameters and command switches:

drive:	specifies the drive containing the disk you want to "defragment."
/F	instructs DOS to remove any empty spaces that exist between files as it defragments a disk.
/U	instructs DOS to defragment the specified files but not eliminate any empty spaces that exist between the files it contains.
/S[:]	is an optional switch that tells DOS to sort the files within their directories during a DEFRAG operations; sort order is indicated by placing one of the following *order* codes after the colon:

	N	Sorts files in alphabetical order by name
	N-	Sorts files in reverse alphabetical order by name
	E	Sorts files in alphabetical order by extension
	E-	Sorts files in reverse alphabetical order by extension
	D	Sorts files by date and time, earliest first
	D-	Sorts files by date and time, latest first
	S	Sorts files by size, smallest first
	S-	Sorts files by size, largest first
/B		instructs DOS to restart your computer after the specified files have been reorganized and defragmented.
/SKIPHIGH		instructs DOS to load DEFRAG into conventional memory; by default, DEFRAG uses upper memory if it is available.
/H		instructs DEFRAG to defragment hidden files.
/LCD		runs DEFRAG using a color scheme compatible with LCD screens, commonly found on laptop and notebook computers.
/BW		runs DEFRAG in monochrome (black and white).
/G0		runs DEFRAG in character-based (nongraphics) mode.

Using DEFRAG

You use the command switches listed above to run DEFRAG directly from the system prompt. DEFRAG also can be started in interactive mode, which allows you to select program options using pull-down menus and option buttons. To run DEFRAG in interactive mode:

Type **DEFRAG** and press **Enter**.

Figure 10.1 shows the opening DEFRAG display. DEFRAG automatically detects the disk drives attached to your system and displays them in the option box in the middle of the display. You use the option box in the middle of the screen to select the drive containing the disk you want optimized. To select drive C:

If necessary, use the arrow keys to highlight C: in your drive listing.

Press **Enter** to select **OK**.

DEFRAG begins by analyzing the selected disk to determine whether it is in need of optimization and, if so, what type of optimization would be most effective. Following this analysis, DEFRAG displays a message box similar to the one shown in Figure 10.2.

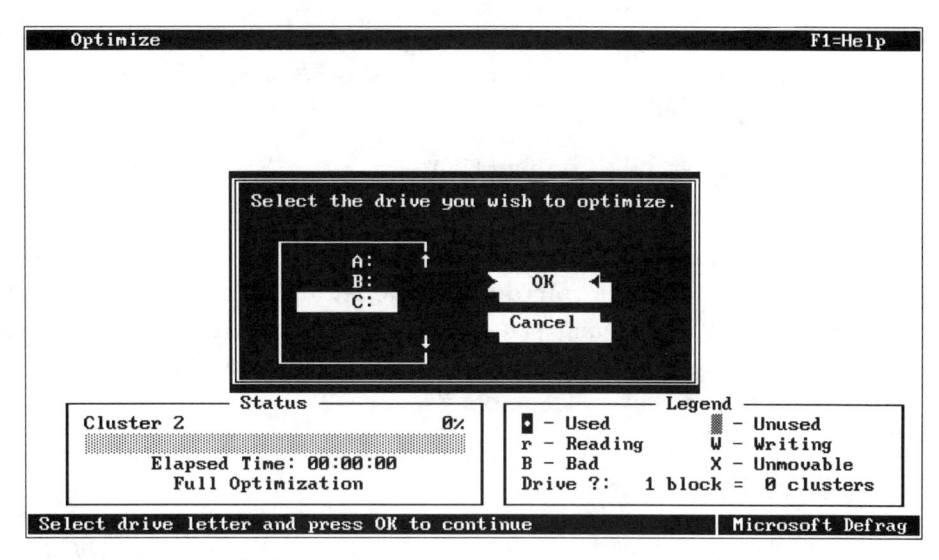

Figure 10.1 DEFRAG optimizes disk performance.

The upper portion of this screen contains a visual representation of the selected disk's contents. The Legend box in the bottom-right corner describes the various symbols used to indicate the contents of each block, which is used to represent the number clusters indicated in the legend. (The number of clusters a block represents differs, depending on the storage capacity of the selected disk.) The box in the lower-left corner of this screen marked Status ultimately will be used to indicate the progress of the defragmentation operation.

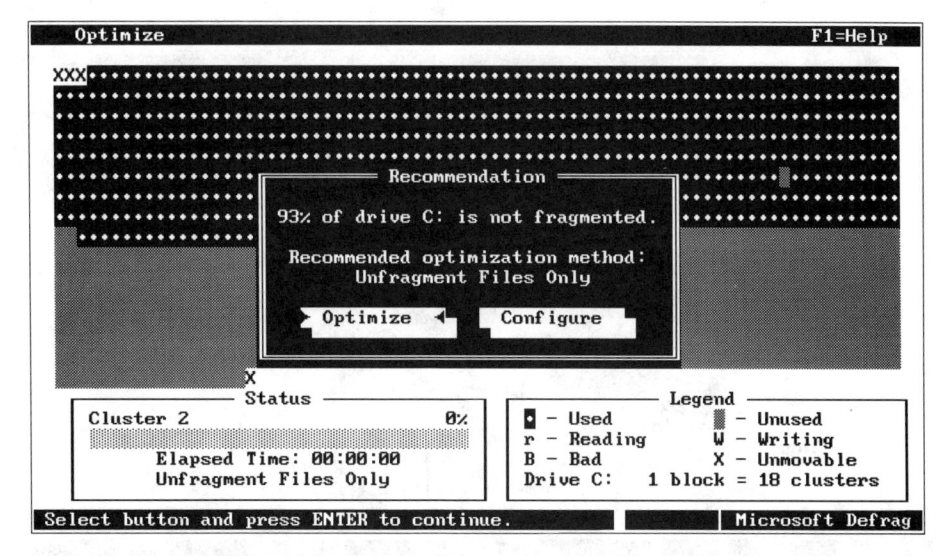

Figure 10.2 DEFRAG reports the results of its analysis, along with optimization suggestions.

Selecting **Optimize** at this point would begin defragmentation, using the suggested parameters. However, these can be overridden, should you desire to do so. To select new settings:

Press **Tab** to select the **Configure** button.
Press **Enter**.

Selecting **Configure** displays the Optimize menu shown in Figure 10.3. The various options on this menu correspond to settings you can specify using the various DEFRAG command parameters and switches. Selecting a Configure option displays an option box containing the choices available for that option. For example, to specify a file sort order:

Use the **Down Arrow** key to highlight **File sort**....
Press **Enter**.

This displays the File Sort option box shown in Figure 10.4. Once again, notice that the options listed here correspond to items specified at the system prompt using the *order* variable. You use the arrow keys and **Spacebar** to select a different sort order. For now:

Press **Esc** to return to the Optimize menu.

For this initial optimization, we'll accept DEFRAG's default settings and begin defragmentation on drive C. To do this:

Use the **Up Arrow** key to highlight **Begin optimization**.
Press **Enter**.

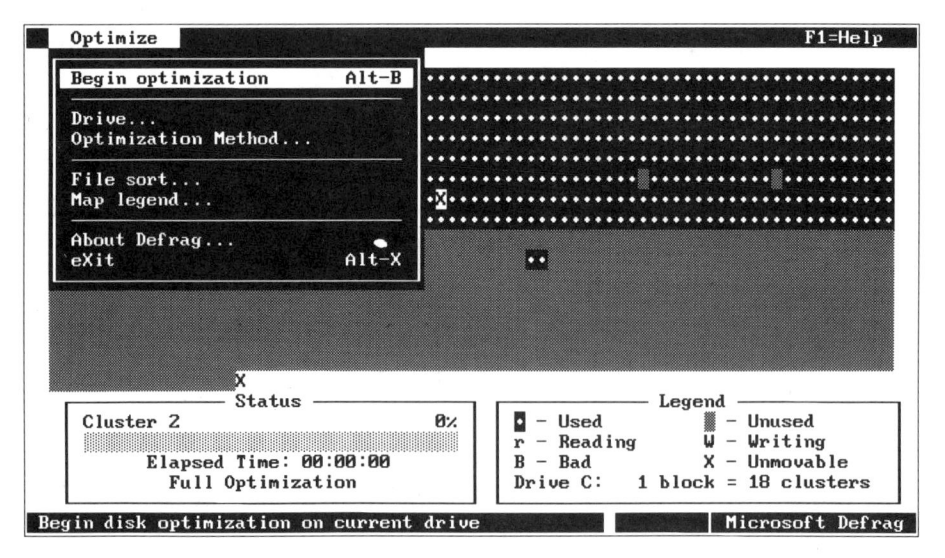

Figure 10.3   You use the Optimize menu to configure DEFRAG.

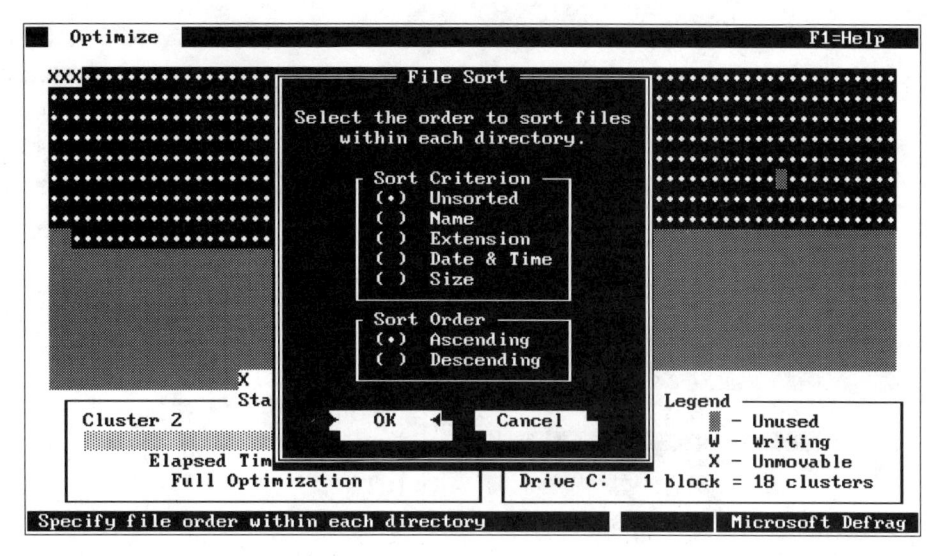

```
┌─ Optimize ──────────────────────────────────────────────────── F1=Help ─┐
│ XXX••••••••••••••••┌────────── File Sort ──────────┐••••••••••••••••• │
│ •••••••••••••••••••│  Select the order to sort files │••••••••••••••• │
│ •••••••••••••••••••│      within each directory.     │••••••••••••••• │
│ •••••••••••••••••••│  ┌─ Sort Criterion ─┐           │•••••••■••••••• │
│ •••••••••••••••••••│  │ (•)  Unsorted    │           │••••••••••••••• │
│ •••••••••••••••••••│  │ ( )  Name        │           │                │
│ ••••••••••••••     │  │ ( )  Extension   │           │                │
│                    │  │ ( )  Date & Time │           │                │
│                    │  │ ( )  Size        │           │                │
│                    │  └──────────────────┘           │                │
│                    │  ┌─ Sort Order ─────┐           │                │
│                    │  │ (•)  Ascending   │           │                │
│                    │  │ ( )  Descending  │           │                │
│              X     │  └──────────────────┘           │                │
│        ┌─ Sta      │                                 │  Legend ─────  │
│        │ Cluster 2 │     ◄ OK ►      Cancel          │  ■ - Unused    │
│        │           │                                 │  W - Writing   │
│        │ Elapsed Tim└─────────────────────────────────┘  X - Unmovable │
│        │ Full Optimization          │ Drive C:  1 block = 18 clusters │
├─ Specify file order within each directory ──┤         │ Microsoft Defrag │
└─────────────────────────────────────────────────────────────────────────┘
```

Figure 10.4 You can select choices from among the various Configure options.

DEFRAG begins by sorting your directory structure using the specified sort order. Once this is completed, the actual defragmentation begins.

During this process, DEFRAG reads each file on your disk into memory, collecting all its data off the various sectors on which that file is stored. After opening up the required space, it then rewrites this data to disk as a contiguous file. The Status box keeps you apprised of DEFRAG's progress.

When the entire process is complete, all of the files on the disk will be contiguous. This, in turn, will improve your disk drive's performance. DEFRAG reports that is has completed optimization (see Figure 10.5). To continue:

Press **Enter** to specify **OK**.

DEFRAG displays the dialog box shown in Figure 10.6. As this dialog box indicates, you can optimize multiple drives in a single DEFRAG session. Alternately, you can select a different configuration and reoptimize the current drive. Finally, you can exit DEFRAG and return to the system prompt. We'll do the latter.

Press **Tab** twice to highlight **Exit DEFRAG**.
Press **Enter**.

This ends the current DEFRAG session and returns you to the DOS system prompt. Used regularly, DEFRAG can dramatically improve the performance of your hard disks. Although utilities have been available for years that accomplish the same thing, Microsoft's inclusion of DEFRAG with MS-DOS 6.0 adds a critical capability to your PC environment without forcing you to look outside of DOS.

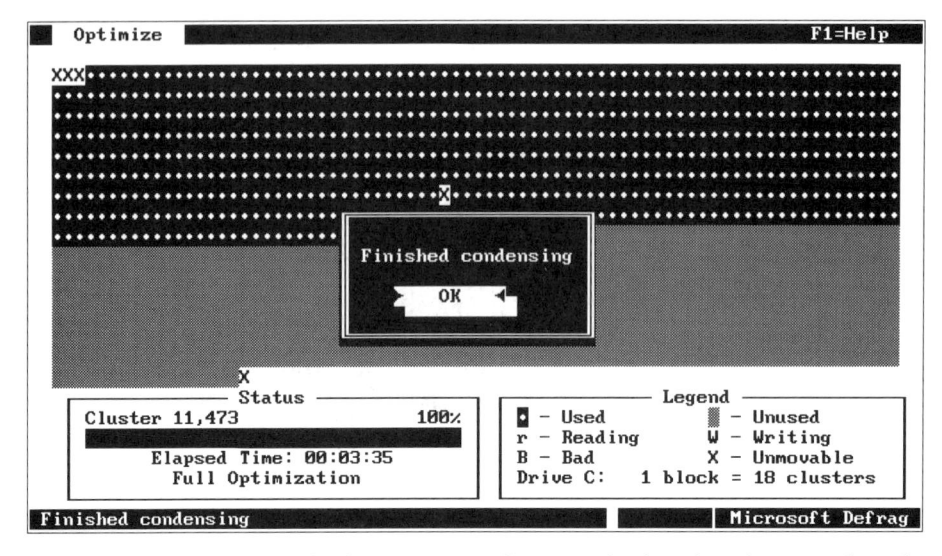

Figure 10.5 DEFRAG informs you when optimization is completed.

A PC Two-fer (The DBLSPACE Utility)

We call them "two-fers" here in the Midwest; you know, those advertising pitches that offer "two-fer the price of one." Boy, does MS-DOS 6.0 have a two-fer, fer you!

How'd you like to double the storage capacity of your disks? Think about it. How would it be if that 60MB hard drive spinning around in your PC suddenly

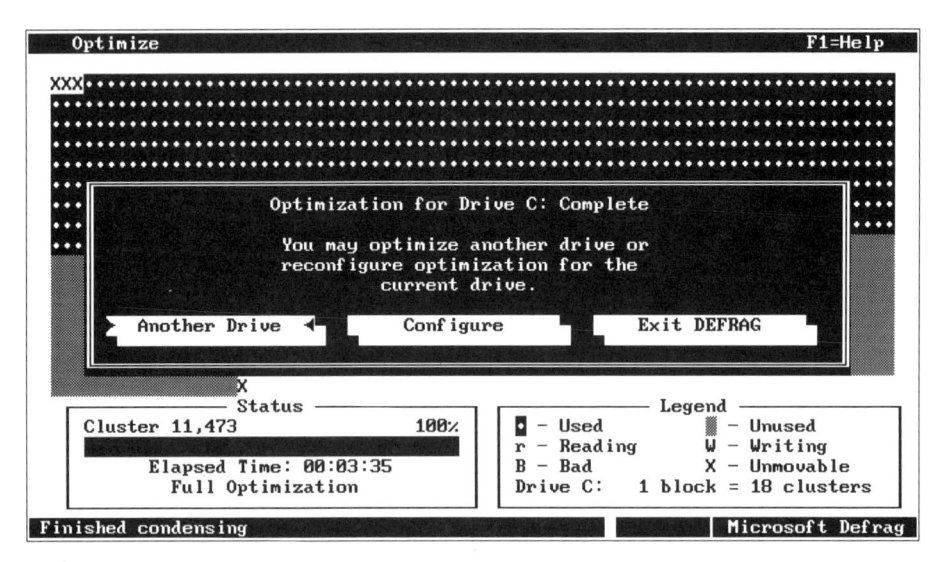

Figure 10.6 You can configure another drive during this DEFRAG session.

could store up to 80MB... 100MB...*120MB* worth of applications and data files? This is exactly what DBLSPACE, another new MS-DOS 6.0 utility, was designed to accomplish.

DBLSPACE adds data compression to DOS. Like file defragmentation, data compression has been available for years, through one of several third-party utilities. Although most of these are quite reliable, there's an inherent danger in "tacking onto" an operating system a technically complex function it was not designed originally to support. Conflicts can, and do, arise. More than one person I know has lost valuable information because of an incorrectly configured data compression scheme. By integrating data compression into DOS, Microsoft has eliminated many of the potential hazards associated with artificially increasing the storage capacity of your disks.

How Data Compression Works

At first glance, the promise of data compression may seem far fetched. After all, how can a disk designed to hold 60MB of data possibly handle more? Isn't this a little like trying to cram the proverbial ten pounds of potatoes into a five-pound bag? Well, yes and no.

Only an idiot would proclaim that ten pounds of just-harvested potatoes could be packed into a five-pound bag. But what if those potatoes were not packaged in their natural state? What if you mashed them first? Now would they fit? You know, they just might.

This is somewhat how DBLSPACE works. It uses a special device driver — remember these from Chapter 6 — to "mash" files before they're stored on disk. Once installed, this same device driver automatically "unmashes" a compressed file, whenever you call it back into memory. But what does DBLSPACE "mash" out of a file? And how does it accomplish this without also destroying some of the information that file contains?

Any file includes superfluous information. Consider, for a moment, the file containing the text of this chapter. Look at all of the blank spaces and empty lines it contains. Or how about the number of times the identical word or sequence of characters appears within it? For example, the indentation at the beginning of each paragraph eats up five successive blank spaces. What if there were some way to represent these five spaces using a single character? How much space could be saved by doing so?

I just counted the number of paragraphs I've written so far in this chapter. (Who says writers don't lead exciting lives?) There are 56 of them. Given that each character in a file requires 8 bits, and there are 5 characters (blank spaces) in each indentation, those 56 paragraphs consume 2240 bits (8 x 5 x 56 = 2240) of space before a first letter ever appears. Replacing those five blank spaces with a single character or symbol would shrink this number to 448 bits (8 x 1 x 56 =

448), for a savings of 1792 bits (2240 - 448 = 1792); or, figuring 8 bits to a byte, 224 bytes (1792 / 8 = 224).

And this is just one example from one portion of one file among many. Feel free to calculate how much my total storage requirements would be reduced if this and other redundancies were eliminated from all of the files comprising this book before they were saved to disk. Or, trust me when I say, it would amount to a lot. DBLSPACE empowers DOS to perform this digital sleight-of-hand automatically each time you write or read selected files to or from a disk.

Setting Up DBLSPACE

Like DEFRAG, DBLSPACE is designed to run in either command or interactive mode. The first time you enter the DBLSPACE command, however, it automatically loads a special utility program that sets up your system to recognize and use data compression. This seems like a logical place to start.

Type **DBLSPACE** and press **Enter**.

Figure 10.7 shows the introductory DoubleSpace message screen, which describes how DoubleSpace works. Notice that the DoubleSpace device driver requires approximately 40K of RAM. DBLSPACE automatically transfers this driver to high memory, if it's available on your system.

Press **Enter** to continue.

At this point, DoubleSpace lets you choose which type of Setup you want to run. You have two options:

```
Microsoft DoubleSpace Setup

        Welcome to DoubleSpace Setup.

        The Setup program for DoubleSpace frees space on your hard
        disk by compressing the existing files on the disk. Setup
        also loads DBLSPACE.BIN, the portion of MS-DOS that provides
        access to DoubleSpace compressed drives. DBLSPACE.BIN
        requires about 40K of memory.

          o To set up DoubleSpace now, press ENTER.

          o To learn more about DoubleSpace Setup, press F1.

          o To quit Setup without installing DoubleSpace, press F3.




 ENTER=Continue   F1=Help   F3=Exit
```

Figure 10.7 A special utility program prepares your system for data compression.

1. **Express Setup**: This method compresses the existing files on drive C and automatically determines what are appropriate DoubleSpace settings for your system.

2. **Custom Setup**: This method gives you greater control over your DoubleSpace configuration. For example, it allows you to create an empty compressed drive on an existing one using free space.

For the most part in these exercises I've opted for the Express option whenever it was offered by a DOS utility. In this case, however, I'm going to make an exception. The reasoning is fairly simple. Once you compress a disk, it can't be "decompressed" without going through some pretty complicated steps. If you were to choose the Express Setup and compress your current files, for example, you would need to copy (or back up) all of them to another disk before you could remove compression from drive C and restore it to its default storage capability. For now, therefore, we'll use the Custom Setup option to have DoubleSpace create a new compressed disk consisting of unused space on drive C. This will give you an opportunity to see how DoubleSpace works without irreversibly affecting your current files.

Press **Down Arrow** to highlight **Custom Setup**.
Press **Enter**.

At the next screen, which is another selection screen:

Press **Down Arrow** to highlight **Create a new empty compressed drive**.
Press **Enter**.

DoubleSpace analyzes your disk drives and displays a screen similar to the one in Figure 10.8. If you have multiple drives on your system, this screen will contain information on each drive it discovers. Notice that DoubleSpace automatically calculates the size of the resulting compressed disk, were you to use all available space on the selected drive. If there are multiple hard drives on your system, you could use the arrow keys to select a driver other then drive C. For now, however:

Press **Enter** to select drive C.

As Figure 10.9 illustrates, you can specify how much space you want DoubleSpace to use for the compress disk. By default, it leaves some of the free space uncompressed, keeping that space available to the current drive. (Figure 10.9 indicates that DoubleSpace plans to leave 2MB on my disk uncompressed and still assigned to drive C.) DoubleSpace automatically sets the compression ratio at 2:1 — that is, it will use a compression ratio of 2:1 to calculate the estimated size of free space on your compressed disk. Finally, it automatically suggests a drive letter to be assigned to your compressed disk.

All of these items are merely suggestions. Each can be changed at your discretion. To see what I mean:

```
Microsoft DoubleSpace Setup

        Select the drive you want to use. DoubleSpace will convert
        that drive's free space into a new compressed drive.

                         Current              Projected Size
            Drive      Free Space            of New Drive

              C          18.2 MB               35.4 MB


        To accept the current selection, press ENTER.

        To select a different drive, press the UP ARROW or DOWN
        ARROW key until the drive you want is selected, and then
        press ENTER. If there are more drives than fit in the
        window, you can scroll the list by pressing the UP ARROW
        DOWN ARROW, PAGE UP, or PAGE DOWN key.

 ENTER=Continue   F1=Help   F3=Exit   ESC=Previous screen
```

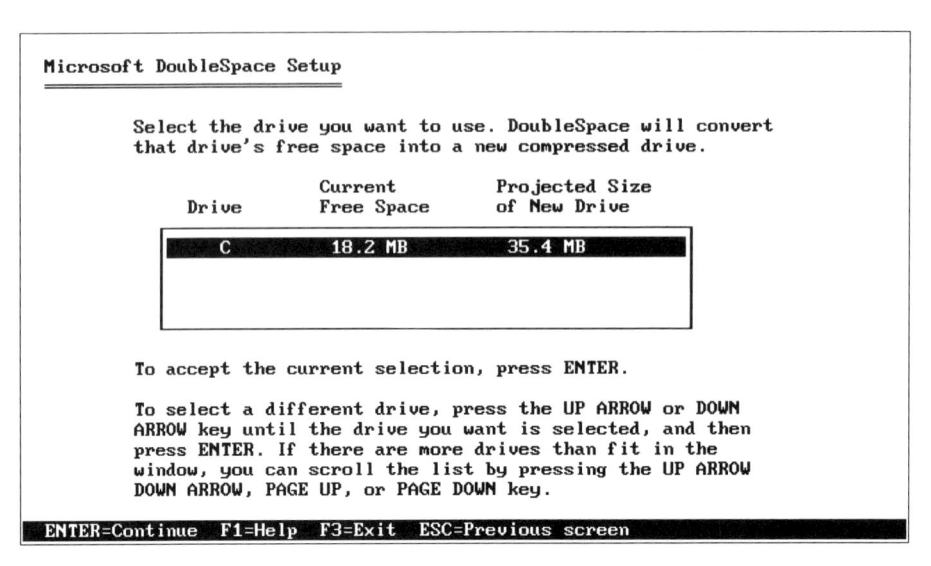

Figure 10.8 DoubleSpace calculates the results of disk compression.

Use the **Up Arrow** key to highlight the drive letter.
Press **Enter**.

DoubleSpace displays a screen that you can use to change the assigned drive letter (see Figure 10.10). I'll be honest, I'm not sure how DoubleSpace decided to suggest H as the drive letter for my system. I have only three drives, A through

```
Microsoft DoubleSpace Setup

        DoubleSpace will use the free space on drive C to create a
        new compressed drive. DoubleSpace creates the new compressed
        drive using the following settings:

        Free space to leave on drive C:        2.00 MB
        Compression ratio of new drive:        2.0 to 1
        Drive letter of new drive:             H:

                                              Continue

        To accept the current settings, press ENTER.

        To change a setting, press the UP or DOWN ARROW key to
        select it. Then, press ENTER to see alternatives.


 ENTER=Continue   F1=Help   F3=Exit   ESC=Previous screen
```

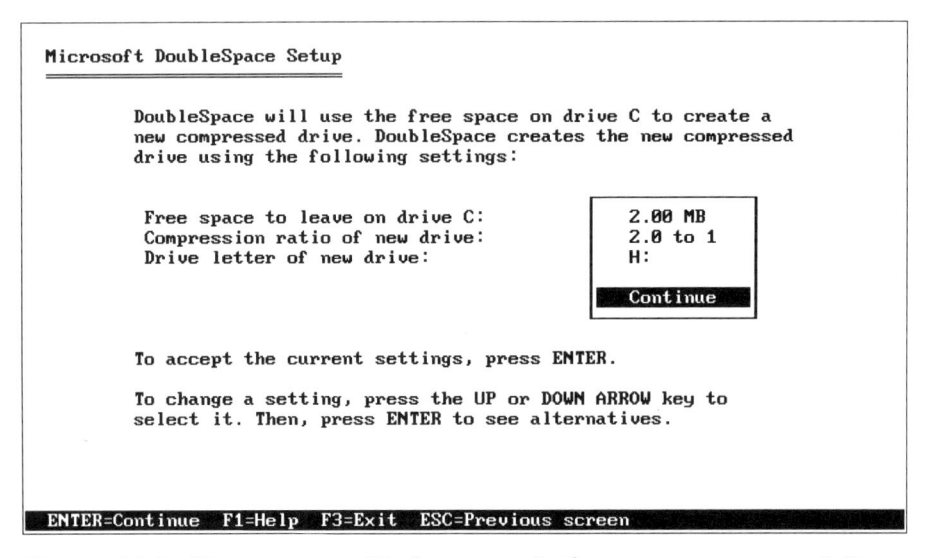

Figure 10.9 You can specify how much free space you want DoubleSpace to use.

```
Microsoft DoubleSpace Setup
═══════════════════════════

        Type the letter you want to assign to the new drive. You can
        specify any letter that is not already being used.

             Drive letter for new drive:   ┌─────┐
                                           │ H:  │
                                           │ I:  │
                                           │ J:  │
                                           │ K:  │
                                           └─────┘

        To accept the current value, press ENTER.

        To enter a different value, type the letter you want, and
        then press ENTER. Or, use the UP and DOWN ARROW keys to
        scroll the list until the letter you want is selected, and
        then press ENTER.



  ENTER=Select   F1=Help   F3=Exit   ESC=Previous screen
```

Figure 10.10 You can modify DoubleSpace's initial suggestions.

C. It would be more convenient, I believe, to create a compressed drive D. To request this, I would:

> Use the **Up Arrow** key to highlight **D:**.
> Press **Enter**.

DoubleSpace returns me to the screen shown in Figure 10-9, replacing its initial suggestion of an H drive letter with my requested value, D.

I'd also like to leave about 5MB of uncompressed space on drive C, rather than the 2MB DoubleSpace recommended. You can request this change using steps similar to those used to specify a different drive letter. Finally, you can request that DoubleSpace use a higher or lower compression ratio to estimate the size of the compressed disk. To do this:

> Use the **Up Arrow** key to highlight the compression ratio.
> Press **Enter**.

Figure 10.11 shows the screen you use to select a compression ratio other than DoubleSpace's default 2:1 setting. Notice that this screen provides a tip as to why you might select a different ratio. Let's assume that you're going to store graphics and text files on the new drive. For these files, it's practical to increase the ratio. So:

> Use the **Down Arrow** to highlight **3.00 to 1**.
> Press **Enter**.

Figure 10.12 shows the Setup screen after all of my suggested changes have been recorded. At this point, we're ready to begin actual disk compression.

```
Microsoft DoubleSpace Setup

        You can select a compression ratio between 1.0 and 16.0.

        If you are planning to store highly compressible files (for
        example, graphics or text files), you might want to choose a
        higher compression ratio. If you are storing less
        compressible files (for example, programs or help files),
        choose a lower compression ratio. For more information about
        choosing a compression ratio, press F1.

        Compression ratio:    ┌─────────────┐
                              │  2.0 to 1   │
                              │  2.1 to 1   │
                              │  2.2 to 1   │
                              └─────────────┘

        To accept the selection, press ENTER.
        To change the selection, press the UP or DOWN ARROW key
        until the compression ratio you want is selected, and then
        press ENTER.

 ENTER=Select   F1=Help   F3=Exit   ESC=Previous screen
```

Figure 10.11 You can choose from a wide range of compression ratios.

Press **Enter** to specify **Continue**.

Before moving on, however, DoubleSpace displays a final message screen (Figure 10.13), indicating what it is about to do. Notice that, as part of setting up disk compression, DoubleSpace must restart your computer. Make certain, therefore, that any floppy disks are removed from your disk drives so that your system will boot from drive C. Then:

```
Microsoft DoubleSpace Setup

        DoubleSpace will use the free space on drive C to create a
        new compressed drive. DoubleSpace creates the new compressed
        drive using the following settings:

        Free space to leave on drive C:        5.00 MB
        Compression ratio of new drive:        3.0 to 1
        Drive letter of new drive:             D:
                                         ┌──────────┐
                                         │ Continue │
                                         └──────────┘

        To accept the current settings, press ENTER.

        To change a setting, press the UP or DOWN ARROW key to
        select it. Then, press ENTER to see alternatives.

 ENTER=Continue   F1=Help   F3=Exit   ESC=Previous screen
```

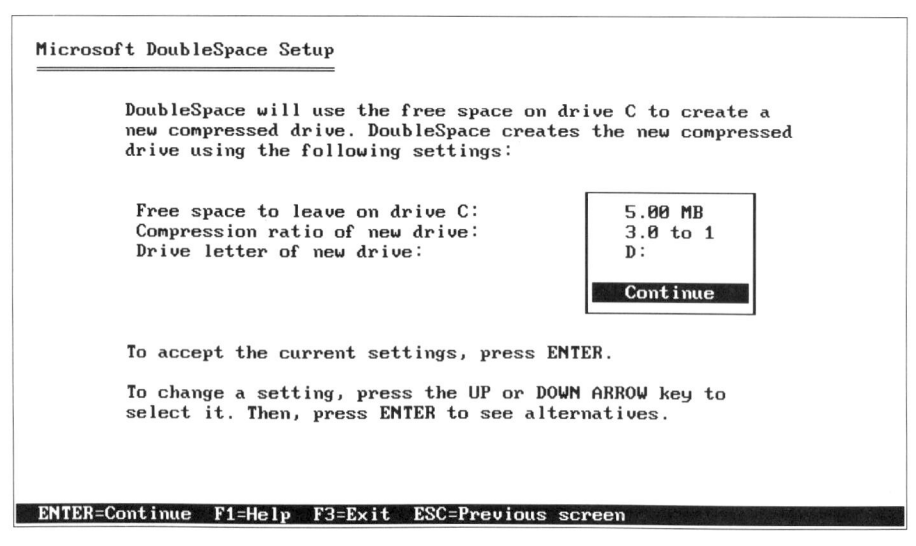

Figure 10.12 DoubleSpace records your modifications before initiating disk compression.

```
Microsoft DoubleSpace Setup

        DoubleSpace is ready to create drive D, a new compressed
        drive, using the free space on drive C. This will take about
        3 minutes.

        During this process, DoubleSpace will restart your computer
        to load DBLSPACE.BIN, the portion of MS-DOS that provides
        access to DoubleSpace compressed drives.


        To create the new compressed drive, press C.
        To return to the previous screen, press ESC.




 C=Continue  F1=Help  F3=Exit  ESC=Previous screen
```

Figure 10.13 You're given one final opportunity to abort disk compression.

Press **C** to begin disk compression.

This sends DoubleSpace merrily on its way, performing the various steps required to create a compressed disk. You'll see a number of messages fly by, each informing you of the program's progress. The final message screen provides a comprehensive report on the results of DoubleSpace's Setup procedure, including the estimated size of your new drive and how long the compression process took. When this screen appears:

Press **Enter** to restart your system with the compressed drive activated.

All of this activity brings you back, ultimately, to the system prompt. Nothing looks that different, does it? Let's see what you accomplished. To learn this:

Type **DBLSPACE** and press **Enter**.

This runs the standard DoubleSpace program — the version of DoubleSpace you'll see after you install at least one compressed drive.

As Figure 10.14 indicates, the previous exercises created a compressed drive on my system with a potential storage capacity of approximately 37MB. Creating this drive increased my disk storage capacity from 40MB, the original size of my hard disk, to almost 65MB — 28MB of uncompressed space on drive C and 37MB of compressed space identified as drive D. Not a bad return on an investment of the few minutes it took to run DBLSPACE.

250   DOS 6.0 HANDBOOK

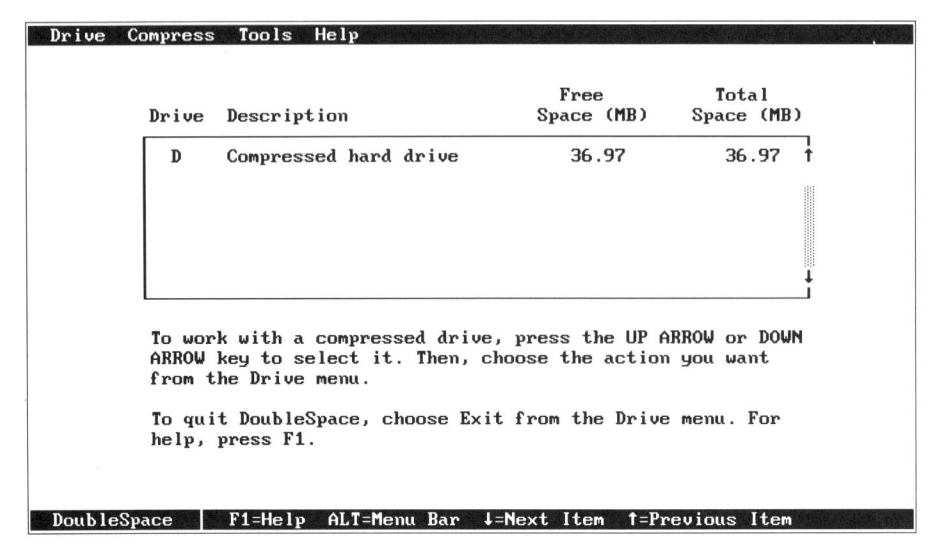

```
┌─Drive  Compress  Tools  Help─────────────────────────────────────┐
│                                           Free         Total     │
│           Drive  Description           Space (MB)   Space (MB)   │
│         ┌──────────────────────────────────────────────────────┐ │
│         │  D    Compressed hard drive    36.97        36.97  ↑│ │
│         │                                                     ▓│ │
│         │                                                     ▓│ │
│         │                                                     ░│ │
│         │                                                     ░│ │
│         │                                                    ↓│ │
│         └──────────────────────────────────────────────────────┘ │
│                                                                  │
│         To work with a compressed drive, press the UP ARROW or DOWN │
│         ARROW key to select it. Then, choose the action you want │
│         from the Drive menu.                                     │
│                                                                  │
│         To quit DoubleSpace, choose Exit from the Drive menu. For│
│         help, press F1.                                          │
│                                                                  │
│                                                                  │
│ DoubleSpace │ F1=Help  ALT=Menu Bar  ↓=Next Item  ↑=Previous Item│
└──────────────────────────────────────────────────────────────────┘
```

Figure 10.14   The DBLSPACE display

✔ ***Note:*** It's important to realize that this 37MB figure represents an *estimate* of how much data the compressed drive will hold, based on the compression ratio you specified. Different kinds of files compress at different ratios. The actual amount of data I ultimately could store on drive D, therefore, may be higher or lower than this figure. It will, however, be more than was possible without compression; that's guaranteed.

Using the DoubleSpace Tools

There are some caveats attached to using DoubleSpace. Primarily, these involve the way certain activities must be performed on a compressed disk, including:

- Defragmentation
- Further compression
- Running CHKDSK

Specifically, these operations should always be run from the DoubleSpace display or, alternately, using the appropriate switch with the DBLSPACE command. You should never run DEFRAG or CHKDSK directly on a compressed disk. To see how this is done:

Press **Alt+T**.

This displays DoubleSpace's pull-down Tools menu, shown in Figure 10.15. Notice that this menu contains special options for each of the activities mentioned earlier. Other pull-down menus can be used to perform additional

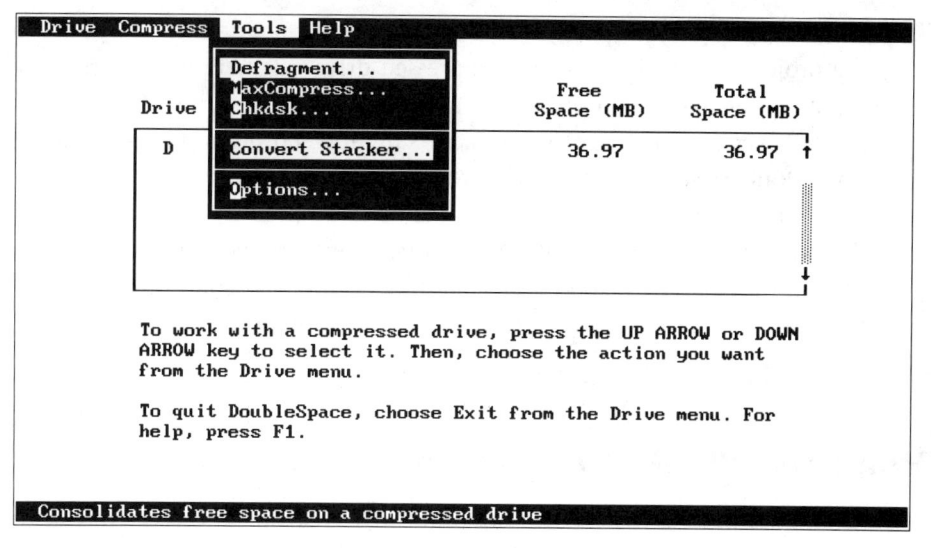

```
 Drive  Compress  Tools  Help
                 ┌──────────────────┐
                 │ Defragment...    │
                 │ MaxCompress...   │         Free         Total
         Drive   │ Chkdsk...        │       Space (MB)   Space (MB)
                 │                  │
           D     │ Convert Stacker..│         36.97        36.97   ↑
                 │                  │
                 │ Options...       │
                 └──────────────────┘


         To work with a compressed drive, press the UP ARROW or DOWN
         ARROW key to select it. Then, choose the action you want
         from the Drive menu.

         To quit DoubleSpace, choose Exit from the Drive menu. For
         help, press F1.


 Consolidates free space on a compressed drive
```

Figure 10.15 The Tools menu

operations relating to disk compression. The Compress menu, for example, contains options for compressing existing files or creating still another compressed disk — the same two options presented the first time you ran DBLSPACE.

Press **Right Arrow** twice to display the Drive menu.

DoubleSpace allows you to perform a number of useful operations on a compressed disk using options on its pull-down Drive menu (see Figure 10.16).

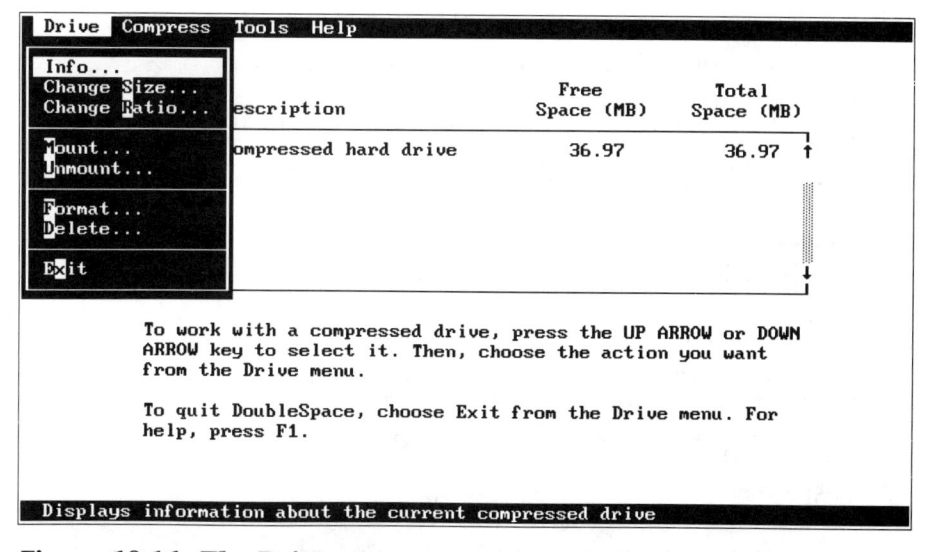

```
 Drive  Compress  Tools  Help
┌──────────────┐
│ Info...      │
│ Change Size..│                Free         Total
│ Change Ratio.│ escription   Space (MB)   Space (MB)
│              │
│ Mount...     │ ompressed hard drive   36.97        36.97   ↑
│ Unmount...   │
│              │
│ Format...    │
│ Delete...    │
│              │
│ Exit         │
└──────────────┘

         To work with a compressed drive, press the UP ARROW or DOWN
         ARROW key to select it. Then, choose the action you want
         from the Drive menu.

         To quit DoubleSpace, choose Exit from the Drive menu. For
         help, press F1.


 Displays information about the current compressed drive
```

Figure 10.16 The Drive menu

You can, for example, specify a different compression ratio, which would change the projected capacity of your compressed drive. (Remember, this figure is an estimate; the actual compression ratio depends on the kinds of files you compress.) Several of the Drive options access highly technical operations relating to how DoubleSpace manages compressed disks. For example, it's possible to unmount a compressed drive, which makes it temporarily unavailable. Some of the operations are potentially destructive; therefore, you should not attempt them until you have a good understanding of how disk compression works. For now, let's exit DoubleSpace and return to the system prompt.

Press **X** to select the **Exit** option.

Running DBLSPACE from the Command Line

As I mentioned earlier, you can perform DBLSPACE operations directly from the system prompt. To see what options are available when you use DBLSPACE in this manner:

Type **DBLSPACE /?** and press **Enter**.

As you can see in Figure 10.17, each of the available command switches corresponds to an option available from within the interactive DoubleSpace display introduced in the previous exercises. Once you become familiar with how DoubleSpace works, it may be more convenient to perform some disk compression related activities directly from the system prompt. The availability of the DBLSPACE command switches makes this relatively easy to do.

```
(C:\) DBLSPACE /?
Creates or configures DoubleSpace compressed drives.

DBLSPACE /CHKDSK [/F] [drive:]
DBLSPACE /COMPRESS drive: [/NEWDRIVE=drive2:] [/RESERVE=size]
DBLSPACE /CONVSTAC=stacvol drive: [/NEWDRIVE=drive2:] [/CVF=sss]
DBLSPACE /CREATE drive: [/NEWDRIVE=drive2:] [/SIZE=size | /RESERVE=size]
DBLSPACE /DEFRAGMENT [drive:]
DBLSPACE /DELETE drive:
DBLSPACE /FORMAT drive:
DBLSPACE [/INFO] drive:
DBLSPACE /LIST
DBLSPACE /MOUNT[=sss] [drive:] [/NEWDRIVE=drive2:]
DBLSPACE /RATIO[=r.r] [drive: | /ALL]
DBLSPACE /SIZE[=size | /RESERVE=size] [drive:]
DBLSPACE /UNMOUNT [drive:]

To set up DoubleSpace or use the DoubleSpace program to manage
compressed drives, type DBLSPACE at the command prompt.

For more information about DoubleSpace command-line options, type
HELP DBLSPACE.

(C:\)
```

Figure 10.17 The DBLSPACE command switches

However you use DBLSPACE, you will find that it provides an invaluable tool for getting the most out of your hard disks — literally. And this makes DBLSPACE a welcome addition indeed to your PC arsenal.

Opening Up the "Black Box" (The MSD Utility)

They used to call computers "black boxes," which implied that it was a dark and mysterious machine, the inner workings of which were beyond the comprehension of all but the most technically proficient digital gurus. In many ways, though, this characterization fits. What *is* going on inside of your PC? Do you know? Odds are you don't. But now you can, thanks to Microsoft Diagnostics, or MSD, a new utility included with MS-DOS 6.0. MSD lets you "peek" inside your PC and examine its various components.

The correct syntax for running MSD is:

```
MSD [/B] [/I][/F[drive:][path]filename][/P[drive:][path]filename]
[/S[drive:][path][filename]]
```

MSD Parameters and Command Switches

MSD accepts the following parameters and command switches:

/B   instructs DOS to run MSD in black-and-white mode.

/I   instructs MSD to bypass its initial analysis of your hardware.

/F   instructs MSD to prompt you for name, company, address, country, phone number, and comments, which it then uses to write a complete MSD report to a file.

The /F switch accepts the following /F parameters:

drive   specifies the drive to which you want to write the report.

path   specifies the directory to which you want to write the report.

filename   specifies the filename you want to assign the report.

/P   writes a complete MSD report to a file, without prompting you for information; the /P switch accepts the same parameters as the /F switch.

/S   writes a summary MSD report to a file, without prompting you for information; the /S switch accepts the same parameters as the /F switch.

254   DOS 6.0 HANDBOOK

> ✔ ***Note:*** If you enter the /F, /P, or /S switches without specifying report parameters, MSD displays the results of its analysis directly to the screen.

Normally, you'll want to have MSD perform its preliminary analysis of your system automatically. Should it have problems running for some reason, however, you can start it with the /I switch, then run the various MSD modules manually once you reach the opening screen. To see the opening screen:

Type **MSD** and press **Enter**.

MSD performs its initial analysis and displays the screen shown in Figure 10.18. Some of the information that was determined during the analysis appears on this opening screen. For example, Figure 10.18 reveals the following:

- MS-DOS 6.0 is running on a 386 system with a Phoenix Basic Input/Output System (BIOS).
- The system contains 640K of conventional RAM, along with both extended and expanded memory.
- A VGA display card that uses a Tseng video BIOS is installed.
- This system is not hooked up to a network.
- The mouse is a serial model.
- The system has four disk drives. (Notice that MSD recognized the compressed disk created in the previous section.)
- There is one parallel (LPT) port and two serial (COM) ports.

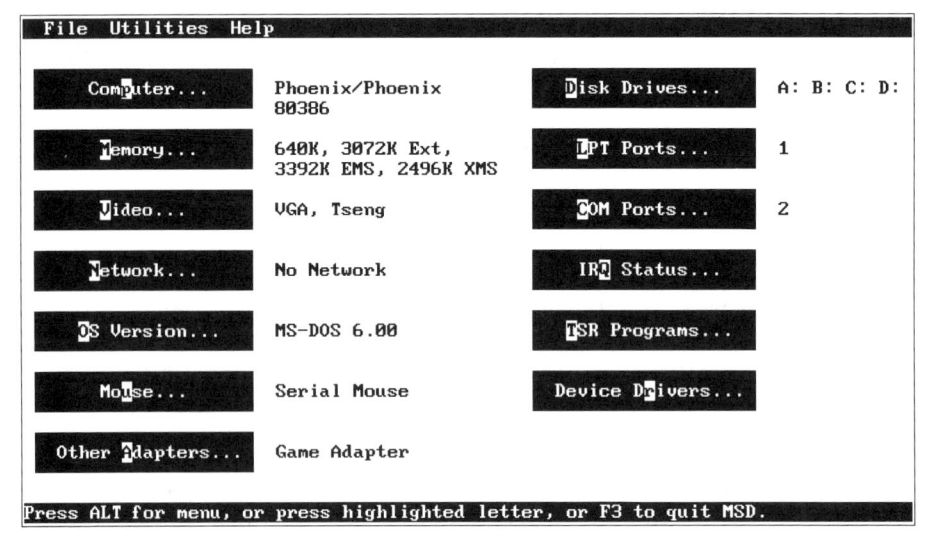

```
File  Utilities  Help

   Computer...      Phoenix/Phoenix        Disk Drives...    A: B: C: D:
                    80386
   Memory...        640K, 3072K Ext,       LPT Ports...      1
                    3392K EMS, 2496K XMS
   Video...         VGA, Tseng             COM Ports...      2

   Network...       No Network             IRQ Status...

   OS Version...    MS-DOS 6.00            TSR Programs...

   Mouse...         Serial Mouse           Device Drivers...

   Other Adapters...  Game Adapter

Press ALT for menu, or press highlighted letter, or F3 to quit MSD.
```

Figure 10.18   MSD reveals a wealth of information about your PC.

This, however, is only a drop in the bucket of information MSD ascertained during its analysis. Notice that every item on the opening screen is followed by an ellipses (...), indicating that each one leads to a secondary screen. To see what I mean:

Press **Q** to select **IRQ Status**.

This displays a report revealing the current status of each interrupt address (IRQ) on your PC (see Figure 10.19). Many add-on devices require an IRQ to work properly. The information on this screen allows you to make certain that no two devices are attempting to use the same IRQ — a definite no-no when you're setting up hardware. To leave the IRQ report and call up a different report:

Press **Enter** to select **OK**.
Press **R** to select **Device Drivers**.

I don't expect you to understand all the information on the Device Drivers report in Figure 10.20. I don't. Notice, however, that it does reveal that several MS-DOS 6.0 device drivers are installed in memory on my system; specifically, DBLSPACE, EMM386, and HIMEM, which is no surprise based on our work in previous chapters. Essentially, DOS is telling us that it knows what we know. Also notice that, as explained in Chapter 6, DOS defines a number of items as devices. In addition to the software drivers I installed, it detected my keyboard and display (CON), serial (COM) ports, parallel (LPT) ports, even my system clock.

Most of the information MSD reveals may seems impenetrable at this stage of your PC education. However, you'll probably quickly grow curious to learn more,

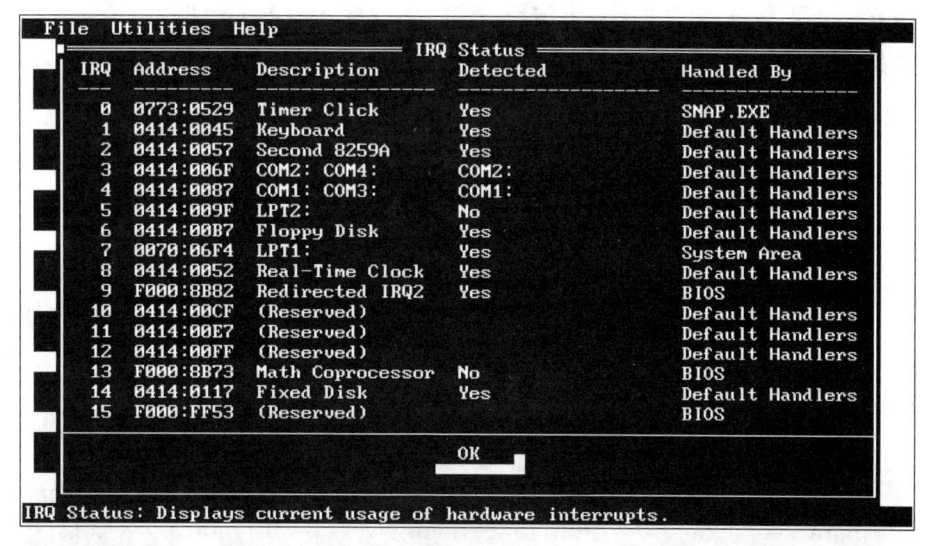

```
 File  Utilities  Help
                              IRQ Status
   IRQ  Address     Description       Detected      Handled By
   ---  ---------   ---------------   --------      ----------------
     0  0773:0529   Timer Click       Yes           SNAP.EXE
     1  0414:0045   Keyboard          Yes           Default Handlers
     2  0414:0057   Second 8259A      Yes           Default Handlers
     3  0414:006F   COM2: COM4:       COM2:         Default Handlers
     4  0414:0087   COM1: COM3:       COM1:         Default Handlers
     5  0414:009F   LPT2:             No            Default Handlers
     6  0414:00B7   Floppy Disk       Yes           Default Handlers
     7  0070:06F4   LPT1:             Yes           System Area
     8  0414:0052   Real-Time Clock   Yes           Default Handlers
     9  F000:8B82   Redirected IRQ2   Yes           BIOS
    10  0414:00CF   (Reserved)                      Default Handlers
    11  0414:00E7   (Reserved)                      Default Handlers
    12  0414:00FF   (Reserved)                      Default Handlers
    13  F000:8B73   Math Coprocessor  No            BIOS
    14  0414:0117   Fixed Disk        Yes           Default Handlers
    15  F000:FF53   (Reserved)                      BIOS

                                  OK

 IRQ Status: Displays current usage of hardware interrupts.
```

Figure 10.19 MSD checks such arcane items as IRQ status.

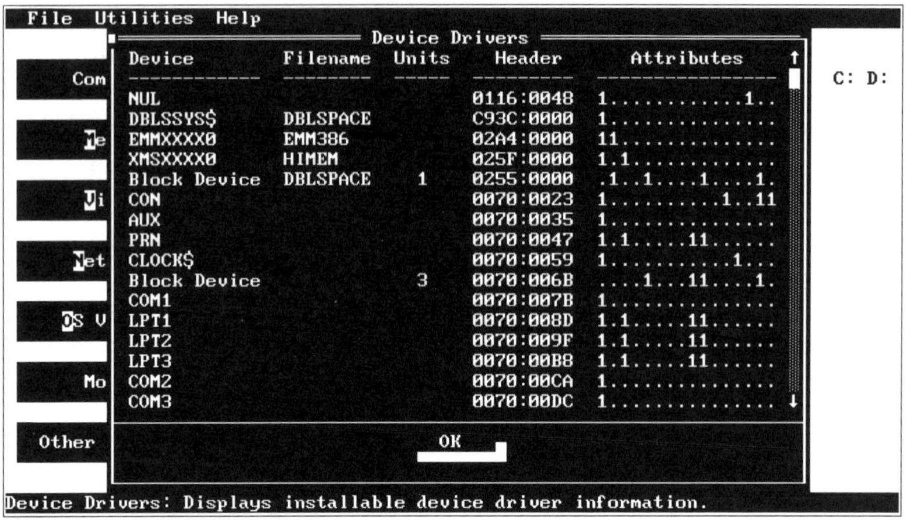

Figure 10.20 The Device Drivers report

and MSD can fulfill the role of mentor in this process. So, although we'll leave MSD for now, I feel certain you'll return.

Press **Alt+F** to display the File menu.
Press X to select **Exit**.

This exits MSD and returns you to the system prompt.

More Than Meets the Eye (Setting Up Multiple Configurations)

Keep in mind that the "P" in PC stands for "personal." That machine in front of you is yours and yours alone, to do with as you please. And trust me, you will do a lot with it. It will grow over time as you add new and even more powerful items to it.

I started out with a simple 8088 machine that had 256K of RAM, a keyboard, a monochrome monitor, and a single 360K disk drive. Today, my main electronic workhorse is a 33MHz 486 with 8MB of RAM. It also includes a 1.2MB, 5.25" disk drive, a 1.44MB, 3.5" drive, two 120MB IDE hard disks, a 15" high-resolution monitor and SVGA video card, a mouse, a CD-ROM drive, an internal fax/modem, a laser printer, a scanner, a sound card and twin speakers.

The price of PC hardware has dropped so dramatically in recent years that many people can now afford to set themselves up with more powerful systems. But don't forget: Every piece of equipment you install on your PC requires, among other things, at least some memory to run. And memory, as I've reiterated throughout this book, is the most valuable resource you have.

There are days that I know I won't be using my sound board; nevertheless, DOS used to require that I load its device driver through my CONFIG.SYS file anyway. With the release of MS-DOS 6.0, this is no longer true.

In many ways I've saved the best new MS-DOS 6.0 feature for last. MS-DOS 6.0 allows you to create a CONFIG.SYS that lets you select from multiple configurations during system startup. In my situation, for example, this means that I no longer need to sacrifice the approximately 14K of RAM my sound driver consumes, if I know I won't be using it on a particular day. That's 14K of memory I'll have available for other uses should I need it. Not loading the drivers for my CD-ROM drive, another item that sometimes sits idle all day, releases over 75K of RAM, a sizable addition to anyone's PC arsenal.

The secret to setting up multiple configurations is knowing how to use those five new CONFIG.SYS commands that were introduced briefly in Chapter 7:

INCLUDE
MENUCOLOR
MENUDEFAULT
MENUITEM
SUBMENU

We'll be discussing these commands in greater detail in a few paragraphs. But first, let's look at the simplest way you can take control of your CONFIG.SYS file, which is by using the question mark (?) to manually pick and choose which features you want loaded at the beginning of a session.

A Personal Question (Using ? in Your CONFIG.SYS File)

Formerly, DOS just breezed through your CONFIG.SYS file, executing each statement it contained with no questions asked. Even when it encountered a statement that made no sense, DOS didn't stop. It merely paused long enough to display a message indicating the line number of the problematic statement and moved on, determined to complete its task.

Now you can slow down DOS long enough so that it can ask you whether or not a specific line should be executed. The key to this extremely useful capability is the simple question mark. Inserting a question mark immediately before the equal sign (=) in any CONFIG.SYS statement that uses the equal sign causes DOS to display the tagged line, followed by a [Y/N]? prompt. The answer you give determines whether DOS executes that statement. For example, Figure 10.21 shows the prompt DOS displayed when I inserted the following line into my CONFIG.SYS file:

```
INSTALL?=C:\DOS\MOUSE.COM /C2
```

This prompt allows me to decide whether I want to load my mouse driver into memory for the current session. If I know I'm only going to be using programs that don't require a mouse, answering No (N) to this prompt bypasses the INSTALL=MOUSE.COM command, freeing up additional memory for other uses.

That was easy, wasn't it? The humble question mark lets you set up an elaborate selection of alternative startup options. But that's nothing compared to what another new addition to MS-DOS 6.0's CONFIG.SYS command stable allows.

Menu Magic (The INCLUDE, MENUCOLOR, MENUDEFAULT, MENUITEM, and SUBMENU Commands)

The question mark works just fine when the decision is simply to load or not to load a single item. Some choices aren't quite this straightforward, however; settings and device drivers in a CONFIG.SYS file can be related to one another.

For example, you may want to load your mouse driver only when you know you'll be using Windows. A sound board may be a second device that's required only by Windows applications. To accomplish this, you could use the question mark, as outlined in the previous section, but then you'd have to trust yourself to remember this relationship each time you started your PC.

A second and more convenient approach is to create a startup menu for CONFIG.SYS using the five special commands listed below. Then DOS itself

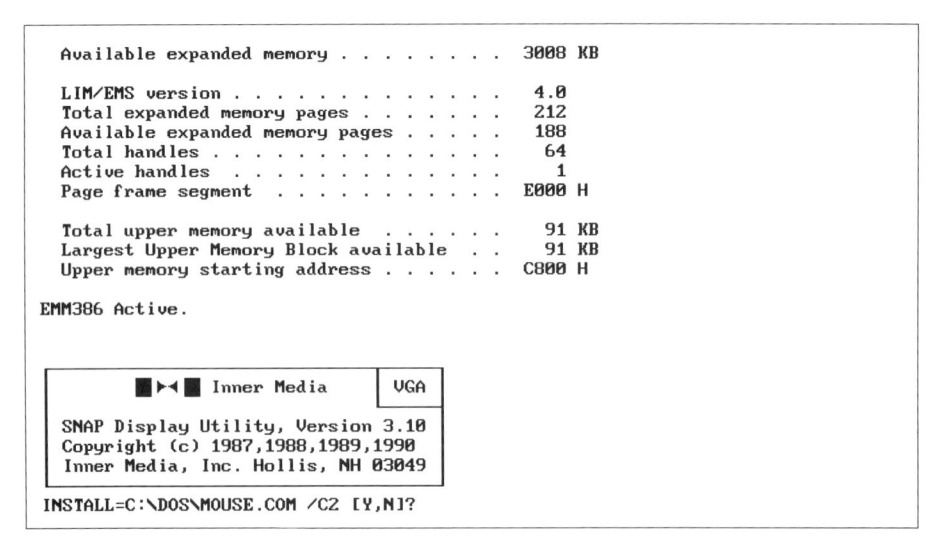

```
Available expanded memory . . . . . . . .  3008 KB

LIM/EMS version . . . . . . . . . . . . .  4.0
Total expanded memory pages . . . . . . .  212
Available expanded memory pages . . . . .  188
Total handles . . . . . . . . . . . . . .   64
Active handles  . . . . . . . . . . . . .    1
Page frame segment  . . . . . . . . . . . E000 H

Total upper memory available   . . . . .   91 KB
Largest Upper Memory Block available . .   91 KB
Upper memory starting address . . . . . . C800 H

EMM386 Active.

        ■►◄■ Inner Media     VGA
SNAP Display Utility, Version 3.10
Copyright (c) 1987,1988,1989,1990
Inner Media, Inc. Hollis, NH 03049
INSTALL=C:\DOS\MOUSE.COM /C2 [Y,N]?
```

Figure 10.21 You can now elect to execute specific CONFIG.SYS statements.

determines which statements to execute, based on the menu item you select. The five commands used to create a startup menu are:

INCLUDE	includes the contents of a configuration block in a startup menu.
MENUCOLOR	sets the text and background colors used in a startup menu.
MENUDEFAULT	specifies the default menu item on a startup menu and optionally, sets a time limit on how long the user has to select a menu item.
MENUITEM	is used to define up to nine items that can appear on a startup menu.
SUBMENU	defines an item on the startup menu that, when selected, displays another set of choices.

To see how these various commands work, let's examine the contents of the following CONFIG.SYS file:

```
[MENU]
MENUITEM base_config,DOS Applications Only
SUBMENU windows,Windows Setup
MENUDEFAULT windows,60

[base_config]
DEVICE=C:\DOS\HIMEM.SYS
DEVICE=C:\DOS\EMM386.EXE RAM HIGHSCAN
INSTALL=C:\COLLAGE\SNAP.EXE /E
DOS=HIGH,UMB
BUFFERS=20,0
FILES=30
LASTDRIVE=E
FCBS=4,0
STACKS=9,256
SHELL=C:\DOS\COMMAND.COM C:\DOS\  /p

[windows]
MENUITEM cd_rom, Load CD-ROM only
MENUITEM scan,Load CD-ROM and Scanner

[cd_rom]
INCLUDE base_config
INSTALL=C:\DOS\MOUSE.COM /C2
DEVICEHIGH=C:\DEV\MTMCDS.SYS /D:MSCD001 /P:340 /A:0 /M:20 /I:2

[scan]
INCLUDE cd_rom
DEVICEHIGH=C:\SCAN\SCAN.EXE

[common]
```

When you turn on your system, MS-DOS begins by reading the [MENU] block and displaying the following menu:

```
MS-DOS 6 Startup Menu
=====================

   1. DOS Applications Only
   2. Windows Setup

Enter a choice: 2                        Time remaining: 60


F5=Bypass startup files    F8=Confirm each CONFIG.SYS line [N]
```

The second selection in this menu, identified as the MENUDEFAULT in line 4 of the CONFIG.SYS file, is highlighted when displayed on your screen. Also, MS-DOS automatically displays and updates the **Time remaining:** information, beginning at the specified 60-second interval. (I'll explain the contents of the bottom line in a few paragraphs.) At this point, you have three options:

1. You can type **1** and press **Enter**. This would cause DOS to execute the commands contained in the [base_config] section.
2. You can type **2** and press **Enter**. This would cause DOS to execute the commands contained in the [windows] section.
3. You could do nothing. If no item is selected within 60 seconds, DOS automatically advances to option 2, the [windows] configuration block, which is identified as the MENUDEFAULT.

If you press 2 or wait for the 60-second input period to elapse, DOS displays the following screen:

```
MS-DOS 6 Startup Menu
=====================

   1. Load CD-ROM only
   2. Load CD-ROM and Scanner


F5=Bypass startup files    F8=Confirm each CONFIG.SYS line [N]
```

At this screen, you have two options:

1. You can type **1** and press **Enter**. This would cause DOS to execute the commands contained in the [cd_rom] section. Notice that the INCLUDE statement causes DOS to include all commands in the [base_setup] section, plus load your mouse and CD-ROM driver.
2. You can type **2** and press **Enter**. This would cause DOS to execute the commands contained in the [scan] section. In this case, the INCLUDE statement causes DOS to include all commands in the [windows] section, which, in turn, runs the [base_setup] commands and then loads the device driver for a scanner.

> ✔ **Note:** It's always a good idea to end a complex CONFIG.SYS file with a [common] block, as in the previous example. This allows application installation programs to append commands to your CONFIG.SYS file, if necessary.

This simple CONFIG.SYS file provides for some complex choices, all of which are presented to you before DOS begins its normal startup procedures. Adapting the procedures used in our sample file for your own system will let you set up a truly personalized PC environment.

There's one final startup feature, also new in MS-DOS 6.0, that we need to cover before we close out this chapter. It relates to the message at the bottom of the initial menu screen shown above, which I promised to explain.

Choices within Choices (Using the F5 and F8 Function Keys)

In the past, you had to be extremely careful when modifying the contents of CONFIG.SYS. If a command was entered incorrectly, or if you inadvertently used conflicting commands, your system could freeze during startup. This could be disastrous unless you had a floppy system disk available from which you could restart your PC successfully.

Now, however, MS-DOS 6.0 recognizes two function key commands that allow you to circumvent a troublesome CONFIG.SYS file, without resorting to a floppy system disk:

1. Pressing **F5** at the beginning of startup causes DOS to bypass CONFIG.SYS and AUTOEXEC.BAT and boot your computer as a "plain vanilla" PC; it takes you directly to the system prompt.
2. Pressing **F8** at startup causes DOS to pause each time it encounters a statement in CONFIG.SYS that involves loading programs or drivers into memory and prompt you as to how it should proceed. In essence, pressing F8 is like telling DOS to insert a question mark into any line within CONFIG.SYS that normally would accept the question mark symbol. (Review my explanation earlier in this chapter of how the question mark works in CONFIG.SYS.)

This ends our "tour de force" of MS-DOS 6.0. In these ten chapters you've seen the various MS-DOS 6.0 commands in action, some of which you'll use quite frequently; others you may never use at all. Still, understanding what DOS is and knowing how the various DOS commands work will help you feel much more comfortable and much less intimidated by that "black box" sitting on the desk before you. It's an incredibly powerful tool, one that, if used wisely, can help you be more productive. So, what are you waiting for? Get started. And have fun.

Part II

Command Reference

Command Reference

Introduction

Permit me, if you will, to put a new spin on an old axiom: "Familiarity breeds conventions." Throughout the previous chapters I've tried to keep our discussion of MS-DOS fairly "user-friendly" — conversational in both tone and content. There seems, however, to be an unwritten law that dictates that any comprehensive book about DOS must include a command reference. Unfortunately, DOS tends to be quite finicky about how you enter commands. For this reason, I'm forced to abandon the informal approach I've attempted to maintain in the preceding pages.

And so, in the pages that follow, you'll find information about virtually every command, statement, function and special utility supported by MS-DOS. This section emphasizes structure over style, form over flavor. And inherent in that structure are several conventions traditionally used to annotate DOS commands, conventions that I, in turn, incorporated into the command descriptions that follow. These include:

uppercase — Identifies specific commands and command switches used to initiate various DOS operations.

lowercase — Identifies variable names, for which you substitute values appropriate to the operation you want to perform. For example, the following annotation,

```
COPY source
```

indicates that the COPY command accepts a variable, *source*, for which you substitute the name of the file or group of files you want to copy to a new location.

brackets ([ ])   Identifies optional parameters or switches associated with a particular command. Items enclosed in brackets do not need to be entered for a DOS command to work properly.

pipes (|)   Indicates when multiple selections are available for a specific command, parameter, or switch. For example, the following annotation

```
ECHO [ON|OFF]
```

signifies that you can include either ON or OFF within an ECHO statement.

Understanding what the various DOS commands do, and how they work, provides you with amazing control over your PC environment. So, dig in. The following section may be somewhat dry, but I can assure you that it will be informative.

ANSI.SYS

ANSI.SYS is a device driver that, when used in CONFIG.SYS, lets you define functions that alter display graphics, provide extended control over cursor movement, or assign new functions to specified keys on your keyboard.

> ✓ **Note:** You can use either the DEVICE or DEVICEHIGH command to load the ANSI.SYS device driver from your CONFIG.SYS file.

Syntax

```
DEVICE=[drive:][path]ANSI.SYS [/X] [/K] [/R]
```

Parameters

`[drive:][path]`

Identifies the location of the ANSI.SYS file.

Switches

`/X`

Used to remap extended keys on a 101-key keyboard.

`/K`

Used to have ANSI.SYS treat a 101-key keyboard like an 84-key keyboard.

> ✓ **Note:** Including this switch when you load ANSI.SYS is similar to using the SWITCHES command with its /K switch. You must load ANSI.SYS with the /K switch if you rely on the SWITCHES=/K command.

`/R`

Adjusts line scrolling to improve readability when ANSI.SYS is used with screen-reading programs (programs designed to make computers more accessible to people with disabilities).

Structuring an ANSI Escape Sequence

Once you load ANSI.SYS, it allows you extensive control over your display and keyboard. Mastering all of the functions supported by ANSI.SYS, however, is no easy task. Your *MS-DOS 6.0 User's Guide* contains extensive information about the various ANSI sequences. For this reason, I'll only provide a couple of simple examples, here.

The following ANSI.SYS escape sequence remaps the F2 function key to display a directory listing whenever it is pressed by redefining the F2 key (0;60) as a string (the "dir" string) followed by the enter key (13p):

```
prompt $e[0;60;"dir";13p
```

The following ANSI.SYS escape sequence changes your default display to white text (37) on a blue background (44):

```
prompt $e[37;44m
```

Related Command

See the SWITCHES command for more information about modifying the operation of a 101-key keyboard.

APPEND

The APPEND command allows DOS to access data files as though they were located in the current directory. After a directory has been APPENDed to the current directory, DOS can search and find all of the files it contains without the file being explicitly referenced with its drive and path information — that is, without the drive and directory being included with the filename.

A familiar metaphor for how APPEND works is the call forwarding feature provided by many of today's phone systems. Just as call forwarding allows your phone to locate you when you're not at home, APPEND automatically lets DOS locate the data files stored in APPENDed directories without their location being spelled out.

The APPEND command, while similar, differs from the PATH command in one fundamental way. The APPEND command will search all specified directories for .HLP (help) files, .TXT (text) files, .DAT (data) files, .OVL (overlay) files, .BIN (binary) files, .DBF/.NDX (database/index) files, and virtually all other nonexecutable files. On the other hand, the PATH command only seeks out executable files with extensions of .COM (small executables), .EXE (complex executables), and .BAT (batch files) once their directories have been specified in the PATH command's parameter list.

Syntax

```
APPEND [[drive:]path[;...]] [ /X[:ON|:OFF] ] [/PATH[:ON|:OFF] ]
[ /E]
```

Parameter

[drive:]path

This parameter specifies the drive (if other than the current drive) and directory/subdirectory that you are APPENDing to the current directory. To specify multiple drives and paths, separate individual entries with a semicolon; for example, APPEND c:\;c:\sys;d:\dos. When used by itself, APPEND ; cancels the existing list of APPENDed directories. DOS will cease to search for files in the canceled directories.

;

When used by itself, the semicolon cancels the existing list of appended directories.

Switches

`/X[:ON|:OFF]`

The /X or X:ON switch includes the APPENDed directories in the PATH. As a result DOS will search the APPENDed directories as well as the directories specified by the PATH command for executable files(.EXE , .COM, and .BAT). When the switch is turned off /X:OFF, DOS will only look to the directories specified by the PATH command for executables, and the directories specified by the APPEND command will be used solely to search for data files. /X:ON is the default.

> ✓ **Note:** The default value for APPEND's /X switch is /X:OFF. When first starting your system, you can use the abbreviation /X to turn on the APPEND to path function. After that, you need to use the entire command (/X:ON and /X:OFF) to change the current state of APPEND.

`/PATH[:ON|:OFF]`

The /PATH:ON switch tells DOS to search the APPENDed directories for data files when an explicit path is specified but the file still cannot be found there. In the event that the path specified is incorrect but the files do exist in an APPENDed directory, the application will still have access to those files. On the other hand, if the switch is set to /PATH:OFF, DOS will search only the drives and directories specified as part of a file's path.

> ✓ **Note:** The default setting for the /PATH switch is /PATH:ON.

`/E`

Ordinarily, the APPEND command maintains a list of APPENDed directories internally; they can be viewed and modified only by using the APPEND command itself. The /E switch, in contrast, stores APPENDed directories to a variable, named APPEND, stored in the DOS Environmental Table. The list of APPENDed directories can bhen be modifed by both the APPEND command and the SET command. The /E switch can only be issued on the first call to the APPEND command.

> 🚫 **Caution:** Never use the APPEND command when working in Microsoft Windows or when running the Windows Setup program.

EXAMPLES

To let DOS treat files in a directory on drive C: called MYDATA as if they were in the current directory:

```
APPEND C:\MYDATA
```

To display the list of APPENDed directories, use the following sysntax:

```
APPEND
```

To cancel the existing list of APPENDed directories, use the following command:

```
APPEND ;
```

To APPEND the WS directory to the current path using the /X switch try the following command:

```
PATH=c:\;c:\dos;c:\apps          //WS is not in the path
APPEND c:\;c:\sys;c:\apps\ws /X  //adds WS to the path
ws                               //calls WS.EXE
APPEND /X:OFF                    //no longer can call WS.EXE
```

The following command demonstrates use of the /PATH:ON|OFF switch.

```
APPEND c:\apps /PATH:ON
TYPE c:\readme.txt    //DOS searches c:\apps for README.TXT,
                      //if README.TXT is not in the root
                      //directory C:\
```

The following command demonstrates use of the /E switch, which tells DOS to search the Environmental Table for directories to APPEND.

```
APPEND /E
APPEND c:\sys;c:\dos;c:\apps /X /PATH:ON
SET              //Lists the environmental table containing
                 //APPEND = C:\SYS;C:\DOS;C:\APPS
```

Related Commands

Use the PATH command to have DOS automatically find executable programs that are not located in the current directory.

For information about environment variables, see the SET command.

ATTRIB

ATTRIB displays or changes file attributes. It displays, sets, or removes the read-only, archive, system, and hidden attributes assigned to files or directories.

Syntax

```
ATTRIB [+R|-R] [+A|-A] [+S|-S] [+H|-H][[drive:][path]filename]
[/S]
```

Parameters

`[drive:][path]filename`

Specifies the location and name of the file(s) you want to process. *filename* recognizes the standard DOS wildcard characters, * and ?.

Switches

`+R`

Sets the read-only file attribute. Although you can call a read-only file into memory, DOS will not allow you to replace the copy of the file that is currently stored on your disk. Read-only files are sometimes referred to as protected files, because they cannot be modified using normal procedures.

`-R`

Assigns a file read/write status by clearing the read-only file attribute. After the read-only attribute is removed, DOS will allow you to save a modified copy of a file back to disk.

`+A`

Assigns the archive attribute to a file. DOS uses the archive attribute to identify files that have been modified since they were last backed up.

`-A`

Clears the archive file attribute.

`+S`

Assigns the system attribute to a file. System files are special files DOS recognizes as critical to its own operations and that are hidden from the user. Files whose system attribute has been set, for example, will not be listed by the DIR command.

`-S`

Clears the system file attribute.

+H

Assigns hidden status to a file or group of files. Hidden files do not show up in file listings displayed using the DOS DIR command.

-H

Removes the hidden-file attribute.

/S

Including the /S switch in an ATTRIB command tells DOS to change or display the attributes not only of files in the current directory, but also of files in any subdirectories it contains.

Examples

To prevent a file called MYDATA.DAT from being displayed in directory listings:

`ATTRIB MYDATA.DAT +H`

To display all attributes of all files in the current directory:

`ATTRIB`

To remove any special attributes assigned to all files in the current directory and its subdirectories:

`ATTRIB *.* -R -A -S -H /S`

Related Commands

For more information about copying files and directories, see the COPY and XCOPY commands.

BACKUP

The BACKUP command creates copies of files in archival format and stores them to a destination drive and path. The format of the archived files is specific to the BACKUP command; they are not readable through conventional means, and in order to process them, it is necessary to convert them back to their original format through the use of the RESTORE command. The BACKUP command can be used to back up the entire hard disk, groupings of directories or subdirectories, individual subdirectories, or just a few selected files in a directory. The destination could be a hard disk drive or a floppy disk. Backups made to floppies are the more common of the two. The DOS BACKUP command will format the destination disk if necessary, and in the case of BACKUPs made from the hard drive to floppies, DOS prompts the user for additional diskettes, if any are needed, while the BACKUP is in progress.

Syntax

```
BACKUP [drive1:][path][filename] [drive2:] [/S] [/M] [/A] [/D]
[/T] [/L:FILENAME] [/F:SIZE]
```

> ***Note:*** The BACKUP command is available in MS-DOS 5.0 and earlier versions. The new MSBACKUP command in MS-DOS 6.0 replaces the BACKUP command from previous DOS versions.

Parameters

`drive1:`

The drive letter (e.g., C:) of the disk containing the file(s) to be backed up.

`path`

The name of a directory or subdirectory containing the files you want to archive (back up); for example, \MYDATA.

`filename`

The name of any files you want to archive. This parameter can contain wildcards (* and ?).

`drive2:`

The target drive — that is, the drive containing the floppy disk or hard drive to which you want the specified files to be archived.

Switches

/S

Backs up the current directory and every subdirectory associated with the specified path. To back up all of the files located on hard disk C: to drive A:

`BACKUP C: A: /S`

The following command backs up files located only in the DOSFILES subdirectory on drive C: to a target disk in drive A:

`BACKUP C:\DOSFILES A:`

It's also possible to back up only individual files or groups of files within a subdirectory. The following command, for example, would back up to a target disk in drive A: all .COM files located in a subdirectory named DOSFILES on C:

`BACKUP C:\DOSFILES\*.COM A:`

/A

Appends any files being archived with the current BACKUP operation to those already stored on the backup disks. The absence of this switch results in all of the existing files on the backup disks being erased or overwritten before the new backup begins.

> *Note:* Archive files are stored in the target root directory if the BACKUP is made to a floppy. They are stored to a target directory \BACKUP (created by the BACKUP command) when the BACKUP is made to a hard disk drive.

/M

Backs up only those files that have been altered since the previous backup. DOS studies the archive attribute bit to determine if it is set. If the archive attribute bit is set (turned on), DOS will back up the file(s).

One popular use of the BACKUP command is to update archive disks by copying only files that have been changed since the last BACKUP operation was performed. The following command tells DOS to BACKUP to drive A: only those files in the MYDATA subdirectory that have been modified since the previous BACKUP was performed:

`BACKUP C:\MYDATA A: /M /A`

> *Caution:* Notice that I included the /A option in this example. This tells DOS to add the newly created archives to the target disk without erasing any previously backed up files it contains.

`/D:date`

Archives only those files that have been modified on or after the date specified in the *date* parameter.

`BACKUP C:\MYDATA A: /D:01-01-92 /A`

`/T:time`

Archives only those files that have been modified since the time specified in the *time* parameter.

`BACKUP C:\MYDATA B: /M /D:02-02-93 /T:12:30a`

> ✓ ***Note:*** The /M, /D, and /T switches bring a greater precision and add control to the BACKUP command, which ultimately saves space and time.

`/L:filename`

Creates a log file denoted by *filename*, in which the path and filename of each backed up file is stored, along with the date and time of the backup. The log also keeps a record of which backup disk(s) contains which archive file. The default filename, if *filename* is not provided along with the /L switch, is BACKUP.LOG.

`/F:size`

Causes the target disk in *drive2* to be formatted to the size specified in the *size* parameter, if necessary, prior to the actual archived file being written to the target disk. The chief advantage of the /F switch is its ability to format diskettes of every size without having to halt the BACKUP process, format the disks, and begin the BACKUP process all over again. This is a real help if you are unable to format disks prior to the BACKUP or if you run out of formatted disks during the BACKUP. Valid /F:*size* options include:

160	160K single-sided 5.25" disk
180	180K single-sided 5.25" disk
320	320K double-sided 5.25" disk
360	360K double-sided 5.25" disk
720	720K double-sided 3.5" disk
1.2	1.2 megabyte high-density 5.25" disk
1.44	1.44 megabyte high-density 3.5" disk
2.88	2.88 megabyte double-sided 3.5" disk

DOS versions 3.3 and higher allows you to format your target disks during a BACKUP operation. The following command, for example, would cause DOS to back up all files on drive C: to drive A:, formatting the target disk (A:) as it does so:

```
BACKUP C: A: /S /F:
```

This command formats the target disk to its default size. To specify a size different from the default, use the following command syntax:

```
BACKUP C: A: / S /F:720
```

Related Command

See the MSBACKUP command for information on how to back up files using MS-DOS 6.0.

BREAK

BREAK tells DOS whether to use or suspend extended CTRL+C checking. DOS allows you to use a BREAK command (CTRL+C) to interrupt a program or an activity — for example, a directory listing. By default, DOS checks whether you've pressed CTRL+C only when it is reading from the keyboard or writing to the screen or a printer. With BREAK set to ON, DOS scans for the CTRL+C command during additional operations, such as when it's reading or writing a disk file.

Syntax

BREAK [ON|OFF]

Parameters

ON|OFF

Turns extended CTRL+C checking on or off. The default setting for BREAK is OFF. Including the BREAK command in your CONFIG.SYS file will enable extended CTRL+C checking each time you start your system.

Examples

Use the following command to have DOS check for CTRL+C only when it is reading from the keyboard or writing to the screen or printer:

BREAK OFF

Use the following command to extend BREAK checking — that is, to specify that DOS should check for CTRL+C during disk read/write activities as well:

BREAK ON

To display the current BREAK setting:

BREAK

Including the following command in your CONFIG.SYS file will turn on extended BREAK checking each time you start your computer:

BREAK=ON

BUFFERS

The BUFFER command is used in the CONFIG.SYS file to reserve memory for a specified number of disk buffers when the computer is started. MS-DOS uses disk buffers in memory to temporarily store data during read and write operations. Each buffer requires 532 bytes of memory; DOS uses 16 bytes for housekeeping purposes and uses the remaining 512 bytes to store data. When an application makes a disk request, DOS searches through the buffers first to see if the information was read in previously and still resides in a buffer. Only if the information isn't in the buffer will DOS access the disk. If DOS has to access the disk, it will read 512 bytes of data into a buffer and then transfer the portion of the data that is currently being requested to the application. The same process occurs in reverse when writing information to a disk: DOS reads 512 bytes of data in to a buffer and then forwards the information to the disk.

Syntax

BUFFERS=n[,m]

Parameters

n

Specifies how many disk buffers you want to created at system startup. The value of *n* must be in the range of 1 through 99.

m

Specifies how many buffers you want created in a secondary buffer cache. The value of *m* must be in the range 0 through 8.

Default Settings

BUFFER is a configuration command that, if it is used, must be placed in the CONFIG.SYS file. If the BUFFER command isn't found in CONFIG.SYS, MS-DOS creates default buffer settings. The number of default buffers varies from system to system, depending on how much memory (RAM) is installed in your computer and the type of disk drive it contains. The following table lists the default BUFFER settings for various combinations:

Configuration	Buffers	Bytes (n)
128K of RAM/360K disk	2	—
128K of RAM/> 360K disk	3	—
128K to 255K of RAM	5	2672
256K to 511K of RAM	10	5328
512K to 640K of RAM	15	7984

If your computer has an 8086 processor, the type used in older PC and PC/XT machines, creating a secondary buffer cache with the (m) parameter can speed up certain disk operations. The default setting for the number of buffers in the secondary cache is 0 — that is, no secondary cache buffers.

If your computer has a processor faster than the 8086 — that is, if it is an AT, 386 or 486 system — you'll experience better results using DOS's SMARTDRV.EXE disk cache, rather than setting up secondary buffers with the (m) parameter.

✔ *Note:* If an invalid value is specified for *n* or *m*, DOS automatically creates the default number of buffers for your computer.

How MS-DOS Uses Buffers

Because MS-DOS uses disk buffers to temporarily store data during read and write operations, increasing the number of buffers available to DOS can speed up certain operations by allowing DOS to access data in memory rather than on slower disk drives.

But since each buffer requires approximately 532 bytes of memory, the more buffers you have, the less memory you have available for programs. In addition, when the number of buffers is set too high, DOS sometimes wastes time reading buffers when it might otherwise go straight to disk.

When you use the DOS=HIGH command to load DOS into the high memory area (HMA), DOS determines if there is enough room in the HMA to accept the specified (or default) number of buffers. If there is, DOS loads them into HMA, thus freeing more conventional RAM for your applications. If there will not be enough room to place your buffers in the HMA, DOS creates them in conventional memory.

Using BUFFERS with SMARTDRV.EXE

If you use the SMARTDRV.EXE disk cache, which stores megabytes of the most recently accessed disk sectors in extended memory, increasing the number of DOS buffers has little or no impact on system performance. To increase the amount of memory available to your applications when using SMARTDrive, you can do one of the following: you can either lower the number of BUFFERS or, alternately, eliminate the BUFFERS command completely from your CONFIG.SYS file.

Example

To create 20 disk buffers each time you start your computer, insert the following command into its CONFIG.SYS file:

```
BUFFERS=20
```

Related Command

The MEM command allows you to see how much memory DOS is using for any disk buffers it has created on your computer.

CALL

You use the CALL command within a batch file to call another batch file without causing the initial batch file — called the parent batch program — to stop. After the called batch file terminates, the parent program continues execution at the line following the CALL command.

Syntax

```
CALL [drive:][path]filename [batch-parameters]
```

Parameters

`[drive:][path]filename`

Specifies the location and name of the batch file you want to execute from within the parent program. The filename must have a .BAT extension.

`batch-parameters`

Specifies any command-line information required by the batch program.

> ✓ *Note:* Valid batch-parameters include almost any information that DOS normally allows you to pass to a batch program, including switches, filenames, the replaceable parameters %1 through %9, and environmental variables such as %baud%. The two major exceptions to this rule are pipes ("|") and redirection symbols ("<<", "<", ">"), which you cannot include as parameters in a CALL command.

Making a Recursive Call

It's possible to create a batch program that calls itself. If you do so, however, be sure to include an EXIT command somewhere within the batch file. Otherwise, the parent and child batch programs — which, in this case, are the same — will loop endlessly.

Examples

To run a batch file called MYBATCH.BAT from another batch program, include the following command in the parent batch program:

```
CALL MYBATCH
```

The following command passes two replaceable parameters to a batch file called MYBATCH.BAT when it is run from the parent program:

```
CALL MYBATCH %1 %2
```

CHCP

CHCP is one of the internationalization commands within MS-DOS. It allows you to display or change the code page, which is a number that represents the lookup table for a particular alternate character set. It contrasts with the other internationalization commands, like COUNTRY, which establishes country preferences (formats for displaying the date and time, for instance), and KEYB, which defines alternate keyboard layouts.

> *Note:* In order to be able to use a character set other than the one that DOS installs by default, you must first execute the NLSFUNC program. NLSFUNC loads country-specific character sets into memory.

Syntax

```
CHCP [nnn]
```

Parameter

This parameter specifies the number of the alternate character set to be used. The code number, and the character set it represents, is shown in the following table:

Page Number	International Character Set
437	United States
850	Multilingual (Latin I)
852	Slavic (Latin II)
860	Portugal
863	Canadian French
865	Norway/Denmark

Examples

To display the current code page, simply type the CHCP command with no parameters, as follows:

```
CHCP
```

For most computers manufactured for sale in the United States, DOS will respond by displaying the number 437. To display the current code page, it is not necessary for NLSFUNC to be executed previously.

Successfully defining and changing the code page requires the following steps:

1. Including a DEVICE=DISPLAY.SYS command in your CONFIG.SYS file.
2. Including the NLSFUNC command in the AUTOEXEC.BAT file to load country-specific information into memory.
3. Including the MODE CON CP PREP command in AUTOEXEC.BAT to load code page information.
4. Entering the CHCP *nnn* command either in the AUTOEXEC.BAT file or interactively at the DOS prompt to change the character set. The following command, for example, makes the French Canadian character set the current code page, assuming that it has already been loaded:

    ```
    CHCP 863
    ```

If *nnn* is not a valid code page, or if code page *nnn* has not been loaded, DOS displays the following error message:

```
Code page 902 not prepared for system
```

Related Commands

For further details on the commands that allow the international customization of DOS, see COUNTRY, DISPLAY, KEYB, MODE, and NLSFUNC.

CHDIR (CD)

CHDIR is used to display the name of the current directory or change to a different directory.

Syntax

CHDIR [drive:][path]|[..]

　or

CD [drive:][path]|[..]

Parameters

[drive:][path]

　Specifies the drive (if other than the current drive) and directory to which you want to change.

[..]

　This is a "shortcut" parameter used to change to the parent directory — that is, the directory immediately above the current directory in your directory tree or hierarchy.

Using the Current Directory from a Different Drive

DOS remembers the active directory for a drive, even when you switch to another drive. If, for example, you are working in the \MYDATA\BUDGET directory on drive D and you change to drive C without changing directories on drive D, you can copy files to and from the \MYDATA\BUDGET directory by specifying only the drive letter, D, without additional directory information.

Examples

To display the current drive letter and directory name, use either of the following commands:

CHDIR
CD

　To return to the root directory — that is, the top of the directory hierarchy for a drive — of the current drive, use one of the following commands:

CHDIR \
CD \

Either of the following commands changes your current directory to the directory named MYDATA:

```
CHDIR \MYDATA
CD \MYDATA
```

To change the current directory on drive D to \MYDATA\BUDGETS, use the following command:

```
CD D:\MYDATA\BUDGETS
```

If your current directory is \MYDATA, use the following command to change to the \MYDATA\BUDGETS directory:

```
CD BUDGETS
```

CHKDSK

This command creates and displays a status report for a disk and, optionally, fixes errors found on the disk. CHKDSK does not verify that the information contained within your files can be read accurately; rather, it reveals logical errors found in the MS-DOS filing system, which consists of the file allocation table and directories.

Syntax

```
CHKDSK [drive:][[path]filename] [/F] [/V]
```

Parameters

drive:

Specifies the drive that contains the disk on which you want to perform a CHKDSK operation.

[path]filename

Specifies the location and name of a file or set of files that you want CHKDSK to check for fragmentation.

> ✔ *Note:* You can use the DOS wildcards (* and ?) with a CHKDSK command to specify multiple files.

Switches

/F

Tells DOS to fix any errors it discovers on a disk during a CHKDSK operation.

> ✔ *Note:* Do not use the /F option when running CHKDSK from within other programs such as Microsoft Windows or the MS-DOS Task Swapper.

/V

Causes DOS to display the name of each file in every directory during a CHKDSK operation, in addition to displaying its usual status report.

Format of status reports

Each time you run CHKDSK, DOS displays a status report similar to the following:

```
Volume MYDISK         created 03-30-93 10:53p
Volume Serial Number is 1735-A60D
```

```
32548864 bytes total disk space
   81920 bytes in 3 hidden files
   75776 bytes in 35 directories
 8978432 bytes in 429 user files
    1024 bytes in bad sectors
23411712 bytes available on disk

    2048 bytes in each allocation unit
   15893 total allocation units on disk
   11432 available allocation units on disk

  647168 total bytes memory
  521168 bytes free
```

Fixing Disk Errors

CHKDSK only corrects disk errors if you specify the /F switch. When you use a CHKDSK /F command, CHKDSK will display a prompt similar to the following:

```
12 lost allocation units found in 4 chains.
Convert lost chains to files?
```

If you press Y, DOS saves each corrupted chain in a file within the root directory and assigns it a name using the format *FILEnnnn*.CHK, where *nnnn* is a four-digit number used to identify each lost chain. You can then use the TYPE command to examine these files and see if you need the data they contain.

Pressing N causes DOS to fix the disk — that is, eliminate the lost chains — but does not save the contents of the lost allocation units to archive files.

Using CHKDSK with Open Files

Do not use CHKDSK on open files. CHKDSK is designed to be used when the files on the disk are in an unchanging state — that is, when they are not open.

DOS does not always update immediately a file it's working on. If you run CHKDSK with the /F parameter while files are open, therefore, it may incorrectly interpret differences between the directory structure and the file allocation tables as errors. This can result in corruption or loss of data.

Also, never run CHKDSK /F from within another program such as Microsoft Windows or the MS-DOS Task Swapper.

Using CHKDSK with Assigned Drives and Networks

The CHKDSK command does not work on drives formed by the SUBST command. You cannot use CHKDSK to check a disk on a network drive.

Bad Disk Sectors

Bad sectors reported by CHKDSK were marked as "bad" when your disk was initially formatted. Because DOS automatically knows not to write files to bad sectors, they pose no danger to your data.

Saving a CHKDSK Status Report to a File

You can use the DOS redirect symbol (>) to save a CHKDSK status report to a disk file. When redirecting output to a disk file, you should not use the /F switch with the CHKDSK command.

Examples

The following command displays the status of the disk in the current drive:

```
CHKDSK
```

The following command displays the status of the disk currently in drive A and fixes any errors CHKDSK discovers:

```
CHKDSK A: /F
```

If DOS encounters any errors, it pauses and displays a message asking how you want to proceed. CHKDSK displays a report showing the status of the disk, once all work is completed.

The following command checks the disk currently in drive B and redirects the resulting report to a file named STATUS:

```
CHKDSK B: > STATUS
```

Because you should not include the /F parameter with CHKDSK when redirecting output, DOS won't repair any errors it encounters during this check. It does, however, include any errors it uncovers within the report file. After reviewing the contents of the STATUS file, you could run CHKDSK a second time, using the /F switch, to correct any errors CHKDSK discovered the first time.

The following command displays the status of the disk along with the names of files in C:\DOCS that do not occupy contiguous blocks:

```
CHKDSK C:\DOCS\*.*
```

Often, defragmenting a disk with large numbers of these noncontiguous files can significantly improve system performance.

CHOICE

You use the CHOICE command within a batch file to request user input. When used in a batch file, CHOICE displays a specified prompt, pauses for the user to choose from among a specified set of keys, and then returns an ERRORLEVEL parameter to the batch program, based on the user's choice. If the user presses an invalid key, the computer beeps.

Syntax

    CHOICE [/C[:]keys] [/N] [/S] [/T[:]c,nn] [text]

Parameters

    text
    "text"

Specifies the text you want displayed when CHOICE pauses and presents the user prompt. If no text is specified, CHOICE displays only the user prompt, providing no additional information about the current operation.

> ✓ *Note:* You only need to include quotation marks within your CHOICE text if you issue the command along with a switch character (/).

Switches

    /C[:]keys

Specifies allowable keys in the prompt. The list of allowable keys should not be separated by commas or spaces. When the specified keys are displayed as part of the prompt to the user, they are separated by commas, and appear within brackets ([ ]), followed by a question mark.

If you don't specify the /C switch to indicate specific keys, CHOICE uses YN (Yes/No) as the default. The colon (:) is optional.

    /N

Causes CHOICE to display only the message you created with the text parameter, not its own user prompt. Any keys specified with the /C switch are still valid when the /N switch is used, but the CHOICE command will simply not indicate to the user what keys are valid. If the /N switch is not used, any text parameter is displayed along with the list of valid keys specified by the /C switch. If neither /N nor *text* is specified, CHOICE will not display a prompt to the user.

/S

    Causes CHOICE to be case-sensitive. When the /S switch is not specified, CHOICE will accept either upper- or lowercase for any of the allowable keys specified with the /C switch.

/Tc,nn

    Tells CHOICE to pause for a specified number of seconds before defaulting to a specified key and continuing execution of the batch file. Use the following values to specify parameters for the /T switch:

c

    Specifies the character to default to after the number of seconds set by *nn*. The character must be in the set of choices specified with the /C switch.

nn

    The number of seconds you want CHOICE to pause execution of the batch file to wait for user input. This period can be from 0 to 99 seconds. Specifying 0 causes CHOICE to default immediately to the value specified with the *c* parameter.

ERRORLEVEL Parameters

CHOICE assigns sequential ERRORLEVEL values to any keys specified with the /C switch. The first key you assign returns a value of 1, the second a value of 2, the third a value of 3, and so on. If the user presses a key that is not among the keys you assigned, CHOICE sounds a warning beep.

    If CHOICE detects an error condition, it returns an ERRORLEVEL value of 255. If the user presses CTRL+BREAK or CTRL+C, CHOICE returns an ERRORLEVEL value of 0.

Example

The following program demonstrates the use of the CHOICE command to allow the user to select from one of three variations of the DIR command:

```
@ECHO OFF

CHOICE /C:ABC /N /T:A,15 "Press A -> DIR,  Press B ->DIR/P, Press C-> DIR /W   "

IF ERRORLEVEL 255 GOTO LABELERR

IF ERRORLEVEL 3 GOTO LABEL3

IF ERRORLEVEL 2 GOTO LABEL2

IF ERRORLEVEL 1 GOTO LABEL1
```

```
        IF ERRORLEVEL 0 GOTO LABELCTRL

:LABEL3
        DIR /W
        GOTO LABELX

:LABEL2
        DIR /P
        GOTO LABELX

:LABEL1
        DIR
        GOTO LABELX

:LABELCTRL
        ECHO YOU PRESSED CONTROL BREAK
        GOTO LABELX

:LABELERR
        ECHO AN ERROR CONDITION HAS BEEN DETECTED
        GOTO LABELX

:LABELX
        ECHO THIS IS THE LAST LINE OF THE PROGRAM
```

Related Command

You can use the returned ERRORLEVEL value in conjunction with an IF statement to initiate specific activities within a batch file.

CLS

CLS is used to clear the screen and display only the DOS command prompt and cursor.

> ✔ ***Note:*** After clearing the screen, CLS positions the cursor at the top-left corner of the display area.

Syntax

```
CLS
```

COMMAND

COMMAND starts a new instance of the MS-DOS command interpreter, COMMAND.COM.

Syntax

```
COMMAND [[drive:]path] [device] [/Cstring] [/E:nnnnn]
[/K:filename] [/P [/MSG]]
```

In your CONFIG.SYS file, use the following syntax:

```
SHELL=[[dos-drive:]dos-path]COMMAND.COM [[drive:]path][device]
[/E:nnnnn] [/P [/MSG]]
```

Parameters

`[drive:]path`

Specifies where the command interpreter is to look for the COMMAND.COM file when the transient part of the program needs to be reloaded. If the COMMAND.COM file is not located in your root directory, you must include this parameter when loading COMMAND.COM for the first time. DOS uses this parameter to set its COMSPEC environment variable.

`device`

Used to specify a different device for command input and output. (See the CTTY command for more information about how to use this parameter.)

`[dos-drive:]dos-path`

Specifies the location of COMMAND.COM.

Switches

`/C string`

When a /C string is specified, DOS immediately executes the command it contains and then exits back to the previous command environment. The space between /C and string is optional.

`/E:nnnnn`

You use this switch to create an environment size other than DOS's default value of 256. This switch specifies the new environment size in bytes, within the range 160 through 32768. DOS automatically rounds this number up to a multiple of 16 bytes.

```
/K filename
```

Runs the specified program or batch file before displaying the DOS system prompt. One popular use of this switch is for specifying a startup file other than C:AUTOEXEC.BAT when you open a DOS window in Windows. (To do this, use the Windows PIF editor to enter the /K switch in the Optional Parameters of the DOSPRMPT.PIF file.) Although you can use the /K switch in a SHELL command line within your CONFIG.SYS file, it is not recommended, as it can cause problems with applications and installation programs that make changes to your AUTOEXEC.BAT file.

✔ *Note:* The /K switch and the filename must be separated by a space.

```
/P
```

The /P switch makes the new copy of the command interpreter permanent. This prevents the EXIT command from stopping the command interpreter. You should only use the /P switch when a SHELL command is issued from within the CONFIG.SYS file. If you do not have a SHELL command in your CONFIG.SYS file, DOS automatically loads COMMAND.COM from the root directory as the permanent environment.

```
/MSG
```

This switch, which specifies that all error messages should be stored in memory, is useful only if you are running MS-DOS from floppy disks. See the extended discussion in "Using the /MSG Switch."

Limits on Environment Size

If *nnnnn* is less than 160 or greater than 32768, MS-DOS uses the default value of 256 bytes and displays the following message:

```
Running multiple command interpreters
```

Starting a new command interpreter causes MS-DOS to create a new command environment — in actuality, a copy of the parent environment. You can change the new environment without affecting the old one. The default size of the new environment is either 256 bytes or the size of the current environment rounded up to the next 16 bytes, whichever is larger. As used here, the current environment refers to the memory actually in use, not the environment size specified with the previous /E switch.

✔ *Note:* You can use the /E switch to override the default and specify a different size for the new environment.

MS-DOS loads the command interpreter in two parts. The resident part is always in memory. DOS loads the transient part of the command interpreter at the top of conventional memory.

> *Caution:* Some programs write over the transient part of COMMAND.COM when they run. Should this happen, the resident part must locate the COMMAND.COM file on disk to reload the transient part of the command interpreter. The COMSPEC environment variable tells DOS where to locate COMMAND.COM on your system.

> *Note:* If COMSPEC is set to a floppy disk drive, MS-DOS will prompt you to insert a disk that contains COMMAND.COM if it cannot find this file on the floppy disk currently in the specified drive.

If your CONFIG.SYS file includes a DOS=HIGH command to load DOS within the HMA, a portion of resident COMMAND.COM is also loaded into the HMA. Doing so makes more conventional memory available for programs.

Using the /MSG Switch

Usually, MS-DOS leaves many error messages in the COMMAND.COM file on the disk instead of using memory to store them. When MS-DOS needs to display one of these messages, MS-DOS retrieves the message from the disk containing COMMAND.COM.

If you are running MS-DOS from floppy disks instead of from a hard disk, MS-DOS cannot retrieve such error messages unless you have the disk containing COMMAND.COM in drive A. If this disk is not present, MS-DOS displays one of the following short messages instead of the full message:

```
Parse error
Extended error
```

You can make sure MS-DOS displays complete error messages by using the /MSG switch with COMMAND. This switch forces MS-DOS to keep these error messages in memory so that they are always available when needed.

Use the /MSG switch with COMMAND if you have a floppy disk system, unless you cannot afford to lose the memory used to store the error messages.

> *Note:* If you use the /MSG switch, you must also specify the /P switch.

Internal vs. External Commands

There are two types of DOS commands:

- internal DOS commands
- external DOS commands

The internal DOS commands are automatically loaded into RAM each time you turn on your PC. Consequently, they are available at any time and from anywhere on your system. External DOS commands, on the other hand, must be loaded into memory from disk before they can be executed.

As a rule, you will use the external DOS commands less frequently than their internal counterparts. For this reason, DOS does not automatically load them into RAM, thus preserving memory — the most valuable commodity installed on your PC — for your application programs.

COMMAND.COM is called a command processor because it processes any commands you enter at the keyboard. If a command can be carried out automatically by COMMAND.COM itself, it is considered an internal command. External DOS commands must be loaded into memory from a disk file and executed just like other programs.

COMMAND.COM automatically implements the following DOS commands, which correspond to the internal DOS commands:

BREAK	ECHO	REM
CALL	EXIT	RENAME (REN)
CHCP	FOR	RMDIR (RD)
CHDIR (CD)	GOTO	SET
CLS	IF	SHIFT
COPY	LOADHIGH (LH)	TIME
CTTY	MKDIR (MD)	TYPE
DATE	PATH	VER
DEL (ERASE)	PAUSE	VERIFY
DIR	PROMPT	VOL

Examples

The following command specifies that DOS is to start a new command interpreter, run a batch file named NEWBAT.BAT, and then return to the parent command interpreter:

```
COMMAND /C NEWBAT.BAT
```

Including the following line in your CONFIG.SYS file accomplishes several things:

```
SHELL=C:\DOS\COMMAND.COM C:\DOS\ /E:1024
```

First, it specifies that COMMAND.COM is located in the DOS directory on drive C. It then directs MS-DOS to set the COMSPEC environment variable to C:\DOS\COMMAND.COM. Finally, this line increases the COMMAND environment from its default size of 256 bytes to 1024 bytes.

> ✔ ***Note:*** Increasing the size of the COMMAND environment is extremely useful if you load several device drivers into DOS at system startup.

COPY

This command copies one or more files to another location. It also can be used to combine files.

Syntax

    COPY [/A|/B] [drive1:]path1 [/A|/B] [/A|/B] [drive2][path2] [/V]

Parameters

drive1

   The drive the files are being copied from.

path1

   The complete filename, including directory path, of the file(s) being copied.

> ✓ **Note:** COPY accepts the DOS wildcard characters, * and ?.

drive2:

   The drive the files are being copied to.

path2

   The directory path and/or filename the file(s) are being copied to.

Switches

/A

   Used to locate an end-of-file marker when copying ASCII files, then terminates the COPY operation once this end-of-file marker is encountered.

/B

   Identifies a non-ASCII (binary) file transfer and tells DOS to read and COPY a number of bytes corresponding to the size of the file being copied.

/V

   Specifies that DOS should verify that the sectors written to the target disk are recorded properly.

Copying to and from Devices

You can substitute a device name for one or more occurrences of the source (*drive1:path1*) or destination (*drive2:path2*).

Using or Omitting the /B Switch when Copying to a Device

When the destination (*drive2:path2*) is a device — for example, COM1 or LPT1 — the /B switch causes MS-DOS to copy data to the device in binary mode. In binary mode, all characters (including special characters such as CTRL+C, CTRL+S, CTRL+Z, carriage returns, and the like) are copied to the device as data. Omitting the /B switch causes MS-DOS to copy data to the device in ASCII mode. In ASCII mode, special characters like those listed above may cause DOS to take special action during the copying process.

Using the Default Destination File

You do not have to specify a destination file. If no destination is specified, MS-DOS creates a copy of the source file using its original name, creation date, and creation time, placing the new copy in the current directory on the current drive.

✔ ***Note:*** You cannot copy a source file in the current directory to the current directory without specifying a different name. Attempting to do this causes DOS to display the following error message:

```
File cannot be copied onto itself
0 File(s) copied
```

Combining Multiple Files with the COPY Command

You can COPY more than one source file by separating entries with a plus sign (+). When used in this manner, COPY combines the specified files into a single, new file.

Another way to combine multiple files into a single file using the COPY command is with wildcards. Using wildcards in the *path1* parameter but specifying a single filename in *path2* causes COPY to combine all files matching the *path1* parameter into a single file, using the filename specified in *path2*.

Copying Files in Subdirectories

To copy all of a directory's files and subdirectories, use the XCOPY command.

Copying Zero-Length Files

COPY does not copy files that are 0 bytes long. Use XCOPY to copy these files.

Examples

The following command copies a file and ensures that an end-of-file character is at the end of the copied file:

COPY MEMO.DOC LETTER.DOC /A

To copy a file named BUDGET93.DAT from the current drive and directory to an existing directory named BUDGETS that is located on drive C, type the following command:

COPY BUDGET93.DAT C:\BUDGETS

> *Caution:* If the BUDGETS directory doesn't exist, DOS copies the file BUDGET93.DAT into a file named BUDGETS that is located in the root directory on the disk in drive C.

The following command copies several files into one file. You may list any number of files as source parameters on the COPY command line. Just separate filenames with a plus sign (+) and specify a filename for the resulting combined file, as the following example shows:

COPY BUDGET89.DAT + BUDGET90.DAT + BUDGET91.DAT BUDGETS.HLD

Separating the source files with a plus sign (+) tells DOS to combine the files named BUDGET89.DAT, BUDGET90.DAT, and BUDGET91.DAT from the current drive and directory into a single file named BUDGETS.HLD, also in the current directory on the current drive.

The following example demonstrates how to use wildcards to combine several files into one:

COPY *.TXT MULTIPLE.DOC

This command combines all files that have the extension .TXT in the current directory on the current drive into one file named MULTIPLE.DOC, also in the current directory on the current drive.

As the following command demonstrates, you can also use the COPY command to copy any text you type at the keyboard into a file:

COPY CON AUTOEXEC.NEW

After you type this command and press ENTER, the cursor advances one line, and waits for you to type the lines that will compose the AUTOEXEC.NEW file. MS-DOS copies everything you type to the file AUTOEXEC.NEW. After entering the contents of this file, pressing CTRL+Z or the F6 function key terminates the COPY operation.

The following command copies any information entered at the keyboard to a printer connected to LPT1:

```
COPY CON LPT1
```

Related Command

For information about copying directories and subdirectories, see the XCOPY command.

COUNTRY

This command allows you to tell MS-DOS that you want to use international time, dates, currency, case conversions, and decimal separators. The COUNTRY command configures DOS to recognize the character set and punctuation conventions observed when using one of the supported languages.

Syntax

COUNTRY=xxx[,[yyy][,[drive:][path]filename]]

Parameters

xxx

Specifies the country code.

yyy

Specifies the code page for the country. The code page determines the particular character set used for the country.

[drive:][path]filename

Specifies the location and name of the file containing country information.

By default, DOS uses annotation common to the United States. Entering the appropriate COUNTRY command in your CONFIG.SYS file lets you change this default setting to that of another country.

The following table lists each country or language supported by DOS. This table also contains the code pages you can use with each country code. For example, if you use country code 055, you can use only code page 850 or 437 for the *yyy* parameter. The default code page is the first of the two code pages listed for each country or language.

Country or Language	Country Code	Code Pages
Belgium	032	850, 437
Brazil	055	850, 437
Canadian-French	002	863, 850
Czechoslovakia	042	852, 850
Denmark	045	850, 865
Finland	358	850, 437
France	033	850, 437
Germany	049	850, 437
Hungary	036	852, 850

International English	061	437, 850
Italy	039	850, 437
Latin America	003	850, 437
Netherlands	031	850, 437
Norway	047	850, 865
Poland	048	852, 850
Portugal	351	850, 860
Spain	034	850, 437
Sweden	046	850, 437
Switzerland	041	850, 437
United Kingdom	044	437, 850
United States	001	437, 850
Yugoslavia	038	852, 850

The country code lets you specify the time and date formats that will be used by the several MS-DOS commands, including BACKUP, DATE, RESTORE, and TIME. The following table lists the date and time formats specified by each country code. Within this table, the Date Format column shows how DOS displays the date January 23, 1991; the Time Format column shows how DOS displays 5:35 P.M., including seconds and hundredths of a second values of 0.

Country or Language	Country Code	Date Format	Time Format
Belgium	032	23/01/1991	17:35:00
Brazil	055	23/01/1991	17:35:00
Canadian-French	002	1991-01-23	17:35:00
Czechoslovakia	042	1991-01-23	17:35:00
Denmark	045	23-01-1991	17.35.00
Finland	358	23.01.1991	17.35.00
France	033	23.01.1991	17:35:00
Germany	049	23.01.1991	17:35:00
Hungary	036	1991-01-23	17:35:00
International English	061	23-01-1991	5:35:00.00p
Italy	039	23/01/1991	17.35.00
Latin America	003	23/01/1991	5:35:00.0p
Netherlands	031	23-01-1991	17:35:00
Norway	047	23.01.1991	17:35:00
Poland	048	1991-01-23	17:35:00
Portugal	351	23-01-1991	17:35:00

Spain	034	23/01/1991	17:35:00
Sweden	046	1991-01-23	17.35.00
Switzerland	041	23.01.1991	17,35,00
United Kingdom	044	23/01/1991	17:35:00.00
United States	001	01-23-1991	5:35:00p
Yugoslavia	038	1991-01-23	17:35:00

Example

Adding the following command to your CONFIG.SYS file converts international currency, time, date, and case to German conventions:

```
COUNTRY=049
```

Related Commands

For information about changing characters and their arrangement on your keyboard, see the KEYB command, or see "Customizing for International Use" in the *MS-DOS User's Guide*.

For information about preparing and selecting code pages, see the MODE (set device code pages) command.

For information about loading country-specific information, see the NLSFUNC command.

For information about defining and changing code pages, see the CHCP command.

CTTY

You use the CTTY command, which changes the terminal device that controls your computer, if you want to use something other than the keyboard and display monitor to manage the input/output of your system.

Syntax

`CTTY device`

Parameter

`device`

Specifies the alternative device you want to use to enter MS-DOS commands. Valid values for the device parameter are PRN, LPT1, LPT2, LPT3, CON, AUX, COM1, COM2, COM3, and COM4.

Setting Up the Serial Port for CTTY

If you use the CTTY command to change the input device to a serial port, you must first use the MODE command to specify the appropriate baud rate, parity, bits, and stop bit for the serial port.

Using CTTY with Programs that Do Not Use MS-DOS to Control I/O

The CTTY command affects only programs that use MS-DOS for reading keyboard input and displaying output. Many programs directly control input or output, bypassing MS-DOS for such operations. These programs will not recognize I/O redirected with the CTTY command.

Examples

Use the following command to redirect control of all input and output from the current device (usually your computer monitor and keyboard) to the COM1 port:

`CTTY COM1`

In this example, a remote terminal device connected to the AUX port controls input and output for your system.

The following command transfers redirected input and output back to the monitor and keyboard:

`CTTY CON`

DATE

DATE is used to view or reset the system date recorded in your computer.

Syntax

    DATE [mm-dd-yy]

Parameter

mm-dd-yy

The date you want recorded in your system. Values for day (dd), month (mm), and year (yy) must be separated by periods (.), hyphens (-), or slash marks (/).

> ✓ *Note:* The date format you should use depends on the COUNTRY setting specified in your CONFIG.SYS file. The following list shows the valid values for the month, day, and year portions of the mm-dd-yy parameter:
>
> | | |
> |---|---|
> | mm | 1 through 12 |
> | dd | 1 through 31 |
> | yy | 80 through 99 or 1980 through 2099 |

Adjusting for Days in a Month

DOS is programmed to automatically recognize the number of days in each month.

Using DATE in Your AUTOEXEC.BAT File

If your system startup procedures include an AUTOEXEC.BAT file, DOS will not automatically display the DATE input prompt. If you want users to record a date each time the computer is started or rebooted, you must include the DATE command (with no parameter) in your AUTOEXEC.BAT file.

Related Commands

See the TIME command for information about changing the current time setting.

See the COUNTRY command for more information on changing the date format used by your computer.

DBLSPACE

DBLSPACE compresses hard disks and floppy disks, effectively doubling the storage capacity of your disks. Once installed, DBLSPACE automatically compresses files as they are stored and decompresses them when they are needed. It accomplishes this feat by removing superfluous information such as spaces and words or characters that recur in a file and replacing them with a single representative character.

DBLSPACE is a utility program that can be run interactively, or it can be executed straight from the command line using parameters and switches. Since the syntax of DBLSPACE can become quite complicated, you should probably focus on running this utility interactively to set up and maintain your compressed disk. In fact, I recommend this so strongly that I will not discuss using DBLSPACE with its command line switches here. For more information on DBLSPACE, see Chapter 10, "Where No DOS Has Gone Before."

When you run DBLSPACE for the first time, it offers you two setup options. Express Setup compresses the existing files and automatically assigns default DBLSPACE settings for your system. Custom Setup, as may have guessed, gives you greater control over your DBLSPACE configuration. You determine where and how your files are stored. In either case, DBLSPACE will create a DEVICE=DBLSPACE.SYS command in your CONFIG.SYS file.

On the other hand, running the DBLSPACE utility when you have already created a compressed drive opens a full-screen program that presents you with a menu containing a number of options. You can get information about your current DLBSPACE drives, change assorted drive attributes (such as the compression ratio or the size of the logical drive), or perform basic disk operations on the compressed drives (such as defragmenting a compressed drive). DBLSPACE also comes with an extensive on-line help facility that makes it easy to use.

DEBUG

This command starts DEBUG, a program that allows you to test and debug executable files. DEBUG serves as a basic machine language monitor.

Syntax

    DEBUG [[drive:][path]filename [testfile-parameters]]

Parameters

    [drive:][path]filename

Specifies the location and name of the executable file you want to test.

    testfile-parameters

Specifies any command-line information required by the executable file you want to test.

DEBUG Commands

DEBUG recognizes the following commands:

?	Displays a list of valid DEBUG commands.
A	Assembles 8086/8087/8088 mnemonics.
C	Compares two portions of memory.
D	Displays the contents of a portion of memory.
E	Enters data into memory starting at a specified address.
F	Fills a range of memory with specified values.
G	Runs the executable file that is in memory.
H	Performs hexadecimal arithmetic.
I	Displays a one-byte value from a specified port.
L	Loads the contents of a file or disk sectors into memory.
M	Copies the contents of a block of memory.
N	Specifies a filename for an L or W command; alternately, specifies the parameters for the file you are testing.
O	Sends a one-byte value to an output port.
P	Executes a loop, a repeated string instruction, a software interrupt, or a subroutine.

Q	Stops the current DEBUG session.
R	Displays or alters the contents of one or more registers.
S	Searches a portion of memory for a specified pattern of one or more byte values.
T	Causes DEBUG to execute a single instruction, after which it displays the contents of all registers, the status of all flags, and the decoded form of the instruction to be executed next.
U	Disassembles bytes and displays the corresponding source statements.
W	Writes the file being tested to a disk.
XA	Allocates expanded memory.
XD	Deallocates expanded memory.
XM	Maps expanded memory pages.
XS	Displays the status of expanded memory.

Caution: As the previous command list suggests, DEBUG is a sophisticated program that provides direct access to the "inner workings" of a computer's memory, BIOS, and other highly technical areas. It should only be used, therefore, if you know exactly what you are doing or, alternately, under the direct supervision of someone who understands what DEBUG is and how it works. With these qualifications, if you are interested in exploring DEBUG, read *Dan Gookin's Guide to Underground DOS 6.0*, also published by Bantam.

DEFRAG

The DEFRAG command is used to reorganize fragmented files into contiguous sectors and clusters on the hard disk, thereby improving system performance. A file is considered fragmented when sections of the file are on different tracks and sectors, and a head seek is required in order to retrieve or store the file.

MS-DOS stores files in contiguous sectors when they are written to a newly formatted disk, and leaves no empty spaces between files. The files are written to the outer sectors first, moving inward towards the inner tracks as each sector is filled. After being initially written, the disk files tend to increase and decrease as they are used. When a file's size is increased, DOS writes as much of the file as possible to the location from which it was retrieved; the balance is stored to an empty sector located nearest the outer rim of the disk. If a file, located on one of the inner tracks, is erased from the hard disk, and a file adjacent to where the erased file previously resided is increased in size, DOS won't write the new file information to the now empty neighboring sector. It will first check the outer rim and store the new data there. Thus we have a disk with empty spaces between files, and files that are not stored in contiguous sectors. The performance of the disk is slowed by constant head seeks to retrieve and store portions of these files. The DEFRAG command temporarily redresses this problem.

Syntax

```
DEFRAG [drive:] [/F] [/S[:]order] [/B] [/SKIPHIGH] [/LCD|BW|G0] [/H]
DEFRAG [drive:] [/U] [/B] [/SKIPHIGH] [/LCD|BW|G0] [/H]
```

Parameter

`drive:`

Specifies the drive that contains the disk you want to optimize.

Switches

`/F`

Defragments files and reorganizes a disk so that no empty spaces exist between the files it contains.

`/U`

Defragments the specified files but does not reorganize the disk to eliminate any empty spaces that exist between the files it contains.

`/S[:]`

Specifies an order for how you want files sorted in their directories.

> ✔ **Note:** If you omit this switch, DEFRAG uses the current order on the disk. The colon (:) is optional.

The following list describes the various parameters you can use when sorting files. In some cases, it's possible to combine multiple sort parameters. When doing so, do not use spaces to separate multiple parameters.

N	Sort files in alphabetic order by name.
N-	Sort files in reverse alphabetic order by name (Z through A).
E	Sort files in alphabetic order by extension.
E-	Sort files in reverse alphabetic order by extension (Z through A).
D	Sort files by date and time, earliest first.
D-	Sort files by date and time, latest first.
S	Sort files by size, smallest first.
S-	Sort files by size, largest first.

`/B`

Use this switch to have DOS restart your computer after the specified files have been reorganized and defragmented.

`/SKIPHIGH`

Loads DEFRAG into conventional memory, rather than upper memory. DOS automatically loads DEFRAG into upper memory, if available.

`/LCD`

Runs DEFRAG on an LCD monitor or emulates an LCD color scheme.

`/BW`

Runs DEFRAG in black-and-white mode.

`/G0`

The default mode for running DEFRAG is a graphics-based mode. The /G0 switch changes DEFRAG from a graphics-based display using character-based symbols for boxes, disk icons, etc., to nongraphics utilizing low-bit characters. /G0 also disables the graphic mouse, displaying the pointer as a block instead of an arrow.

`/H`

The /H switch allows you to defragment and move hidden/system files. New to DOS with the release of DOS 6.0 is the ability to store system files on sectors other than the first sectors of the disk, thus further reducing the chances of defragmenting hidden/system files.

DEFRAG vs. CHKDSK

Information reported by DEFRAG differs from information that CHKDSK reports. DEFRAG reports hidden and user files as a single number; CHKDSK reports figures for each. Also, DEFRAG counts the root as a directory; CHKDSK does not. Finally, DEFRAG does not include a disk's volume label as a file; CHKDSK does.

Using DEFRAG with FASTOPEN

If you run the FASTOPEN.EXE program to speed up disk access, you should always include the /B switch with a DEFRAG command. This causes DOS to restart your computer after any files are reorganized with DEFRAG.

> *Caution:* Never run DEFRAG from within another program, such as Microsoft Windows or the DOS Shell. Doing so may result in lost data.

DEFRAG Exit Codes

DEFRAG uses a series of error codes to inform you of its progress or, alternately, any complications it encounters during a DEFRAG operation. The following list describes the meaning of the various DEFRAG codes:

0	The defragmentation was successful.
1	An internal error occurred.
2	The disk contained no free clusters. (DEFRAG requires at least 1 free cluster to operate successfully.)
3	The user pressed CTRL+C to stop the process.
4	A general error occurred.
5	DEFRAG encountered an error while reading a cluster.
6	DEFRAG encountered an error while writing a cluster.
7	An allocation error occurred. To correct the error, use the CHKDSK command with the /F switch.
8	A memory error occurred.
9	There was insufficient memory to defragment the disk.

> ✔ ***Note:*** You can use an ERRORLEVEL command in conjunction with IF commands within a batch file to process the error codes returned by DEFRAG.

Example

The following command will load DEFRAG into conventional memory, defragment all files on drive C — removing any spaces between files for optimum performance — and then sort these files, by extension, in ascending alphabetical order.

```
DEFRAG C: /F /SE /SKIPHIGH
```

DEL (Erase)

You use DEL to delete (erase) specified files.

Syntax

```
DEL [drive:][path]filename [/P]
ERASE [drive:][path]filename [/P]
```

Parameter

`[drive:][path]filename`

Specifies the location and name of the file or set of files you want to delete.

Switch

`/P`

Prompts you for confirmation before deleting the specified file.

Deleting More Than One File at a Time

To delete all the files in a directory, enter the DEL command using the [drive:]path parameter, with no individual filenames. DEL supports the DOS wildcards (* and ?). Wildcards can be used to delete multiple files in a single DEL operation, as shown in the following example:

```
del *.*
```

DEL displays the following prompt:

```
All files in directory will be deleted! Are you sure (Y/N)?
```

Press Y and then ENTER to erase all files in the current directory. To cancel the DEL command, press N and then ENTER.

> *Caution:* Use wildcards in a DEL command carefully. A good practice is to issue a DIR command first, using the desired wildcards, to verify that only the files you want will be affected.

Using the /P Switch

Including the /P switch causes DEL to display the following prompt for each file before deleting it:

```
filename, Delete (Y/N)?
```

Pressing Y confirms that you want this file deleted. If you press N, DOS cancels the DEL command for the current file. DOS then displays the name of the next file, if you requested a multiple-file DEL operation.

> ✔ ***Note:*** Pressing CTRL+C at this prompt terminates the DEL command and returns you to the DOS system prompt.

> 🚫 ***Caution:*** Although DOS provides an UNDELETE command, it is reliable only if no subsequent disk activities have not modified any of the disk clusters that contained a file. Therefore, if you ever accidentally delete a file that you want to keep, you should stop what you are doing and immediately use the UNDELETE command to retrieve it.

Examples

The following command will delete all files with an extension of .BAK in the DOCUMENT directory on drive C:

```
DEL C:\DOCUMENT\*.BAK
```

Either of the two following commands will delete all the files in a directory named HOLD on drive D:

```
DEL D:\HOLD
DEL D:\HOLD\*.*
```

Related Commands

See the UNDELETE command for information about retrieving a deleted file.
See the RMDIR command for information about removing a directory.

DELOLDOS

Deletes the OLD_DOS directory. The OLD_DOS directory is created during the installation of the upgrade to DOS 6.0. It stores all of the files necessary to revert to your old DOS version. Once you've used the DELOLDOS command, you won't be able to use the UNINSTALL utility to return you to your previous version of DOS.

Syntax

```
DELOLDOS /Y
```

Switch

/Y

Instructs the DELOLDOS command not to prompt you for verification before deleting the OLD_DOS directory.

> ✔ *Note:* In order for the DELOLDOS command to run you need to be in the directory above the OLD_DOS directory.

Example

The following command deletes the OLD_DOS directory and its files:

```
DELOLDOS /Y
```

Related Commands

For information on deleting files, see the DEL and ERASE commands.

For information on deleting directories, see the RMDIR (RD) and DELTREE commands.

DELTREE

Deletes a parent directory and all of the files and subdirectories contained within it. The DELTREE command is a combination of the DEL, ERASE, and RMDIR(RD) commands.

Syntax

```
DELTREE [/Y] [drive:]path
```

Parameter

`drive:path`

　Specifies the name and location of the directory you want to delete. If the directory is a parent directory, not only will the directory and its file(s) be deleted, but all child subdirectories and their files will also be deleted.

Switch

`/Y`

　DELTREE deletes the directory without prompting for confirmation when the /Y switch is included. Otherwise, DELTREE displays the following message:

```
Delete directory "directory" and all of its subdirectories? (y/n)
```

> *Caution:* Files deleted using the DELTREE command can't be retrieved using the UNDELETE command.

Example

In the following example, the TREE command is used to display the directory tree for the MYTAXES\92TAXES directory, and the DELTREE command deletes MYTAXES and all of its subdirectories, including 92TAXES.

```
TREE \MYTAXES\92TAXES
DELTREE /Y \MYTAXES
```

DEVICE

DEVICE is used to load device drivers into memory during system startup.

Syntax

    DEVICE=[drive:][path]filename [dd-parameters]

Parameters

[drive:][path]filename

Specifies the location and name of the device driver you want to load.

[dd-parameters]

Used to pass on to DEVICE any command-line information required by the device driver being loaded.

Using Standard Device Drivers

MS-DOS provides a number of standard installable device drivers. These include:

ANSI.SYS	EMM386.EXE	POWER.EXE
DISPLAY.SYS	HIMEM.SYS	RAMDRIVE.SYS
DRIVER.SYS	INTERLNK.EXE	SETVER.EXE
DBLSPACE.SYS	MSCDEX.EXE	SMARTDRV.EXE
EGA.SYS		

> *Caution:* The files COUNTRY.SYS and KEYBOARD.SYS, although they end with the SYS extension, are not device drivers. Rather, they are data files used when you issue the COUNTRY or KEYB command, respectively. Should you attempt to load either of these files with the DEVICE command, your system will halt and you will not be able to restart MS-DOS.

Installing Device Drivers for Other Products

Manufacturers of mice, scanners, CD-ROM drives and many other devices include device-driver software with their products. To install a third-party device driver, you'll need to specify its location and name on a DEVICE command line within your CONFIG.SYS file.

Installing a Third-Party Console Driver

Some consoles (display and keyboard combinations) require their own device drivers. If you use one of these third-party console drivers in conjunction with DOS's own DISPLAY.SYS driver, the third-party device driver must be installed first. If you reverse this order — that is, loading DISPLAY.SYS first — loading the third-party device driver may disable the already installed copy of DISPLAY.SYS.

The previous scenario is only one example of when multiple device drivers must be installed in a specific order. DOS's own EMM386.EXE memory manager, for instance, requires HIMEM.SYS to work properly. The line loading HIMEM.SYS must precede the EMM386 command in your CONFIG.SYS file. It's always a good idea to read any instructions accompanying a device driver carefully before inserting its command line in CONFIG.SYS.

Example

The following command loads the DOS ANSI device driver, which lets you use ANSI escape sequences to control your screen and keyboard:

```
DEVICE=C:\DOS\ANSI.SYS
```

✔ ***Note:*** This command assumes that the ANSI.SYS file is located in the DOS directory of drive C.

Related Commands

For information about loading device drivers into the upper memory area, see the DEVICEHIGH command.

For information about loading COUNTRY.SYS, see the COUNTRY command.
For information about loading KEYBOARD.SYS, see the KEYB command.

DEVICEHIGH

You use this command, in conjunction with the DOS=UMB statement, to load device drivers into the upper memory area. Doing so frees additional conventional RAM for other programs.

> ✔ *Note:* If no upper memory is available, the DEVICEHIGH command operates identically to the DEVICE command and automatically loads the specified device driver into conventional RAM.

Syntax

```
DEVICEHIGH [drive:][path]filename [dd-parameters]
```

The following command syntax allows you to specify the region(s) of upper memory into which you want a device driver loaded:

```
DEVICEHIGH= [/L:region1[,minsize1][;region2[,minsize2]...]
[/S]] [drive:][path]filename [dd-parameters]
```

Parameters

[drive:][path]filename

Specifies the location and name of the device driver you want to load into the upper memory area.

[dd-parameters]

Used to pass on to DEVICEHIGH any command-line information required by the device driver being loaded.

Switches

/L:region1[,minsize1][;region2[,minsize2]...]

This switch lets you force DOS to load a device driver into one or more specific regions of memory. The optional *region* and *minsize* parameters are used to identify the upper memory block (UMB) region you want a device to occupy and, when appropriate, the minimum amount of memory within this UMB you want DOS to set aside for that device.

/S

Shrinks the UMB to its minimum size while the driver is loading.

DEVICEHIGH Tips and Techniques

By default, MS-DOS loads a device driver into the largest upper memory block (UMB) available, while making all other UMBs available for the driver's use. Using the /L switch to load the device driver into a specific region of memory or to specify which region(s) you want to make available to a specific driver can help you use your system's RAM more efficiently. Including a region number after the /L switch forces DOS to load that particular driver into the largest block in the specified region.

Certain device drivers use more than one area of memory. For these drivers, you can specify multiple regions by separating the individual UMB numbers with a semicolon (;).

As a rule, DOS loads a device driver into the specified region only if that region contains a UMB larger than the driver's load size. The required size usually corresponds to size of the executable program file. Some drivers require additional memory while running beyond that used to load them initially. When this is the case, the *minsize* parameter allows you to make certain that a driver will not be loaded into a UMB that is too small for it to function in properly. Specifying a *minsize* value causes DOS to load the driver into that region only if it contains a UMB that is larger than both the driver's load size and the *minsize* value.

Including the /S switch in a DEVICEHIGH statement allows you to make the most efficient use of memory. First, use DOS's MemMaker utility to analyze a device driver's precise memory requirements and determine whether the /S switch is compatible with that driver. Because the /S switch affects only UMBs for which a minimum size was specified, it requires that you include the /L switch in a DEVICEHIGH statement.

Using the DOS=UMB Command

If you want to use the DEVICEHIGH command, you'll need to include a DOS=UMB command in your CONFIG.SYS file. If the UMB parameter is not specified, the DEVICEHIGH command functions identically to the DEVICE command in that it loads all device drivers into conventional memory.

Installing HIMEM.SYS and a UMB Provider

DEVICEHIGH requires extended memory. If extended memory exists, first use the DEVICE command once to install DOS's HIMEM.SYS device driver. You can then use DEVICE to install an upper memory block (UMB) provider, if your system requires one. Computers with an 80386 or 80486 processor can use DOS's EMM386.EXE as the UMB provider.

> ✓ **Note:** The HIMEM.SYS and UMB provider must be loaded before the first DEVICEHIGH command in your CONFIG.SYS file.

Examples

Including the following commands in your CONFIG.SYS file causes MS-DOS to load a device driver named NEWDRIV.SYS into the upper memory area of an 80386 computer:

```
DEVICE=C:\DOS\HIMEM.SYS
DEVICE=C:\DOS\EMM386.EXE RAM
DEVICEHIGH=NEWDRIV.SYS DOS=UMB
```

Including the following command in your CONFIG.SYS file causes MS-DOS to load a mouse driver (MOUSE.SYS) into UMB 2 within the upper memory area:

```
DEVICEHIGH=/L:2 MOUSE.SYS
```

You can use the following command to load NEWDRIV.SYS into region 1 of upper memory and also make region 3 available to it, if needed:

```
DEVICEHIGH=/L:1;3 NEWDRIV.SYS
```

The following command loads NEWDRIV into upper memory regions 1 and 3 only if each region contains at least 30K of free memory:

```
DEVICEHIGH=/L:1,30;3,30 NEWDRIV.SYS
```

Related Commands

See the DEVICE command for information about loading device drivers into conventional RAM.

See the LOADHIGH command for information about loading programs into the upper memory area.

See the MEMMAKER command for information about using the MemMaker program to move programs to the upper memory area.

DIR

DIR displays a list of a directory's files and subdirectories. Using DIR without parameters or switches displays the disk's volume label and serial number, followed by one directory or filename per line. Directory and filename listings include the filename extension, the file size in bytes, and the date and time the file was last modified. Summary information at the end of a directory listing includes the total number of files listed, their cumulative size, and the free space (in bytes) remaining on the disk.

Syntax

```
DIR [drive:][path][filename] [/P] [/W]
[/A[[:]attributes]][/O[[:]sortorder]] [/S] [/B] [/L] [C]
```

Parameters

[drive:][path]

Specifies the drive and directory for which you want to see a file listing.

[filename]

Specifies a particular file or group of files for which you want to see a file listing.

Switches

/P

Causes DOS to display a directory listing one screen at a time. DOS prompts you to press any key to continue the listing.

/W

Displays the listing in wide format, showing filenames only. The wide format allows DOS to include as many as five filenames or directory names on each line.

/A[[:] attributes]

Used to display only the names of directories and files that match any attributes you specify. Omitting this switch causes DIR to display the names of all files except hidden and system files. The following list describes each of the values you can use for attributes. If you're including multiple attributes in a DIR command, do not place spaces between the individual attributes.

- -H   Hidden files
- -H   Files that are not hidden
- -S   System files
- -S   Files other than system files

	-D	Directories
	-D	Files only (not directories)
	-A	Files ready for archiving (backup)
	-A	Files that have not changed since the last backup
	-R	Read-only files
	-R	Files that are not read-only

`/O[[:] sortorder]`

Used to specify the order in which you want DIR to sort and display directory information. Omitting this switch causes DOS to organize its file display using the order in which filenames occur within the directory. The following list describes each of the values you can use for *sortorder*. When sorting on multiple criteria, do not place spaces between the individual attributes.

	-N	In alphabetic order by name
	-N	In reverse alphabetic order by name (Z through A)
	-E	In alphabetic order by extension
	-E	In reverse alphabetic order by extension (Z through A)
	-D	By date and time, earliest first
	-D	By date and time, latest first
	-S	By size, smallest first
	-S	By size, largest first
	-G	With directories grouped before files
	-G	With directories grouped after files
	-C	By compression ratio, lowest first.
	-C	By compression ratio, highest first.

`/S`

Lists every occurrence of the specified filename within the specified directory and any subdirectories it contains.

`/B`

Lists only filenames and extensions, one per line, but does not include heading information and file summaries. (Note: The /B switch overrides the /W switch.)

`/L`

Converts the directory listing to lowercase.

`/C`

Displays information on the compression ratio of files stored on Dblspace volumes. DOS ignores the /C switch if it is used with the /W or /B switch.

Using Wildcards with DIR

The DOS wildcards (? and *) allow you to identify a group of files or subdirectories that you want included in a directory listing. (The Examples section includes an example of how to use wildcards in a DIR command.)

Specifying File Display Attributes

Using the /A switch with multiple attributes causes DIR to display only those files that match all of the specified attributes. Entering either of the following commands, DIR/A-RH or DIR/AH-R, tells DOS to display the names of hidden files that are not write-protected.

Specifying Filename Sorting

Using the /O switch with multiple *sortorder* values causes DIR to sort the filenames multiple times, beginning with the first criterion listed. For example, the following command, DIR/OE-S, tells DOS to first sort the directory listing using the extensions of directories and filenames. A second pass then sorts the files by size, placing the largest files first.

Using Redirection Symbols and Pipes

You can use a redirection symbol (>) or pipe (|) to redirect a directory listing to a device other than your computer monitor, its default destination. The Examples section contains an example of how this is accomplished.

> ***Caution:*** Before using a pipe (|) for redirection, be sure to set the TEMP environment variable in your AUTOEXEC.BAT file. Otherwise, the temporary file will appear in the directory listing.

Presetting DIR Parameters and Switches

Most people like to see a directory listing presented in a certain way. For example, I like mine sorted by extension and filename. One way to accomplish this is to always enter the DIR command in the following format:

```
DIR /OEN
```

This works, but after a while, typing in the required switches grows tedious. DOS provides an easy way around this problem: Including a DIRCMD command in your AUTOEXEC.BAT file allows you to set a default format for your directory listings. You can use any valid combination of DIR parameters and switches with the SET DIRCMD command, including the location and name of a file.

To set the DIRCMD environment variable to my preference each time I start my system, therefore, I simply added the following command to my AUTO-EXEC.BAT file:

```
SET DIRCMD=/OEN
```

For a single use of the DIR command, I can override this new default format by including the sort order on the DIR command line, but preceding it with with a minus sign, as shown in the following example:

```
DIR /-O
```

You can change the DIRCMD default settings by typing the SET command at the command prompt with a new parameter or switch after the equal sign (=). The new default settings remain in effect for all subsequent DIR commands, until you use SET DIRCMD again on the command line or until you restart MS-DOS.

The following command clears all DIRCMD settings and returns your system to the default directory format:

```
SET DIRCMD=
```

Use the following command to view the current settings of the DIRCMD environment variable:

```
SET
```

DOS displays a list of environment variables and their settings, including the DIRCMD variable if it has been defined.

Examples

The following command displays all files and directories in a directory, including hidden or system files:

```
DIR /A
```

A DIR command can be as easy or complex as you like. Suppose, for example, that you want to see the contents of every directory on your disk, pausing the display each time the screen is filled. Furthermore, you'd like this listing to be sorted by file size, largest to smallest. Moving to the root directory and typing in the following command accomplishes all of this:

```
DIR /S/O-S/P
```

DIR lists the name of the root directory and the names of the files in the root directory, starting with the largest one. (Because subdirectories have a file length of zero, they would be shown at the end of the root directory listing.) DIR then lists this same information for every subdirectory on the active disk.

To alter the preceding example so that DIR displays the filenames and extensions but omits the directory names, type the following command:

```
DIR /S/O-S/P/A:-D
```

You can use the redirection symbol to send a directory listing to another device. The following command prints a copy of a directory listing to your system printer:

```
DIR > PRN
```

Specifying PRN on the DIR command line causes the directory listing to be sent to the printer attached to the LPT1 port, the default printer port on most computers. If your printer is attached to a different port, replace PRN with the name of the correct port for your system.

To redirect a directory listing to a file, simply replace PRN with a filename, including path information if necessary, as in the following example:

```
DIR > \MYDOCS\DIR.LST
```

If the MYDOCS directory exists but DIR.LST does not, DOS creates it. If the MYDOCS directory does not exist, DOS displays the following message:

```
File creation error
```

To display a list of all the filenames with the BAT extension in all directories on drive C, type the following command:

```
DIR C:\*.BAT /O/S/P
```

DIR displays an alphabetized list of all files on your disk with a BAT extension, pausing each time the screen fills.

Related Commands

For information about displaying the directory structure of a path or disk, see the TREE command.

For information about compressing disks, see the DBLSPACE command.

For more information about setting environment variables, see the SET command.

DISKCOMP

You use this command to compare the contents of two floppy disks.

Syntax

```
DISKCOMP [drive1: [drive2:]] [/1] [/8]
```

Parameters

drive1:

Specifies the drive containing one of the floppy disks you want compared.

drive2:

Specifies the drive containing the second floppy disk.

Switches

/1

Compares only the first sides of the disks, even if the disks are double-sided and the drives can read double-sided disks.

/8

Compares only the first 8 sectors per track, even if the disks contain 9 or 15 sectors per track.

DISKCOMP Messages

DISKCOMP works only with floppy disks. It cannot be used with a hard disk. If you specify a hard disk drive for *drive1* or *drive2*, DISKCOMP displays the following error message:

```
Invalid drive specification
Specified drive does not exist or is non-removable
```

If all tracks on one disk are identical to their counterpart on the other disk, DISKCOMP displays the following message:

```
Compare OK
```

✓ *Note:* DISKCOMP ignores a disk's volume number when it makes the comparison.

If the tracks are not the same, DISKCOMP displays a message similar to the following:

```
Compare error on side 1, track 2
```

When DISKCOMP completes the comparison, it displays the following message:

```
Compare another diskette (Y/N)?
```

Press Y and DISKCOMP prompts you to insert disks for the next comparison. Pressing N exits DISKCOMP and returns you to the DOS system prompt.

Omitting Drive Parameters

Omitting the *drive2* parameter causes DISKCOMP to use the current drive for *drive2*. Omitting both drive parameters causes DISKCOMP to use the current drive for both.

During single-drive DISKCOMP operations, DOS prompts you to swap disks when appropriate.

Using One Drive for the Comparison

You can specify the same floppy disk drive for both *drive1* and *drive2*. Doing so causes DISKCOMP to perform a comparison using the single drive. It prompts you to insert the appropriate disk when necessary. You might have to swap the disks more than once, depending on the capacity of the disks and how much memory is free on your system.

Comparing Different Types of Disks

You can only use DISKCOMP to compare disks of identical format. If the disk in *drive1* is not of the same type as the disk in *drive2*, DISKCOMP displays the following message:

```
Drive types or diskette types not compatible
```

Using DISKCOMP with Networks and Redirected Drives

DISKCOMP will not work on a network drive or on a redirected drive created with the SUBST command.

Comparing an Original Disk with a Copy

DISKCOMP checks to see whether two disks are identical to one another. It compares the disks' structure, as well as their content. For this reason, DISKCOMP cannot be used to compare a disk created with the COPY command against the original. If you attempt this, DISKCOMP may display a message similar to the following:

```
Compare error on side 0, track 0
```

This error can occur even though the files on the two disks are identical. Although the COPY command copies the contents of files, it does not necessarily place them in the same location on the destination disk.

DISKCOMP Exit Codes

DISKCOMP generates various exit codes, based on the result of a disk comparison. The following list contains each exit code and a brief description of its meaning:

0	The disks were identical.
1	DISKCOMP discovered differences in the contents of the two disks.
2	The user pressed CTRL+C and aborted the process.
3	A critical error occurred.
4	An error occurred during initialization.

You can use the ERRORLEVEL parameter on the IF command line in a batch program to process exit codes returned by DISKCOMP.

Example

Use the following command to compare two disks on a single-floppy system:

```
DISKCOMP A: A:
```

DISKCOMP prompts you to insert each disk, as required.

Related Command

See the FC command for information about comparing two files.

DISKCOPY

You use this command to copy the contents of one floppy disk to a second floppy disk. The target disk can be either formatted or unformatted.

Syntax

```
DISKCOPY [drive1: [drive2:]] [/1] [/V]
```

Parameters

`drive1:`

Specifies the drive containing the disk you want to make a copy of, called the source disk.

`drive2:`

Specifies the drive containing the disk you want to copy to, called the target disk.

Switches

`/1`

Copies only the first side of a disk.

`/V`

Verifies that the information is copied correctly. Use of this switch slows the copying process.

> *Caution:* DISKCOPY destroys the existing contents of the target disk as it copies the new information to it.

Invalid Drive for DISKCOPY

DISKCOPY works only with removable disks, such as floppy disks. It cannot be used with a hard disk. If you specify a hard disk drive for *drive1* or *drive2*, DISKCOPY displays the following error message:

```
Invalid drive specification
Specified drive does not exist or is non-removable
```

DISKCOPY Messages

During a DISKCOPY, DOS prompts you to insert the source and target disks when appropriate and waits for you to press any key before continuing. After the copy is completed, DISKCOPY displays the following message:

```
Copy another diskette (Y/N)?
```

Press Y and DISKCOPY prompts you to insert disks for the next copy operation. Pressing N exits DISKCOPY and returns you to the DOS system prompt.

You can use DISKCOPY to copy information to an unformatted target disk. When the target disk is unformatted, DISKCOPY formats it using the same number of sides and sectors per track as are on the source disk. During the process, DISKCOPY displays the following message:

```
Formatting while copying
```

If the capacity of the source disk is greater than that of the target disk and your computer can detect this difference, DISKCOPY displays the following message:

```
TARGET media has lower capacity than SOURCE
Continue anyway (Y/N)?
```

If you press Y, DISKCOPY tries formatting the target disk as it copies files from the source disk.

If you attempt a DISKCOPY between disks of dissimilar formats, DISKCOPY displays the following error message:

```
Drive types or diskette types
not compatible
Copy process ended
```

Omitting Drive Parameters

Omitting the *drive2* parameter causes DISKCOPY to use the current drive as the target drive. Omitting both drive parameters causes DISKCOMP to use the current drive for both the source and target drives.

During single-drive DISKCOPY operations, DOS prompts you to swap disks when appropriate.

Using One Drive for Copying

You can specify the same floppy disk drive for both *drive1* and *drive2*. Doing so causes DISKCOPY to use the same drive. If the disks contain more information than available memory can hold, DISKCOPY will be unable to read all of the information at once. After reading as much information as fits in memory at one time from the source disk, DOS prompts you to insert the target disk. DISKCOPY then writes the information in memory to the target disk, after which DOS prompts you to reinsert the source disk so it can read in the next group of data. This process continues until the entire disk has been copied. The number of times you will need to repeat this process depends on the capacity of the disks and how much memory is free on your system.

Avoiding Disk Fragmentation

If the source disk is fragmented, DISKCOPY requires additional time to find, read, or write files. Also, any fragmentation on the source disk will be replicated on the target disk. (Fragmentation is the presence of small areas of unused disk space between existing files on a disk.) The COPY or XCOPY commands transfer data sequentially. This eliminates fragmentation and speeds up processing on the target disk.

Copying Startup Disks

You should always use DISKCOPY to replicate a startup disk — that is, a disk containing the DOS system files. Because DISKCOPY creates a clone of the source disk, your target disk also will be a startup disk. Using COPY or XCOPY to copy a startup disk does not, however, guarantee that the DOS system files will be located in the appropriate place. A copied disk, therefore, usually will not work properly as a startup disk.

DISKCOPY Exit Codes

DISKCOPY generates various exit codes based on the result of a disk copy. The following list contains each exit code and a brief description of its meaning:

  0   The copy operation was successful.
  1   A nonfatal read/write error occurred.
  2   The user pressed CTRL+C and aborted the process.
  3   A critical error occurred.
  4   An error occurred during initialization.

You can use the ERRORLEVEL parameter on the IF command line in a batch program to process exit codes returned by DISKCOPY.

Example

Use the following command to make an exact copy of one disk on another disk, using a single floppy drive.

```
DISKCOPY A: A:
```

DISKCOPY prompts you to insert each disk, as required.

Related Commands

See the COPY command for information about copying one or more files.

See the DISKCOMP command for information about comparing two disks to see if they are identical.

See the XCOPY command for information about copying directories and subdirectories.

DISPLAY.SYS

This device driver supports code-page switching for the console; it allows international character sets to be displayed on the screen. If used, it is loaded by the DEVICE configuration command in the CONFIG.SYS file.

Syntax

    DEVICE=[drive:][path]DISPLAY.SYS CON[:]=(type[,[hwcp][,n]])
    DEVICE=[drive:][path]DISPLAY.SYS CON[:]=(type[,[hwcp][,(n,m)]])

Parameters

[drive:][path]

Specifies the location of the DISPLAY.SYS file.

type

Specifies the display adapter you are using. Valid values include:

- EGA (used to support both EGA and VGA display adapters)
- LCD

If you omit the type parameter, DISPLAY.SYS checks the hardware to determine what kind of display adapter you have.

> ✓ *Note:* It's possible to specify CGA or MONO as values for *type*. Because code-page switching is not enabled for these devices, however, doing so has no effect.

hwcp

Specifies the number of the code page that your hardware supports. The following list indicates the code pages supported by MS-DOS, along with the country and language for each:

437	United States
850	Multilingual (Latin I)
852	Slavic (Latin II)
860	Portuguese
863	Canadian-French
865	Nordic

n

Specifies the number of code pages your hardware supports, in addition to the primary code page specified for the *hwcp* parameter. Valid values for *n* are in the range 0 through 6:

- For EGA display adapters, the maximum value allowable for *n* is 6.
- For LCD display adapters, the maximum value allowable for *n* is 1.

m

Specifies the number of subfonts the hardware supports for each code page. The default value is 2 if *type* is EGA, and 1 if *type* is LCD.

Using DISPLAY.SYS with Monochrome or CGA Display Adapters

Because monochrome and CGA display adapters do not support code-page switching, using DISPLAY.SYS with either type of adapter has no effect.

Installing a Third-Party Console Driver

Some consoles (display and keyboard combinations) require their own display drivers. If you use one of these third-party console drivers in conjunction with DISPLAY.SYS, the third-party driver must be installed first. Reversing this order — that is, loading DISPLAY.SYS first — may disable the copy of DISPLAY.SYS that has already been installed.

Example

The following command causes DISPLAY.SYS to support an EGA display adapter with the United States hardware code page (437) and the potential for two additional MS-DOS code pages:

```
DEVICE=C:\DOS\DISPLAY.SYS CON=(EGA,437,2)
```

DOS

When used within the CONFIG.SYS file, this command instructs MS-DOS to load a portion of itself into the high memory area (HMA) and manage upper memory blocks (UMBs) created by an upper memory block manager.

Syntax

```
DOS=HIGH|LOW[,UMB|,NOUMB]
DOS=[HIGH,|LOW,]UMB|NOUMB
```

Parameters

HIGH|LOW

Instructs DOS whether or not it should load a portion of itself into the high memory area (HMA). The HIGH parameter tells MS-DOS to attempt to load itself into the HMA; the LOW parameter loads all of MS-DOS in conventional RAM. The default setting is LOW.

UMB|NOUMB

Instructs MS-DOS whether or not it should manage upper memory blocks (UMBs) created by an UMB provider such as EMM386.EXE. The UMB parameter specifies that, if UMBs exist, DOS should manage them. The NOUMB parameter instructs MS-DOS not to manage UMBs, even if they exist. The default setting is NOUMB.

For the DOS command to work properly, it must find the HIMEM.SYS device driver or another extended memory manager in memory. If your computer has an 80386 or 80486 processor, you can use EMM386.EXE for memory management and to provide UMBs.

Using the HIGH Parameter

Specifying the HIGH parameter causes DOS to attempt to load a portion of itself into the HMA. Doing so frees additional conventional memory for programs and data.

If you attempt to load DOS HIGH and no HMA is available, the following message appears:

```
HMA not available Loading DOS low
```

Using the UMB Parameter

Specifying the DOS=UMB command allows you to load programs and device drivers into the upper memory area. Doing so frees additional space in conventional RAM for programs and data.

If you attempt to use the UMB parameter and no UMBs are available, DOS does not display an error message.

Examples

The following command loads a portion of DOS into HMA, if it is available:

```
DOS=HIGH
```

It's possible to use both parameters in the same DOS statement. To do so, separate them with a comma, as in the following example:

```
DOS=HIGH,UMB
```

The DOS command can be placed anywhere in your CONFIG.SYS file.

Related Commands

See the DEVICEHIGH command for information about loading a device driver into the upper memory area.

See EMM386.EXE for more information about managing memory on an 80386 or 80486 system.

See the LOADHIGH command for information about loading a program into the upper memory area.

DOSKEY

You use this command to run the DOSKEY utility, which can be used to recall recently executed DOS commands, edit command lines, and create macros. DOSKEY is a terminate-and-stay-resident program, which means that, once loaded, it remains in memory until you turn off your computer. When installed, DOSKEY occupies about 4 kilobytes of resident memory.

Syntax

```
DOSKEY [/REINSTALL] [/BUFSIZE=size] [/MACROS]
[/HISTORY][/INSERT|/OVERSTRIKE] [macroname=[text]]
```

Parameter

`macroname=[text]`

When used, this parameter creates a DOSKEY macro that, once it exists, can be used to carry out one or more DOS commands. *macroname* specifies the name you want to assign to the macro. *text* specifies the commands you want to record. Thereafter, whenever you enter the command *macroname*, DOS executes the command or commands specified in *text*.

Switches

`/REINSTALL`

Used to install a new copy of the DOSKEY program. You can install a second copy of DOSKEY, even if one is already running. If you're installing a second copy of DOSKEY, /REINSTALL also clears the buffer — the area of memory reserved for storing the command line history and DOS macros. Each instance of DOSKEY, however, consumes an extra 4K of memory.

`/BUFSIZE=size`

Creates a buffer of the specified size, which DOSKEY uses to store commands and macros. The minimum buffer size is 256 bytes. The default buffer size is 512 bytes.

`/MACROS`

Displays a list of all current DOSKEY macros. Using a redirection symbol (>) with the /MACROS switch sends this list to a file. /MACROS can be abbreviated as /M.

`/HISTORY`

Displays a list of all commands stored in memory. Using a redirection symbol (>) with the /HISTORY switch sends this list to a file. The /HISTORY switch can be abbreviated as /H.

`/INSERT|/OVERSTRIKE`

Used to switch between insert and overstrike mode when editing text on the DOS command line. The /INSERT switch causes any new text that you type on a line to be inserted into old text (as if you had pressed the INSERT key). The /OVERSTRIKE switch causes new text to replace old text. The default setting is /OVERSTRIKE. Pressing the INSERT key also toggles between insert and overstrike mode.

Recalling a Command

The following keys allow you to recall a command after loading DOSKEY into memory:

UP ARROW	Recalls the MS-DOS command you used before the one currently displayed.
DOWN ARROW	Recalls the MS-DOS command you used after the one currently displayed.
PAGE UP	Recalls the oldest MS-DOS command you used in the current session.
PAGE DOWN	Recalls the most recent MS-DOS command you used.

Editing the Command Line

DOSKEY allows you to edit the current command line. The following list describes the DOSKEY editing keys and their functions:

LEFT ARROW	Moves the cursor back one character.
RIGHT ARROW	Moves the cursor forward one character.
CTRL+ LEFT ARROW	Moves the cursor back one word.
CTRL+ RIGHT ARROW	Moves the cursor forward one word.
HOME	Moves the cursor to the beginning of the line.
END	Moves the cursor to the end of the line.
ESC	Clears the command from the display.

COMMAND REFERENCE **341**

F1	Sends a single letter from the most recently entered DOS command to your display screen.
F2	Lets you automatically re-enter the last DOS command up to a specified character.
F3	Recalls any letters remaining in the DOS command line used to execute the most recent DOS operation.
F4	Deletes characters, beginning with the current character position, up to a character you specify.
F5	Copies the current command to the temporary command buffer and clears the command line.
F6	Places an end-of-file character (CTRL+Z) at the current position on the command line.
F7	Displays all commands stored in memory, along with their associated numbers. DOSKEY sequentially assigns numbers to previously executed commands, beginning with 1 for the first (oldest) command stored in memory.
ALT+F7	Deletes all commands stored in memory.
F8	Searches memory for a command that you want DOSKEY to display. After typing the first character or first few characters of the command you want to find, press F8. DOSKEY displays the most recent command that begins with the text you typed. Press F8 repeatedly to cycle through all the stored commands that begin with the characters you specified.
F9	Prompts you for a command number and displays the command associated with the number you specify.
ALT+F10	Deletes all macro definitions.

Creating a Macro

DOSKEY lets you create macros that carry out one or more MS-DOS commands. The following special characters control command operations when defining a macro:

$G or $g	Use either of these characters to redirect output to a device or file, instead of to the screen. When used in a macro, this character is equivalent to the DOS redirection symbol (>).
GG or gg	Use either of these double characters to append output to an existing file, rather than to create a new file that replaces the older one. These characters are equivalent to the DOS append redirection symbol (>>).

$L or $l	Use either of these characters to read input from a file or a device other than the keyboard. This character is equivalent to the DOS input redirection symbol (<).
$B or $b	Using one of these characters is equivalent to using the DOS pipe (|) on a command line.
$T or $t	Use either of these characters to separate multiple commands while creating macros or typing commands on the DOSKEY command line.
$1 through $9	Represents user-specified command-line information that will be entered when you run a macro. These characters resemble batch parameters (%1 through %9), which allow you to enter different data in the command line each time you run a macro.
$*	Represents all command-line information you want to specify when you enter the macro name. This character also resembles the batch parameters $1 through $9, with one very critical difference: Everything you type on the command line following the macro name is substituted for the $* within the macro.
$$	Use this symbol to specify the dollar sign character ($). (You need a double dollar sign because DOS interprets a single dollar sign to identify other special characters, as outlined in the previous examples.)

The following command line is an example of a macro created with DOSKEY:

```
DOSKEY QF=FORMAT $1 /Q /U
```

This macro performs a quick and unconditional format of a disk. It uses the replaceable parameter $1 to let you specify the drive containing the disk you want to format at execution time.

Running a Macro

To run a macro, simply type the macro name at the DOS system, starting at the first position on the command line. If the macro contains $* or a batch parameter ($1 through $9), insert a space between the macro name and the first parameter. Spaces must separate any replaceable parameters you specify.

The following command runs the QF macro created in the previous example and formats a disk in drive A:

```
QF A:
```

Creating a Macro with the Same Name as an MS-DOS Command

It's possible to create a macro that has the same name as an MS-DOS command. Use the following procedures to specify whether you want to run the macro or the MS-DOS command of the same name:

- To run the macro, begin typing the macro name immediately after the command prompt, with no space between the prompt and the command name.
- To execute the DOS command, insert one or more spaces between the prompt and the command name.

Examples

The next command starts the DOSKEY program using the default settings:

```
DOSKEY
```

The following command creates a batch program named MACINIT.BAT that includes all DOSKEY macros:

```
DOSKEY /MACROS > MACINIT.BAT
```

Before using the MACINIT.BAT file, you'll need to use a text editor to include the DOSKEY command at the beginning of each macro line.

The following command creates a batch program named TMP.BAT, which contains recently used commands:

```
DOSKEY /HISTORY >  TMP.BAT
```

The next command defines a macro containing multiple commands:

```
DOSKEY TX=CD\MYDIR$TDIR/W $*
```

✔ *Note:* In the previous example, the $T character is used to separate individual commands. Once created, this macro changes the current directory to MYDIR and then displays a directory listing using the wide display format.

The following command creates a macro that uses a batch parameter to let the user specify a new directory name:

```
DOSKEY MC=MD $1$TCD $1
```

✔ *Note:* In the previous example, the $1 parameter is used to let the user enter a new directory name. When executed, the macro first creates a new directory using the user-defined name and then changes to this new directory from the current directory.

Typing the following command would cause the preceding macro to create a new directory called NEWDIR and then change to that directory:

```
MC NEWDIR
```

The following command creates a macro that uses batch parameters to move a file or group of files:

```
DOSKEY MV=COPY $1 $2 $T DEL $1
```

The user enters a source path and filename ($1) and a destination path or filename ($2). The command copies the file or files from the source to the destination directory. It then deletes the source files.

DOSSHELL

You use this command to start the DOS Shell, a graphical interface that provides easy access to most MS-DOS commands.

Syntax

```
DOSSHELL [/T|/G[:res[n]]] [/B]
```

Parameters

res

Used to specify the screen resolution you want to use. (The default value of *res* depends on your hardware.) Valid *res* values are:

L	low resolution
M	medium resolution
H	high resolution

n

Specifies a screen resolution when there is more than one choice within a category. (The default value of *n* depends on your hardware.)

Switches

/T

Runs MS-DOS Shell in text mode.

/G

Runs MS-DOS Shell in graphics mode.

/B

Runs MS-DOS Shell using a black-and-white color scheme. This can be useful if your system uses an LCD display, as is the case for most laptop or notebook computers.

Running MS-DOS Shell with Microsoft Windows

You should never run Microsoft Windows from within the DOS Shell. To use both Microsoft Windows and DOS Shell, start the DOS Shell from within a Windows session.

Memory Requirement

Your computer must have at least 384K of available conventional memory to run the DOS Shell.

Adjusting Screen Resolution

You can adjust screen resolution from within the DOS Shell using the Display command within the pull-down Options menu. Selecting Display opens a dialog box listing the mode (text or graphics), the number of lines, the resolution category, and the specific number within each category for all possible screen-resolution modes available for your computer.

The DOSSHELL.INI File

DOS stores your current Shell settings for program items and groups, options, screen resolution, colors, and so on within a file called DOSSHELL.INI. DOS automatically updates the DOSSHELL.INI file whenever you make a change or start a program item. For this reason, DOSSHELL.INI must be stored on a drive that is not write-protected.

Setting the Location to Store Temporary Files

DOS creates temporary files in the directory where DOSSHELL.EXE is located each time you run a program from the DOS Shell. To specify a different location for these temporary files, use the SET command to create a TEMP environment variable in your AUTOEXEC.BAT file.

Example

To start the MS-DOS Shell in graphics mode, type the following command:

```
dosshell /g
```

DRIVER.SYS

When used in CONFIG.SYS, this device driver creates a logical drive that allows you to access a physical floppy disk drive.

> ✔ **Note:** A logical drive is nothing more than a pointer that identifies a physical disk drive in your system. The logical drive is associated with a drive letter (for example, A or B).

Syntax

```
DEVICE=[drive:][path]DRIVER.SYS /D:number [/C] [/F:factor]
[/H:heads] [/S:sectors] [/T:tracks]
```

Parameter

`[drive:][path]`

Identifies the location of the DRIVER.SYS file.

Switches

`/D:number`

Used to specify the number of the physical floppy disk drive. Valid settings for this number are 0 through 127.

> ✔ **Note:** DOS identifies the first physical floppy disk drive in a system, usually drive A, as drive 0 and the second disk drive as drive 1. (A third floppy disk drive, if one exists, must be external and is assigned the number 2.) If your computer has one floppy disk drive, both drives A and B are numbered 0. If your computer has multiple floppy disk drives, drive B is numbered 1.

`/C`

Indicates that the physical disk drive can detect whether its drive door is closed.

`/F:factor`

Specifies the type of disk drive. Valid settings for *factor* are as follows:

0	a 160K/180K or 320K/360K, 5.25" disk drive
1	a 1.2 megabyte, 5.25" disk drive
2	a 720K, 3.5" disk or other drive type
7	a 1.44 MB, 3.5" disk drive
9	a 2.88 MB, 3.5" disk drive

The default value for *factor* is 2. Refer to your drive's documentation to determine the appropriate values for these settings.

> ✓ ***Note:*** As a rule, using the /F switch eliminates the need to include the /H, /S, and /T switches in the DRIVER.SYS statement. Before doing so, however, you should check the default values for these switches to make sure that they are correct for your disk drive. Conversely, specifying the /H, /S, and /T switches allows you to omit the /F switch.

```
/H:heads
```

Specifies the number of heads in the disk drive. Valid settings for *heads* are 1 through 99. The default value for *heads* is 2. Refer to your drive's documentation to determine the appropriate values for this setting.

```
/S:sectors
```

Specifies the number of sectors per track. Valid settings for *sectors* are 1 through 99. The default value for *sectors* depends on the value of /F:*factor*, as follows:

/F:0	/S:9
/F:1	/S:15
/F:2	/S:9
/F:7	/S:18
/F:9	/S:36

Refer to your drive's documentation to determine the appropriate values for this setting.

```
/T:tracks
```

Specifies the number of tracks per side on the block device. Valid settings for *tracks* are 1 through 999. The default value for *tracks* is 80, unless /F:*factor* is 0, in which case the default value is 40. Refer to your drive's documentation to determine the appropriate values for this setting.

Disk Drive Change-Line Support

The term "change-line support" means that a disk drive is able to detect whether its drive door is opened and closed. Change-line support allows faster MS-DOS operation with floppy disks. Specifying the /C switch indicates to DOS that the physical disk drive can support change-line error detection. Refer to your drive's documentation to determine whether it supports change-line detection.

Examples

The following line, when included in your CONFIG.SYS file, adds an external 720K drive to your system:

```
DEVICE=DRIVER.SYS /D:2
```

Since no location is specified, MS-DOS searches for DRIVER.SYS in the root directory of your startup drive.

The properly structured DRIVER.SYS statement will allow you to use a single 1.44-megabyte external disk drive to copy files from one floppy disk to another. Accomplishing this requires adding two identical DEVICE commands for DRIVER.SYS in your CONFIG.SYS file, as shown in the following example:

```
DEVICE=DRIVER.SYS /D:2 /F:7
DEVICE=DRIVER.SYS /D:2 /F:7
```

✔ *Note:* This procedure assigns two logical drive letters to the same physical drive. DOS will prompt you to swap disks in this single drive, as needed, during the copying process.

Related Commands

See the DRIVPARM command for information about modifying the parameters of a physical disk drive that is supported by your hardware.

See the SUBST command for information about substituting a logical drive letter for a hard disk drive.

DRIVPARM

When included in a CONFIG.SYS file, this command defines parameters for physical devices such as disk drives each time you start your system.

> ✓ **Note:** Unlike DRIVER.SYS, which you use to create and manage logical drives, the DRIVPARM command affects a physical drive. Settings specified in the DRIVPARM command override the driver definitions for an already existing device.

Syntax

    DRIVPARM=/D:number [/C] [/F:factor] [/H:heads] [/I]
    [/N][/S:sectors] [/T:tracks]

Switches

/D:number

   Used to specify the physical drive number. Valid values for this switch are 0 through 255.

/C

   Specifies that the drive can detect whether or not its drive door is closed.

/F:factor

   Specifies the drive type. Valid settings for *factor* are as follows:

0	a 160K/180K or 320K/360K, 5.25" disk drive
1	a 1.2 megabyte, 5.25" disk drive
2	a 720K, 3.5" disk drive
5	Hard disk
6	Tape
7	a 1.44 MB, 3.5" disk drive
8	Read/write optical disk
9	a 2.88 MB, 3.5" disk drive

   The default value for *factor* is 2.

/H:heads

   Specifies the maximum number of heads on the device. Values for *heads* must be in the range 1 through 99. The default value depends upon the value you specify for /F:*factor*.

`/I`

> Specifies an electronically compatible 3.5" floppy disk drive.

✔ *Note:* To be "electronically compatible," an installed drive must be able to use your existing disk controller. The /I switch is designed to work around an older ROM BIOS that does not support 3.5" floppy disk drives.

`/N`

> Specifies a nonremovable device.

`/S:sectors`

> Specifies the number of sectors per track that the device supports. Values for *sectors* must be in the range 1 through 99. The default value depends upon the value you specify for /F:*factor*.

`/T:tracks`

> Specifies the number of tracks per side that the device supports. The default value depends upon the value you specify for /F:*factor*.

Disk Drive Change-Line Support

The term "change-line support" means that a physical disk drive is able to detect whether its drive door is opened or closed. Change-line support improves performance by letting DOS know when you have replaced the floppy disk within a drive. Specifying the /C switch indicates to DOS that the physical disk drive can support change-line error detection.

✔ *Note:* Refer to your drive's documentation to determine whether it supports change-line detection.

Example

Adding the following command to a CONFIG.SYS file would reconfigure an already existing tape drive identified as drive E to write 10 tracks of 99 sectors each:

```
DRIVPARM=/D:4 /F:6 /H:1 /S:99 /T:10
```

✔ *Note:* Remember, DRIVPARM does not create a new logical drive; rather, it modifies the parameters of an existing physical drive.

ECHO

ECHO is used in a batch file to specify whether command echoing and message display are turned on or off.

Syntax

ECHO [ON|OFF] [message]

Parameters

ON|OFF

Used to turn the command echoing feature on or off.

message

Used to specify text that you want MS-DOS to display on the screen. When you run a batch program, DOS normally displays on the screen the commands that the batch program contains as they are executed; this is called echoing. An ECHO OFF command disables echoing: Commands are still executed, but DOS does not display them on the screen.

> ✔ *Note:* To display the current ECHO setting, use the ECHO command without a parameter.

Using ECHO to Display Messages from a Batch File

The ECHO command provides a convenient way to include messages in a batch file, even when command echoing is turned off.

Hiding the Command Prompt

If you use the ECHO OFF command on the command line, the command prompt does not appear on your screen. To redisplay the command prompt, type ECHO ON.

Preventing MS-DOS from Echoing a Line

Inserting an at (@) sign at the beginning of a command line within a batch program prevents MS-DOS from echoing that line to the display.

Echoing a Blank Line

Typing the ECHO command followed immediately by a period (.) causes MS-DOS to display a blank line on the screen. This technique is especially useful when formatting messages generated by a batch file.

✔ **Note:** Do not include a space between the ECHO command and the period.

Displaying Pipes and Redirection Characters

The ECHO command will not display a pipe (|) or redirection character (< or >).

Examples

Ordinarily, DOS displays the names of batch file commands as it is executing them. Suppose, however, that you do not want DOS to display the command it is executing, but that you do want it to display a message in your batch file that is several lines long. One way to accomplish this is to turn ECHO off, then generate the desired message using individual ECHO lines. The following example shows a section of a batch program that turns off command echoing, then displays a three-line message, followed by a blank line:

```
@ECHO OFF
ECHO This batch program
ECHO formats and checks
ECHO new disks
ECHO.
```

✔ **Note:** The first line in the previous example uses the at (@) sign to suppress display of the ECHO OFF command.

The ECHO command is somewhat unique in that it does not have to be the first word in the batch file line in order to be executed. When used with an IF statement, ECHO may appear later in the command line, as illustrated in the following example:

```
IF EXIST *.RPT ECHO The report has arrived.
```

This command line displays the specified message only if a file with an RPT extension exists in the current directory.

Related Command

See the PAUSE command for information about suspending the execution of a batch program.

EDIT

EDIT runs the MS-DOS Editor, which can be used to create and modify ASCII text files. Editor is a full-screen editor used to create, edit, save, and print standard text (ASCII) files. Editor is an interactive program — that is, it allows you to choose commands from pull-down menus and specify information and preferences with dialog boxes. This makes it much easier to use than the EDLIN program provided with earlier versions of DOS. Editor even includes an on-line Help feature, which provides information about MS-DOS Editor techniques and commands.

Syntax

EDIT [[drive:][path]filename] [/B] [/G] [/H] [/NOHI]

Parameter

[drive:][path]filename

Used to specify the location and name of the file you want to edit. If the specified file already exists, Editor opens it and displays its contents on the screen. If the specified file does not exist, Editor creates it and displays its menu bar and a blank screen, which you use for text input.

Switches

/B

Used to run Editor in black and white. This option is especially useful if the Editor screen is difficult to read on a monochrome monitor or — more typically — on the LCD display found in most laptop and notebook computers.

/G

Provides the fastest screen updating for a CGA monitor.

/H

Tells Editor to display the maximum number of lines possible for your monitor.

/NOHI

Allows you to use 8-color monitors with Editor. Usually, DOS uses 16 colors.

> ***CAUTION:*** Editor does not work if DOS cannot find a file called QBASIC.EXE, the MS-DOS QBasic programming language. For this reason, QBASIC.EXE must be in the current directory, included in your search path, or located in the same directory as the file EDIT.COM. Therefore, if you delete QBASIC.EXE to free up space on your hard disk, you cannot use the MS-DOS Editor.

> ✓ ***Note:*** Some monitors may not support the display of shortcut keys by default. If your monitor does not display shortcut keys, use the /B switch (for CGA monitors) and the /NOHI switch (for systems that do not support bold characters).

Related Command

See the EDLIN command for a brief overview of the text editor included with early releases of MS-DOS.

EDLIN

This command runs EDLIN, the text editor included with MS-DOS 5.0 and earlier DOS releases.

Syntax

    EDLIN [[drive:][path]filename]

Parameter

[[drive:][path]filename]

The name of the ASCII file, including its complete path information, that you want to edit. If the file specified by *filename* already exists, EDLIN automatically loads this file into memory for editing. If the specified file does not exist, EDLIN reserves the name you specify for a subsequent Save operation, at which time it will be created.

The EDLIN Commands

The following list contains the EDLIN commands, which you use to perform all of your editing operations:

Command	Function
a	Appends a line
c	Copies a line or lines
d	Deletes a line or lines
e	Ends an EDLIN session and saves your file to disk
i	Inserts lines into the current file
l	Lists a range of lines
m	Moves a range of text to a specified line
p	Pages through a file, 23 lines at a time
q	Ends an EDLIN session without saving the file to disk
r	Replaces text
s	Searches for specified text
t	Transfers the contents of another file into the file being edited
w	Writes specified lines to disk
line number	Displays the specified line and prepares that line for editing
Ctrl-C	Terminates the current operation

Related Command

See the EDIT command for information on the MS-DOS Editor, a more powerful text editor that replaces EDLIN in MS-DOS versions 5.0 and higher.

EGA.SYS

This device driver saves and restores an EGA display when running the Task Swapper from within DOS Shell. The Task Swapper allows multiple applications to be open at the same time, although it does not allow them to execute concurrently.

Syntax

```
DEVICE=[drive:][path]EGA.SYS
```

Parameters

```
[drive:][path]
```

Specifies where the EGA.SYS file is stored on your hard disk.

> *Caution:* If you have an EGA monitor, you must install the EGA.SYS device driver before running Task Swapper from within the DOS Shell.

> *Note:* If your system includes both a mouse and an EGA monitor, installing EGA.SYS before the mouse driver will increase the amount of memory available to DOS and your application programs.

EMM386

This command is used on computers with an 80386 or higher processor to enable or disable EMM386 expanded-memory support. (The EMM386 command also can be used to enable or disable support for a Weitek coprocessor.)

> *Caution:* The EMM386 command is only supported on systems that have an 80386 or higher processor. Attempting to execute the EMM386 command on a PC/XT or 80286 (AT) system causes MS-DOS to display the following message:
>
> ```
> EMM386 driver not installed
> ```

Syntax

```
EMM386 [ON|OFF|AUTO] [W=ON|W=OFF]
```

Parameters

ON|OFF|AUTO

Activates or suspends expanded-memory support once the EMM386.EXE device driver has been installed in memory.

- The ON parameter activates expanded-memory support. (The default value is ON.)
- The OFF parameter deactivates expanded-memory support.
- The AUTO parameter configures EMM386.EXE to auto mode. (In auto mode, EMM386.EXE enables expanded-memory support only when a program calls for it.)

W=ON|W=OFF

Enables or disables Weitek coprocessor support. The default value is W=OFF. The W=ON parameter enables Weitek coprocessor support even when expanded-memory support is disabled using the EMM386 OFF command.

> *Caution:* DOS uses the high memory area (HMA) to enable Weitek coprocessor support. Loading MS-DOS into the HMA with a DOS=HIGH command may interfere with Weitek coprocessor support.

> **Note:** For the EMM386 command to work properly, the EMM386.EXE driver must be installed in memory, using the appropriate statement in your CONFIG.SYS file.

Examples

The following command enables expanded-memory support if EMM386.EXE has been installed successfully from CONFIG.SYS:

```
EMM386 ON
```

The following command disables expanded-memory support if EMM386.EXE has been installed successfully from CONFIG.SYS:

```
EMM386 OFF
```

> **Note:** With EMM386 expanded-memory support turned off, DOS changes the EMM386 device driver to prevent programs from accessing expanded memory. Doing so allows you to load non-VCPI compliant programs, such as Windows 3.0 running in standard mode.

The following command enables support for a Weitek coprocessor, providing EMM386.EXE has been installed successfully from CONFIG.SYS:

```
EMM386 W=ON
```

The following command disables support for a Weitek coprocessor, providing EMM386.EXE has been installed successfully from CONFIG.SYS:

```
EMM386 W=OFF
```

> **Note:** If you specify the W=ON or W=OFF parameter and no Weitek coprocessor is installed in your computer system, MS-DOS displays the following error message:
>
> ```
> Weitek Coprocessor not installed
> ```

The following command displays the current status of EMM386 expanded-memory support:

```
EMM386
```

Related Command

See EMM386.EXE for information on how to install and configure the MS-DOS EMM386.EXE device driver.

EMM386.EXE

EMM386.EXE converts extended memory into expanded memory, providing access to the upper memory area on a computer that has an 80386 or higher processor.

Syntax

```
DEVICE=[drive:][path]EMM386.EXE [ON|OFF|AUTO] [memory]
[MIN=size] [W=ON|W=OFF] [Mx|FRAME=address|/Pmmmm] [Pn=address]
[X=mmmm-nnnn] [I=mmmm-nnnn] [B=address] [L=minXMS] [A=altregs]
[H=handles] [D=nnn] [RAM=mmmm-nnnn] [NOEMS] [NOVCPI] [HIGHSCAN]
[VERBOSE] [WIN=mmmm-nnnn] [NOHI] [ROM=mmmm-nnnn] [NOMOVEXBDA]
[ALTBOOT]
```

> **Caution:** To enable expanded memory management, your CONFIG.SYS file has to include the following statement, which must appear in CONFIG.SYS before the line that installs EMM386.EXE:
>
>   DEVICE=HIMEM.SYS

Parameters

[drive:][path]

Specifies the location of the EMM386.EXE file.

[ON|OFF|AUTO]

Activates and deactivates the EMM386.EXE device driver.

- The ON parameter activates expanded-memory support.
- The OFF parameter deactivates expanded-memory support.
- The AUTO parameter configures EMM386.EXE to auto mode. (In auto mode, EMM386.EXE enables expanded-memory support and upper memory block support only when a program calls for it.)

The default value is ON, but you can use the EMM386 command to change this value once EMM386.EXE is installed from your CONFIG.SYS file.

memory

Used to specify the maximum amount of extended memory that you want EMM386.EXE to convert to expanded/Virtual Control Program Interface memory (EMS/VCPI).

Values for memory are indicated in kilobytes and must be within a range from 64 through the lesser of the following two values:

- 32768
- the amount of extended memory available when DOS installs EMM386.EXE through CONFIG.SYS

> ✔ **Note:** The default value is the amount of free extended memory. EMM386.EXE rounds the specified value down to the nearest multiple of 16.

Switches

`MIN=size`

Used to specify the minimum amount of EMS/VCPI memory you want EMM386.EXE to provide. Setting a value with this switch guarantees the availability of EMS/VCPI memory by preventing other programs from using the memory it sets aside.

Values for MIN are indicated in kilobytes and must be within a range from 0 through the value specified by the MEMORY parameter.

- The default value is 256.
- If you specify the NOEMS switch, the default value is 0.
- If the value of MIN is greater than the value of MEMORY, EMM386.EXE uses the value specified by MIN.

`W=ON|W=OFF`

Enables or disables support for the Weitek coprocessor. The default setting is W=OFF.

`Mx`

Specifies the address at which you want DOS to establish a page frame for managing EMS. Valid settings for *x* are 1 through 14. Each setting indicates a different page frame address, as illustrated in the following list:

1	C000h
2	C400h
3	C800h
4	CC00h
5	D000h
6	D400h
7	D800h
8	DC00h
9	E000h

10	8000h
11	8400h
12	8800h
13	8C00h
14	9000h

> ✔ **Note:** You should only use values of 10 through 14 if your computer has at least 512K of installed RAM.

FRAME=address

Used to specify directly an address for the page-frame segment base. Valid settings for address are in the ranges 8000h through 9000h and C000h through E000h, using increments of 400h.

> 🚫 **Caution:** The following command provides expanded memory but disables the page frame:
>
> FRAME=NONE
>
> Be aware, however, that disabling the page frame can cause some programs that require expanded memory to work improperly.

/Pmmmm

Specifies the address of the page frame. Valid settings for *mmmm* are in the ranges 8000h through 9000h and C000h through E000h, using increments of 400h.

Pn=address

Specifies the segment address of a specific page, where *n* is the number of the page you are specifying, and *address* is the segment address you want. Valid settings for *n* are 0 through 255. Valid settings for *address* are in the ranges 8000h through 9C00h and C000h through EC00h, using increments of 400h.

Using the Mx switch, the FRAME switch, or the /Pmmmm switch precludes you from specifying addresses for pages 0 through 3 with the /Pmmmm switch.

> 🚫 **Caution:** To maintain compatibility with version 3.2 of the Lotus/Intel/Microsoft Expanded Memory Specification (LIM/EMS), you must specify contiguous addresses for pages 0 through 3.

`X=mmmm-nnnn`

Excludes the specified address range from EMM386.EXE control. Valid values for *mmmm* and *nnnn* are in the range A000h through FFFFh and are rounded down to the nearest 4-kilobyte boundary.

> ✔ **Note:** The X switch takes precedence over the I switch if the two ranges overlap.

`I=mmmm-nnnn`

Makes the specified address range available to EMS386.EXE for an EMS page or UMBs. Valid values for *mmmm* and *nnnn* are in the range A000h through FFFFh and are rounded down to the nearest 4-kilobyte boundary.

`B=address`

Used to specify the lowest segment address you want made available for EMS "banking" — that is, swapping 16-kilobyte pages in and out of memory. Valid values are in the range 1000h through 4000h. The default value is 4000h.

`L=minXMS`

Ensures that the specified amount of extended memory will still be available after you load EMM386.EXE. The default value is 0, and *min* is specified in kilobytes.

`A=altregs`

Used to specify how many fast alternate register sets, which DOS uses for multitasking, you want to allocate to EMM386.EXE. Valid values are in the range 0 through 254. The default value is 7.

> ✔ **Note:** Each alternate register set you specify increases by approximately 200 bytes the amount of memory required by EMM386.EXE.

`H=handles`

Specifies how many handles EMM386.EXE should set aside to manage EMS. Valid values are in the range 2 through 255. The default value is 64.

`D=nnn`

Specifies how many kilobytes of memory you want EMM386 to reserve for buffered direct memory access (DMA). Valid values for *nnn* are 16 through 256. The default value is 16.

```
RAM=mmmm-nnnn
```

Specifies a range of segment addresses you want EMM386 to configure as upper memory blocks (UMBs).

> *Note:* If no RAM is specified, EMM386.EXE uses all available extended memory.

```
NOEMS
```

Provides EMM386 access to the upper memory area but does not convert extended memory to expanded memory.

```
NOVCPI
```

Disables support for VCPI applications. This reduces the amount of extended memory allocated.

> *Caution:* This switch must be used with the NOEMS switch. If you specify the NOVCPI switch without also including the NOEMS switch, EMM386.EXE does not disable VCPI support.

> *Note:* Specifying both switches causes EMM386.EXE to disregard the MEMORY parameter and the MIN switch.

```
HIGHSCAN
```

Forces EMM386.EXE to use an additional check to determine the availability of upper memory for use as UMBs or EMS windows. Specifying this switch on some computers may have no effect, or may cause EMM386 to incorrectly identify upper memory areas as available when they are not. As a result, your computer might stop responding to your instructions.

```
VERBOSE
```

Instructs EMM386.EXE to display status and error messages when it is loaded from the CONFIG.SYS file.

```
WIN=mmmm-nnnn
```

Removes a specified range of addresses from control of EMM386.EXE and reserves that range for use by Windows. Valid settings for *mmmm* and *nnnn* are in the range A000h through FFFFh. EMM386.EXE rounds any entered range down to the nearest 4-kilobyte boundary.

> **Note:** The X switch takes precedence over the WIN switch if the two ranges overlap. The WIN switch takes precedence over the RAM, ROM, and I switches if their ranges overlap.

`[NOHI]`

Prevents EMM386.EXE from loading into the upper memory area. Specifying this switch decreases the amount of conventional RAM available to DOS and your application programs, while increasing the upper memory area available for UMBs.

`[ROM=mmmm-nnnn]`

Specifies a range of segment addresses that EMM386.EXE uses for shadow RAM — random-access memory set aside for read-only memory (ROM). Valid settings for *mmmm* and *nnnn* are A000h through FFFFh. EMM386.EXE rounds an entered value down to the nearest 4-kilobyte boundary. Specifying this switch can improve performance on systems that do not already have shadow RAM.

`NOMOVEXBDA`

The NOMOVEXBDA parameter prevents EMM386.EXE from moving the extended BIOS data into upper memory; instead, it remains in conventional memory.

`ALTBOOT`

In the event your computer doesn't respond to warm booting (pressing the CTRL+ALT+DEL key combination) when EMM386.EXE is loaded, include the ALTBOOT parameter. ALTBOOT forces EMM386.EXE to use an alternate handler to restart your computer.

> **CAUTION:** Use the preceding EMM386.EXE parameters and switches carefully. Installing EMM386.EXE incorrectly can disable your computer during system startup. If this occurs, you'll need to reboot your computer from a floppy disk and then edit CONFIG.SYS before attempting to restart your system.

Using EMM386.EXE with Windows 3.1

When EMM386.EXE is used with Windows 3.1, the following switches take precedence over certain settings in the Windows SYSTEM.INI file:

```
I
X
NOEMS
Mx
Pnnnn
FRAME
```

Settings in the Windows SYSTEM.INI file over which these switches take precedence include:

EMMINCLUDE
EMMEXCLUDE
EMMPAGEFRAME

> ✔ **Note:** Changing these settings within the SYSTEM.INI file has no effect on Windows performance, if EMM386.EXE is loaded during system startup.

If you have a small computer system interface (SCSI) or enhanced system device interface (ESDI) hard disk or other device, SMARTDRV double buffering may be required to use EMM386.EXE. Adding the following to your CONFIG.SYS file enables SMARTDRV double buffering:

```
DEVICE=SMARTDRV.EXE /DOUBLE_BUFFER
```

You'll need to add this line before any DEVICEHIGH statements and before any statements that load installable device drivers that use expanded memory.

Examples

Adding the following statements to your CONFIG.SYS file starts EMM386 as an expanded-memory emulator, using its default values:

```
DEVICE=HIMEM.SYS
DEVICE=EMM386.EXE
```

> ✔ **Note:** Unless noted otherwise, the examples here presume that HIMEM.SYS and EMM386.EXE are located in the root directory of the boot disk. If this is not the case on your system, you'll need to include the appropriate path information for these commands to work properly.

Adding the following line to your CONFIG.SYS file instructs EMM386.EXE to allocate a maximum of 2948K of memory and a guaranteed 256K of memory (the default value) to expanded memory management:

```
DEVICE=EMM386.EXE 2048
```

Adding either of the following lines to your CONFIG.SYS file instructs EMM386.EXE to emulate expanded memory, using the segment-base address D000h for the EMS page frame and allocating 1024K of memory for expanded memory management:

```
DEVICE=EMM386.EXE 1024 FRAME=D000
DEVICE=EMM386.EXE 1024 P0=D000 P1=D400 P2=D800 P3=DC00
```

Adding the following line to your CONFIG.SYS file preserves the settings from the previous exercise. It also prevents EMM386 from using the segment addresses C000h through CC00h and specifies that it should use 10 handles:

```
DEVICE=EMM386.EXE 1024 FRAME=D000 X=C000-CC00 H=124
```

Adding the following line to your CONFIG.SYS file instructs EMM386.EXE to provide access to the upper memory area and create EMS/VCPI memory:

```
DEVICE=EMM386.EXE RAM
```

EXIT

You use this command to exit the COMMAND.COM program (the command interpreter) and return to the program that started COMMAND.COM, if one exists.

Syntax

```
EXIT
```

Some applications provide temporary access to an MS-DOS command interpreter. (Opening an MS-DOS window from within the Windows environment is one example of such an application.) The EXIT command allows you to close the secondary command interpreter and return to the application from which it was started or to the original command interpreter.

Including the /P switch with the SHELL statement in your CONFIG.SYS file disables the EXIT command. Doing so ensures that you will not be able to quit the initial command interpreter.

> *Caution:* Failure to include the /P switch in the command statement within CONFIG.SYS when loading COMMAND.COM leaves the EXIT command enabled. This creates the potentially troublesome situation of allowing you to quit your initial command interpreter. Should this happen, and should the SHELL statement in the CONFIG.SYS file not indicate the location of COMMAND.COM, the only way to restart the command interpreter is to specify at the command prompt the location of the COMMAND.COM file.

Related Command

See COMMAND.COM for information on starting and using a second command interpreter.

EXPAND

The EXPAND command decompresses a compressed file. Compressed files can't be viewed or executed without first using the EXPAND command to decompress them. This command can be used to retrieve one or more files from the setup disks that accompany MS-DOS 6.0.

Syntax

    EXPAND [drive:][path]filename [[drive:][path]filename[...]]
    destination

Parameters

[drive:][path]filename

Specifies the location and name of a compressed file or group of files to be expanded.

✔ *Note:* EXPAND doesn't accept the DOS wildcard characters (* and ?).

destination

Used to specify a target location and/or name for the file(s) that is being decompressed.

✔ *Note:* If you're decompressing a single file, the destination can include a drive letter and colon, a directory name, a filename, or any combination of these items. When decompressing multiple files, DOS automatically assigns a filename to each destination file.

Retrieving Files from the Setup Disks

To limit the number of DOS distribution disks, Microsoft compresses most of the files on the installation or update disks provided with MS-DOS 6.0. Compressed files on the distribution disks use a file extension that ends with an underscore character (_). The DOS installation or upgrade program automatically decompresses these files as it copies them to you system. You must use the EXPAND command to retrieve additional files from the distribution disks following initial installation or they will not run properly. EXPAND prompts you automatically for any information it requires during a decompression operation.

Examples

Decompressing a Single File

In the following example, I'll assume you accidentally deleted the CHKDSK.EXE file from your DOS directory on drive C. The only way to re-create this file is to decompress and copy the original file CHKDSK.EX_, which can be found on your DOS 6.0 installation or upgrade disks. First, you'll need to determine which disk contains CHKDSK.EX_. To do this, use EDIT to view the contents of a file called PACKING.LST, which can be found on Setup disk 1 of your distribution disks. The PACKING.LST file identifies which disk contains the various DOS distribution files. After inserting the appropriate disk into drive A, the following command can be used to decompress and transfer the CHKDSK file to your DOS directory.

```
EXPAND A:\CHKDSK.EX_ C:\DOS\CHKDSK.EXE
```

Decompressing Multiple Files

The following command will decompress three files on a distribution disk in drive A and copy them to the DOS directory on drive C.

```
EXPAND A:\CHKDSK.EX_ A:\SETUP.BA_ A:\UNDELETE.EX_
```

Running EXPAND Interactively

If you omit the parameters when using the EXPAND command, it will prompt you for the location and name of compressed files and the destination you have in mind for the EXPANDed versions of these files, as follows:

```
Enter the name and/or path for the compressed file:
```

If, as in our previous example, you want to decompress and copy the CHKDSK.EX_ file from the Setup disk in drive A, type the following:

```
A:\CHKDSK.EX_
```

Next, EXPAND provides the following prompt:

```
Enter the name and/or path for the decompressed file:
```

If your DOS files are located in the C:\DOS directory, you would respond with the following:

```
C:\DOS\CHKDSK.EXE
```

Using this information, EXPAND would then complete the requested decompression operation.

FASTHELP

You use this command to request on-line information about the MS-DOS version 6.0 commands. The information displayed by FASTHELP is less detailed than information provided by the HELP command.

Syntax

```
FASTHELP [command]
[command /?]
```

Parameter

`command`

Used to identify the command about which you want information. If this parameter is not included, FASTHELP lists and briefly describes every command available in MS-DOS 6.0.

Switch

`/?`

When the command name appears on a line by itself, without FASTHELP but followed by the /? switch, DOS interprets it as the equivalent of the FASTHELP [command] command.

Examples

Either of the following two commands will display information about the XCOPY command:

```
FASTHELP XCOPY
XCOPY /?
```

You can request on-line help about a specific command in one of two ways. The first method, shown above, is to specify the name of the command on the FASTHELP command line. The second method, also shown above, requires that you type both the name of the command and a /? switch at the command prompt; this method is slightly faster.

Related Command

See the HELP command for another method of obtaining on-line assistance with DOS commands.

FASTOPEN

This command can be used from the DOS system prompt or from within your CONFIG.SYS file to run the FASTOPEN program. By tracking the location of files on a hard disk and storing this information in memory, where it is easily accessible, FASTOPEN decreases the amount of time needed to open frequently used files.

Syntax

```
FASTOPEN drive:[[=]n] [drive:[n][...]] [/X]
```

Use the following syntax to load FASTOPEN with your CONFIG.SYS file:

```
INSTALL=[[dos-drive:]dos-path]FASTOPEN.EXE drive:[[=]n]
[drive:[[=]n][...]] [/X]
```

Parameters

`drive:`

Used to specify a hard disk drive for which you want FASTOPEN to track the location of files.

`n`

Used to specify the number of files FASTOPEN can track concurrently. Valid values for *n* are 10 through 999. The default value is 48.

`[dos-drive:]dos-path`

Indicates the location of FASTOPEN.EXE.

Switch

`/X`

Creates a name cache in expanded memory, rather than conventional memory. The name cache is a special area of memory that MS-DOS uses to store (cache) the names and locations of opened files.

> ***Caution:*** To avoid losing data, do not run a disk-compacting program such as Norton Speed Disk or Microsoft Defrag while FASTOPEN.EXE is loaded.

FASTOPEN works only on hard disks. It cannot be used with floppy disks, network drives, or other storage devices. FASTOPEN can manage up to 24 hard-disk partitions concurrently. FASTOPEN tracks the number of files specified by the *n* parameter for each partition, up to a maximum of 999 files in all partitions.

Only one copy of FASTOPEN can be run at any given time. The only way to modify the FASTOPEN settings, once FASTOPEN has been installed, is to restart your computer and reload MS-DOS.

> ***Caution:*** Do not use the FASTOPEN command from within the MS-DOS Shell. Doing so can lock up your machine.

FASTOPEN requires approximately 48 bytes of memory for each file that it tracks.

Example

Adding the following line to your CONFIG.SYS file instructs DOS to track the location of up to 75 files on drive C:

```
INSTALL=C:\DOS\FASTOPEN.EXE C:=75
```

> ***Note:*** This example assumes FASTOPEN.EXE is located in the DOS directory of drive C. If this is not the case on your system, you'll need to adjust the command structure accordingly.

FC

FC compares the contents of two files and reports on their differences.

Syntax

The following syntax performs an ASCII comparison:

```
FC [/A] [/C] [/L] [/LBn] [/N] [/T] [/W]
[/nnnn] [drive1:][path1]filename1 [drive2:][path2]filename2
```

The following syntax performs a binary comparison:

```
FC /B [drive1:][path1]filename1 [drive2:][path2]filename2
```

Parameters

[drive1:][path1]filename1

Specifies the location and name of the first file to be compared.

[drive2:][path2]filename2

Specifies the location and name of the second file to be compared.

Switches

/A

Abbreviates the results of an ASCII comparison. By default, FC displays all lines that are different. The /A switch instructs FC to display only the first and last line for each set of differences.

/C

Ignores the case of letters. For example, with the /C switch selected, FC considers t and T to be the same.

/L

Compares the files in ASCII mode.

> ✓ **Note:** ASCII mode is the default mode for comparing files that do not have extensions of .EXE, .COM, .SYS, .OBJ, .LIB, or .BIN.

/LBn

Specifies how many lines you want to use for an internal line buffer, which FC uses to store consecutive lines in which differences exist.

> **Note:** The default length of the FC line buffer is 100 lines. If the files being compared have more than this number of consecutive differing lines, FC cancels the comparison and returns you to the system prompt. (Notice that this value represents consecutive lines in which difference are detected, *not* the number of lines in the files.)

/N

Displays the line numbers for reference during an ASCII comparison.

/T

Suppresses the default FC procedure of expanding tabs to spaces during an ASCII file comparison.

/W

Compresses tabs and spaces during the comparison. If a line contains many consecutive spaces or tabs, specifying the /W switch instructs FC to ignore tabs and spaces at the beginning and end of a line.

/nnnn

Specifies how many consecutive lines must match before FC considers the two files it is comparing to be resynchronized. The default is 2; if the number of matching lines in the files is less than this number, FC displays the matching lines as differences.

/B

Compares the files in binary mode. When running in binary mode, FC compares the specified files byte by byte. It does not attempt to resynchronize the files after finding a mismatch.

> **Note:** Binary mode is the default mode for comparing files that have extensions of .EXE, .COM, .SYS, .OBJ, .LIB, or .BIN.

MS-DOS uses the following format to report mismatches found during a binary comparison:

```
xxxxxxxx: yy zz
```

The value of *xxxxxxxx* specifies the relative hexadecimal address for the pair of bytes, measured from the beginning of the file. The hexadecimal values for *yy* and *zz* represent the mismatched bytes from filename1 and filename2, respectively.

You can include wildcards (? and *) in one or the other filename specified with the FC command, but not both. The results of a wildcard search are as follows:

- Including a wildcard in *filename1* instructs FC to compare all files matching the search parameters to the file identified as *filename2*.

- Including a wildcard in *filename2* instructs FC to use whatever value is in the corresponding position in *filename1*.

Examples

The following command initiates an ASCII comparison of two text files named BUDGET.RPT and EXPENSE.RPT, displaying the results in abbreviated format:

```
FC /A BUDGET.RPT EXPENSE.RPT
```

The following command performs a binary comparison of two batch files named MENU.BAT and PROGRAMS.BAT:

```
FC /B MENU.BAT PROGRAMS.BAT
```

The following command compares every .BAT file in the current directory with the file MODEL.BAT:

```
FC *.BAT MODEL.BAT
```

The following command compares the file MY.BAT on drive C with the file MY.BAT on drive D:

```
FC C:MY.BAT D:*.BAT
```

FCBS

When used in a CONFIG.SYS file, the FCBS command specifies the number of file control blocks that MS-DOS can have open at any given time.

Syntax

    FCBS=x

Parameter

x

Specifies the number of file control blocks that MS-DOS can have open at one time. Valid settings for *x* are 1 through 255. The default value is 4.

> ✔ ***Note:*** A file control block stores information about a file. File control blocks are a throwback to the early days of the PC revolution. Today's applications no longer rely on file control blocks. Therefore, you should only include an FCBS statement in your CONFIG.SYS file if a specific program you use requires it.

Example

Adding the following statement to your CONFIG.SYS file instructs MSDOS to allow ten file control blocks to be open concurrently:

    FCBS=10

Related Command

Most programs use file handles. See the FILES command for more information about setting up file handles.

FDISK

This command runs FDISK, which helps you prepare a hard disk for use with MS-DOS.

Syntax

FDISK [/STATUS]

Switch

/STATUS

Displays information about the partitions on your computer's hard disk(s) without actually running the FDISK program. You use FDISK to perform the following tasks:

- Create a primary MS-DOS partition
- Create an extended MS-DOS partition
- Set a partition to active
- Delete a partition
- Display partition data
- Select the next hard disk for partitioning, if a system has multiple hard disks.

FDISK works only on hard disks physically installed on your computer. It will not work on a drive formed by using the SUBST command (which allows you to assign a drive name to a directory); nor will FDISK work on a network drive.

Caution: FDISK has the potential of destroying all the data on your hard disk. For this reason, you should never experiment with the FDISK command.

Examples

The following command runs FDISK and allows you to prepare your hard disk for use:

FDISK

After you issue this command, FDISK displays a series of menus designed to help you create partition(s) on a hard disk.

The following command does not run FDISK, but rather displays information about the partitions on your hard disk:

FDISK /STATUS

FILES

You use this command in a CONFIG.SYS file to indicate the number of files that MS-DOS can access concurrently.

Syntax

    FILES=x

Parameter

x

Specifies the number of files that MS-DOS can access at one time. Valid settings for *x* are in the range 8 through 255. The default value is 8. Three of these files are automatically reserved for use by DOS.

> ✔ ***Note:*** The default setting of 8 files is, quite honestly, inadequate. One of the first things you should do, therefore, is add a line to your CONFIG.SYS file increasing this number. For each additional file that DOS can open, the amount of memory available to your programs is decreased by approximately 64 bytes.

Example

To specify that MS-DOS can access up to 20 files at one time, add the following line to your CONFIG.SYS file:

    FILES=20

FIND

FIND searches for a specified text string within a file or files.

Syntax

```
FIND [/V] [/C] [/N] [/I] "string" [[drive:][path]filename[...]]
```

Parameters

`"string"`

Specifies the text string (group of characters) that you want to find. This text must be enclosed within quotation marks, as shown in the syntax statement, above.

`[drive:][path]filename`

Specifies the location and name of the file FIND should search when looking for the specified string. *Filename* cannot contain DOS wildcard characters.

Switches

`/V`

Displays all lines that do not contain the specified string.

`/C`

Does not display lines containing the specified text but, rather, displays a count of the number of lines in which it appears.

> ✔ *Note:* If you include both the /C and /V switches in a single FIND command, FIND displays a count of the lines that do not contain the specified string.

`/N`

Precedes each line in which the specified text string exists with a line number indicating its relative position within the file.

> ✔ *Note:* If you include both the /C and /N switches in the same FIND command, FIND ignores the /N switch.

`/I`

Specifies that the search is not to be case-sensitive. With the /I switch selected, for example, FIND does not differentiate between t and T.

Find and Special Characters

To include quotation marks in the search, enter two sets of quotation marks for each set of quotation marks contained within the string, as in the following example:

```
FIND """Drive,"" he said." C:\TEXT\DIALOG
```

FIND does not recognize carriage returns. When using FIND to search a file that includes carriage returns, you must limit the search string to text that is not likely to include a carriage return. For example, FIND will not report a match for the string "dining room" wherever a carriage return occurs between the "dining" and "room".

Searching Multiple Files

You cannot use wildcards (* and ?) in a FIND command. However, you can use FIND with the FOR command, which allows you to search multiple files with a single command line. The following command, for example, uses this method to search the current directory for files that have the extension .TXT; in each file found, the command searches for the string "Nimersheim":

```
FOR %F IN (*.TXT) DO FIND "Nimersheim" %F
```

Examples

The following command displays all lines from a file called MENU.BAT that contain the string "echo":

```
FIND "echo" MENU.BAT
```

The following command displays all lines from a file called MENU.BAT that contain the string "echo", whether that word is written in upper- or lowercase letters:

```
FIND /I "echo" MENU.BAT
```

Related Command

See the FOR command for information about how to specify multiple files for a text search.

FOR

FOR runs a specified command for each file in a set of files.

Syntax

```
FOR %variable|%%variable IN (set) DO command
[command-parameters]
```

Parameters

`%variable or %%variable`

Represents a replaceable variable. The FOR command replaces the %%*variable* in a batch file — or the %*variable* when entering the FOR command directly from the keyboard — with each text string in the specified set until the command (which is specified with the command parameter) processes all the files.

`(set)`

Identifies the files, group of files, or text string that you want to process with the specified command. You must enclose the set parameter within parentheses (( )).

`command`

Specifies the command that you want to carry out on each file identified by the set parameter.

`command-parameters`

Specifies any parameters or switches that you want to use with the specified command (if the specified command uses any parameters or switches).

> ✔ *Note:* IN and DO are not parameters, but they are required in the FOR command. Omitting either of these keywords causes MS-DOS to display an error message.

Using the Replaceable Variable

To avoid confusion with the batch file parameters %0 through %9, FOR lets you substitute any character for its variable except the numerals 0 through 9. It's possible to use multiple values for the variable in complex batch programs; you cannot, however, enter multiple FOR commands on the same command line.

Specifying a Group of Files

By using the DOS wildcards (* and ?) in the *set* parameter, you can perform a FOR operation on a group of files or multiple groups of files. The following examples all represent valid file sets:

```
(*.doc)
(*.doc *.txt *.me)
(jan*.doc jan*.rpt feb*.doc feb*.rpt)
(ar??1991.* ap??1991.*)
```

Examples

The following command uses the replaceable variable %T and the TYPE command to display the contents of all the files in the current directory that have the extension .BAT or .TXT.

```
FOR %T IN (*.BAT *.TXT) DO TYPE %T
```

✔ *Note:* If you're using this command in a batch file, replace every occurrence of %T with %%T.

FOR statements can include command switches, pipes, and redirection symbols. The following command, for example, redirects the output of the previous FOR example to LPT1, your first parallel port:

```
FOR %T IN (*.BAT *.TXT) DO TYPE %T > LPT1
```

FORMAT

This command formats the disk in the specified drive to accept MS-DOS files.

Syntax

```
FORMAT drive: [/V[:label]] [/Q] [/U] [/F:size][/B|/S]
FORMAT drive: [/V[:label]] [/Q] [/U] [/T:tracks /N:sectors] [/B|/S]
FORMAT drive: [/V[:label]] [/Q] [/U] [/1] [/4] [/B|/S]
FORMAT drive: [/Q] [/U] [/1] [/4] [/8] [/B|/S]
```

Parameter

drive:

Identifies the drive containing the disk you want to format.

Switches

/V:label

Specifies a volume label for the disk being formatted. The maximum allowable length for a volume label is 11 characters.

✔ *Note:* If you omit the /V switch or use it without specifying a volume label, MS-DOS prompts you for the volume label after it finishes formatting the disk.

/Q

Tells DOS to perform a quick format on the disk. When performing a quick format, FORMAT merely deletes the file allocation table (FAT) and the root directory of a previously formatted disk. The disk is not scanned for bad sectors.

✔ *Note:* Use the /Q switch to reformat previously formatted disks that you know are in good condition.

/U

Specifies an unconditional format operation for a floppy or hard disk. Unconditional formatting destroys all existing data on the disk. This prevents you from using an UNFORMAT command to recover data on a disk that is accidentally formatted.

/F:size

Specifies the size of the floppy disk to format. The following list describes the valid *size* parameters you can use with the /F switch:

160 or 160k or 160kb
160K, single-sided, double-density, 5.25" disk

180 or 180k or 180kb
180K, single-sided, double-density, 5.25" disk

320 or 320k or 320kb
320K, double-sided, double-density, 5.25" disk

360 or 360k or 360kb
360K, double-sided, double-density, 5.25" disk

720 or 720k or 720kb
720K, double-sided, double-density, 3.5" disk

1200 or 1200k or 1200kb or 1.2 or 1.2m or 1.2mb
1.2-MB, double-sided, quadruple-density, 5.25" disk

1440 or 1440k or 1440kb or 1.44 or 1.44m or 1.44mb
1.44-MB, double-sided, quadruple-density, 3.5" disk

2880 or 2880k or 2880kb or 2.88 or 2.88m or 2.88mb
2.88-MB, double-sided, extra-high-density, 3.5" disk

> ✔ **Note:** The /F switch is available only in DOS versions 4.0 and higher. Whenever possible, use the /F switch instead of the /T and /N switches to specify disk size and format.

/B

Formats the disk but leaves enough space to allow that disk to accept the three system files for any version of MS-DOS.

> ✔ **Note:** The /B switch is maintained in MS-DOS version 6.0 for compatibility reasons only, because previous releases of MS-DOS required that you reserve this space prior to using the SYS command to copy the system files to the disk.

/S

Automatically copies the DOS system files on a disk following formatting.

/T:tracks

Specifies the number of tracks that should be created on this disk.

> ✔ ***Note:*** Whenever possible, use the /F switch instead of this switch. If you use the /T switch, you must also use the /N switch; together, these two switches provide the same information represented by a single /F switch. The /F and /T switches cannot be used in the same FORMAT command.

/N:sectors

Specifies the number of sectors per track.

> ✔ ***Note:*** Whenever possible, use the /F switch instead of this switch. If you use the /N switch, you must also use the /T switch; together, these two switches provide the same information represented by a single /F switch. The /F and /N switches cannot be used in the same FORMAT command.

/1

Formats a disk for use in a single-sided floppy disk drive.

/4

Formats a standard 360K double-sided, double-density floppy disk in a 1.2MB high-density disk drive.

> 🚫 ***Caution:*** Some 360K drives cannot reliably read disks formatted with this switch.

/8

Formats a 5.25" disk to contain 8 sectors per track. Use this switch to format a floppy disk to be compatible with MS-DOS versions prior to 2.0.

Formatting a Hard Disk

When you use the FORMAT command to format a hard disk, MS-DOS displays a message of the following form before attempting to format the hard disk:

```
WARNING, ALL DATA ON NON-REMOVABLE DISK
DRIVE x: WILL BE LOST!

Proceed with Format (Y/N)?_
```

To format the hard disk, press Y. Pressing N cancels the FORMAT operation and returns you to the DOS system prompt.

Format Messages

After formatting the disk, MS-DOS displays a message listing the total disk space, any space found to be defective, the total space used by the operating system — if you used the /S or /B switch — and how much space remains available for your files.

If you specify the /U switch or any switch that changes the size of the disk, FORMAT performs an unconditional format operation by deleting all data on the disk.

Quick Formatting

Specifying the /Q switch speeds up the formatting process. For even faster formatting, use both the /Q and /U switches.

> *Caution:* Use the /Q switch only if you have *not* received read or write errors on the disk being formatted.

FORMAT Exit Codes

The following list shows each exit code and a brief description of its meaning:

0	The format operation was successful.
3	The user pressed CTRL+C or CTRL+BREAK to stop the process.
4	A fatal error occurred (any error other than 0, 3, or 5).
5	The user pressed N in response to the prompt "Proceed with Format (Y/N)?" to stop the process.

You can check these exit codes by using the ERRORLEVEL condition with the IF batch command. For an example of a batch program that supports ERRORLEVEL conditions, see the CHOICE command.

> *Caution:* Formatting a disk destroys any data that the disk previously contained.

Examples

Use the following command to format a new floppy disk in drive A, using the default size:

```
FORMAT A:
```

Use the following command to perform a quick format operation on a previously formatted disk in drive A:

`FORMAT A: /Q`

Use the following command to format a floppy disk in drive B, completely deleting all data on the disk:

`FORMAT B: /U`

Use the following command to format a 720K system disk in drive B:

`FORMAT B: /F:720 /S`

Use the following command to format a floppy disk in drive A and assign it the volume label "MY_DATA":

`FORMAT A: /V:MY_DATA`

Related Commands

See the UNFORMAT command for information about restoring disks after using the FORMAT command.

See the DIR, LABEL, and VOL commands for more information about disk volume labels.

GOTO

GOTO specifies program branching within a batch file. You use the GOTO command within a batch program to change the order in which the lines it contains are executed. If current conditions indicate that program branching should occur, MS-DOS finds the section of the batch file identified with the specified label, and it processes the commands beginning on the next line.

Syntax

    GOTO label

Parameter

   label

   A label used to identify where the batch file should branch to.

> ✓ **Note:** A label may be up to 8 characters long. It may include spaces but not other separators, such as commas, semicolons, or equal signs.

MS-DOS identifies as a label any line in a batch program that begins with a colon (:). Recognizing that a label line is used only as a marker, DOS ignores any commands it contains.

If you specify a label that does not exist, DOS terminates the batch and displays the following message:

    Label not found

Using GOTO for Conditional Operations

The GOTO command by itself unconditionally transfers control to a label within a batch file. However, it is possible to create a "smart" GOTO that can decide whether or not it should skip to a particular label. This is accomplished by combining GOTO with the IF batch command.

Briefly, IF allows a condition to be tested. If the condition is true, then the command following IF and the clause containing the condition will be executed. The IF command can be used in this way to test for such things as the existence of a file, a particular parameter entered at the command line, or an error condition.

Example

The following file uses a series of GOTO statements to automatically select the correct disk drive in which to format a disk based on the drive letter entered by the user when he or she executes the batch program:

```
@ECHO OFF
CLS
IF %1 == A: GOTO ABRANCH
IF %1 == a: GOTO ABRANCH
IF %1 == B: GOTO BBRANCH
IF %1 == b: GOTO BBRANCH
GOTO END
:ABRANCH
FORMAT A: /S
GOTO END
:BBRANCH
FORMAT B: /S
GOTO END
:END
CLS
```

> ✔ *Note:* As this example illustrates, GOTO is often used on the same command line with other commands to perform conditional operations.

Related Command

See the IF command for more information about conditional operations.

GRAPHICS

GRAPHICS is a special utility that allows MS-DOS to print the contents of a graphics or color display.

Syntax

```
GRAPHICS [type] [[drive:][path]filename] [/R] [/B] [/LCD]
[/PRINTBOX:STD|/PRINTBOX:LCD]
```

Parameters

type

Specifies the type of printer connected to your computer's PRN port. The following list contains the valid choices for this parameter and provides a brief description of each printer type:

COLOR1
An IBM Personal Computer Color Printer with black ribbon

COLOR4
An IBM Personal Computer Color Printer with RGB (red, green, blue, and black) ribbon

COLOR8
An IBM Personal Computer Color Printer with CMY (cyan, magenta, yellow, and black) ribbon

HPDEFAULT
Any Hewlett-Packard PCL printer

DESKJET
A Hewlett-Packard DeskJet printer

GRAPHICS
An IBM Personal Graphics Printer, IBM Proprinter, or IBM Quietwriter printer

GRAPHICSWIDE
An IBM Personal Graphics Printer with an 11-inch-wide carriage

LASERJET
A Hewlett-Packard LaserJet printer

LASERJETII
A Hewlett-Packard LaserJet II printer

PAINTJET
A Hewlett-Packard PaintJet printer

QUIETJET
A Hewlett-Packard QuietJet printer

QUIETJETPLUS
A Hewlett-Packard QuietJet Plus printer

RUGGEDWRITER
A Hewlett-Packard RuggedWriter printer

RUGGEDWRITERWIDE
A Hewlett-Packard RuggedWriterwide printer

THERMAL
An IBM PC-convertible Thermal Printer

THINKJET
A Hewlett-Packard ThinkJet printer

`[drive:][path]filename`

Identifies the location and name of the file containing information about all supported printers. If this parameter is omitted, DOS looks for its default printer file, GRAPHICS.PRO, in both the current directory and the directory containing the GRAPHICS.COM file.

Switches

`/R`

Prints the image using reversed print mode — that is, white characters on a black background. (The default print method is black letters on a white background.)

`/B`

Prints the background in color. This switch is valid only for COLOR4 and COLOR8 printers.

`/LCD`

Prints an image by using the liquid crystal display (LCD) aspect ratio instead of the CGA aspect ratio. The effect of this switch is the same as specifying the /PRINTBOX:LCD switch.

`/PRINTBOX:STD|/PRINTBOX:LCD`

Selects the print-box size. (You may abbreviate PRINTBOX as PB.)

> ✔ ***Note:*** The GRAPHICS command supports the CGA, EGA, and VGA graphics display modes.

Printing the Contents of the Screen

Once GRAPHICS.COM is installed, pressing Shift+PrintScrn initiates a print operation.

> 🚫 ***Caution:*** You cannot use the SHIFT+PRINT SCREEN key combination to print the contents of a screen to a PostScript printer.

Example

Use the following command to prepare to print a graphics screen on your printer:

```
GRAPHICS
```

With the information you want to print displayed on your screen, press Shift+PrintScrn. DOS scans the current display and sends it to the printer.

Related Command

See the PRINT command for information about printing text files.

HELP

You use HELP to display MS-DOS's on-line Help messages.

Syntax

```
HELP [command]
```
or
```
HELP [/B] [/G] [/H] [/NOHI] [command]
```

Parameter

`command`

Use this optional parameter to bypass the HELP index and immediately display information on a specific command or topic.

Switches

`/B`

Use this switch if your screen display is a monochrome monitor equipped with a graphics card.

`/G`

Speeds the update of data on a CGA monitor.

`/H`

Monitors usually display 25 lines per screen, but if you include this switch, the maximum number of lines possible for your hardware will be exhibited on screen.

`/NOHI`

For use with monitors lacking high-intensity support.

Example

The following command displays the HELP index:

`HELP`

The following command bypasses the HELP index and displays information about the DOS FORMAT command:

`HELP FORMAT`

Related Command

See the FASTHELP command for information about displaying abbreviated Help messages for DOS commands.

HIMEM.SYS

HIMEM.SYS is the MS-DOS extended-memory manager. This driver, when loaded from the CONFIG.SYS file, coordinates the use of any extended memory (the memory above one megabyte) installed on your computer.

Syntax

```
DEVICE=[drive:][path]HIMEM.SYS [/A20CONTROL:ON|OFF]
[/CPUCLOCK:ON|OFF] [/EISA] [/HMAMIN=m] [/INT15=xxxx]
[/NUMHANDLES=n] [/MACHINE:xxxx] [/SHADOWRAM:ON|OFF] [/VERBOSE]
```

Parameter

`[drive:][path]`

Specifies the location of the HIMEM.SYS file.

> ✓ *Note:* You can omit the drive and path information if HIMEM.SYS is stored in the root directory of your startup drive.

Switches

`/A20CONTROL:ON|OFF`

Specifies whether HIMEM should take control of the A20 line. The A20 handler gives your computer access to the high memory area (HMA). The default setting is /A20CONTROL:ON. Specifying /A20CONTROL:OFF causes HIMEM to take control of the A20 line only if A20 was off when HIMEM was loaded.

`/CPUCLOCK:ON|OFF`

Instructs HIMEM whether or not it should manage the clock speed of your computer. With some computers, loading HIMEM causes the system to switch to a different clock speed. If this happens on your system, specifying /CPUCLOCK:ON may correct the problem. The default setting is /CPUCLOCK:OFF.

> ✓ *Note:* Enabling the CPUCLOCK option slows down HIMEM.

`/EISA`

This switch is used only on an EISA (Extended Industry Standard Architecture) system with more than 16MB of RAM. On such systems, the /EISA switch allocates all available extended memory.

`/HMAMIN=m`

Specifies how many kilobytes of memory an application must require for HIMEM to give that application use of the high memory area (HMA). *m* can range from 0 to 63, which represents the number of kilobytes in the HMA.

> ✓ ***Note:*** The /HMAMIN switch is optional. If you omit this switch — or set it to its default value of 0 — HIMEM allocates the HMA to the first application that requests it, regardless of how much of the HMA the application is going to use. In addition, the /HMAMIN switch has no effect when the computer is running Windows in 386 Enhanced mode.

`/INT15=xxxx`

Allocates the amount of extended memory (in kilobytes) to be reserved for the Interrupt 15h interface. Valid settings for *xxxx* range from 64 to 65535. If you specify a value less than 64, *xxxx* is set to 0, which is its default value.

> ✓ ***Note:*** Some older applications use the Interrupt 15h interface, rather than the standard extended memory specification, to allocate extended memory. Setting *xxxx* to 64KB ensures that enough memory is available to applications that use Interrupt 15h.

`/NUMHANDLES=n`

Specifies the maximum number of extended memory block (EMB) handles that can be used simultaneously. Valid settings for NUMHANDLES range from 1 to 128. The default value is 32.

`/MACHINE:xxxx`

Specifies what type of computer you are using.

> ✓ ***Note:*** HIMEM normally detects automatically the type of system on which it is being installed. If it can't, HIMEM uses the default system type: IBM AT or compatible. If you have trouble loading HIMEM, try choosing a system type from the following list.

The value for *xxxx* can be any of the codes or corresponding numbers listed in the following table:

at	1	IBM AT or 100% compatible
ps2	2	IBM PS/2
ptlcascade	3	Phoenix Cascade BIOS
hpvectra	4	HP Vectra (A & A+)
att6300plus	5	AT&T 6300 Plus
acer1100	6	Acer 1100
toshiba	7	Toshiba 1600 & 1200XE
wyse	8	Wyse 12.5 Mhz 286
tulip	9	Tulip SX
zenith	10	Zenith ZBIOS
at1	11	IBM PC/AT (alternative delay)
at2	12	IBM PC/AT (alternative delay)
css	12	CSS Labs
at3	13	IBM PC/AT (alternative delay)
philips	13	Philips
fasthp	14	HP Vectra
ibm7552	15	IBM 7552 Industrial Computer
bullmicral	16	Bull Micral 60
dell	17	Dell XBIOS

/SHADOWRAM:ON|OFF

The setting of this switch determines whether HIMEM should enable or disable shadow RAM, assuming that it is available on your computer.

Some computer systems automatically copy code from ROM into the much faster RAM at startup. This technique of making use of shadow RAM makes the system run faster, but also reduces the amount of extended memory available to applications. Ordinarily, HIMEM.SYS will not interfere with a system's use of shadow RAM. However, on systems with less than 2MB of RAM, HIMEM.SYS will automatically attempt to disable the use of shadow RAM, thereby creating more extended memory for itself to allocate. However, this can tend to slow system performance unacceptably. In this case, the default behavior of HIMEM.SYS can be changed by using the /SHADOWRAM:ON switch.

/VERBOSE
/V

Instructs HIMEM.SYS to display status and error messages as it is loaded into memory from the CONFIG.SYS file. You may abbreviate /VERBOSE as /V. An alternative method of displayin status messages is to depress the ALT key as HIMEM.SYS is loaded.

Installing HIMEM.SYS

As a rule, you will not need to specify any of the above command-line options. The default HIMEM values are appropriate for most computers.

You install HIMEM by adding a DEVICE command for HIMEM.SYS to your CONFIG.SYS file. The HIMEM command line must come before any commands that start applications or device drivers that use extended memory; for example, HIMEM.SYS must come before the EMM386 command line.

Examples

Adding the following statement to your CONFIG.SYS file loads HIMEM, using its default values:

```
DEVICE=HIMEM.SYS
```

This statement assumes HIMEM.SYS is stored on the root directory of your startup drive. If HIMEM.SYS is located in another directory on your system, be sure to include the necessary path information in your CONFIG.SYS file.

The following statements install HIMEM.SYS and load DOS into HMA:

```
DEVICE=HIMEM.SYS
DOS=HIGH
```

> ✓ *Note:* HIMEM.SYS or another XMS driver must be installed from CONFIG.SYS before you attempt to load MS-DOS into the high memory area (HMA). The DOS=HIGH command can appear anywhere in your CONFIG.SYS file after HIMEM.SYS is installed.

IF

IF performs conditional processing from within a batch file.

Syntax

```
IF [NOT] ERRORLEVEL number command
IF [NOT] string1==string2 command
IF [NOT] EXIST filename command
```

Parameters

`NOT`

Instructs MS-DOS to carry out the specified command only if the condition evaluated by the IF statement is false.

`ERRORLEVEL number`

Specifies a true condition only if the most recently returned exit code is equal to or greater than the specified number.

`command`

Indicates the command that MS-DOS should execute if the condition specified in the preceding IF statement is met.

`string1==string2`

Used to compare strings or batch variables (%1 through %9). If the two values being compared are equal, IF returns a true condition. You do not need to enclose literal strings in quotation marks.

`EXIST filename`

Returns a true condition if the specified filename exists. MS-DOS carries out the command following an IF statement only if the condition specified in the IF statement is true. If this condition is false, DOS ignores the command.

Examples

The following statement displays the message "Can't find data file" only if MS-DOS doesn't find a file called TEST.TXT:

```
IF NOT EXIST TEST.TXT ECHO Test file not found
```

The following set of statements displays an error message only if an error occurs during disk formatting:

```
:BEGIN
@ECHO OFF
FORMAT A: /S
IF NOT ERRORLEVEL 1 GOTO END
ECHO An error occurred during formatting.
:END
ECHO End of batch program.
```

✔ *Note:* When a program stops, it returns an exit code to MS-DOS. For example, a value of 1 is typically used to indicate that DOS could not complete the specified operations. In the previous example, this exit code (ERRORLEVEL=1) was used to display the error message.

INCLUDE

This command is used in a CONFIG.SYS file to include the contents of a configuration block in an optional startup menu.

Syntax

INCLUDE=blockname

Parameter

`blockname`

Specifies the name of the configuration block to include in a particular set of startup options.

> ✔ *Note:* The INCLUDE command is one of five special CONFIG.SYS commands used for defining multiple configurations within a single CONFIG.SYS file.

Examples

The following CONFIG.SYS file defines three configurations:

```
[menu]
menuitem base_config,Base configuration only
menuitem full_config,Normal configuration
menuitem net_config, Normal configuration with network

[base_config]
dos=high
device=c:\dos\himem.sys

[full_config]
include=base_config
dos=umb
device=c:\dos\emm386.exe ram
devicehigh=c:\dos\ramdrive.sys 512

[net_config]
include=full_config
devicehigh=c:\net\network.sys

[common]
```

This CONFIG.SYS file contains three configuration blocks. Each subsequent block uses an INCLUDE statement to incorporate all features of the blocks that precede it.

The [base_config] block contains two typical CONFIG.SYS commands:

```
DOS=HIGH
DEVICE=C:\DOS\HIMEM.SYS
```

The [full_config] block includes the commands in [base_config] plus the following three statements:

```
DOS=UMB
DEVICE=C:\DOS\EMM386.EXE RAM
DEVICEHIGH=C:\DOS\RAMDRIVE.SYS 512
```

The third configuration, [net_config], includes all the commands in [full_config] (which in turn includes those in [base_config]) plus the following statement, which loads a network driver:

```
DEVICEHIGH=C:\NET\NETWORK.SYS
```

> *Note:* It's always a good idea to end a complex CONFIG.SYS file with a [common] block, as in the previous example. This allows application installation programs to append commands to your CONFIG.SYS file, if necessary.

Related Commands

The INCLUDE command is one of five special CONFIG.SYS commands for defining multiple configurations. With multiple configurations, you define a menu that appears when your computer starts. Each menu item corresponds to a block of commands, or "configuration block," in your CONFIG.SYS file.

The other four commands used to create a startup menu are:

MENUCOLOR	Used to specify foreground and background colors for a startup menu
MENUDEFAULT	Used to specify the default menu item
MENUITEM	Used to define an item on the menu
SUBMENU	Used to define a submenu

INSTALL

This command is used in a CONFIG.SYS file to install executable, memory-resident programs into RAM each time you start your computer. INSTALL does not create an environment for a program it loads. Therefore, slightly less memory is used if you load a program with INSTALL rather than from your AUTOEXEC.BAT file.

> *Caution:* Some programs may not run properly when loaded with an INSTALL statement.

Syntax

    INSTALL=[drive:][path]filename [command-parameters]

Parameters

    [drive:][path]filename

Specifies the location and name of the memory-resident program you want to run.

    command-parameters

Used to enter any command parameters required by the program specified with filename.

Example

The following statement installs DOS's FASTOPEN.EXE program from your CONFIG.SYS file specifying that FASTOPEN be configured to allow up to 75 files to be open concurrently:

    INSTALL=C:\FASTOPEN.EXE C:=75

KEYB

KEYB configures your keyboard for a specific language.

Syntax

```
KEYB [xx[,[yyy][,[drive:][path]filename]]] [/E] [/ID:nnn]
```

Use the following syntax to load KEYB from a CONFIG.SYS file:

```
INSTALL=[[dos-drive:]dos-path]KEYB.COM
[xx[,[yyy][,[drive:][path]filename]]] [/E] [/ID:nnn]
```

Parameters

xx

Specifies the keyboard code. (See the table following this listing for a list of valid settings for *xx*.)

yyy

Specifies the code page. If this value is not specified, KEYB uses the current code page. (See the table following this listing for a list of valid settings for *yyy*.)

[drive:][path]filename

Specifies the location and name of the keyboard definition file. You can omit path information if KEYBOARD.SYS is located in a directory included in your PATH statement.

[dos-drive:]dos-path

Specifies the location of the KEYB.COM file.

Switches

/E

Specifies that an enhanced keyboard is installed. You need this switch only if you are using an enhanced keyboard with a PC/XT (8086) computer.

/ID:nnn

Specifies the keyboard in use. This switch is only required for three countries: France, Italy, and the United Kingdom. These countries support more than one keyboard layout for the same language. (See the table following this listing for a list of valid settings for *nnn*.)

Values for xx, yyy, and nnn

The following table shows the valid values for *xx*, *yyy*, and *nnn* for each country or language:

Country or Language	Keyboard code (*xx* value)	Code Page (*yyy* value)	Keyboard Id (MI*nnn*D value)
Belgium	be	850, 437	
Brazil	br	850, 437	
Canadian-French	cf	850, 863	
Czechoslovakia (Czech)	cz	852, 850	
Czechoslovakia (Slovak)	sl	852, 850	
Denmark	dk	850, 865	
Finland	su	850, 437	
France	fr	850, 437	120, 189
Germany	gr	850, 437	
Hungary	hu	852, 850	
Italy	it	850, 437	141, 142
Latin America	la	850, 437	
Netherland	sn	850, 437	
Norway	no	850, 865	
Poland	pl	852, 850	
Portugal	po	850, 860	
Spain	sp	850, 437	
Sweden	sv	850, 437	
Switzerland (French)	sf	850, 437	
Switzerland (German)	sg	850, 437	
United Kingdom	uk	850, 437	166, 168
United States	us	850, 437	
Yugoslavia	yu	852, 850	

Implementing KEYB

You can load KEYB in one of three ways:

1. Enter the appropriate KEYB command at the DOS system prompt.
2. Include an INSTALL statement to load KEYB.COM from your CONFIG.SYS file.
3. Include the appropriate KEYB command in your AUTOEXEC.BAT file.

Examples

Use the following command to specify a German keyboard if your KEYBOARD.SYS file is in the DOS directory on drive C:

```
KEYB GR,,C:\DOS\KEYBOARD.SYS
```

Use the following command to have DOS display the current keyboard settings:

```
KEYB
```

Switching Between Keyboard Configurations

To switch from a KEYB-loaded keyboard configuration to the default keyboard configuration: press CTRL+ALT+F1.

To return to a memory-resident keyboard configuration: press CTRL+ALT+F2.

Related Command

See the CHCP command for information about using different character sets.

LABEL

LABEL creates, changes, or deletes the volume label (name) of a disk.

Syntax

```
LABEL [drive:][label]
```

Parameters

`drive:`

Specifies the location of the disk you want to name.

`label`

Specifies the new volume label. You must include a colon (:) between the drive parameter and volume label.

Volume Label Name Limitations

A volume label may contain as many as 11 characters and may include spaces. Consecutive spaces are interpreted as a single space.

> **Caution:** A volume label cannot include the following characters: * ? / \ | . , ; : + = [ ] ( ) & ^ < > " Also, LABEL will not work on a drive created with the ASSIGN, JOIN, or SUBST command.

Examples

The following command runs the LABEL program in interactive mode:

```
LABEL
```

When entered in this manner, DOS displays a message in the following format:

```
Volume in drive A is (volume name, if one currently exists)
Volume Serial Number is (volume serial number)
Volume label (11 characters, ENTER for none)?
```

Enter the following to assign the name "MY DATA" to this disk:

```
MY DATA
```

Entering the following command at the DOS system prompt would accomplish the same result, bypassing the interactive LABEL prompt:

```
LABEL A:MY DATA
```

Related Commands

See the DIR or VOL command for information about displaying the current disk label.

See the VOL command for information about displaying a disk's volume serial number.

LASTDRIVE

LASTDRIVE is used in your CONFIG.SYS file to specify the maximum number of drives or other storage devices you can access.

Syntax

```
LASTDRIVE=x
```

Parameter

x

Specifies the highest drive letter in the range A through Z that you want assigned to a storage device on your computer. By default, MS-DOS sets the value of LASTDRIVE to the letter following the letter of the last physical drive.

Effect on Memory

MS-DOS sets aside approximately 512 bytes of RAM for each drive letter set aside with a LASTDRIVE statement. Therefore, you should specify the minimum number of devices your system requires.

Example

The following command sets the last drive to N, giving your computer access to 14 logical drives:

```
LASTDRIVE=N
```

LOADFIX

This command loads a program above the first 64K of memory.

Syntax

```
LOADFIX [drive:][path]filename [program-parameters]
```

Parameters

`[drive:][path]`

Specifies the drive and directory containing the program you want to run.

`filename`

Specifies the name of the program you want to run.

`program-parameters`

Used to include any parameters you would normally enter at the system prompt when starting this program.

Some applications display a "Packed file corrupt" message when you attempt to load them. This generally occurs when you install DOS or device drivers in the HMA, thus freeing up portions of conventional RAM for other uses. Certain older programs were designed to begin loading their program code above 64K, a memory address that did not interfere with early DOS releases. Some of these programs will not run successfully if a portion of their code ends up in low memory previously occupied by DOS. The LOADFIX command "tricks" a program into loading at the 64K address for which it was designed, even if lower memory is available.

Example

The following command begins loading a program called MYPROG.EXE at the 64K memory address, thus eliminating the "Packed file corrupt" message it displays when run without LOADFIX:

```
LOADFIX C:\MYPROG.EXE
```

LOADHIGH (LH)

This command loads a program into the upper memory area.

Syntax

    LOADHIGH|LH [drive:][path]filename [parameters]

The following syntax is used to specify that a program be loaded into a particular region or regions of memory:

    LOADHIGH|LH [/L:region1[,minsize1][;region2[,minsize2]...] [/S]]
    [drive:][path]filename [parameters]

Parameters

    [drive:][path]filename

Specifies the location and name of the program you want to load into high RAM.

    parameters

Specifies any command-line information required by the program you're loading into high memory.

Switches

    /L:region1[,minsize1][;region2[,minsize2]...]

This switch lets you force DOS to load a program into one or more specific regions of memory. The optional *region* and *minsize* parameters are used to identify the upper memory block (UMB) region you want a program to occupy and, when appropriate, the minimum amount of memory within this UMB you want DOS to set aside for that program.

    /S

Shrinks the UMB to its minimum size while the program is loading.

LOADHIGH Tips and Techniques

By default, MS-DOS loads a program into the largest upper memory block (UMB) available, while making all other UMBs available for the program's use. Using the /L switch to load the program into a specific region of memory or to specify which region(s) you want to make available to a specific program can help you use your system's RAM more efficiently. Including a region number after the /L switch forces DOS to load that particular program into the largest block in the specified region.

Certain programs use more than one area of memory. For these programs, you can specify multiple regions by separating the individual UMB *region* numbers with a semicolon (;).

As a rule, DOS loads a program into the specified region only if that region contains a UMB larger than the program's load size. The required size usually corresponds to the size of the executable program file. Some programs require additional memory while running, beyond that used to load them initially. When this is the case, the *minsize* parameter allows you to make certain that a program will not be loaded into a UMB that is too small for it to function in properly. Specifying a *minsize* value causes DOS to load the program into that region only if it contains a UMB that is larger than both the program's load size and the *minsize* value.

Including the /S switch in a LOADHIGH statement allows you to make the most efficient use of memory. First, use DOS's MEMMAKER utility to analyze a program's precise memory requirements and determine whether the /S switch is compatible with that program. Because the /S switch affects only UMBs for which a minimum size was specified, it requires that you include the /L switch in a LOADHIGH statement.

Although the LOADHIGH command can be executed interactively from the DOS prompt, it is best placed in the AUTOEXEC.BAT file.

Using the DOS=UMB Command

If you want to use the LOADHIGH command, you'll need to include a DOS=UMB command in your CONFIG.SYS file. If the UMB parameter is not specified, the LOADHIGH command functions identically to the DEVICE command, in that it loads all device drivers into conventional memory.

Installing HIMEM.SYS and a UMB Provider

LOADHIGH requires extended memory. If extended memory exists, first use the DEVICE command once to install DOS's HIMEM.SYS device driver. You can then use DEVICE to install an upper memory block (UMB) provider, if your system requires one. Computers with an 80386 or 80486 processor can use DOS's EMM386.EXE as the UMB provider.

✔ *Note:* The HIMEM.SYS and UMB provider must be loaded before the first LOADHIGH command can be executed.

Examples

The following command loads the DOSKEY program, which is located in the DOS directory of drive C, into the upper memory area and specifies that MS-DOS should load the driver into region 2:

```
LOADHIGH /L:2 C:\DOS\DOSKEY
```

The following command loads a program called TESTPROG.EXE into conventional RAM — referred to as region 0 — and also gives it access to upper memory region 2:

```
LH /L:0;2 C:\TESTPROG.EXE
```

Related Commands

See the DEVICEHIGH command for information about loading device drivers into upper memory.

See the DOS command for more information about the DOS=UMB command.

See the MEMMAKER command for information about using the MEMMAKER program to move programs to the upper memory area.

MEM

You use MEM to display the amount of used and free memory in your system.

Syntax

```
MEM [/C|/D|/F|/M modulename] [/PAGE]
```

Switches

/C (Classify)

Displays a list of the programs currently loaded into RAM and shows information about the memory used by each. This list also summarizes overall memory use and lists the largest free memory blocks. You may use the /C switch with the /P switch, but not with other MEM switches.

/D (Debug)

Lists the programs and internal drivers currently loaded into RAM. This list displays each module's size, segment address, and module type. It also summarizes overall memory use and displays other information that programmers will find useful. You may use the /D switch with the /P switch, but not with other MEM switches.

/F (Free)

Displays a list of the free areas of conventional and upper memory available on your system. This list shows the segment address and size of each free area of conventional memory. It also shows the largest free upper memory block in each region of upper memory. You may use the /F switch with the /P switch, but not with other MEM switches.

/M (Module) programname

Shows how a program module is currently using RAM. You must specify a program name after the /M switch. MEM /M lists the areas of memory allocated to the specified program module and the address and size of each area. You may use the /M switch with /P switch, but not with other MEM switches.

/P

Pauses the display after each screen of output. Note: This switch may be used with any of the other MEM switches. It can also be specified as /PAGE

Examples

The following command displays a comprehensive summary of how your system is currently utilizing RAM:

```
MEM /C
```

The results might look similar to the following:

```
Modules using memory below 1 MB:
Name         Total            =   Conventional   +   Upper Memory
MSDOS        15984    (16K)       15984   (16K)       0       (0K)
COMMAND      8052     (8K)        8052    (8K)        0       (0K)
EMM386       4256     (4K)        4256    (4K)        0       (0K)
HIMEM        1072     (1K)        1072    (1K)        0       (0K)
SMARTDRV     28304    (28K)       28304   (28K)       0       (0K)
win386       35152    (34K)       29088   (28K)       6096    (6K)
WIN          1600     (2K)        1600    (2K)        0       (0K)
ANSI         4192     (4K)        0       (0K)        4192    (4K)
DOSKEY       4128     (4K)        0       (0K)        4128    (4K)
MOUSE        17280    (17K)       0       (0K)        17280   (17K)
Free         560480   (646K)      560480  (553K)      92      (92K)

Memory Summary:

Type of Memory    Total            =    Used              +    Free
Conventional      655360   (640K)       94880    (93K)         560480   (547K)
Upper             127296   (124K)       127296   (124K)        0        (0K)
Extended (XMS)    7733248  (7552K)      6684672  (6528K)       1048576  (1024K)
Expanded (EMS)    1048576  (1024K)      0        (0K)          1048576  (1024K)
Total memory      9564480  (9340K)      6906848  (6745K)       2657632  (2595K)

Total under 1 MB  782656   (764K)       222176   (217K)        560480   (547K)

Largest executable program size       560480   (547K)
Largest free upper memory block       92       (92K)
MS-DOS is resident in the high memory area.
```

> ✓ **Note:** "Largest executable program size" is the largest contiguous block of conventional memory available for a program. "Largest free upper memory block" is the largest area of upper memory available for a program. "MS-DOS is resident in the high memory area" indicates that MS-DOS is running in the first 64K of extended memory, rather than in conventional memory.

The following command displays information about the current memory use of a specific program module:

```
MEM /M MSDOS
```

If you requested information on MSDOS, the results might look similar to the following:

```
MSDOS is using the following memory:
Segment     Region       Size                 Type
00116                    5072     (5K)        System Data
004A9                      80     (0K)        System Program
00553                      80     (0K)          Free
01BDD                  541232     (529K)        Free
Total size:            545464     (534K)
```

> ✔ ***Note:*** Some program modules, such as MSDOS, allocate more than one area of memory. The MEM /M command displays all the areas of memory allocated to the specified program, including the segment address and size of each allocation. For upper memory blocks, MEM /M also shows the region number. The Type column shows how the program is using that particular area of memory. The "Total size," in this case 35152 bytes (33K), shows the total amount of memory allocated by MS-DOS for the specified program.

Related Command

See the CHKDSK command for information about checking the amount of space available on a disk.

MEMMAKER

This command starts the MEMMAKER program, which can be used to increase the amount of conventional RAM — RAM below the 640K memory address — available to application programs by moving device drivers and memory-resident programs to upper memory. MEMMAKER works only on computers with an 80386 or 80486 microprocessor and extended memory.

Syntax

```
MEMMAKER [/B] [/BATCH] [SESSION] [/SWAP:drive] [/T] [/UNDO]
[/W:size1,size2]
```

Switches

/B

Use the /B switch if your monochrome monitor isn't displaying MEMMAKER correctly.

/BATCH

Causes MEMMAKER to run in batch mode — that is, unattended — accepting the default values for all prompts.

> ✔ *Note:* If any errors occur during processing, MEMMAKER creates a special file, MEMMAKER.STS, containing information about any problems it encountered. The contents of this file can be viewed using the DOS EDIT program. Before aborting, MEMMAKER restores your previous CONFIG.SYS and AUTOEXEC.BAT files.

/SESSION

Is exclusive to MEMMAKER during the memory optimization process.

/SWAP:drive

Specifies the letter of the drive that was originally your startup disk drive. This switch is necessary only if the drive letter of your startup disk drive has changed since your computer started, as might be the case if you use disk-compression software that employs disk swapping. You do not need this switch if you are using Stacker 2.0.

/T

Computers with IBM Token Ring networks might encounter problems when running MEMMAKER. The /T switch disables the detection of IBM Token Ring networks.

/UNDO

Uses a special archive file to to reverse the most recent changes MEMMAKER has made to your system configuration. This switch provides a safeguard, should you encounter any problems after running MEMMAKER.

/W:size1,size2

Specifies how much upper memory space DOS should reserve for Windows translation buffers. MEMMAKER normally sets aside two 12K regions of upper memory for Windows translation buffers. On non-Windows systems, specifying /W:0,0 prevents MEMMAKER from using this memory.

> *Caution:* Never run MEMMAKER from within other programs, like Microsoft Windows or the DOS Shell.

Examples

The following command runs MEMMAKER in batch mode and directs it to not reserve any upper memory for Windows translation buffers:

MEMMAKER /BATCH /W:0,0

The following command instructs MEMMAKER to restore your previous system configuration:

MEMMAKER /UNDO

The following command allows MEMMAKER to work with a disk-compression program that assigns another drive letter to the drive containing your DOS system files after you turn on your system:

MEMMAKER /SWAP:D

This command tells MEMMAKER that drive D now contains your CONFIG.SYS and AUTOEXEC.BAT files.

Related Commands

See the DEVICEHIGH command for information about loading device drivers into upper memory.

See the LOADHIGH command for information about loading programs into upper memory.

MENUCOLOR

MENUCOLOR sets the text and background colors for a startup menu created in the CONFIG.SYS file.

Syntax

MENUCOLOR=x[,y]

Parameters

x

Specifies the color of the menu text. Choose a color code for *x* from the table later in this section.

y

Specifies the color of the screen background. Choose a color code for *y* from the table later in this section. If you do not specify a *y* value, MS-DOS uses a black background.

> ✔ **Note:** MENUCOLOR must appear within a menu block in the CONFIG.SYS file.

Color Values

The following table lists the valid color choices for the MENUCOLOR command:

0	Black
1	Blue
2	Green
3	Cyan
4	Red
5	Magenta
6	Brown
7	White
8	Gray
9	Bright blue
10	Bright green
11	Bright cyan
12	Bright red
13	Bright magenta
14	Yellow
15	Bright white

> **Caution:** Never specify the same values for *x* and *y*; if you do, the menu will not be readable.

Example

The following MENUCOLOR command sets the menu text to bright white and the screen background to blue:

```
MENUCOLOR 15, 1
```

Related Commands

The MENUCOLOR command is one of five special CONFIG.SYS commands for defining multiple configurations. With multiple configurations, you define a menu that appears when your computer starts. Each menu item corresponds to a block of commands, or "configuration block," in your CONFIG.SYS file.

The other four commands used to create a startup menu are:

INCLUDE	Used to include the contents of one configuration block in another
MENUDEFAULT	Used to specify the default menu item
MENUITEM	Used to define an item on the menu
SUBMENU	Used to define a submenu

MENUDEFAULT

You use this command to specify the default menu item on a startup menu. You may also use it optionally to set a time limit on how long the user has to select a menu item.

Syntax

MENUDEFAULT=blockname[,timeout]

Parameters

blockname

Specifies the default menu item by name, that is, the name you assigned the corresponding configuration block in your CONFIG.SYS file.

> ✓ *Note:* When MS-DOS displays the startup menu, the specified configuration block is highlighted and its number appears as a default value after the "Enter a choice" prompt.

timeout

Indicates how many seconds MS-DOS should wait before starting the computer with the default configuration. You can specify a *timeout* value from 0 to 90 seconds. A *timeout* of 0 forces automatic selection of the default, effectively bypassing the menu display.

> 🚫 *Caution:* If you do not specify a *timeout* value, MS-DOS halts startup until the ENTER key is pressed.

Example

The following statements, when included in a CONFIG.SYS file, define three menu items, set the colors to bright white text on a blue background, set the default item to the "cd-rom" configuration block, and set the *timeout* to 60 seconds:

```
[MENU]
MENUITEM=base_config,Base configuration only
MENUITEM=full_config,Standard configuration
MENUITEM=cd_rom,Standard configuration with CD-ROM device
MENUCOLOR 15,1
MENUDEFAULT=cd_rom,60
```

When MS-DOS starts and reads this menu block, it displays the following menu:

```
MS-DOS 6 Startup Menu
=====================
   1. Base configuration only
   2. Standard configuration
   3. Standard configuration with CD-ROM device
Enter a choice: 3              Time remaining: 60
```

MS-DOS waits 60 seconds after displaying this menu. If no other item is selected, MS-DOS starts the computer using the commands in the [cd-rom] configuration block.

Related Commands

The MENUDEFAULT command is one of five special CONFIG.SYS commands for defining multiple configurations. With multiple configurations, you define a menu that appears when your computer starts. Each menu item corresponds to a block of commands, or "configuration block," in your CONFIG.SYS file.

The other four commands used to create a startup menu are:

INCLUDE	Used to include the contents of one configuration block in another
MENUCOLOR	Used to specify foreground and background colors for a startup menu
MENUITEM	Used to define an item on the menu
SUBMENU	Used to define a submenu

MENUITEM

MENUITEM defines an item on a startup menu. You may have up to 9 menu items per menu.

Syntax

    MENUITEM=blockname[,menu_text]

Parameters

    blockname

Specifies the name of the associated configuration block. This is the name you'll use elsewhere in the CONFIG.SYS file to define the configuration block containing the statements you want executed when this menu item is selected. The block name may be up to 70 characters long and may contain most printable characters. It may not, however, include spaces, backslashes (\) and forward slashes (/), commas, semicolons (;), equal signs (=), or square brackets ([ ]).

    menu_text

Identifies the text you want MS-DOS to display in the startup menu for this menu item. If you don't specify any menu text, MS-DOS displays the block name as the menu item. The menu text may be up to 70 characters long and may contain any display characters available in the ASCII character set.

How MS-DOS Manages the Startup Menu

MS-DOS automatically numbers startup menu items, displaying them in the order in which they appear in the menu block. The first menu item specified in the menu block is assigned the number 1. You may specify up to 9 menu items. If you need to define more, you must use the SUBMENU command.

Example

Adding the following menu block to a CONFIG.SYS file defines a startup menu that includes two items, Normal Configuration and Network Configuration, and assigns menu text to each:

    [MENU]
    MENUITEM normal_config,Normal Configuration
    MENUITEM network_config,Network Configuration

When you start your computer, the following startup menu appears:

```
MS-DOS 6 Startup Menu
=====================
1. Normal Configuration
2. Network Configuration
Enter a choice: 1
```

In this menu, the first item corresponds to the [normal_config] configuration block and the second to the [network_config] block.

Related Commands

The MENUITEM command is one of five special CONFIG.SYS commands for defining multiple configurations. With multiple configurations, you define a menu that appears when your computer starts. Each menu item corresponds to a block of commands, or "configuration block," in your CONFIG.SYS file.

The other four commands used to create a startup menu are:

INCLUDE	Used to include the contents of one configuration block in another
MENUCOLOR	Used to specify foreground and background colors for a startup menu
MENUDEFAULT	Used to specify the default menu item
SUBMENU	Used to define a submenu

See the SUBMENU command for information on how to define submenus options within a menu block.

MKDIR (MD)

MKDIR creates a directory.

Syntax

```
MKDIR [drive:]path
MD [drive:]path
```

Parameters

`drive:`

Specifies the drive on which the new directory is being created. This parameter is not required if you are creating a directory on the current drive.

`path`

Specifies the complete path name for the new directory. The maximum allowable length of any single path from the root directory to the final directory is 63 characters, including backslashes (\).

Examples

The following command creates a new directory named MYTAXES directly below the root directory on the current drive:

```
MD \MYTAXES
```

You do not need to include complete path information if the new directory is located directly below the current directory. If you're in the MYTAXES directory, for example, the following command would create a subdirectory named 92TAXES directly below it:

```
MKDIR 92TAXES
```

Related Commands

See the RMDIR command for information about deleting a directory. See the CHDIR command for information about changing directories.

MORE

You use MORE to display the output of a DOS command or file one screen at a time.

Syntax

```
command-name | MORE
MORE < [drive:][path]filename
```

> ✔ *Note:* When using the pipe (|), MORE controls the output of DOS commands such as DIR, SORT, and TYPE. When using the redirection character (<), you must specify a filename as the source; MORE will then display it on the screen.

> 🚫 *Caution:* Before using a pipe for redirection, you should set the TEMP environment variable in your AUTOEXEC.BAT file.

Parameters

command-name

Specifies the command that supplies the information you want to display one screen at a time.

[drive:][path]filename

Specifies the location and name of a file that supplies data you want to display.

Examples

Either of the following commands reads in the contents of a file called MYTEXT.ASC and displays it on your monitor one screen at a time:

```
MORE < MYTEXT.ASC
TYPE MYTEXT.ASC | MORE
```

Either of these MORE commands displays the first screen of information from MYTEXT.ASC, after which it prompts you with the following message:

```
-- More --
```

Pressing any key displays the next screen of information.

Related Command

See the TYPE command for information about displaying the contents of a file.

MOVE

The MOVE command moves a file or group of files to a directory of your choice. It also allows you to rename directories.

Syntax

```
MOVE [drive:][path]filename[,[drive:][path]filename[...]]
destination
```

Parameters

`[drive:][path]filename`

Specifies the name and location of the file or group of files that are to be moved. If no filename is specified, *drive* and *path* represent the directory you want renamed.

> ✓ **Note:** MOVE accepts the DOS wildcard characters * and ?.

> ✓ **Note:** When renaming directories, you cannot also move the directory to another location in the directory tree.

`destination`

Specifies the new name for the directory or the destination to which the file or files are to be moved. The *destination* parameter may consist of the drive and path to which the files are to be moved. If a filename, different from the source, is included as part of the *destination*, MOVE renames the file. If the filename specified in the *destination* exists in the destination directory, MOVE will overwrite the file with the contents of the source file.

> ✓ **Note:** Include the filename in the *destination* parameter only if you're moving one file. If more than one file is being moved, the *destination* must be a directory name. If you do specify a filename when moving more than one file, DOS will display the following message:
>
> ```
> Cannot move multiple files to a single file
> ```

MOVE Error Codes

In addition to visually displaying information on the files it has moved, the MOVE command returns an error code when it has completed its operation. If

MOVE executed successfully, it returns an ERRORLEVEL of 0. If an error occurred in moving one or more files, MOVE returns an ERRORLEVEL of 1.

Examples

To change the name of the C:\DOS directory to DOS6, enter the following command:

MOVE C:\DOS C:\DOS6

To move MEMO1.DOC from C:\DOCS to C:\DOCS\MEMOS, use the following command:

MOVE C:\DOCS\MEMO1.DOC C:\DOCS\MEMOS

To move MEMO1.DOC and LETTER3.DOC from C:\DOCS\MEMOS and C:\DOCS\LETTERS, respectively, to C:\PROJECT\DOSBOOK, use the following variation of the MOVE command:

MOVE C:\DOCS\MEMOS\MEMO1.DOC,C:\DOCS\LETTERS\LETTER3.DOC C:\PROJECT\DOSBOOK

To move the file REF.DOC from C:\DOC to C:\PROJECT\DOSBOOK and simultaneously change its name to CMDREF.DOC, use the following command:

MOVE C:\DOC\REF.DOC C:\PROJECT\DOSBOOK\CMDREF.DOC

Finally, the following command moves the files MEMO1.DOC through MEMO9.DOC from C:\DOC to C:\DOC\MEMOS:

MOVE C:\DOC\MEMO?.DOC C:\DOC\MEMOS

Related Command

For more information on renaming files, see the RENAME (REN) command.

MSAV

This command reduces the possibility of a computer virus damaging your computer's memory and disks.

Syntax

MSAV [[drive:] | [path]] [/S | /C] [/R] [/A] [/L] [/N] [/P] [/F] [/VIDEO]

Parameters

drive:

Specifies the drive that MSAV scans for viruses. MSAV will scan memory and the entire drive.

path

Specifies the location of the files you want to scan. MSAV will scan memory and the files in the specified directory.

> ✔ *Note:* The undocumented *path* parameter allows you to specify the directory that you want MSAV to scan for viruses. However, if you also attempt to provide a file specification for the individual file or files that you would like MSAV to scan, the command will return an error message.

Switches

/S

Scans the disk specified by *drive:* and the files on those disks, but does not remove viruses that MSAV finds. MSAV uses this switch by default.

/C

Scans the disk specified by *drive:* and the files on those disks, and removes viruses that MSAV finds.

/R

Creates an MSAV.RPT file that lists the number of files MSAV checked for viruses, the number of viruses it found, and the number of viruses it removed. By default, MSAV does not create a report.

/A

Scans all drives except drive A and drive B.

/L

Scans all drives except network drives.

/N

If this switch is used, MSAV will first look for a file named MSAV.TXT in the directory that contains the MSAV.EXE program. If it finds it, it will display it. MSAV will then scan the specified drive or directory using its command-line interface. If MSAV detects a virus, it will return an exit code of 86, rather than displaying a message to the screen.

/P

Executes MSAV using a command-line interface rather than the default graphical interface.

/F

Turns off the display of filenames that have been scanned. Use this switch only with the /N or /P switch.

/VIDEO

Displays a list of the switches that affect the appearance and operation of MSAV. This list consists of all of the remaining switches given below.

/25	Sets the screen to a 25-line display; this is the default setting.
/28	Sets the screen to a 28-line display. This switch will work with VGA displays only.
/43	Sets the screen to a 43-line display. This switch will work with both EGA and VGA adapters.
/50	Sets the screen to a 50-line display. /50 works with VGA adapters only.
/60	Sets the screen to a 60-line display. This switch is supported only by a Video 7 display adapter.
/IN	Runs MSAV using a color scheme, even if a color adapter is not detected.
/BW	Runs MSAV using black-and-white colors.
/MONO	Runs MSAV using a monochromatic color scheme.
/LCD	Runs MSAV using an LCD color scheme.
/FF	Allows for the fastest screen updating on computers with CGA display adapters. The disadvantage of this switch is that it may decrease video quality.
/BF	Uses the computer's BIOS to handle the video display.
/NF	Disables the use of alternate fonts.

/BT	Allows the use of a graphics mouse in Windows.
/NGM	Runs MSAV using the default mouse character instead of the graphics character.
/LE	Exchanges the left and right mouse buttons.
/PS2	Resets the mouse if the mouse cursor disappears or locks up.

Example

The following command starts MSAV using a monochrome color scheme, checking all all drives except the two floppy drives, A and B:

```
MSAV /MONO /A
```

Related Command

While MSAV executes a program that scans memory and a hard disk for existing viruses, VSAV is a terminate-and-stay-resident utility that attempts to prevent a virus from being written to the hard disk or establishing itself in memory.

MSBACKUP

The MSBACKUP command, newly introduced in DOS 6.0, replaces the BACKUP command familar to users of previous versions of DOS. MSBACKUP offers a good deal of flexibility in backing up files from hard drives and restoring files that have been archived on floppy drives. MSBACKUP is capable of backing up the entire hard disk drive or just selected files in individual subdirectories. You can schedule backups to be done automatically or on a regularly timed basis. All files backed up using the MSBACKUP command can also be restored using MSBACKUP, whereas restoring files backed up with versions of DOS prior to 6.0 requires a separate utility, RESTORE.

Syntax

```
MSBACKUP [setup_file] [/BW|/LCD|/MDA]
```

Parameter

`setup_file`

Used to specify a setup file. This file identifies the files you want to back up, the type of backup (full, incremental, or differential) to be performed, and the destination medium for the backup. All setup files must have a .SET extension. If you do not specify a setup file, MSBACKUP uses DEFAULT.SET.

Switches

`/BW`

Starts MSBACKUP using a black-and-white color scheme.

`/LCD`

Starts MSBACKUP using a video mode compatible with laptop displays.

`/MDA`

Starts MSBACKUP using a monochrome display adapter.

Type of Backup

Specifies the type of backup you want to perform.
The following list describes types of backups. You can specify only one type.

- F (full backup) Backs up all files specified in the setup file.
- I (incremental backup) Backs up only those files that have changed since the last full or incremental backup.
- D (differential backup.) Backs up all files specified in the setup file that have changed since the last full backup.

Example

The following command loads a setup file named WEEKLY.SET (which could be used to define a weekly full backup procedure on specified files):

```
msbackup weekly
```

Related Commands

For more information on the old MS-DOS BACKUP command, see BACKUP. For more information on restoring files backed up using the old BACKUP command in previous versions of DOS, see the RESTORE command.

MSD

Use this special Microsoft utility to obtain detailed technical information about your computer.

Syntax

Use the following syntax to run the MSD program using its interactive menu options.

```
MSD [/B][/I]
```

Use the following syntax to instruct MSD to create a report containing information about your system components:

```
MSD [/I][/F[drive:][path]filename][/P[drive:][path]filename]
[/S[drive:][path][filename]]
```

Switches

```
/B
```

Runs MSD in black and white instead of color. Use the /B switch when you have a monitor that does not correctly display MSD in color.

```
/I
```

Specifies that MSD should bypass its initial analysis of your hardware. Use the /I switch if you are having problems starting MSD or if MSD is not running properly.

```
/F[drive:][path]filename
```

Prompts you for name, company, address, country, phone number, and comments, then writes a complete MSD report to a file. The /F switch accepts the following /F parameters:

[drive]	Specifies the drive to which you want to write the report.
[path]	Specifies the directory to which you want to write the report.
filename	Specifies the filename you want to give the report.

```
/P[drive:][path]filename
```

Writes a complete MSD report to a file, without prompting you for information. The /P switch accepts the following parameters:

[drive]	Specifies the drive to which you want to write the report.
[path]	Specifies the directory to which you want to write the report.
filename	Specifies the filename you want to give the report.

```
/S[drive:][path][filename]
```

Writes a summary MSD report to a file, without prompting you for information. The /S switch accepts the following parameters:

[drive]   Specifies the drive to which you want to write the report.

[path]   Specifies the directory to which you want to write the report.

[filename]   Specifies the filename you want to give the report.

> ✔ **Note:** If you do not specify any report parameters, MSD displays the results of its analysis directly to the screen.

Information Provided by MSD

MSD Options

The following is a brief description of the options available when MSD is run in interactive mode:

Computer	Displays your computer's manufacturer, processor type, and bus type; ROM BIOS manufacturer, version and date; keyboard type; DMA controller configuration; and math coprocessor status.
Memory	Displays a map of the upper memory area (UMA) — memory address between 640K and 1024K.
Video	Shows your video card manufacturer, model and type, video BIOS version and date, and current video mode.
Network	Displays information about a network, if one is installed on your system.
Operating System	Displays the operating system version, location of MS-DOS in memory, the drive the computer was started from, the current environment settings, and the path from which MSD was run.
Mouse	Shows the MS-DOS mouse driver version, mouse type, mouse interrupt (IRQ) number, and other information specific to the configuration of the mouse.
Other Adapters	Displays the game card status for up to two game devices or joysticks.
Disk Drives	Displays the size and number of bytes free for all disk drives, local and remote, installed on your system.
LPT Ports	Displays the port addresses and status of any parallel ports installed on your system.

COM Ports	Displays the port addresses, current communications parameters and status of any serial ports installed on your system.
IRQ Status	Displays the configuration of your hardware interrupts, or IRQs.
TSR Programs	Displays the name, location in memory, and size of any terminate-and-stay-resident (TSR) program loaded in memory at the time MSD was run.
Device Drivers	Displays the names of any device drivers installed on your system at the time MSD was run.

Examples

The following command runs MSD in interactive mode, configured for a monochrome monitor:

```
MSD /B
```

The following command runs MSD and automatically creates a report named MYSYSTEM.TXT containing the results of its analysis:

```
MSD /P MYSYSTEM.TXT
```

NLSFUNC

You use this command to load country-specific information for national language support (NLS).

Syntax

Use the following syntax to run NLSFUNC from the DOS system prompt:

```
NLSFUNC [[drive:][path]filename]
```

Use the following syntax to include NLSFUNC in a statement within your CONFIG.SYS file:

```
INSTALL=[[dos-drive:]dos-path]NLSFUNC.EXE [country-filename]
```

Parameters

```
[drive:][path]filename or country-filename
```

Specifies the location and name of the file containing country-specific information. If you use this parameter in a CONFIG.SYS file, you must include the drive and directory information.

> ✔ *Note:* The default value for [drive:][path]filename is defined by the COUNTRY command in your CONFIG.SYS file. If no COUNTRY command exists in CONFIG.SYS, NLSFUNC looks for COUNTRY.SYS in the root directory of the startup drive.

```
[dos-drive:]dos-path
```

Specifies the location of NLSFUNC.EXE.

Examples

Enter the following command to use the default country-specific information found in the COUNTRY.SYS file:

```
NLSFUNC
```

Use the following command to get country-specific information from a file called NEWINFO.SYS:

```
NLSFUNC NEWINFO.SYS
```

NUMLOCK

NUMLOCK is used in a CONFIG.SYS file during system startup to specify whether NUMLOCK is initially set to ON or OFF.

Syntax

NUMLOCK=[ON|OFF]

Parameters

ON|OFF

Turns NUM LOCK ON and OFF, respectively.

Example

If you use a startup menu, including the following command in the MENU block of your CONFIG.SYS file would ensure that NUM LOCK is always ON when the startup menu appears:

NUMLOCK=ON

PATH

This command specifies the search path DOS uses to find executable files — files ending with an extension of .EXE, .COM, or .BAT.

Syntax

```
PATH [;] [[drive:]path[;...]]
```

Parameters

`[drive:]path`

Specifies a drive, directory, and any subdirectories to search. You must use a semicolon (;) to separate multiple directories included in a PATH statement.

`;`

Entering a PATH command with a semicolon as its only parameter clears all path settings and instructs MS-DOS to search only the current directory for executable files, including external DOS commands.

> *Caution:* The maximum length of the PATH command is 127 characters. If your search path requires more directories than this limit allows, use the SUBST command to substitute logical drive names for some directories.

DOS uses three different methods to find the instructions associated with any commands you enter:

1. DOS first checks to see whether the command you issued is an internal DOS command — that is, a command that was loaded into memory by COMMAND.COM when you first started your system.
2. If the entered command is not an internal command, DOS attempts to find the corresponding executable file in the current directory.
3. If DOS can't find the requested file in the current directory, it begins an organized search of any directories included in your PATH statement, starting with the first directory listed.

> *Note:* The order in which directories are listed in a PATH statement affects how quickly DOS finds an executable file. Therefore, you should place any directories containing frequently used files near the beginning of the PATH statement.

Examples

The following command displays the current search path:

```
PATH
```

The following command clears all search-path settings:

```
PATH ;
```

The following command tells MS-DOS to automatically search three directories (DOSFILES, BATCH, and PROGRAMS) for executable programs and external commands:

```
PATH C:\BATCH;D:\DOSFILES;C:\PROGRAMS
```

Related Commands

See the APPEND command for information about setting a search path for data files.

See the SUBST command for information on substituting drive letters for path names.

PAUSE

PAUSE suspends execution of a batch program until a key is pressed.

Syntax

```
PAUSE
```

Example

The following batch file sets up a situation that prompts a user to change disks in drive B at the appropriate time:

```
@ECHO OFF
:BEGIN
COPY B:*.*
ECHO Please put a new disk into drive B
ECHO When all disks have been copied,
ECHO press Ctrl+C to terminate this batch file
PAUSE
GOTO BEGIN
```

This batch file begins by copying all the files on a disk in drive B to the current directory. It then pauses and prompts the user to either insert a new disk in drive B or terminate the batch file by pressing Ctrl+C.

> ✔ *Note:* The echoed message in lines 3 and 4 provides these instructions; PAUSE automatically displays a message telling the user to
>
> ```
> "Press any key to continue ..."
> ```

POWER

You use POWER to adjust the power-consumption settings on your system components after the POWER.EXE device driver has been loaded.

Syntax

```
POWER [ADV[:MAX|REG|MIN]|STD|OFF]
```

Parameters

ADV[:MAX|REG|MIN]

Indicates that you want to use advanced power-consumption management. The ADV parameter lets you choose from the following settings:

MAX	Used to specify maximum power conservation
REG	Used to balance power conservation with application and device performance. REG is the default setting.
MIN	Used if the performance of an application or device deteriorates when you specify MAX or REG

STD

What the STD parameter accomplishes depends on the type of computer you have: On computers that support the Advanced Power Management (APM) specification, STD uses its built-in power-management features to conserve power. On computers that do not support the APM specification, STD disables power management.

OFF

Disables power management.

> *Caution:* Before using the POWER command, you must install the POWER.EXE driver with a DEVICE command in your CONFIG.SYS file.

Examples

The following command displays the current power setting:

```
POWER
```

The following command activates POWER's advanced features and specifies that it should use maximum power-consumption management:

```
POWER ADV:MAX
```

> ✔ ***Note:*** The MAX setting adversely affects performance on some computers. If the MAX option slows down your system but you still want to conserve power, try using the MIN setting.

Related Command

See the POWER.EXE command for information about the POWER device driver.

POWER.EXE

This is a device driver you load from within your CONFIG.SYS file to reduce the power consumption of various system components when applications and devices are idle.

Syntax

    DEVICE=[drive:][path]POWER.EXE [ADV[:MAX|REG|MIN]|STD|OFF] [/LOW]

Parameters

    drive:path

Specifies the location of the POWER.EXE file.

    ADV[:MAX|REG|MIN]

Indicates that you want to use advanced power-consumption management. The ADV parameter lets you choose from the following settings:

- MAX   Used to specify maximum power conservation.
- REG   Used to balance power conservation with application and device performance. REG is the default setting.
- MIN   Used if the performance of an application or device deteriorates when you specify MAX or REG.

    STD

What the STD parameter accomplishes depends on the type of computer you have: On computers that support the Advanced Power Management (APM) specification, STD uses its built-in power-management features to conserve power. On computers that do not support the APM specification, STD disables power management.

    OFF

Disables power management.

Switch

    /LOW

Loads the POWER.EXE device driver into conventional memory, even if the upper memory area is available.

> ✓ **Note:** If HIMEM or EMM386.SYS are installed on your system, DOS automatically loads POWER.EXE into the upper memory area.

Example

Insert the following statement into your CONFIG.SYS file to load POWER.EXE into conventional memory, using its maximum power-consumption setting:

```
DEVICE=C:\DOS\POWER.EXE /ADV:MAX /LOW
```

Related Command

See the POWER command for information about modifying the initial POWER.EXE setting.

PRINT

This command lets you print a text file in the background as you use other MS-DOS commands.

Syntax

    PRINT [/D:device] [/B:size] [/U:ticks1] [/M:ticks2] [/S:ticks3]
    [/Q:qsize] [/T] [[drive:][path]filename[...]] [/C] [/P]

Parameter

[drive:][path]filename

Specifies the file or group of files that you want printed in the background. You may include up to ten files in a single PRINT command. Multiple filenames may be separated by a space or a comma.

Switches

/D:device

Identifies which port your printer is attached to. /D options include:

LPT1 (Parallel port 1)

LPT2 (Parallel port 2)

LPT3 (Parallel port 3)

COM1 (Serial port 1)

COM2 (Serial port 2)

COM3 (Serial port 3)

COM4 (Serial port 4)

PRN (the default device, usually LPT1)

The /D switch must precede any filename used on the command line.

/B:size

Creates an internal print buffer of the specified size. The maximum allowable size of the print buffer is 16,384 bytes; the default size, 512 bytes, is the minimum buffer size.

Caution: Although increasing the size of the print buffer speeds up the PRINT command, it decreases the amount of memory available for other purposes.

`/U:ticks1`

Indicates the maximum number of processing cycles — or clock ticks, which occur approximately 18 times per second — that PRINT should wait for the printer to be available. Settings for this switch must be in the range 1 through 255; the default setting is 1. If the printer is not available within the time specified, PRINT cancels the current print job.

`/M:ticks2`

Indicates the maximum number of clock ticks allocated to print a character on the printer. Settings for this switch must be in the range 1 through 255; the default setting is 2. If PRINT takes too long to print a character, DOS displays an error message.

`/S:ticks3`

Indicates the number of clock ticks MS-DOS allocates for background printing. Settings for this switch must be in the range 1 through 255; the default setting is 8. Increasing this value speeds up printing, but slows down other activities.

`/Q:qsize`

Indicates the maximum number of files you can place in the print queue. Settings for this switch must be in the range 4 through 32; the default value is 10.

`/T`

Removes all files from the print queue.

`/C`

Selectively removes files from the print queue. The /C switch removes from the print queue any files that are listed after it. If no files follow the /C switch, PRINT removes from the print queue the file immediately preceding it. If a /P switch appears after the /C switch, PRINT removes from the queue all files following the /C switch except the file immediately preceding the /P switch.

`/P`

Adds files to the print queue. The /P switch adds to the print queue any files that are listed after it. If no files follow the /P switch, PRINT adds to the print queue the file immediately preceding it. If a /C switch appears after the /P switch, PRINT adds to the queue all files following the /P switch except the file immediately preceding the /C switch.

Length of a PRINT Queue Entry

Each print queue entry may contain a maximum of 64 characters, including the drive letter and path information.

Limitations on Switches

You must specify the desired /D, /B, /U, /M, /S, and /Q switches the first time you use the PRINT command after starting MS-DOS. The only way to modify these switch settings after running PRINT the first time is to restart your computer.

Examples

Use the following command to view the current status of the print queue:

```
PRINT
```

MS-DOS displays the name of the file currently being printed, the names of any files still in the print queue, and any error messages generated by PRINT during the current print cycle.

Use the following command to create a print queue for printing on LPT2:

```
PRINT /D:LPT2
```

The following command removes one file, LETTER.ONE, from the print queue and adds another file, LETTER.TWO, at the same time:

```
PRINT LETTER.ONE /C LETTER.TWO /P
```

The following command increases the maximum number of files allowed in the print queue from the default value of 10 to 25:

```
PRINT /Q:25
```

PROMPT

You use this command to change the appearance of the MS-DOS system prompt.

Syntax

```
PROMPT [text]
```

Parameter

text

Specifies any text or other information you want included in your system prompt. DOS provides several special system prompt characters, including:

Characters	Resulting prompt information
$q	the = character
$$	$ character
$t	the current time
$d	the current date
$p	the currently active disk drive and directory
$n	the default drive
$v	the version number of your DOS release
$g	a "greater than" symbol (>)
$l	a "less than" symbol (<)
$b	a "pipe" character (|)
$_	a linefeed/carriage return
$s	a blank space
$e	ASCII escape code (code 27)
$h	Backspace (used to delete a character that has been written to the prompt command line)

Examples

The following command sets the system prompt to display the current drive and path, enclosed in parentheses, followed by a greater than symbol (>):

```
PROMPT ($p)$g
```

The following command sets the system prompt to show the current date and time, then display a second line containing the active directory, enclosed in parentheses, and a greater than symbol (>):

```
PROMPT $d $t $_($p)$g $s
```

Related Commands

See the DATE command for information about setting the current date.
See the TIME command for information about setting the current time.

QBASIC

This command runs the QBasic programming language.

Syntax

    QBASIC [/B] [/EDITOR] [/G] [/H] [/MBF] [/NOHI]
    [[/RUN][drive:][path]filename]

Parameter

    [drive:][path]filename

Identifies a program you want loaded with the QBasic language.

Switches

    /B

Sets the QBasic display to black and white.

✔ **Note:** Try using the /B switch if the QBasic shortcut keys do not show up on your display.

    /EDITOR

Runs Editor, a QBasic-based text editor included with DOS. Using this switch is the same as entering EDIT at the system prompt.

    /G

Improves QBasic's performance on a system with a CGA monitor.

    /H

Adjusts the QBasic screen to use the maximum number of lines possible for your display.

    /MBF

Automatically converts several built-in QBasic functions.

    /NOHI

Allows the use of a monitor that does not support high-intensity video.

✔ **Note:** Try using the NOHI switch if the QBasic shortcut keys do not show up on your display.

> ***Caution:*** The NOHI switch should never be used with a COMPAQ laptop computer.

/RUN

Runs the specified QBasic program before displaying it. This switch requires a filename.

Using the MS-DOS Text Editor

The QBASIC.EXE file must be in the current directory, a directory included in your search path, or the same directory as the EDIT.COM file for MS-DOS Editor (EDIT.COM) to load successfully.

RAMDRIVE.SYS

Creates a virtual (RAM) drive in memory. The RAM drive simulates a hard drive and can perform any of the operations you would normally do using a hard disk drive. The RAM drive is assigned the next available drive letter (for example, D: if C: is the only hard drive assigned).

The advantage of a RAM drive is increased speed, since DOS accesses memory much faster than it does a physical drive. On the other hand, since RAMDRIVE.SYS uses your computer's RAM to create the virtual drive, all information contained on the RAM drive is lost when the system is shut down or restarted; so, be sure to save all pertinent data files to a hard drive or floppy before shutdown. In addition, unless you create your RAM drive in extended or expanded memory, it reduces the amount of memory available to your applications.

Syntax

```
DEVICE=[drive:][path] RAMDRIVE.SYS [DriveSize SectorSize
[NumEntries]] [/E | /A]
```

> ✓ **Note:** You can create multiple RAM drives by adding other DEVICE=RAMDRIVE.SYS command lines to your CONFIG.SYS file.

Parameters

`[drive:][path]`

Specifies the drive letter and path to the RAMDRIVE.SYS file.

`DriveSize`

Used to specify the size of the virtual (RAM) drive in kilobytes. RAM drives can range in size from 4K to 32,767K. Since this is an optional parameter, RAMDrive will create a 64K virtual drive if *DriveSize* isn't specified.

> ✓ **Note:** RAMDRIVE.SYS won't create the RAM drive if insufficient memory is available.

`SectorSize`

If you use the *DriveSize* parameter, you can use this parameter to denote the disk sector size in bytes. Although the default *SectorSize* value is 512, acceptable values include 128 bytes and 256 bytes.

454   DOS 6.0 HANDBOOK

```
NumEntries
```

Limits the number of files and directories you can create in the virtual drive's root directory. The files and directories can be limited to anywhere between 2 and 1024 entries. If there is sufficient memory to create the RAM drive but *NumEntries* isn't specified, a default limit of 64 entries is imposed. If there is insufficient memory to support the number of files and directories specified by the *NumEntries* parameter, RAMDrive will attempt to allow 16 entries in the root.

> ✔ **Note:** Using the *NumEntries* parameter requires that the *DriveSize* and *SectorSize* parameters also be used.

Switches

```
/E
```

Creates the RAM drive in extended memory. This assumes that your system is configured for extended memory and possesses an extended memory manager such as HIMEM.SYS, which can be loaded by the DEVICE= command in your CONFIG.SYS file.

> ✔ **Note:** If you use the /E switch, the DEVICE=HIMEM.SYS command must precede the DEVICE=RAMDRIVE.SYS command in your CONFIG.SYS file.

```
/A
```

Creates the RAM drive in expanded memory. This assumes that your system is configured for expanded memory and possesses an expanded memory manager such as EMM386, 386MAX, CEMM, or QEMM, which is loaded by the DEVICE command in your CONFIG.SYS file.

> ✔ **Note:** If you use the /A switch, the DEVICE=EMM386 command must precede the DEVICE=RAMDRIVE.SYS command in your CONFIG.SYS file.

Creating RAMDRIVE.SYS in Conventional Memory

As a rule, you shouldn't create a RAM drive in conventional memory simply because it reduces the amount of memory available for your applications. But rules are made to be broken. One reasonable exception to this rule occurs when your system doesn't possess extended memory or expanded memory, and you lack a hard drive and are using a floppy drive system. The increased speed you'll gain when accessing your application will compensate for the loss of conventional memory.

The correct syntax for creating a RAM drive in conventional memory is as follows:

`DEVICE=RAMDRIVE.SYS`

This RAMDrive was created without specifying the /E or /A switch, and will be referred to by the next available drive letter.

> ✔ *Note:* Be sure to use the LASTDRIVE command to set aside additional drive letters.

Using RAMDRIVE.SYS with Extended Memory

Specify the /E switch to create the RAM drive in extended memory. Your system must be configured for extended memory, for which you'll need an extended memory manager, such as HIMEM.SYS, that conforms to the Lotus/Intel/Microsoft/AST eXtended Memory Specification (XMS). The DEVICE command to install the extended memory manager must precede the DEVICE command to install RAMDRIVE.SYS.

Using RAMDRIVE.SYS with Expanded Memory

Specify the /A switch to create the RAM drive in expanded memory. Your system must be configured for expanded memory. In order to create one or more virtual drives in expanded memory, you'll need an expanded memory manager, such as EMM386.SYS, that conforms to the Lotus/Intel/Microsoft Expanded Memory Specification (LIM EMS). The DEVICE command to install the expanded memory manager must precede the DEVICE command to install RAMDRIVE.SYS.

Increasing Efficiency with a RAM drive

Defining a TEMP environmental variable and setting it to one of the directories on the RAM drive will increase the overall performance of many disk operations. Also, if you're running WINDOWS, create a RAM drive that contains at least 2MB of memory, thus ensuring there is enough space to create temporary files and to handle printing.

Example

To create a RAMDrive in expanded memory and allocate 640K of expanded memory, a sector size of 512, and root directory entries of 80, use the following syntax:

DEVICE=C:\SYS\RAMDRIVE.SYS 640 512 80 /A

Related Command

See the LASTDRIVE command for further information on setting aside drive letters for devices.

REM

This command lets you include REM lines — non-executable comments — in a CONFIG.SYS or a batch file.

Syntax

    REM [comment]

Parameters

    comment

Specifies the text you want included in CONFIG.SYS or a batch file as a comment.

> ✔ *Note:* You cannot include the DOS redirection characters (> or <) or a pipe (|) in a REM line.

Examples

The following batch file includes remarks for both explanations and vertical spacing:

    @ECHO OFF
    REM This batch program formats and checks disks in drive A.
    REM It is named FORMATA.BAT.
    REM
    ECHO Insert a new disk in drive A.
    PAUSE
    FORMAT A: /V
    CHKDSK A:

> ✔ *Note:* In general, the intention of REM is to display comments within a batch file that will not be seen by the user. However, unless ECHO is OFF, all REM statements will still be displayed to the screen.

Related Command

See the ECHO command for information about displaying messages in CONFIG.SYS or a batch file.

RENAME (REN)

RENAME is an internal DOS command used to rename a file or group of files. RENAME does not, however, allow you to specify a new drive or path.

Syntax

```
RENAME [drive:][path]filename1 filename2
REN [drive:][path]filename1 filename2
```

Parameters

`[drive:][path]filename1`

Specifies the location and name of the file or group of files you want to rename.

> ✔ *Note:* You may use the DOS wildcards (* and ?) to rename groups of files with similar filenames.

`filename2`

Specifies a new name for the file or group of files you want to rename.

> 🚫 *Caution:* DOS aborts a RENAME operation if a file with *filename2* already exists in the current directory and displays the following error message:
>
> ```
> Duplicate filename or file not found
> ```

Examples

The following command changes all HLD extensions in the current directory to SAV:

```
REN *.HLD *.SAV
```

The following command renames the PROJBUDG.DAT file on a floppy disk in drive A to REALBUDG.DAT:

```
REN A:PROJBUDG.DAT REALBUDG.DAT
```

The newly renamed file REALBUDG.DAT remains on drive A.

Related Commands

See the COPY command for information about renaming files as you copy them to a different drive or directory.

See the LABEL command for information about renaming a disk.

See the XCOPY command for information about copying entire directories to a new location.

REPLACE

This command replaces files in a destination directory or group of directories with files in the source directory that have the same name.

Syntax

```
REPLACE [drive1:][path1]filename [drive2:][path2]
[/A][/P][/R][/S][/W][/U]
```

Parameters

[drive1:][path1]filename

Specifies the location and name of the source file or group of files.

> ✔ *Note:* When specifying a filename, you may use the DOS wildcard characters (* and ?).

[drive2:][path2]

Specifies a destination directory or group of directories for the source file or group of file.

> ✔ *Note:* You cannot specify a filename for files you replace. The REPLACE command always replaces files with files of the same name.

Switches

/A

Adds new files to the destination directory instead of replacing existing files. You cannot use the /A switch with the /S or /U switch.

/P

Asks you to confirm an operation before REPLACE copies the source file to the specified destination.

/R

Replaces both unprotected and read-only files.

> 🚫 *Caution:* If you attempt to replace a read-only file and do not specify the /R switch, DOS aborts the REPLACE operation.

/S

    Searches all subdirectories of the destination directory and replaces matching files. You cannot use the /S switch with the /A switch.

/W

    Instructs DOS to wait until a disk is inserted in a floppy drive before searching for source files and initiating the REPLACE operation. This allows you to switch floppy disks during the REPLACE operation.

/U

    Instructs DOS to replace files on the destination directory only if a newer version exists on the source directory. You cannot use the /U switch with the /A switch.

> **Caution:** You cannot use the REPLACE command to update hidden files or system files such as IO.SYS and MSDOS.SYS.

REPLACE Exit Codes

Besides a two-line summary that it displays after it has completed operation, REPLACE uses a series of error codes to inform you of its progress or, alternately, any complications it encounters during a REPLACE operation. The following list describes the meaning of the various REPLACE codes:

    0   REPLACE successfully replaced or added the files.

    1   The version of MS-DOS is incompatible with the version of REPLACE.

    2   REPLACE could not find the source files.

    3   REPLACE could not find the source or destination path.

    5   The user does not have access to the files you want to replace.

    8   There is insufficient system memory to carry out the command.

    11   The user used the wrong syntax on the command line.

> **Note:** You may use an ERRORLEVEL command in conjunction with IF commands within a batch file to process the error codes returned by REPLACE.

Examples

One convenient use for the REPLACE command is to make certain that any version of the same file stored in different locations on a disk are identical to one another. The following command replaces every file called MYDATA.DAT on drive C with the version of that file currently on a disk in drive B:

```
REPLACE B:\MYDATA.DAT C:\ /S
```

The following command transfers newer font (FON) files from a disk in drive A to a directory named PRINT on drive C, which already contains older versions of these files:

```
REPLACE A:*.FON C:\PRINT /U
```

Related Commands

See the ATTRIB command for information about changing file attributes.
See the COPY command for information about copying files.
See the RENAME (REN) command for information about renaming files.

RESTORE

You use this command to restore files that were backed up by using any version of BACKUP from MS-DOS versions 2.0 through 5.0.

> ✔ **Note:** To restore files backed up using DOS 6.0, you must use the MSBACKUP utility.

Syntax

```
RESTORE drive1: drive2:[path[filename]] [/S] [/P] [/B:date]
[/A:date][/E:time] [/L:time] [/M] [/N] [/D]
```

Parameters

drive1:

A required drive letter indicating the drive containing the archived file(s) to be restored.

drive2:

The target drive — that is, the hard disk to which the archived file(s) should be restored.

path

The name of a directory or subdirectory that originally contained the files being restored.

filename

The names of the archived file(s) you want to restore.

Switches

/S

Restores any subdirectories associated with the specified path.

/M

Restores only those files that have been altered since the previous backup.

/B:date

Restores only those files that have been modified on or before the specified date.

/A:date

Restores only those files that have been modified on or after the specified date.

`/E:time`

Restores only those files last modified on or earlier than the specified time. The format of time varies according to the COUNTRY setting in your CONFIG.SYS file. (For information about specifying time, see the TIME command.)

`/L:time`

Restores only those files last modified on or later than the specified time.

`/P`

Causes RESTORE to display a special prompt whenever it encounters a file on the target disk that has changed since the last backup or is marked as a read-only file. You are then given the option of either replacing the existing version or telling RESTORE to bypass that file.

`/N`

Restores only those files that are not already present on the target disk.

`/D`

Displays a list of the files on the backup disk that match the names specified in filename without restoring any files. However, even though no files are being restored, you must specify *drive2* when you use /D.

Limitations on RESTORE

You cannot use the RESTORE command to restore system files (IO.SYS and MSDOS.SYS), and RESTORE does not work with drives that have been redirected with the ASSIGN or JOIN command.

Determining Whether RESTORE Was Successful

When it completes its operation, the RESTORE command returns an exit code that determines whether all files have been restored successfully or whether RESTORE encountered an error. You can create a batch file in which the ERRORLEVEL parameter is used in a series of IF commands to process the possible exit codes returned by RESTORE. These exit codes are as follows:

0	RESTORE successfully restored the file or files.
1	RESTORE could not find the files to restore.
3	The user pressed CTRL+C to stop the RESTORE operation.
4	RESTORE stopped because of an error.

Examples

The following command restores the file MYDATA.DAT from an archive disk in drive B to the FILES directory on drive C:

`RESTORE B: C:\FILES\MYDATA.DAT`

The following command restores all files on an archive disk in drive A that were backed up from the directory \BUDGETS\DATA on drive D:

`RESTORE A: D:\BUDGETS\DATA\*.*`

You must use the *.* wildcard notation in the previous command to indicate a full restore. Omitting this notation causes the RESTORE command to attempt to restore a file named DATA in the BUDGETS directory.

The following command performs a complete hard disk restore for drive D from archive disks placed in drive A:

`RESTORE A: D:\*.* /S`

The /S switch and the wildcards (*.*) in the previous example specify that RESTORE is to restore all backed up files to their original directories and subdirectories on drive D.

Related Commands

See the MSBACKUP command for information about backing up and restoring files with MS-DOS 6.0.

See the BACKUP command for information about backing up files with versions of MS-DOS prior to MS-DOS 6.0.

RMDIR (RD)

You use RMDIR to delete (remove) a directory.

Syntax

RMDIR|RD [drive:]path

Parameter

[drive:]path

Specifies the DOS path notation for the directory you want to remove.

> *Caution:* The RD command works only on an empty directory — that is, a directory in which no files are stored and which has no subdirectories. Attempting to delete a directory that still contains files or directories causes DOS to display the following message:
>
>   Invalid path, not directory, or directory not empty

> *Caution:* You cannot delete a directory if it is the current directory. If you attempt to do this, DOS displays the same error message as it does when you attempt to remove a directory that is not empty.

Example

The following commands both delete a directory named \DOSFILES\HOLD:

    RMDIR \DOSFILES\HOLD
    RD \DOSFILES\HOLD

Related Commands

See the ATTRIB command for information about hidden files.
See the MKDIR command for information about creating a directory.

SET

This command displays, sets, or removes MS-DOS environment variables.

Syntax

```
SET [variable=[string]]
```

Parameters

`variable`

Specifies the environment variable you want to set or modify.

`string`

Specifies the string you want associated with the specified variable. Environment variables allow you to modify certain elements of your DOS working environment, hence, the name. For example, if you customize your system prompt using the PROMPT command, DOS stores the new setting in a variable called, appropriately enough, PROMPT. Likewise, changing the default appearance of directory listings adds a new variable called DIRCMD to your DOS environment. Also, many programs use environment variables to identify where to find certain information they need to run properly.

If you specify only a variable and an equal sign (without a string) for the SET command, MS-DOS removes that variable from your environment.

> ***Caution:*** After you use a SET command, MS-DOS might display the following message:
>
> ```
> Out of environment space
> ```
>
> This message indicates that the available environment space is insufficient to hold the new variable definition. It's possible to increase the amount of environment space in your system by inserting the appropriate SHELL command statement into your CONFIG.SYS file.

Examples

The following command displays the current environment settings:

```
SET
```

The following command removes a previously defined variable called TEMP from your DOS environment:

```
SET TEMP=
```

The following command sets the environment variable TEMPFILE to a directory called TEMP on drive D:

```
set TEMPFILE=D:\TEMP
```

Related Commands

See the PATH, PROMPT, SHELL, and DIR commands for information about setting environment variables that MS-DOS uses to control its own operations.

See the COMMAND command for information on how to increase your environment space.

SETVER

SETVER changes the MS-DOS version number that MS-DOS 6.0 reports to a program or device driver. It requires that SETVER.EXE was previously loaded by a DEVICE= statement in your CONFIG.SYS file.

Syntax

    SETVER [drive:path][filename [n.nn]] [/DELETE [/QUIET]]

Parameters

`[drive:path]`

Specifies the location of the SETVER.EXE file.

`filename`

Specifies the name of the program file (usually an .EXE or .COM file) that you want to add to the version table.

> ✔ *Note:* You cannot use wildcard characters (* or ?) with the SETVER command.

`n.nn`

Indicates the MS-DOS version (for example, 3.3 or 4.01) that MS-DOS 6.0 reports to the specified program file.

Switches

`/DELETE`

Deletes the version table entry for the specified program file. You may abbreviate this switch as /D.

`/QUIET`

Suppresses the message DOS normally displays when it deletes an entry from the version table.

> ✔ *Note:* Changes to SETVER take effect only after the computer has been restarted.

Why Use SETVER?

Some programs designed to run with a previous version of MS-DOS will not run properly under MS-DOS 6.0. In some cases, nothing can be done about this except to request an upgrade from the program's manufacturer. Quite often, however, the problem can be solved by adding its name to the SETVER version table. Doing so "tricks" the program into believing that your computer is running a version of MS-DOS for which it was designed, even though you're really using MS-DOS 6.0.

> *Caution:* Although this works with many programs, it does not eliminate incompatibilities with all applications. SETVER will not solve the problem if the program is indeed incompatible with MS-DOS 6.0.

Loading the Version Table into Memory

Before you can use the SETVER command, you must load the version table into memory by including a SETVER statement in your CONFIG.SYS file. During installation, the MS-DOS Setup program modifies your CONFIG.SYS file to include the SETVER statement.

SETVER Confirmation

If you make changes to the version table and no errors are detected, MS-DOS displays the following message:

```
WARNING - Contact your software vendor for information about
whether a specific program works with MS-DOS 6.0. It is
possible that Microsoft has not verified whether the program
will successfully run if you use the SETVER command to change
the program version number and version table. If you run the
program after changing the version table in MS-DOS 6.0, you may
lose or corrupt data or introduce system instabilities.
Microsoft is not responsible for any loss or damage, or for
lost or corrupted data.

Version table successfully updated. The version change will
take effect the next time you restart your system.
```

SETVER Error Codes

SETVER uses a series of error codes to inform you of its progress or, alternately, any complications it encounters during a SETVER operation. The following list describes the meaning of the various SETVER codes:

 0   SETVER successfully completed its task.
 1   The user specified an invalid command switch.
 2   The user specified an invalid filename.
 3   There is insufficient system memory to carry out the command.

4	The user specified an invalid version-number format.
5	SETVER could not find the specified entry in the version table.
6	SETVER could not find the SETVER.EXE file.
7	The user specified an invalid drive.
8	The user specified too many command-line parameters.
9	SETVER detected missing command-line parameters.
10	SETVER detected an error while reading the SETVER.EXE file.
11	The SETVER.EXE file is corrupt.
12	The specified SETVER.EXE file does not support a version table.
13	There is insufficient space in the version table for a new entry.
14	SETVER detected an error while writing to the SETVER.EXE file.

> ✔ *Note:* You may use an ERRORLEVEL command in conjunction with IF commands within a batch file to process the error codes returned by SETVER.

Examples

The following command modifies the version table so that DOS reports it is version 4.1 whenever you run a program called MYPROG.EXE:

```
SETVER MYPROG.EXE 4.1
```

The following command deletes the MYPROG.EXE entry from the version table:

```
SETVER MYPROG.EXE /DELETE
```

The following command lists the contents of the version table for drive C:

```
SETVER C:
```

SETVER.EXE

SETVER.EXE is a device driver that loads the MS-DOS version table into memory. During installation, the MS-DOS Setup program modifies your CONFIG.SYS file to include the SETVER statement.

Syntax

`DEVICE=[drive:][path]SETVER.EXE`

Parameters

`[drive:][path]`

   Specifies the location of the SETVER.EXE file.

> ***Caution:*** If you use SETVER to report a different MS-DOS version for a device driver, the DEVICE statement that loads SETVER.EXE must appear earlier in your CONFIG.SYS file than the DEVICE command used to load the troublesome device driver.

SHELL

SHELL specifies the name and location of the command interpreter you want MS-DOS to use.

Syntax

    SHELL=[[drive:]path]filename [parameters]

Parameters

    [[drive:]path]filename

Specifies the location and name of the command interpreter you want MS-DOS to use.

    parameters

Specifies any command-line parameters or switches that can be used with the new command interpreter.

> ✔ *Note:* The SHELL command is the preferred method of using COMMAND to increase the size of the environment.

Examples

The following command loads a command interpreter called NCOM.COM, rather than COMMAND.COM, which is located in the directory named NU on your startup drive:

    SHELL=\NU\NCOM.COM

The following command shows the same NCOM.COM command interpreter being loaded, but this time using the switches /C, /P, and /E:

    SHELL=\NU\NCOM.COM /C /P /E

The following command loads a second version of COMMAND.COM and increases the environment size to 256 bytes:

    SHELL=COMMAND.COM /E:256 /P

Related Commands

See the COMMAND command for information about COMMAND.COM switches.

See the SET command for information about how DOS uses environment variables.

SHIFT

You use SHIFT in a batch file to change the position of replaceable parameters.

Syntax

SHIFT

The SHIFT command allows you to increase the number of variables that can be used within a batch file. SHIFT also can be used to change the values of the replaceable parameters %0 through %9 by copying each parameter into the previous one — copying the value of %1 to %0, the value of %2 to %1, and so forth. This amounts to shifting each replaceable parameter one position to the left. This second technique can be useful when you're writing a batch file that performs the same operation on any number of parameters.

> **Caution:** There is no command to restore variables displaced by the SHIFT command. After executing a SHIFT command, the first parameter (%0) that existed before the SHIFT cannot be recovered.

Example

The following batch file, MULTICOPY.BAT, illustrates how the SHIFT command can be used with any number of parameters. It copies several files to a specified directory with a single command. The replaceable parameters in this batch file are filenames entered by the user.

```
@ECHO OFF
REM MULTICOPY.BAT copies any number of files
REM to a directory.
REM Use the following command to run this batch file:
REM mycopy dir file1 file2... file-n
SET todir=%1
:GETFILE
SHIFT
IF "%1"=="" GOTO END
COPY %1 %todir%
GOTO getfile
:END
SET todir=
ECHO The requested COPY operation has been completed.
```

> **Note:** MULTICOPY.BAT cycles through any filenames entered by the user, assigning each one to the %1 replaceable parameter, until all specified files have been copied to the new directory.

SMARTDRV

This command creates a disk cache in extended memory. The purpose of a disk cache is to speed system performance by anticipating what data the system will need to retrieve from your hard disk. SMARTDrive assumes that the program code or data that will be needed next can be found in the same general area as that read previously. By loading all the data immediately surrounding the required data, the system frequently can read and write data subsequently from the high-speed cache rather than the significantly slower hard disk. It is best included in your AUTOEXEC.BAT file.

Syntax

SMARTDrive can be started either interactively from the DOS prompt or from within your AUTOEXEC.BAT file by using the following syntax:

```
[drive:][path]SMARTDRV.EXE [[drive[+|-]]...] [/E:ElementSize]
[InitCacheSize][WinCacheSize][/B:<BufferSize>] [/C] [/R] [/L]
[/Q] [/V] [/S]
```

Once SMARTDrive is running, you can use the following syntax to control its operation:

```
SMARTDRV [[drive[+|-]]...] [/C] [/R]
```

Parameters

`[drive:][path]`

Specifies the location of the SMARTDRV.EXE file.

`drive[+|-]`

Enables or disables caching, using the following procedures:

1. Specifying a drive letter without a plus or minus sign enables read-caching and disables write-caching.
2. Specifying a drive letter followed by a plus sign (+) enables both read-caching and write-caching.
3. Specifying a drive letter followed by a minus sign (-) disables both read-caching and write-caching.

You can control caching for multiple drives by separating them with a space.

`/E:ElementSize`

Specifies in bytes how much of the cache's contents SMARTDrive moves each read/write cycle. Valid settings for the /E switch are 1024, 2048, 4096, and 8192;

the default is 8192. The larger this value, the more conventional memory SMARTDrive requires.

`InitCacheSize`

Specifies the cache size in kilobytes when SMARTDrive begins running under DOS. How large a cache you specify influences how efficiently SMARTDrive runs. As a rule, the larger the cache, the less frequently SMARTDrive has to read information from the disk, resulting in better performance. If you do not specify an *InitCacheSize* value, SMARTDrive sets this value according to how much memory your system has, as reflected in the following list:

Extended	**InitCacheSize**
Up to 1 MB	All extended
Up to 2 MB	1 MB
Up to 4 MB	1 MB
Up to 6 MB	2 MB
6 MB or more	2 MB

`WinCacheSize`

Specifies, in kilobytes, how much SMARTDrive should reduce its disk cache size when you're working in the Microsoft Windows environment. If you do not specify a *WinCacheSize* value, SMARTDrive sets this value according to how much memory your system has, as reflected in the following list:

Extended	**WinCacheSize Memory**
Up to 1 MB	Zero (no caching) memory
Up to 2 MB	256K
Up to 4 MB	512K
Up to 6 MB	1 MB
6 MB or more	2 MB

> ✓ **Note:** When you start Windows, SMARTDrive reduces the size of the cache to recover memory for Windows' use. When you quit Windows, the cache returns to its normal size. *WinCacheSize* specifies the smallest size to which SMARTDrive will reduce the cache. If you specify a value for *InitCacheSize* that is smaller than the value specified for *WinCacheSize*, *InitCacheSize* is set to the same size as *WinCacheSize*.

`/B:BufferSize`

Specifies the size of the read-ahead buffer. The setting of this buffer can be any multiple of *ElementSize*; its default size is 16K.

> **Note:** A read-ahead buffer is additional information that SMARTDrive reads when an application reads information from the hard disk. For example, if an application reads 512K of information from a file, SMARTDrive then reads the amount of information specified by *BufferSize* and saves it in memory. The next time the application needs to read information from that file, it can read it from memory instead.

/C

Writes all cached information from memory to the hard disk. You might use this option if you are going to turn off your computer and want to make sure all cached information has been written to the hard disk. (SMARTDrive automatically writes all cached information to the hard disk whenever you restart your computer by pressing CTRL+ALT+DELETE.)

> **Caution:** SMARTDrive does not write cached information to the hard disk if you simply turn off the power or press your computer's reset button.

/R

Clears the contents of the existing cache and restarts SMARTDrive.

/L

Prevents SMARTDrive from automatically loading into upper memory blocks (UMBs), even if there are UMBs available.

> **Note:** If you are using SMARTDrive's double-buffering feature and your system appears to be running slowly, try loading SMARTDrive with the /L switch.

/Q

Prevents SMARTDrive from displaying error and status messages when it starts. This is the default value. It cannot be used at the same time as the /V switch.

/S

Displays additional information about the status of SMARTDrive. SMARTDrive is started by the SMARTDRV command in your AUTOEXEC.BAT file. (However, if you use EMM386.EXE or run Windows in 386 enhanced mode, you may need to use the double-buffering feature of SMARTDrive, which is installed by using a DEVICE command in your CONFIG.SYS file.)

```
/V
```
    Causes SMARTDrive to display status and error messages when it starts. (By default, SMARTDrive displays messages only if an error occurs). The /V switch cannot be used at the same time as the /Q switch.

Using Extended Memory

For SMARTDRV.EXE to use extended memory, you must first install HIMEM.SYS or another extended-memory manager that conforms to the Lotus/Intel/Microsoft/AST eXtended Memory Specification (XMS).

Loading SMARTDrive into the Upper Memory Area

If the upper memory area is available through MS-DOS, SMARTDrive will automatically load into upper memory. You do not need to use the LOADHIGH command with SMARTDRV.EXE.

SMARTDrive and Compressed Drives

By default, SMARTDrive does not cache compressed drives, but does cache the physical drive on which the compressed volume file is located. Although SMART-Drive is capable of caching compressed drives, doing so is not recommended because it slows down your system. If SMARTDrive were to cache both the compressed drive and the physical drive on which the compressed volume file is located, information would have to pass through SMARTDrive's disk cache twice.

Examples

Adding the following command to your AUTOEXEC.BAT file creates a 256K disk cache, the default SMARTDrive configuration:

```
C:\DOS\SMARTDRV.EXE
```

Adding the following, more typical, command to your AUTOEXEC.BAT file creates a 3MB (3072K) disk cache and ensures that programs cannot reduce the size of this cache to less than 1MB (1024K):

```
C:\DOS\SMARTDRV.EXE 3072 1024
```

The following command tells SMARTDrive to write all cached information from memory to the hard disk:

```
C:\DOS\SMARTDRV.EXE /C
```

> ***Caution:*** You should always issue this command before turning off your computer or pressing its reset button.

SMARTDRV.EXE

With some hard disks, SMARTDrive may have to be installed with double buffering. In this case, a DEVICE=SMARTDRV.EXE statement must also appear in your CONFIG.SYS file. For details, see Chapter 7, "Have it Your Way: Fine-Tuning Your System."

SORT

This command sorts data from a variety of input devices and writes the results to the screen, a file, or another device.

Syntax

    SORT [/R] [/+n] [<] [drive1:][path1]filename1 [> [drive2:][path2]filename2]

    [command |] SORT [/R] [/+n] [> [drive2:][path2]filename2]

Parameters

    [drive1:][path1]filename1

Specifies the location and name of the file containing the data you want to sort.

    [drive2:][path2]filename2

Specifies the location and name of a file in which you want the sorted output stored.

    command

Specifies a DOS command you want executed, with SORT organizing its output.

Switches

    /R

Specifies a reverse sort — that is, from Z to A, then from 9 to 0. SORT does not distinguish between uppercase and lowercase letters.

    /+n

Sorts the file according to the character in column n; the default is column 1.

SORT and Piping and Redirection

SORT supports the standard DOS redirection symbols. The pipe (|) or the less than sign (<) will redirect data through SORT from a DOS command or other sources. The MORE command allows you to display SORTed information one screen at a time. Finally, you can use the greater than sign (>) to direct the sorted output to a file or other device.

> ***Caution:*** Before using a pipe for redirection, you should set the TEMP environment variable in your AUTOEXEC.BAT file.

Examples

The following command reads the file MYDATA.TXT and sorts it in reverse order, displaying the results on your screen one screen at a time:

```
SORT /R < MYDATA.TXT | MORE
```

Related Command

See the MORE command for information about displaying information one screen at a time.

STACKS

This command supports the dynamic use of data stacks to handle hardware interrupts.

Syntax

STACKS=n,s

Parameters

n

Specifies the number of stacks. Valid values for n are 0 and numbers in the range 8 through 64.

s

Specifies the size (in bytes) of each stack. Valid values for s are 0 and numbers in the range 32 through 512.

If you do not specify any parameters, STACKS uses the following default settings:

Computer	Stacks
IBM PC, IBM PC/XT, IBM PC-Portable	0, 0
Other	9, 128

Caution: If DOS ever displays a "Stack Overflow" or "Exception error 12" message, try increasing the number or size of the stacks.

Example

The following command allocates 9 stacks of 265 bytes each for hardware-interrupt handling, a common setting on Windows systems:

stacks=9,256

SUBMENU

SUBMENU defines an item on the startup menu that, when selected, displays another set of choices.

Syntax

    SUBMENU=blockname[,menu_text]

Parameters

    blockname

Specifies the name of the associated configuration block. This is the name you'll use elsewhere in the CONFIG.SYS file to define the configuration block containing the statements you want executed when this submenu item is selected. Unlike the "main" menu block, which must have the block name MENU, a menu block for a submenu may have any name you want. The block name may be up to 70 characters long and may contain most printable characters. However, the block name may not include spaces, backslashes (\) and forward slashes (/), commas, semicolons (;), equal signs (=), or square brackets ([and]).

    menu_text

Identifies the text you want MS-DOS to display in the startup menu for this submenu item. If you don't specify any menu text, MS-DOS displays the block name as the menu item. The menu text may be up to 70 characters long and contain any display characters available in the ASCII character set.

Examples

The following statements, when included in a CONFIG.SYS file, define a main startup menu with one submenu, set the default item to the submenu, and specify a 60-second time-out for the user to make a selection:

    [MENU]
    MENUITEM base_config,Base configuration only
    MENUITEM full_config,Standard configuration
    SUBMENU cdmenu, Standard configuration with CD-ROM device
    MENUDEFAULT cdmenu,60

    [cdmenu]
    MENUITEM cd_rom, Load CD-ROM driver only
    MENUITEM scan, Load CD-ROM and scanner drivers

Each time you start your computer, MS-DOS displays the following menu:

```
MS-DOS 6 Startup Menu
=====================
1. Base configuration only
2. Standard configuration
3. Standard configuration with CD-ROM
Enter a choice: 3
```

If item 3 is selected, MS-DOS displays the following menu instead:

```
MS-DOS 6 Startup Menu
=====================
1. Load CD-ROM driver only
2. Load CD-ROM and scanner drivers
Enter a choice: 1
```

Related Commands

The SUBMENU command is one of five special CONFIG.SYS commands for defining multiple configurations. With multiple configurations, you define a menu that appears when your computer starts. Each menu item corresponds to a block of commands, or "configuration block," in your CONFIG.SYS file. For more information on defining configuration blocks, see the INCLUDE command.

The other four commands used to create a startup menu are:

INCLUDE	Used to include the contents of one configuration block in another
MENUCOLOR	Used to specify foreground and background colors for a startup menu
MENUDEFAULT	Used to specify the default menu item
MENUITEM	Used to define an item on the menu

SUBST

SUBST associates a path with a drive letter.

Syntax

```
SUBST [drive1: [drive2:]path]
SUBST drive1: /D
```

Parameters

drive1:

Specifies the virtual drive to which you want to assign a path. The drive letter you assign represents a virtual drive, because you can use the drive letter in commands as if it represented a physical drive.

> *Caution:* The *drive1* parameter must be within the range specified by the LASTDRIVE command. If you specify a drive letter outside the LASTDRIVE range, DOS displays the following error message:
>
> ```
> Invalid parameter - drive1:
> ```

drive2:

Specifies the physical drive that contains the specified path (if different from the current drive).

path

Specifies the path that you want to assign to a virtual drive.

Switch

/D

Deletes a virtual drive.

> *Caution:* The following commands should never be used on drives that have been reassigned with a SUBST command:
>
> | *ASSIGN | DISKCOMP | FORMAT | RECOVER |
> |---------|----------|--------|---------|
> | BACKUP | DISKCOPY | LABEL | RESTORE |
> | CHKDSK | FDISK | *MIRROR | SYS |
> | DEFRAG | | | |
>
> *Commands from DOS 5.0 and earlier versions

Why Use Subst?

The chief advantage of the SUBST command is convenience. Rather than continually referencing a lengthy path to a directory with which you work frequently, you can refer to that directory by using a single drive letter. Hence, for example, rather than having to constantly refer to a directory named C:\TMP\PROJECTS\PROJECT1\BILLING, you can instead refer to it as D:.

In addition, the PATH statement is limited to 127 characters; by reassigning one or more directories to logical drives, this limitation can sometimes be effectively overcome. For example, imagine that adding the directory C:\WORDPROC\PROGRAMS\WINWORD2 to the PATH would make the PATH statement more than 127 characters long. If the SUBST command were used, this directory could be referred to simply as D:\, for example.

Using SUBST with Microsoft Windows

You should never use the SUBST command to create or delete virtual drives while working in the Windows environment. Use the following steps to modify virtual drives for Windows operations:

1. Exit Windows.
2. Create or delete the virtual drive.
3. Restart Windows.

Examples

Use the following command to display the names of the virtual drives in effect on your system:

```
SUBST
```

Use the following command to create a virtual drive M for the path C:\FINANCE\BUDGETS:

```
SUBST M: C:\FINANCE\BUDGETS:
```

You can now reach this directory by typing the letter of the virtual drive, followed by a colon, rather than the full path name, as illustrated in the following example:

```
M:
```

> ✓ ***Note:*** This example works only if you have included the line LASTDRIVE=Z in your CONFIG.SYS file to define M or a higher letter as the highest letter that MS-DOS recognizes as a disk drive.

Related Command

See the LASTDRIVE command for information about increasing the number of drive letters available on your system.

SWITCHES

SWITCHES is used in a CONFIG.SYS file to specify special options in MS-DOS.

Syntax

SWITCHES=/W /K /N /F

Switches

/W

Specifies that the WINA20.386 file has been moved to a directory other than the root directory. Use this switch only if you run Microsoft Windows 3.0 in enhanced mode and have moved the WINA20.386 file from the root directory to another directory.

/K

Forces an enhanced keyboard to behave like a conventional keyboard.

/N

Prevents the user from pressing F5 or F8 to bypass startup commands.

/F

Instructs DOS to eliminate the 2-second delay that normally follows display of the "Starting MS-DOS ..." message.

Examples

Adding the following statement to your CONFIG.SYS file causes MS-DOS to use conventional keyboard functions, even though your computer has an enhanced keyboard:

SWITCHES=/K

Adding the following statement to your CONFIG.SYS file instructs DOS that you have moved the WINA20.386 file to a directory other than the root directory:

SWITCHES=/W

SYS

SYS copies the MS-DOS system files and the MS-DOS command interpreter (COMMAND.COM) to create a startup disk.

Syntax

    SYS [drive1:][path] drive2:

Parameters

    [drive1:][path]

Specifies the location of the system files. The default location for these files is the root directory on the current drive.

    drive2:

Specifies the drive to which you want to copy the system files. Because system files can be copied only to a root directory, this parameter does not include path information.

> ***Caution:*** The SYS command does not work on network drives or on drives that have been redirected by using the SUBST command. Nor does it work on drives that have been redirected with ASSIGN or JOIN, two commands that were available with versions of DOS prior to DOS 6.0.

Examples

The following command copies the MS-DOS system files and command interpreter from the disk in the current drive to a disk in drive B:

    SYS B:

The following command copies the MS-DOS system files and command interpreter from a disk in drive E to a disk in drive A:

    SYS E: B:

Related Commands

See the COPY and XCOPY commands for information about copying files.

TIME

You use TIME to view the system time or reset your computer's internal clock. MS-DOS uses time information to update the directory whenever you create or change a file.

Syntax

    TIME [hours:[minutes[:seconds[.hundredths]]][A|P]]

Parameters

hours

Specifies the hour. Valid values are 0 through 23.

minutes

Specifies minutes. Valid values are 0 through 59.

seconds

Specifies seconds. Valid values are 0 through 59.

hundredths

Specifies hundredths of a second. Valid values are 0 through 99.

A|P

Specifies A.M or P.M. for the 12-hour time format. If you type a valid 12-hour time but do not type A or P, TIME uses A (for A.M.).

Using the TIME command in AUTOEXEC.BAT

If your system startup procedures include an AUTOEXEC.BAT file, DOS will not automatically display the TIME input prompt. If you want users to record a time each time the computer is started or rebooted, you must include the TIME command (with no parameter) in your AUTOEXEC.BAT file.

Examples

Either of the following commands will set your computer's clock to 3:25 P.M.:

    TIME 15:25
    TIME 3:25p

Use the following command to display the current time or to display a prompt by which you can change the current time:

```
TIME
```

Related Commands

See the DATE command for information about changing the current date setting.

See the COUNTRY command for more information on changing the date format used by your computer.

TREE

TREE displays the directory structure of a disk or path.

Syntax

```
TREE [drive:][path] [/F] [/A]
```

Parameters

drive:

Identifies the drive containing the disk for which you want to display a directory tree.

path

Specifies the directory for which you want to display a TREE listing.

> ✔ *Note:* The structure TREE displays depends upon the parameters you specify on the command line. If you do not specify a drive or path, TREE displays the tree structure beginning with the current directory of the current drive.

Switches

/F

Displays the names of the files in each directory, along with the names of directories.

/A

Instructs TREE to use text characters, rather than graphic characters, to display the lines linking subdirectories. Use this switch with display cards that do not support graphic characters, or if you send output to a nongraphic printer.

Examples

The following command displays the names of all the subdirectories on the disk in your current drive, along with any files they contain:

```
TREE \ /F
```

The following command prints the same list that the previous example displayed:

```
TREE \ /F >PRN
```

The following command displays, one screen at a time, all the directories on drive D:

```
TREE D:\ | MORE
```

Caution: Before using a pipe for redirection, you should set the TEMP environment variable in your AUTOEXEC.BAT file.

Related Command

See the DIR command for information about displaying the contents of a directory.

TYPE

TYPE displays a text file without modifying its contents.

Syntax

TYPE [drive:][path]filename

Parameter

[drive:][path]filename

Specifies the location and name of the file that you want to view.

> ✓ *Note:* Using TYPE to display a binary file or a file created by a program will produce unusual characters on the screen, including form feed characters and escape-sequence symbols. As a rule, you should use the TYPE command to display files that contain text only.

Examples

The following command displays the contents of a file named MYDATA.TXT:

TYPE MYDATA.TXT

The following command displays the same file, but pauses after the screen is filled:

TYPE MYDATA.TXT | MORE

> *Caution:* Before using a pipe (|) for redirection, you should set the TEMP environment variable in your AUTOEXEC.BAT file.

Related Commands

See the DIR command for information about displaying filenames and file sizes.
See the MORE command for information about displaying text files one screen at a time.

UNDELETE

This command restores files previously deleted with the DEL command.

Syntax

```
UNDELETE [[drive:][path]filename] [/DT|/DS|/DOS]
UNDELETE [/LIST|/ALL|/PURGE[:drive]|/STATUS|/LOAD|/UNLOAD
|/S[:drive]|/Tdrive[-entries]]
```

Parameter

[drive:][path]filename

Specifies the location and name of the file or set of files you want to recover.

> ✔ **Note:** By default, UNDELETE restores all deleted files in the current directory.

Switches

/DT

Recovers only those files listed in the deletion-tracking file. DOS requests confirmation before recovering each file.

/DS

Recovers only those files listed in the SENTRY directory. DOS requests confirmation before recovering each file.

/DOS

Recovers only those files that are internally listed as deleted by MSDOS. DOS requests confirmation before recovering each file. If a deletion-tracking file exists, this switch causes UNDELETE to ignore it.

/LIST

Lists deleted files that DOS determines can be recovered with an UNDELETE command. The *[drive:][path]filename* parameter and the /DT, /DS, and /DOS switches determine the contents of this list.

/ALL

Automatically recovers deleted files without user intervention.

`/PURGE[:drive]`

Deletes the contents of the SENTRY directory. (See "Types of UNDELETE protection," below.)

> ✓ ***Note:*** By default, UNDELETE searches the current drive for the SENTRY directory.

`/STATUS`

Displays the type of delete protection set up for each drive.

`/LOAD`

Loads the terminate-and-stay-resident (TSR) portion of UNDELETE.

`/UNLOAD`

Unloads the TSR portion of UNDELETE from memory. This switch disables DOS's ability to restore deleted files. UNLOAD may be abbreviated to /U.

`/S[:drive]`

Enables the delete sentry level of protection and loads the TSR portion of the UNDELETE program, using the settings defined in the UNDELETE.INI file. If you do not specify a drive, using this switch enables the delete sentry level of protection on the current drive.

`/Tdrive[-entries]`

Enables the delete tracker level of protection and loads the TSR portion of the UNDELETE program. You must specify the *drive* parameter, which identifies the drive containing the disk for which you want UNDELETE to save information about deleted files.

The *entries* parameter is optional. If used, this setting must be a value in the range 1 through 999, indicating the maximum number of entries in the deletion-tracking file.

The default value for entries depends upon the type of disk being tracked. The following list shows each disk size, its default number of entries, and its corresponding file size:

Disk	Entries	File size
360K	25	5K
720K	50	9K
1.2 MB	75	14K
1.44 MB	75	14K
20 MB	101	18K
32 MB	202	36K
32 MB	303	55K

> **Caution:** If you use the ASSIGN command to redirect disk operations, you must do so before installing deletion tracking for the ASSIGNed drive. Deletion tracking cannot be used on drives that have been redirected with the JOIN or SUBST command. ASSIGN and JOIN are redirection commands available only with DOS versions prior to 6.0.

Types of UNDELETE Protection

UNDELETE provides three levels of file protection:

1. Delete sentry, the highest level of protection, ensures that you can recover deleted files. The TSR portion of delete sentry requires approximately 14K of memory.
2. Delete tracker provides an intermediate level of protection. The TSR portion of delete tracker requires approximately 14K of memory.
3. The third and least effective protection level, MS-DOS, which requires no memory, is automatically available on all systems.

> **Note:** UNDELETE will not recover directories deleted with an RMDIR (RD) command or the DELTREE command.

> **Caution:** Although the UNDELETE command will usually recover deleted files, it can guarantee success only if run *immediately* after a file was deleted.

Examples

Use the following command to UNDELETE all deleted files in the current directory, instructing DOS to request confirmation before each UNDELETE operation:

```
UNDELETE
```

Use the following command to automatically UNDELETE any deleted files in the DATA directory of drive C that had an extension of HLD:

```
UNDELETE C:\DATA\*.HLD /ALL
```

The following command loads SENTRY, the highest level of UNDELETE protection, using drive D to keep track of any deleted files:

```
UNDELETE /SD
```

The TSR portion of SENTRY requires approximately 14K of memory.

UNFORMAT

This command restores the contents of a disk following a FORMAT operation.

Syntax

`UNFORMAT drive: [/L] [/TEST] [/P]`

Parameter

`drive:`

Specifies the drive containing the disk on which you want to perform an UNFORMAT operation.

Switches

`/L`

Displays a list of every file and subdirectory UNFORMAT finds on the target disk before restoring its contents. Pressing Ctrl+S pauses the list; pressing any key continues the scroll.

`/TEST`

Displays a report indicating how UNFORMAT would re-create the target disk, but does not initiate an UNFORMAT operation.

`/P`

Sends any messages generated by UNFORMAT to a printer connected to LPT1.

Limitations on the UNFORMAT Command

1. UNFORMAT cannot restore a disk that was formatted using the /U switch.
2. UNFORMAT cannot be used to restore data on network drives.
3. UNFORMAT will not recover fragmented files — that is, files whose contents are stored in discontiguous sectors of a disk. When it encounters a fragmented file, UNFORMAT asks whether you want recover only the first part or delete it altogether.

Examples

The following command determines whether UNFORMAT can restore a formatted disk in drive B:

`UNFORMAT B: /TEST`

The following command restores a formatted disk in drive A, listing all files and subdirectories before actually initiating an UNFORMAT operation:

```
UNFORMAT A: /L
```

Related Commands

See the FORMAT command for information about formatting a disk.

See the UNDELETE command for information about recovering deleted files.

VER

VER displays the MS-DOS version number.

Syntax

VER

Example

The following command displays the version number of the MS-DOS release installed on your computer.

VER

VERIFY

This command instructs MS-DOS to verify that your files are written correctly to a disk.

Syntax

VERIFY [ON|OFF]

Switch

ON|OFF

Enables or disables file verification, respectively. To verify that files are copied correctly, you can also use the /V switch with the COPY or XCOPY commands. For more information about the /V switch, see these commands.

> ✔ **Note:** The VERIFY command can be placed in your CONFIG.SYS file or AUTOEXEC.BAT file, or it can be issued interactively at the DOS prompt.

Examples

The following command enables file verification:

VERIFY ON

The following command displays the current status of file verification:

VERIFY

Related Command

See the CHKDSK command for information about checking a disk for bad sectors.

VOL

You use this command to display a disk's volume label and serial number.

Syntax

    VOL [drive:]

Parameters

   drive:

   Specifies the drive that contains the disk for which you want to display the volume label and serial number.

> ✔ ***Note:*** DOS versions 4.0 and later automatically generate a serial number whenever a disk is formatted.

Example

The following command displays the volume label and serial number assigned to the disk in drive B:

    VOL B:

Related Commands

See the FORMAT and LABEL commands for information about assigning a volume label to a disk.

VSAFE

This terminate-and-stay-resident (TSR) utility guards your computer against viruses.

Syntax

VSAFE /[option[+ | -] ...] /NE /NX /Ax /Cx /N /D /U

Switches

option[+|-]

Uses one of the following values to specify how VSAFE should perform virus checking:

1 Issues a warning if a virus attempts to format a hard disk; the default setting is "on."

2 Issues a warning if a program attempts to stay in memory; the default setting is "off."

3 Automatically prevents a program from writing to disk; the default setting is "off."

4 Performs a virus check each time you load an executable file; the default setting is "on."

5 Checks the boot sector of all your disks for viruses; the default setting is "on."

6 Issues a warning whenever a program attempts to write to the boot sector or partition table of your hard disk; the default setting is "on."

7 Issues a warning whenever a program attempts to write to the boot sector of a floppy disk; the default setting is "off."

8 Issues a warning whenever an attempt is made to modify an executable file; the default setting is "on."

The plus or minus sign (+ or -) switch is used to turn on or off an option, respectively.

/NE

Instructs VSAFE not to load itself into expanded memory.

/NX

Instructs VSAFE not to load itself into extended memory.

`/Ax`

Specifies a hot key for VSAFE, using the Alt key in combination with whatever key is specified by *x*.

`/Cx`

Specifies a hot key for VSAFE, using the Ctrl key in combination with whatever key is specified by *x*.

`/N`

Allows network drivers to be loaded after VSAFE is started and checks them for viruses.

`/D`

Disables checksumming as a protection technique.

`/U`

Removes the TSR portion of VSAFE from memory.

Example

The following command instructs VSAFE to warn you when any attempt is made to format a hard disk or write to the boot sector of a floppy disk:

`VSAFE /1 /7+ /Cv`

The /Cv switch defines Ctrl+V as the hot key used to display the VSAFE screen.

Related Command

See MSAV for more information on virus detection and eradication.

XCOPY

XCOPY copies files from multiple directories in a single operation.

Syntax

    XCOPY source [destination] [/A|/M] [/D:date] [/P] [/S [/E]]
    [/V] [/W]

Parameters

    source

Specifies the names and locations of the files you want to copy. Source must include either a drive or a path.

    destination

Specifies where you want to copy files to. The destination parameter can include a drive letter and colon, a directory name, a filename, or any combination of these items.

Switches

    /A

Copies only source files that have their archive file attributes set. When you use this switch, XCOPY does not modify the archive attribute byte of the source file.

    /M

Copies source files that have their archive file attributes set and, unlike the /A switch, turns off each file's attribute after it is copied.

    /D:date

Copies source files only if they have been modified on or after the specified date. The format of date depends on the COUNTRY setting you are using.

    /P

Instructs DOS to prompt you before each file is copied.

    /S

Copies specified files located in the source directory and all of its subdirectories, unless any are empty. Omitting this switch causes XCOPY to work like the COPY command, in that it will only copy files from a single directory.

/E

Copies all subdirectories, even ones that are empty. You must use the /S switch with this switch.

/V

Instructs DOS to verify that the sectors written to the target disk are recorded properly.

/W

Displays the following message before initiating the XCOPY operation:

```
Press any key to begin copying file(s)
```

Caution: Older versions of XCOPY copied all files, even hidden and system files, if instructed to do so. The XCOPY included with MS-DOS 6.0 does not copy hidden and system files to the destination disk.

Specifying Destination as a File or Directory

XCOPY displays the following prompt if the destination parameter does not end with a backslash (\) and does not specify an existing directory:

```
Does destination specify a filename
or directory name on the target
(F = file, D = directory)?
```

There are two responses to this prompt:

1. Press F if you want the file(s) to be copied to a file.
2. Press D if you want the file(s) to be copied to a directory.

XCOPY Error Codes

XCOPY uses a series of error codes to inform you of its progress or, alternately, of any complications it encounters during a SETVER operation. The following list describes the various XCOPY codes:

0	Files were copied without error.
1	No files were found to copy.
2	The user pressed CTRL+C to terminate XCOPY.
4	Initialization error occurred. There is not enough memory or disk space, or you entered an invalid drive name or invalid syntax on the command line.
5	Disk write error occurred.

✔ **Note:** You can use an ERRORLEVEL command in conjunction with IF commands within a batch file to process the error codes returned by XCOPY.

Examples

The following command copies all the files and subdirectories, including empty subdirectories, from a source disk in drive A to a destination disk in drive B:

`XCOPY A: B: /S /E`

The following example uses the /D: switch to copy from drive B to drive A only those files last modified on or after January 1, 1992:

`XCOPY B: A: /D:01/01/92 /S /V`

✔ **Note:** The /S switch instructs DOS to copy files from subdirectories. The /V switch instructs DOS to verify that the files on both disks are identical following each XCOPY operation.

Related Commands

See the COPY command for information about copying individual files.

See the COUNTRY command for information on date formats used by the /D switch.

See the ATTRIB command for information about how to set the archive file attribute.

Appendix A

Installing MS-DOS 6.0

This appendix walks you through the steps required to install MS-DOS 6.0 on your PC. It begins by describing how to protect your DOS distribution diskettes against accidental damage. You'll then learn how to run the MS-DOS 6.0 Setup utility, a special program that transfers the MS-DOS 6.0 files from Microsoft's distribution diskettes either to your hard disk or a floppy startup disk.

What You Will Need

To perform the procedures outlined in this chapter you will need:

- the Microsoft MS-DOS 6.0 distribution diskettes, the disks on which MS-DOS 6.0 was originally shipped.
- one extra disk, if you are replacing a previous version of DOS with MS-DOS 6.0.
- at least 4MB of unused disk space, if you're installing MS-DOS 6.0 on a hard disk. (This number could be as high as 8MB, depending on which optional DOS or Windows utilities you decide to include in your MS-DOS configuration.)
- three floppy disks (1.2MB or 1.44MB) if you're installing MS-DOS 6.0 on a floppy disk system.

Write-Protecting Floppy Disks

Floppy disks are extremely portable; files can be easily copied onto a floppy disk and then transferred to another PC. Floppy disks also are reusable; they can be reformatted and reused, virtually forever. There is a down side to these conveniences. Unless you take the proper precautions, the contents of a floppy disk could be erased accidentally. To help guard against this, you should always protect important disks against inadvertent disk-write operations. Certainly, the original disks shipped with MS-DOS 6.0 fall into this category. Both 5.25" and 3.5" disks provide built-in write-protection, which allows you to prevent any new data from being written to them.

Write-Protecting 5.25" Disks

Figure A.1 shows a typical 5.25" floppy disk. Notice the small notch near the upper right-hand corner of this disk. Each time DOS attempts to write to a 5.25" disk, a special mechanism within the disk drive checks to see whether or not this notch is covered. If the notch is not covered, DOS performs the requested write operation; if this notch is covered, however, DOS identifies the disk as write-protected and aborts the write operation.

Most 5.25" disks ship with small adhesive tabs called write-protect tabs. To protect a disk against accidental erasure, simply take one of these tabs and fold it over the write-protect notch, as illustrated in Figure A.2.

Write-Protecting 3.5" Disks

Figure A.3 shows a typical 3.5" disk, sometimes called a *microfloppy*. The plastic case of a 3.5" disk includes a built-in write-protection device.

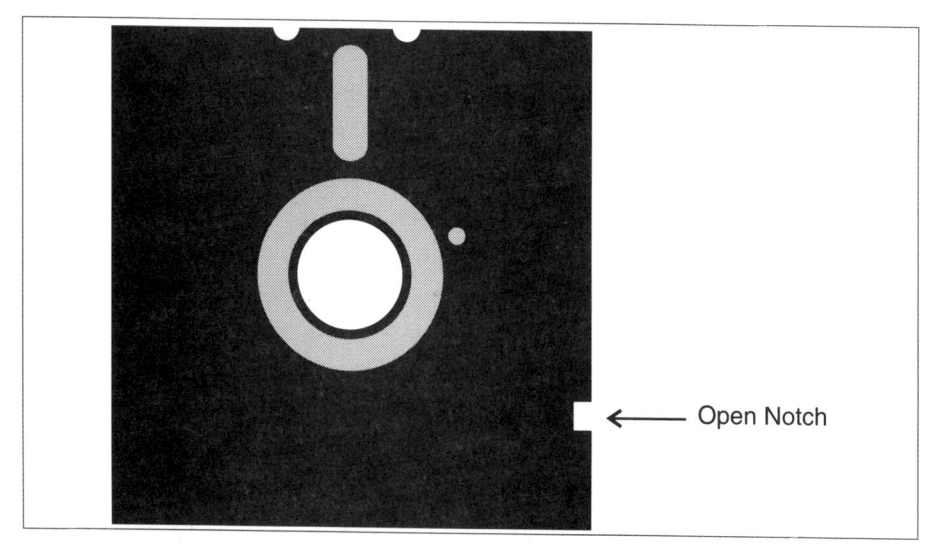

Figure A.1   All 5.25" disks include a write-protect notch.

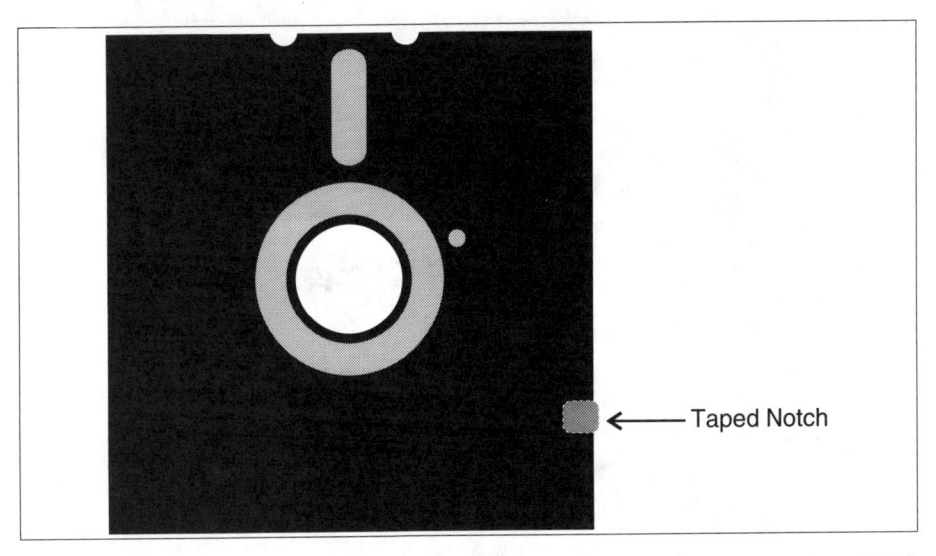

Figure A.2 Special adhesive tabs are used to write-protect a 5.25" disk.

Write-protection for a 3.5" disk works exactly the *opposite* of how it does on a 5.25" disk, which means a microfloppy is write-protected when this hole is *not* covered. To write-protect a 3.5" disk, therefore, you slide the built-in plastic tab toward the bottom of the disk. This exposes the write-protect hole, as illustrated in Figure A.4.

Figure A.3 Write protection is built into 3.5" disks.

Figure A.4 To record data on a 3.5" microfloppy, you must slide the plastic tab over its write-protect hole.

Write-Protecting Your MS-DOS 6.0 Distribution Disks

Before proceeding with the actual installation of DOS, let's write-protect the original MS-DOS distribution disks. This will prevent them from being accidentally erased or damaged during installation. To write-protect your DOS distribution disks, do one of the following:

1. If your DOS distribution disks were shipped in the 5.25" format, fold a write-protect tab over the notch in each disk.

2. If you are using 3.5" distribution disks, slide back the plastic tab on each disk to expose the write-protect hole.

Your disks are now protected against accidental damage. So, let's begin installing MS-DOS 6.0 on your PC system.

Getting Ready

The actual steps necessary to install DOS depend on whether you are installing it on a brand new computer or replacing a previous release of DOS with this newest version. In the next section, therefore, there are two different methods outlined for starting the MS-DOS 6.0 installation procedure. Follow the instructions appropriate for your situation.

The MS-DOS 6.0 Setup Utility

Microsoft designed a special Setup utility that completely automates the installation of MS-DOS 6.0. All you have to do is start Setup, answer a few simple questions, swap a few disks at the appropriate time (which you'll be prompted to do), and DOS takes care of everything else. In truth, installing MS-DOS 6.0 with the Setup utility is almost "idiot-proof," meaning there's very little chance of errors creeping into your DOS installation.

> ***Caution:*** As was true of its immediate predecessor, MS-DOS 5.0, the MS-DOS 6.0 files cannot be run directly from their distribution disks. You *must* use the Setup program to install MS-DOS 6.0 successfully on your system.

If you're upgrading to MS-DOS 6.0 from an earlier version, you'll be glad to hear that Setup is a *nondestructive* procedure. It preserves any files previously stored on your hard disk, including all application programs and data files. Setup even includes a special feature that allows you to "uninstall" this newest DOS release and return to your previous version of DOS, should you encounter any problems following installation.

Regardless of whether you're upgrading from a previous version of DOS or installing it for the first time, you will be asked to answer the following questions or verify certain information about your system during the installation process:

- Is your PC is hooked up to a network?
- Specify a path name to indicate where you want the installation program to place the MS-DOS 6.0 files.
- Do you want to automatically load the DOS 6.0 Shell program each time you start your PC? (For more information about this program, see "Using the DOS Shell" in Chapter 2, and Appendix B, "Going Graphic: An Introduction to the DOS Shell.")
- What type of display is installed on your system (CGA, EGA, or VGA)?

> ***Note:*** If you're upgrading to MS-DOS from another operating system, you'll also need to know what kind of DOS it is — whether it's Microsoft DOS or a version of DOS licensed to another manufacturer.

Take a moment before we get started to make certain that you have this information available. You'll then be able to enter it at the appropriate time as specified by Setup.

Okay. I think I've covered all the preliminary bases. So let's get started installing MS-DOS 6.0 on your PC.

> ✓ *Note:* Throughout this appendix, my assumption will be that you're installing DOS onto a hard disk. Most PCs sold these days include one. If your system has only floppy disk drives, don't worry. The Setup screen messages and instructions include information about installing DOS onto floppy disks.

Installing MS-DOS 6.0 on a New System

If you are installing DOS on a new system, one that you've just purchased and that does not have DOS already set up on its hard disk, you may be pretty nervous. That's understandable. The first few moments sitting at a computer keyboard can be quite an intimidating experience, coupled with the fact that you're about to partition and format a hard disk — a fairly complex undertaking for anyone. If your first inclination is to forget the whole thing and keep making do with pencil, paper, calculator, and all those other familiar but inefficient tools a computer replaces, don't. Installing MS-DOS 6.0 is no more difficult than turning on a light switch. I'm serious. Here's what you do:

Insert Disk 1 of your DOS distribution diskettes in whatever disk drive is identified as drive A on your system. (If you're using a 5.25" disk, you may need to close the drive latch.)

Turn on your PC.

There you go. You've finished the hard part. Really. From now on, all you have to do is follow the instructions that Setup displays on your monitor. (You did turn on your monitor, didn't you?) They'll keep you apprised of what Setup is doing, as well as what *you* must do to get MS-DOS 6.0 up and running on your PC. Read each screen carefully and follow any directions it contains. Very shortly, you'll be ready to begin reading Chapter 1 of this book — the first step in familiarizing yourself with your new computer and the operating system that makes it work.

Upgrading to MS-DOS 6.0 from a Previous Version

If a previous version of DOS already exists on your hard disk, upgrading to this newest version is a simple matter of running the special Setup program included on Disk 1 of the MS-DOS 6.0 distribution diskettes. Before actually running Setup, however, make sure you have a blank disk available to hold the various files DOS 6.0 creates as a safeguard, in the unlikely event that you find it necessary to revert to your previous DOS version.

APPENDIX A: INSTALLING MS-DOS 6.0   513

> *Note:* Although Setup can be run from either drive A or B, Setup automatically creates your "uninstall" on drive A. Make certain, therefore, that the disk you select for this purpose is the proper size for your A drive.

> *Tip:* Back Up before Setup
> Although the DOS 6.0 Setup program is designed to preserve any files currently stored on your hard disk, it's always a good idea to back up those files before performing any procedure that modifies your hard disk system files in any way. Since you are replacing a current version of DOS, I'll assume you know how to accomplish this and recommend that you do so, prior to running the DOS 6.0 Setup program.

To replace your current DOS version with DOS 6.0:

Start your system using its current version of DOS.

Place Disk 1 of the MS-DOS distribution diskettes in drive A or B, whichever is appropriate for your system.

Type **A:** or **B:** (whichever is appropriate) and press **Enter**.

Type **SETUP** and press **Enter**.

After a few seconds, you'll see the screen shown in Figure A.5, which gives you three options: proceed with Setup, learn more about Setup, or abort the procedure. For now, press **Enter** to set up MS-DOS 6.0.

Figure A.6 shows the next message Setup displays. This message reminds you that you will need one or more disks to save the files that DOS requires to "uninstall" MS-DOS 6.0 at some later time, should this be necessary. Remember, this "uninstall" disk must be the appropriate size for drive A on your system.

> *Note:* Remember, the messages shown here are those that appear when you are installing MS-DOS 6.0 on a hard disk. If Setup determined that you were using a floppy disk system, you would see slightly different messages at certain times during the installation process. Read each message carefully and you should have no trouble installing MS-DOS 6.0 on floppy disks.

To continue installation:

Press **Enter**.

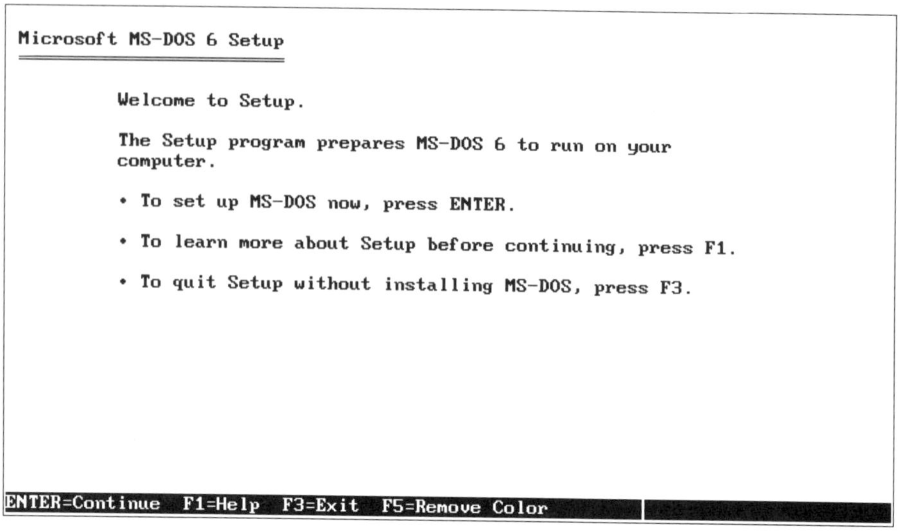

```
Microsoft MS-DOS 6 Setup

        Welcome to Setup.

        The Setup program prepares MS-DOS 6 to run on your
        computer.

          • To set up MS-DOS now, press ENTER.

          • To learn more about Setup before continuing, press F1.

          • To quit Setup without installing MS-DOS, press F3.




ENTER=Continue   F1=Help   F3=Exit   F5=Remove Color
```

Figure A.5 You use the Setup utility to upgrade to MS-DOS 6.0 from a previous version.

At this point, Setup analyzes your hardware and makes its "best guess" as to your system hardware. Figure A.7 shows the system settings that Setup returned for my computer. Obviously, the specific items listed in this message screen for your system may differ from the ones shown here. If Setup's analysis of your system is correct:

Press **Enter**.

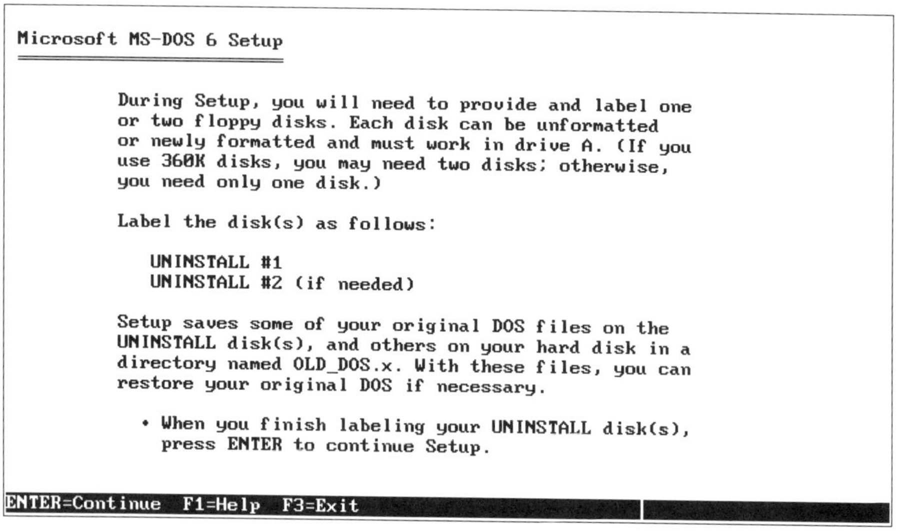

```
Microsoft MS-DOS 6 Setup

         During Setup, you will need to provide and label one
         or two floppy disks. Each disk can be unformatted
         or newly formatted and must work in drive A. (If you
         use 360K disks, you may need two disks; otherwise,
         you need only one disk.)

         Label the disk(s) as follows:

            UNINSTALL #1
            UNINSTALL #2 (if needed)

         Setup saves some of your original DOS files on the
         UNINSTALL disk(s), and others on your hard disk in a
         directory named OLD_DOS.x. With these files, you can
         restore your original DOS if necessary.

           • When you finish labeling your UNINSTALL disk(s),
             press ENTER to continue Setup.

ENTER=Continue   F1=Help   F3=Exit
```

Figure A.6 MS-DOS 6.0 includes an "uninstall" feature that allows you to easily revert to your previous version of DOS, if necessary.

APPENDIX A: INSTALLING MS-DOS 6.0   515

```
Microsoft MS-DOS 6 Setup
========================

    Setup will use the following system settings:

    ┌─────────────────────────────────────┐
    │ DOS Type:      MS-DOS               │
    │ MS-DOS Path:   C:\DOS               │
    │ Display Type:  VGA                  │
    │                                     │
    │ The settings are correct.           │
    └─────────────────────────────────────┘

    If all the settings are correct, press ENTER.

    To change a setting, press the UP ARROW or DOWN ARROW key until
    the setting is selected. Then press ENTER to see alternatives.




ENTER=Continue   F1=Help   F3=Exit
```

Figure A.7 Setup attempts to determine your system settings.

If there is an incorrect entry in Setup's analysis:

Use the **Up Arrow** to highlight the incorrect value.
Press **Enter**.

Setup displays a screen containing additional options for the selected item. For example, Figure A.8 shows a screen containing the various types of displays Setup recognizes. To select a different setting, highlight it using the arrow keys, and

```
Microsoft MS-DOS 6 Setup
========================

    MS-DOS can use the following display types:

    ┌─────────────────────────────────────┐
    │ Monochrome                          │
    │ CGA                                 │
    │ EGA                                 │
    │ EGA Monochrome                      │
    │ VGA                                 │
    │ VGA Monochrome                      │
    │ Hercules                            │
    │ MCGA                                │
    │ 8514                                │
    └─────────────────────────────────────┘

    To accept the current selection, press ENTER.

    To change the selection, press the UP ARROW or DOWN ARROW key
    until the item you want is selected, and then press ENTER.

ENTER=Continue   F1=Help   F3=Exit   ESC=Previous Screen
```

Figure A.8 Setup lets you change the default settings it selects.

then press Enter. Setup returns you to the initial setting screen with the new value you selected entered in the appropriate field. To continue:

Press **Enter**.

At this point, Setup offers you the option of installing three additional utilities not included in its default configuration. They are:

1. Backup: Used to archive files from your hard disk to floppy disks.
2. Undelete: Used to create a special table DOS then uses to restore accidentally erased files.
3. Anti-Virus: Used to identify and remove over 1,000 different computer viruses, those potentially destructive codes that can disrupt your system.

Each of these utilities comes in two versions, one that you can use with DOS, and a second version designed to run under Windows, Microsoft's popular graphics-based user interface. You use the screen shown in Figure A.9 to tell Setup if you want to install these optional utilities. If you do, you can further instruct Setup to install them for DOS, Windows, or both operating environments. Because Setup found a copy of Windows on my system, Figure A.9 suggests that the utilities be installed to run under Windows only. I'm going to change this. You can use the same procedure to modify the settings on this screen for your system.

```
Microsoft MS-DOS 6 Setup

        The following programs can be installed on your computer.

                      Program for                Bytes used

          Backup:      Windows only              1,081,344
          Undelete:    Windows only                262,144
          Anti-Virus:  Windows only              1,392,640
          Install the listed programs.

          Space required for MS-DOS and programs:   6,936,128
          Space available on drive C:              23,332,864



          To install the listed programs, press ENTER.  To see a list
          of available options, press the UP or DOWN ARROW key to
          highlight a program, and then press ENTER.

ENTER=Continue   F1=Help   F3=Exit
```

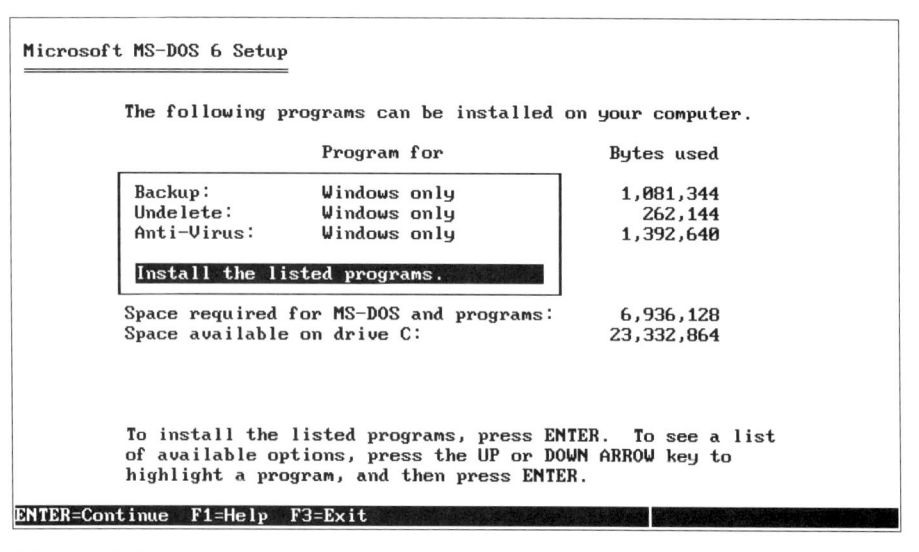

Figure A.9 Setup asks if you want to install the optional MS-DOS 6.0 utilities.

APPENDIX A: INSTALLING MS-DOS 6.0   **517**

> ✓ ***Note:*** As Figure A.9 illustrates, Setup calculates how much disk storage each optional utility requires. It also lets you know the amount of free space on your disk. You can use these figures to verify that your hard disk has enough room to hold any utilities you select.

To change the settings for the Backup utility:

Press the **Up Arrow** key three times to highlight **Backup:**.
Press **Enter**.

Setup displays the screen shown in Figure A.10. You use this screen to indicate which version or versions of the selected utility you want to install. To change the current setting:

Use the arrow keys to highlight the setting you want.
Press **Enter**.

Figure A.11 shows the results of my choice to have all three optional utilities installed for both DOS and Windows. Notice that the disk requirements in the far-right column have been adjusted to reflect my selections.

With all these preliminary steps completed, Setup is ready to begin actually installing MS-DOS 6.0. To do this:

With the "Install the listed programs." option highlighted, press **Enter**.

```
Microsoft MS-DOS 6 Setup

         Backup for:

         ┌─────────────────────────────────────────┐
         │ Windows and MS-DOS                      │
         │ Windows only                            │
         │ MS-DOS only                             │
         │ None                                    │
         └─────────────────────────────────────────┘

         If you want to install the highlighted program, press ENTER.
         To select a different option, press the UP or DOWN ARROW
         key to highlight the program you want. Then press ENTER to
         choose it.




ENTER=Continue   F1=Help   F3=Exit   ESC=Previous Screen
```

Figure A.10 The optional utilities can be configured to run under DOS, Windows, or both.

```
Microsoft MS-DOS 6 Setup

       The following programs can be installed on your computer.

                    Program for                Bytes used
       Backup:      Windows and MS-DOS          1,949,696
       Undelete:    Windows and MS-DOS            262,144
       Anti-Virus:  Windows and MS-DOS          1,703,936
       Install the listed programs.

       Space required for MS-DOS and programs:  8,115,776
       Space available on drive C:             23,332,864


       To install the listed programs, press ENTER. To see a list
       of available options, press the UP or DOWN ARROW key to
       highlight a program, and then press ENTER.

ENTER=Continue  F1=Help  F3=Exit
```

Figure A.11 Setup records your selections, after which you can continue installation.

> ✓ *Note:* Depending on which utility options you specified, Setup may display some additional screens requesting more information. If this is the case, read each screen and respond appropriately.

As Figure A.12 demonstrates, Setup is extremely cautious. It asks you to verify, one more time, that you want to install MS-DOS 6.0 on your system. To indicate Yes:

Press **Y**.

At this point, Setup copies several preliminary files from the MS-DOS 6.0 distribution disks to your hard disk in preparation for final installation. It also does some quick housekeeping, preparing itself to create an archive copy of your current DOS system files. When Setup completes these preliminary steps, it displays the message shown in Figure A.13, instructing you to place an UNINSTALL disk in drive A. To create the UNINSTALL disk:

If necessary, remove the MS-DOS 6.0 Setup disk from drive A.

Insert a blank disk in drive A and, if necessary, close the drive latch.

Press **Enter**.

If you're installing MS-DOS 6.0 from drive A, after Setup copies all the files it needs to this disk, it instructs you to remove the UNINSTALL disk from drive A and reinsert Disk 1 of the DOS distribution disks. If you're installing MS-DOS

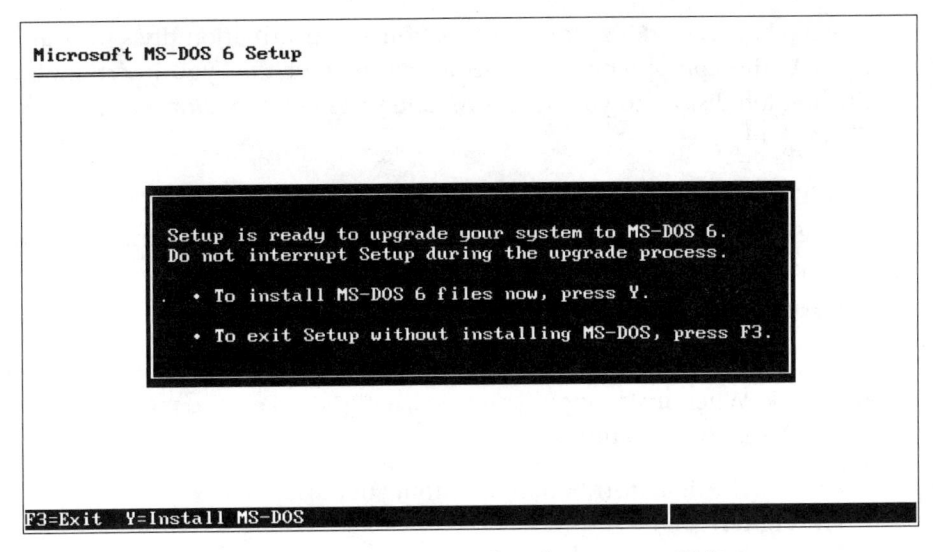

```
Microsoft MS-DOS 6 Setup


       ┌─────────────────────────────────────────────────────┐
       │                                                     │
       │  Setup is ready to upgrade your system to MS-DOS 6. │
       │  Do not interrupt Setup during the upgrade process. │
       │                                                     │
       │    • To install MS-DOS 6 files now, press Y.        │
       │                                                     │
       │    • To exit Setup without installing MS-DOS, press F3. │
       │                                                     │
       └─────────────────────────────────────────────────────┘




F3=Exit  Y=Install MS-DOS
```

Figure A.12 Setup does not proceed unless you tell it to.

6.0 from drive B, Setup continues the installation procedure automatically after it creates the UNINSTALL disk. If Setup pauses after it creates the UNINSTALL disk:

Remove the UNINSTALL disk from drive A.

Insert MS-DOS distribution disk #1 in the appropriate drive and, if necessary, close the drive latch.

Press **Enter**.

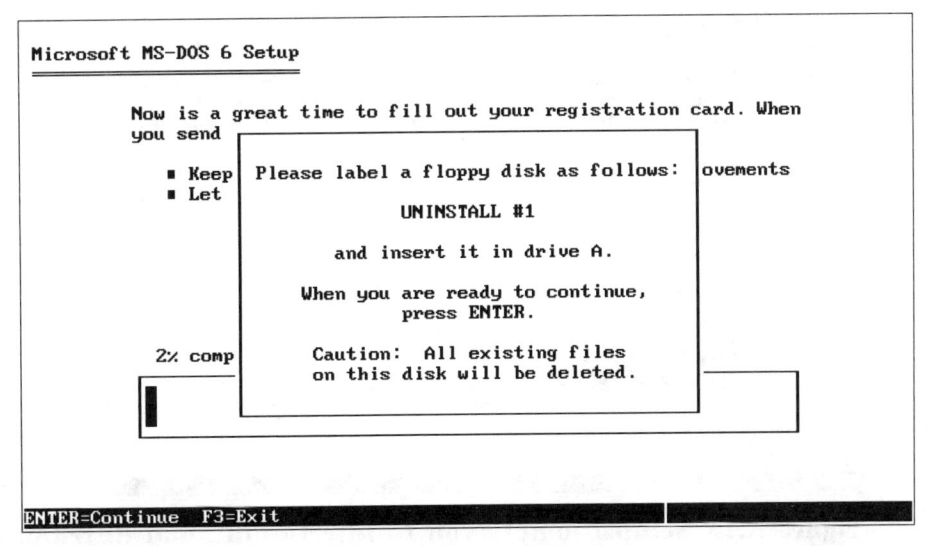

```
Microsoft MS-DOS 6 Setup


       Now is a great time to fill out your registration card. When
       you send
              ┌──────────────────────────────────────────┐
         ■ Keep│  Please label a floppy disk as follows:  │ovements
         ■ Let │                                          │
              │              UNINSTALL #1                │
              │                                          │
              │         and insert it in drive A.        │
              │                                          │
              │     When you are ready to continue,      │
              │              press ENTER.                │
         2% comp│                                          │
              │     Caution:  All existing files         │
              │     on this disk will be deleted.        │
         │    └──────────────────────────────────────────┘


ENTER=Continue  F3=Exit
```

Figure A.13 Setup automatically prepares the UNINSTALL disk.

Setup begins working, copying files from the distribution disks to your hard disk. At the appropriate times, Setup will request that you insert additional distribution disks into your disk drive and press Enter to continue, as shown in Figure A.14.

Remove the current distribution disk from drive A.

Insert the requested distribution disk in the appropriate drive and, if necessary, close the drive latch.

Press **Enter**.

This continues until all of the MS-DOS 6.0 files have been copied onto your hard disk. When installation is finished, Setup displays the message shown in Figure A.15. To end Setup:

Remove the final distribution disk from your disk drive.
Press **Enter**.

Setup displays one final message, shown in Figure A.16, informing you that it has saved your CONFIG.SYS and AUTOEXEC.BAT files on the UNINSTALL disk, if they existed previously. It then instructs you how to end the installation and restart your computer, which will now be running under MS-DOS 6.0. To exit the Setup program and start MS-DOS 6.0:

Press **Enter**.

After a few seconds, you'll see the infamous C> DOS system prompt. Congratulations! You have successfully installed MS-DOS 6.0 on your com-

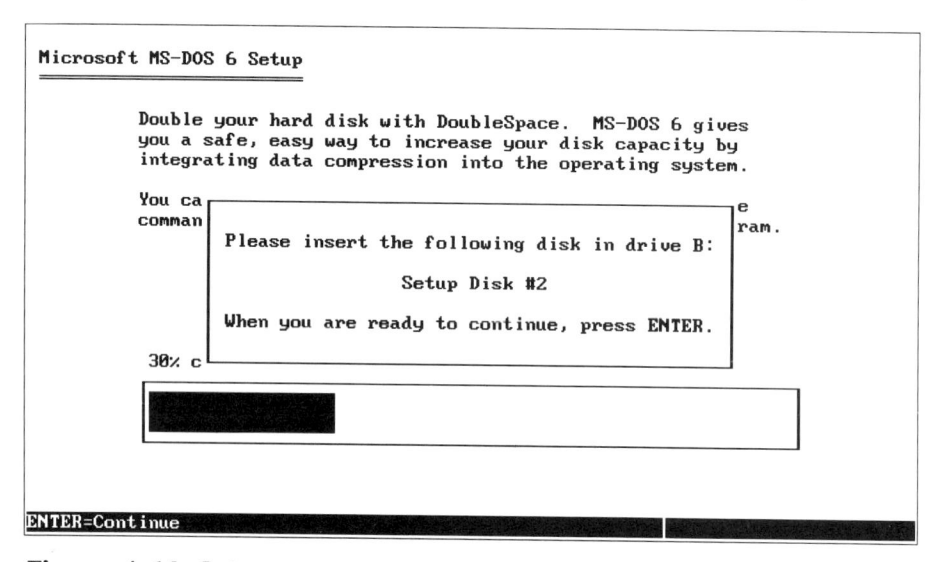

```
Microsoft MS-DOS 6 Setup

        Double your hard disk with DoubleSpace.  MS-DOS 6 gives
        you a safe, easy way to increase your disk capacity by
        integrating data compression into the operating system.

        You ca┌─────────────────────────────────────────────┐e
        comman│                                             │ram.
              │  Please insert the following disk in drive B:│
              │                                             │
              │              Setup Disk #2                  │
              │                                             │
              │  When you are ready to continue, press ENTER.│
        30% c └─────────────────────────────────────────────┘


        ▮▮▮▮▮▮▮▮▮▮

ENTER=Continue
```

Figure A.14 Setup prompts you to insert additional distribution disks, as needed.

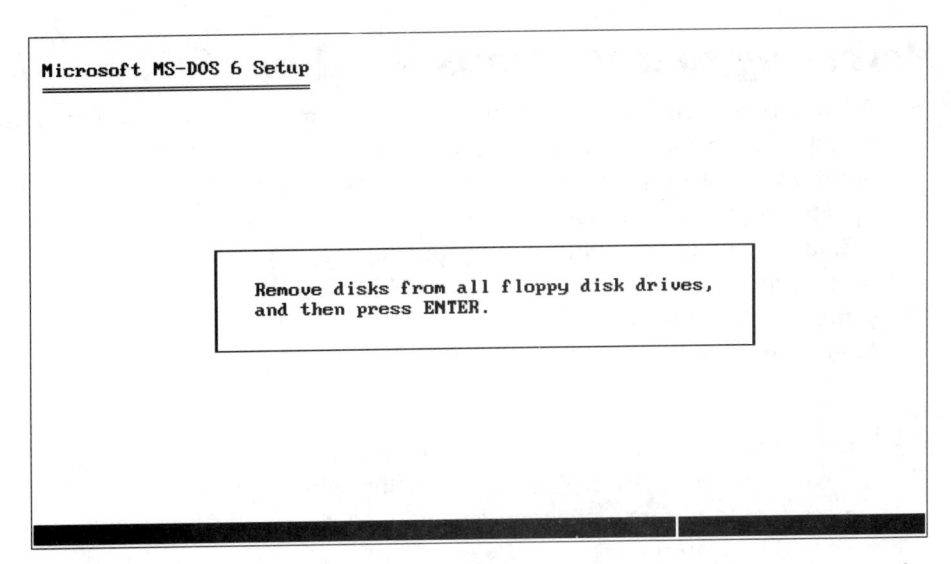

```
Microsoft MS-DOS 6 Setup
═══════════════════════




                    ┌─────────────────────────────────────────┐
                    │                                         │
                    │  Remove disks from all floppy disk      │
                    │  drives, and then press ENTER.          │
                    │                                         │
                    └─────────────────────────────────────────┘
```

Figure A.15 Once installation is complete, Setup instructs you to remove any distribution disks from your drive.

puter. Now, head back to Chapter 1 and see what DOS has to offer. Well, not quite yet, come to think of it. First read the next section, which explains how you can restore your previous version of DOS using the UNINSTALL disk, if necessary.

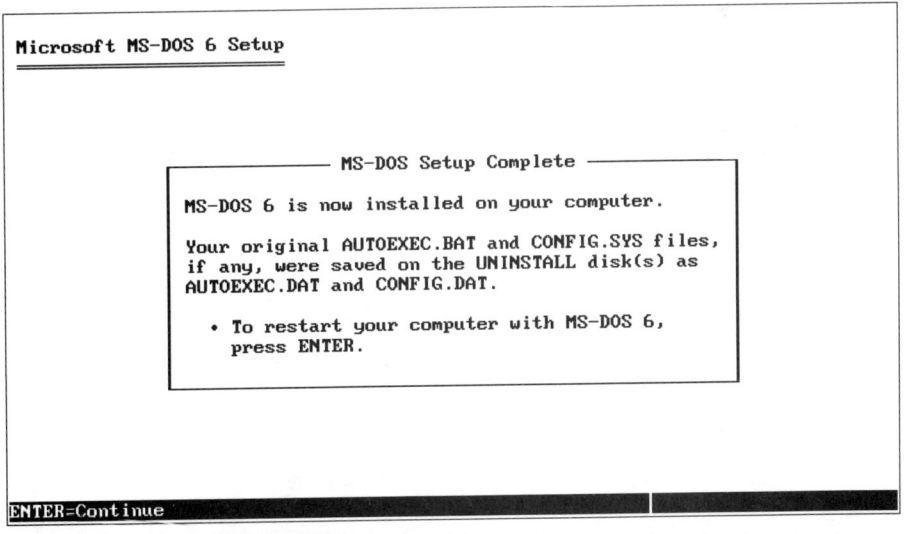

```
Microsoft MS-DOS 6 Setup
═══════════════════════


               ┌────────────── MS-DOS Setup Complete ──────────────┐
               │                                                   │
               │  MS-DOS 6 is now installed on your computer.      │
               │                                                   │
               │  Your original AUTOEXEC.BAT and CONFIG.SYS files, │
               │  if any, were saved on the UNINSTALL disk(s) as   │
               │  AUTOEXEC.DAT and CONFIG.DAT.                     │
               │                                                   │
               │    • To restart your computer with MS-DOS 6,      │
               │      press ENTER.                                 │
               │                                                   │
               └───────────────────────────────────────────────────┘



 ENTER=Continue
```

Figure A.16 Setup automatically preserves your previous CONFIG.SYS and AUTOEXEC.BAT files.

Reverting to a Previous Version of DOS

As mentioned earlier, it's possible (though highly improbable) that you may have trouble running some older programs under version 6.0 of DOS. Should this occur, the most logical solution is to replace the troublesome program with an updated version that's compatible with DOS 6.0. If this is not possible and you absolutely *must* use the problematic program, you may find it necessary to revert back to an older release of DOS. The UNINSTALL disk Setup created greatly simplifies this process. This disk contains all of the files required to replace MS-DOS 6.0 with whatever version of DOS you used previously.

> ***Caution:*** The following exercise is included merely to demonstrate how the UNINSTALL disk works. Do not actually perform it, unless you find it necessary to restore a previous version of DOS to your system, and then it should be a last resort.

To revert from DOS 6.0 to your previous version:

Insert the UNINSTALL disk created by Setup into drive A and close the drive latch. (You must run this disk from drive A.)

Turn on your PC.

DOS provides on-screen instructions on how to continue the recovery procedure, after which your system will once again be running under the version of DOS you were using prior to upgrading to DOS 6.0.

Appendix B

Going Graphic: An Introduction to the DOS Shell

This appendix introduces some of the main features associated with working within the DOS Shell, the graphical user interface (GUI) included with MS-DOS 6.0. As explained in Chapter 2, the DOS Shell replaces the standard DOS system prompt with an interactive, graphics-based environment. When working in this environment you initiate most DOS operations using menus and dialog boxes. Dialog boxes are special windows that appear on your display requesting additional information about a given procedure.

If you're new to DOS, starting out in the DOS Shell can help you familiarize yourself with basic concepts and procedures without also having to learn immediately precise and often complex commands. Then, as you grow more comfortable with your PC, you can begin weaning yourself off the DOS Shell, gradually moving over to the faster and more efficient system prompt.

Starting the DOS Shell

During installation, Setup automatically creates a PATH to the DOS directory. This allows you to run programs in that directory, including the DOS Shell, from anywhere on your system. From the DOS system prompt:

Type **DOSSHELL**.
Press **Enter**.

This loads the DOS Shell and displays a screen similar to the one in Figure B.1.

> **Note:** Your DOS Shell will differ significantly from Figure B.1, which shows DOS Shell running on my computer. Specifically, your screen will include different directories and filenames.

The DOS Shell Display

The DOS Shell display is divided into several sections. These include:

Menu bar	Used to select and display the DOS Shell pull-down menus.
Drive listing	Used to select the active disk drive.
Directory tree	Used to display and select directories on the active drive.
File listing	Used to select and work with files stored in the current directory.
Program group window	Used to select and run programs and utilities you've set up using the DOS Shell.
Status line	Shows the current time, as well as displaying any special commands currently available in the DOS Shell.

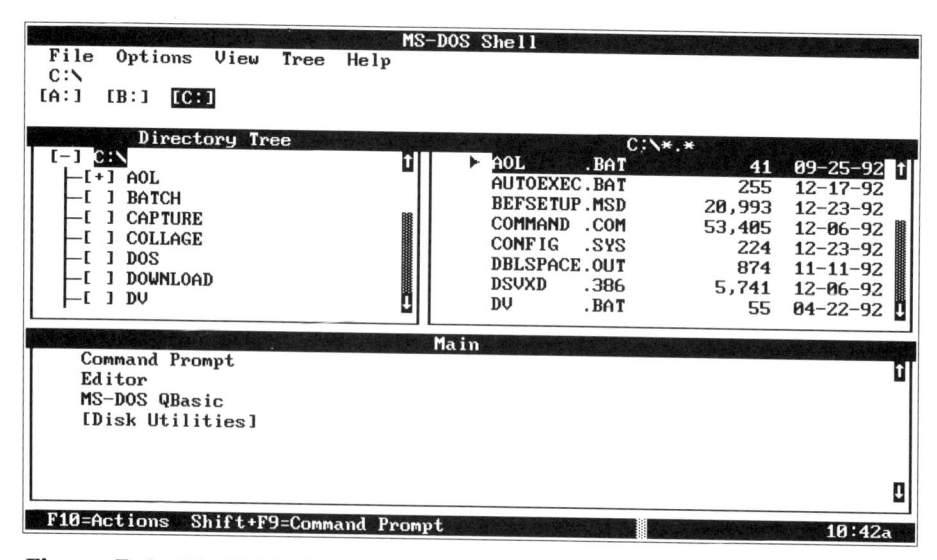

```
                          MS-DOS Shell
 File   Options   View   Tree   Help
 C:\
 [A:]    [B:]    [C:]
─────────Directory Tree──────────    ─────────C:\*.*──────────
 C:\                                 ▶ AOL     .BAT       41  09-25-92
  ├─[+] AOL                            AUTOEXEC.BAT      255  12-17-92
  ├─[ ] BATCH                          BEFSETUP.MSD   20,993  12-23-92
  ├─[ ] CAPTURE                        COMMAND .COM   53,405  12-06-92
  ├─[ ] COLLAGE                        CONFIG  .SYS      224  12-23-92
  ├─[ ] DOS                            DBLSPACE.OUT      874  11-11-92
  ├─[ ] DOWNLOAD                       DSVXD   .386    5,741  12-06-92
  └─[ ] DV                             DV      .BAT       55  04-22-92
────────────────────────────Main──────────────────────────────
  Command Prompt
  Editor
  MS-DOS QBasic
  [Disk Utilities]

 F10=Actions   Shift+F9=Command Prompt                   10:42a
```

Figure B.1 The DOS Shell replaces the system prompt with a graphics-based display.

Navigating the DOS Shell

You can run the DOS Shell either from the keyboard or with a mouse. Most people find the latter method, a mouse, more convenient. If your PC includes an electronic rodent, therefore, it's the more logical way to go. (The documentation that accompanied your mouse will explain how to get DOS to recognize that a mouse is attached to your computer.)

I'll discuss using a mouse in a few paragraphs. First, however, let me detail the keys that will allow anyone working from the keyboard to navigate the DOS Shell.

Running the DOS Shell from the Keyboard

The DOS Shell recognizes the following keyboard commands:

Arrow keys	Used to move the highlight bar within the currently active portion of the display.
Enter key	Used to select a highlighted option.
Esc key	Used to cancel a selected option.
Tab key	Used to switch between the different areas of the DOS Shell display.
PgUp key	Used to view previous sections of information that are too large to fit in a single display window.
PgDn key	Used to view subsequent sections of information that are too large to fit in a single display window.

Using the DOS Shell with a Mouse

Mouse users need to be familiar with the following common mouse operations:

Point	The process of maneuvering your mouse until the on-screen mouse pointer indicates an item on the DOS Shell display.
Click	Pressing and releasing the mouse button.
Click on	Pointing to an item on the screen and then clicking the mouse button.
Double-click	Pressing and releasing the mouse button twice in quick succession.
Drag	Holding down the mouse button as you move the pointer around the DOS Shell display.

As I stated earlier, most people who use a mouse find it to be more intuitive and convenient than controlling a computer exclusively from the keyboard. So, if you have a mouse, I recommend that you use it, but I'll include both keyboard and mouse procedures as we check out some of the DOS Shell's main features.

> **Note:** Look back at Figure B.1. Do you see the small, white vertical rectangle in the Status bar, just to the left of the time? This is the initial DOS Shell mouse cursor. If this rectangle appears anywhere on your display, DOS Shell recognizes that your system includes a mouse. If you've loaded your mouse driver and don't see the mouse cursor, something is wrong, in which case, you have two options: either continue on, using the keyboard or exit the DOS Shell and try reloading your mouse driver.

Switching the DOS Shell to a Graphic Display

Regardless of your PC hardware, the DOS Shell is initially set up to run in character mode. In this mode DOS Shell uses letters, numbers, symbols, and so forth, to emulate a graphic display. Notice, for example, the braces ([ ]) around the disk drive letters and directory names in Figure B.1. Telling the DOS Shell to use a true graphics display will allow you to take full advantage of your computer's capabilities. Let's do this.

If you have a mouse, use the following procedures to switch over to the DOS Shell graphics display:

Point to the word **Options** in the menu bar.
Click the left mouse button. (This displays the pull-down Options menu.)
Point to the Display option.
Click the left mouse button.

If your system does not include a mouse, use the following keyboard sequence to display the Screen Mode dialog box:

Press **Alt+O** to display the Options menu.
Press **D** to select Display.

Either of these two methods causes the DOS Shell to display a dialog box similar to the one shown in Figure B.2. You use this dialog box to tell the DOS Shell the type of display you want to use.

> **Note:** The specific options listed in the Screen Display Mode dialog box shown in Figure B.2 depend on the type of display monitor you have. (The dialog box shown here is for a VGA display.)

Figure B.2 You use the Display option to choose the display that the DOS Shell should use on your system.

To change to a different display:

Point to the desired mode. (I find the 25-line display to be quite legible.) Double-click the left mouse button.

or

Use the arrow keys to highlight a graphics display mode.
Press **Enter**.

This switches DOS Shell over to a true graphics display. Notice in Figure B.3, for example, that the brackets have been replaced with stylized representations of the items they indicate: disk drives, file folders, sheets of paper, and so forth. These representations are called *icons*.

Selecting Items on the DOS Shell Display

The real advantages associated with using a mouse in a GUI like the DOS Shell surface when you begin selecting items from the display. In fact, a GUI like the DOS Shell allows you to do some things standard DOS doesn't.

For example, although DOS lets you use wildcards to perform certain operations (DIR, COPY, DEL, and so forth) on multiple files, the names of these files must be similar to one another. By contrast, completely unrelated files can be selected from the DOS Shell display for additional processing. To see what I mean:

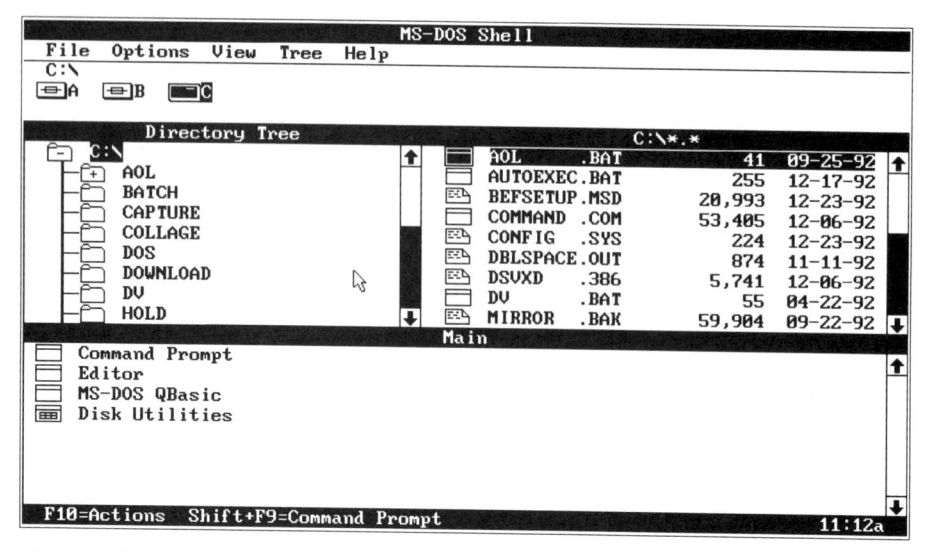

Figure B.3 Selecting a graphics display mode alters the DOS Shell's appearance.

Click on the filename at the top of your current directory listing.
Point to the third filename listed in the current directory.
Hold down the **Ctrl** key.
Click the left mouse button.
Point to the fourth filename listed in the current directory.
With the **Ctrl** key still depressed, click the left mouse button.
Release the **Ctrl** key.

or

Press **Tab** to make the file listing active.
Press **Shift+F8** to switch file selection to Add mode.
Use the arrow keys, if necessary, to position the highlight bar on the first filename.
Press **Spacebar** to select this file.
Press **Down Arrow** twice to position the highlight bar on the third filename.
Press **Spacebar** to select this file.
Press **Down Arrow** to position the highlight bar on the fourth filename.
Press **Spacebar** to select this file.
Press **Shift+F8** to turn off Add mode.

Either of these two techniques selects the three specified files, as shown in Figure B.4, even though the names of these files have nothing in common. This would be impossible using only the DOS wildcards. Once you've selected multiple files, the DOS Shell makes them available for additional processing. The

APPENDIX B: AN INTRODUCTION TO THE DOS SHELL   529

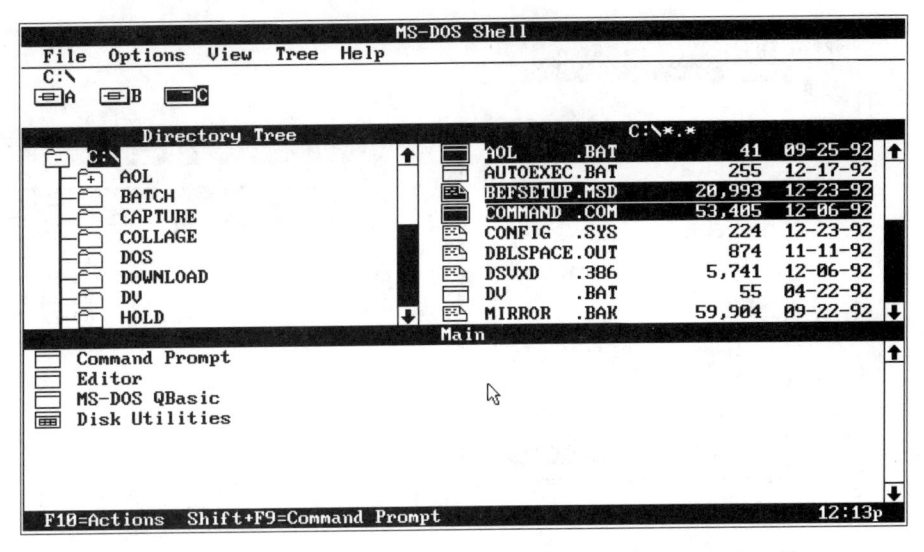

```
┌─────────────────────────── MS-DOS Shell ───────────────────────────┐
│ File  Options  View  Tree  Help                                    │
│ C:\                                                                │
│  A     B     C                                                     │
│ ┌──── Directory Tree ─────┐         ┌────── C:\*.* ──────┐         │
│ │ C:\                     │ │   AOL       .BAT      41  09-25-92│ │
│ │   ├── AOL               │ │   AUTOEXEC  .BAT     255  12-17-92│ │
│ │   ├── BATCH             │ │   BEFSETUP  .MSD  20,993  12-23-92│ │
│ │   ├── CAPTURE           │ │   COMMAND   .COM  53,405  12-06-92│ │
│ │   ├── COLLAGE           │ │   CONFIG    .SYS     224  12-23-92│ │
│ │   ├── DOS               │ │   DBLSPACE  .OUT     874  11-11-92│ │
│ │   ├── DOWNLOAD          │ │   DSVXD     .386   5,741  12-06-92│ │
│ │   ├── DV                │ │   DV        .BAT      55  04-22-92│ │
│ │   └── HOLD              │ │   MIRROR    .BAK  59,904  09-22-92│ │
│ ├─────────────────────── Main ────────────────────────────────────┤│
│ │ Command Prompt                                                   ││
│ │ Editor                                                           ││
│ │ MS-DOS QBasic                                                    ││
│ │ Disk Utilities                                                   ││
│                                                                    │
│ F10=Actions  Shift+F9=Command Prompt                       12:13p  │
└────────────────────────────────────────────────────────────────────┘
```

Figure B.4   It's easy to select multiple files in the DOS Shell.

three disparate files in Figure B.4 could be copied, deleted, moved, or used in conjunction with any of a dozen other DOS Shell procedures.

Viewing Storage Requirements for Multiple Files

To see what I mean, let's ask the DOS Shell to show us the total storage requirements for these three files. We can do this easily, using the Show Information option in the pull-down Options menu.

Click on the **Options** selection of the DOS Shell menu bar.
Click on the **Show Information** option.

or

Press **Alt+O** to display the Options menu.
Press **Alt+S** to select the Show Information option.

This displays the Show Information message window as shown in Figure B.5. I've positioned the mouse pointer to indicate those values that reflect information for all three selected files. After reviewing this information, use either of the following procedures to close the Show Information message box and return to the DOS Shell display:

Click on **Close**.

or

Press **Esc**.

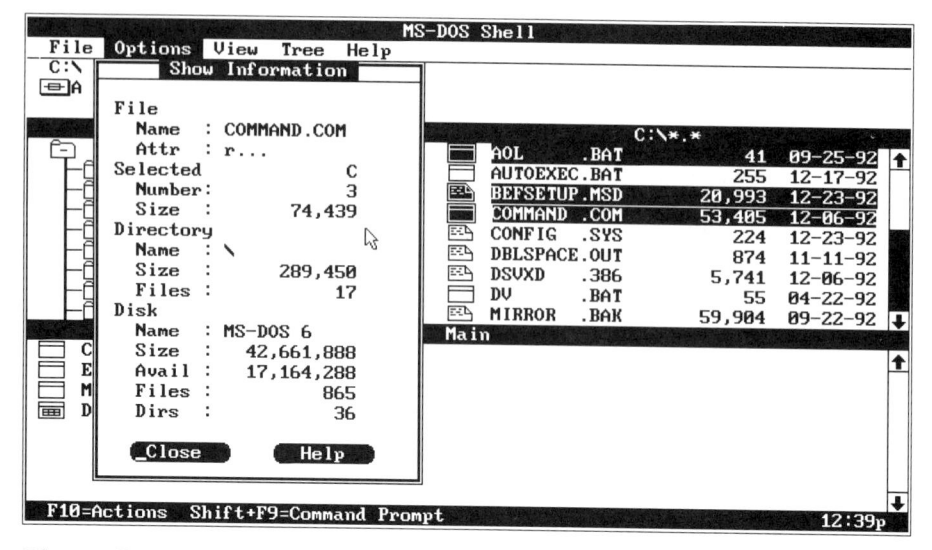

Figure B.5 Commands are carried out using the selected files.

Canceling a Multiple File Selection

The three files selected earlier are still highlighted on your display. You can use the following steps to return to a single-file selection:

Click on any filename without depressing the Ctrl key.

or

Press **Spacebar**.

This returns the DOS Shell to a single-file selection.

Task Switching

For all of its strengths, and it has many, DOS possesses one major weakness. At its heart, DOS is designed to do one thing at a time. It is, in the PC vernacular, a *single-tasking environment*. The DOS Shell strives to sidestep this inherent weakness of DOS by allowing you to load multiple programs concurrently and then switch between them from within the DOS Shell.

What Is Task Switching?

Task switching allows you to load more than one application program — that is, perform multiple tasks — from within the DOS Shell. Try as you might, you can't do this from the standard DOS prompt. Rather, if you're running one application and need to use a another application, you must quit the first program completely before DOS will allow you to load the second.

Task switching emulates the way people, rather than PCs, work. Think about it. How many times during an average day do you find yourself doing one thing then suddenly switching your concentration over to something else that requires your attention. You may, for example, be halfway through writing a letter and suddenly remember that you need to send out the payment for this month's electric bill. When you temporarily stop working on the letter and pull out your checkbook, you have switched tasks.

Task switching from the DOS Shell works in much the same manner. You can, for example, be using one program — writing a letter with your word processor, for instance — and then immediately switch to a second program — say, a personal finance program like Quicken — to pay your electric bill. After writing the check (or, more correctly, having Quicken write it for you), you can recall the DOS Shell's Active Task List and return to your word processing, which still holds the draft of your letter exactly as you left it. This is a powerful and extremely useful capability, and one that's available only from within the DOS Shell.

Enabling Task Switching

In its default configuration, the DOS Shell is set up for single-tasking. Before you can load multiple programs into memory concurrently, therefore, you must enable the DOS Shell Task Swapper. To enable task switching:

Point to **Options** in the DOS Shell menu bar.
Click the left mouse button.
Point to the **Enable Task Swapper** option.
Click the left mouse button.

or

Press **Alt+O** to display the Options menu.
Press **E** to choose Enable Task Swapper.

Enabling the Task Swapper opens up a new window named Active Task List in your DOS Shell display. (Once again, in Figure B.6, I've used the mouse pointer to highlight this new window.)

The Active Task List window is empty when you first open it. As I pointed out, you can't begin task switching until this capability is enabled. Now that we've done so, let's see how the DOS Shell supports task swapping.

Adding Programs to the Task List

To add a program to the Active Task List you simply start that program with task switching enabled. How's that for easy to use? There are three ways to run a program from within the DOS Shell:

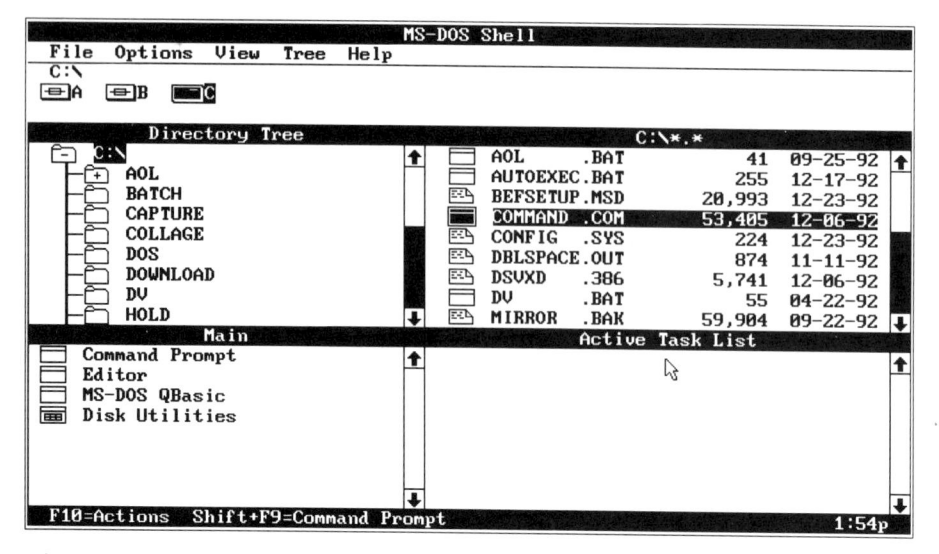

Figure B.6 Task switching is enabled if the Active Task List window appears on your DOS Shell display.

1. Use the Run option on the File menu.
2. Double-click on that program's filename within the directory tree.
3. Highlight a program's filename within the directory listing and then press Enter.

We'll use the last two methods to add the MS-DOS Editor to our Active Task List. If you're using a mouse:

Point to **Editor** in the Main window of the DOS Shell display.
Double-click the left mouse button.

If you're using the keyboard:

Press **Tab** to activate the Main window.
Use the arrow keys to highlight **Editor**.
Press **Enter**.

The DOS Shell displays the dialog box shown in Figure B.7. This dialog box asks you to identify the file you want to edit. Entering the name of an already existing file in this box would start the DOS Editor and automatically load that file into memory. If the filename you enter doesn't exist, Editor creates it. Let's do this.

Type **TESTFILE.TXT** and press **Enter**.

After a few seconds you'll be advanced to Editor's text editing screen. (For more information on Editor, see Chapter 7.) At this point, you're ready to begin

APPENDIX B: AN INTRODUCTION TO THE DOS SHELL 533

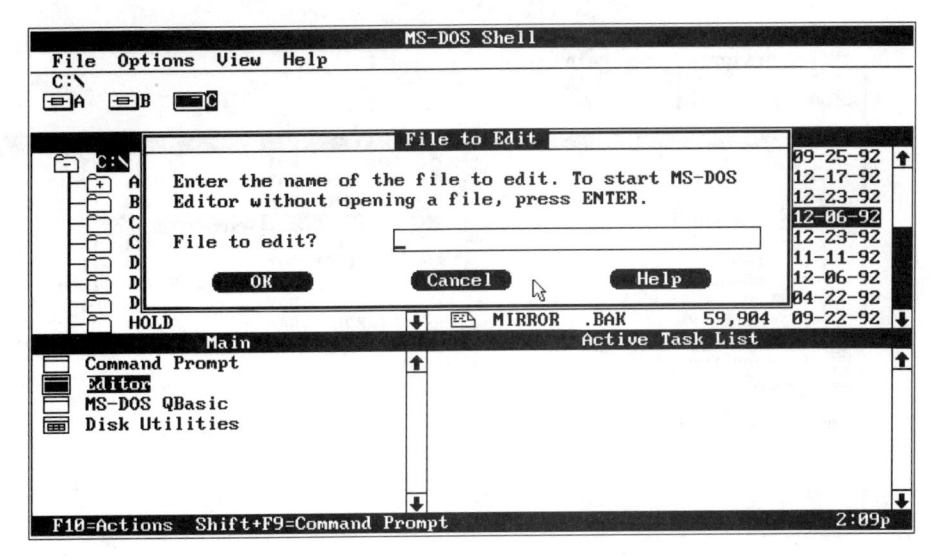

Figure B.7 It's easy to run programs from within the DOS Shell.

creating a file, just as you would if it were running independently under DOS. Remember, though, that we're working in the Task List. Let's return to the DOS Shell and see what this means.

Press **Alt+Tab**.

✓ *Note:* There is no mouse alternative for this command.

The Alt+Tab key combination cycles you through multiple programs running in a task switching session. Because Editor is the only program currently open, you were immediately returned to the DOS Shell. (Notice, however, that an item marked Editor has been added to the Active Task List window, as shown in Figure B.8.)

The DOS Shell cycles you through open applications in a "round-robin" fashion. The sequence of this cycle is the reverse order of use, i.e., the last program you were using will be the first program accessed if you press Alt+Tab at the DOS Shell. Subsequent Alt+Tab keystrokes will cycle you "back" through any other applications running under task switching until you return to the DOS Shell.

Removing Programs from the Task List

The safest way to close a program running under task switching is to make that application the active program and then issue the command normally used to close it. When you exit an application, it's automatically removed from the Active Task List.

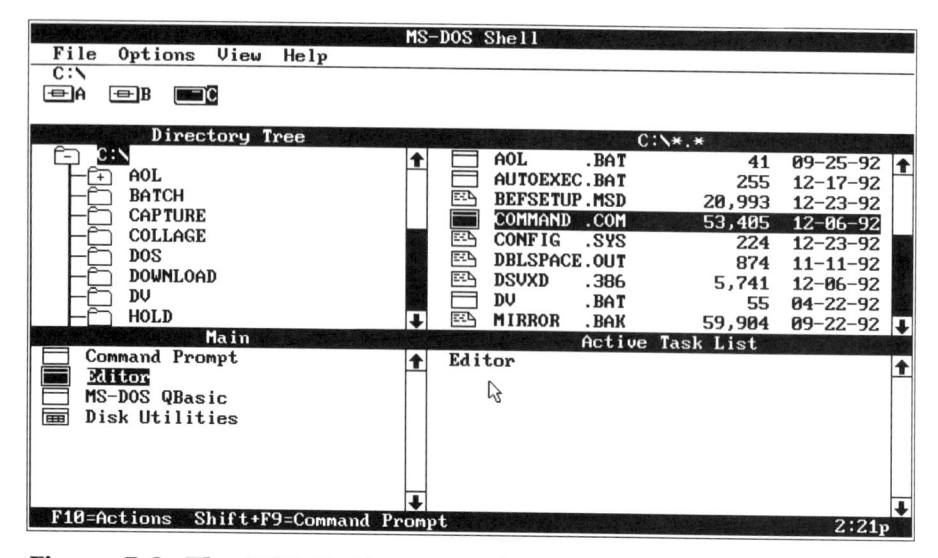

```
┌─────────────────────────────────────────────────────────────┐
│                        MS-DOS Shell                         │
│  File   Options   View   Help                               │
│  C:\                                                        │
│  [=]A   [=]B   [■]C                                         │
├─────────────────────────────────────────────────────────────┤
│       Directory Tree              │          C:\*.*         │
│  ┌─ C:\                        ↑  │ AOL      .BAT     41  09-25-92 ↑│
│    ├─ AOL                         │ AUTOEXEC.BAT    255  12-17-92  │
│    ├─ BATCH                       │ BEFSETUP.MSD 20,993  12-23-92  │
│    ├─ CAPTURE                     │ COMMAND .COM 53,405  12-06-92  │
│    ├─ COLLAGE                     │ CONFIG  .SYS    224  12-23-92  │
│    ├─ DOS                         │ DBLSPACE.OUT    874  11-11-92  │
│    ├─ DOWNLOAD                    │ DSVXD   .386  5,741  12-06-92  │
│    ├─ DV                          │ DV      .BAT     55  04-22-92  │
│    └─ HOLD                     ↓  │ MIRROR  .BAK 59,904  09-22-92 ↓│
├──────────── Main ─────────────────┼───── Active Task List ─────────┤
│    Command Prompt              ↑  │ Editor                       ↑ │
│ ■  Editor                         │                                │
│    MS-DOS QBasic                  │    ▷                           │
│ □  Disk Utilities                 │                                │
│                                ↓  │                              ↓ │
├─────────────────────────────────────────────────────────────┤
│ F10=Actions  Shift+F9=Command Prompt                  2:21p │
└─────────────────────────────────────────────────────────────┘
```

Figure B.8 The DOS Shell automatically adds Editor to its Active Task List.

There may be times, however, when you find yourself in the position of having to manually delete an application from the Active Task List. This could happen, for example, if a particular program "freezes up" during a task switching session. Although Editor is working just fine, let's manually delete it from the Active Task List so that you know how when you need to. To manually delete Editor from the Active Task List:

Use either the mouse or the keyboard to highlight Editor in the Active Task List.

Press **Alt+F** or click on File in the menu bar to display the pull-down File menu.

Press **D** or click on the **Delete** option.

DOS displays the warning message shown in Figure B.9. As this message implies, you should only use this method to modify your Active Task List as a last resort — that is, if all other attempts to quit a program using its normal procedures for doing so fail. To close Editor and remove it from the Active Task List:

Click on **OK**.

or

Press **Tab** to move the cursor from Cancel to OK.

Press **Enter**.

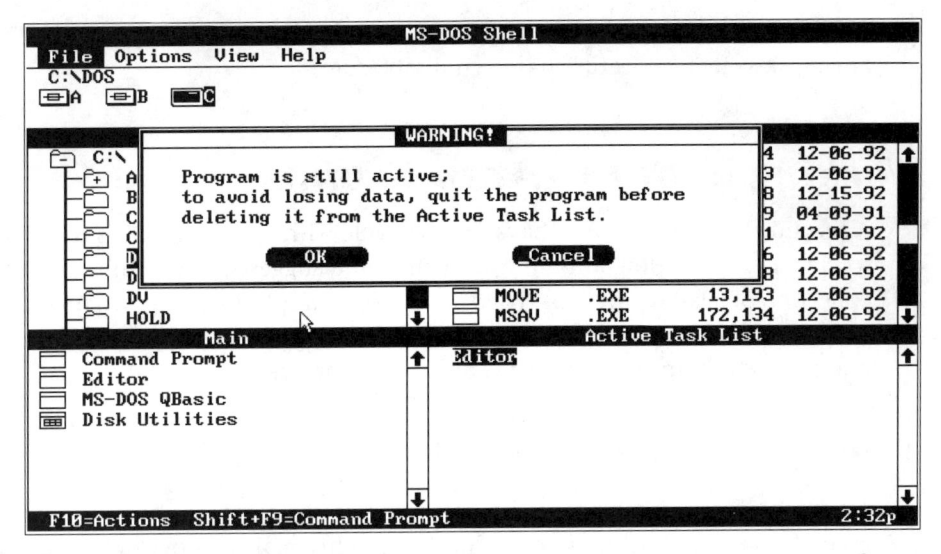

Figure B.9 The Delete option can be used to remove programs from your Active Task List.

> ***Caution:*** If you ever are forced to use the Delete option to remove a problematic program from the Active Task List, it's generally a good idea to immediately close any other applications in the Active Task List using the normal exit procedures. As an added precaution you should also exit the DOS Shell and reboot your system. Doing so eliminates the possibility that a prematurely exited application will cause problems later in your task switching session.

Ending Task Switching

It's just as easy to end a task switching session as it was to start one. In fact, both activities involve the same steps:

Point to **Options** in the DOS Shell menu bar.
Click the left mouse button.
Point to the **Enable Task Swapper** option.
Click the left mouse button.

or

Press **Alt+O** to display the Options menu.
Press E to choose Enable Task Swapper.

This removes the Active Task List from your display, indicating that the DOS Shell task switching feature has been disabled.

Working with Program Groups

A second DOS Shell feature that's not available with standard DOS is the ability to create and use program groups. As its name suggests, a program group is a collection of related programs. This sounds fairly simple, I'll admit; what program groups represent, however, is a totally different approach to organizing your PC operations than the standard DOS directory structure.

What Are Program Groups?

Traditionally, people have used DOS directories to organize their PC environment by application program or file type. This makes perfect sense if your primary concern is the "physical" location of files. And at the disk level, that's exactly what you should be concerned about. When creating a disk structure it's logical to place all the necessary files to run Microsoft Word, for example, in one directory, Lotus 1-2-3 files in a second directory, DOS files in a third directory, and so forth. If you think about how you normally work, however, you'll see where the logic in this structure breaks down.

How often do you work on a project that can be completed with a single program? Not often, I'd guess. To write this book, for example, I've relied at various times on my word processor, a screen capture utility, a graphics package (to print out the figures), DOS itself and, once or twice, a communications program. It would be nice, therefore, if I could gather together these various programs and place them in some kind of cabinet, metaphorically speaking, that contains all of the tools required to complete this job. It essence, this is precisely what a program group allows you to do.

To move this discussion out of the conceptual and into the real world, let's examine the program groups that already exist within your DOS Shell.

The Initial Program Groups

Setup automatically created four program groups within your DOS Shell environment during installation and placed them in a display window called Main. These four initial program groups are:

- Command prompt
- Editor
- MS-DOS QBasic
- Disk Utilities

A quick glance at each group name provides a clue to its purpose. As you may suspect, for example, the Editor group is designed to give you quick access to the Editor program introduced earlier in this appendix and, by extension, the text files created with it. Similarly, the Disk Utilities group contains several DOS programs that perform disk-related tasks. To see what I mean:

Double-click on **Disk Utilities** in the Main window.

or

Use the **Tab** and arrow keys to highlight **Disk Utilities** in the Main window. Press **Enter**.

Figure B.10 shows the various items Setup placed within the Disk Utilities program group. As you can see, each performs some operation relating to disks. In this particular example, the actual programs that perform these tasks are in a single directory, the DOS directory Setup created during installation. But, they don't have to be; they can be spread hither and yon across your disk. This ability to gather related programs, regardless of where they are physically stored in a disk's directory structure, is a program group's greatest strength.

To more clearly illustrate how this works, we'll create our own program group, one designed to hold some additional MS-DOS utilities that could come in handy as you work in the DOS Shell.

Creating a Program Group

You create a program group using the New command, one of the options listed in the DOS Shell File menu. (The New command is only available when you are

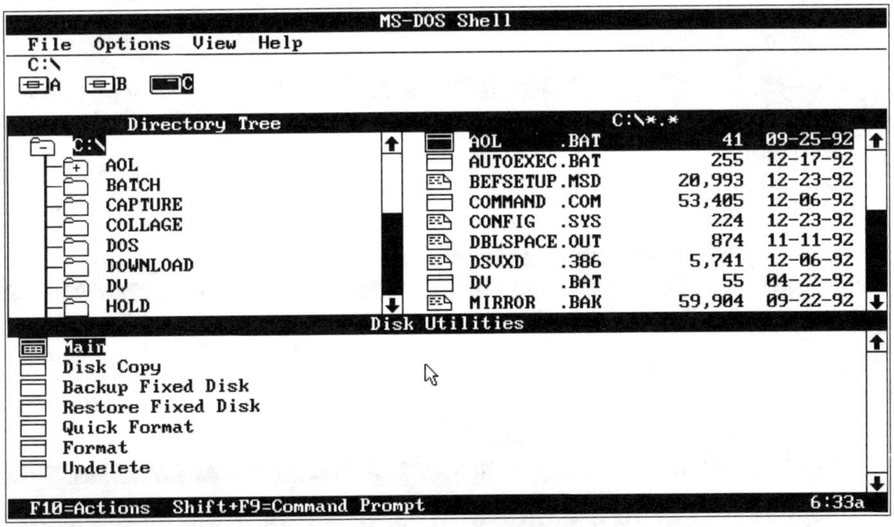

Figure B.10 Program groups contain related items.

actually working within the Program Group window.) We want our utilities group to be its own option from within the Main window, so let's exit Disk Utilities and return to the Main program group:

Double-click on the **Main** icon in the Disk Utilities window.

or

Use the **Tab** and arrow keys to highlight **Main**.
Press **Enter**.

Now that we're where we want to be, let's begin creating our new program group.

Point to **File** in the DOS Shell menu bar.
Click the left mouse button.
Point to the **New** option.
Click the left mouse button.

or

Press **Alt+F** to display the File menu.
Press **N** to select New.

This displays the New Program Object dialog box shown in Figure B.11. Like most DOS Shell operations, creating a new program group is an interactive procedure — that is, the DOS Shell requests the information it needs to create a new group.

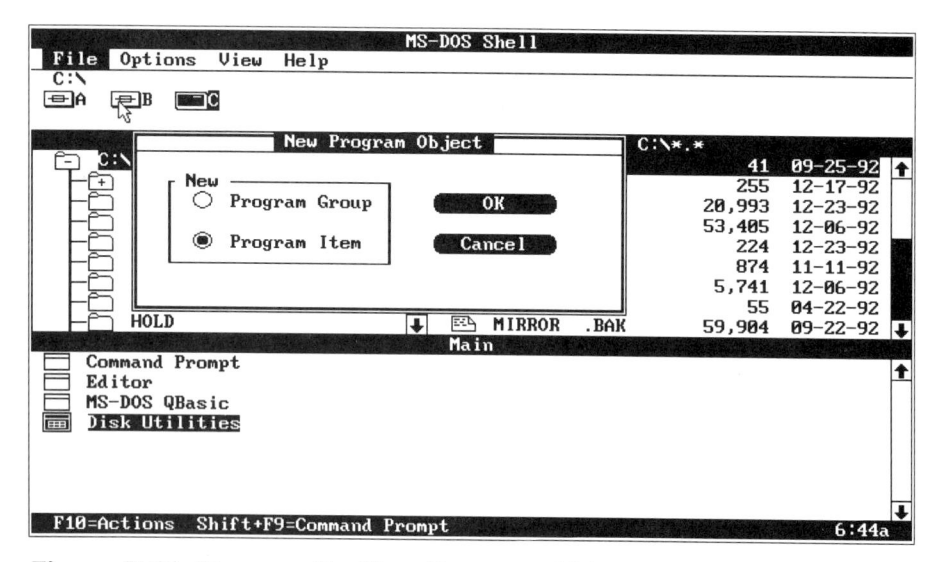

Figure B.11 You use the New Program Object dialog box to supply initial information about your new program group.

To start things off, the DOS Shell needs to know whether you want to create an entirely new program group or add a new item to a program group that already exists. To begin creating a new group:

Point to the circle to the left of **Program Group**.
Click the left mouse button.
Click on **OK**.

or

Press the **Up Arrow** key to "check" **Program Group**.
Press **Tab** to move the cursor to the **OK** option.
Press **Enter**.

This displays the Add Group dialog box (see Figure B.12). You use this dialog box to provide DOS with initial information about your new program group. The Title field is used to specify the name you want to appear in the Main window of your DOS Shell. Let's go ahead and assign a name to our new program group.

Type **Additional Utilities** and press **Enter**.

> *Tip:* **Name to Fit the Function**
> Group names are not limited by the eight-character filenaming convention; they may be up to 74 characters long. This makes it easy to select a group name that identifies that group's function. Keeping group names short, however, helps conserve space within your DOS Shell display.

This adds a new listing, Additional Utilities, to the Main program group window. Once a group exists, you can begin identifying the items you want it to contain. To add items to the Additional Utilities program group:

Double-click on **Additional Utilities**.
Point to **File** in the DOS Shell menu bar.
Click the left mouse button.
Select **New**.
At the New Program Object dialog box, select **Program Item**.
Select **OK**.

or

Press **Alt+F** to display the File menu.
Press **N** to select New.

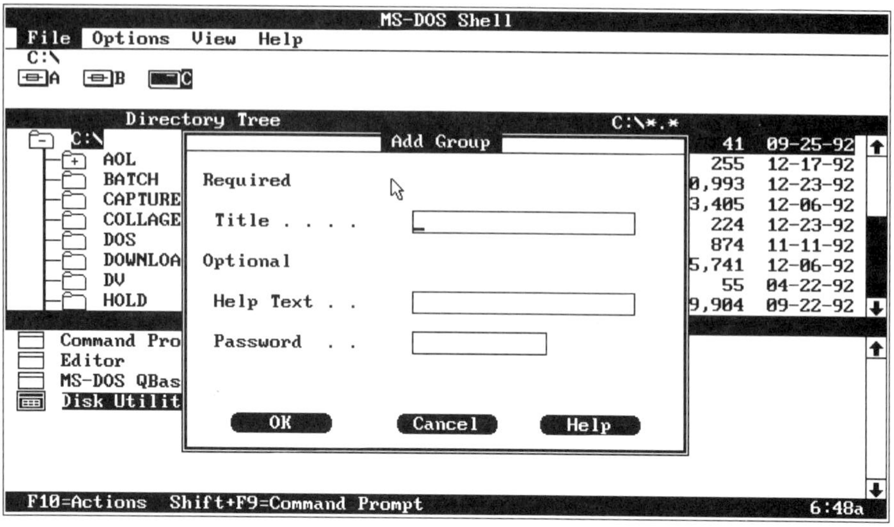

Figure B.12 DOS requests information about the new group you're creating.

If necessary, use the arrow keys to "check" **Program Item**.
Press **Tab** to move the cursor to the **OK** option.
Press **Enter**.

This displays the Add Program dialog box shown in Figure B.13, which is used to enter information required to perform the task associated with the item you're creating. To see how this works:

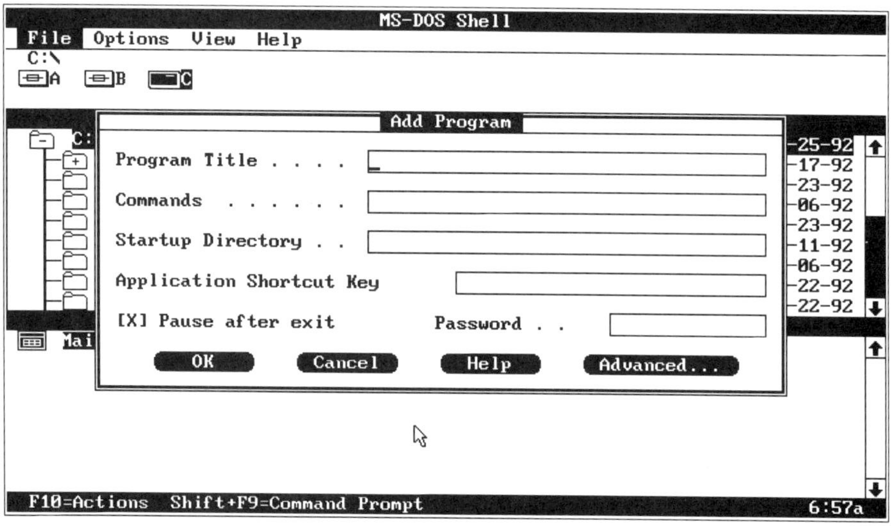

Figure B.13 The Add Program dialog box

APPENDIX B: AN INTRODUCTION TO THE DOS SHELL 541

Type **Display Memory Status** and press **Tab**.
Type **MEM.EXE /C /P** and press **Tab**.
Type **C:\DOS** and press **Tab** four times.
Press **Enter**.

> ✔ *Note:* If Setup placed your DOS files in a directory other than C:\DOS, enter the appropriate directory location in step 3 above accordingly.

This creates a program item called Display Memory Status and places it in the Additional Utilities program group we created earlier (see Figure B.14).

Running a Program

Now that the MEM.EXE program is accessible directly from the DOS Shell (we hope), let's run it.

Double-click on Display Memory Status in the Additional Utilities window.

or

Press **Tab** until the highlight bar is located in the Additional Utilities program group window.

Press **Down Arrow** to highlight **Display Memory Status**.

Press **Enter**.

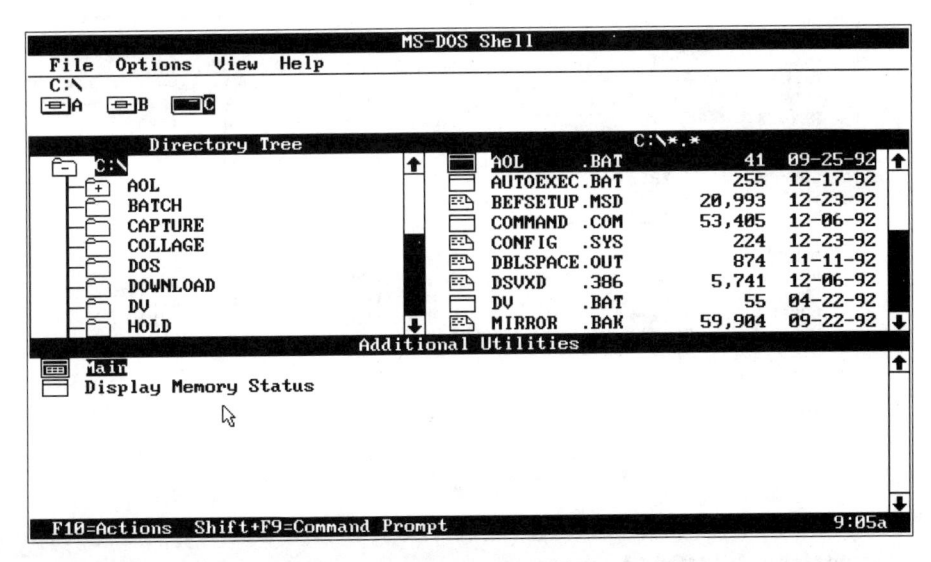

Figure B.14 DOS adds the new item to the current program group.

Selecting this new item runs MEM.EXE, the MS-DOS 6.0 utility program that analyzes your PC's memory and returns a message similar to the one shown in Figure B.15.

> ✓ ***Note:*** The actual values on your display will differ from the ones shown here, which reflect the results of a memory analysis performed on my own 386 system.

Including the /P switch causes DOS to pause temporarily after a full screen of information appears. To continue the MEM display:

Press any key.

This time when MEM pauses, you'll see the following message:

```
Press any key to return to MS-DOS Shell
```

This message is not normally associated with the MEM command; rather, it was generated by the DOS Shell, based on the fact that we left the "Pause after exit" option active in the Add Program dialog box for this program item. Selecting this option lets you review on-screen information displayed by a program executed from the DOS Shell, prior to returning to Shell's GUI. Now that we've seen this message, let's leave MEM.EXE:

Press any key.

```
Modules using memory below 1 MB:

  Name         Total       =    Conventional   +   Upper Memory
  -------      -----            ------------       ------------
  MSDOS        15453  (15K)     15453  (15K)           0  (0K)
  SETVER         704   (1K)       704   (1K)           0  (0K)
  HIMEM         1104   (1K)      1104   (1K)           0  (0K)
  EMM386        3120   (3K)      3120   (3K)           0  (0K)
  COMMAND       2912   (3K)      2912   (3K)           0  (0K)
  SNAP         77632  (76K)     77632  (76K)           0  (0K)
  MARK          1680   (2K)      1680   (2K)           0  (0K)
  COMMAND       3488   (3K)      3488   (3K)           0  (0K)
  MOUSE        17088  (17K)     17088  (17K)           0  (0K)
  DOSSHELL      2288   (2K)      2288   (2K)           0  (0K)
  SMARTDRV     27232  (27K)         0   (0K)       27232  (27K)
  DOSKEY        4144   (4K)         0   (0K)        4144   (4K)
  Free        567248 (554K)    529920 (518K)       37328  (36K)

Memory Summary:

  Type of Memory        Total       =      Used      +      Free
  --------------        -----              ----             ----
  Conventional         655360 (640K)    125440 (123K)    529920 (518K)
Press any key to continue . . .
```

Figure B.15 You can now check the status of your PC's memory from within the DOS Shell.

Congratulations! You've just created the beginning of a program group. Once a program group item exists, it can be modified and made even more useful.

Modifying a Program Group Item

Suppose, for example, that someone other than you will be using the memory status item. You could create an on-line help message for anyone who doesn't know how MEM.EXE works. To create an on-line Help message for MEM.EXE:

Select **File** or press **Alt+F**.
Select **Properties** or press **P**.
Select **Advanced** or **Tab** to the Advanced button and press **Enter**.

The DOS Shell displays the Advanced dialog box shown in Figure B.16. You can use this dialog box to specify the following options within a program group:

Help Text A Help message is information you want displayed when a user accesses on-line Help for this program group or item. Help messages may be up to 256 characters long.

Conventional Memory This field is used to indicate the *minimum* RAM required for this program. Generally, this number should correspond to the memory requirements (in KB) specified by the manufacturer. Use this field if you repeatedly run out of memory when running programs from the program manager.

XMS Memory You use this field to indicate the amount of extended memory, if any, that you want this program to use.

Video Mode This option is used to specify whether a program displays text or graphics.

Reserve Shortcut Keys These keys are used to activate (not checked) or deactivate (checked) the normal DOS Shell hot keys when you're working with this program group item. For example, checking the Alt+Tab option stops this key combination from cycling you out of this program into another application when the Active Task List is enabled.

Prevent Program Switch Activating this option turns off program switching, forcing you to exit the current application before you can access another program running in the DOS Shell.

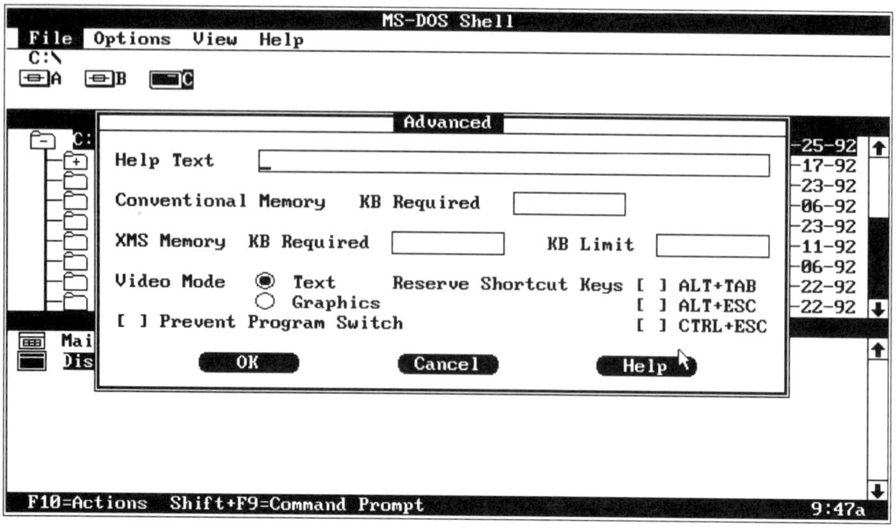

Figure B.16 The Advanced dialog box

We'll use the Advanced dialog box to create a Help message for MEM.EXE. To do this:

Type **This utility lets you check the current status of any memory installed on your PC.**

Press **Enter** to close the Advanced dialog box.

Press **Enter** a second time to store the Properties and return to the DOS Shell display.

Let's see what MS-DOS did with your Help message. With Display Memory Status highlighted:

Press **F1**.

This displays the Help message created in the previous exercise (see Figure B.17). To exit Help:

Select **Close**.

or

Press **Esc**.

Removing a Program Group Item

Now that we've gone through all this trouble to create the Display Memory Status item, let's get rid of it. This was, after all, only an example of how to use program

```
                    MS-DOS Shell
 File  Options  View  Help
 C:\
  A    B    C
                    MS-DOS Shell Help
              Help For Display Memory Status
         This utility lets you check the current status of any memory
         installed on your PC.


         Close        Back        Keys      Index        Help

 F10=Actions  Shift+F9=Command Prompt                      9:58a
```

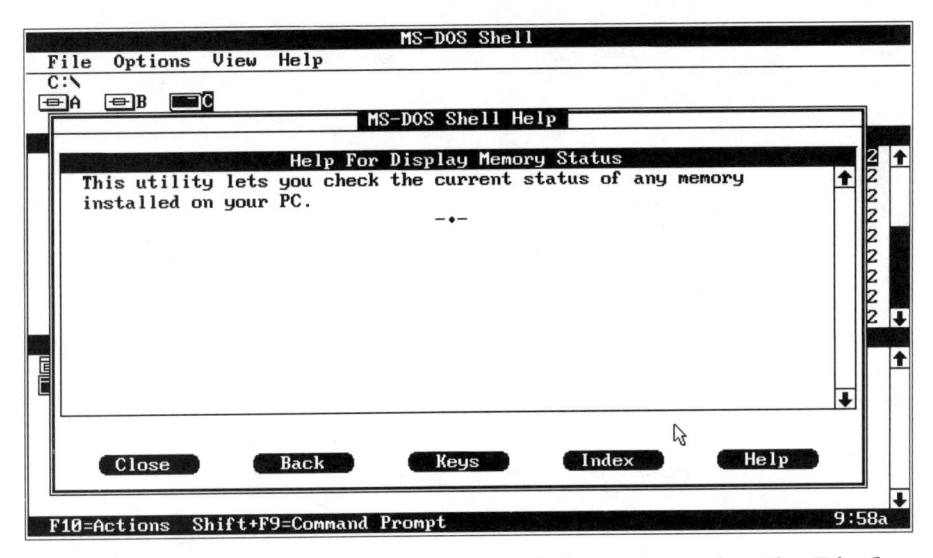

Figure B.17 The DOS Shell created a Help message for the Display Memory Status item.

groups. Undoubtedly, you'll want to create your own using items that match your needs. To eliminate Display Memory Status:

   Use the mouse or the arrow keys to highlight **Display Memory Status**.
   Press the **Delete** or **Del** key.

When the Delete Item dialog box appears:

   Press **Enter** to select **Delete this item**, the default option.

Poof! DOS deletes the Display Memory Status item from your Additional Utilities program group.

   As this simple example demonstrates, the DOS Shell's ability to create and maintain program groups allows you to establish a customized environment for your PC operations, which is the greatest advantage associated with the DOS Shell. I don't think I'd want to work exclusively in the DOS Shell, as standard DOS commands tend to be faster once you master them. Used wisely, however, the DOS Shell can supplement, even if it doesn't supplant, MS-DOS itself.

   This ends our brief foray into the DOS Shell. Stick around for a while and experiment, if you like. When you've finished, simply select the Exit option in the File menu. This will return you to standard DOS.

Appendix C

Glossary

application program

A program that performs a specific function. An electronic spreadsheet, for example, is an application program used to perform complex calculations with a personal computer.

ASCII

An abbreviation for American Standard Code for Information Interchange. In standard ASCII code, individual alphanumeric characters and control codes are represented by a numeric value between 0 and 255; for example, the ASCII code for an uppercase "A" is 65.

AUTOEXEC.BAT

A special batch file that DOS looks for each time your system is booted up. If AUTOEXEC.BAT exists, DOS automatically executes any commands it contains as part of its startup procedures.

bit

Short for binary digit. A bit is the smallest piece of information possible. In the case of a computer, it is represented by a 0 or 1, indicating the off or on state of an electronic switch, respectively.

batch files

ASCII-formatted files that can be executed by DOS. Generally, batch files are used to automate a series of commands that can be entered at the DOS system prompt.

booting up

The process of starting your PC. During boot up, DOS loads a portion of itself into RAM and then displays the DOS system prompt or executes any commands it finds in the CONFIG.SYS and AUTOEXEC.BAT files. (See cold boot and warm boot.)

branching

Transferring control or execution of a batch file to another statement within that file. Branching is usually initiated based on the results generated by some type of conditional testing. (See conditional testing.)

CD-ROM

CD-ROMs are massive data storage devices capable of holding over 500MB of information. They are read-only mediums that require the use of a CD-ROM drive to retrieve the information stored to the disk. Information is written and sealed at the factory, and only damage done to the surface can alter the data stored to the CD-ROM from that point on. CD-ROMs are ideal storage devices for the distribution of software requiring numerous floppy disks.

byte

The primary unit of measurement for computer memory. A byte, which consists of 8 bits, is capable of representing one character.

cold boot

The process of starting your PC by turning on its power switch.

COMMAND.COM

The DOS command processor. The contents of this file, which include the DOS internal commands, are loaded into memory each time you start your system. At various times during processing, DOS may need to reload a portion of the COMMAND.COM code to complete a particular operation. In these situations, DOS looks for COMMAND.COM on the root directory of the disk from which it was started.

command line

The line on which you enter DOS commands. You use the command line to enter the desired command and any valid parameters or switches you want associated with that command during execution.

conditional testing

The process of verifying whether a condition is TRUE or FALSE. For example, the conditional test IF 3 < 2 will return a FALSE condition, since 2 is not a lower value than 3. Conditional testing is often used to control branching within a batch file. (See branching.)

APPENDIX C: GLOSSARY 549

CONFIG.SYS

> A system file containing configuration information about your system. If a CONFIG.SYS file exists, DOS executes the statements it contains each time you start your computer.

CPU

> Central Processing Unit. The main chip that executes all instructions entered into your PC. MS-DOS computers are built around the Intel 8xxxx family of CPUs and CPUs that emulate the instruction set of the Intel microprocessors.

cursor

> The blinking line or highlight box indicating where the next input will be accepted by a PC.

default

> The standard value assigned to a variable or setting on your system. For example, the default DOS prompt is a C> symbol, assuming drive C is the currently active drive.

device name

> The logical name DOS uses to identify a device. For example, the device name LPT1 is used to identify the first parallel port of your PC, if one is available.

device driver

> A special file that must be loaded into memory for DOS to manage a given hardware component or procedure. Device drivers are generally installed from the CONFIG.SYS file during system startup.

directory

> A grouping of disk files identified by their logical (not physical) location on the disk. For example, you could copy all the files shipped with DOS to a directory called DOSFILES.

disk file

> A collection of program code or related data sets which are stored as a single unit on a floppy or hard disk.

DOS (Disk Operating System)

> A group of programs and utilities designed to manage the hardware components of a computer system and coordinate the execution of application programs on that system.

DOS prompt

> See system prompt.

drive identifier

The device name assigned to represent a disk drive. DOS generally assigns the letters A and B to floppy disks; letters C through P can be assigned to any hard disks that system contains. (See device name.)

EDIT

The DOS text editor. You can use EDIT to create and modify ASCII files, such as CONFIG.SYS or AUTOEXEC.BAT. (See ASCII.)

expansion cards

Circuit boards that can be installed in your PC to add features or capabilities it did not previously possess. For example, installing a modem card allows your PC to communicate with other computers over a standard telephone line.

expansion slots

The connectors used to install expansion cards in your PC. On most MS-DOS computers, the expansion slots are located across the back of the motherboard.

external commands

Commands that DOS executes after first loading them from an external disk file. To save memory, DOS does not load its external commands into RAM at system startup.

File Allocation Table (FAT)

A table used to identify the sectors stored on a disk. DOS automatically creates a FAT during formatting. Information in the FAT indicates whether a specific sector is good, bad, available, or in use.

filename

The unique name used to identify individual files on your disks.

filter

A program that takes input, processes that input, and then modifies it in some way prior to output. The MORE filter, for example, is used to display information one screen at a time.

fixed disk

See hard disk.

floppy disk

A magnetic storage medium that uses flexible disks. Floppy disks are removable storage devices, meaning they can be removed from one system and transferred to another. Most floppy disks used on an MS-DOS system come in one of two sizes: 5.25" and 3.5". Currently, the storage capacity of floppy disks compatible with MS-DOS systems ranges from 180K to 2.99 MB.

formatting

The process of preparing a disk to store data. During formatting, DOS creates sectors, tracks, a directory, and a file allocation table (FAT) on a disk.

function keys

A series of 10 or 12 keys set aside for special operations by DOS and application programs.

GUI

A graphical user interface. Uses visual displays to initiate certain activities. The DOS Shell included with DOS versions 4.0 and higher is a GUI, as is Microsoft Windows.

hard disk

A mass storage device found in many MS-DOS systems. Hard disks can store much greater amounts of data than floppy disks. Currently, the storage capacity of hard disks ranges from 10 MB to over 300 MB. Versions of DOS prior to 4.0 were able to access a maximum of 32 MB on a single hard disk partition.

hardware

The physical components of a PC system.

hidden files

Files that do not appear in a directory listing, although they do exist on a disk. DOS places two hidden files on any disk you format as a system disk: IO.SYS and MSDOS.SYS. (These filenames will be different for other versions of DOS.)

internal commands

Commands DOS loads into memory each time your system is started. Internal DOS commands are always available to the user and do not need to be loaded from a disk file prior to execution.

key combination

When two or more keys are pressed concurrently to execute a command or procedure. For example, you use a Ctrl+Alt+Del key combination to warm boot your PC. (See warm boot.)

kilobyte (KB)

1024 bytes

megabyte (MB)

1024 kilobytes

monitor

The device used to display text or images generated by your PC; also called a display screen.

mouse

A device used to manipulate a pointer around your display and then initiate actions by pressing a mouse button.

MS-DOS

A disk operating system for IBM-compatible personal computers produced by Microsoft and licensed through third-party manufacturers. (See DOS.)

parameter

Information appended to a DOS command that indicates something about how that command should be executed. For example, in the command FORMAT A:, the A: is a required parameter that tells DOS, in this case, that you want to format a disk in drive A.

path

Notation indicating the location of a file. The path generally includes the drive letter, along with the directory (and any associated subdirectories) on which that file resides.

PC DOS

The version of MS-DOS licensed and sold by IBM for use on that company's personal computers. (See DOS and MS-DOS.)

peripheral

Any physical device attached to your PC. Examples of peripherals include monitors, printers, external disk drives, CD-ROM devices and external monitors, among others.

port

An input/output (I/O) address through which your PC interacts with external devices. A modem, for example, is generally connected to a serial port.

RAM

Random Access Memory. Memory whose contents are constantly changed and updated during processing.

redirection

Causing output that would normally go to one device to be rerouted to a different device. You can, for example, redirect the results of a DIR listing from your system monitor to a disk file.

APPENDIX C: GLOSSARY 553

ROM

Read-only memory. Memory whose contents are not changed during processing.

root directory

The top level directory on any disk.

software

The programs and instructions that control what happens inside your PC.

system disk

A disk that can be used to boot your system. DOS places certain files on a disk during formatting, if you specify that disk is to be a system disk.

system prompt

A symbol DOS displays to signify that it is prepared to accept user input. The default system prompt for DOS is the device name assigned to the currently active disk drive, followed by a greater than symbol (>). For example, C> would be a default system prompt indicating that drive C: is currently active. The system prompt can be modified using the DOS PROMPT command.

virus

Potentially destructive code that's normally hidden in a file used for other purposes. MS-DOS 6.0 includes a special utility, VSAFE, that is designed to discover and, in some cases, eliminate viruses.

volume label

An identifying label or name written to a disk. Generally, volume labels are specified when a disk is formatted. Alternately, you can use the LABEL command to create a volume label after a disk has been formatted. A DOS volume label is limited to 11 characters.

warm boot

The process of restarting your computer with a Ctrl-Alt-Del key combination.

wildcard characters

Special characters DOS allows as substitutes for other characters in a DIR or COPY operation. The two valid DOS wildcard characters are the asterisk (*) and question mark (?).

write protection

The process of protecting a disk against being written to. This is accomplished by attaching a special tab to a 5.25" disk. On a 3.5" disk, the write protection device is built into the disk's plastic case.

Index

A

Active Task List
 adding programs to, 531–533
 caution, 535
 removing programs from, 533–535
Advanced Power Management
 (APM), 137
Alt key, 15, 16
American National Standards Institute
 (ANSI), 140
ANSI (American National Standards
 Institute), 140
ANSI codes, 140–141
ANSI display color and attribute codes,
 141–142
ANSI.SYS device driver, 137, 140–142,
 267–268
APM (Advanced Power
 Management), 137
APPEND command, 269–271
 fooling DOS, 97
 parameters and switches, 100–101
 syntax, 100
Application programs, 24, 547
Applications, 24
Application software, 20, 21
Archive attribute, files, 212–213, 215
ARC file extension, 107
ASCII, 547
ASSIGN command, 99, 101

Asterisk (*), wildcard, 83–84
ATTRIB command, 272–273
 file attributes, 212
 parameters and switches, 212–213
 tip, 214
 using, 213–215
Attribute codes, 141–142
Attributes, files, 212–215
AUTOEXEC.BAT file, 138–139,
 183–184, 547
 DIRCMD variable, 188–189
 during boot up, 548
 SMARTDRV command, 159
 verify on statement, 127

B

BACKUP command, 274–277
 caution, 99
 command options, 209
 format codes, 210
 parameters and switches, 208–210
 replaced by MSBACKUP utility, 207
BAK file extension, 107
Basic Input/Output System (BIOS), 8,
 11, 21
Batch files, 26, 219, 547
 branching within file, 226
 commands, 221–222
 creating a batch file, 222–226
 how a batch file works, 221

replaceable parameters, 224–225
running a batch file, 228–229
testing conditions, 225–226
using, 219–222
Batch processing, 183–184
BATCH subdirectory, 26
BAT file extension, 106, 108
Binary digit (Bit), 50, 547
BIN file extension, 107
BIOS (Basic Input/Output System), 8, 11, 21
Bit (binary digit), 50, 547
Boot disk, 138, 139
Booting up, 548
   cold, 548
   warm, 187, 551, 553
Branching, 226, 548
BREAK command, 278
Bubble memory, 13
BUFFERS command, 279–281
   improving disk performance, 156, 157, 159
Buffers, disk
   BUFFERS command, 156, 157, 159, 279–281
   double-buffering, 158–160
   in the HMA, 158
   recommended number, 157
   required memory, 158
   secondary buffer, 157
Byte, 10–11, 50, 548

C

CALL command, 222, 282
CapsLock key, 17
CD-ROM, 13, 548
Central Processing Unit (CPU), 8, 9–10, 549
CGA (Color Graphics Adapter), 17
CHCP command, 283–284
CHDIR (CD) command, 285–286
   internal command, 25
   parameters, 85
   syntax, 85
   using, 85–87
   using on other drives, 87–89
CHKDSK command, 287–289
   analyzing a disk, 56–61
   caution, 99
   deleting bad sectors, 59
   external command, 26
   include a file analysis, 58–59
   parameters and switches, 57
   recovering lost clusters, 59–60
   running, 57–58, 61
   syntax, 57
CHKSTATE.SYS, 137, 139
CHOICE command, 290–292
   batch file command, 222
   parameters and switches, 227
   syntax, 227
Clearing monitors, 84–85
Click, mouse, 37
Click on, mouse, 37
CLS command, 292
Clusters, recovering, 59–60
Codes, color and attribute, 140–141
Cold boot, 548
Color codes, 140, 141
Color Graphics Adapter (CGA), 17
COM file extension, 106, 108
COMMAND COM file, 21, 53, 139, 548
COMMAND command, 293–297
Command conventions, 265–266
Command line, 548
Command modifiers, 27
Command Reference. *See also* individual commands
   ANSI.SYS device driver, 267–268
   APPEND command, 269–271
   ATTRIB command, 272–273
   BACKUP command, 274–277
   BREAK command, 278

INDEX 557

BUFFERS command, 279–281
CALL command, 282
CD (CHDIR) command, 285–286
CHCP command, 283–284
CHDIR (CD) command, 285–286
CHKDSK command, 287–289
CHOICE command, 290–292
CLS command, 292
COMMAND command, 293–297
COPY command, 298–301
COUNTRY command, 302–304
CTTY command, 305
DATE command, 306
DBLSPACE utility, 307
DEBUG command, 308–309
DEFRAG command, 310–313
DEL (ERASE) command, 314–315
DELOLDOS command, 316
DELTREE command, 317
DEVICE command, 318–319
DEVICEHIGH command, 320–322
DIR command, 323–327
DISKCOMP command, 328–330
DISKCOPY command, 331–334
DISPLAY.SYS device driver, 335–336
DOS command, 337–338
DOSKEY utility, 339–344
DOSSHELL command, 345–346
DRIVER.SYS device driver, 347–349
DRIVPARM command, 350–351
ECHO command, 352–353
EDIT command, 354–355
EDLIN command, 356
EGA.SYS device driver, 357
EMM386 command, 358–359
EMM386.EXE, 360–367
ERASE command, 314–315
EXIT command, 368
EXPAND command, 369–370
FASTHELP command, 371
FASTOPEN command, 372–373
FC command, 374–376

FCBS command, 377
FDISK command, 378
FILES command, 379
FIND command, 380–381
FOR command, 383–383
FORMAT command, 384–388
GOTO command, 389–390
GRAPHICS utility, 391–393
HELP command, 394
HIMEM.SYS device driver, 395–398
IF command, 399–400
INCLUDE command, 401–402
INSTALL command, 403
KEYB command, 404–406
LABEL command, 407–408
LASTDRIVE command, 409
LH (LOADHIGH) command, 411–413
LOADFIX command, 410
LOADHIGH (LH) command, 411–413
MD (MKDIR) command, 425
MEM command, 414–416
MEMMAKER command, 417–418
MENUCOLOR command, 419–420
MENUDEFAULT command, 421–422
MENUITEM command, 423–424
MKDIR (MD) command, 425
MORE command, 426
MOVE command, 427–428
MSAV command, 429–431
MSBACKUP command, 432–433
MSD utility, 434–436
NLSFUNC command, 437
NUMLOCK command, 438
PATH command, 439–440
PAUSE command, 441
POWER command, 442–443
POWER.EXE, device driver, 444–445
PRINT command, 446–448
PROMPT command, 449–450
QBASIC command, 451–452
RAMDRIVE.SYS, 453–456
RD (RMDIR) command, 465

REM command, 457
REN (RENAME) command, 458
RENAME (REN) command, 458
REPLACE command, 459–461
RESTORE command, 462–464
RMDIR (RD) command, 465
SET command, 466–467
SETVER command, 468–470
SETVER.EXE device driver, 471
SHELL command, 472
SHIFT command, 473
SMARTDRV command, 474–477
SMARTDRV.EXE, 478
SORT command, 479–480
STACKS command, 481
SUBMENU command, 482–483
SUBST command, 484–486
SWITCHES statement, 487
SYS command, 488
TIME command, 489–490
TREE command, 491–492
TYPE command, 493
UNDELETE command, 494–496
UNFORMAT command, 497–498
VER command, 499
VERIFY command, 500
VOL command, 501
VSAFE utility, 502–503
XCOPY command, 504–506
Commands, recalling, 230–234
Computer viruses, 6, 553
  VSAFE utility, 215–218, 502–503
Conditional testing, 548
CONFIG.SYS file, 138–140,
    257–258, 549
  ANSI.SYS, 267
  contents of, 154–156
  creating, 149–150
  during boot up, 548
  miscellaneous commands, 181–183
  setup utility, 142
Contiguous files, 236

COUNTRY command, 302–304
  COUNTRY.SYS file, 138
COUNTRY.SYS file, 138
COPY command, 298–301
  internal command, 25
  parameters and switches, 108–109
  to create a file, 111–112
  to duplicate files, 109–111
  wildcard characters, 298, 553
COPY CON command, 112
CPU (Central Processing Unit), 8,
    9–10, 549
Ctrl key, 15, 16
CTTY command, 305
Cursor, 549

D

Daisywheel printers, 18–19
Data, 22
  compression, 242–253
  protection, 191–218
DATE command, 25, 306
DBLSPACE utility, 307
  DBLSPACE.SYS, 137
  double storage capacity, 242–243
  how data compression works,
    243–244
  running from the command line,
    252–253
  setting up, 244–250
  using the DoubleSpace tools,
    250–252
DBLSPACE.SYS, 137
DEBUG command, 308–309
Default, 549
  directory, 87
  startup disk, 139
DEFRAG command, 310–313
  caution, 99
  parameters and switches, 237–238
  syntax, 237
  using, 238–242

what it accomplishes, 237
why it is needed, 236–237
DEL (ERASE) command, 314–315
   caution, 116
   internal command, 25
   parameters and switches, 116
   syntax, 116
   using, 116–117
   warnings, 116
   what it does, 115–116
DELOLDOS command, 316
   caution, 148
   what it does, 147–149
DELTREE command, 317
   caution, 96
   parameters and switches, 96
   remove directory trees, 95–97
   syntax, 96
   using, 96
DEVICE command, 318–319
Device driver, 37, 133, 549
   ANSI.SYS, 137, 140–142, 267–268
   CHKSTATE.SYS, 137, 139
   COUNTRY.SYS, 138
   DBLSPACE.SYS, 137, 139
   DISPLAY.SYS, 137
   DRIVER.SYS, 137, 139–140, 347–349
   EGA.SYS, 137, 139, 357
   EMM386.EXE, 137, 139, 168–171, 360–367
   HIMEM.SYS, 137, 139, 150, 166–167, 168, 395–398
   INTERLNK.EXE, 137, 139
   KEYBOARD.SYS, 138
   POWER.EXE, 137, 444–445
   RAMDRIVE.SYS, 137, 453–456
   SETVER.EXE, 138, 139, 142–145, 471
   SMARTDRV.EXE, 138, 280–281, 478
DEVICEHIGH command, 320–322
   increase available RAM, 162
   parameters and switches, 181
   what it does, 180–181

Device name, 549
Devices, 133–145
   device drives, 137–138
   DOS devices, 135
   main categories, 134
   redirecting input and output, 135–137
   what it is, 134–135
Dialog boxes, 35–36
DIR command, 323–327
   caution, 136
   displaying contents of a directory, 78
   example, 26, 27, 28
   F3 key, 118
   initial DIR Help message, 41
   internal command, 25
   parameters and switches, 79–80
   syntax, 78
   using, 80–81
   using switches, 81–82
   using wildcards, 81–82
   wildcard characters, 82–84, 553
   /? switch, 38–39
DIRCMD variable, 188–189
Directories, 73–101, 549
   append subdirectories, 76
   changing active directories, 85–89
   changing active disk drives, 84
   clearing your display, 84–85
   creating, 77–78
   customizing system prompt, 89–92
   default directory, 86, 87
   designing a logical structure, 74–76
   display directory structure, 92–93
   displaying contents, 78–84
   fooling DOS, 97–101
   hidden files, 551
   listing, 551
   parent directories, 87
   pathfinder, 76–77
   removing directories, 93–95
   removing directory trees, 95–97

root directory, 74, 533
typical structure, 75
Disk buffers
    BUFFERS command, 156, 157, 159, 279–281
    double buffering, 158–160
    in the HMA, 158
    recommended number, 157
    required memory, 158
    secondary buffer, 157
DISKCOMP command, 328–330
    caution, 99
    external command, 26
    parameters and switches, 65
    running, 65–66
DISKCOPY command, 331–334
    caution, 64, 99
    parameters and switches, 63
    running, 63–65
Disk file, 549
Disks, 47–71
    analyzing, 56–61
    checking a volume label, 62
    comparing, 65–66
    copying, 63–65
    directory, 52
    duplicating, 63–66
    error correction, 57
    file, 549
    floppy disks, 13, 49, 51, 139–140, 550
    floppy disks vs. hard disks, 49
    formatting, 51–52, 53–56
    generate file status report, 57
    hard disks, 14, 49, 51, 68–71, 73–74, 551
    how they work, 49–51
    improving performance, 156–158
    increase storage capacity, 242–243
    labeling, 61–62
    partitioning a hard disk, 68–71
    preparing a disk for work, 51–52
    restoring accidentally formatted disks, 66–68
    storage capacity, 550, 551
    storage space information, 58
Display adapters, 17–18
Display resolutions, 18
Display screen, 552
    to change color, 140
DISPLAY.SYS device driver, 137, 335–336
DLL file extension, 107
DOS (Disk Operating System), 549
    faces of, 5–7
    first introduced, 5
    introduction, 23–45
    version 1.0, 6
    version 4.1, 6
    version 5.0, 6
    version 6.0, 6
    what it is, 4–5
DOS command, 162, 168, 337–338
DOS command line, 25, 27
DOS High, 168
DOSKEY utility, 339–344
    creating macros, 232–234
    parameters and switches, 230
    recalling command lists, 231
    saving macros, 234
    using, 230
    using the command list, 232
    what it does, 230
DOS SHELL, 24, 28–31, 523–545
    canceling a multiple file selection, 530
    changing the active area, 32–33
    device driver, 37
    dialog boxes, 35–36
    display, 31–32
    EGA.SYS, 137
    GUI, 551
    mouse, 36–37, 525–526
    navigating, 32, 525–526

pull-down menu, 33–34
quitting, 37–38
requesting help, 34–35
required MS-DOS version, 31
running from the keyboard, 525
selecting items on the display, 527–530
starting, 31, 523–524
switching to a graphic display, 526–527
task switching, 530–536
using, 28–38
using speed keys, 34
using the keyboard, 33
viewing storage requirements, 529
working with program groups, 536–545
DOSSHELL command, 345–346
DOS system prompt, 29
DOS=HIGH command, 6, 158
Dot matrix printers, 18
Double-buffering, 158–160
Double-click, mouse, 37
Double storage capacity, 242–253
Drag, mouse, 37
Drive identifier, 550
Drive letter, 76
   ASSIGN command, 101
   SUBST command, 98, 99–101
DRIVER.SYS device driver, 347–349
   what it does, 137, 139–140
DRIVPARM command, 350–351
DRV file extension, 107
Duplicating disks, 63–66
Duplicating files, 108–112, 129–131

E

ECHO command, 352–353
   what it does, 222
EDIT command, 354–355
   caution, 152
   create and modify text files, 151, 550

parameters and switches, 151–152
starting, 151
syntax, 151
using, 152–154
EDLIN command, 356
EGA (Enhanced Graphics Adapter), 12, 17, 18
EGA.SYS device driver, 137, 139, 357
Electronic mail, modem, 19
EMM386 command, 162, 358–359
EMM386.EXE, 137, 139, 360–367
Enhanced Graphics Adapter (EGA), 12, 17, 18
ERASE command, 115–116, 314–315
Erasable optical disks, 13
Escape codes, 140, 141
EXE file extension, 106, 108
EXIT command, 368
Exiting
   DOS Shell, 37–38
   help, 45
EXPAND command, 369–370
Expanded memory, 163–164
   location, 165
Expansion cards, 550
Expansion slots, 8, 12, 550
   motherboard, 9
Extended memory, 137, 163
   location, 165
External commands, 25–26, 550
External files, 161

F

FASTHELP command, 371
FASTOPEN command, 372–373
FAT (File Allocation Table), 52, 119, 236
   formatting, 551
FC command, 374–376
   parameters and switches, 123–124
   syntax, 123
   using, 124

562 INDEX

FCBS command, 377
FDISK command, 378
  caution, 70, 99
  external command, 26
  options, 70
  partitioning a hard disk, 68–69
  running, 69–71
  switches, 69
File Allocation Table (FAT), 52, 119, 236, 550
File attributes, 212–215
  Archive, 212
  Hidden, 212
  Read-only, 212
  System, 212
File extensions
  ARC, 107
  ASC, 107
  BAK, 107
  BAT, 106, 108
  BIN, 107
  COM, 106, 108
  DLL, 107
  DRV, 107
  EXE, 106, 108
  FNT, 107
  HLP, 107
  INI, 107
  PCX, 107
  SYS, 107
  TXT, 107
  ZIP, 107
Filename, 550
Files, 103–131
  comparing files, 123–124
  contiguous vs. noncontiguous, 236
  copying, 108–112, 129–131
  deleting, 115–119
  external, 161
  file types, 104–105
  hidden, 551
  modifying file attributes, 212–215
  moving, 127–129
  naming conventions, 106–108
  noncontiguous, 236, 237
  organizing long listings, 114–115
  path notation, 108
  recovering deleted files, 119–123
  redirecting output to, 136–137
  renaming, 124–126
  reorganize fragmented files, 237–242
  to protect from erasure, 214
  using COPY command to create, 111–112
  verifying file copies, 126–127
  viewing the contents, 112–114
FILES command, 156, 158, 159, 379
Filters, 26, 27, 114, 550
FIND command, 380–381
Fine-tuning your system, 147–190
  AUTOEXEC.BAT, 183–184
  CONFIG.SYS, 181–183
  contents of CONFIG.SYS, 154–156
  creating and modifying text files, 151–154
  creating a virtual disk, 160–161
  creating CONFIG.SYS, 149–150
  improving disk performance, 156–158
  increasing number of drives, 161–162
  loading DOS High, 168
  making the most of memory, 162–167
  mega-memory management, 168–180
  pathfinder, 184–187
  setting MS-DOS 6.0 in stone, 147–149
  upper memory, 180–181
  using double-buffering with SMARTDRV, 158–160
Fixed disk, 550

Floppy disk, 13, 49, 51, 550
  advantage, 13
  disadvantages, 13
  DRIVER.SYS for older PCs, 139–140
  storage capacity, 550
Floppy disk drives, 13
FNT file extension, 107
Fooling DOS, 97–101
FOR command, 383–383
  what it does, 222
FORMAT command, 384–388
  caution, 54, 99
  external command, 26
  FORMAT.EXE program, 105, 138
  formatting a system disk, 54–56
  parameters and switches, 53–54
  syntax, 53
  what it does, 51–52
FORMAT.EXE program, 105, 138
Formatting, 551
  assigned serial number, 63
Fragmented files, reorganizing, 236–242
Function keys, 15, 16, 117–118, 551
  F1, 117
  F2, 117
  F3, 117
  F5, 261
  F7, 117
  F8, 261
  F9, 117

G

GOTO command, 389–390
  syntax, 226
  what it does, 222
Graphical User Interface (GUI), 18, 29, 551
GRAPHICS utility, 391–393
GUI (Graphical User Interface), 18, 29, 551

H

Hard disks, 14, 49, 51, 73–74, 551
  drawback, 14
  increase storage capacity, 242–253
  partitioning, 68–71
  storage capacity, 551
Hardware, 7–20, 551
  additional hardware options, 18–20
  monitors and display adapters, 17–18
  PC keyboards, 14–17
  secondary storage devices, 12–14
  system unit, 8–12
HELP command, 394
  elements of Help display, 40
  exiting Help, 45
  introduced, 38
  navigating the Help display, 40–41
  new and improved, 39–40
  requesting Help for a command, 41–43
  searching Help on a topic, 43–45
  speed keys, 45
  /? switch, 38–39
Help Display, 40–43
  exiting, 45
  searching a topic, 43–45
Hercules monochrome graphics, 17
Hidden attribute, files, 212–215
Hidden files, 551
High Memory Area (HMA), 165
  location, 165
HIMEM.SYS device driver, 137, 139, 150, 166–167, 395–398
  loading, 168
HLP file extension, 107
HMA (high memory area), 165
  buffers, 158
  location, 165

I

IF command, 222, 225–226, 399–400
INCLUDE command, 401–402
   menu magic, 258
   what it does, 259
INI file extension, 107
Input devices, 134
Input/Output devices, 134
Input/Output ports, 8, 11–12
INSTALL command, 181–182, 403
   caution, 182
   parameters, 182
   syntax, 182
Installing MS-DOS 6.0, 507–522
   caution, 511
   getting ready, 510
   installing on a new system, 512
   reverting to a previous version, 522
   setup utility, 511–522
   upgrading, 512
   what you need, 507
   write-protecting distribution disks, 510
   write-protecting floppy disks, 507–508
   write-protecting 5.25" disks, 508, 509
   write-protecting 3.5" disks, 508–509, 510
Internal commands, 25–26
International characters, 137
INTERLNK.EXE, 137, 139
IO.SYS file, 21, 53, 139
   hidden file, 551

J

JOIN command, 101
Joysticks, 19

K

KEYB command, 138, 404–406
Keyboard, 14–17
   function keys, 15
   fundamental design, 14
   modify performance of, 140
   mouse, 19
   numeric keypad, 16–17
   shift keys, 15–16
   system keys, 17
KEYBOARD.SYS, 138
Key combinations, 28, 551
Keypad, 16
Keys, 28
   ANSI.SYS, 140
Kilobyte (KB), 10–11, 551

L

LABEL command, 407–408
   caution, 61, 99
   parameters, 61
   running, 61–62
   syntax, 61
   volume label, 61, 553
Laptop computers, 16
Laser printers, 18–19
LASTDRIVE command, 409
   caution, 99
   increases number of devices, 161–162
LOADFIX command, 410
LOADHIGH (LH) command, 411–413
   parameters and switches, 190
   syntax, 190
   what it does, 189–190
Logical drives, 69, 71
LPT1, 135, 136
LPT2, 135

M

Macros
   creating, 232–234
   saving, 234
Mapping, memory, 164
MDA (Monochrome Display Adapter), 17, 18

INDEX 565

Megabyte (MB), 10–11, 551
Mega-memory management, 168
MEM command, 414–416
MEMMAKER command, 417–418
MEMMAKER.EXE, memory
    management utility, 137
MemMaker Utility, 171–180
Memory, 134
    amount required by a buffer, 158
    basic units, 10
    expanded memory, 163–164
    extended memory, 163
    history of, 162–165
    HMA (high memory area), 158, 165
    making the most of, 162–167
    mapping, 164
    mega-memory management,
        168–180
    system memory, 8, 10–11
    types of memory and locations, 165
    upper memory, 164–165, 180–181
Memory board, 12
Memory mapping, 164
MENUCOLOR command, 419–420
    menu magic, 258
    what it does, 259
MENUDEFAULT command, 421–422
    menu magic, 258
    what it does, 259
MENUITEM command, 423–424
    menu magic, 258
    what it does, 259
Menu magic, 258–261
Mice. *See* Mouse
Microsoft Disk Operating System. *See*
    MS-DOS
Microsoft Windows, 18
    caution, 270, 287
    GUI, 551
Mirror command, 99
MKDIR (MD) command, 425
    internal command, 25

parameters, 78
    syntax, 77
    using, 78
Mnemonic, 33
Modem card, 550
MODE command, 26
Modems, 19–20, 135
    port, 552
Modifiers, 27
Monitors, 17–18, 552
    clearing, 84–85
    modify performance of, 140
Monochrome Display Adapter (MDA),
    17, 18
MORE filter, 426
    caution, 115
    parameters, 114
    syntax, 114
    using, 114–115
    what it does, 550
Motherboard, 8, 9, 12, 550
MOUSE, 19, 135, 552
    click, 37
    click on, 37
    DOS Shell, 36–37
    double-click, 37
    drag, 37
    point, 37
Mouse pen, 19
MOVE command, 427–428
    caution, 129
    parameter, 127–129
    renaming directories, 128–129
    syntax, 127
    using, 127–129
MSAV command, 429–431
MSBACKUP command, 432–433
MSBACKUP utility, 192
    caution, 197, 207
    creating setup files, 201–205
    ending MSBACKUP session, 207
    parameters and switches, 193

566 INDEX

running, 193–201
saving setup file, 205–206
MSD utility, 434–436
   parameters and switches, 253
   syntax, 253–254
   using, 254–256
MS-DOS (Microsoft Disk Operating System). See also DOS versions, 5–6
   what it is, 4–5
MS-DOS task swapper, 287
MSDOS.SYS file, 21, 53, 139
   hidden file, 551
Multiple configurations, 256–257
MYFORMAT.BAT, 227–229

N

New features, 235–261
   DBLSPACE utility, 242–253
   DEFRAG command, 236–242
   F8 function key, 261
   F5 function key, 261
   INCLUDE command, 258, 259
   MENUCOLOR command, 258, 259
   MENUDEFAULT command, 258, 259, 260
   MENUITEM command, 258, 259
   MSD utility, 253–256
   multiple configurations, 256–257
   SUBMENU command, 258, 259
   using ? in CONFIG.SYS file, 257–258
NLSFUNC command, 437
Noncontiguous files, 236
Notebook computers, 16
Numeric keypad, 16–17
NUMLOCK command, 182, 438
NumLock key, 17

O

On-line Help for DOS commands, 24
Optional command parameters, 27–28
Options, 26, 27

Output devices, 134
Overlays, 161

P

Parameters, 26, 27, 552
Parent directory, 87
Path, 76–77
   caution, 185
   elements in a path statement, 77
   maximum length, 78
PATH command, 439–440, 552
   caution, 185
   internal command, 25
   parameter and switch, 185
   pathfinder, 184–187
   syntax, 185
   tip, 185
Path notation, 108
PAUSE command, 222, 441
PC DOS, 6, 552
PC keyboards, 14–17
   function keys, 15
   fundamental design, 14
   mouse, 19
   numeric keypad, 16–17
   shift keys, 15–16
   system keys, 17
PC software. See Software
PCX file extension, 107
Pen tablets, 19
Performance
   disk, 156–158
   monitors, 140
Peripheral, 552
PgUp key, 17
Pixel, 18
Pointing devices, 19
Point, mouse, 37
Port, 135, 552
POWER command, 442–443
Power consumption, reducing, 137

POWER.EXE, device driver, 137, 444–445
Previous version, reverting to, 522
PRINT command, 446–448
Printers, 18–19
   caution, 136
   daisywheel, 18–19
   dot matrix, 18
   laser, 18, 19
Program groups, 536–545
   creating a program group, 537–541
   initial program groups, 536–637
   modifying an item, 543–544
   removing a program group item, 544–545
   running a program, 541–543
   what are they?, 536
Programs
   adding to task list, 531–533
   applications, 24, 547
   removing from task list, 533–535
   software, 20–21
PROMPT command, 449–450
   assign a text value to a key, 141
   display color change, 140
   note, 92
   parameters, 89
   special symbols, 90–92
   syntax, 89
   using, 89–90
Protection, data
   BACKUP command, 207–210
   modifying file attributes, 212–215
   MSBACKUP utility, 192–207
   RESTORE command, 207, 210–212
   VSAFE utility, 215–218
PrtSc (Print Screen) key, 17
Pull-down menu, 33–34

Q

QBASIC command, 451–452
QBASIC.EXE, 152

Question mark (?), wildcard, 83–84
Qwerty layout, 14, 15

R

RAM (Random Access Memory), 8, 10–11, 12, 26, 137, 150, 162, 552
   conventional RAM location, 165
   during boot up, 548
   external commands, 550
RAM disk, 160–161
   should you create one?, 161
RAMDRIVE.SYS, 453–456
   parameters and switches, 160
   should you create one?, 161
   syntax, 160
   what it does, 137
Random Access Memory (RAM), 8, 10–11, 12, 26, 137, 150, 162, 548, 550, 552
Read-only attribute, files, 212–214
Read-Only Memory (ROM), 8, 10–11, 553
RECOVER command, 99
Redirection, 552
REM command, 222, 457
Removable disks, 13
RENAME (Ren) command, 458
   internal command, 25
   parameters, 125
   syntax, 124–125
   using, 125–126
   wildcards, 126
REPLACE command, 459–461
RESTORE command, 462–464
   caution, 99
   messages, 212
   options, 211
   parameters and switches, 210–211
   replaced by MSBACKUP utility, 207
   syntax, 210
RMDIR (RD) command, 465
   internal command, 25

568 INDEX

parameters, 94
sample directory tree, 93
syntax, 93–94
using, 94–95
ROM (Read-Only Memory), 8, 10–11, 553
Root directory, 74, 553

S

Screen echo, 222
Secondary storage devices, 12–14
    bubble memory, 13
    CD-ROMs, 13, 548
    erasable optical disks, 13
    floppy disks, 12, 13, 49, 51, 550
    hard disks, 12, 14, 49, 51, 68–71, 73–74, 242–253, 551
    RAM cards, 13
    tape devices, 12
    Write-Once Read-Many (WORM) devices, 13
Sectors, deleting, 59
Sentry method, UNDELETE, 120–121
Serial number, assigned, 63
SET command, 466–467
    example, 188
    parameters, 187
    syntax, 187
SETUP, installation utility, 142
SETVER command, 468–470
    caution, 144
    parameters and switches, 143–144
    SETVER.EXE, 142
    syntax, 143
SETVER.EXE device driver, 138, 139, 142–143, 471
SETVER table, 142–143, 145
SHELL command, 472
SHIFT command, 222, 473
Shift keys, 15–16, 17
SMARTDRV command, 474–477
    double-buffering, 156, 158–159

SMARTDRV.EXE, 138, 280–281, 478
Software, 20–21, 553
    application, 20, 21
    system, 20–21
    utilities, 20, 21
SORT command, 479–480
Speed keys, 34, 45
Subdirectories, appending, 76
STACKS command, 481
Storage capacity
    floppy disk, 550
    hard disk, 551
    how to double, 242–253
Storage requirements, multiple files, 529
Structuring commands, 27–28
SUBMENU command, 482–483
    menu magic, 258
    what it does, 259
SUBST command, 484–486
    caution, 99
    difference between SUBST and APPEND, 101
    fooling DOS, 97–98
    parameters and switches, 98–99
    removing a SUBST assignment, 99–100
    syntax, 98
    using, 99
Super VGA (SVGA), 17, 18
SVGA (Super VGA), 17, 18
Switches, 26, 27. *See also* Command Reference entries
    option [+/–], VSAFE, 216
    /nnnn, FC, 124
    /A
        BACKUP, 209
        COPY, 109
        FC, 123
        RAMDRIVE, 160
        TREE, 92
        XCOPY, 129

/ALL, UNDELETE, 119
/Ax, VSAFE, 216
/A:, DIR, 79
/A:date, RESTORE, 211
/B
  COPY, 109
  DEFRAG, 237
  DIR, 80
  EDIT, 152
  FC, 124
  FORMAT, 53
  MSD, 253
/BUFSIZE=, DOSKEY, 230
/BW
  DEFRAG, 237
  MSBACKUP, 193
/C
  FC, 124
  DIR, 80
/Cx, VSAFE, 216
/C:keys, CHOICE, 227
/D
  SETVER, 144
  SUBST, 98
  VSAFE, 216
/DOS, UNDELETE, 119
/DS, UNDELETE, 119
/DT, UNDELETE, 119
/D:date
  BACKUP, 209
  XCOPY, 130
/E
  APPEND, 101
  RAMDRIVE, 160
  XCOPY, 130
/F
  CHKDSK, 57
  DEFRAG, 237
  MSD, 253
  TREE, 92
/F:size
  BACKUP, 209

FORMAT, 53–54
/G, EDIT, 152
/GO, DEFRAG, 237
/H
  DEFRAG, 237
  DOSKEY, 230
  EDIT, 152
/HISTORY, DOSKEY, 230
/I, MSD, 253
/INSERT, DOSKEY, 230
/L
  DIR, 90
  FC, 124
  UNFORMAT, 67
/LBn, FC, 124
/LCD
  DEFRAG, 237
  MSBACKUP, 193
/LIST, UNDELETE, 119
/L:, DEVICEHIGH, 181
/L:filename, BACKUP, 209
/L:region1,minsize1, LOADHIGH, 190
/L:time, RESTORE, 211
/LOAD, UNDELETE, 120
/M
  BACKUP, 209
  DOSKEY, 230
  RESTORE, 211
  XCOPY, 129
/MACROS, DOSKEY, 230
/MDA, MSBACKUP, 193
/N
  CHOICE, 227
  FC, 124
  RESTORE, 211
  VSAFE, 216
/NOHI, EDIT, 152
/NE, VSAFE, 216
/NX, VSAFE, 216
/N:sectors, FORMAT, 54
/OVERSTRIKE, DOSKEY, 230
/O:, DIR, 79

/P
  DEL, 116
  DIR, 79
  MSD, 253
  RESTORE, 211
  UNFORMAT, 67
  XCOPY, 130
/PATH, APPEND, 100, 101
/PURGE[:drive], UNDELETE, 120
/Q, FORMAT, 54
/QUIET, SETVER, 144
/REINSTALL, DOSKEY, 230
/S
  ATTRIB, 213
  BACKUP, 209
  CHOICE, 227
  DEVICEHIGH, 181
  DIR, 80
  FORMAT, 54
  LOADHIGH, 190
  MSD, 253
  RESTORE, 211
  XCOPY, 130
/S[:], DEFRAG, 237
/S[:drive], UNDELETE, 120
/SKIPHIGH, DEFRAG, 237
/STATUS
  FDISK, 69
  UNDELETE, 120
/T, FC, 124
/Tdrive[-entries], UNDELETE, 120
/TEST, UNFORMAT, 67
/T:c,nn, CHOICE, 227
/T:time, BACKUP, 209
/T:tracks, FORMAT, 54
/U
  DEFRAG, 237
  FORMAT, 54
  UNDELETE, 120
  VSAFE, 216
/V
  CHKDSK, 57
  COPY, 109
  DISKCOPY, 63
  XCOPY, 130
/V:label, FORMAT, 54
/W
  FC, 124
  XCOPY, 130
/X, APPEND, 100
/Y, DELTREE, 96
/1
  DISKCOMP, 65
  DISKCOPY, 63
  FORMAT, 53
/4, FORMAT, 53
/8
  DISKCOMP, 65
  FORMAT, 53
/? switch, 38–39
+A, ATTRIB, 213
+H, ATTRIB, 213
+R, ATTRIB, 213
+S, ATTRIB, 213
–A, ATTRIB, 213
–H, ATTRIB, 213
–R, ATTRIB, 213
–S, ATTRIB, 213
SWITCHES statement, 487
System attribute, files, 212
System date, 25
SYS command, 488
  caution, 99
SYS file extension, 107
System disk, 553
System files
  COMMAND.COM, 53
  IO.SYS, 53
  MSDOS.SYS, 53
System keys, 17
System memory, 8, 10–11
  RAM, 8, 10–11, 12, 26, 137, 150, 162, 165, 548, 550, 552
  ROM, 8, 10–11, 553

INDEX **571**

System prompt, 553
  customizing, 89–92
System printer, redirecting output to, 135–136
System software, 20–21
System unit, 7, 8–14
  Basic Input/Output System (BIOS), 8, 11
  central processing unit (CPU), 8, 9–10
  expansion slots, 8, 12
  Input/Output Ports, 8, 11–12
  motherboard, 8, 9
  system memory (RAM and ROM), 8, 10–11

T

Tape devices, 12
Task switching, 530–536
  adding programs to the task list, 531–533
  enabling, 531
  ending, 535–536
  removing programs from the task list, 533–535
  what is it?, 530–531
Text files, creating and modifying, 151–154
TIME command, 489–490
  internal command, 25
Trackball, pointing device, 19
Tracker method, UNDELETE, 120–211
TREE command, 491–492
  parameters and switches, 92
  syntax, 92
  using, 92–93
TXT file extension, 107
TYPE command, 493
  internal command parameters, 112
  syntax, 112
  using, 113–114

U

UNDELETE command, 494–496
  levels of protection, 120
  parameters and switches, 119–120
  syntax, 119
  using, 121–123
UNFORMAT command, 497–498
  limitations, 68
  parameters and switches, 67
  running, 67–68
  syntax, 66–67
UNINSTALL disk, 522
UNIX, 4
Upper memory, 164–165, 180–181
User interface, 29
Utilities, 20, 21

V

Variables, 27
VER command, 499
VERIFY command, 500
  automatic verification, 127
  parameter, 126
  syntax, 126
VGA (Video Graphics Array), 17, 18
VGA display, 12, 139
Video Graphics Array (VGA), 17, 18
Virtual disk, creating, 160–161
Virus, 553
  protection, 6
  VSAFE utility, 215–218, 502–503
VOL command, 501
  automatically assigned serial number, 63
  character limitation, 62
  parameters, 62
  running, 62
  syntax, 62
  tip, 62
Volume label, 553
  checking, 62

VSAFE utility, 502–503
  do you need it?, 218
  parameters and switches, 216
  syntax, 215
  using, 216–217
  virus, 553

W

Warm booting, 187, 553
  caution, 187
  key combination, 551
Wildcards
  asterisk (*), 83–84
  caution, 144
  characters, 553
  CHKDSK command, 287
  combining, 84
  COPY command, 298
  DIR command, 82–84
  question mark (?), 83–84
  RENAME command, 126
Windows setup program, 270
WORM (Write-Once Read-Many), 13
Write-Once Read-Many (WORM)
  devices, 13
Write protection, 553
  floppy disks, 507–510
  5.25" disks, 508, 509
  3.5" disks, 508–509, 510

X

XCOPY command, 504–506
  parameters and switches, 129–130
  syntax, 129
  using, 130–131

Z

ZIP file extension, 107